THIS BOOK BELONGS TO:

JANET
GRACE

STORY

THE ROBERT S. KAPLAN SERIES IN MANAGEMENT ACCOUNTING

■ *Robert S. Kaplan, Consulting Editor*

MANAGEMENT ACCOUNTING
  Atkinson / Banker / Kaplan / Young

THE DESIGN OF COST MANAGEMENT SYSTEMS
  Cooper / Kaplan

MANAGEMENT CONTROL SYSTEMS (1997)
  Merchant

ADVANCED MANAGEMENT ACCOUNTING, 2/E
  Kaplan / Atkinson

MANAGEMENT ACCOUNTING

ANTHONY A. ATKINSON
University of Waterloo

RAJIV D. BANKER
University of Minnesota

ROBERT S. KAPLAN
Harvard University

S. MARK YOUNG
University of Southern California

PRENTICE HALL, Englewood Cliffs, NJ 07632

Library of Congress Cataloging-in Publication Data

Management accounting / Anthony A. Atkinson . . . [et al.].
    p.   cm. — (The Prentice-Hall series in accounting)
  Includes indexes.
  ISBN 0-13-016809-2
  1. Managerial accounting. I. Atkinson, Anthony A. II. Series.
HF5657.4.M328 1995   94-32832
658.15'11—dc20   CIP

Acquisitions editor: Bill Webber
Development editor: Leslye Givarz
Editor in Chief, Development: Stephen Deitmer
Managing editor: Joyce Turner
Assistant editor: Diane de Castro
Editorial/production supervision: Linda Pawelchak
In-house production liaison: Penelope Linskey
Interior and cover design: Suzanne Behnke
Design director: Linda Fiordilino
Copy editing: JaNoel Lowe
Photo editor: Lori Morris-Nantz
Photo research: Chris Pullo
Page layout: Maureen Eide
Production assistant: Renée Pelletier
Manufacturing buyer: Vincent Scelta
Manufacturing manager: Patrice Fraccio
Conceptual electronic art: Boston Graphics
Permissions editor: Mary Helen Fitzgerald
Proofreading: Maine Proofreading Services
Cover photos: Vladimar Pcholkin / FPG;
Walter Hodges / Allstock; Arnold
Zann; Ovak Arslanian; John
Abbot Photography; Frank
Siteman / Rainbow

© 1995 by Prentice-Hall, Inc.
A Simon & Schuster Company
Englewood Cliffs, New Jersey 07632

Printed in the United States of America
10 9 8 7 6 5 4 3 2

ISBN: 0-13-016809-2

Prentice-Hall International (UK) Limited, *London*
Prentice-Hall of Australia Pty. Limited, *Sydney*
Prentice-Hall Canada Inc., *Toronto*
Prentice-Hall Hispanoamericana, S.A., *Mexico*
Prentice-Hall of India Private Limited, *New Delhi*
Prentice-Hall of Japan, Inc., *Tokyo*
Simon & Schuster Asia Pte. Ltd., *Singapore*
Editora Prentice Hall do Brasil, Ltda., *Rio de Janeiro*
Prentice-Hall, Englewood Cliffs, *New Jersey*

This Book Is Dedicated to Our Parents and Families

BRIEF CONTENTS

CONTENTS

2|17|96

2

MANAGING ACTIVITIES   38

3

COST CONCEPTS 90

4

COST BEHAVIOR 134

5

BUDGETING FOR OPERATIONS   190

5·37   3/30/96

6

BASIC PRODUCT COSTING SYSTEMS   240

2/2/96

7

TWO-STAGE ALLOCATIONS AND ACTIVITY-BASED COSTING SYSTEMS   276

8

PRICING AND PRODUCT MIX DECISIONS   324

9

PROCESS AND ACTIVITY DECISIONS   366

9/33   3/1/96

10

CAPITAL BUDGETING   404

4/12/96

11

PLANNING AND CONTROL   440

11-39 4/12/96

2/30

12

FINANCIAL CONTROL   486

12.44   3/30/96

4/12/96

13

COMPENSATION   534

13-47   4/12/96

14

BEHAVIORAL AND ORGANIZATIONAL ISSUES IN MANAGEMENT ACCOUNTING AND CONTROL SYSTEM DESIGN   572

read Ch 14   4/27/96

14.49 4/27/96

14.51 4/27/96

PREFACE

Management Accounting was written to introduce students to the new role for management accounting and control information in organizations. Management accountants in organizations traditionally served as scorekeepers; they maintained and reported the financial consequences of events that occurred in past periods. The reports were derived from the aggregate financial statements of total enterprise performance. They were frequently delayed, highly aggregated, and, increasingly in recent years, distorted from the actual technology and economies of the organization.

Today, management accountants must play a much more central role in the management and control of organizational performance. Measures of the economic condition of the enterprise—such as the cost and profitability of the organization's products, services, and customers—are available only from management accounting systems. The information produced by management accountants must support both the operational and strategic needs of the enterprise. Historically used to *control* workers and employees, management accounting information must now be more detailed and more timely so that employees can receive rapid feedback on their performance, enabling them to learn from the recent past so that they can improve for the future. Management accounting information, by measuring the economic performance of decentralized operating units—such as business units, divisions, and departments—provides feedback to senior management about the units' performance and also serves as the linkage between the strategy of the organization and the execution of that strategy in individual operating units.

Management Accounting was written with a focus on organizational activities—the collection of tasks performed by the organization's employees to create value for customers. Chapter 1 introduces the nature of management accounting information and how it must be customized to the different needs of operators, middle managers, and senior executives. It contrasts the historical with the newly emerging contemporary role for management accounting in manufacturing and service organizations. Chapter 2 focuses on the organization's goals—including satisfying the expectations of multiple stakeholders—and how these goals determine the organization's strategy. The primary focus is on creating value for customers with performance measures derived to signal how organizational activities are contributing to customer value creation. *Benchmarking* and *continuous improvement* are introduced as important measurement tools to help organizations improve their performance for customers.

Chapter 3 introduces basic cost concepts within an activity framework. This chapter integrates recent advances in the foundations of activity-based costing into a general framework for describing cost behavior. Chapter 4 builds on this activity framework to describe cost behavior. Material in this chapter highlights the distinction between spending on organizational resources and the consumption of organizational resources to produce products and services for customers. Thus cost behavior is embedded in a general management framework arising from the demands for organizational resources, the nature of contracting for organizational resources, and management actions that, over time, adjust the supply of organizational resources to current and anticipated demands. Chapter 5, on budgeting, shows how organizations make decisions about the supply of resources, and associated spending on resources, based on forecasted demands by customers for products and services.

Chapter 6 introduces the basics of product costing, such as job order and process cost systems. This material is developed using the foundation of activity costing introduced in Chapters 3 and 4. Chapter 7 builds upon this foundation by introducing activity-based cost (ABC) systems, including the two-stage process of assigning service department costs to production departments and activities, and then from cost centers and activities down to products and services. The chapter identifies the distortions arising from traditional costing systems that rely only on volume-related cost drivers. ABC systems use unit, batch, and product-sustaining cost drivers to avoid these distortions. Selling and distribution costs also are treated as components of product and customer costs. With the foundations of product and customer costing established in Chapters 6 and 7, Chapter 8 illustrates the managerial uses of the information from these systems for strategic decisions, such as short- and long-term pricing and product-mix decisions. Chapter 9 continues the analysis of managerial decisions using cost information to study decisions about processes and activities. Thus Chapter 9 focuses on activity-based management—that is, how managers use managerial accounting information to enhance profitability through improved performance of activities and processes. This chapter integrates management accounting information with organizational improvement initiatives, such as total quality management and cycle time (just-in-time) management.

Chapters 1–9 represent a new approach to teaching management accounting. These chapters derive the demand for managerial accounting information from an integrated treatment of organizational objectives, an orientation to customers, and a focus on activities as the unit of analysis for measurement of cost, quality, and time.

Chapter 10 presents capital budgeting, the process used to acquire long-lived organizational assets. Chapter 11 revisits the fundamental organizational task, introduced in Chapter 2, of how the organization develops goals for multiple stakeholders and implements planning and control systems to enable the organization to achieve its desired goals. Chapter 12 deals with the particular issues arising from the use of financial controls, including responsibility centers and associated performance measurement systems, such as flexible budgets and return-on-investment metrics. The strengths and limitations of financial control systems are discussed. Chapter 13 introduces compensation systems in the context of aligning employees' motivation, incentives, and rewards with overall organizational goals.

Chapter 14 concludes the text by discussing the behavioral aspects of management accounting and control systems. This chapter helps to bring together several important topics related to effective implementation and use of management accounting and control systems. It stresses not just the provision of accurate, timely, and relevant information for managers' decisions and control processes, but also the impact of the design of such systems on managers' motivation and incentives.

The entire text provides a blend of contemporary theory with practical applications and actual company experiences. A supplementary readings book, specifically designed to complement and support *Management Accounting* and described later in the preface, will enable students and instructors to study important issues in greater depth.

EMPHASIS ON REAL-WORLD EXAMPLES

Recognizing that today's students respond best to material drawn from actual events at actual companies, we have made a concerted effort to support our text with examples wherever possible.

The emphasis on actual business settings goes well beyond the use of examples within the textual narrative: The text is also well illustrated with full-color and black-and-white illustrations taken from the annual reports and newsletters of over 150 companies. These photos add to the richness of the text's real-world flavor and emphasize that management accounting information has actual, tangible applications in a variety of workplace settings. These settings cover the spectrum of service and manufacturing companies alike, from Fireman's Fund insurance to McDonnell Douglas aircraft to Magma Copper and on to many, many more businesses.

Consider This . . . features are boxed inserts that focus on a particular point of interest. Some of these features look at current or emerging practices in management accounting, such as ethics in budgeting. Other Consider This . . . boxes offer an insight into an actual company's operations. Management accounting comes alive in these features, which look at AT&T, Photon International Technology, the Pittsburgh Pirates, and scores of other businesses.

The text is supplemented with a set of **videotapes** containing actual footage of operations supplied by Fortune 500 service and manufacturing companies. Videos are also available containing excerpts from a variety of ABC News programs that deal with management accounting topics.

The text is also supplemented on a semi-annual basis by the popular **Themes of the Times** newspaper, which provides important news articles on management accounting topics from *The New York Times*.

SPECIAL FEATURES

Each chapter begins with a set of **Learning Objectives** to give students a preview of what material the chapter covers. These learning objectives appear again in the margins of the text adjacent to where the objectives are first addressed. They serve as a roadmap for the first read and for quick reference in review.

Key terms are displayed in bold-face type when first introduced in the text. Marginal definitions are provided for these key terms, which also serve as a vehicle for student review.

Chapters end with a **Summary**, which reinforces important topics. The **Key Term** list, with the terms referenced to the page where they are defined, follows. We then present the **Assignment Material**, which offers a range of Questions, Exercises, Problems, and Cases.

The end of the book offers a complete glossary and company and subject indexes.

SUPPLEMENTS AND SERVICES FOR THE INSTRUCTOR

The Prentice Hall Accounting and Taxation Hotline. Professors in need of a copy of this text or any supplement may call our toll-free telephone number, 1-800-227-1816 and place an order through Patti Dant, Prentice Hall's Director of Accounting and Taxation Customer Service.

Annotated Instructors Edition with annotations by S. Mark Young. The Annotated Instructors Edition is a special version of the regular textbook enhanced by the addition of Teaching Tips and Points to Stress printed in the margin.

Instructors Manual by S. Mark Young. For each text chapter, this supplement contains a chapter overview, chapter outlines, 10-minute quiz, ties from the text to the *Readings in Management Accounting* supplement, and suggested Harvard Business School cases.

Solutions Manual by Anthony A. Atkinson, Rajiv D. Banker, Robert S. Kaplan, and S. Mark Young. Provides solutions for all questions, exercises, problems, and cases in the text. Each solution has been triple-checked for accuracy.

Solutions Transparencies consist of the solutions for all questions, exercises, problems, and cases in the text on acetate transparencies. Masters of these transparencies can be found in the Solutions Manual.

Test Item File by Rajiv D. Banker, Marvin L. Bouillon, and S. Mark Young. Includes 1100 questions for quizzes and tests. Each chapter of the Test Item File contains about 15 true-false questions, 50 multiple-choice questions, 10 exercises and problems, and 5 essay questions (which require students to use their critical thinking skills).

Prentice Hall Test Manager. This computerized version of the Test Item File allows instructors to create exams by manually or randomly selecting questions. Selection can be done according to question type, level of difficulty, table-based, or previously used questions. The question editing feature allows existing Test Item File questions to be edited or new question to be inserted. Tests can be previewed onscreen before printing and saved to one of the word processing files. The program prints multiple variations of the same test, scrambling the order of questions and multiple choice answers. A comprehensive, fully-indexed desktop reference guide is included, which is easy to use and includes helpful tutorials, illustrations, and examples.

ABC News/Prentice Hall Video Library for Management Accounting. Prentice Hall and ABC News are working together to produce the best and most comprehensive video ancillaries available in the college market. Through its wide variety of award-winning programs—*Nightline, Business World, On Business, This Week with David Brinkley,* and *World News Tonight*—ABC offers a resource for feature and documentary-style videos related to text concepts and applications. The programs have extremely high production quality, present substantial content, and are hosted by well-versed, well-known anchors. The Publisher and the author team have worked together to select videos on topics that will work well in Management Accounting courses and have provided teaching notes on how to use them in the classroom in the special Media Guide supplement.

In addition to the ABC News videos, a special video cassette has been prepared containing company-specific **plant tours** selected from videos provided by hundreds of Fortune 500 service and manufacturing companies. These segments were carefully previewed and edited by the authors to bring actual shop-floor footage into the classroom to support concepts found in the text. Again, teaching notes for these segments can be found in the Media Guide.

Themes of the Times. *The New York Times* and Prentice Hall are sponsoring *Themes of the Times,* a program designed to enhance student access to current information of relevance in the classroom. Through this program, the core subject matter provided in the text is supplemented by a collection of time-sensitive articles from one of the world's most distinguished newspapers, *The New York Times.* These articles demonstrate the vital, ongoing connection between what is learned in the classroom and what is happening in the world around us. Teaching notes offering suggestions on how to bring these articles into the classroom are offered in the Media Guide.

To enjoy the wealth of information of *The New York Times* daily, a reduced subscription rate is available. For information, call toll-free: 1-800-631-1222.

Internet Mailing Lists. For adopters connected to the Internet, we are offering two mailing lists to support the textbook. The first one, ABKYI-L@WATARTS.UWATERLOO.CA, moderated by Anthony Atkinson, will be open only to professors who are using the text in their classrooms. It will provide adopters with a means of asking questions and exchanging ideas. Through this means the authors will provide examples of contemporary practice to illustrate ideas in the text.

The second mailing list, ABKYD-L@WATARTS.UWATERLOO.CA, will be open and unmoderated. It is intended to provide students and other interested parties with a forum to raise and discuss issues and problems related to the topics discussed in the text.

Information about these important services may be obtained through the Prentice Hall Accounting and Taxation Hotline or through your local Prentice Hall representative.

Check Figures. A list of check figures gives key amounts for all exercises, problems, and cases. The check figures are available in quantity for the classroom by contacting the Prentice Hall Accounting and Taxation Hotline.

SUPPLEMENTS FOR THE STUDENT

Study Guide by S. Mark Young. For each chapter in the text, the Study Guide provides a chapter overview, chapter review, and self-test to help students prepare for examinations.

Spreadsheet Templates by Albert Fisher. This software can be used to solve an average of four exercises and problems per chapter. The selected exercises and problems are identified by a diskette icon in the margin of the text and are designed to focus students on learning and applying the accounting concepts discussed in the text chapters. Diskettes are available from the Publisher and can be freely copied for students upon adoption of the textbook.

Readings in Management Accounting by S. Mark Young is a compilation of recent business press and academic articles that parallel the contents of the book and are taken from *The Journal of Cost Management, Management Accounting, The Wall Street Journal, Fortune Magazine, The Harvard Business Review,* and other sources. Each section of the book is introduced to the student with a summary of the articles and their overall contribution to the topic. Each reading concludes with a set of questions designed to provide thought and analysis on the part of the student. In addition, both the Instructors Manual and the Annotated Instructors Edition detail at what juncture each of the articles can be used with the main textbook.

ACKNOWLEDGMENTS

We would like to take this opportunity to thank the many professors who reviewed portions of this textbook at various stages of its development:

Onker Basu	The University of Akron
Jacob Birnberg	University of Pittsburgh
Donald Bostrom	The University of North Dakota
George Gardner	Bemidji State University
Paul Gemmiti	SUNY College at Cobelskill
Edward Goodhart	Shippensburg University

Dolan Hinson	The University of North Carolina at Charlotte
Fred Jacobs	Michigan State University
Zafar Khan	Eastern Michigan University
Leslie Kren	The University of Wisconsin at Milwaukee
Alan Larris	The University of Akron
Robert Lin	California State University at Hayward
Frank Lordi	Widener University
Kenneth Merchant	University of Southern California
Gerald Myers	Pacific Lutheran University
Richard Rivers	Southern Illinois University at Carbondale
Michael Shields	University of Memphis
Kimberly Smith	The College of William and Mary
Donn Vickery	The University of San Diego
Joseph Weintrop	Baruch College of the City University of New York

We would also like to thank the following professors for class-testing prepublication versions of this textbook and providing many valuable suggestions:

Felix Amenkhienan	Radford University
Hsihui Chang	National Chengchi University
Timothy Farmer	The University of Missouri at St. Louis
Sanford Gunn	The State University of New York at Buffalo
Scott Jones	The University of Delaware
Debra Hua Lu	St. Cloud State University
Gerald Myers	Pacific Lutheran University
Linda Staniszewski	The University of Southern Mississippi
Scott Stovall	Harding University
Audrey Taylor	Wayne State University

We want to express our sincere thanks and appreciation to the many people at Prentice Hall who provided invaluable assistance to us during this project. Joe Heider provided the initial encouragement to develop the ideas and format in this book. Bill Webber skillfully managed the difficult coordination activities needed to produce a multiauthor text that included many forms of material contributed by many different organizations. Stephen Deitmer's skills in keeping track of all the development material and guiding it through the production process amazed us all and earned our profound gratitude. Linda Pawelchak, Leslye Givarz, and JaNoel Lowe made invaluable editorial suggestions that improved the clarity of the manuscript. We are also grateful to Linda Albelli, Suzanne Behnke, John Chillingworth, Patti Dant, Diane deCastro, Linda Fiordilino, Patrice Fraccio, David Gillespie, Dan Griffin, Amy Hinton, Vincent Scelta, Lori Morris-Nantz, Chris Pullo, Melinda Reo, Sandy Steiner, Natasha St. Hill, Penny Linskey, and Joyce Turner for the many contributions each made to this book.

We are grateful to the following organizations that provided material we used to develop the examples used in this text: Abbott Laboratories; Alberto-Culver Company; Allegheny Ludlum Corporation; Allied-Signal Inc.; AM International; Amdahl; Amerada Hess Corporation; American Greetings Corporation; American Home Products Corporation; AMETEK, Inc.; Amoco Corporation; Amoskeag Company; Anacomp, Inc.; Anheuser-Busch Companies, Inc.; Archer Daniels Midland Company; Arco; Aristech Chemical Corporation; ARMCO Inc.; Armstrong World Industries, Inc,; Ashland Oil, Inc.; Avondale Industries, Inc.; Baker Hughes Incorporated; Ball Corporation; Bausch & Lomb Incorporated; Bayer USA Inc.; Becton Dickinson and Company; Bethlehem Steel Corporation; The Black & Decker Corporation; The Boeing Company; Boise Cascade Corporation; Borden, Inc.; Bowater Incorporated; Briggs & Stratton Corporation; Brunswick Corporation; Cabot Corporation; Carlisle Companies Incorporated; Central Soya Company.; CertainTeed Corporation; Chemed Corporation; Chrysler Corporation; Cincinnati Milacron; The Coca-Cola Company; Coca-Cola Enterprises Inc.; Colgate Palmolive Company; Commerce Clearing House, Inc.; Compaq Computer Corporation; ConAgra, Inc.; Conner Peripherals; Consolidated Papers, Inc.; Control Data; Cooper Industries; Coors Brewing Company; Corning Incorporated; The Coastal Corporation; CPC International Inc.; Crown Cork & Seal Company, Inc.; Cummins Engine Company Inc.; Cyprus Minerals Company; Data General Corporation; Deere & Company; Deluxe Corporation; The Dexter Corporation; R.R. Donnelley & Sons Company; Doskocil Companies Inc.; Dover Corporation; Dow Chemical Company; Dow Corning Corporation; Eaton Corporation; Echlin; EG&G Inc.; Emerson Electric Co.; Federal-Mogul Corporation; Ferro Corporation; First Brands Corporation; Flowers Industries, Inc.; Ford Motor Company; Freeport-McMoRan Inc.; Gannett Co., Inc.; GenCorp, Inc.; General Dynamics Corporation; General Electric Company; General Mills, Inc.; General Motors Corporation; General Signal Corporation; Georgia Gulf Corporation; Georgia-Pacific Corporation; The Gillette Company; Gitano Group, Inc.; P.H. Glatfelter Company; The Goodyear Tire & Rubber Company; W.R. Grace & Company; Harley-Davidson, Inc.; Harris Corporation; Harsco Corporation; M.A. Hanna Company; H.J. Heinz Company; Helene Curtis, Inc.; The Henley Group, Inc.; Hercules Incorporated; Hershey Foods Corporation; Hewlett-Packard Company; Hillenbrand Industries; Hoechst Celanese; Hubbell Incorporated; Hudson Foods, Inc.; Illinois Tool Works Inc.; IMC Fertilizer Group, Inc.; IMCERA Group Inc.; Interco Incorporated; Interface Inc.; Intergraph Corporation; International Business Machines Corporation; International Multifoods Corporation; J&L Specialty Products Corporation; Johnson Controls, Inc.; Johnson & Johnson; Jostens, Inc.; Kaman Corporation; Kerr-McGee Corporation; Kimball International, Inc.; Kimberly-Clark Corporation; Kellwood Company; Eastman Kodak Company; Lafarge Corporation; The Leslie Fay Companies Inc.; Lockheed Corporation; Lone Star Technologies, Inc.; Longview Fibre Company; The Louisiana Land and Exploration Company; Louisiana-Pacific Corporation; Lukens Inc.; Lyondell Petrochemical Company; Magma Copper Company; MagneTek, Inc.; MAPCO Inc.; Martin Marietta Corporation; Masco Corporation; Masco Industries; Matel, Inc.; Maytag Corporation; McCormick & Company, Incorporated;

Mcdonnell Douglas Corporation; The Mead Corporation; Media General, Inc.; Medtronic, Inc.; Merck & Co., Inc.; Meredith Corporation; Millipore; Minnesota Mining and Manufacturing Company; Mitchell Energy & Development Corp.; Mobil Corporation; Molex Incorporated; Morton International; NACCO Industries, Inc.; Nalco Chemical Company; National Gypsum Company; NCR Corporation; NERCO, Inc.; Newmont Mining Corporation; Nortek, Inc.; North American Philips Corporation; Ocean Spray Cranberries, Inc.; Olin Corporation; Outboard Marine Corporation; Owens/Corning Fiberglas; Paccar; Pentair, Inc.; The Perkin-Elmer Corporation; Pennzoil Company; Phelps Dodge Corporation; Philip Morris Companies Inc.; Phillips Petroleum Company; Pitney Bowes; Polaroid Corporation; Pope & Talbot, Inc.; Potlatch Corporation; PPG Industries, Inc.; Premark International, Inc.; The Procter & Gamble Company; Quaker State Corporation; Ralston Purina Company; Raytheon Company; The Reader's Digest Association, Inc.; Reliance Electric Company; Reynolds Metals Company; Rexene Corporation; Rockwell International Corporation; Savannah Foods & Industries, Inc.; Sara Lee Corporation; Schering-Plough Corporation; The Seagram Company Ltd.; Sequa Corporation; Shell Oil Company; The Sherwin-Williams Company; A.O. Smith Corporation; Snap-on Tools Corporation; Southdown, Inc.; SPX Corporation; St. Joe Paper Company; Standard Commercial Corporation; The Standard Products Company; The Stanley Works; Storage Technology Corporation; Sun-Diamond Growers of California; Tambrands Inc.; Tandem Computers Incorporated; Tecumseh Products Company; Texas Instruments Incorporated; Thermo Electron Corporation; Thomas & Betts Corporation; Time Warner Inc.; Tosco Corporation; Tredegar Industries; Tri Valley Growers; Tribune Company; Tyco Laboratories, Inc.; Tyler Corporation; Unilever; Union Camp Corporation; Universal Corporation; Universal Foods Corporation; Unisys Corporation; Unocal Corporation; The Upjohn Company; USG Corporation; Valero Energy Corporation; Varian Associates, Inc.; Vulcan Materials Company; Wang Laboratories, Inc.; Warner-Lambert Company; The Washington Post Company; Weirton Steel Corporation; Western Digital Corporation; Western Publishing Group, Inc.; Westinghouse Electric Corporation; Westvaco Corporation; Wheelabrator Technologies Inc.; Wheeling-Pittsburgh Corporation; Whirlpool Corporation; Wickes Companies, Inc.; Witco Corporation; Worthington Industries; Wm. Wrigley Jr. Company; Xerox Corporation; Zenith Electronics Corporation.

Many organizations provided us with photographs and those are acknowledged specifically in the text. Other organizations provided us with videos of plant tours and these organizations are acknowledged in the video guide.

ANTHONY A. ATKINSON

is currently Deloitte & Touche Professor and Management Accounting Area Head at the University of Waterloo. Atkinson received a Bachelor of Commerce and M.B.A. degrees from Queen's University in Kingston, Ontario, M.S. and Ph.D. in Industrial Administration degrees from Carnegie-Mellon University in Pittsburgh, and the designation of Certified Management Accountant in Nova Scotia. He has written or co-authored a text, five monographs, and over 30 articles on performance measurement and costing. In 1989, the Canadian Academic Accounting Association awarded Atkinson the Haim Falk Prize for Distinguished Contribution to Accounting Thought for his monograph that studied transfer pricing practice in six Canadian companies. He has served on the editorial boards of two professional and five academic journals and has been a member of the Canadian government's Cost Standards Advisory Committee, for which he developed the costing principles it now requires of government contractors.

RAJIV D. BANKER

is the Arthur Anderson & Co./Duane R. Kullberg Chair in Accounting and Information Systems at the Carlson School of Management, University of Minnesota. Banker graduated from the University of Bombay at the top of his class and received a doctorate in business administration from Harvard University. He received two awards for teaching excellence at Carnegie Mellon University and the Outstanding Teacher Award at the University of Minnesota.

Banker has published more than 70 articles in leading research journals in accounting, information systems, computer science, operations management, management science, and economics, including articles in the *Accounting Review, Journal of Accounting and Economics,* and the *Journal of Accounting Research.* He has received three awards for his research articles. Banker's current research in management accounting includes issues pertaining to strategic cost management, activity-based costing, costs of quality, and value of performance-based incentive plans, among other issues. His research is supported by the National Science Foundation, the Institute of Management Accountants, and several leading corporations.

ROBERT S. KAPLAN

is the Arthur Lowes Dickinson Professor of Accounting at the Harvard Business School. Formerly, he was on the faculty of the Graduate School of Industrial Administration at Carnegie Mellon University and served as Dean of that school from 1977 to 1983. He received a B.S. and M.S. in Electrical Engineering from MIT and a Ph.D. in Operations Research from Cornell University. Author of more than 90 papers, Kaplan received the Outstanding Accounting Educator Award in 1988 from the American Accounting Association (AAA). He also received the 1987 AICPA/AAA Notable Contributions to Accounting Literature Award for his Accounting Review paper, "Measuring Manufacturing Performance," the 1984 McKinsey Award for "Yesterday's Accounting Undermines Production," in the *Harvard Business Review*, and the AICPA Accounting Literature Award in 1971.

Kaplan consults on the design of performance and cost management systems with many leading companies in North America and Europe.

S. MARK YOUNG,

Associate Professor at the School of Accounting at the University of Accounting at the University of Southern California, is Associate Editor of *The Accounting Review*, the major research journal of the American Accounting Association. Young received an A.B. from Oberlin College, an M. Acc. from Ohio State University, and a Ph.D. from the University of Pittsburgh. He is the recipient of four outstanding teaching awards at the undergraduate and graduate levels, including the 1994 Golden Apple teaching award from the MBA Program at USC. He has published over 30 papers and presented many research papers in Europe, Asia, Australia, and the United States. Young has been a KPMG Peat Marwick faculty fellow and has received research grants from the National Science Foundation and the Consortium for Advanced Manufacturing International. For a paper co-authored with Frank Selto, Young won the Management Accounting Association's (AAA) Notable Contribution to the Literature Award for 1994.

MANAGEMENT ACCOUNTING: INFORMATION THAT CREATES VALUE

LEARNING OBJECTIVES

This chapter will introduce you to:

1. the role for management accounting information in organizations

2. the differences between management accounting and financial accounting

3. career opportunities for those who study management accounting

4. the different demands for management accounting information for different people in the organization

5. the reasons that management accounting information includes both financial and nonfinancial information

6. historical and contemporary views of how management accounting creates value for organizations: its relation to operations, marketing, and strategy

7. the role for management accounting in service organizations

8. the importance of understanding activities as the primary focus for measuring and managing performance

Beck's Motors: How to Supply Good Management Accounting Information

Pete Littleton, an employee in a local public accounting firm, was interviewing for a new job as a management accountant at Beck's Motors, a large automobile dealership in Gotham City. Barry Beck, founder and president, had spent several hours explaining to Pete why his company now needed a management accountant:

> I started out as an automobile mechanic. After gaining some experience, I wanted to work for myself, so I opened my own garage, repairing cars with expired warranties. Then I branched out and bought used cars from customers and auctions, made needed repairs, and advertised and sold them. Because of my reputation for high-quality repairs and ethical business dealings, my business flourished. When a local dealership for Worldwide Motors became available, I applied and was awarded the franchise.

> My business is now a lot more complex than when I was just repairing cars or even when I started out selling used cars. I now have nearly 50 employees, working in four major business divisions: new car sales, used car sales, car repairs and service, and parts sales. The financial statements at the end of the year indicate that I am making some money, but I don't know which aspects of my business are generating the income. Some expenses are easy to trace to one of the four business lines, but we have a lot of common expenses for the dealership, like the building, parking lot, telecommunications, administrative staff, and computing. If I understood the economics of the business better, I would be able to decide which aspects I should expand and which areas require my attention for improvement. It's not as easy as it seems. Most of our new car sales require that we take a used car as a trade-in. Before we can resell many of these used cars, we have to repair them, which often includes installing new parts. I don't know how much each of our business divisions contributed to the profitability of this entire transaction.

(© Mark Richards)

3

The total profit eventually reaches our income statement, but that doesn't help me evaluate and reward the performance of my employees in each of the four business divisions.

I would also like to know which of my managers are doing a good job and who needs to make significant improvements. And the managers keep telling me that they need better information to understand which of their employees are most efficient and effective. Ideally, I would like to have information provided to every employee in the dealership that would help them understand how what they do contributes to the overall success of the dealership. Just showing them an annual income statement for Beck's Motors won't tell them how they are contributing to our overall success and whether they are improving in their job performance.

Your job, should you decide to accept it, will be to design management accounting systems that will help me and everyone else at Beck's Motors understand how they are contributing to the overall success of the company, and how they can do their jobs even better.

Pete Littleton wondered whether his previous training and experience had prepared him for the challenging tasks Barry Beck had presented to him.

Management accounting system
An information system that collects operational and financial data, processes it, stores it, and reports it to users (workers, managers, executives).

Management accounting information
Output from a management accounting system (e.g., calculated cost of a product, an activity, or a department in a recent time period).

Management accounting
The process of producing financial and operating information for organizational employees and managers. The process should be driven by the informational needs of individuals *internal* to the organization and should guide their operating and investment decisions.

OBJECTIVE 1.1
The role for management accounting information in organizations

The challenges Pete Littleton faces will lead him to examine what the term *management accounting* means and how management accounting information can improve decisions and management controls in organizations. This book has been created to inform students about the design of **management accounting systems.** These are systems that collect, process, store, and report operational and financial information for a variety of vital operational and managerial decisions.

MANAGEMENT ACCOUNTING INFORMATION

The **management accounting information** produced by a management accounting system can include, for example, the expenses incurred in an operating department or the calculated cost of a product, service, or activity. Management accounting information is one of the primary informational sources for organizations. **Management accounting** produces information that helps workers, managers, and executives in organizations make better decisions (see Appendix 1A for a comprehensive definition and description of management accounting). Traditionally, management accounting information has been financial; that is, it has been denominated in a currency such as dollars or deutschmarks, but the domain of management accounting increasingly has expanded to encompass operational or physical (nonfinancial) information, such as quality and process times, as well.

Measures of the *economic condition* of the enterprise—the cost and profitability of the organization's products, services, customers, and activities—

The role of management accountants is to provide decision makers at all levels of the organization help with the information they need to discharge their assigned responsibilities. This help can include developing, gathering, and interpreting the information. *(Courtesy Impact Images)*

are available only from management accounting systems. Management accounting information also measures the *economic performance* of decentralized operating units, such as business units, divisions, and departments. These measures of economic performance provide a linkage between the strategy of the organization and the execution of the strategy by individual operating units. Management accounting information is also one of the primary means by which operators/workers, middle managers, and executives receive *feedback* on their performance, enabling them to learn from the past and to improve in the future.

Ultimately, organizations will succeed and prosper by designing products and services that customers value, producing these products and services and distributing them to customers with efficient operating processes, and marketing and selling the organization's outputs effectively to customers. Although management accounting information cannot guarantee success in these critical organizational activities, inadequate and distorted signals from management accounting systems will cause companies to encounter severe difficulties. Effective management accounting systems can create considerable value by providing timely and accurate information about the activities that are required for the success of today's organizations.

MANAGEMENT ACCOUNTING: DIFFERENT FROM FINANCIAL ACCOUNTING

Many students using this book already will have taken a financial accounting course. **Financial accounting** deals with reporting and communicating economic information about an organization to *external* constituencies: shareholders, creditors (such as bankers and bondholders), regulators, and governmental tax authorities. Financial accounting information communi-

Financial accounting
The process of producing financial statements for external constituencies, such as shareholders, creditors, and governmental authorities. This process is heavily constrained by standard-setting, regulatory, and tax authorities and the auditing requirements of independent accountants (contrast with management accounting).

OBJECTIVE 1.2
The differences between
management accounting
and financial accounting

cates to outsiders the consequences of the decisions and process improvements made by managers and employees. The financial accounting process is constrained by external regulatory authorities, such as the Financial Accounting Standards Board (FASB) and the Securities and Exchange Commission (SEC) in the United States, and by governmental tax agencies. As a consequence, financial accounting tends to be rule driven, and students of financial accounting study the journal entries that generate the mandated financial statements.

In contrast, management accounting deals with providing economic information to *internal* constituencies: operators/workers, middle managers, and senior executives. Companies have great discretion in the design of their management accounting systems. These systems should be designed to provide information that helps an organization's employees make good decisions about products, processes, and customers. The information from management accounting systems also should help employees learn how to improve the quality, lower the cost, and increase the responsiveness of their operations for customer needs. Therefore, management accounting students have to learn about the decisions and informational needs of organizational participants, not about rules and journal entries. Exhibit 1–1 provides an overview of the basic features of financial and management accounting.

From this brief description, it may seem logical that the accounting process should start by determining the information needed for internal purposes and then consider how to explain and aggregate the economic impact

EXHIBIT 1–1
Financial and Management Accounting: Basic Features

	FINANCIAL ACCOUNTING	MANAGERIAL ACCOUNTING
AUDIENCE	External: Stockholders, creditors, tax authorities	Internal: Workers, managers, executives
PURPOSE	Report on past performance to external parties; contracts with owners and lenders	Inform internal decisions made by employees and managers; feedback and control on operating performance
TIMELINESS	Delayed; historical	Current, future oriented
RESTRICTIONS	Regulated; rules driven by generally accepted accounting principles and government authorities	No regulations; systems and information determined by management to meet strategic and operational needs
TYPE OF INFORMATION	Financial measurements only	Financial, plus operational and physical measurements on processes, technologies, suppliers, customers, and competitors
NATURE OF INFORMATION	Objective, auditable, reliable, consistent, precise	More subjective and judgmental; valid, relevant, accurate
SCOPE	Highly aggregate; report on entire organization	Disaggregate; inform local decisions and actions

of internal decisions for external constituencies. Indeed, in the 19th century, companies' accounting systems were designed to meet the decision-making and control needs of managers (see Consider This . . . Management Accounting in 19th-Century Enterprises). During the past century, however, accounting for external constituencies became quite demanding because of external regulations (from the FASB and SEC) and shareholder and creditor expectations, so many organizations reversed their prior emphasis on developing information for internal purposes and switched to place external demands as the highest priority. *This book,* however, *will focus exclusively on the production and interpretation of information for internal purposes.* The practices described in this book derive only from the information and decision needs of an organization's employees.

WHO SHOULD STUDY MANAGEMENT ACCOUNTING?

Several audiences will find the study of management accounting principles to be interesting and valuable. First, obviously, are individuals who expect to become management accountants. Historically, public practice with professional accounting and auditing firms was the "glamour field" for accounting students. Now, the challenging new environment for manufacturing, service, not-for-profit, and governmental organizations has created exciting opportunities for management accountants. Until quite recently, financial people in organizations played staff roles. They were scorekeepers, sitting apart from the action, making sure that the organization's records complied with external regulatory procedures. They also issued periodic retrospective reports on internal operations.

Today's competitive environment enables management accountants to become part of the organization's value-added team to participate in the process of strategy formulation and implementation, to translate strategic intent into operational and managerial measures, and to move away from merely being the caretaker of data to the designer of the organization's critical management information systems. For individuals aspiring for an initial career in management accounting, this book will provide a valuable perspective on the various ways in which the measures and information they produce can create value in organizations.

OBJECTIVE 1.3
Career opportunities for those who study management accounting

Scientists and engineers also will find the study of management accounting valuable. The work of technical people in organizations will be monitored, evaluated, and informed by management accounting information. Management accounting information will measure the impact and success of engineers' and scientists' product and process designs. Investment in new products, new projects, and new equipment will be viewed through the lens of the organization's management accounting system. Knowing the rules of the measurement game and being able to understand and explain when organizational management accounting systems are hindering the company's goal for technological excellence and innovation will be powerful assets for technologists.

The third, and perhaps most important, audience consists of the individuals who expect to become managers, either general managers who run organizations or the leaders of staff positions, such as market research,

CONSIDER THIS . . .

Management Accounting in 19th-Century Enterprises

TEXTILE INDUSTRY   The demand for management accounting information can be traced back to the early stages of the industrial revolution—in textile mills, in armories that built weapons, and in other manufacturing operations. In these organizations, workers were hired by owners to perform various tasks in the manufacturing process. The owners developed managerial accounting information, such as the cost per yard of woven cotton, both to control the work performed by the hired workers and to inform pricing and product mix decisions. For example, records of early 19th century textile mills show that mill managers received information about the hourly cost of converting raw material (cotton) into intermediate products (thread and yarn) and finished products (fabric) and the cost per pound of output by departments and for each worker. This information enabled the manager to assess the efficiency with which raw cotton was being converted into finished yarn and fabric. The cost information, for operational control, enabled managers to compare productivity among workers and to track the productivity of individual workers over several periods of time.

Such information could be used to provide additional compensation for the most productive workers and to serve as targets that less productive workers could be encouraged to achieve. The cost information helped managers evaluate the efficiency of internal processes, to make sure that efficiencies were maintained and improved, and to signal where additional purchases of machinery might be worthwhile. The cost information, for product costing and profitability purposes, was used to set piecework wages for the workers and to establish target prices for selling fabric or yarn, particu-larly for items that were specialized and customized for individual orders.

RAILROAD INDUSTRY   Railroad organizations developed in the United States in the mid-19th century. These were enormous and complex enterprises that could not have functioned effectively without extensive management accounting information to provide summary measures of performance for decentralized and dispersed managers. These measures enabled the local managers to take actions, based on the unique information they had about local conditions, that were consistent with maximizing the economic performance (that is, profits) of the entire railroad. The railroads developed measures such as cost per ton-mile for individual commodity types and for each geographic segment of operations. The operating ratio, the ratio of operating expenses to revenues, was developed both for operational control—to evaluate the efficiency of operations of local managers—and for product costing—to measure the profitability of various types of business—passenger versus freight, region by region.

OTHER INDUSTRIES: RETAIL, STEEL, MACHINE TOOLS   Other 19th-century enterprises also developed specific management accounting information to guide their productivity activities and to assist product-related decisions. Retail organizations, such as Marshall Field, Sears Roebuck, and Woolworth, measured *gross margin* (selling revenues less purchase and operating costs) of merchandise by department to measure the profitability of individual lines of business, and *inventory stock turns* (the ratio of annual cost of sales to average inventory levels) to assess capital

investment analysis, human resource management, research and development, information systems, and strategic planning. These individuals will benefit from a modern management accounting course by helping them understand the active role they must play in demanding excellence from their organization's management accounting systems. Managers must understand that the design of management accounting systems is too important to be left solely to management accountants. For many years, nonfinancial managers were intimidated by the professional training and certification of the accounting people. The nonfinancial managers were passive consumers of the

Many costing tools used in management accounting today were developed in the middle to late 19th century by the people who managed railroad operations and who used detailed cost information to monitor operations and to quote prices to potential customers. The goal of using this information was to help the railroad improve its profitability. *(The Bettmann Archive)*

efficiency. The gross margin and stock turn information guided the managers' decisions about which type of merchandise generated the highest profitability and signaled when particular lines of merchandise needed to have higher prices, lower purchase costs, or more rapid sales turnover to reach company standards. Steel mills, such as those owned and operated by Andrew Carnegie, measured daily the cost of material, labor, and energy inputs used to produce steel and rails. Carnegie used the cost information to evaluate the performance of department managers, foremen, and workers and to check the quality and mix of raw materials, the operational control function. The cost information also was used to evaluate improvements in processes and products. For nonstandardized products,

such as steel for bridges, the cost information was the basis for pricing decisions. The company would not accept a contract unless it had a careful analysis and estimate of the costs involved.

Companies in the 19th century that manufactured discrete items, such as machine tools, had to understand the costs of resources used to produce each item. This information was needed to determine the profitability of producing different product lines and to help determine the prices that would be offered, particularly for customized products, to prospective customers.

Engineers in the scientific management movement, such as Frederick Taylor, developed procedures to measure in considerable detail the quantity of materials and the labor and machine time required to manufacture individual products. This information was collected primarily to improve and control the efficiency of production operations but also served as an input to product costing calculations. The work of the scientific management engineers was the origin of standard cost systems in which the costs of direct materials, direct labor, and factory overhead (such as the costs of purchasing, materials handling, quality control, maintenance, and scheduling departments) were assigned to individual products. The costing techniques developed at this time persisted for many decades and still can be found in many of today's organizations.

A major theme of this book will be to introduce some newly developed ideas in product costing that are more relevant for today's production environment than the procedures that were designed for and worked well in the early part of the 20th century.

Source: This section draws on material in Chapters 2 and 3 of H. Thomas Johnson and Robert S. Kaplan, *Relevance Lost: The Rise and Fall of Management Accounting* (Boston: Harvard Business School Press, 1987).

information produced by their organization's accounting system. While recognizing that the information was generally late, reported at too aggregate a level, plagued with arbitrary allocations, and frequently distorted,[1] it was the only accounting system they had, and they had learned to live with it. They expressed their feelings toward their accounting system by describing it as "a system designed by accountants for accountants."

[1] We will describe these limitations of traditional management accounting systems later in this chapter.

Competitive challenges today make such passivity dangerous to the enterprise. Management accounting systems must function effectively for managers, not for their accounting staff. Managers should learn how management accounting systems can provide timely, accurate, and relevant information for them and should insist that their management accounting staff redesign systems that do not meet these criteria. Thus, this book is intended for general and staff managers, for engineers and scientists, and for individuals aspiring to become management accounting professionals.

DIVERSITY OF MANAGEMENT ACCOUNTING INFORMATION

We can illustrate the diverse uses for management accounting information with a relatively simple example. Consider the operation of an automobile dealership. Who uses operational and financial information in this type of organization?

■ Automotive Repair Mechanic—Description of Task and Information Needs

Dennis Mitchell is an automobile mechanic who repairs and maintains cars. Dennis performs many standard activities for which much prior knowledge already exists; for example, he frequently replaces brakes, installs a new muffler or exhaust system, lubricates the car, changes the oil and oil filter, or performs a tune-up. These tasks have been done thousands of times before by mechanics at this dealership and at auto repair facilities all over the world. Thus, standards probably exist for the amount of time Dennis should take to perform each of these tasks as well as for the quantity of materials and supplies required for the maintenance or repair. Since Dennis's efficiency in performing maintenance and repairs is evaluated after each job, we may want to provide him with information on the actual time he required and the actual parts and materials he used so that he can determine whether he is performing at the normal efficiency assumed in establishing the standards for this activity. In addition to the materials and labor time input, some repair jobs may require that the automobile be tested on specialized equipment or that special equipment be used to help in the repair itself. Dennis will find it helpful to know how much time each job required on specialized equipment.

Dennis is frequently asked to do some nonstandard work, for example, to fix an engine that is not working when the cause for the malfunction has not yet been determined. Or he may be repairing a car that has suffered considerable damage in an accident. In these cases, the full extent of the damage and required repairs are not known until he starts working on the car. Dennis will record how much time he actually spent on the job as well as the quantity and identity of parts and materials he used to bring the car back into working condition. This information will be used to determine the price charged to the customer for the nonstandard repairs.

After Dennis finishes a maintenance or repair procedure, he performs a quality check by starting the car and testing whether it runs properly. If he finds a defect, he replaces the faulty part (either a bad part or a badly installed

Paper moves through a modern paper machine at about 14 meters per second. Tiny holes in the web of paper can create costly problems. Mead Corporation, a paper maker, designed a computer-based artificial intelligence system that uses 1,200 sensing devices and computer systems to control some 750 process variables in paper making. *(Courtesy William Taufic)*

part) and continues to work on the car until all detected defects have been eliminated.

INFORMATIONAL SUMMARY FOR OPERATORS   Let us summarize the information generated for Dennis Mitchell, the employee who produces the service. The information includes data on the quantity of materials, supplies, and labor and on the amount of machine time he used to produce the service. It also includes data on the quantity of outputs he produced (the number of repair jobs completed). Finally, it includes quality information, such as the proportion of repairs successfully completed without additional rework or the number of defects detected while producing the service.

At this simple level, we can see the role for a wide variety of quantitative information for employees such as Dennis Mitchell, but so far not much of a role for financial information. This is typical of traditional organizations. Employees and operators have been directed to perform prescribed tasks; they can be given quantitative summaries of their performance but are told little about the economic or financial consequences of the work they perform. We will return to this issue later, but, for now, let us assume that *production and service workers primarily need operational, not financial, data.*

INFORMATIONAL FREQUENCY FOR OPERATORS   In addition to the amount and type of information provided to Dennis, what frequency of information will be most useful to him? He is not likely to think it very useful to get only a monthly report that provides summary and aggregate information about (1) total parts and materials used in car repairs; (2) total time used during the month to repair cars, including both actual time and the difference between actual and standard times allowed for the repairs; and (3) total time spent reworking defects during the month. He will find it difficult to relate such a *highly aggregated* and *delayed* report to each of the repair jobs he performed during the month. Dennis, like other employees who produce outputs such as repaired cars continually throughout the day, needs daily, or even individual, job summaries for learning how well he is performing and where opportunities for improvement may exist.

To summarize, at the operational level, the relevant information will be *accurate quantitative* information about inputs used (labor and machine time, parts and supplies), outputs produced, and the *quality* of the service or production process. The information should be *timely,* which means daily or after each job, so that any discrepancies from standard or historical records can be noted at the time. Operators have little apparent need for financial or cost data.

■ Manager of the Automotive Service Department— Description of Task and Information Needs

Consider now the information needs of Jennifer Green, the manager of the service department. Jennifer supervises the two dozen mechanics who work in the department and is also responsible for the service representatives who discuss proposed maintenance and repairs with customers and who return repaired cars to them.

Jennifer will be interested in information about the use of the service department's resources. Since mechanics are paid for an 8-hour shift, whether they are working on jobs or not, she will want a report that compares hours actually spent repairing and maintaining cars with the hours for which mechanics are paid. This will help her to see whether the department currently has unused capacity or whether it is operating at full capacity. If productive work is consistently below *capacity,* Jennifer can consider reducing the size of the service department; if the department is consistently working at capacity, she can contemplate adding additional resources, such as extra mechanics and another service bay, to handle the higher demand. To assess the *efficiency* of the mechanics, as measured by the quantity of resources used for maintenance and repairs, she may want to compare the actual labor times, machine times, and quantity of materials and supplies used on individual jobs to the standards established for those jobs. She will want to determine which mechanics are working more efficiently than others to accomplish a given type and amount of work and which are using more resources than expected. She also will monitor the *quality* of the work performed—which jobs or mechanics are generating defects, rework, and customer complaints.

In addition to monitoring *capacity use, efficiency,* and *quality* of work performed, Jennifer may need information on the *profitability* of the service operation. She will receive a weekly or monthly report on the profit or loss generated by the service department. In addition to this aggregate report, she may want a report on the profitability according to the type of service performed, such as muffler repairs, tune-ups, oil changes, and brake replacements. This report requires an accurate linkage of total service department costs with the revenues generated by individual service jobs. Jennifer can use the information on this report to modify prices, to choose an appropriate product mix— perhaps certain jobs can be performed more efficiently by subcontracting to local mechanics in the area rather than being handled internally—and to establish marketing and promotion policies to attract more maintenance and repair business to the service department. If certain types of jobs appear to be losing money, Jennifer can work with the mechanics to see how these jobs can be performed at lower cost.

Jennifer also needs to know the accurate cost for each of the repair services since she may be asked to estimate repair costs for used cars that the auto dealership acquires as trade-ins when customers purchase new cars. Cost information also helps Jennifer make decisions about whether to acquire additional equipment to enable existing jobs to be performed using less mechanic time or to allow mechanics to perform certain jobs that are not possible currently with existing equipment. In summary, Jennifer will use information on the cost of individual types of maintenance and repair jobs to inform her decisions on *pricing*, *product mix* (which repair jobs are more profitable to promote), *capacity expansion* (adding service bays, mechanics, or new equipment), *contraction* (reducing the number of mechanics), *outsourcing* (contracting with local repair shops for certain types of service work rather than doing this work internally), *process improvement* (performing service jobs faster and using fewer supplies and materials), and *bidding* for new business. These all represent important decisions made by middle- and upper-level managers in organizations that require accurate economic (financial) information about current and future operations.

■ Manager of the Automobile Dealership— Description of Task and Information Needs

Barry Beck is the president of Beck's Motors, the auto dealership where Dennis Mitchell and Jennifer Green are employed. Barry is obviously concerned with the overall profitability of the dealership but has less need than Dennis or Jennifer for information to monitor hourly and daily operations or the profit and loss on individual jobs and car sales. Barry receives a monthly, perhaps weekly, report on the dealership profitability, broken down by its major operating departments: new car sales, used car sales, car repairs and service, and parts sales. This report requires a reasonable assignment of dealer expenses to the individual operating departments; that is, how much of Beck Motor's people, building, and equipment resources are devoted to the various lines of business: new car sales, fleet sales, used car sales, repairs and service, and sales of parts. Barry also will want to see financial and operating statistics on **critical success factors,** that is, those factors that indicate whether the organization is creating long-term value and profitability. For example, critical success factors include the number of cars sold and the margins on car sales by type of vehicle, revenue per employee in the service department, customer satisfaction indexes, and number of customer complaints. This information will enable Barry to monitor whether any operating department is falling short of its profit plan. It will highlight the likely causes for unexpected shifts in profitability, such as variations in volume, mix, quality, and pricing. Barry also will want to compare the performance of his dealership with that of similar dealerships in terms of volume, efficiency, and profitability. This creates a demand for external data about the best practices of competitors or other

Critical success factors
The elements, such as quality, time, cost reduction, customer service, or product performance, that create long-term profitability for the organization.

Benchmarking
Studying how other best-performing organizations, either internal or external to the firm, perform similar activities and processes.

Strategic information
Information that guides the long-term decision making of the organization. Strategic information can include the profitability of products, services, and customers; competitor behavior; customer preferences and trends; market opportunities and threats; and technological innovations.

Operational control
The process of providing feedback to employees and their managers about the efficiency of activities being performed.

Product costing
The process of measuring and assigning the costs of the activities performed to design and produce individual products (and services, for nonmanufacturing companies).

Customer costing
The process of assigning marketing, selling, distribution, and administrative costs to individual customers so that the cost of serving each customer can be calculated.

Management control
The process of providing information about the performance of managers and operating units.

Operations-level employees in continuous process industries like steelmaking use detailed real-time information to control the process. In the background of this picture, an operator in the cold mill at Armco Incorporated's Butler Works is using real-time, computer-based information to control the ongoing production process in the mill. The supervisors in the foreground of this picture, whose role is to evaluate and suggest improvements in the mill's operations, rely on summarized production and cost information about the mill's activities. (*Courtesy Armco Incorporated*)

comparable organizations, a practice now referred to as **benchmarking.** The information used by a senior executive like Barry Beck—the profitability of products, services, and customers; market opportunities and competitive threats; and technological innovations—are examples of **strategic information,** information that is critical for informing and guiding the decisions of a company's senior executives.

FUNCTIONS OF MANAGEMENT ACCOUNTING

The automobile dealership example illustrates several important principles of management accounting information. First, management accounting information serves several functions—**operational control, product costing, customer costing,** and **management control**—as shown in Exhibit 1–2.

The demand for management accounting information differs, depending on the level of the organization. At the operator level, where raw materials or purchased parts are converted into finished products and where services are performed for customers, information is needed primarily to control and improve operations. The information is disaggregate and frequent; it is more physical and operational than financial and economic. As one moves higher in the organization, where work is supervised and where decisions about products, services, and customers are made, information may be received less frequently and is more aggregate and strategic. It is used more to give an overall picture of the organization, to provide a broader understanding of the entity, and to send a warning signal if some aspect of operations is different from expectations.

The information at higher organizational levels summarizes transactions and events that occur at the individual operator or customer level. At these levels, more financial information is used so that managers can assess the economics of events occurring at the operator level of the organization. At the highest level of the organization, the information is even more strategic and less frequent. A much higher proportion of such information is financial, with only a few key operational variables used to report on critical success factors for the overall organization. Exhibit 1–3 summarizes the different types of information used at different levels of the organization. Thus, management accounting information must be tailored to provide what employees and managers need at each level. This important theme will appear throughout the book.

OBJECTIVE 1.4
The different demands for management accounting information for different people in the organization

OBJECTIVE 1.5
The reasons that management accounting information includes both financial and nonfinancial information

EXHIBIT 1-3
Traditional Informational Needs at Different Levels of Organization

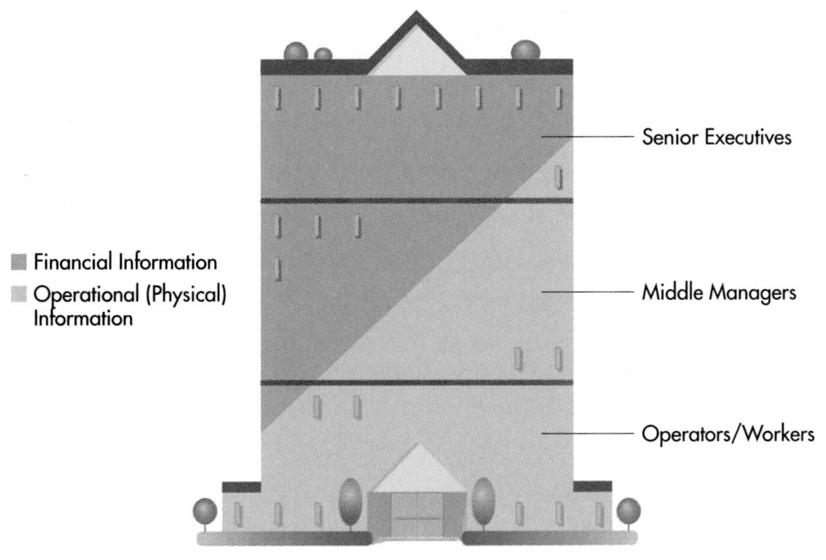

Financial Information
Operational (Physical) Information

Senior Executives

Middle Managers

Operators/Workers

OBJECTIVE 1.6
Historical and contempo-
rary views of how manage-
ment accounting creates
value for organizations: its
relation to operations, marketing, and strategy

TWENTIETH-CENTURY DEVELOPMENTS IN MANAGEMENT CONTROL

■ DuPont, One of the First Diversified Corporations

Many innovations in management accounting systems occurred in the early decades of the 20th century to support the growth of multiple-division, diversified corporations. The DuPont Company was the prototype of a vertically integrated manufacturing organization, where raw materials were acquired and processed through several stages to produce a diversified mix of chemical products that companies in several different industries used. The 19th-century industrial and service enterprises focused on a single type of product (textiles, steel, railroad services, retailing) so that aggregate operating and financial statistics were adequate for performance measurement and management decisions. The senior managers of the more diversified DuPont Company had to devise advanced techniques to coordinate operating activities in their different divisions. These techniques included **operating budgets,** the document that forecasts revenues and expenses during the next operating period, such as monthly forecasts of sales, production, and operating expenses (a topic that will be covered in depth in Chapter 5), and **capital budgets,** the management document that authorizes spending for resources with multiyear useful lives, such as plant and equipment (a topic that will be covered in depth in Chapter 10).

DuPont's headquarters office collected daily and weekly data on sales, payroll, and manufacturing costs from all of the company's mills and branch sales offices. This information was used for several managerial purposes. It helped to rationalize operations and to monitor production and sales efficiencies. It helped the senior management team plan the growth among the company's diverse activities. It also was a means to evaluate and control the performance of the company's three main functional operating departments: manufacturing, distribution, and purchasing.

Perhaps the most enduring of the innovations introduced at the DuPont Corporation was the development of the **return-on-investment (ROI)** performance measure. The ROI measure combined both a profitability measure (Return on Sales = Operating Income/Sales) and an asset or capital utilization measure (Sales/Investment) into a single number:

Operating budget
The document that forecasts revenues and expenses during the next operating period, typi-cally a year. The operating budget also authorizes spending on discretionary activities, such as research and development, advertising, maintenance, and employee training.

Capital budget
The management document that authorizes spending for resources, such as plant and equipment, that will have multiyear useful life-times.

Return on investment
The calculation that relates the profitability of an organizational unit to the investment required to generate that profitability. Often written as the return on sales multiplied by the ratio of sales to assets (or investment) employed.

$$\text{ROI} = \frac{\text{Operating Income}}{\text{Investment}} = \frac{\text{Operating Income}}{\text{Sales}} * \frac{\text{Sales}}{\text{Investment}}$$

DuPont used the ROI figure as the single best performance measure to plan, evaluate, and control the profits being earned for the company's owners.[2] The senior managers of the DuPont Company used the new types of eco-

---

[2] Details on the DuPont innovations in management accounting can be found in Chapter 4 of Johnson and Kaplan, *Relevance Lost*. The use of return on investment as a performance measurement and control signal is described in Chapter 11 of this text.

nomic information, such as the ROI measure, to help them decide which of their divisions should receive additional capital to expand capacity.

For example, consider the following operating statistics of the two divisions:

	Division 1	Division 2
Operating Income	$ 800,000	$ 300,000
Investment	$20,000,000	$3,000,000
Return on investment (ROI)	4%	10%

At first glance, Division 1 looks much more profitable than Division 2 since its operating income of $800,000 is nearly three times higher than Division 2's $300,000 income. But the ROI calculation shows that Division 1 required nearly 7 times the investment as Division 2 to generate its operating income. On an ROI basis, Division 2 is $2^1/_2$ times more profitable than Division 1. In evaluating the profitability of a division, an investment, or even a savings account, we would not want to just look at the absolute level of income being earned; we would want to know how much had been invested to generate that income and to compare the return on investment with other investment alternatives.

■ Management Accounting Systems at General Motors

DuPont's management innovations were extended when its senior financial manager, Donaldson Brown, left to become the chief financial officer for the General Motors company around 1920 when it was reorganized under a new chief executive, Alfred Sloan. General Motors introduced many management accounting initiatives to accomplish what Donaldson Brown described as the company's guiding operating philosophy, "centralized control with decentralized responsibility." **Decentralized responsibility** refers to the authority that local division managers had to make decisions on pricing, product mix, customer relationships, product design, acquisition of materials, and appropriate operating processes, based on their superior access to information about local opportunities and operating conditions, without having to seek higher approval for their decisions. **Centralized control** refers to the financial information that corporate managers received periodically about divisional operations and profitability that assured the senior managers that their division managers were making decisions and taking actions that were contributing to overall corporate goals.

Brown and Sloan's management accounting systems at General Motors included

➤ *An annual operating budgeting process:* The process ensured consistency between top management's financial goals and each division manager's operating targets. This process determined whether the plans of each division were consistent and coordinated with the plans of the other divisions; that is, a sales division did not expect to sell more than a manufacturing division expected to produce. The annual budgeting process

Decentralized responsibility
Senior corporate managers give local division managers the rights to make decisions on pricing, product mix, customer relationships, resource acquisition, materials sourcing, and operating processes without having to seek approval from higher-level managers. Decentralized responsibility allows local managers to make decisions rapidly based on their superior access to information about local opportunities and threats.

Centralized control
The management process by which senior executives receive periodic information about decentralized divisional operations to ensure that division managers are making decisions and taking actions that contribute to overall corporate goals.

also identified the capital requirements of the various divisions and made decisions about how the funds would be generated and subsequently allocated to the divisions.

➤ *Weekly sales reports and monthly flexible budgets:*[3] The sales reports indicated promptly if actual sales were deviating from the estimates used to prepare the budget and operating plan. **Flexible budgets** provided forecasts of what expenses *should* have been given the actual volume and mix of production and sales in the most recent period. The system of weekly sales reports and flexible budgets provided feedback to division managers about current operations so they could take actions to adjust quickly to changes in the company's operating environment.

➤ *Annual divisional performance reports, including return on investment:* The annual performance report gave top management information that enabled them to allocate both resources and management compensation among divisions, using uniform and agreed-to performance criteria, such as return on investment. Sloan greatly valued the ROI (rate of return) measure stating, "No other principle with which I am acquainted serves better than rate of return as an objective aid to business judgment."

The GM management accounting system enabled a complex organization to plan, coordinate, control, and evaluate the operations of multiple, somewhat independent operating divisions, such as Chevrolet, Pontiac, and Fisher Body. It enabled the managers of these divisions to pursue aggressively their individual financial, operating, design, and marketing objectives while contributing, in a coherent fashion, to the overall wealth of the corporation. The Alfred Sloan and Donaldson Brown initiatives played a critical role in creating an enormously successful enterprise during the 1920–1970 time period. The senior managers of General Motors in the latter decades of the 20th century experienced severe difficulties, however, when they failed to use these procedures effectively and to adapt them to the new competitive challenges from European and Japanese car makers.

SERVICE ORGANIZATIONS

The major changes that manufacturing companies have experienced in recent years have also occurred in virtually all types of service organizations. Service companies have existed for hundreds of years, and their importance in modern economies has increased substantially during the 20th century. See Exhibit 1–4 for examples of service industries and companies.

■ Environment of Service Companies

Service companies, like manufacturing companies, need accurate, relevant, and timely management accounting information. Service companies differ from manufacturing companies in several ways. The most obvious difference

Flexible budget
A forecast of what expenses should have been given the actual volume and mix of production and sales.

OBJECTIVE 1.7
The role for management accounting in service organizations

---

[3] Flexible budgets forecast expected expenses at the volume and mix of production and sales that actually occurred in a period. Flexible budgets are discussed in Chapter 11 of this text.

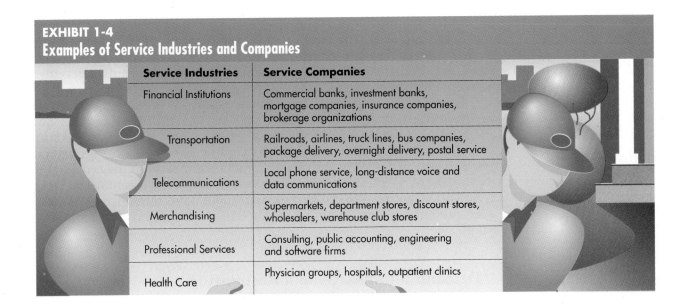

EXHIBIT 1-4
Examples of Service Industries and Companies

Service Industries	Service Companies
Financial Institutions	Commercial banks, investment banks, mortgage companies, insurance companies, brokerage organizations
Transportation	Railroads, airlines, truck lines, bus companies, package delivery, overnight delivery, postal service
Telecommunications	Local phone service, long-distance voice and data communications
Merchandising	Supermarkets, department stores, discount stores, wholesalers, warehouse club stores
Professional Services	Consulting, public accounting, engineering and software firms
Health Care	Physician groups, hospitals, outpatient clinics

is that service companies do not produce a product. Less obvious, service companies have more direct contact with customers. Thus, in addition to price, service companies must be especially sensitive to the timeliness and the quality of the service they provide to their customers. Service companies can produce no inventory in advance of the customer's need but generally deliver in real time directly to the customer. Also, inspectors in manufacturing companies can check the quality of products before they are shipped to customers so that manufacturing errors can be detected and corrected. In service companies, frequently an employee delivers the service directly to the customer so that defects are more likely, more noticeable, and the consequences more severe as dissatisfied customers choose alternative suppliers after an unhappy experience.

Despite this challenging environment for service companies, they historically have used management accounting information less intensively than have manufacturing companies. Service companies did use financial information to budget and control spending in their functional departments. Even though service companies were frequently as complex and diversified as manufacturing companies, they made little attempt to measure accurately the costs of the services they produced and delivered, or of serving different types of customers. This lack of accurate information about service cost and customer profitability probably occurred because most service companies operated in benign, noncompetitive markets. Almost all service companies operated in highly regulated environments. In Canadian and European countries, many of these organizations, such as the railroads, airlines, and telecommunications companies, were not even private companies. They were government-owned and -operated monopolies. Either as highly regulated companies operating in the private sector or as government-supplied monopolies, the service organizations had little demand to measure the cost of individual products, services, or customers. Nor were there strong pressures for efficiency and productivity improvements. The government typically set prices for regulated companies based on aggregate actual operating costs incurred and assets employed. The return was calculated across all the products and services offered by the company, not at the individual service level. Aggressive, perhaps more efficient, competitors were frequently prevented from entering the markets in which the regulated companies operated.

For example, until the 1970s, regulation and law prevented banks from paying interest on certain products such as demand deposits—checking accounts—and were limited in the rate they could pay on time deposits such as saving accounts. Banks could not expand outside their local geographic area and were restricted in the types of products and services they could offer consumers. At the same time, for many years, many other organizations, such as brokerage and investment houses, and finance and insurance companies, were prevented from offering banking-like services in competition with banks.

■ Demand for Management Accounting Information in Service Companies

In the former, highly regulated environments of service companies, where regulators set prices to cover the operating costs of inefficient companies, or in government-operated companies, where taxpayer funds subsidized any losses, managers were not under great pressure to lower costs, improve the quality and efficiency of operations, introduce new products that made profits, or eliminate products and services that were incurring losses. Since such decisions and actions were not being made, the demand for information to inform such decisions and actions was virtually nonexistent. Consequently, the management accounting systems in most service organizations were simple: budget expenses by operating department and measure and monitor actual spending against these functional departmental budgets. Service com-

---

Service companies find information about customer tastes particularly useful in identifying the nature and trend of customer expectations. A major challenge facing management accountants, who have traditionally focused on financial information such as costs and profits, is to help decision makers develop systematic information about customer service requirements and the organization's success in meeting those requirements. *(Roger Foley/Photo Researchers, Inc.)*

panies were not the hothouses for management accounting innovations that occurred in 19th-century railroad, steel, and machine tool companies, as well as in the emerging 20th-century industrial giants such as DuPont and General Motors.

CHANGING COMPETITIVE ENVIRONMENT

During the last quarter of the 20th century, the competitive environment for both manufacturing and service companies has become far more challenging and demanding. As a consequence, today's companies demand different and better management accounting information. Let us explore the changes both in competition and in the nature and type of the new requirements for management accounting information.

■ Deregulation of Service Companies

The deregulation movement in North America and Europe during the 1970s and 1980s has completely changed the ground rules under which service companies operate. Pricing, product mix, and geographic and competitive restrictions have been virtually eliminated in the financial services industry. Transportation companies are now permitted to enter and leave markets and to determine the prices at which they offer services to customers. Telecommunications companies, instead of having prices set to achieve allowable returns based on costs incurred and assets employed, now compete aggressively on price, quality, and service. Health care reimbursement is also shifting away from pure cost recovery schemes. Even government monopolies, such as the postal service, are today experiencing competition from private companies, such as Federal Express and UPS, that offer overnight delivery of letters and packages; from telecommunication companies that allow documents to be sent via facsimile transmission; and from new technologies that permit messages and documents to be transmitted on international electronic mail networks. Information to improve the quality, timeliness, and efficiency of the activities they perform and to understand accurately the cost and profitability of individual products, services, and customers has now become critical to the success of all these service organizations.

■ Manufacturing and Service Organizations in the Global Environment

Starting in the mid-1970s, manufacturing companies in North America and Europe encountered severe competition from overseas companies that offered high-quality products at low prices. Global networks for raising and disbursing capital, for acquiring and transporting raw materials, and for distributing finished goods allowed the best manufacturers, in whatever country they were located, to access local, domestic markets throughout the world. No longer was it sufficient for a company to have cost and quality parity against its domestic competitors. A company could survive and prosper only if its costs, quality, and product capabilities were as good as those of the best companies in the world.

With a much more competitive environment, the demands become much higher to have accurate, relevant information on a company's actual costs. This information is needed to

➤ Help engineers design products that could be produced efficiently

➤ Signal where improvements in quality, efficiency, and speed were needed in manufacturing operations

➤ Guide product mix decisions

➤ Choose among alternative suppliers

➤ Negotiate about price, product features, quality, delivery, and service with customers

Due to a confluence of circumstances, however, companies' management accounting systems were inadequate for this task.

Service companies' previously regulated and protected environment provided little incentive for them to develop accurate information on the costs of their products or of the cost of servicing individual customers. Thus, completely new systems had to be created to measure the cost and profitability of their product lines, market segments, and individual products and customers. New operational control systems also were required to enhance the cost improvement, quality improvement, and process time reduction activities of the people in these organizations.

The traditional systems that manufacturing companies had used for decades to measure product costs were now supplying highly distorted infor-

CONSIDER THIS . . .

Companies Under Attack

The global battles for industry supremacy are now well documented. In the 1970s and continuing through the 1980s, most large North American and European steel companies began to lose cost and quality advantages to companies in Japan and South Korea. The U.S. auto manufacturers, General Motors, Ford, and Chrysler, suffered devastating market share losses to Japanese manufacturers such as Toyota, Honda, and Nissan before they stabilized share through huge process and quality improvements and better product designs. Japanese luxury cars including Lexus, Acura, and Infiniti threatened the comfortable niches of German luxury car manufacturers, Mercedes-Benz, BMW, and Porsche. Caterpillar, a world leader in off-road vehicles, saw its position challenged by Komatsu; Xerox was undermined by Canon; Hewlett-Packard and Tektronix by Japanese instrument companies such as Hitachi; and producers of semiconductor memory chips, including Texas Instruments, Siemens, and Intel, lost quality and cost leadership to Japanese and South Korean producers.

Facing intense competition from Komatsu, a Japanese manufacturer of off-road vehicles, Caterpillar Corporation had to rethink its entire approach to manufacturing. Process improvement activities aimed at reducing costs and increasing quality relied heavily on management accounting information. Moreover, Caterpillar set out to improve its flexibility in handling unusual customer requests. Caterpillar painted this grader white, instead of the traditional Caterpillar yellow, for a paving contractor. *(Courtesy Fitzgerald Grading, Inc.)*

mation, however. These systems failed to assign accurately the large and growing indirect and support expenses that were now required to design, produce, market, sell, and deliver products and services. The errors introduced by costing systems that no longer reflected the economics of contemporary operations were causing managers, designers, and operators to make incorrect decisions. Product engineers were designing automobiles and electronic instruments with too many special and unique components and too many options. These designs greatly raised purchasing, materials handling, and manufacturing costs. Companies attempted to reach new market segments and new geographic regions, but the additional revenues from these initiatives failed by substantial amounts to cover the extra costs required to design, produce, deliver, sell, and service products for the new segments and regions.

■ Role for Activity-Based Cost (ABC) Systems

One of the central themes of this book is the design and use of **activity-based costing** concepts. Activity-based costing (or ABC, as it is frequently called) is now being introduced in many manufacturing and service organizations to overcome the inability of traditional cost systems to accurately assign overhead costs. With many manufacturing companies now having overhead costs more than 5 or 10 times their direct labor costs, management accounting systems that allocate overhead based on direct labor distort enormously the costs assigned to products and customers.

ABC systems avoid arbitrary allocations and subsequent cost distortions by *assigning the costs of organizational resources to the activities being performed* by the resources and, then, assigning activity costs to the *products, services, and customers that are creating the demand for or benefiting from the activities being performed.* That is, the cost of purchasing is assigned to the items being purchased, the cost of designing products is directly assigned to the new products being designed, and the cost of assisting customers is assigned to the individual customers. Several chapters in the book will be devoted to developing the theory (Chapters 3 and 4) and application (Chapters 6 to 8) of activity-based costing for management decision making.

Activity-based costing A procedure that measures the costs of objects, such as products, services, and customers. Activity-based costing (ABC) first assigns resource costs to the activities performed by the organization. Then activity costs are assigned to the products, customers, and services that benefit from or are creating the demand for the activities.

■ Activity-Based Management (ABM)

Managers' decisions based on activity-based cost information is called **activity-based management,** or ABM. ABM includes decisions to modify pricing, product mix, and customer mix; to change supplier and customer rela-

Activity-based management
The management processes that use the information provided by an activity-based cost analysis to improve organizational profitability. Activity-based management (ABM) includes performing activities more efficiently, eliminating the need to perform certain activities that do not add value for customers, improving the design of products, and developing better relationships with customers and suppliers. The goal of ABM is to enable customer needs to be satisfied while making fewer demands on organizational resources.

tionships; and to improve the design of products and services. Activity-based management also includes performing activities more efficiently and eliminating the need to perform certain activities that do not create any customer value. For example, companies can reengineer and improve their business processes and invest in new technologies that reduce the cost of performing critical activities.

■ Improvement of Operational Control Systems

The product costing system was not the only management accounting system that proved inadequate in the changed competitive and technological environment. Operational control systems, with their extensive monthly summaries of financial performance, were sending reports too late for corrective actions to be taken and were too aggregate to signal causes of unfavorable performance. Recall the information that Dennis Mitchell, the mechanic in the automobile dealership, needed to monitor and improve his work activities: actual resource (time and materials) usage by individual job and actual usage compared to established standards after each job was performed. This information needed to be timely—available shortly after the repair job was finished—and disaggregated—reporting on the resources used for each individual job, not the sum of all resources used for all jobs performed during a month.

The monthly performance reports of many operating departments also had become filled with cost allocations, so that managers were being held accountable for performance that was neither under their control nor traceable to them. The costs of corporate- or factory-level resources, such as the heat and lighting in the building or the landscaping outside, were being allocated arbitrarily to individual departments even though the departments were not responsible for these costs and their incurrence could not be traced to the actions taken at the individual departments. For example, referring again to the bowling alley scenario, think about having the accountants, after a ball is thrown down each of an establishment's 35 bowling lanes, counting all the pins knocked down in the entire establishment, dividing by 35, and reporting back the average, say 8.25714,[4] to

---

C ONSIDER THIS . . .

Bowling for dollars

One financial officer remarked, "To understand the problem of delayed and aggregate financial information, you could think of the department manager as a bowler, throwing a ball at pins every minute. But we don't let the bowler see how many pins he has knocked down with each throw. At the end of the month we close the books, calculate the total number of pins knocked down during the month, compare this total with a standard, and report the total and the variance back to the bowler. If the total number is below standard, we ask the bowler for an explanation and encourage him to do better next period. We're beginning to understand that we won't turn out many world-class bowlers with this type of reporting system."

Source: R. S. Kaplan, "Texas Eastman Company," Harvard Business School Case #9-130-039, pp. 6–7.

---

[4] Many accountants like to report all results using 6 significant digits. It makes them feel that they are very accurate. In truth, they are merely being precise but are usually quite inaccurate (the first digit may be wrong). In management accounting, we prefer to be vaguely accurate (get the first digit correct) rather than precisely wrong.

every bowler. Such a number may be quite accurate (it does represent the mean number of pins knocked down per alley), but it is completely useless to every individual bowler. Each bowler wants to see the number of pins she has knocked down, so that she might improve on the next toss. The bowler does not want this number contaminated or influenced by the actions of others over which she has no control.

◼ Changing the Nature of Work: From Controlling to Informing

The distorted and delayed signals from management accounting systems were symptomatic of even deeper changes occurring in organizations. The very nature of work was undergoing radical transformations. Work standards and standard costs were innovations established a century ago by engineers in the scientific management movement (see Consider This . . . Management Accounting in 19th-Century Enterprises, p. 8). The system of work and cost standards represented a philosophy by which engineers and managers determined operators' tasks. Operators were instructed to keep following these procedures, and the system of measurement (comparing actual results to the predetermined standards) was used to check whether the workers had followed the procedures in which they had been instructed. In the current vigorous global competition that companies were now confronting, however, performance against historical standards was no longer adequate. **Continuous improvement** of performance was necessary to match or stay ahead of leading global competitors. *Continuous improvement* refers to ongoing processes by which employees problem solve and search for methods to reduce and eliminate waste, improve quality, and reduce defects.

Managers came to realize that perhaps their best source of new ideas for continually improving performance would come from their operators, the people who were closest to the work being performed and who could see, firsthand, the types of defects that were occurring and the principal causes of these defects. Allowing employees to take such actions, without explicit authorization from middle managers and senior executives, has come to be known as **employee empowerment.** Companies practicing employee empowerment encourage their employees to solve problems and to devise new approaches for performing work and satisfying customers. To implement such improvements, however, the local operators could not be held strictly to predetermined standards. They needed freedom to experiment with solutions to fix the root causes of defects. They also needed information—first to identify the source and likely causes of defects and, subsequently, to see immedi-

CONSIDER THIS . . .

Measuring quality

U.S. companies failed to see superior Japanese quality coming [because] they lacked the proper instruments on their corporate dashboards. The indicators they were watching didn't measure quality. The Japanese indicators did. . . . Japanese companies evolved means of measuring customer satisfaction, competitive quality, performance of major processes (such as cycle time for product development). These measures found a place on the corporate instrument panel and contributed to CEO decision making.

American CEOs focused instead on financial reports, and their decisions reflected that focus. Xerox is probably the best example of how a financially powerful company allowed itself to be taken completely by surprise. . . . In the 1960s, Xerox executives could look at their instruments and see sales, costs, and profits at a glance. But they had no meter showing customer satisfaction. If they had, it would have set off a vital alarm.

Source: Reprinted by permission of *Harvard Business Review*. An excerpt from "Made in U.S.A.: A Renaissance in Quality, by Joseph M. Juran, July/August 1993. Copyright © 1993 by the President and Fellows of Harvard College; all rights reserved.

Continuous improvement
The ongoing processes by which employees continually problem solve and search for methods to reduce and eliminate waste, improve quality and reduce defects, shorten response and cycle times, and design products that are simpler to manufacture, deliver, and service.

Employee empowerment
Managers give employees who are closest to operating processes, customers, and suppliers the rights to make decisions. Employees are encouraged to solve problems and devise creative new approaches for performing work and satisfying customers.

Total quality
A management philosophy that attempts to eliminate all defects, waste, and activities that do not add value to customers; also refers to an organizational commitment to customer satisfaction.

ately the consequences from attempts to fix the causes of the defects. In this **total quality** philosophy, operators became problem solvers. They were now part of the process that helped to find solutions for eliminating defective output, waste, and activities that do not add value to customers. Thus, the role of operators changed from following standard operating procedures and monitoring the machines that were producing output to a role of quickly identifying problems as they arose, devising countermeasures for the problems, implementing the countermeasures, and testing and validating that the problems had been solved by these countermeasures. For this task, information was needed to *inform* their problem-solving activities, not to *control* them against preset and soon-to-become-obsolete standards. *Management accounting information is shifting away from its historical emphasis on controlling the actions of employees. The information is now being used to inform and empower the employees to facilitate their continuous improvement activities.*

■ Role for Nonfinancial Information

Nonfinancial information about activities being performed has become critical. Employees must focus not just on reducing costs but also on how to improve quality, reduce cycle times, and satisfy customer needs. For these efforts, the employees need performance data on activities, such as defects, rework, scrap, yields, on-time delivery, customer lead times, and returns. Such data must be supplied frequently if employees, managers, and executives are to take effective action to improve performance. The data to be supplied are driven from the organization's operational and strategic objectives that will make it more competitive in global markets. LSI Logic, a designer and manufacturer of high-performance semiconductors, uses what it calls "the cycle of quality" to improve process performance. The cycle of quality at LSI Logic involves 4 steps: (1) identifying the problem, (2) monitoring the problem to assess its severity, (3) analyzing the problem to find its causes, and (4) correcting the problem.

As Exhibit 1–5 shows, nonfinancial information about cycle time, quality, safety, and management culture plays an important role in focusing and evaluating cycle of quality activities. The percentages in this pie chart are the proportion of cycle of quality activities that were devoted to each area of the business.

■ Employee Empowerment: Sharing Financial Information

Among the many interesting changes underway in providing relevant information to assist operators in their quality and process improvement activities is an expanded role for financial information. Previously, operators received, at best, only operational or physical information: quantities of inputs used, time required to complete a task, quality of work accomplished. Such operating or nonfinancial information, of course, becomes even more important to

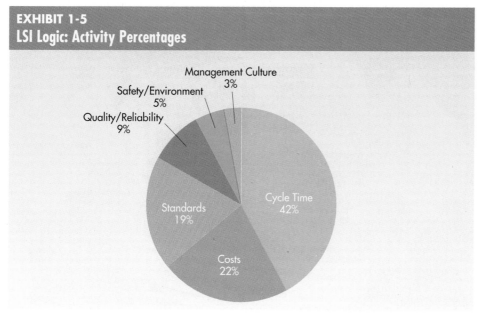

EXHIBIT 1-5
LSI Logic: Activity Percentages

- Management Culture 3%
- Safety/Environment 5%
- Quality/Reliability 9%
- Standards 19%
- Cycle Time 42%
- Costs 22%

Source: LSI Logic Corporation, 1992 Annual Report, page 6.

local operators as they engage in quality and process improvement activities. The operators can also benefit from seeing cost and expense information about the resources they are using. For example, they can decide whether to replace the tooling in a machine so that the output has more consistent quality. As operators modify and redesign processes, they should be concerned not only with improving cycle times, quality, yields, and productivity, but also with lowering the cost of performing work. For this purpose, several innovating organizations are now sharing, for the first time, financial information with operators to enable them to:

➤ Identify the opportunities for significant cost reduction
➤ Set priorities for improvement projects
➤ Make trade-offs among alternative ways to improve operations
➤ Evaluate proposed investments to improve operations
➤ Assess the consequences of their improvement activities

Thus, another new and important theme for this book is the role for *management accounting information to provide information to employees for their problem-solving and continuous improvement activities*. The book will stress the use of financial and nonfinancial information to *inform* local decision making and deemphasize the traditional role for cost accounting information to *control* operator performance. This shift in emphasis mirrors the shift occurring in practice: from a command-and-control philosophy to an inform-and-improve philosophy for an organization's employees.

Understanding how activities cause costs and what activities are necessary to provide customers with what they want can help organizations save money. By studying the inspection and adjustment activities for new cars performed at the factory and at dealerships, this group of Chrysler Corporation employees identified redundancies and developed a procedure to prepare new cars for customers. This revised procedure is expected to save Chrysler Corporation about $42 million dollars annually. *(Courtesy Chrysler Corporation)*

■ Measuring and Managing Activities

OBJECTIVE 1.8
The importance of understanding activities as the primary focus for measuring and managing performance

Finally, the themes of activity-based cost systems, operational control systems, and expanded use of nonfinancial information for guiding employees' continuous improvement activities can all be integrated by viewing *activities* as the central focus of the organization. *The measurement of activities will be the key organizing principle for studying management accounting information.* Activities should be viewed as the mechanism by which organizational resources and employees accomplish work. *Operational control information provides financial and nonfinancial information on the cost, quality, and time required to perform activities.* In turn, the operational control information is used to develop performance measures and targets that will signal how well individual activities are contributing to the complete set of processes that are performed to satisfy customer needs. Activities also are the unit of measurement for cost information, leading naturally to the use of activity-based cost systems. *Activities provide the linkage between organizational spending on resources* (people, equipment, materials and supplies, and energy) *and the products and services that are produced and delivered to customers.*

BEHAVIORAL IMPLICATIONS OF MANAGEMENT ACCOUNTING INFORMATION

We have stressed the role for management accounting information to *inform* the decisions and problem-solving activities of operators and managers. Information is never neutral, however. Just the act of measuring and informing affects the individuals involved. This principle occurs even in physical phenomena in which the Heisenberg uncertainty principle notes that the act of measuring the position or velocity of a particle affects the particle's position or velocity. The intrusive effect of measurement is even more pronounced when dealing with humans rather than particles. As measurements are made on operations and, especially, on individuals and groups, the behavior of the individuals and groups are affected. People react to the measurements being made. They will focus on those variables or the behavior being measured and spend less attention on variables and behavior that are not measured. In addition, if managers attempt to introduce or redesign cost and performance measurement systems, people familiar with the previous systems will resist. These people have acquired expertise in the use (and occasional misuse) of the old system and will be concerned with whether their experience and expertise will be transferable to the new system. People may also feel committed to the decisions and actions that were taken based on the information the old system produced—decisions and actions that may no longer seem valid under the light produced by the information from a newly installed management accounting system.

Management accountants must understand and anticipate the reactions of individuals to information and measurements. The design and introduction of new measurements and systems must be accompanied with an analysis of the likely reactions to the innovations. The final chapter (Chapter 14) in the book will address these behavioral and organizational issues that are critical to the success of a management accountant.

BECK'S MOTORS AND PETE LITTLETON REVISITED

Pete Littleton, the accountant we encountered at the opening of this chapter, now understands the challenges he would face as the new management accountant for Beck's Motors. He must design systems that will inform organizational employees about the efficiency, cost, and profitability of their activities. This information will serve several business purposes as shown in Exhibit 1–6.

In addition, as the company's management accountant, Pete Littleton will formulate operating and capital budgets that will help Barry Beck and his business unit managers plan their business for the coming year and for several years into the future. These budgets become the quantitative expression of the auto dealership's strategy for growth and future profitability.

EXHIBIT 1–6
Business Purposes of Management Accounting Information

BUSINESS PURPOSE	ROLE FOR MANAGEMENT ACCOUNTING INFORMATION
Operational control	Provide feedback information about the quality, timeliness, and efficiency of tasks performed and the performance of individuals and of operating units. This information is needed daily by mechanics like Dennis Mitchell as well as by salespersons in the new car, used car, and parts departments to help them improve their day-to-day activities.
Product and customer costing	Measure the costs of resources used to produce a product or service and to market and deliver the product/service to customers; assess the profitability of the organization's products and services by linking resources generated, that is, revenues from the sale of the products and services to the costs of resources required for their design, production, sales, delivery, and service. The managers of each of Beck's Motors' operating units will have detailed information on the cost and profitability of their individual product and service lines. Customer profitability by retail customer, fleet accounts, and corporate accounts also will be available so that the dealership's marketing people can target particularly profitable segments and managers can take actions to improve the profitability of currently unprofitable accounts.
Organizational performance measurement	Develop performance measures for decentralized organizational units to promote organizational performance that is consistent with business unit strategy and will facilitate coordination with other business units. Summary financial measures will enable Barry Beck, president of Beck's Motors, to assess the relative profitability of his four operating units: new car sales, used car sales, car repairs and service, and parts sales. Nonfinancial measures will provide indicators of quality, customer satisfaction, and time required to perform key activities.

SUMMARY

Management accounting has become an exciting discipline that is undergoing major changes to reflect the challenging new environment that organizations all over the world now face. Accurate, timely, and relevant information on the economics and performance of organizations will be crucial to organizational success. This chapter has introduced the different informational needs for operators/workers, middle managers, and senior executives and for the different tasks that are informed by management accounting information: operational control, product and customer costing, and management control. Individuals will use both financial and nonfinancial information as they perform their tasks. The focus on the costs incurred and the value created by organizational activities will provide a central focus for management accounting information. The design of management accounting systems and the use and interpretation of the management accounting information that is the output from these systems are now critical to the success of both manufacturing and service organizations in today's globally competitive and technologically challenging environment. This textbook introduces students to the opportunities for enhancing organizational performance through effective design and use of management accounting systems.

KEY TERM LIST

activity-based costing, p. 23

activity-based management, p. 24

benchmarking, p. 14

capital budget, p. 16

centralized control, p. 17

continuous improvement, p. 25

critical success factors, p. 13

customer costing, p. 14

decentralized responsibility, p. 17

employee empowerment, p. 25

financial accounting, p. 5

flexible budget, p. 18

management accounting, p. 4

management accounting information, p. 4

management accounting system, p. 4

management control, p. 14

operating budget, p. 16

operational control, p. 14

product costing, p. 14

return on investment, p. 16

strategic information, p. 14

total quality, p. 26

APPENDIX 1.1

Definition of Management Accounting

Management accounting has been defined by the Institute of Management Accountants as *the process of identification, measurement, accumulation, analysis, preparation, interpretation, and communication of financial information used by management to plan, evaluate, and control within an organization and to assure appropriate use of and accountability for its resources.*[5]

Identification	Recognition and evaluation of business transactions and other economic events for appropriate accounting action.
Measurement	Quantification, including estimates, of business transactions or other economic events that have occurred or forecasts of those that may occur.
Accumulation	Disciplined and consistent approaches to recording and classifying appropriate business transactions and other economic events.
Analysis	Determination of the reasons for the reported activity and its relationship with other economic events and circumstances.
Preparation and interpretation	Meaningful coordination of accounting and/or planning data to provide information, presented logically, which includes, if appropriate, the conclusions drawn from those data.
Communication	Reporting pertinent information to management and others for internal and external uses.
Planning	Quantifying and interpreting the effects of planned transactions and other economic events on the organization. The planning responsibility, which includes strategic, tactical, and operating aspects, requires that the accountant provide quantitative historical and prospective information to facilitate planning. It includes participation in developing the planning system, setting obtainable goals, and choosing appropriate means of monitoring the progress toward the goals.

[5] *Statements on Management Accounting 1A,* "Definition of Management Accounting" (National Association of Accountants, March 19, 1981). The Institute of Management Accountants (formerly known as the National Association of Accountants) is the U.S. professional society of practitioners and academics who are interested in the design and operations of management accounting systems in organizations.

Evaluating	Judging implications of historical and expected events and helping to choose the optimum course of action. Evaluating includes translating data into trends and relationships. Management accountants must communicate effectively and promptly the conclusions derived from the analyses.
Controlling	Assuring the integrity of financial information concerning an organization's activities and resources; monitoring and measuring performance and inducing any corrective actions required to return the activity to its intended course. Management accountants provide information to executives operating in functional areas who can use it to achieve desirable performance.
Assuring accountability resources	Implementing a system of reporting that is aligned with organizational responsibilities. This reporting *of* system will contribute to the effective use of resources and measurement of management performance. The transmission of management's goals and objectives throughout the organization in the form of assigned responsibilities is a basis for identifying accountability. Management accountants must provide an accounting and reporting system that will accumulate and report appropriate revenues, expenses, assets, liabilities, and related quantitative information to managers. Managers will then have better control over these elements.
External reporting	Preparing financial reports based on generally accepted accounting principles, or other appropriate bases, for nonmanagement groups such as shareholders, creditors, regulatory agencies, and tax authorities. Management accountants should participate in the process of developing the accounting principles that underlie external reporting.

ASSIGNMENT MATERIAL

QUESTIONS

1–1 Why do operators, middle managers, and senior executives have different informational needs?

1–2 Why do a company's operators, managers, and executives have different informational needs than do shareholders and external suppliers of capital?

1–3 Why may financial information alone be insufficient for the informational needs of operators, managers, and executives?

1–4 What forces have caused management accounting systems designed decades ago to become less relevant and less valuable for organizational employees in today's globally competitive environment?

1–5 How does the role for management accounting systems change as the environment becomes more competitive?

1–6 What is the impact of shifting the role of management accounting information from *controlling* workers and operators to *informing* the continuous improvement activities of these workers and operators?

1–7 What information do employees need about the activities performed in the organization?

1–8 How does measuring the cost of activities differ from the traditional cost accounting function of allocating costs to products for inventory valuation?

1–9 What, if any, are the differences between the management accounting information needed in manufacturing organizations and those needed in service organizations?

EXERCISES

1–10 Consider the operation of a fast-food company with hundreds of retail outlets scattered about the country. Identify the management accounting information needs for

(a) The manager of a local fast-food outlet that prepares food and serves it to customers who walk in or pick it up in a drive-by window

(b) The regional manager who supervises the operations of all the retail outlets in a three-state region

(c) Senior management located at the company's corporate headquarters. Consider specifically the information needs of the president and the vice presidents of operations and marketing

Be sure to address the content, frequency, and timeliness of information needed by these different managers.

1–11 Consider the operation of a hospital. Identify the management accounting information needs for

(a) The managers of (1) a patient unit where patients stay while being treated for illness or recuperating from an operation and (2) the radiology department where patients obtain X rays and receive radiological treatment

(b) The manager of the nursing service who hires and assigns nurses to all patient units and to specialty services such as the operating room, emergency room, recovery room, and radiology room

(c) The chief executive officer of the hospital

Be sure to address the content, frequency, and timeliness of information needed by these different managers.

PROBLEMS

1–12 Many German companies have their management accounting department report to and located within manufacturing operations rather than structure it as part of the corporate finance department. These companies operate two separate accounting departments. One performs financial accounting functions for shareholders and tax authorities; the other maintains and operates the costing system for manufacturing operations.

REQUIRED:

What are the advantages and disadvantages of having separate departments for financial accounting and management accounting?

1-13 The controller of a German machine tool company believed that historical cost depreciation was inadequate for assigning the cost of using expensive machinery to individual parts and products. Each year he estimated the replacement cost of each machine. Depreciation, based on the machine's replacement cost, was included in the machine-hour rate used to assign machine expenses to the parts produced on that machine. Additionally, the controller included an interest charge, based on 50% of the machine's replacement value, into the machine-hour rate. The interest rate was an average of the 3- to 5-year interest rate on government and high-grade corporate securities. As a consequence of these two decisions (charging replacement cost rather than historical cost and imputing a capital charge for the use of capital equipment), the product cost figures used internally by company managers were inconsistent with the numbers that were needed for inventory valuation for financial and tax reporting. A tedious reconciliation process was required at the end of each year to back out the interest and replacement value costs from the cost of goods sold and inventory values so that the financial statements could be prepared.

REQUIRED:

(a) Why would the controller introduce additional complications into the company's costing system by assigning replacement value depreciation costs and imputed interest costs to the company's parts and products?

(b) Why should management accountants create extra work for the organization by deliberately adopting policies for internal costing that violate the generally accepted accounting principles that must be used for external reporting?

1-14 A recent article on the decline of a U.S. corporation described the information provided and the reward structure of senior managers: "Summarized data on sales and sales growth were displayed on senior executives' instrument panels and the managerial reward system gave generous weight to sales volume. In contrast, the senior executives' dashboard lacked summarized information on field failures, their effect on customer relations, the performance of competing machines, the growing cancer of failure-prone features, and the extent of customer defections."[6]

REQUIRED:

(a) Shouldn't senior executives be responsible for delivering excellent financial performance to shareholders, leaving the details of customer relations, engineering design, and manufacturing operations to the vice presidents and managers of these various departments?

(b) Are financial measures alone sufficient to measure the performance of an organization during a period and to use as a basis for compensating the senior executives of an organization? Why or why not?

(c) What problems, if any, arise from monitoring and rewarding senior executives by a combination of financial and nonfinancial measures?

[6] J. Juran, "Made in U.S.A.: A Renaissance in Quality," *Harvard Business Review* (July–August 1993).

CASES

1–15 A U.S. automobile components plant had recently been reorganized so that quality and employee teamwork were to be the guiding principles for all managers and workers. One production worker described the difference:

> In the old production environment, we were not paid to think. The foreman told us what to do, and we did it even if we knew he was wrong. Now, the team decides what to do. Our voices are heard. All middle management has been cut out, including foremen and superintendents. Management relies on us, the team members, to make decisions. Salary people help us make these decisions; the production and manufacturing engineers work for us. They are always saying, "We work for you. What do you need?" And they listen to us.

The plant controller commented:

> In traditional factories, the financial system viewed people as variable costs. If you had a production problem, you sent people home to reduce your variable costs. Here, we do not send people home. Our production people are viewed as problem solvers, not as variable costs.[7]

REQUIRED:

(a) What information needs did the production workers have in the old environment?

(b) What information do you recommend be supplied to the production workers in the new environment that emphasizes quality, defect reduction, problem solving, and teamwork?

1–16 The manager of a large semiconductor production department expressed his disdain for the cost information he was presently supplied with:

> Cost variances are useless to me. [We will study about cost variances in later chapters. For purposes of working this problem, it is sufficient to recognize that a cost variance represents the difference between the cost actually assigned to a production department and the cost that was expected or budgeted for that department.] I don't want to ever have to look at a cost variance, monthly or weekly. Daily, I look at sales dollars, bookings, and on-time delivery (OTD)—the percent of orders on time. Weekly, I look at a variety of quality reports including the outgoing quality control report on items passing the final test before shipment to the customer, in-process quality, and yields. Yield is a good surrogate for cost and quality. Monthly, I do look at the financial reports. I look closely at my fixed expenses and compare these to the budgets, especially on discretionary items like travel and maintenance. I also watch headcount.

> But the financial systems still don't tell me where I am wasting money. I expect that if I make operating improvements, costs should go down, but I don't worry about the linkage too much. The organizational dynamics make it difficult to link cause and effect precisely.[8]

REQUIRED:

Comment on this production manager's assessment of his limited use for financial and cost summaries of performance. For what purposes, if any, are

---

[7] R. S. Kaplan and Amy Sweeney, "Romeo Engine Plant," Harvard Business School Case #9-194-932.

[8] R. S. Kaplan, "Analog Devices: The Half-Life System," Harvard Business School Case #9-190-061.

cost and financial information helpful to operating people? How should the management accountant determine the appropriate blend between financial and nonfinancial information for operating people?

√ 1–17 An article in *The Wall Street Journal* (June 23, 1993) reported on the major changes occurring in General Motors. Its new CEO, John Smith, had been installed after the board of directors requested the resignation of Robert Stempel, the previous CEO.

> Last year [John Smith's] North American Strategy Board identified 30 components that could be simplified for 1994 models. Currently, GM has 64 different versions of the cruise control/turn signal mechanism. It plans to pare that to 24 versions next year, and the following year to just 8. The tooling for each one costs GM's A.C. Rochester division about $250,000. Smith said, "We've been talking about too many parts doing the same job for 25 years but we weren't focused on it." [Note that the tooling cost is only one component of the cost of proliferating components. Other costs include the design and engineering costs for each different component, purchasing costs, setup and scheduling costs, plus the stocking and service costs for every individual component in each automobile dealership (including Beck's Motors) around the country.]

> GM's proliferation of parts is mind-boggling. GM makes or buys 139 different hood hinges, compared with 1 for Ford. . . . Saginaw's Plant Six juggles parts for 167 different steering columns—down from 250 last year but still far from the goal of fewer than 40 by decade's end.

> This approach increased GM's costs exponentially. Not only does the company pay far more engineers than competitors to design steering columns, but it needs extra tools and extra people to move parts around, and it has suffered from quality glitches when workers confused one steering column with another.

REQUIRED:

(a) How could an inaccurate and distorted product costing system have contributed to the overproliferation of parts and components that General Motors executives have only recently recognized?

(b) What characteristics should a new cost system have that would enable it to signal accurately to product designers and market researchers about the cost of customization and variety?

MANAGING ACTIVITIES

This chapter will introduce you to:

1. the organization, its components, purpose, and major stakeholders
2. the idea of the organization as a sequence of activities or a value chain
3. the role of the customer in defining the focus of the activities in the value chain and the nature of value-added and nonvalue-added activities
4. the role of performance measures in helping organization members to manage the value chain
5. benchmarking and continuous improvements as tools to improve organization performance
6. the relationship between organization activities and costs
7. the concept of just-in-time as a means to improve organization performance

CHAPTER 2

◼ Timber River Metal Windows: The Dilemma

Timber River Metal Windows, a manufacturer of metal windows for the home housing market, was in trouble and everyone in the company knew it. Sales had been falling for 5 years, and, to make matters worse, the company's ratio of costs to sales seemed to be out of line with that of its competitors. Several improvement programs that urged employees to work harder and not waste time and money had initial successes, but none of these successes seemed to last; costs soon returned to their old levels after the program wound down. The sales staff had spoken to customers to identify the cause of declining sales and came back with a consistent story: The company's windows cost too much, took too long to arrive, and often had defects. The employees at Timber River Metal Windows knew that they had to do something if the company was to survive.

The Timber River Metals example illustrates the type of challenges facing decision makers in today's organizations. The focus of this chapter is on the organization itself: its purpose, constituencies or stakeholders, and especially its activities. The role of management is to develop and use information to guide the organization's sequence of activities in a way that uses the fewest possible resources in meeting the objectives of the organization's constituents. Let's consider some fundamental features of organizations to better understand how Timber River Metal Windows can identify and address the challenges it faces to survive.

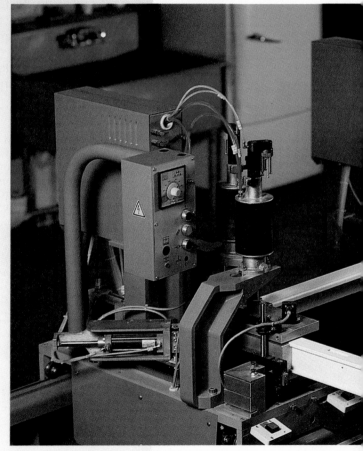

(Rob Crandall/Stock Boston, Inc.)

WHAT ARE ORGANIZATIONS?

Organizations are collections of people, equipment, and capital. They come in all sizes and forms (for example, government agencies, fast-food chains, religious groups, multinational automobile manufacturers, student societies or interest groups, and performing arts groups). There are many things that organizations do *not* have in common, but *all* organizations share one thing: a purpose.

WHAT IS AN ORGANIZATION'S PURPOSE?

It might be strange to think of a collection of people, equipment, and capital as having a purpose, but having a well-defined and well-understood purpose is one of the most important ingredients for organization success. Since management's role is to create organization success by guiding activities that meet constituents' objectives using the fewest possible resources, it follows that management has a vital stake in defining the organization's purpose and making sure that everyone understands the organization's commitments. This chapter begins by identifying the people, or groups, who determine an organization's broad purposes, or **objectives**.

Objectives
The broad purposes of an organization or process. Objectives reflect the stakeholder requirements that the organization is committed to achieving, such as employee safety, profitability, and customer satisfaction.

This employee at Potlatch Corporation, a diversified forest products company, is using a reducing band saw to cut a squared log, or cant, into lumber. Employees at Potlatch have continuously refined and improved sawing so that the saw operator, using specially designed monitors and computers, can obtain the largest value of desired products from a given piece of raw material at the lowest possible cost to the company. *(Courtesy Tom Tracy)*

WHO ARE THE ORGANIZATION'S STAKEHOLDERS?

Stakeholders are the people with a legitimate claim on having the organization's objectives reflect their requirements; they define the organization's objectives. Most organizations have 5 groups of stakeholders: the employees, the partners, the owners, the community, and, most important, the customers.

■ Stakeholder Contributions

Each stakeholder group contributes something to the organization and expects something in return. Each group's contribution helps the organization pursue its objectives and defines what it expects from the organization in return for its contribution. These expectations place constraints on the organization's operations by consuming resources or by limiting the range of acceptable organization behaviors.

Employees contribute their knowledge and time and expect rewards,[1] interesting jobs, economic security, and proper treatment from the organization. Employee time and knowledge create opportunities for the organization to undertake activities that require people. Employees' expectations define the types of jobs, income, and personnel practices that the organization must provide to attract and keep the employees it wants.

Partners[2] provide the materials and services that the organization needs to achieve its objectives but does not, or cannot, provide itself. In return, business partners expect to earn a fair return on their investment of time and money in the relationship and to be treated fairly. Business partners place economic demands on the organization by specifying the prices that they demand for their products; they constrain the organization's choice of business practices to those they deem fair.

As the residual providers of funds, *owners* give the organization—whether it is a profit-seeking entity, a charity, or a government department—the capital it needs to operate. Like business partners, business owners expect a return on their investment that is commensurate with the risk they take by investing in the organization. The owners' return requirements constrain operations by limiting the ventures in which the company can engage to those that are expected to provide returns exceeding the owners' minimum return requirements.

Stakeholders
Groups of people who have a legitimate claim on having an organization's objectives reflect their requirements. Stakeholders include customers, employees, partners, owners, and the community.

Partners
The suppliers and distributors that an organization uses to achieve its objectives.

---

[1] Rewards can be extrinsic (such as compensation) or intrinsic (such as satisfaction with a job well done). Most employees seek a mix of both types of rewards.

[2] Partners are often called *suppliers* and include organizations that provide materials, services, components, equipment, people, and ideas. We use *business partners* in this book to imply that effective organizations work more closely with suppliers than the word *suppliers* suggests.

EXHIBIT 2-1
Broadening Disclosure to Reflect Community Concerns

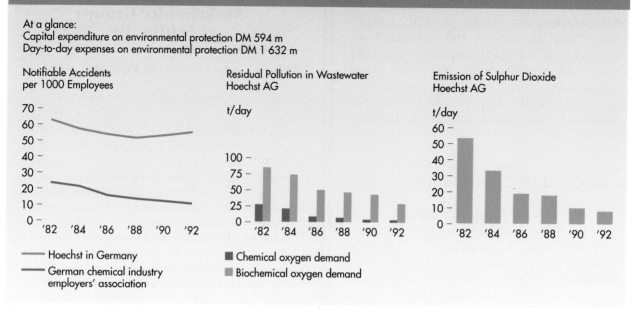

At a glance:
Capital expenditure on environmental protection DM 594 m
Day-to-day expenses on environmental protection DM 1 632 m

The annual report of the Hoechst AG Group, a manufacturer of chemical products, contains these exhibits reporting on the organization's safety and environment performance—a measure of Hoechst's community related performance. *(Courtesy Hoechst AG Group)*

The analogues of the owner in profit-oriented organizations are the patrons in not-for-profit organizations who donate money or time and the legislative authority in government that authorizes expenditures. Patrons in not-for-profit organizations and legislatures in government expect the organization to use the funds they provide to pursue its stated objectives. These expectations constrain the scope of the organization's acceptable activities.

Community
Defines the legal, moral, and social norms that constrain an organization's activities.

The **community** allows the organization to operate within its midst. In return, the community expects the organization to act ethically, particularly in its dealings with customers, employees, and government. It also expects the organization to be socially responsible by observing society's laws and conventions and, perhaps, even to be progressive by doing things such as protecting the environment and making contributions to social causes (see Exhibit 2–1). The expectations of the community constrain the range of activities that the organization can undertake by describing what activities are acceptable or unacceptable and by placing claims on the organization's resources through expectations of required and voluntary contributions.

The requirements of employees, partners, owners, and the community *define the environment and the general constraints that the organization must recognize* in its operations.

OBJECTIVE 2.2
The idea of the organization as a sequence of activities or a value chain

The discussion now turns to the group that determines the focus and objectives of an organization's activities, its customers. Exhibit 2–2 summarizes these groups, their contributions, and what they often expect from an organization.

Special Role of Customers

Organizations undertake activities to meet customer requirements. Customers define the fundamental reason for any organization to exist. Because the objective of any organization can be defined as meeting the needs of its customers within the operating constraints defined by its other stakeholders, we will focus on the customer when we evaluate the type and sequence of activities that the organization undertakes.

THE ORGANIZATION AS A SEQUENCE OF ACTIVITIES OR VALUE CHAIN

Consider the activities at Mike's Fast Foods, a restaurant that serves fast foods primarily to customers who take out the food to eat. Michael Rooney, the owner, is concerned about declining sales and profits and wonders what he can do to reverse these trends.

The major activities at Mike's Fast

EXHIBIT 2–2
Contributions and Requirements of the Organization's Stakeholders

GROUP	CONTRIBUTION	REQUIREMENTS	COMMENTS
Employees	Effort, skills, information	Rewards, interesting jobs, economic security, proper treatment	Employee requirements define the constraints that the system of activities designed to meet customer requirements must fulfill.
Partners	Goods, services, information	Financial rewards commensurate with the risk taken	Same as the comments for employees.
Owners	Capital	Financial rewards commensurate with the risk taken	Same as the comments for the employees.
Community	Allows the organization to operate or does not oppose its operation	Conformance to laws, good corporate citizenship and, perhaps, social leadership	Same as the comments for the employees.
Customers	Financial resources and/or the defined need served by the organization	Service, quality, value	This group's requirements define the purpose and focus of the system of activities designed and used by the organization.

Johnson Controls, a manu-
facturer of electronic components, communicates its
critical success factors to all
employees using a pin that
signifies its four key success
factors of quality, service,
productivity, and time com-
pression. *(Courtesy Johnson
Controls, Inc.)*

Foods include acquiring raw materials, hiring and training employees, making the products that the customers buy, serving customers, and responding to customer complaints. We will use Mike's Fast Foods to illustrate many of the ideas that we develop in this chapter.

It is useful to think of the organization as performing a sequence of activities whose output is a good or service[3] that is delivered to the organization's customer. For example, a library gives its customers a needed book or information, a government employment agency helps a client find a job, a theater group provides its audience with entertainment, and a computer manufacturer provides its customers with computers. Some people call a sequence of activities that creates a good or service a **value chain** since each step in the chain *should add something that the customer values* to the product.

Value chain
A sequence of activities whose objective is to provide a product to a customer or provide an intermediate good or service in a larger value chain.

Activity
A unit of work, or task, with a specific goal. Examples of activities are grading a student's examination, issuing a medicare check, and painting an automobile.

■ Activities

An **activity** is a unit of work, or task, with a specific goal. Examples are assembling a hamburger in a restaurant, interviewing a client in a welfare office, or setting up a machine in a factory.

[3] The discussion that follows applies equally to goods or services. Therefore, we will use the word *product* in the following discussion with the understanding that the product can be a good or service. Moreover, the discussion that follows applies equally to profit-seeking, not-for-profit, and government organizations.

There are four broad classes of activities in the value chain. See Exhibit 2–3, which depicts the items noted here.

1. *Activities relating to getting ready to make the product*, which include research and development, hiring and training employees, and buying raw materials, components, and equipment (input activities)

2. *Activities related to making the product*, which include operating the machines or using the tools to make the product, moving work in process around the facility, storing work in process, and inspecting partly completed work (processing activities)

3. *Activities related to dealing with the customer*, which include selling activities, billing activities, service activities, and distribution activities (output activities)

4. *Other activities that support the first three activities*, such as activities undertaken by the administrative functions, including personnel, accounting, and the general administrative offices (administrative activities)

■ Customer Perspective as a Means to Focus the Value Chain

Because the value chain exists to provide a product to the customer, it makes sense to evaluate the activities in the value chain from the customer's perspective. In fact, if we think of the value chain ending with the final customer, we can think of each link in the value chain as the customer of the previous link. If each link in the value chain focuses on meeting the needs of its customers, the organization will deliver the product that the final customer wants. This is a simple, but powerful, way to provide focus and coordination in an organization that may have literally thousands of activities in the value chain.

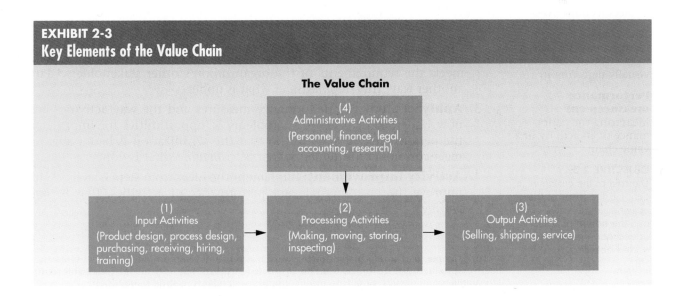

EXHIBIT 2-3
Key Elements of the Value Chain

The Value Chain

(4) Administrative Activities (Personnel, finance, legal, accounting, research)

(1) Input Activities (Product design, process design, purchasing, receiving, hiring, training)

(2) Processing Activities (Making, moving, storing, inspecting)

(3) Output Activities (Selling, shipping, service)

Listening to Stakeholders at Boeing Corporation

Faced with falling sales, increased competition, and declining employee morale caused by layoffs expected to total more than 20,000, Boeing Corporation had to change. The world's largest aircraft manufacturer has been forced to examine its management and production practices, some of which have been in place since 1945. Significant changes include involving customers in the design of Boeing's new 777, employee empowerment, adopting the philosophy of continuous improvement in operations, and moving to just-in-time manufacturing. These changes have been significant in a company that observers have characterized as authoritarian and imperial, and there are signs the company has been successful. In early 1994, Boeing's chairman announced that the company was halfway toward its goal of cutting costs by 25%. Industry observers expect that Boeing's new attitude and practices will result in making the 777 a commercial success.

Source: "Banking on a Big Bird," *The Economist*, March 12, 1994, pp. 73–74.

Effective
A process that meets its objectives.

Efficient
A process that uses the fewest possible resources to meet its objectives.

Charting
Identifying each activity in the value chain and visually depicting it.

Performance measurement
Measuring the performance of an activity or a value chain.

OBJECTIVE 2.3
The role of the customer in defining the focus of the activities in the value chain and the nature of value-added and nonvalue-added activities

■ Process Measurement and Improvement

So far, we have discussed the need for an organization to have a purpose that is defined by its stakeholders. The organization's purpose defines the focus and the objectives, or constraints, that the activities should achieve or that limit it. In addition, organizations need information to identify the current performance of their activities and to suggest opportunities for improvement.

At Mike's Fast Foods, if the customer wants a product that has a consistent quality, is delivered quickly, and costs less than the comparable products offered by competitors, the people undertaking each activity (such as those responsible for cleaning, ordering, customer service, and cooking) in the value chain can think of how to improve the performance of their respective activities in order to improve quality, service, and cost.

The most important role of the organization's employees is to manage the chain of activities in a way that is both effective and efficient. We say that an organization is **effective** if it achieves its purposes or objectives. We say that an organization is **efficient** if it uses the fewest resources possible to achieve its objectives.

Employees improve effectiveness and efficiency by performing these four general steps regarding the organization's activities:

1. **Charting:** Identify each activity in the process (value chain) that delivers the product to the customer, that is, *identifying and depicting* what is done.

2. **Performance measurement:** Measure the performance of each activity in the process (value chain) from the perspective of customer requirements while assuring that the overall performance of activities meets the requirements of the organization's other stakeholders.[4] Put another way, this step *measures* what is done.

3. **Analyze:** Study the performance measures and the way activities are now undertaken to identify problems or opportunities for improving the performance of activities so that the organization is better able to meet customer requirements, that is, *evaluating* what is done.

4. **Activity improvement:** Implement the ideas from step 3, analysis, to improve the customer-relevant performance of activities, that is, *improving*.

[4] For example, it is unacceptable for the organization to develop a sequence of activities that delivers products that customers want but is unsafe to workers, fails to provide a reasonable return to suppliers and owners, or fails to meet community standards relating to pollution.

While the responsibilities of management accountants can differ significantly, depending on the organization, one of their most important roles is to support completion of step 2 by developing the information or performance measures that organization members can use in each of these four steps.

PERFORMANCE MEASURES

Organizations must develop performance measures, called **critical performance indicators**, to assess performance on their critical success factors—the elements of performance that are required for success in meeting stakeholders' requirements. The three critical success factors that relate to the ability of the operations of most organizations to meet customer requirements are service, quality, and cost.

■ Service

Service refers to the product's tangible features, such as performance, taste, and functionality, and its intangible features, such as how people are treated when making the purchase decision and the amount of time it takes to deliver the product to the customer after it is ordered. In short, service is everything about the product that the customer values. *Therefore, an element of service is the organization's choice of what products to offer to its customers.* Some people call service the product's *value in use.* Giving good service means giving the customer what he wants.

Service is what the organization promises the customer to promote the purchase decision. It is the bundle of expectations that the customer has about all the facets surrounding the product's purchase and use. Therefore, service is what the customer pays for; what she is willing to pay for the product reflects the service she expects from it. For Mike's Fast Foods, service means everything that the customer expects when she comes through the door and includes restaurant layout, the behavior of the sales staff, the cleanliness, and the food selection.

Some elements of service are difficult to measure directly since they reflect the customer's subjective valuation of the package of product attributes. Therefore, performance on intangible service features is often measured indirectly using a performance measure such as sales volume, a measure of revealed customer valuation. Performance on other features can be measured directly, however. For example, Mike might keep track of how long it takes to serve a customer at Mike's Fast Foods during peak time or the number of times that he sees litter on the restaurant floor, as a measure of service. Developing measures of service performance is a major role of management accounting.

CONSIDER THIS . . .

Data Analysis in Action at Shell Oil

Shell Oil's Taft plant was having recurring problems with process water overflowing into the plant's chemical sewage basin. Using standard modeling and data analysis tools that isolated the characteristics of overflow situations, a plant employee discovered that the problem was being caused by a filter that was not working properly. The filter was repaired and the number of overflows dropped, saving the plant about $18,000 per year.

Quality
The similarity between the promised and the realized level of service.

Organizations find out about the type of service that customers expect by asking them. This provides information about changes and trends and helps identify what most customers want.[5] Many organizations have made the mistake of assuming that they know what their customers want without confirming this information directly with them.

■ Quality

Quality is defined relative to service. Service is everything that the customer is promised about the product. Quality relates to how well the organization delivers on its service commitments and means different things to different people. In the context of this text, **quality** means giving the customer what was promised; it is defined as conformance to specifications.

Many organizations believe that quality and efficiency are related because a process that produces high-quality products usually has high efficiency ratings. A plant engineer at H.J. Heinz observed, "The days we have the best quality are also the days we make the most product."

Once we have defined quality as conformance to specifications, we can see the basis for the remarks made by the plant engineer at Heinz. When quality is bad, production either has to be reworked or destroyed and the cost per unit of good production increases. As quality goes up, scrap and rework fall, as do costs. Think of it this way: In a given situation,[6] how can it ever be less expensive to do something incorrectly and then have to fix it rather than to do it right the first time?

Many people associate the quality of a product with its performance, attributes, or features. For example, many people believe that a Rolls Royce has higher quality than a Buick because it has more features. In this book, the differences between the performance, attributes, and features of a Buick and a Rolls Royce result in their classification as products with different services rather than as the same product, a car, with different qualities. When we define quality as conformance to specifications, Buicks actually have higher quality than Rolls Royces because, on average, customer surveys report that Buicks have fewer defects per vehicle than do Rolls Royces.

Quality is important to customers because they expect to get what they have paid for. What you pay for determines your expectations, and quality is

---

[5] Since most organizations cannot ask every customer what he wants, they must rely on sample information to make inferences about what the customer population wants.

[6] We are assuming that all elements in the processing system are fixed. Organizations may deliberately incur costs for improved raw materials, better equipment, better product design, better process layout, and employee training to reduce the incidence of defective production. These organizations are replacing the cost of finding and fixing bad production with the cost of preventing it.

Red Lobster, a chain of seafood restaurants, requires its suppliers to inspect every piece of fish they supply. Inspection ensures that all raw materials meet Red Lobster's high quality standards. Candling, which involves using a lighted background to inspect fish fillets, identifies imperfections such as blood spots, bones, and parasites in a fish fillet. (*Courtesy Greg Edwards*)

judged relative to your expectations. For example, you expect more from a meal in a 5-star restaurant than you do from a meal in a fast-food restaurant. Quality has to do with how each product lives up to your expectations. In the case of Mike's Fast Foods, quality relates to the attributes of the meal and its presentation. High quality means that the customer has a low risk of being disappointed. As organizations get better at keeping promises to customers, quality goes up.

■ Cost

Cost reflects the organization's ability to minimize the use of resources given the objectives that it seeks. Accomplishing the same things with fewer resources and, therefore, lower costs, means that the organization is becoming more efficient. Cost is important because of the relationship between a product's cost and its price. In the long run, the price an organization receives for a product must cover its costs or it will go out of the business of making that product. Since customers will buy the product with the lowest price, all other things being equal, keeping costs low provides an organization with a strong competitive advantage.

At the same time, in choosing among all the products that provide them with the services and quality they want, customers will buy the product that provides them with the preferred mix of services, quality, and price. If two products provide the same services and quality, however, the customer will choose the product with the lower price.

The return expectations of owners requires also that the difference between the revenue generated by the organization's products and their costs (the organization's profit) must be sufficient to meet the owners' return

Cost
Efficiency to the provider of a product; that is, using minimum resources to achieve objectives, and price paid to the purchaser of a product.

requirements. Therefore, to keep prices low and to meet the owners' return requirements, organizations must keep their costs low.

■ Overall Performance—Stakeholder Monitoring

If customers value service, quality, and cost performance, the organization must measure all these attributes to manage the performance of its activities. Exhibit 2–4 summarizes these important performance measures (indicators) for these critical success factors.

Recall that customer performance measures, or performance indicators, are important because they are made and evaluated on a continuous basis. The focus on customer performance measures does not mean, however, that performance measures related to meeting the needs of the organization's other stakeholders are unimportant and should be ignored.

For example, measures such as employee and partner satisfaction, employee and partner turnover, return on owners' investment, and the organization's image in the community are critical performance indicators for the organization to monitor. Performance on these other factors, with the exception of employee safety considerations, however, are usually monitored less frequently. In such cases, less frequent monitoring is appropriate since these factors are influenced by longer-term periodic decisions (such as the design of the production process or the organization) or discretionary expenditures (such as a donation to a charity) rather than the short-term, continuous decisions relating to operating a process controlling a sequence of events.

Sometimes there are exceptions to the general rule of continuously monitoring customer-related measures of organization performance, such as for high-risk systems that can cause serious problems for the organization. For example, (1) because the working environment provides a high potential for personal injury, most steel mills continuously monitor and report accidents involving personal injury; (2) because their facilities provide a high potential for environmental damage, most paper mills continuously monitor and report environmental incidents, such as accidental spills; and (3) because

EXHIBIT 2–4
Customer Performance

CRITICAL SUCCESS FACTOR	EXAMPLES OF CRITICAL PERFORMANCE INDICATORS
Service	Customer retention rate, number of customers, amount of purchases per customer, percent of customers served during peak period in the target service time, customer satisfaction surveys
Quality	Number of customer complaints per 1,000 orders filled, customer satisfaction surveys
Cost	Ratio of costs to revenues, ratio of material in final product to material purchased, ratio of labor allowed for work done to total labor, sales per hour during peak operations

their environment provides a high potential for political damage, most political parties continuously monitor and report political incidents, such as reported misdeeds by party members.

Suppose that Mike Rooney can purchase a stove for Mike's Fast Foods that will reduce costs by using less fuel. This is attractive because it would reduce costs, thereby allowing Mike to lower his prices and still improve profit performance. This option is attractive to both customers and owners. The stove may be dangerous in a fast-food environment, however, and may represent an unacceptably high risk to employees. Issues relating to meeting employee, partner, owner, and community needs are usually affected by long-term decisions that create the environment within which people operate the production systems and are considered when a process is designed or improved, which is a periodic decision requiring frequent, rather than continuous, reporting of information.

PERFORMANCE MEASUREMENT

Performance measurement is perhaps the most important, most misunderstood, and most difficult task in management accounting. An effective system of performance measurement contains critical performance indicators (performance measures) that (1) consider each activity and the organization itself from the *customer's perspective*, (2) evaluate each activity using *customer-validated* measures of performance, (3) consider all facets of activity performance that affect customers and, therefore, are *comprehensive*, and (4) provide *feedback* to help organization members identify problems and opportunities for improvement.

OBJECTIVE 2.4
The role of performance measures in helping organization members to manage the value chain

■ Reflection of the Customer's Perspective

Performance measures should summarize the things that are critical to the organization's success in meeting customer requirements. This attribute is very basic, yet many organizations fail to measure systematically what their customers want and value. Customer-focused performance measures help organization members manage activities by concentrating their attention on improving what matters to the customer. If all employees at Mike's Fast Foods know that customers require fast service in a clean environment and products that are delivered consistently, and at a low price, they can all manage their activities accordingly, even if they do not deal directly with customers. For example, maintenance personnel can interpret these objectives to mean that equipment should be maintained so that it will prepare the food consistently and will not fail during use.

■ Reflection of the Customer's Validation

Performance measures should be external, or customer validated, rather than internal and should reflect an understanding of the difference between the output and outcome of activities. This requires the ability to define precisely what customers value.

Output
A physical measure of production or activity, such as the number of units produced or the amount of time spent doing something.

Outcome
The value attributed to output by the customer, for example, the number of good units of production and the amount of client satisfaction generated by a service.

An **output** is a physical measure of activity such as the number of units produced or the amount of time spent doing something. An **outcome** is how the customer values the result of the activity, such as the number of good units of production or the amount of client satisfaction generated by a service. For example, in a government office that helps people find jobs, output is the number of hours spent counseling clients and outcomes are the number of jobs found that meet clients' legitimate expectations. In a university, output is the numbers of credit hours of instruction given to a student and outcome is what the student learned in the course.[7]

Most organizations measure outputs (such as number of pieces made, number of words typed, number of shipments delivered) rather than outcomes (such as number of pieces made that met customer requirements, number of good words typed, number of shipments delivered without damage and on time). *The critical difference between outcome and output measurement is that outcome focuses on effectiveness in meeting customer requirements but output does not. Therefore, an organization that focuses on improving outputs fails to distinguish between what is done and what is done that is valuable.*

■ Reflection Comprehensive Information

An effective program of performance measurement assesses all facets of relevant performance so that the decision maker will not trade off relevant, but unmeasured, facets of performance for performance on measured facets. Organizations must avoid falling into the trap of thinking "if we can't measure what we want, then we will want what we can measure."[8]

When Domino's Pizza promised its customers it would deliver pizzas to their homes within 30 minutes or it would provide a $3 refund, it was both defining and guaranteeing its service. What Domino's did not envision, or intend, was that young, often inexperienced drivers would race through the streets to meet the 30-minute service commitments. Consumers began to complain about this guarantee and told Domino's Pizza that they would

---

[7] This assumes that the student's objective is to acquire knowledge. If the student's objective is strictly to get course grades to support finding a job, grades are the outcomes.

[8] The difficulty of finding performance measures that are aligned with intended performance and the problems created if an appropriate performance measure is not found are well known in the organization behavior literature. For example, see Steven Kerr, "On the Folly of Rewarding A, While Hoping for B," *Academy of Management Journal* 18, no. 4 (1975), pp. 769–783.

rather wait longer for their pizzas and have these delivery people drive more slowly. The people running the individual Domino's Pizza outlets felt the same way and were willing to break the service guarantee and pay customers the $3. By focusing only on one facet of performance—speed—Domino's Pizza sent the message to its employees that speed alone, and not any other important facet, like safety, counted. This issue reached a conclusion in December 1993 when a jury awarded $99 million to a woman who suffered head and spine injuries after she was broadsided by a Domino's Pizza driver who ran a red light. Shortly after, Domino's discontinued its promise of a 30-minute delivery.

As another example of how focusing attention on a single performance measure can lead to dysfunctional behavior, suppose that the counter staff at Mike's Fast Foods is told to take and fill orders quickly to improve the rate of servicing customers. Customers who are unable to communicate their orders quickly (for example, they may be new to the restaurant and unfamiliar with the menu or they may have language or hearing problems) will frustrate the employees who may be evaluated on their rate of sales. In turn, the employees might be rude to, or even ignore, customers they believe might impede their productivity. Therefore, the counter staff at Mike's Fast Foods should be told to focus on providing good service first and then working to improve speed.

■ Provision of Feedback

Performance measures should be understandable and tailored to the people who manage the activity. An effective performance measurement program should help the people managing the process to identify problems and suggest solutions to them. This attribute reflects the purposeful nature of performance measurement in assessing operations and providing a guide for improvement.

WARNING SIGNALS   A **signal** is information provided to a decision maker. Performance measures usefully provide two types of signals. The first type is a *warning* that something is wrong, in the same way that an increase in a person's temperature signals a problem. The warning signal triggers an investigation to uncover its cause in order to correct the problem.

In business, warning signals are usually provided by profit or cost measures and are used by supervisory management to monitor ongoing operations for which they are responsible but do not operate directly. For example, at Mike's Fast Foods, declining sales and a declining profit as a percentage of sales would be a signal to the store manager that there are underlying problems relating to attracting customers and controlling costs that require identification and correction.

DIAGNOSTIC SIGNALS   The second type of signal is *diagnostic* and suggests what the problem is and, perhaps, a path to follow to solve it. For example, many automobiles have monitoring systems that can sense a loss of pressure in the braking system. If the monitoring system detects a problem, it stores a code in its memory to indicate the problem that it has identified and

Signal
Information provided to a decision maker. There are two types of signals: (1) a warning that there is a problem and (2) a diagnostic that identifies the problem.

signals the driver with a warning light that service is required. The driver, who might have little or no mechanical ability, has been warned that something is wrong that requires an expert's attention. Then the service mechanic can use a tool to access the stored code, which is a diagnostic signal that identifies why the monitoring system turned on the warning light.

In response to declining sales, which is a warning signal, the manager at Mike's Fast Foods might undertake a customer survey that identifies, among other things, that cleanliness is a problem in the restaurant. This specific, or diagnostic, information focuses attention on cleaning activities.

People who directly manage activities need both warning and diagnostic information to identify problems that require attention. Unfortunately, most diagnostic information is expensive to gather systematically, and organizations usually use warning information, particularly financial information, to trigger the gathering of diagnostic information.

PERFORMANCE MEASURES AS AIDS IN OPERATIONS CONTROL

We can summarize the role of performance measures by saying that they are a critical part of operations control. **Control** is the set of methods and tools that organization members use to keep the organization on track toward achieving its objectives.

Control
The set of methods and tools that organization members use to keep the organization on track toward achieving its objectives.

The organization's customers determine operations' objectives within the context of the constraints defined by the organization's other stakeholders. Control may be exercised by (1) developing standard procedures or (2) hiring qualified people who understand the organization's objectives, telling

Many organizations use quality boards, which summarize quality-related performance and information in a prominent place. The idea of quality boards is to signal to employees that quality is important. The boards provide diagnostic information that employees can use to identify and solve quality problems.
(Courtesy Tony Atkinson)

them to do whatever they think is best to help the organization achieve its objectives, and using the control system to evaluate the resulting performance, thereby assessing how well they have done. For example, to illustrate the point made in (1), Mike's Fast Foods might develop a standard way to make a hamburger and require that all hamburgers be cooked using this method and to enforce compliance with that method. To illustrate the point made in (2), Mike's Fast Foods might hire a manager who is told to do whatever is necessary to achieve the owner's objectives.

Information is important in both of these systems of exercising control. When control is used to *ensure compliance with standard operating procedures*, information is used to motivate people to follow rules and to verify that they follow them. When control is used *to motivate people to be creative in meeting* customer objectives, information is used to inform people and help them choose a course of action that helps the organization achieve its objectives.

PERFORMANCE STANDARDS

Once the organization has decided what critical performance indicators to monitor and has developed a system to capture these measurements, it must evaluate performance. Part of the performance evaluation process is to compare realized, or actual, performance with some standard or target. A discrepancy between the actual and planned performance levels, for example, failing to meet sales targets at Mike's Fast Foods, signals a problem that, in turn, invokes a problem-solving exercise to solve it.

Organizations develop performance standards in many different ways. A number of organizations set performance standards for a process based on its estimated potential. For example, an engineer might study a bottling machine and conclude, based on its design and operating characteristics, that it should be able to fill 1,500 bottles per hour. Based on experience, the manager at Mike's Fast Foods might believe that a food preparer should be able to make a hamburger in 20 seconds. Performance would be evaluated relative to these standards of performance potential.

Other organizations set performance targets based on improving past performance. For example, a study of past performance might reveal that tailors complete 20 shirts per hour. Based on this information, the target for current performance might be set at 21 shirts per hour.

The problem with basing performance standards either on potential or on past performance is that these standards provide no sense of urgency because they do not reflect what is going on in the world outside the organization. These standards usually are intended to encourage people to work harder or faster, not smarter, because the emphasis is on improving the way that things are done and eliminating things that do not improve the product's attributes. Pressures to work harder will create organization frictions if the people subjected to these standards challenge them quietly or openly.

Today many organizations are taking a different approach to evaluating performance that reflects a broader management approach to operations. That philosophy is called *continuous improvement*, which involves continu-

Competitive benchmarking
An organization's search for, and implementation of, the best way to do something as practiced by another organization.

OBJECTIVE 2.5
Benchmarking and continuous improvements as tools to improve organization performance

ously reevaluating and improving ongoing activities. Part of this philosophy of continuous improvement includes a tool called *competitive benchmarking*.

COMPETITIVE BENCHMARKING AND CONTINUOUS IMPROVEMENT

Competitive benchmarking is an organization's search for, and implementation of, the best way to do something as practiced in other organizations. Many observers credit Xerox, the manufacturer of copying equipment, with developing the systematic approach to benchmarking that many organizations use today. During the 1970s, Xerox was shocked to discover how poor its manufacturing performance was compared to that of Fuji-Xerox, its Japanese subsidiary. Xerox set out to improve its practices by comparing them to those of its foreign subsidiaries, its competitors, and organizations in other industries. For example, to improve its inventory handling and shipping practices, Xerox visited L.L. Bean, a mail-order retailer with an inventory management process that industry analysts considered to be the best in the business. Xerox learned many things from L.L. Bean that helped improve Xerox's inventory operations. Along the same lines, the manager at Mike's Fast Foods might visit competitors to study how they perform customer service activities, organize their kitchens, design their products, buy raw materials, and manage staffing in order to design better ways of doing things at Mike's Fast Foods.

Benchmarking attempts to identify an activity, such as billing, that needs to be improved, find an organization that is doing that job well, study its process, and then put that process, or an improved version of it, into operation.

Because best practices are always changing, benchmarking is associated with the philosophy of always looking to do things better, which is part of the philosophy of continuous improvement. *Continuous improvement* is the relentless search to (1) document, understand, and improve the activities that the organization undertakes to meet its customers' requirements, (2) eliminate processing activities that do not add product features that customers value, and (3) improve the performance of activities that increase customer value or satisfaction.

Because competitive benchmarking is both expensive and time consuming, the main source of process improvement ideas is ongoing internal problem solving and improvement activities conducted by organization members. Today many organizations are using systems of employee involvement or empowerment to encourage employees to use their ideas to improve activity performance.

CONSIDER THIS . . .

Benchmarking at Chrysler Corporation

Many people see benchmarking as an effective way to remain competitive. An interviewer asked Robert Eaton, the incoming chairman of Chrysler Corporation, if benchmarking was a big priority. Eaton replied,

Without a doubt, I've felt for many years that if you don't know where you are and where you're going, then any route will do. You must know where you are in relation to the best and where you're trying to go—and that's to exceed the best in the world, or to be right among them. If you don't know those two things, you're unquestionably not going to be there. You won't make it.

The **Deming Wheel** has been proposed as a means of organizing process improvements.[9] The Deming Wheel, shown in Exhibit 2–5, involves a *continuous* cycle of

1. *Planning:* developing specific objectives and using measures of past performance to evaluate past results relative to those objectives
2. *Doing:* putting improvements identified during the planning phase into effect
3. *Checking:* identifying, by using performance measures, whether the plan has had its intended effect
4. *Action:* preventing the reoccurrence of the corrected problem by ensuring that successful process revisions become permanent for each task in the organization

The idea is to *continuously* monitor and analyze a task's results and to look for a better way to do that task.

Many people believe that this drive for continuous improvement is best accomplished by training and empowerment of the person doing the task to evaluate the performance results and to develop needed process improvements. This idea is based on the belief that the person doing the task has the best mix of skills and detailed knowledge of the operation to make improvements.

[9] Kaizen, Masaaki Imai, *The Key to Japan's Competitive Success* (New York: McGraw-Hill, 1968), pp. 60–65.

Deming Wheel
A means to organize process improvements, which involves a continuous cycle of planning, doing, checking, and action.

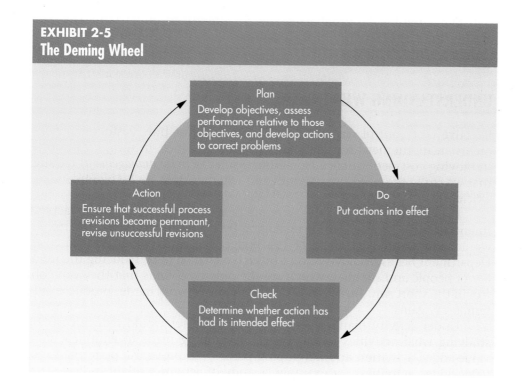

EXHIBIT 2-5
The Deming Wheel

Plan
Develop objectives, assess performance relative to those objectives, and develop actions to correct problems

Do
Put actions into effect

Action
Ensure that successful process revisions become permanant, revise unsuccessful revisions

Check
Determine whether action has had its intended effect

ORGANIZATION PERFORMANCE MEASURES—A SUMMARY

Let us now turn from our general discussion of performance measures and continuous improvement to focus specifically on more details of cost as a performance measure. Although costs seem to be a straightforward topic, some aspects related to costs require careful consideration.

COSTS AND MANAGING BY THE NUMBERS

In the past, cost information supported a process called *managing by the numbers*. If the company is managed by the numbers, planners will decide how much costs need to be reduced and then they will reduce each facility's or department's budget by that amount.

Managing by the numbers has three problems: (1) It is ineffective, (2) it assumes that cost is the only relevant measure of an activity's performance, and (3) it does not recognize the reasons that costs exist in an organization.

In response to a budget cut, in the short run, each group will work a little harder to cope with its cutback because it is trying to do the same things with less money. This pace quickly tires people out however, and, before long, there will be pressures to rehire the people who were laid off. For example, Mike's Fast Foods might react to its low profits by reducing the number of people employed. In the short run, the staff might respond by working harder and, perhaps, even by staying after their shift to catch up on cleaning, stocking, and other activities that can be postponed when the customers are in the restaurant.

Managing by the numbers makes no attempt to understand *why* costs exist in the organization; rather, it assumes that costs are bad and should be eliminated.

OBJECTIVE 2.6
The relationship between organization activities and costs

UNDERSTANDING WHAT CAUSES COSTS

Effective cost control requires an understanding of how customer requirements create the need for activities and how activities, in turn, create costs. Improving cost performance (sometimes called *activity management*) requires that we study the need for activities and whether they are being undertaken efficiently.

For example, consider the activities of a clothing manufacturer facing a financial crisis. In a system of managing by the numbers, each department would be allocated its share of the budget cut and told to reduce costs. Department heads usually respond to such a challenge by reducing the number of people and supplies, which are the only cost items that they can control in the short run. However, asking everyone to work harder produces only temporary gains.

Under activity management, the manufacturer would reduce costs by studying what activities it undertakes, developing plans to eliminate non-value-added activities, and developing plans to improve the performance of value-added activities. For example, a study of activities might indicate that

50% of labor costs in the factory relate to handling work in process, which adds nothing to the attributes of the product that customers value. Instead, handling activities reflect organization constraints, poor product design, and a poor factory layout. If this organization took the time to redesign the product, to simplify the processing needed to make each one, and to rearrange the layout of its factory to reduce the need for handling, many of these handling costs would be eliminated permanently without any effect on the value of the product to the customer. Relative to competitors who continue to undertake those handling activities, this organization would acquire a permanent cost advantage. In the short run, other organizations that had not eliminated those handling activities might sprint, as the employees might do in Mike's Fast Foods in response to a cut in personnel. The sprint cannot be maintained over the long run, however, because people eventually tire of working harder to make up for inefficient product or process designs.

Eliminating activities that do not improve the product attributes that customers value is a very effective way to cut costs. Philip Crosby, one of the noted quality gurus of the 1980s, argued that "quality is free." Crosby believes that $1 spent in preventing defective production will result in savings of at least $1, and usually more, in the costs of detecting and fixing quality problems. At Mike's Fast Foods, for example, spending $10 to train an employee how to avoid common mistakes is likely to repay itself many times over by reducing customer ill-will caused by those mistakes.

INFORMATION ABOUT ACTIVITIES

Because of the performance improvement potential resulting from improved activity management, many experts have argued that organizations should develop activity data, such as the amount of time taken to make and deliver a product or service, the amount of materials handled, storage space used on the factory floor, and rework done, and then manage by using these activity data rather than cost data. These activity data would not only identify problems but also, in many cases, suggest an approach to solve problems. Many organizations are now developing activity information, which is used as diagnostic information to improve performance. At the same time, organizations are developing information about activity costs to use as warning signals of the cost of nonvalue-added activities and to prioritize improvement efforts.

WHY ORGANIZATIONS USE COST PERFORMANCE MEASURES

Consider the relationships in Exhibit 2–6, which shows how activities create costs from left to right. The activities that organizations undertake to make a product and deliver it to the customer create a demand for resources—materials, labor, and equipment. The acquisition and consumption of these resources create costs, which the accounting system measures.

The most primitive level of control is simply to try to reduce costs, which we called *managing by the numbers*. For example, one strategy, which is common in government, is to institute a hiring freeze. This reduces costs in the short run because the hiring freeze reduces the amount of labor that the organization unit is allowed to employ and pay in the short run. A hiring freeze does nothing to control costs in the long run, however, because nothing has been done to reduce the underlying demand for labor by eliminating the need for the activity that causes the demand for it.

■ Value-Added and Nonvalue-Added Activities and Cost Performance

Once we begin to study the activities that create costs, we begin to get insights into how to reduce costs. Exhibit 2–5 shows four types of activities, each of which has two indices. The first index identifies whether the activity is either value added or nonvalue added. A **value-added activity** is an activity that, if eliminated, would reduce the product's service to the customer in the long run. For example, acquiring the raw materials to make a product is a value-added activity because, without them, the organization would be unable to make the product. Painting an automobile is a value-added activity because

Value-added activity
An activity that, if eliminated, would reduce the product's service to the customer in the long run.

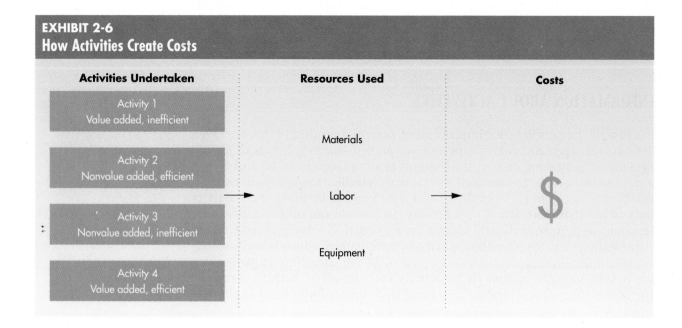

EXHIBIT 2-6
How Activities Create Costs

Activities Undertaken	Resources Used	Costs
Activity 1 — Value added, inefficient	Materials	
Activity 2 — Nonvalue added, efficient	Labor	$
Activity 3 — Nonvalue added, inefficient		
Activity 4 — Value added, efficient	Equipment	

At the end of the sugar refining process, liquid sucrose is heated in a vacuum. After the heating is completed, the vacuum is broken and the residual material, called massecuite, is separated into sugar crystals. This executive at Savannah Foods installed a continuous pan to replace the batch vacuum pan. In the new process, liquid sucrose goes in and massecuite is pumped out in a continuous process. There is no cleaning, the vacuum is never broken, and there is no wasted time. Eliminating two nonvalue-added activities (breaking the vacuum and cleaning) results in savings, greater productivity, and higher quality. *(Courtesy Colonial Sugars)*

customers want painted cars. We evaluate each value-added activity by how it contributes to the final product's service, quality, and cost.

We call any activity that cannot be classified as value added a **nonvalue-added activity**.[10] Nonvalue-added activities are characterized by their negativeness because they have the potential to reduce the organization's results on every facet of performance that the customer values.[11]

An organization performs nonvalue-added activities because the current product design or process design requires them. As previously mentioned, poor facility layout requires that the work in process be moved during production. Since a customer neither knows nor cares about how many times the product was moved around the facility while it was being made, moving work

Nonvalue-added activity
An activity that presents the opportunity for cost reduction without reducing the product's service potential to the customer.

[10] Some people call the costs created by nonvalue-added activities and the costs created by the poor design of value-added activities *chronic waste* because these costs can be reduced only by eliminating the need to perform nonvalue-added activities or by redesigning activities to eliminate inefficiencies. *Sporadic waste* refers to inefficiencies created by the improper operation, rather than the design, of activities.

[11] Because they invariably involve handling work in process and because handling often leads to damage, nonvalue-added activities often degrade, but never improve, quality. Because they are not done instantaneously, nonvalue-added activities decrease service by increasing cycle time and by increasing the amount of time it takes to discover mistakes, thereby increasing the number of mistakes that are made. Nonvalue-added activities usually reflect the organization's limitations and constraints and, therefore, they often reduce, but never increase, flexibility. Because they are never costless, nonvalue-added activities increase costs.

in process around an office, a store, or a factory adds nothing to the value that the customer assigns to the product.

Organizations cannot just eliminate nonvalue-added activities; they must instead change the underlying process that makes nonvalue-added activities necessary. To eliminate nonvalue-added activities, organizations must improve the underlying process so that they are no longer required. Therefore, a longer and more accurate definition of a nonvalue-added activity is *an activity that presents the opportunity for cost reduction without reducing the product's service potential to the customer.* Classifying an activity as nonvalue added reflects judgment about whether or not it will ever be possible to reduce and eventually eliminate the activity and, therefore, its cost by improving the product design or process layout. The drive to reduce and eliminate nonvalue-added activities is important because, by doing so, the organization permanently reduces the costs it must incur to make its goods or services without affecting the value the customer assigns to the product.

Some activities are tricky to classify. For example, the law may require that a factory not pollute its environment. Therefore, we might classify pollution abatement equipment and activities as value added. If we designed a process or used raw materials or equipment that created no pollution, however, we could avoid the cost of pollution abatement equipment.

We always should be careful when we assume that an activity is value added. For example, in wine making, classifying storing as a value-added activity assumes that the only way to make fine wine is to store it and allow it to age. Think of the advantage that someone would have if she discovered a way to make wine that tasted as good as conventionally aged wine but did not require long storage periods.

■ Efficient and Inefficient Activities and Cost Performance

Exhibit 2–6 also uses an index to classify the activity as either efficient or inefficient. Recall from our earlier discussion that *efficient* means that the activity is being done with no excess consumption of resources. We can determine whether an activity is being done relatively efficiently by comparing our performance against other organizations. *Inefficient* means that the activity uses more resources than it should to produce the desired outcome.

Return to Exhibit 2–6. Activities 2 and 3 should be eliminated in the long run because they add nothing to the product that the customer values. When we eliminate activities 2 and 3, we also eliminate activities that demand resources that, in turn, create costs. Therefore, by deleting nonvalue-added activities, we reduce the organization's long-term cost structure.

In the short run, however, when we cannot change the process or product design that creates the need for these nonvalue-added activities, we might try to improve the efficiency of type 3 activities to reduce costs while keeping in mind that our ultimate goal is to eliminate the need to perform these activities. Mike's Fast Foods, for example, might have a supervisor who inspects each product before it is packaged to ensure that it is complete and looks acceptable. This inspection cost is incurred because the employees have not been trained or are not trusted to inspect their own work. If the employees were taught how to inspect their own work and were motivated to do the inspection properly, Mike would eliminate the need for the supervisor. Until the employees have been trained to undertake self-inspection, however, Mike must use the supervisor and look for ways to improve the efficiency of the supervisor's inspection activities.

Next we consider activity 1, a value-added activity that is being poorly done. We might find that one reason it is taking so long to accomplish is that the employee's work area is poorly laid out and, therefore, people have to wait for parts they need to complete their task. For example, General Motors decided to improve the process that assemblers used to make the complicated front seats for its Cadillacs. The assemblers were given worktables on wheels; in addition, the assemblers could adjust the height of the worktables so that they could see well and work comfortably. The process of supplying the parts that went into the seats also was redesigned. The parts were put into bins along a U-shaped path about 10 meters long. The shape and length of the path minimized the distance the assembler had to travel. The bins highlighted inventory levels which, in turn, permitted the factory to minimize the amount of parts inventory it carried. At the same time, it provided a signal concerning when parts had to be restocked. The assembler pushed the worktable along the path, taking needed parts from the bins and assembling them into the seat. These simple changes improved both the efficiency of the assembly process and the quality of the seats.

Based on a study of competitor's practices, the manager at Mike's Fast Foods might reorganize the kitchen to minimize the movement of people who prepare the food. The layout could be redesigned so that the food preparers do not have to move from one spot to another when preparing the food for cooking.

Making such improvements implies an understanding of how activities create the demand for resources and, in turn, how resources consume costs. We get a warning signal that something is wrong when we benchmark our costs. The manager at Mike's Fast Foods may find out that, on average, the cost to make a hamburger at Mike's Fast Foods is 5% higher than a competitor's costs.

Costs are warning signals, not diagnostic signals, because they indicate the presence, but not the cause, of excess costs. To understand and improve processes, we need to understand how costs behave so that we can attack the root causes of excess costs. Cost information is important, however, to help organization members identify the cost of activities so that efforts to eliminate nonvalue-added activities or improve value-added activities and nonvalue-added activities that cannot be eliminated in the short run can be prioritized.

After studying costs, the manager at Mike's Fast Foods might estimate that the cost of food waste resulting from inefficient practices in ordering food is $5,000 per week and the estimated cost of labor wasted from inefficient layout of the kitchen is $2,000 per week. Both of these activities should be improved, but the food-ordering practices would be tackled first because they promise higher cost savings if resolved.

■ The Importance of Other Stakeholders' Criteria on Classifying Activities

So far we have classified activities as value added or nonvalue added and as efficient or inefficient. This discussion requires an important qualification. To this point, we have considered only the customer's perspective in classifying activities. We must be careful when we are classifying activities to recall that other stakeholders also define constraints that organizations must meet and that some activities may reflect some of the constraints defined by other stakeholders.

For example, customers may want products at the lowest possible price. To keep costs low, an organization might spend as little as possible on employee safety and, consequently, provide a dangerous working environment. Even if a dangerous work environment did *not* affect employee attitudes and performance, most governments consider dangerous working conditions socially undesirable and have passed laws that regulate work environments. Therefore, dangerous working conditions would fail to meet community expectations about the type of work environment that organizations should provide.

Similarly, although inspection is usually viewed as an nonvalue-added activity, sometimes the law requires it. For example, government contracting usually requires 100 percent inspection of parts critical to aircraft. Consumer product safety laws require 100 percent inspection of the formulation of batches of chemicals used to prepare prescription drugs that are critical to a patient's life. Therefore, we always must be careful to evaluate whether an activity is value added and efficient within the constraints that the organization's stakeholders define for the organization's operations.

ACTIVITY, OR VALUE, ANALYSIS

Activity analysis
An approach to operations control that involves the application of steps of continuous improvement to an activity; also known as *value analysis*.

Activity analysis is an approach to operations control that began to enjoy extensive use during the 1980s. An activity is any discrete task that an organization undertakes to make or deliver a product or service. Specifically, activity analysis has four steps:

1. *Identify the process objectives* that are defined by what the customer wants, or expects, from the process.
2. *Record by charting*, from start to finish, the activities used to complete the product or service.[12]
3. *Classify* all activities as value added or nonvalue added.
4. *Continuously improve* the efficiency of all activities and develop plans to eliminate nonvalue-added activities.

[12] Sometimes (1) and (2) are combined and referred to as *charting*. The important consideration is that activities must be identified in order to be charted, or depicted. (Refer to the related discussion of the general steps employees perform regarding an organization's activities on p. 46.)

Exhibit 2–7 summarizes these steps. Activity analysis has proved very useful in helping organizations to identify opportunities to reduce costs and to improve quality and processing time in a systematic way.

Activity analysis represents a systematic way for organizations to think about the processes that they use to provide products to their customers.

■ Storyboards: A Structured and Comprehensive Approach to Charting

Storyboarding describes an individual activity in a process on a card or piece of paper that is then tacked onto a large board. When each of the process activities has been described on a card, the sequence of the individual cards on the storyboard is a process flowchart. Writers and animators at the Walt Disney studios began using storyboards in the 1930s and 1940s as they designed the sequence of events in full-length animated feature films.

Storyboards provide a visual, practical, and low-cost tool to use in activity analysis. They provide a ready means to involve all the people who work on activities in the process of identifying and describing those activities.

EXHIBIT 2-7
Steps in Activity Analysis

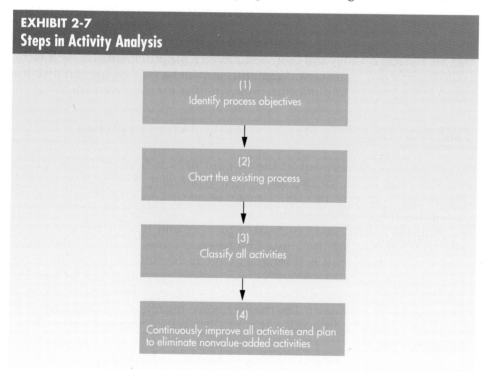

(1) Identify process objectives

(2) Chart the existing process

(3) Classify all activities

(4) Continuously improve all activities and plan to eliminate nonvalue-added activities

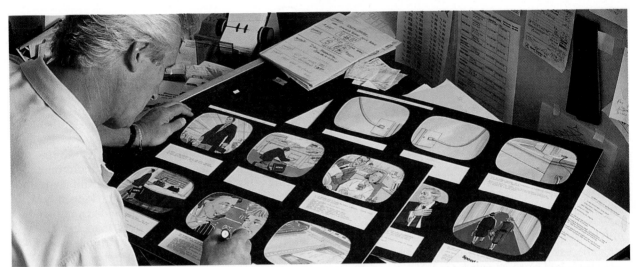

This illustrator is developing the storyboad for a television commercial. The idea behind the storyboard is to develop the story line using a series of illustrations. During the design phase, the storyboard provides a vehicle through which all project participants can contribute their ideas. During the implementation phase, the story board provides the basis for a common understanding of what is to be undertaken. In the same way, organizations use storyboards to ensure a broad participation in identifying the sequence of activities the organization uses to make a good or service and as a basis for identifying process improvement opportunities.

After the process has been depicted on the storyboard by individual cards, the next step is to identify how each activity on the storyboard contributes to the organization's success. For example, activities deemed to be value added could be presented on green cards. Activities identified as non-value added could be presented on red cards, which makes them highly visible targets for potential elimination. If the organization's critical success factors are service, quality, and cost, performance measurements for each factor could be recorded on its card. Again, this provides a very visible and practical approach to identify and prioritize opportunities for improvement.

TIME REQUIREMENTS FOR ACTIVITIES AND CYCLE TIME

Organizations are interested in the amount of time it takes to undertake a sequence of activities for two reasons. First, although there is no systematic information to support this belief, many people believe that a number of the costs of nonproduction personnel, equipment, and supplies vary proportionally with the time it takes to make a product and that these costs can be reduced by eliminating the causes of long cycle times. Intuitively this makes sense because whether it is storing, moving, inspecting, or processing that is added to cycle time, that activity will cost money. Second, in many instances, customers value a prompt response, and therefore a short process time, to their request for a product. For these reasons, organizations have started to express an interest in measuring the time it takes to complete a sequence of activities, or cycle.

■ Cycle Time

Some analysts have proposed classifying activities into four types: (1) processing, (2) moving, (3) storing (also called *waiting*), and (4) inspecting. Analysts call the sum of the times spent on all four activities, which is the total time that the organization takes to make the good or produce the service, the product's manufacturing **cycle time**. The interest in cycle time reflects the widespread belief that a product's service, quality, and cost are all roughly related to cycle time: Service and quality are thought to go down as cycle time goes up and cost is thought to go up as cycle time increases.

On the surface, a relationship between cycle time and some of the organization's costs makes sense. As the efficiency of value-added activities improves, the number of people and the amount of equipment, materials, and supplies used to make a product decreases, as does the cycle time because the number of activities decreases or the time for each activity diminishes. As nonvalue-added activities related to moving, inspecting, and storing are reduced, the number of people and the amount of equipment, materials, and supplies used in the process decrease and cycle time decreases because there are fewer activities. Therefore, we would expect that as we improve the efficiency of value-added activities or eliminate nonvalue-added activities, the process cycle time and cost will fall. Many people use cycle time as an index of the amount of waste in the process.

Cycle time
The total time the organization needs to complete an activity or a process.

■ Manufacturing Cycle Efficiency

A popular measure for assessing process efficiency is **manufacturing cycle efficiency (MCE)**:

Manufacturing cycle efficiency =

$$\frac{\text{Processing time}}{\text{Processing time} + \text{Moving time} + \text{Storing time} + \text{Inspection time}}$$

Manufacturing cycle efficiency
The ratio of the time required by value-added activities in a value chain to the total time required by all activities in the value chain.

Exhibit 2–8 summarizes the results of a cycle time study of the process that a furniture company used to make a batch of stereo component cabinets.

EXHIBIT 2–8
Cycle Time Results

ACTIVITY	TIME TAKEN (HOURS)
Processing	23
Moving	12
Storing	475
Inspecting	5
Total	515

The manufacturing cycle efficiency for this product was

$$\text{Manufacturing cycle efficiency} = \left[\frac{23}{23 + 12 + 475 + 5} \right] = 4.5\%$$

You might wonder why the time taken for storing is so large relative to the time spent actually working on the product. Moreover, you might be surprised to know that most organizations have a manufacturing cycle efficiency below 10 percent. The reason for this is the batch nature of most manufacturing and many service operations, which we now consider.

FACILITIES LAYOUT

Process layout
A means of organizing a production activity so that all similar equipment or functions are grouped together, for example, a university where faculty are housed by department.

To understand why inventories pile up in conventional processing systems, thereby creating cycle time, you have to understand the conventional way that facilities, whether they are factories or offices, are organized. In a **process layout**, all similar equipment or functions are grouped together. For example, at most universities, the offices of staff in the same department or faculty are close together. Most large automobile service stations are organized so that mufflers are fixed in one area, wheel alignments are done in another area, body work and painting in another area, and mechanical work

This picture shows a manufacturing cell in an ITW DeVilbiss factory that makes air-spray equipment. The cellular approach to manufacturing minimizes the amount of work-in-process moving and handling by locating the equipment needed to make a product in a single area in the factory. Cellular manufacturing helps the company to improve quality, reduce cycle times, and reduce costs. The bins in the right foreground, are called *KanBan bins* and indicate which parts are needed by the assembly cell. Work in this machining cell is triggered by the return of empty bins from the assembly cell. *(Courtesy ITW)*

in still another area. In most printing shops, similar machines are grouped together.

Process layouts tend to be used by organizations in which production is done in small batches of unique products. In a process layout, the product is moved from area to area while it is being made. Work in process is stored in each area in a process layout as it waits to be worked on.

In a **product layout**, equipment is organized to accommodate making a specific product (e.g., an automobile assembly line or a packaging line for cereal or milk). Product layouts are used for high-volume products. In a product layout, the product is moved along the assembly line and the parts that are added to it are stored along the line. In large cities, some hospitals become specialized, and then the people requiring a particular specialty go to such a designated hospital. The resulting volume of specialized patients justifies a product layout for treating that specialty.

A third approach to layout is a hybrid approach that is often called **cell manufacturing**. In cell manufacturing, different machines are grouped together to make products that have roughly similar processing requirements. The machines are usually flexible and can be adjusted easily, or even automatically, to make the different products. The result is a product layout line in the middle of a factory or office that otherwise has a process layout.[13]

Product layout
A means of organizing a production activity so that equipment or functions are organized to make a specific product, for example, an automobile assembly line.

Cell manufacturing
A means of organizing a production activity so that all the equipment needed to make a good or service is grouped together.

■ Process Layout Systems: An Example

In a process layout, which most organizations use, work in process follows a serpentine path, usually in batches, through the factories and offices that create it. Along this path are processing stations that perform some activity as the good or service passes. For example, the process associated with a loan application at a bank might be as follows. The customer goes to the bank (a moving activity). The bank takes the loan application from a customer (a processing activity). Loan applications are accumulated (a storage activity) and passed (a moving activity) to a loan officer for approval (both a processing activity and an inspection activity). Loans that violate standard loan guidelines are accumulated (a storage activity) and then passed (a moving activity) to regional supervisor for approval (a processing activity). The customer is contacted when a decision has been made (a processing activity) and, if the loan is approved, the loan proceeds are deposited in the customer's account (a processing activity).

If you were to observe this process at this bank, you would see work in process piled up at each of the processing points, or stations, as they are usually called. Loan applications might be piled on the bank teller's desk, the loans officer's desk, and the regional supervisor's desk. This work-in-process inventory accumulates at processing stations in a conventional organization for three reasons.

Handling work in batches is the first, and most important, cause of inventory in a process layout system. Organizations use batches to reduce set-

[13] For example, hospitals sometimes have clinics that focus on treating a single ailment such as a hearing problem. During a clinic, the people and equipment needed to treat the ailment are moved to one area so that the patients can be diagnosed and treated both effectively and efficiently. When the clinic hours end, the equipment and staff disband.

ting up,[14] moving, and handling costs. Batch processing increases the inventory levels in the system because, at each processing station, all the items in the batch must wait until the entire batch is processed.

Second, if the rate at which each processing area handles work is not balanced, either because one processing area is slower or another area has stopped working due to problems with equipment, materials, or people, work will pile up at the slowest processing station. Such scheduling delays create another reason that inventory levels increase in a process layout system.

Third, since supervisors evaluate many processing area managers on their ability to meet production quotas, the processing station managers try to avoid having their facility starved for work. Therefore, these managers might deliberately store incoming work in process so that they can continue to work even if the processing area that feeds them is shut down. Similarly, to avoid starving the next processing station and suffering recriminations, processing station managers might store finished work to continue to supply the stations further down the line when their station is shut down because of problems. This is the risk-avoiding reason for increasing inventory in a process layout system.

Some organizations have developed innovative approaches to eliminate many of the costs relating to moving and storing—which are significant non-value-added costs associated with process layout systems. Exhibit 2–9 illustrates the system that Gannett Corporation, the United States' largest newspaper publisher, has developed. By using computers and electronic communication, the electronic pagination process reduces cycle time and costs in a process layout system by eliminating the physical movement of work in process between the processing points used to create a newspaper layout.

■ Product Layout Systems: An Example

Product layout systems store inventory along the production line. Because there is a single dominant flow, planners are able to coordinate the use of inventory with the line's flow rate. Because there are costs of acquiring the parts or materials, however, they often are acquired in batches. Suppose that an assembly line is scheduled to assemble 600 cars on a given day. The purchasing group knows that these 600 cars will require 2,400 regular tires and 600 spare tires and can arrange for these tires to be delivered. Under ideal conditions, these tires would be delivered to the assembly line just as they are required. The costs of transporting the tires from the supplier, however, might suggest that several days' worth of tires be delivered at a time.[15]

---

[14] *Setting up* refers to the activities related to getting ready to do something. Common setting up activities are cleaning and setting a machine prior to using it, inserting a tool in a machine before using it, getting a pile of invoices to work on, looking up and dialing a telephone number before you can talk to someone, and turning on a computer and accessing a program that is required for the job about to be done. Note that costs that vary with the number of batches, like many moving costs, are indirectly determined by the batch size (since, given a level of production, choosing the batch size simultaneously defines the number of batches). Therefore, like setting up costs, moving costs that are related to the number of batches create a motivation to produce in large batches.

[15] In this case, the setup cost would be the cost of the truck and the driver used to transport the tires. The costs of loading and unloading the tires are not setup costs because they would be incurred regardless of the size of each batch of tires. Setup costs can be reduced by reducing the distance between the supplier and the assembler, using smaller and less expensive trucks, and arranging for delivery by a truck that will be making the trip anyway (such as an independent courier or a shuttle truck that continuously cycles around a loop between suppliers and buyers).

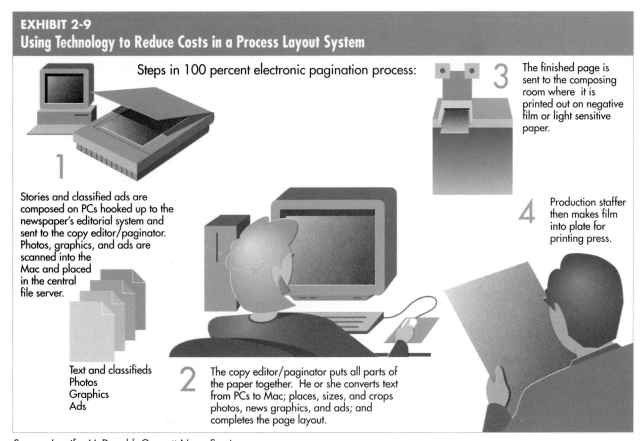

EXHIBIT 2-9
Using Technology to Reduce Costs in a Process Layout System

Steps in 100 percent electronic pagination process:

1 Stories and classified ads are composed on PCs hooked up to the newspaper's editorial system and sent to the copy editor/paginator. Photos, graphics, and ads are scanned into the Mac and placed in the central file server.

Text and classifieds
Photos
Graphics
Ads

2 The copy editor/paginator puts all parts of the paper together. He or she converts text from PCs to Mac; places, sizes, and crops photos, news graphics, and ads; and completes the page layout.

3 The finished page is sent to the composing room where it is printed out on negative film or light sensitive paper.

4 Production staffer then makes film into plate for printing press.

Source: Jennifer McDonald, Gannett News Service.

Think of a cafeteria. People pass by the containers of food and take what they want. Employees watch the containers of food and organize the food preparation activities so that the containers are refilled just as they are emptied. Note that the containers are not filled one unit at a time. For example, the cook does not make one bowl of soup at a time because setup costs of making soup this way would be prohibitively expensive. If we can reduce setup costs, however, we can reduce the batch sizes (the size of the containers) along the line, thereby reducing the level of inventory in the system, reducing costs, and improving quality. The ultimate goal is to reduce setup costs to zero and to reduce processing time to close to zero, so that individual products can be provided instantly upon request.

■ Inventory-Related Costs

Demands for inventory create huge costs in organizations, including the cost of moving, handling, and storing the work in process and its cost when it becomes obsolete or is damaged. Moreover, many organizations have found that layouts and inefficiencies that create the motivation to hold work in process also hide problems that create excessive costs relating to rework.

For example, in batch operations, workers near the end of a process (downstream) often find problems in the way that workers earlier in the process (upstream) have done their jobs. When work is prepared and presented in batches, many items in the batch often are defective and must all be reworked. When work is prepared continuously, however, one item at a time, an upstream problem is detected almost immediately and can be corrected with a minimal level of rework cost.

■ Inventory and Process Cycle Time

Not only does the inventory created by batch production create costs, but the delays associated with storing and moving inventory increase cycle times, thereby reducing service to customers by causing delays. These delays can happen at any stage of the production cycle, even before manufacturing starts. For example, because of high setup costs, a manufacturer might require that a product be manufactured in some minimum batch size. If a customer order is less than the minimum batch size and if the order cannot be filled from existing finished goods inventory, then the customer must wait until enough orders have accumulated to meet the minimum batch size requirement.

It might take a loan officer only 5 minutes to read and approve a loan application. The application might wait for several hours, or even several days, however, to be taken to the loan officer on the grounds that it is too expensive to have a clerk running back and forth with each loan application.

OBJECTIVE 2.7
The concept of just-in-time as a means to improve organization performance

JUST-IN-TIME MANUFACTURING

To avoid the types of costs and service problems associated with conventional manufacturing and facilities layouts, some organizations produce upon demand or just-in-time. The following are examples:

1. Coca-Cola Enterprises, Inc., the largest U.S. bottler of Coca-Cola, has developed just-in-time sales centers that carry no inventory. This reduces costs and speeds the flow of finished product to customers.
2. Fast-food operators understand that making food when required by the customer, rather than before, improves quality and lowers costs.
3. In 1921, at Ford Motor Corporation's River Rouge plant, the total time taken from steel making to completing the Model T automobile was 4 days. This was accomplished by balancing the production line so that materials and components were made available just-in-time.
4. To serve as a just-in-time supplier to large automobile assembly plants, PPG, a glass manufacturer, locates its automobile glass manufacturing plants close to its customers.

Just-in-time or JIT
Making a good or service only when the customer, who may be internal or external, requires it.

Just-in-time or **JIT** means making a good or service only when the customer, internal or external, requires it. You can think of just-in-time production as attempting to make the manufacturing cycle efficiency equal 1. Just-in-time production requires a product layout with a continuous flow (no delays) once production starts. It means that setup costs must be reduced substantially to eliminate the need to produce in batches, and it means that processing systems must be reliable.

Just-in-time production is a philosophy rather than a tool or set of tools. Just-in-time production is based on the elimination of all nonvalue-added activities to reduce cost and time. It is an approach to improvement that is continuous and involves employee empowerment and involvement. Just-in-time production encompasses all facets of making the good or service, including developing the design, acquiring the factors of production, making the good or service, delivering it to the customer, and following up after the delivery. Critical performance indicators in just-in-time systems are inventory levels (which should be as low as possible); failures, whether these are material, people, or machine failures (with a goal of zero); moving (with a goal of zero); and storing[16] (with a goal of zero).

■ Implications of Just-in-Time

Just-in-time is simple in theory but hard to achieve in practice. Many organizations are nervous about just-in-time because a problem anywhere in the system can stop all production. For this reason, organizations that use just-in-time must eliminate all the sources of failure in the system. The production process must be redesigned so that it is not prohibitively expensive to process one or a small number of items at a time. This usually means reducing the distance over which work in process has to travel and using very flexible people and equipment that can handle all types of jobs. Production people must be better trained so that they carry out their activities without mistakes. Suppliers must be trained to provide defect-free materials or components precisely when they are required. Equipment must be maintained so that machine failures are eliminated.

The lending process at the bank is an interesting application of these ideas. One way to reduce the cost of moving would be to process loan applications on a computer so that the loan application could be moved instantly over any distance. The bank clerk might take the loan application on a computer or the bank might even allow customers with computing capabilities to submit loan applications electronically, eliminating the need for the customer to come into the bank and reducing the clerical time used.

The loan application might be processed by a computer program that would scan consumer credit databases to immediately reject or flag applications by customers who have credit problems. Simple loan applications might be approved on the spot, pending verification of the client's claims. This would improve service and reduce the amount of loan officer time spent approving simple loan applications. Complex loan applications could be called out of the database instantly by loan officers many miles away. At that point, they could be reviewed and approved almost as quickly as simple loan applications. By moving away from a physical loan application that must be moved between people, the process would have been made more efficient and faster. Moreover, by eliminating the need to batch loan applications to accumulate enough to make it worthwhile to move them and for a loan officer to

16 Storage includes both deliberate storage and work in process waiting to be processed.

set up to review them, a centrally located loan officer could be provided with a constant stream of loan applications from many branches.

It is interesting to consider how just-in-time might be used at Mike's Fast Foods. Some fast-food restaurants use a just-in-time, continuous flow product layout while others use batch production in a process layout. In fact, some fast-food restaurants combine both approaches. During rush hours, these hybrid systems use a batch approach to production and keep inventories at predefined levels (for example, the restaurant might use racks or bins to hold food ready to be sold to the customer and tell the employees to start another batch of production when the existing inventory falls below a line drawn on the bin or rack) and at off-peak times, they may produce to order. The motivation to use just-in-time is to improve the quality of the food and to reduce waste by eliminating the need to throw out food that has been sitting too long. The motivation to use batch production is to sustain a certain level of inventory to reduce the time the customer has to wait for an order. As processing time and setup costs drop, the organization can move closer to just-in-time.

■ Just-in-Time Manufacturing and Management Accounting

Just-in-time manufacturing has two major implications for management accounting. First, management accounting must support the move to just-in-time manufacturing by monitoring, identifying, and communicating to decision makers the sources of delay, error, and waste in the system. Defect rates, cycle times, percentage of time that deliveries are on time, order accuracy, actual production as a percentage of planned production, and actual machine time available compared to planned machine time available are all important measures of the system's reliability, which is critical to just-in-time. Machine and labor use statistics, which are common under conventional production systems, are an anathema to just-in-time production systems in which operators are expected to produce only what is requested, when it is requested, and on time, in contrast to operating processes merely to use available machine and labor capacity. Second, the clerical process of management accounting is simplified by just-in-time manufacturing because there are fewer inventories to monitor and report.

TIMBER RIVER METAL WINDOWS REVISITED

Let's see how the ideas in this chapter might affect Timber River Metal Windows, which we introduced at the beginning of this chapter.

■ The Problem at Timber River Metal Windows

First, consider the existing production processes at the company. Timber River Metal Windows manufactured aluminum windows for the home housing market. Because of the long and unpredictable lead times in making windows, the company manufactured windows to keep in stock as inventory. Customer orders drew down existing inventory. Each window type had a reorder point, which was usually about 10 windows. When inventory fell to that level, the company manufactured a new batch of windows, usually between 30 and 40 windows.

Window production began when the production scheduler issued an order for a batch of production. The employees removed the aluminum need to fill the order from the raw materials storage area and, using a large container, moved it to the cutting area to await a free operator and machine. When the machine was ready, all the pieces for the batch were cut into the required lengths.

The workers then put the pieces back into the container and moved them to the painting area where they waited their turn in the painting booth. At the painting area, workers batched the containers by color—white, green, and brown. Because of the time and cost to change the painting booth from one color to another, the painters liked to have a large batch of one color ready before they began painting. Usually they waited for between 3 and 5 batches of one color before they set up for it.

After the painters had painted the pieces for a batch and dried them in a drying booth, they put the pieces for a batch back into a container and moved it to the assembly area where the materials waited to be assembled. Once the pieces for a batch reached the assembly area, the assembly group ordered the glass needed to complete that batch. When the glass arrived, usually in 2 or 3 days, process controllers scheduled the batch for assembly.

Predictable and recurring problems such as incorrectly cut pieces (usually this meant that the operator set the cutting machine improperly and cut every piece improperly), pieces that the painters mixed up with other batches, and improperly painted pieces, slowed the assembly process, increasing cycle time and costs. If the assemblers observed any of these problems, employees set the entire batch aside to await the rework of the required items.

After the windows were assembled, the employees tested them for appearance and air leaks, rejecting any that failed those tests. The company sold those windows to a local building supplies company as rejects. Exhibit 2–10 summarizes production information for a typical batch of production.

EXHIBIT 2-10
Timber River Metal Windows Production Batch Summary

Item	Amount
Batch average total cycle time	12 working days
Average manufacturing cycle efficiency	5.7%
Percentage of windows requiring rework	32%
Material yield	78%
Labor yield	64%

The outcomes reported in Exhibit 2–10 reflected a poorly organized, poorly scheduled, and inefficient batch production process that produced poor quality, poor service, and unnecessarily high costs as described previously. These data implied a host of problems for the company, which then attacked and solved them systematically over a period of about 4 years.

■ The Solution at Timber River Metal Windows

To eliminate the moving and storing problems caused by batch production and highlighted by the manufacturing cycle efficiency ratio, this company reorganized its production into small work cells. In these cells, one worker, never moving more than several meters from her worktable, assembled an entire window from pieces cut on a machine that was controlled by a computer programmed to make the cuts precisely. This machine, purchased to improve the material yield, cut parts for several orders at a time to maximize its use of metal, which was purchased in large sheets. The company eliminated the painting department and purchased painted aluminum from a supplier that had modern dry paint facilities. These changes reduced the final inspection defects from 8% to 2%, reduced inventory-related costs from 35% of sales to 5% of sales, cut rework by 80%, improved manufacturing cycle efficiency to 75%, and reduced total cycle time to 6 hours. Employee morale improved considerably as management asked employees to take control of running and improving the manufacturing process.

The move to using a computer-controlled cutting machine allowed the company to fill orders for any size of window, eliminating the requirement that customers order standard-size windows. The company moved to just-in-time production and freed up virtually all its finished goods storage area and about half of the factory floor space.

The situation in Timber River Metal Windows illustrates the advantages of continuous flow operations, which is the style of organization toward which activity analysis moves most organizations. The example also shows how measures of the organization processes can be used to identify and suggest improvements to process problems. In summary, Timber River Metal Windows improved its performance by

1. Improving its ability to respond quickly to customer requests and manufacture custom orders

2. Reducing inventory-related costs, including the opportunity costs of funds invested in inventory; floor space; insurance; special equipment such as storage racks and forklifts; warehouse employees; damage; obsolescence; and theft

3. Avoiding a large amount of rework by producing smaller batches and getting immediate feedback about product and process deficiencies

SUMMARY

In this chapter, we developed the idea of an organization as a collection of people, equipment, and capital with a purpose. The organization's purpose is defined by its major stakeholders—customers, employees, partners, owners, and the community—who pursue their individual objectives by collaborating with other stakeholders through the medium of the organization. A major role of management is to balance the sometimes conflicting objectives of the organization's different stakeholders and to identify a set of organization objectives.

We argued that it is useful to think of the organization pursuing its objectives, or purpose, by undertaking a sequence of activities designed to deliver a product (a physical good or a service) to its customers. This sequence of activities must be evaluated from the customers' perspective because they are the ones who ultimately judge the acceptability of what is delivered to them. We argued that service, quality, and cost are almost universal attributes that customers use to judge products. The organization's other stakeholders define constraints on this process in terms of what it requires of, or promises to, them as the process meets customers' requirements.

Organization members need information about process details, including time, quality, and cost, to manage this sequence of activities in a way that the organization uses the fewest possible resources to meet its objectives. Helping organization members to develop the systems to capture and interpret this information defines a natural and useful role for management accountants in organizations.

We discussed the role of charting process activities and labeling activities as value added or nonvalue added. The underlying idea here is that organization members should constantly strive to improve the service, quality, and cost performance of all activities and should plan, in the longer run, to eliminate activities that provide the opportunity for cost reduction without reducing the product's service potential to customers.

The activity perspective developed in this chapter provides the foundation concept for the balance of this book. The remainder of the book develops the ideas and methods that people use to measure, assess, and improve the organization's activities.

KEY TERM LIST

activity, p. 44

activity analysis, p. 64

activity improvement, p. 47

cell manufacturing, p. 69

charting, p. 46

community, p. 42

competitive benchmarking, p. 56

control, p. 54

cost, p. 49

critical performance indicators, p. 47

cycle time, p. 67

Deming Wheel, p. 57

effective, p. 46

efficient, p. 46

just-in-time or JIT, p. 72

manufacturing cycle efficiency, p. 67

nonvalue-added activity, p. 61

objectives, p. 40

outcome, p. 52

output, p. 52

partners, p. 41

performance measurement, p. 46

process layout, p. 68

product layout, p. 69

quality, p. 48

service, p. 47

signal, p. 53

stakeholders, p. 41

value chain, p. 44

value-added activity, p. 60

ASSIGNMENT MATERIAL

QUESTIONS

2–1 What is an activity? Give an example.

2–2 What is charting? What is its purpose?

2–3 What is cost? Why is it important?

2–4 What is cycle time?

2–5 What does *effective* mean?

2–6 What does *efficient* mean?

2–7 What is a critical performance indicator? Give an example of one for a university.

2–8 What are organization objectives?

2–9 What do *outcome* and *output* mean? Are they related?

2–10 What do *service* and *quality* mean? Are they related?

2–11 What is a signal?

2–12 What are stakeholders?

2–13 What is a value chain? Give an example.

2–14 What is a value-added activity? Give an example.

EXERCISES

2–15 Can you think of something other than service, quality, and cost that is important to a customer? Explain.

2–16 Can you think of a product where one or several of the elements of service, quality, and cost are unimportant to the customer? Explain.

2–17 For each of the following products, what are the three most important elements of service?

(a) Television set

(b) University course

(c) Meal in an exclusive restaurant

(d) Meal that is taken away from a restaurant

(e) Container of milk

(f) Visit to the doctor

(g) Trip on an airplane

(h) Pair of jeans

(i) Novel

(j) University text

2–18 For each of the following products, suggest three measures of quality:

(a) Television set

(b) University course

(c) Meal in an exclusive restaurant

(d) Meal that is taken away from a restaurant

(e) Container of milk

(f) Visit to the doctor

(g) Trip on an airplane

(h) Pair of jeans

(i) Novel

(j) University text

2–19 Give examples of three activities or processes for which cycle time is important (for example, the time it takes an ambulance to respond to a call). Explain why cycle time is important in each activity or process.

2–20 Can you think of any product for which cost is not an issue? When we say that cost is not an issue, we mean that the customer will invest little or no effort to investigate opportunities to buy the required product at the lowest possible price.

2–21 Describe how you might use competitive benchmarking to improve your studying habits.

2–22 Some people call continuous improvement *continuous hassles* because the pressure never lets up. Suppose that, as a manager, you were committed to the philosophy of continuous improvement. Explain how you might create an environment in which your subordinates did not feel that continuous improvement meant continuous hassles.

2–23 Briefly describe, using a process flowchart, any process with which you are familiar. Identify two activities in the process that you think are nonvalue added and explain why you think that they are. You need not make this complicated. Describing something simple such as borrowing a book from the library is good enough (but do not use this example).

2–24 If inspection activities are nonvalue added, auditing should be classified as a nonvalue-added activity. Explain why you agree or disagree.

2–25 How would you classify the layout of a large grocery store? Why do you think it is laid out this way? Can you think of any way to improve the layout of a conventional grocery store?

2–26 Production people often say that inventory is a liability, not an asset. Why do accountants call inventory an asset? Why might production people think of inventory as a liability?

PROBLEMS

2–27 Describe the value chain in a university. Make sure that you identify each of the activities that a university undertakes and how it relates to the university's customers.

2–28 What are the key activities in a hospital? What are the critical success factors in a hospital and how might they be used to evaluate the key activities?

2–29 Describe the value chain in a business that sells gas to a customer. What are the critical success factors and how might they be used to evaluate the key activities?

2–30 Can you think of any type of organization for which the customer's perspective is not critical in evaluating performance of its activities? If you can think of such an organization, why is the customer's perspective not important? If you cannot think of such an organization, why is the customer's perspective always critical in evaluating performance?

2–31 Many organizations publish rankings of universities, and many of the universities complain about the way that these rankings are developed.

REQUIRED:

    (a) Identify a university's critical success factors and construct a performance measurement system for a university's business school that reflects those critical success factors.

    (b) Based on the university's critical success factors, construct a performance measurement system for students enrolled in a university's business school.

2–32 Because of the competitiveness of the industry, monitoring performance in a fast-food restaurant business is critical for success.

REQUIRED:

    (a) Identify a fast-food restaurant's critical success factors.

    (b) Identify a fast-food restaurant's major activities.

    (c) Construct a performance measurement system for each activity that reflects the restaurant's critical success factors.

2–33 Because of the competitiveness of the airline industry, monitoring performance is critical for success.

REQUIRED:

    (a) Identify an airline's critical success factors.

    (b) Identify an airline's major activities.

    (c) Construct a performance measurement system for each activity that reflects the airline's critical success factors.

2–34 Identify critical success factors for a manufacturer of personal computers and construct a performance measurement system that reflects those critical success factors.

2–35 For any activity or process that you can think of, define an output and an outcome. (Do not use an example from the text.) Explain how using the outcome measure would be more effective in promoting activity improvement efforts than using the output measure.

2–36 For any activity or process that you can think of, define a performance measurement system that looks at only a part of what the process contributes to the organization. Explain how assessing performance on only a part of what the process contributes to the organization might promote inappropriate behavior.

2–37 Consider the process of examinations in a university setting.

REQUIRED:

    (a) What are the main activities in the examination process?

    (b) What resources does each main activity in the examination process consume?

    (c) Suppose that the university was faced with a cutback and reduced the available levels of the resources that you believe examinations consume. Explain what you think would happen.

2–38 Think of any process that you have observed directly.

REQUIRED:

    (a) Draw the process flowchart for this process.

    (b) Is this process organized using a process layout or a product layout?

    (c) Why do you think the process is laid out the way it is?

    (d) What opportunities do you see to improve the process layout?

    (e) Why are these improvement opportunities important?

2–39 Think of going to a movie. The theater has three key processing stations: the booth where you buy your ticket, the counter where you buy refreshments, and the entry point into the movie area where the usher takes your ticket.

REQUIRED:

(a) Identify the reason that inventory (people) builds up at each of these stations.

(b) For each station, identify two strategies that might be used to reduce processing time and reduce the inventory level.

(c) What performance measures might be used to identify the effect of inventory levels on customers?

2–40 Some people call conventional manufacturing systems *just-in-case* systems because they hold inventories just in case the processing system fails.

REQUIRED:

(a) Describe any processing system that you have seen where inventory is held just in case some component in the system fails.

(b) What strategy might be used to eliminate the need (motive) to hold inventory just in case the system fails?

CASES

2–41 Bob Eaton, Chrysler Corporation's vice-chairman, made the following observation about Chrysler employees whose job is to answer calls from customers with problems or complaints:

> The people who answer these phones have one of the most important jobs in the company. They are our front lines. They can have a more direct effect on sales than anyone else.

After noting that it can cost as much 5 times more to get a new customer than it costs to keep one, and that, on average, a satisfied customer will recount his experience to 5 people and an unsatisfied customer to 35, Mr. Eaton went on to say:

> Even the best salespeople sell only 2 or 3 cars a day. Our people on the phones deal with dozens of customers every day. How well they take care of our customers is critical.

REQUIRED:

Design a performance measurement system for the Chrysler staff that takes these customer calls.

2–42 Nalco Chemical Company makes industrial chemicals. The following material appeared in the December 1991 edition of the *Nalco News*, the company's employee newsletter.

> Our customers are concerned with just-in-time delivery, safe chemical delivery, and shorter lead times—in addition, many customers are setting higher requirements for us.

> Since 1985, our order volume has increased significantly. We hired an outside consultant to help us put all of our delivery functions under one umbrella called Operation Excellence. They helped us design a strategy to deliver products 100 percent of the time within the time frame that we agree upon with the customer. We want to improve overall delivery time by delivering 80 percent of our U.S. pounds to customers in 7 days or less. Right now we ship about 800 million pounds a year domestically, so that's a pretty tall order.

This past July we shipped 16 percent of our orders within 7 days. . . . In October it was 40 percent. . . . In January we should reach 60 percent, and by April we are determined to reach our goal of 80 percent.

[Currently,] 98.6% of our 7-day deliveries are on time; 94% of our 14-day deliveries are on time; and 97.5% of our 21-day deliveries are on time. Of course, our goal is to be 100% on time in all 3 categories within 6 months.

To achieve these goals we are manufacturing certain products closer to the customers and are streamlining manufacturing processes so they are more cost effective. We are building a centralized finished goods warehouse at Clearing to help us more efficiently handle the large numbers of domestic orders—40%—that are shipped from that facility.

We also are installing a warehouse management software program to track all orders on a real-time basis, as well as installing a product-package forecasting system to predict what customers will be ordering. This means we can adjust our manufacturing to meet their needs. This will allow us to order raw materials more cost effectively, and we will have the time to get the right type of container to the plant to meet our manufacturing schedule.

Finally, all products will be bar coded and forklift trucks will have a video display screen to help select products at each location and minimize shipping errors. We have heard from our customers and we are responding. Quality is defined by excellent customer service, and this is our driving force toward excellence. We must never forgot that the reason we are here is to serve our customers in a quality manner. *(Courtesy Nalco Chemical Company)*

REQUIRED:

(a) What competitive strategy does Nalco Chemical Company seem to have adopted?

(b) What do you think of the manner and level of the goals that Nalco Chemical Company has set for itself?

(c) What do you think about the way that the company has gone about improving service to its customers?

2–43 In 1990, McDonnell Douglas Space Systems Company (MDSSC) used three primary strategic business objectives (SBOs):

(a) Customer-focused—to become the preferred supplier in our key market segments

(b) Cultural—to become a company that is the embodiment of total quality management

(c) Financial—to achieve sales growth greater than 6% per year. To increase after-tax return on investment from 16.4% to 20% over the next 10 years. MDSSC made the following statement about performance measurement:

We can measure our performance as a company against our SBOs. To achieve the goals that we have set, we need everyone to be involved. We need a road map created from objectives, flowing down throughout the organization, to identify all the tasks we need to reach our stated goals. Measuring our performance against those goals will help us to see how well we are doing.

The process at MDSSC was for senior management to create broad business unit objectives and then for each business unit to set its objectives to support the objectives of the larger group. In this way, objectives would flow down through the organization. Unit leaders were told the following:

Your team's objectives should be set high enough to challenge the group, but not so high that they cannot be reached.

For example, the Business and General Support group had the following Strategic Objectives:

(a) Improve the quality of information and services by a factor of 5 in 3 years leading toward 100% quality

(b) Reduce all cycle times by 50%

(c) Reduce costs by 30% in 3 years

The measurement process for each of these SBOs was defined as follows:

(a) Customer feedback

(b) Cycle time measurement systems

(c) Cost measurement systems

REQUIRED:

    (a) What do you think of this system?

    (b) How would you measure customer feedback, cycle time, and costs?

    (c) Identify how this system might be used in your university or college to improve operations. Your discussion should identify strategic business objectives and include specific measurements.

2–44 Consider the process of registering for courses at your university or college.

REQUIRED:

    (a) Draw a process flowchart that describes the process of registering for courses at your university or college.

    (b) As a customer, what are the key criteria that you use to evaluate the registration process?

    (c) Label each activity that you have identified in the process as value added or nonvalue added.

    (d) How might the registration process be reorganized to eliminate the non-value-added activities?

    (e) How might the activities be reorganized to improve performance on the evaluative criteria that you think are important?

    (f) Which activity would you improve first? Why?

2–45 The fishing products industry has 5 critical success factors: (1) keep costs down so that prices can be kept down; (2) ensure that products meet stated, or expected, quality standards; (3) ensure that the assigned quota of each specie is harvested; (4) ensure that the fish that are harvested are handled and processed in a way that maximizes their retail value; and (5) continue to develop new products that are appealing to customers to ensure growth.

Several unique conditions affect the fishing industry. Harvesting is constrained by two factors. A government regulatory agency sets quotas for each specie of fish. The quotas specify the maximum amount of each specie of fish that can be caught and the permissible fishing period. Because of equipment failure, weather conditions, and stock depletion, most firms are unable to catch their assigned quota of any given specie.

Care must be taken at each step in the process of harvesting and transporting the fish. During harvesting, too many fish in the nets can crush and bruise the fish, resulting in a loss of quality. Fish begins to deteriorate the moment it is caught. Therefore, the fish must be packed in ice in the ship's hold. Discharging the fish from the ship's hold into the processing plant must be done carefully to ensure that the fish is not damaged or bruised.

Within the processing plant, care must be taken to ensure that the fish is processed rapidly (to prevent deterioration), carefully (to ensure that quality standards relating to color, form, and lack of parasites are met), effectively (to ensure that bones, skin, and blood are not left in the fish and, conversely, that excessive amounts of flesh are not removed with the bone), and efficiently (since many of the operations are manual, labor costs are significant).

The Down East Fishing Products Company (DEFPC) is organized into three responsibility units: *harvesting* (this consists of the fleet of 12 ships and their crews used to harvest various specie of fish); *processing* (processing plants that are used to process the raw fish into the fresh, frozen, and cooked products demanded by the company's customers); and (3) *marketing* (responsible for creating the demand for the company's products).

The performance of each of the responsibility units is now evaluated as follows:

(a) *Harvesting:* tons of fish caught

(b) *Processing:* costs relative to flexible budget standards

(c) *Marketing:* sales increases over the previous year

REQUIRED:

Assess the current system used to evaluate the performance of each responsibility center at DEFPC. Make suggestions for improvements.

2–46 Speedy Copy operates a chain of copy centers located throughout North America. Usually located close to college and university campuses, Speedy Copy provides a variety of services organized into 6 business areas: (1) normal copying, (2) color copying, (3) binding, (4) graphics services (such as posters and business cards), (5) preparing readings packages for university courses (including obtaining copyright permissions), and (6) basic word processing services.

Speedy Copy's approach to business is captured in its motto: *"Provide value to the customer while doing it right and fast."* The company's operations manual explains that market surveys suggest that success in the copy business depends on (1) providing services that customers value, (2) providing a fast response to a customer request, (3) providing clear copies, (4) providing accurate duplication services (for example, ensure that a readings package is not missing any pages and that copies are complete and properly aligned), and (5) doing all of the above at a competitive cost.

You have recently been appointed the manager of a Speedy Copy center located near the campus of a small university (about 1,800 students) in a small town (population about 6,000) in a predominantly rural area. You and 27 other center managers report to a regional manager. You are paid a salary and a bonus that depends on the measured performance of your center.

Each quarter, every center manager negotiates performance targets (which reflect local conditions and opportunities) with the center manager's regional manager in each of the following areas:

(a) Sales for each of the 6 business areas mentioned above.

(b) Costs as a percentage of sales in each of the 6 business areas.

(c) Product quality as determined by a random audit of output conducted during a surprise visit by a team from the regional office.

(d) Service as determined by the time required to complete a sample of jobs chosen by the audit teams (all jobs are logged in and out on the computer terminal at the customer service counter).

(e) Customer satisfaction as determined by a quarterly survey of faculty and students at the nearby university. (The content of the survey is approved jointly by the center manager and the center manager's regional manager. The survey is conducted by the regional manager's staff).

A performance score is computed as follows: (1) a score is determined for each of the 5 items of performance and (2) the scores on these 5 items are summed to compute a total score. The center manager's bonus is based on the total score. The performance score on each of the 5 items of performance is determined as follows:

(a) Three points for meeting the target, plus or minus 3%

(b) Two points for missing target by between 3% and 5%

(c) One point for missing target by between 5% and 8%

(d) Four points for exceeding the target by between 3% and 5%

(e) Five points for exceeding the target by between 5% and 8%.

Performance that varies by more than 8% of target is excluded from the evaluation and is subjected to an immediate investigation by a committee comprising (1) the center manager, (2) the regional manager, and (3) the regional controller.

REQUIRED:

(a) Evaluate this performance measurement system by indicating why you like, or dislike, each of its relevant features.

(b) As part of your efforts to improve the quality of your products and the services provided to your customers, you have decided to develop a product and service quality monitoring system for your copy center. Suggest what type of system might be useful and why.

2–47 Woodpoint Furniture Manufacturing manufactures various lines of pine furniture. The plant uses a functional layout, which is summarized in Exhibit 2–11; that is, it is organized so that all similar functions are performed in one area. Most pieces of furniture are made in batches of 10 units.

EXHIBIT 2-11

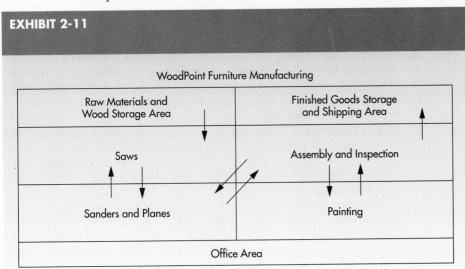

Raw materials are ordered and stored in the raw materials storage area. When an order is issued for a batch of production, the wood for that batch is withdrawn from the raw materials area and taken to the saw area where it is sawed into the pieces that are required for the production lot.

The pieces are then transferred to the sanding and planing area where they are stored awaiting processing in that area. When the machines are free, any sanding or planing is done on all the pieces in the batch. Any pieces that are damaged by the planing or sanding are reordered from the saw area. The other pieces in the lot are set aside in a storage area when pieces have to be reordered from the saw area.

When all the pieces have been sanded or planed, they are transferred to the assembly area where they are placed in a large bin to await assembly. Pieces are withdrawn from the bin as assembly proceeds. Any defective or missing pieces are returned to the saw or sand and plane area to be remanufactured.

As assembly proceeds or is completed (depending on the product), any required painting or staining is done in the painting area. Pieces to be stained or painted are transferred back and forth between the assembly and paint area on a trolley. There is a storage area in the paint department for pieces awaiting painting. When assembly is halted to await pieces that have been sent for painting and staining, the rest of the pieces in that batch are put into the storage bin.

When assembly is completed, the product is checked by the quality inspector. Any defective products are returned to the appropriate department for rework. When the product is approved, it is packaged and put into final storage to await an order by the customer.

REQUIRED:

(a) Identify the activities undertaken to make furniture in WoodPoint Furniture Manufacturing by drawing a process flowchart for a typical piece of furniture. Classify each activity on your process flowchart as a value adding or nonvalue-added activity.

(b) What critical performance indicators would you use to evaluate the performance of this manufacturing operation?

2–48 Consider Exhibit 2–12, next page. It summarizes the activities at Bethlehem Steel Corporation's Sparrows Point Plant. The blast furnaces make the iron that is refined into steel. The basic oxygen furnaces and open hearth furnaces refine the iron into steel. The mix of iron, scrap, and alloys used to make the steel and the characteristics of the furnace determine the steel's properties, which include formability, strength, toughness, hardenability, and corrosion resistance. The continuous slab caster uses the steel from the basic oxygen furnace to make slabs of steel. The steel from the open hearth furnace is poured into ingot molds for cooling.

When it has cooled and hardened, the steel ingot, weighing between 11,000 and 80,000 pounds, is removed from the mold and stored. When required, the ingots are reheated and moved to the blooming or slabbing mills, which transform the ingots into blooms (square or rectangular shape) or slabs (wide and flat shape), depending on the final product that the ingot will be used to make. This operation also improves the properties of the steel. The billet mill reduces blooms into 4-inch square billets that are shipped to the rod mill, which produces coils of rod that are then transformed into finished items such as wire. Plates are rolled from reheated slabs in the plate mill. The plates must be cut on all sides to the desired dimensions after rolling. Slabs are also used to make strip steel, which is either made into some final products directly or is subjected to finishing operations to make steel sheet or tinplate.

EXHIBIT 2-12
From Modest Beginnings to Quality Steel Products

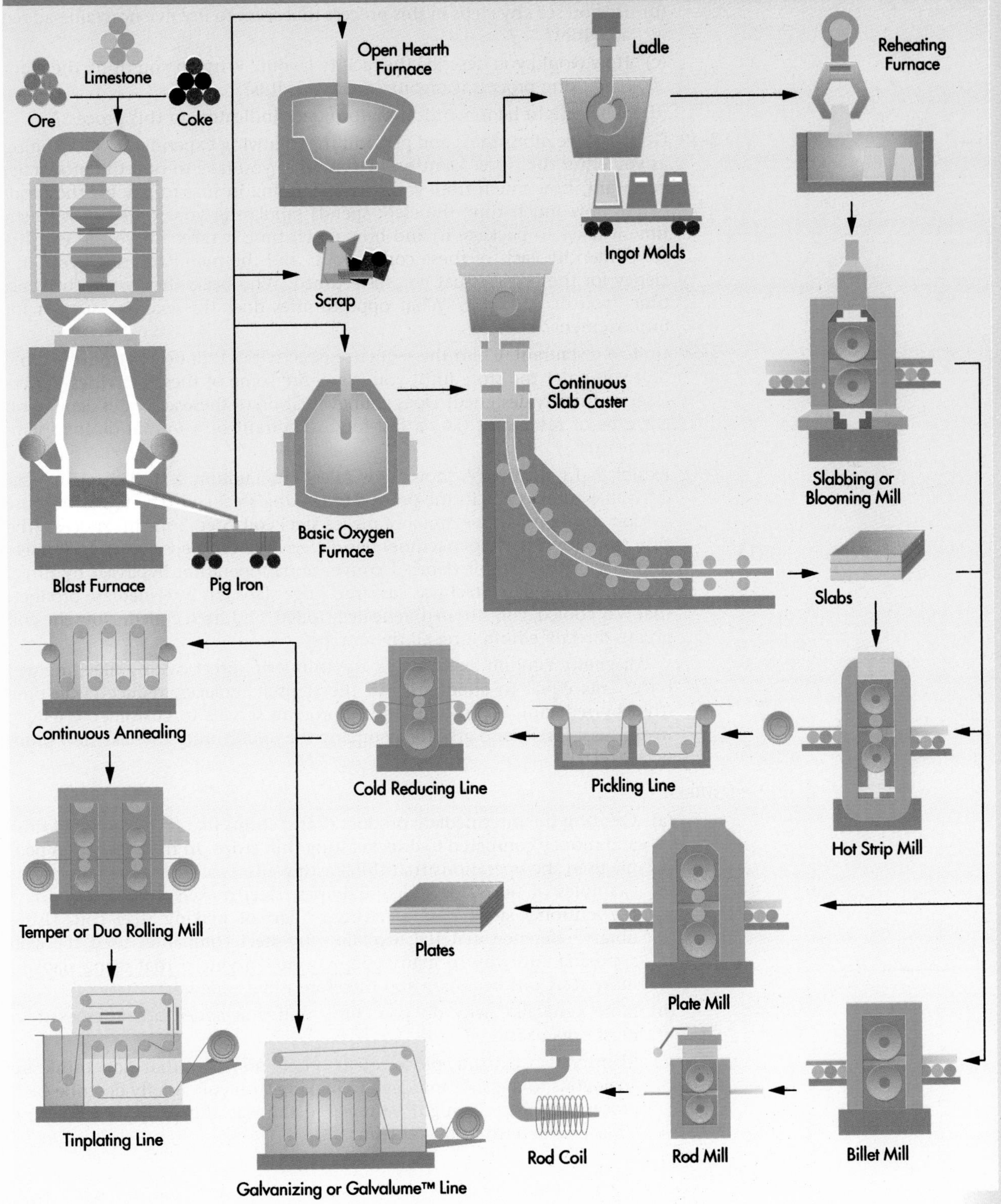

Limestone

Ore

Coke

Open Hearth Furnace

Ladle

Reheating Furnace

Ingot Molds

Scrap

Continuous Slab Caster

Slabbing or Blooming Mill

Blast Furnace

Pig Iron

Basic Oxygen Furnace

Slabs

Continuous Annealing

Cold Reducing Line

Pickling Line

Hot Strip Mill

Temper or Duo Rolling Mill

Plates

Plate Mill

Tinplating Line

Galvanizing or Galvalume™ Line

Rod Coil

Rod Mill

Billet Mill

Courtesy Bethlehem Steel Corporation.

REQUIRED:

(a) What do you think is critical to the customer in making a purchasing decision?

(b) Do you see any steps in this process that seem to involve nonvalue-added activities?

(c) How would you describe the facility layout? Why do you think the manufacturing process is organized the way it is?

(d) What might be the critical performance indicators in this process?

2–49 Go to a store or business and perform the following experiment. Start timing as you enter the store. Identify the time that you take to find the product(s) you want, how much time you spend standing in line to pay for the product(s), how much time the clerk spends tabulating your order, how much time it takes to package it, and how much time it takes for you to exit the store. Identify each of these components and the manufacturing cycle efficiency for the process that you have timed. Who bears the cost of the cycle time—you or the store? What opportunities does this exercise suggest for improvement?

2–50 Go to a restaurant. Chart the sequence of activities that occurs from the time that you enter the store until you leave. Are some of these activities unnecessary or poorly designed? Does your evaluation of these activities depend on the type of restaurant (i.e., a fast-food restaurant or a formal dining establishment)?

2–51 Exhibit 2–13, next page, shows how Allegheny Ludlum, a steel company, cut nonvalue-added steps in the process of making steel coil. The top line in the exhibit shows how the company makes steel coil. Step 3 in this process (the thin strip direct casting machine) has replaced all the steps shown in the second line of the exhibit (labeled conventional operation bypassed by direct casting). In the past, steel was cast into huge slabs (an intermediate product) that was cooled, conditioned, reheated, rolled, and then coiled. Now the coil is cast, directly eliminating all these steps.

Allegheny Ludlum expects that the thin strip direct casting machine will have costs equal to about 25% of the steps it replaces, reduce cycle time (thereby reducing inventories and improving service to customers), reduce investment levels, and give the company the opportunity to make new products.

REQUIRED:

(a) Creating the intermediate product (slabs) seems like such a waste of time and money compared to direct casting thin strips. In the past, when people used the operations that thin casting allows steel makers to avoid as examples of nonvalue-added activities, steel makers argued that these conventional steps were a necessary part of making steel coil. Using library reference material, explain why steel companies used the slab approach and why so many people were convinced that using slabs to make steel was necessary and therefore value added.

(b) More generally, why do you think nonvalue-added activities exist in most organizations?

(c) Identify two existing processes in other industries that you think are analogous to the slab approach to making steel coil. Briefly describe each process and how it might be replaced the way thin strip direct casting replaced the need to make slabs.

EXHIBIT 2-13
New Coilcast™ Production Process

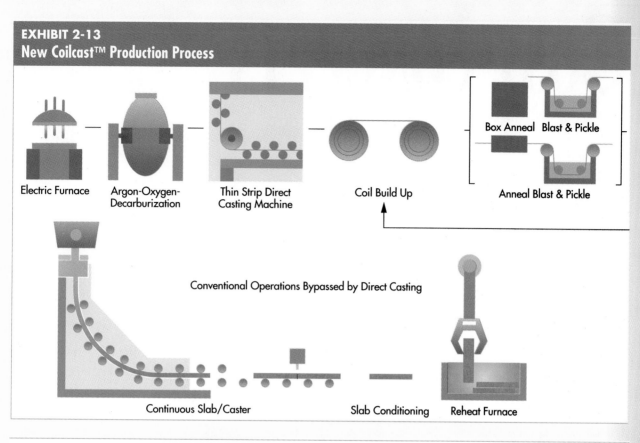

Electric Furnace

Argon-Oxygen-Decarburization

Thin Strip Direct Casting Machine

Coil Build Up

Box Anneal   Blast & Pickle

Anneal Blast & Pickle

Conventional Operations Bypassed by Direct Casting

Continuous Slab/Caster

Slab Conditioning

Reheat Furnace

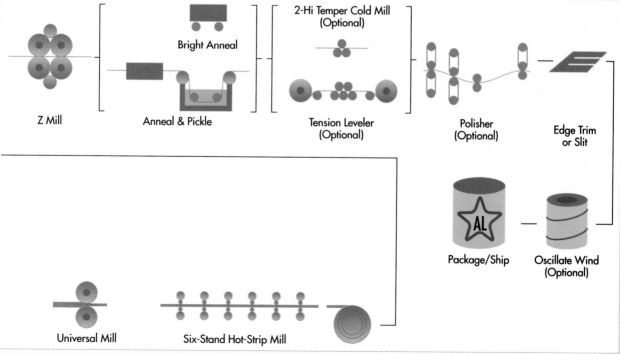

Z Mill

Bright Anneal

Anneal & Pickle

2-Hi Temper Cold Mill (Optional)

Tension Leveler (Optional)

Polisher (Optional)

Edge Trim or Slit

Package/Ship

Oscillate Wind (Optional)

Universal Mill

Six-Stand Hot-Strip Mill

Courtesy Allegheny Ludlum Corporation.

COST CONCEPTS

LEARNING OBJECTIVES

This chapter will introduce you to:

1. how costs are classified based on function
2. the difference between direct and indirect costs
3. how overhead costs arise
4. the difference between unit-related, batch-related, product-sustaining, and facility-sustaining activity cost drivers
5. how cost relations with activities and their drivers are expressed as equations
6. how information is collected to estimate activity costs
7. how cost concepts extend to service organizations
8. how standard costs are determined
9. uses and limitations of standard cost systems

Ellora Electric Company: Let's Talk About Costs

"Don, please prepare an analysis of how our decision to replace the old spray painting machines with the new automated machines will affect costs," said Mike Manley. After having worked for 10 years in production engineering, Donald Dent just joined the management group at the Grand Rapids plant of Ellora Electric Company, as an assistant to Michael Manley, manager in charge of the plant.

Mike continued: "The new machines should reduce *direct labor costs* considerably because they will require only one worker from now on. I also expect to see efficiency gains in *direct materials* because of the new machines' greater accuracy. I want you to pay special attention to *manufacturing overhead costs*. Although *facility-sustaining* costs, such as depreciation and insurance, will no doubt increase, we should obtain savings in other *overhead* costs, such as supervision, maintenance, materials handling, work-in-process inventory storage, and quality inspection."

Donald Dent headed straight for the library to check out a book on management accounting and make sure that he understood precisely what Mike meant when he used cost terms such as *direct labor*, *direct materials*, and *manufacturing overhead costs*. He also wanted to check the plant's accounting records to find out how much the different types of costs had changed when the new automated spray painting machines were installed.

Don's situation is not unusual. Today's organizations require well-informed decision makers who must be knowledgeable about the information on which they are basing their decisions.

(Tobey Sanford/Courtesy G.E.)

NEED FOR COST INFORMATION

Managers often require cost information to help them make decisions. The following are examples:

➤ Product managers at Compaq Computer Corporation evaluated market demand and product cost data for their own and their competitors' personal computer models before deciding to cut their prices in early 1992.

➤ Comparing manufacturing costs of various facilities was an important step in General Motor's selection of plants that needed to be closed in 1993 and 1994.

➤ Periodic decisions about routes and fares require managers at American Airlines to weigh the costs of deploying aircraft and personnel on a route against competitive market demand conditions that determine revenues.

➤ The *gain-sharing incentive plan*[1] at Whirlpool Corporation's washer and dryer component plants calls for paying bonuses to workers for reductions in the ratio of *manufacturing costs* to **production volume**.

➤ Successful control of hospital operations at Humana Corporation, Inc., requires its managers to maintain a close check on both the amount of costs budgeted versus the amount spent by each department and on reimbursement of costs from insurance companies.

Production volume
Overall measure, such as number of units, of various products manufactured in a given time period.

[1] Gain-sharing incentive plans are designed to share productivity gains between workers and owners. They are based on an agreed-upon formula to quantify and share the gains.

Helping decision makers understand the nature and behavior of costs in organizations, including this ice cream manufacturing facility, is one of the most important roles played by management accountants.
(Courtesy Ben & Jerry's)

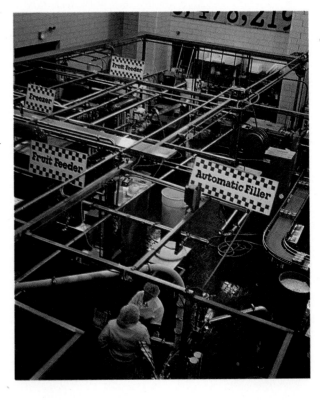

During 1992 employees at Allegheny Ludlum submitted more than 1,150 ideas, which saved the company over $1.4 million. This group of employees received an award of $7,500 for an idea that reduced costs and improved productivity. *(Courtesy Allegheny Ludlum Steel)*

In each case, different types of costs needed to be reported so that managers could make the appropriate tradeoffs for different decisions.

Most cost accounting systems calculate product costs to use as an input to managers' *product pricing and mix decisions*. Costs are also monitored to ensure that they are kept under control and that resources are used efficiently. In addition, costs may need to be analyzed especially for nonroutine decisions, such as plant closures or additions of new airline routes. Therefore, it is important to understand a number of different cost concepts so that the information generated by a cost accounting system can be used as required for different decisions.

This chapter presents 3 basic frameworks useful for understanding the design of cost accounting systems operating in different organizations. First, we describe how cost accounting systems were designed traditionally to analyze costs *by function*, such as manufacturing, selling or administration, to value inventory for external financial reporting. Second, we describe how costs are classified *by activities* in many systems designed recently and how costs of activities are expressed and estimated in terms of cost equations. (Remember that Chapter 2 defined organizations as a sequence of activities.) Finally, we describe the basic structure of standard cost accounting systems, used by many firms to estimate and control costs.

FUNCTIONAL COST CLASSIFICATIONS

Accounting systems collect and analyze cost data to support managerial decision making. *Cost* is defined as the monetary value of goods and services expended to obtain current or future benefits. All costs are not necessarily the

OBJECTIVE 3.1
How costs are classified based on function

Period costs
Costs treated as expenses in the period in which they are incurred because they cannot be associated with the manufacture of products.

Product costs
Costs associated with the manufacture of products.

same as expenses. *Expenses* are reported in the income statement. They represent either costs for which benefits were already derived in the current fiscal period, such as cost of goods sold, or **period costs**, such as advertising, whose benefits cannot be matched easily with the products or services sold in a specific fiscal period. **Product costs** are all costs incurred for the manufacture of different products. The portion of product costs assigned to the products sold in a period appears as expenses in the income statement; the remaining portion assigned to the products in inventory appears as assets in the balance sheet.

■ Traditional Cost Classification

Traditionally, the basic structure of cost accounting systems has reflected the need to determine *product costs* based on external financial reporting requirements imposed by corporate, securities, or income tax laws. These external requirements specify which costs are assigned to products, which costs are included in the inventory valuation disclosed in the balance sheet, and which costs are expended as cost of goods sold and included in the income statement. In principle, cost accounting systems to support managerial decision making can be designed independently of such external reporting requirements. Systems designed in the past, however, economized on information-processing costs by adopting the structure imposed by external reporting requirements. Therefore, most cost accounting systems we observe in business firms today tend to focus on the determination of product costs for inventory valuation and cost of goods sold.

Manufacturing costs
All costs of transforming raw materials into finished product.

Nonmanufacturing costs
All costs other than manufacturing costs.

Traditional cost accounting systems classify costs into **manufacturing costs** and **nonmanufacturing costs**, based on functions (see Exhibit 3–1):

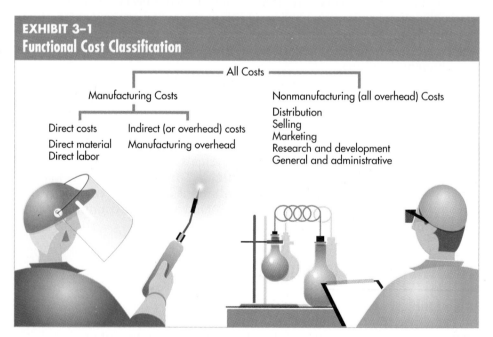

EXHIBIT 3–1
Functional Cost Classification

All Costs

Manufacturing Costs

Direct costs
Direct material
Direct labor

Indirect (or overhead) costs
Manufacturing overhead

Nonmanufacturing (all overhead) Costs
Distribution
Selling
Marketing
Research and development
General and administrative

➤ Manufacturing

1. *Manufacturing costs*, which include all costs of transforming raw materials into a finished product, for example, direct costs (direct materials, direct labor) and indirect costs (manufacturing overhead)

➤ Nonmanufacturing

2. *Distribution costs*, which include costs of delivering finished product to customers

3. *Selling costs*, which include sales personnel salaries and commissions, and other sales office expenses

4. *Marketing costs*, which include advertising and publicity expenses

5. *Research and development costs*, which include expenditures for designing and bringing new products to the market

6. *General and administrative costs*, which include expenses such as chief executive officer's salary, and legal and accounting office costs that do not fall under any of the above categories

For external reporting purposes, only manufacturing costs are included in the valuation of finished goods inventories. Traditional cost accounting systems, therefore, analyze these costs in great detail to assign them to products. Nonmanufacturing costs are all treated as period costs and are reported as expenses, without any additional analysis.

OBJECTIVE 3.2
The difference between direct and indirect costs

Manufacturing costs are classified into *direct* and *indirect* costs, as noted. **Direct costs** can be traced directly to a product. These costs are assigned to products directly based on the measured quantity of the resources consumed for their manufacture. Examples of direct manufacturing costs are

Direct costs
Costs that can be traced easily to the product manufactured or service rendered.

1. *Direct material costs*, which include the costs of all materials and parts that can be traced in the final product. For instance, if the manufacture of an automobile chassis requires 120 pounds of steel, and the steel price is $11 per pound, the direct material cost per chassis is Price/Pound * Number of pounds of steel per chassis, or, $1,320 (120 * $11) per automobile chassis.

2. *Direct labor costs*, which include the wages and fringe benefits paid to workers involved directly in manufacturing a product. If 6 workers spend 45 minutes each and the wage rate, including benefits, is $32 per hour, the direct labor cost is Wage rate/Hour * Number of direct labor hours, or, $144 (6 * $32 * 45/60) per automobile chassis.

In general, direct costs can be expressed symbolically in terms of cost equations of the following form:

$$C = P * Q \qquad (3.1)$$

where
C = cost of input resource
P = price per unit of resource
Q = quantity (number of units) of resource

CONSIDER THIS . . .

The Costs of Staying Airborne

Cost analysis is important in the airline industry, a major worldwide service industry. Airline managers need to decide whether to add new routes, discontinue existing routes, or adjust the number of daily flights on a route. The identification of costs with specific flights, however, is difficult for all airline firms. The proportion of indirect costs is large in cost accounting systems designed to estimate the costs of each flight. It is possible to identify costs such as fuel and the salaries of pilots and flight attendants directly with individual flights. But it is difficult to trace other costs—such as airplane depreciation; general administration; and the salaries of promotion and sales people, ground service personnel, and maintenance staff—directly to individual flights. A study of 28 major U.S. airlines by Banker and Johnston indicates that only about 37.5% of the operating costs were direct costs. (Compare the classification of costs for this service industry with those for manufacturing firms, described on page 100.)

Following the deregulation of the U.S. airline industry, many airlines have pursued new operating strategies. Airlines such Northwest, U.S. Air, and Delta schedule many of their flights through their hubs in Minneapolis, Pittsburgh, and Atlanta, respectively, because of the cost advantage that this strategy offers. Banker and Johnston find that the operating cost per passenger seat-mile is lower for airline firms routing their flights through hubs. This cost advantage is even greater when the airline dominates the hub (controlling more than 60% of the flights from the airport), as Northwest, U.S. Air, and Delta do at their hubs. Careful analysis of costs also helps managers make decisions about scheduling more flights per week on existing routes. Banker and Johnston find that adding a flight on an existing route results in

lower flying operations costs and passenger service costs per passenger seat-mile, but this cost advantage is offset partially by higher promotion and sales costs and traffic and servicing costs per passenger seat-mile.

Cost categories used in the Uniform System of Accounts for airlines to file financial data with Department of Transportation	Percentage of total operating cost in 1981–85	
Direct		
1. Fuel and oils	24.37%	
2. Flying operations labor (pilots, copilots, navigators and flight engineers)	8.57	
3. Passenger service (flight attendants)	<u>4.60</u>	37.54%
Indirect cost		
4. Aircraft traffic and servicing (ground servicing of aircraft and handling passengers at the gates, baggage and cargo)	8.86%	
5. Maintenance labor (maintenance of flight equipment and ground property and equipment)	6.95	
6. Maintenance materials and tools	2.06	
7. Ground property and equipment (depreciation, rentals and landing fees)	12.52	
8. Flight equipment (depreciation and rental expenses	8.42	
9. Promotion and sales (advertising, publicity, reservation and sales)	9.03	
10. General overhead (administration, utilities, insurance, communications)	<u>14.62</u>	<u>62.46</u>
		100.00%

Source: Banker, R. D., and H. H. Johnston, "An Empirical Study of Cost Drivers in the U.S. Airline Industry," *The Accounting Review*, July 1993, pp. 576–601.

OBJECTIVE 3.3
How overhead costs arise
Indirect costs
Costs that cannot be traced easily to products or services produced; also referred to as *overhead costs.*

All other manufacturing costs are classified as **indirect costs**. Such costs are also referred to as *manufacturing overhead* or *burden. Indirect costs* cannot be easily identified with individual products and are usually assigned to products by using accounting conventions—methods traditionally sanctioned for use in practice by authoritative accounting groups—for the allocation of overhead costs. Manufacturing overhead costs include wages and benefits paid to production supervisors and to workers engaged in support activities that cannot be traced readily to individual products. Such support activities include purchasing and receiving materials; scheduling and expediting production; setting up machines; moving and storing raw materials and *work in process*; performing *quality inspections*; and providing packaging and shipping, machine maintenance, process and product engineering, plant upkeep, and janitorial services. Each of these activities is essential to the functioning of the plant, and most support workers help in producing several product lines. Because these activities are not performed specifically for manufacturing a unit of a product, it is generally difficult to find a direct quantity measure to assign their costs to individual product units.

■ Ellora Electric Revisited: Let's Talk Again About Costs

Recall the introductory conversation at Ellora Electric in which the boss, Michael Manley, asked Donald Dent to estimate the impact of changeover to new automated spray painting machines on manufacturing costs.

First, Don checked the meaning of the relevant basic cost terms in a management accounting textbook. Next, he examined the cost accounting records at Ellora Electric's Grand Rapids plant. He determined the direct material cost as the cost of paint consumed in the spray painting department. He identified the workers responsible for the spray painting activity and measured direct labor costs as the wages and benefits earned by these workers. Cost accounting records also indicated the amount of overhead costs assigned to the spray painting department. Thus, Don was able to compile the information in Exhibit 3–2 for the monthly costs of the spray painting department, analyzed by function, both before and after the new automated machines were installed.

EXHIBIT 3–2
Ellora Electric Company: Spray Painting Department Costs

	BEFORE	AFTER	CHANGE
Direct material (paint)	$22,400	19,900	$(2,500)
Direct labor	18,700	14,100	(4,600)
Overhead costs:			
Supervision	3,100	2,800	(300)
Material handling	4,000	2,900	(1,100)
Storage	3,600	2,100	(1,500)
Inspection	3,000	2,000	(1,000)
Machine maintenance	2,600	3,800	1,200
Depreciation	5,700	9,100	3,400
Insurance	1,100	1,500	400
Total costs	$64,200	$58,200	$(6,000)

Don determined that production volume had remained the same in the 3 months after the installation of the new machines as in the 3 months before. He was now in a position to estimate the impact of the machine changeover on various costs categorized by function.

Don attributed the $6,000 net reduction in costs to the efficiencies gained with the installation of the automated machines. In particular, there is now less waste of paint material and less need for machine operators. In addition, the process is now faster and more reliable, and nonvalue-added activities (described in Chapter 2), such as materials handling and storage, are reduced. The net savings from these activities more than offset the increases in machine maintenance, depreciation, and insurance costs.

■ Cost Structure Today

The composition of manufacturing costs has changed substantially in recent years. In the early 1900s when many businesses first installed formal cost systems, direct labor represented a large proportion, sometimes 50% and more, of the total manufacturing costs. As a result, cost accounting systems were designed to focus on measuring and controlling direct labor, and they served their purpose adequately.

In today's industrial environment, however, direct labor is only a small portion of manufacturing costs. In the electronics industry, for instance, direct labor cost is estimated to be between 5% and 15% of the total manufacturing cost, yet the cost of direct materials remains important, representing about 40% to 60% of the costs in many plants.

One notable change in cost structure is that the share of overhead costs has become increasingly important. This change has occurred because of the shift toward greater automation (which requires more production engineering, scheduling, and machine setup activities), the emphasis on better customer service, and the proliferation of multiple products. In addition to

Standard Products Company, which manufactures automobile components, makes facia moldings for automobile bumpers. The moldings have 7 clips that had to be positioned by hand before the molding was cut. By devising an automated method to position and hold the 7 clips, thereby replacing direct labor costs with overhead costs, output was increased and scrap and rework were reduced. *(Courtesy Standard Products Company)*

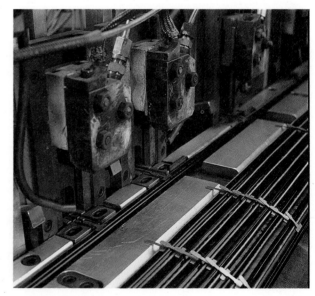

What Drives Manufacturing Overhead Costs

Manufacturing executives indicate that overhead costs rank behind only quality and getting new products out on schedule as their primary concern. Overhead costs as a percentage of value added in manufacturing have been increasing steadily over the past 100 years, and the proportion of direct labor costs has been decreasing. ("Value added in manufacturing" equals direct labor plus manufacturing overhead costs.) Production managers have been paying increased attention to overhead costs in today's environment because these people have more leverage on improving productivity through cutting overhead than they do through pruning direct labor.

The critical step for managers in controlling overhead costs lies in developing a model that identifies the forces driving these costs. Miller and Vollman (1985) in a classic paper suggest that overhead costs in a plant are driven not by production volume but by the following four types of manufacturing transactions:

1. *Logistical transactions*, which involve ordering, executing, and confirming the movement of materials from one location to another. These transactions are processed, transcribed, and analyzed by people on the shop floor as well as by people in receiving, expediting, shipping, data entry, and accounting departments.

2. *Balancing transactions*, which ensure that the supplies of materials, labor, and capacity are equal to the demand for these resources. Personnel in purchasing, production and materials planning, production scheduling and control, and labor requirements planning take part in these transactions.

3. *Quality transactions*, which comprise quality control, including inspection and rework; quality improvement, including worker training, engineering, and supplier certification; and field support, including warranty repairs.

4. *Change transactions*, which update manufacturing information systems to accommodate changes in engineering designs, schedules, routings, standards, materials specifications, and bills of material.

Source: Miller, J. G., and T. E. Vollman, "The Hidden Factory," *Harvard Business Review*, September–October 1985, pp. 142–150.

indirect manufacturing costs becoming more important, overhead costs associated with distribution, selling, marketing, and administrative activities have increased as direct labor costs have continued to decline in recent years.

An important consequence of this change in cost structure is that cost systems designed for manufacturing activities with high direct labor content are fast becoming obsolete. When direct material and direct labor costs are substantial, cost systems are designed to monitor them in detail to ensure that they are traced correctly to the individual products. When overhead costs are small, it is not crucial to understand how they arise or how to assign them carefully to products because overhead assignments would be unlikely to lead to large distortions. When overhead costs contribute a significant part of the total costs, however, it is important to understand them. Therefore, designers of new cost accounting systems now pay special attention to overhead costs.

ACTIVITY-BASED ANALYSIS OF COSTS

It is relatively easy to understand how direct material and direct labor costs are incurred because they can be traced directly to the products manufactured or services rendered by the organization. But to understand why overhead costs are incurred, we first need to analyze why a variety of activities are performed in an organization to support the production of goods and services.

Consider two plants located in Massachusetts that are operated by Jim and Barry's Ice Cream Company. The first plant, located in Springfield, manufactures only vanilla ice cream. The second plant, located in Worcester, produces a variety of ice cream flavors. Last year, the Springfield plant manufactured 600,000 gallons of vanilla ice cream. The Worcester plant also manufactured a total of 600,000 gallons, but it produced eight different flavors: 90,000 gallons each of chocolate, strawberry, coffee, and raspberry ice cream and 60,000 gallons each of raisins and nuts, orange, butterscotch, and pecan ice cream. Although both plants produce the same volume of ice cream using the same manufacturing process, there are differences between the two plants. Both use about the same amount of direct materials, such as cream and flavorings, and about the same number of direct labor hours and machine hours, yet the manufacturing costs for the Worcester plant are much higher than those for the Springfield plant.

Manufacturing overhead costs are higher at the Worcester plant because more indirect labor is required to perform support activities such as setting up the machines and quality testing ice cream color and flavor when changing from one batch of an ice cream flavor to another flavor, supervising the production and machine setup labor during and after changeover, storing and handling different materials, purchasing materials required for the manufacture and packing of different products, scheduling and expediting production, servicing different customer orders, and providing engineering support for different products. Overhead costs increase with the volume of activities required to support production, and because the Worcester plant requires a greater volume of activities, it incurs higher manufacturing overhead.

■ Types of Production Activities

Production activities are classified into four categories: unit-related, batch-related, product-sustaining, and facility-sustaining activities.

Unit-related activities are those whose volume or level is associated with the number of units produced or other measures, such as direct labor hours and machine-hours, that relate directly to the number of units produced. The indirect labor required for quality inspection that checks every item (or checks, say, 10% or 20% of items) is evidently associated with the number of units produced. Uniform supervision of all activities performed by direct workers requires supervisory effort that is associated with the number of direct labor hours. Consumption of lubricating oil and the power required to work the machines, as well as the scheduled maintenance of machines after every 20,000 hours of use (or after any specified amount of use), results in overhead costs that are associated with machine-hours. Since direct labor hours and machine-hours themselves increase with the number of units produced, the use of many activities supporting production increases with the level of production.

Batch-related activities are associated with the number of batches produced, rather than with the number of units manufactured. Machine setups, for instance, are required when beginning the production of a new batch of products. Once the machine has been set up, no additional setup

---

Manufacturing overhead costs
Indirect cost of transforming raw materials into finished product; indirect manufacturing costs.

OBJECTIVE 3.4
The difference between unit-related, batch-related, product-sustaining, and facility-sustaining activity cost drivers

Unit-related activities
Activities whose levels are related to the number of units produced.

Batch-related activities
Activities whose levels are related to the number of batches produced.

effort is required, whether we produce a batch of 100 units or 1,000 units of the product. Since the *in-process materials* for a batch are moved together from one work center to the next, the cost of materials handling also tends to be associated with the number of batches rather than with the size of the batches. Similarly, because *first-item quality inspections* (inspecting only the first unit in each batch) involve testing a fixed number of units in a batch, rather than a percentage, indirect labor for such inspection is also associated with the number of batches.

Clerical effort expended to issue purchase orders or to receive materials from suppliers is an overhead activity associated with the number of purchase orders, or with the number of deliveries, rather than with the quantity of materials ordered. The cost of the purchased materials, such as cream and flavors at Jim and Barry's, depends on the quantity of materials, but the overhead cost of processing the paperwork for purchases depends on the number of orders. Production scheduling is also considered a batch-related activity because it is associated more with the number of production runs that need to be scheduled in a plant rather than with the number of units produced in each run.

Product-sustaining activities are performed to support the production and sale of individual products. The higher the number of products and product lines, the higher is the cost of product-sustaining activities. Examples include administrative efforts required in maintaining drawings and routings of parts, product engineering efforts to maintain coherent specifications for individual products (and their component parts) and their routing through different work centers in the plant, and the process engineering required to implement engineering change orders (ECOs). Engineering efforts to design and test process routines for products and to perform product enhancements are also other examples of product-sustaining activities. The need to expedite production orders also increases as the number of products and customers serviced by a plant increases. Costs of obtaining patents or regulatory approval, such as Food and Drug Administration approval for new pharmaceutical drugs or food products, also increase with the number of products.

At Jim and Barry's, product-sustaining activities include designing new ice cream flavors; developing, maintaining, and improving recipes; and designing packaging and marketing materials for individual ice cream flavors. The demand for these activities increases with the number of products but is independent of their production volumes.

Facility-sustaining activities are required to support the upkeep of the plant and the associated managerial infrastructure that makes production possible. These activities are not related to the number of individual products, the number of production runs, or the number of units manufactured. Examples include plant rental and depreciation, plant maintenance, insurance and taxes, housekeeping, landscaping, lighting, and security. Plant administration comprises these activities and those performed by the plant manager, plant accountants, and personnel managers.

Exhibit 3–3 displays the four categories of production-related activities in a hierarchical diagram (as well as related activity cost-driver information, which is discussed in subsequent sections). Facility-sustaining activities are at the top of this hierarchy, followed by product-sustaining activities, batch-related activities, and, finally, unit-related activities, which are at the bottom.

Product-sustaining activities
Activities performed to support the production of individual products.

Facility-sustaining activities
Activities performed to provide the managerial infrastructure and to support the upkeep of the plant.

This hierarchy reflects the fact that the costs of batch-related activities are independent of unit-related activities, the costs of product-sustaining activities are fixed relative to both batch-related and unit-related measures, and finally, the costs of facility-sustaining activities are independent of the number of products, batches, or units produced. This type of classification of activities raises a question about the identification of measures associated with the costs of these different types of activities. These measures, known as **activity cost drivers**, are addressed in the next section.

Activity cost driver
Unit of measurement for the level (or quantity) of the activity performed.

■ Activity Cost Drivers

OBJECTIVE 3.5
How cost relations with activities and their drivers are expressed as equations

Earlier in this chapter, we expressed the costs of direct materials and direct labor in terms of the following equations:

Cost of steel = Price of steel per pound * Number of pounds of steel

Cost of direct labor = Wage rate per hour * Direct labor hours

Recall that, symbolically, equation (3.1) depicts these equations as

$$C = P * Q$$

where

cost of input resource
P = price per unit of resource
Q = quantity (in units) of resource

Although this equation works well for direct costs, such precise and specific quantity measures often are not available conveniently or at a reasonable cost for most overhead activities. For instance, supervisors' salaries are usually regarded as indirect costs. In theory, we could require the supervisors to maintain detailed logs recording the actual time that they spend supervising the production of specific batches of products, which would allow these costs to be assigned *directly* to product units or batches. However, because they spend time on numerous batches in a day, recording the detailed information is cumbersome and takes much of their valuable time.[2]

Most designers of cost accounting systems, therefore, prefer to attribute such overhead costs indirectly by developing alternative surrogate quantity measures that are available more readily. For example, if supervisors spend their time supervising activities of direct workers more or less uniformly across all batches being produced, the amount of their time spent on different batches is likely proportional to the direct labor hours worked on those batches. Cost accounting systems, therefore, often use direct labor hours as a surrogate quantity measure (cost driver) for supervisory effort. In other words, the supervision cost equation

[2] In contrast, partners in accounting firms and legal firms record the time they spend consulting with clients in meticulous detail, because such records are required to bill the clients and no alternatives or surrogate measures of the partners' effort expended on different clients will suffice for this purpose.

Supervision activity cost =
   Supervision wage rate * Supervision hours

is expressed instead as

Supervision activity cost =
   Supervision activity overhead rate per DLH *
   Direct labor hours (DLH)

or symbolically, as

$$C = R * X \qquad (3.2)$$

where

R = the *overhead rate* for the activity
X = the surrogate *cost driver* measure for the
   activity

Thus, activity cost drivers are either direct measures, such as the number of supervision hours, or indirect surrogate measures, such as direct labor hours, that are used to reflect the quantity of activity performed.

Turn back now to Exhibit 3–3. It lists activity cost drivers for unit-related activities that are unit-level measures, cost drivers for batch-related activities that are batch-level measures, and so on. In choosing the appropriate cost driver, system designers consider how well the measure relates to the quantity of the activity performed and the convenience of collecting the information. For instance, setup hour is commonly used as the cost driver for the machine set up activity. If, however, all batches of products require about the same number of hours to setup the machines, we could use the more convenient number of setups as the activity cost driver because it is proportional to setup hours.

An additional point requires further attention. We expressed $C = R * X$ to represent the activity cost equation. The activity overhead rate, R, however, is usually not readily available.

CONSIDER THIS . . .

The Cost of Manufacturing Transactions

A recent study of 32 plants in the electronics, machinery, and automobile-components industries by Banker, Potter, and Schroeder (1994) reveals that manufacturing overhead costs, on average, were approximately three times the direct labor costs. Direct material costs contributed the largest part of total manufacturing costs.

Components of Manufacturing Costs

	Electronics	Machinery	Automobile Components
Direct labor	8.4%	10.8%	7.8%
Direct material	65.2	63.6	67.5
Manufacturing overhead	26.4	25.6	24.7%
Total	100.0%	100.0%	100.0%

For this sample of 32 plants, manufacturing overhead costs are strongly correlated to direct labor costs. But manufacturing overhead is more strongly correlated to measures of manufacturing transactions, as described by Miller and Vollman (see "Consider This . . . What Drives Manufacturing Overhead Costs," on page 99. In this study, the number of logistical transactions was measured by the average area for the movement and storage of work-in--process materials, and the number of balancing transactions by the number of personnel assigned to purchasing and production planning activities. Quality transactions were measured by the number of personnel assigned to quality control and improvement activities, and change transactions were measured by the number of engineering change orders.

Source: Banker, R. D., G. Potter, and R. G. Schroeder, "An Empirical Study of Manufacturing Overhead Cost Drivers," Journal of Accounting and Economics, November 1994.

By examining past accounting records, we can determine the values of C, the total cost of performing the activity, and X, the total number of units of the cost driver for that activity. The activity overhead rate, R, is then calculated from this information using the following equation:

$$R = \frac{C}{X} \qquad (3.3)$$

The estimated activity overhead rate, R, can then be used to assign activity costs to products. For instance, if the overhead rate for setup activity is $32

EXHIBIT 3-3
Categories of Activities and Their Activity Cost Drivers

CATEGORIES	REPRESENTATIVE ACTIVITIES	ACTIVITY COST DRIVERS
Facility-sustaining activities	• Plant management • Accounting and personnel • Housekeeping, lighting • Rent, depreciation	• Square feet of space • Number of workers
↓ ↓ ↓		
Product-sustaining activities	• Product design • Parts administration • Engineering • Expediting production orders	• Number of products • Number of parts • Number of ECOs
↓ ↓ ↓		
Batch-related activities	• Machine setup • First-item inspections • Purchase ordering • Materials handling • Production scheduling	• Setup hours • Inspection hours • Number of orders • Number of material moves • Number of production runs
↓ ↓ ↓		
Unit-related activities	• Every-item inspection • Supervision of direct labor • Consumption of power and oils to run machines	• Number of units • Direct labor hours • Machine hours

per setup hour, and if 200 setup hours were used for the production of Product A in January, then $6,400 ($32 * 200) of setup activity costs can be assigned to Product A in January. In such assignment of costs to products, overhead rates and activity cost driver values are comparable to the price and quantity of a direct cost.

CONSIDERATION OF MULTIPLE ACTIVITIES   To make production possible, numerous activities are commonly performed in a plant. The principles described earlier apply directly to such situations involving multiple activities. For example, suppose that a production process requires five activities. We can determine a separate overhead rate for each of these five activities, as described above, so that we have

$$R_1 = \frac{C_1}{X_1},\ R_2 = \frac{C_2}{X_2},\ R_3 = \frac{C_3}{X_3},\ R_4 = \frac{C_4}{X_4},\ \text{and } R_5 = \frac{C_5}{X_5} \tag{3.4}$$

The total of the overhead costs for the plant comprises the costs of each of the five activities. Therefore, we can write the total overhead costs, C, as

$$\begin{aligned} C &= C_1 + C_2 + C_3 + C_4 + C_5 \\ &= R_1X_1 + R_2X_2 + R_3X_3 + R_4X_4 + R_5X_5 \end{aligned} \tag{3.5}$$

Notice that the total overhead cost is a *function of all five activity cost drivers* X_1, X_2, X_3, X_4, and X_5. Suppose that we use only one cost driver, for example, X_1, instead to describe the cost equation and determine an alternative overhead rate, R', so that

$$R = \frac{C}{X_1} = \frac{C_1 + C_2 + C_3 + C_4 + C_5}{X_1} \qquad (3.6)$$

If we write $C = R'X_1$ and use it for the estimation of costs, the estimates will be distorted when the values of the remaining cost drivers, X_2, X_3, X_4, and X_5, change in a different proportion than the selected driver X_1.

COST DISTORTION WITH ONE DRIVER To illustrate how the use of only one cost driver distorts the estimation of costs, consider the following example. The true cost equation has two activity cost drivers:

$$X_1 = \text{direct labor hours}$$
$$X_2 = \text{setup hours}$$

and is given by $C = \$70X_1 + \$500X_2$.

The activity cost driver values, in total, for February 1994, are

$$X_1 = 1{,}000 \text{ direct labor hours}$$
$$X_2 = 60 \text{ setup hours}$$

and, therefore, the total costs are $100,000 ($70 * 1000 + $500 * 60). If the second cost driver, X_2 (setup hours) is not recognized and the cost accounting system is based on only one cost driver, X_1, direct labor hours, then the cost equation is estimated as

$$C = R_1' * X_1 \text{ where } R_1' = \$100 \ (\$100{,}000/1{,}000).$$

This cost per direct labor hour is the apparent activity overhead rate because all costs are allocated (for simplicity) by just this one cost driver.

Assume that the cost equation estimated using February 1994 data is applicable to March 1994 production. The values of the activity cost drivers associated with the production of a Product A planned in March 1994 are

$$X_1 = 90 \text{ direct labor hours}$$
$$X_2 = 7 \text{ setup hours}$$

The cost equation based on only the first cost driver estimates the costs of Product A as follows:

$$\text{Estimated cost of Product A} = R_1' * X_1 = \$100 * 90 = \$9{,}000$$

This estimate distorts the value of costs that should be attributed to Product A because, in fact, the costs are

$$
\begin{aligned}
\text{True cost of Product A} &= \$70X_1 + \$500X_2 \\
&= \$70 * 90 + \$500 * 7 \\
&= \$6{,}300 + \$3{,}500 \\
&= \$9{,}800
\end{aligned}
$$

Montex Company: Departmental Costs for Two Representative Departments

DEPARTMENT	MACHINE SETUPS	QUALITY INSPECTIONS
Manager	Roger Smith	David Carlson
Wages and benefits	$406,000	$476,000
Tools, supplies, and other costs	110,000	26,000
Initial total costs	$516,000	$502,000
Add: Engineer's wages		
(based on interview with Mr. Carlson)	—	38,000
Revised total costs	$516,000	$540,000

Such distortions always occur unless the values of the omitted cost driver (setup hours, in this case) vary *exactly* in proportion to the values of the included cost driver (direct labor hours).

The challenging task before us, therefore, is to identify all the principal activities performed in an organization and the appropriate cost drivers for each of these activities.

■ Identifying Activity Costs: Montex Company Illustration

OBJECTIVE 3.6
How information is collected to estimate activity costs

Activity overhead rate
Ratio of the cost of resources to provide an activity to the level of the capacity made available by those resources.

To identify activity costs, select a cost driver measure, and determine the **activity overhead rate**, it is necessary to perform observations in detail, to examine cost accounting records, and to interview knowledgeable and experienced managers. These actions provide a good understanding of the activities performed by different organizational units.

Consider the study conducted by Linda Collins, manager in charge of cost analysis and planning at Montex Company. Montex makes steel and brass pumps at its four plants located in Minnesota, Indiana, Illinois, and Michigan. Linda first examined the accounting and payroll records at the Minnesota plant. She organized payroll costs, including benefits, by department and analyzed expenditure records to identify tools, supplies, and other costs with individual departments. Exhibit 3–4 shows the cost associated with two departments, machine setup and quality inspections, and the names of the managers in charge of each of them.

After collecting the departmental cost information, Linda next interviewed the departmental managers to identify what activities were performed by the personnel in each department. Edited versions of these interviews with salient information appear below.

The first interview was with Roger Smith, who has been with Montex Company for 26 years, and is now the manager of the machine setup department.

Linda Collins: How many people do you have in your department?

Roger Smith: I supervise 8 people. We had 7 until last June, but because of the high workload, we had to add Steve Swanson in the second half of last year. Steve is now a permanent worker in our department.

Linda Collins: What work do they do?

Roger Smith: All my people are responsible for setting up the machines.

Linda Collins: What drives the amount of work that they do?

Roger Smith: Well, setups are required each time they begin a production run. When the machine is available for the production run, our people go and set up the machine and inspect the first item produced to make sure that the machine is set up right.

Linda Collins: So it is the number of production runs or batches that drives your work, not how large a run is?

Roger Smith: Yes, that is really the case. Setting up the machine takes about the same time even if a batch is for 60 pumps instead of 30 pumps.

Linda Collins: Do the setups for all batches take about the same amount of time?

Roger Smith: No. There are big differences, depending on the product for which we have to set up the machines. There are some products with very complex specifications that require about 3 hours of setup time. For simple products, such as P101, we can set up the machine in only one-half hour.

Linda Collins: So the number of setup hours is perhaps the best measure of how much work you setup people put into the manufacture of a product.

Roger Smith: Yes.

Linda Collins: How many hours of setup work can your crew perform in a year?

Roger Smith: Well, I expect about 1,800 hours of productive time from each of my people. Last year we had $7\frac{1}{2}$ workers on average, so there were a total of 13,500 hours available for setup. This year we have 8 workers, we will provide a total of 14,400 possible hours for setup.

Linda next interviewed David Carlson, an 18-year veteran at Montex, now in charge of the quality inspection department.

Linda Collins: How many people do you have in the quality inspection department?

David Carlson: I have 12 people. Three of them are responsible for inspecting materials received from our suppliers. The remaining 9 are responsible for the final inspection of all our production. I supervise all of their work, so I spend about 25% of my time on receipt inspection and 75% on final inspection.

Linda Collins: Hmm. Let me see. Our payroll records indicate that there are only 11 people reporting to you in your department.

David Carlson:	Yes, but Jon Wang from the production engineering department is now permanently assigned to me to help us with our final product inspections.
Linda Collins:	[checking her payroll records] That means I need to add another $38,000 in wages and benefits to your department and subtract it from the production engineering department. Your departmental costs, therefore, are $540,000. (See Exhibit 3–4.)
David Carlson:	Yes.
Linda Collins:	Let me move on. What determines the amount of work for your people inspecting material receipts?
David Carlson:	We inspect every lot of materials we receive, so I suppose it is the number of material receipts.
Linda Collins:	Does the amount of inspection time depend on the size of the lot?
David Carlson:	Not unless it is an exceptionally large lot that we receive only once or twice a year. You see, we randomly inspect incoming materials and normally take only about 1 hour to record, inspect, and store each lot we receive.
Linda Collins:	How many lots can you receive and inspect in a year with your present staff?
David Carlson:	We can do up to 100 per week. Since the plant works 50 weeks in a year, I suppose it means that we can inspect 5,000 materials receipts in a year.
Linda Collins:	What drives the work done by your people responsible for the final inspection of your production?
David Carlson:	Company policy requires us to inspect every unit we produce, so it is the total number of units produced at the plant.
Linda Collins:	Do all products require the same number of inspection hours?
David Carlson:	Yes. We follow the same procedures for all our pumps.
Linda Collins:	How many pumps can your crew inspect in a year?
David Carlson:	We can inspect 5,000 pumps in a week, so it means that we can inspect 250,000 pumps in a year. You should realize, of course, that during some weeks when the production level is low in the plant, we do not inspect 5,000 pumps, and sometimes during peak production periods we work overtime to get the job completed.

■ Determining Overhead Rates for Montex

How can we assimilate all this information to determine the overhead rates for the activities performed by these two departments? The analysis requires five steps for each department:

1. Identify the activities performed by the organization.

2. Determine the cost of performing each activity.

3. Identity a cost driver for each activity.

4. Determine the number of units of the cost driver made available by the resources committed to each activity.

5. Divide the activity cost by the number of cost driver units made available to determine the activity overhead rate.

Linda Collins next determined activity overhead rates as follows:

MACHINE SETUP ACTIVITY OVERHEAD RATE

STEP 1 Roger Smith's department performs machine setups.

STEP 2 Last year, the cost of the activity resources was $516,000. (See Exhibit 3–4.)

STEP 3 The appropriate cost driver in this case is the number of setup hours, rather than the number of setups, because the setup time is different for different products.

STEP 4 The activity cost of $516,000 made 13,500 hours available for machine setups (see discussion with Smith).

STEP 5 The overhead rate for the activity, therefore, is $38.22 per setup hour ($516,000/13,500).

Based on Smith's estimates for this year, 14,400 setup hours will be available. If we expect the costs of both wages and benefits and tools and supplies

Companies using paper products reduce inventories and costs by acquiring the paper they use at press time. Therefore, providing paper just as the customer needs it is a key success factor for companies such as Bowater Incorporated. This customer service requires special mill runs, which, in turn, require complex scheduling systems and a need to monitor closely the distribution system. The company must determine whether the costs of these special customer service activities are exceeded by the profits resulting from the sales generated by this service. *(Courtesy Mason Morfit)*

to increase proportionally with the number of setup hours made available, we would expect the total activity cost this year to be $550,368 ($38.22 * 14,400).

MATERIAL RECEIPTS ACTIVITY AND FINAL INSPECTION ACTIVITY OVERHEAD RATES

STEP 1 David Carlson's department performs 2 different activities (inspecting materials received from suppliers and inspecting materials produced by Montex).

STEP 2 Linda Collins identified the people working on each of these two activities and apportioned David Carlson's salary and other costs between the 2 activities. She determined that last year total department costs were $540,000 (see Exhibit 3–4), the material receipts inspection activity cost $135,000, and the final inspection activity cost $405,000.

STEP 3 Linda selected the number of material receipts as the cost driver for the first activity (inspection of materials from suppliers), and the number of units produced as the cost driver for the second activity (inspection of pumps produced).

STEP 4 It is possible to inspect 5,000 material receipts with the resources made available for this activity last year, while there is the capacity to inspect 250,000 finished pumps with the resources available for inspection at present.

STEP 5 The overhead rate is $27.00 ($135,000/5,000) per material receipt for the first activity. The overhead rate is $1.62 ($405,000/250,000) per pump for the second activity.

See Exhibit 3–5 for a summary of overhead rates at Montex. Recall that these are only three *representative* activities performed at Montex Company, but if the three were the *only* activities, overhead costs at Montex could be written as

Overhead cost =
$38.22 * Setup hours + $27.00 * Material receipts + $1.62 * Finished pumps

This represents the more general version of the cost equation described in equation (3.5).

EXHIBIT 3–5
Montex Company: Overhead Rates for Three Representative Activities

ACTIVITY	MACHINE SETUP	MATERIAL RECEIPTS INSPECTION	FINISHED PRODUCT INSPECTION
Total cost	$516,000	$135,000	$405,000
Cost driver	Setup hours	Number of receipts	Number of pumps
Capacity made available	13,500 hours	5,000 receipts	250,000 pumps
Overhead rate	$38.22 per setup hour	$27.00 per receipt	$1.62 per pump

An important concept needs to be highlighted here by referring to the machine setup department. Notice that the expenditure for each activity depends on the *amount of driver capacity made available, not the actual use of the capacity,* so long as this capacity for 13,500 setup hours is adequate for actual demand. The wages and benefits for the 7½ setup workers and their supervisor and the associated costs of the tools, supplies, and other resources they require total $516,000. The total expenditure for this activity would have been the same amount even if the setup crew had been used for only 13,120 hours and had remained idle for the remaining 380 (13,500 — 13,120) hours. The cost for this activity, therefore, depends on the *capacity* that is made available, rather than on its actual use. This issue is discussed in more detail in Chapter 4 when we examine how costs vary with the level of the activity.

COST CONCEPTS FOR SERVICE ORGANIZATIONS

OBJECTIVE 3.7
How cost concepts extend
to service organizations

So far we have discussed cost concepts in the context of manufacturing organizations. How can we apply these concepts to service organizations, including both for-profit and not-for-profit organizations, that are not engaged in manufacturing activities?

Among the services offered by Caremark International, Inc., to its customers is a mail-order drug program that serves 30 million customers in 700 companies. The Caremark employee on the right in this picture is discussing the prescription-drug benefit management program—which helps its corporate customers monitor, understand, and manage the cost of their prescription-drug benefit plans—with a benefit insurance analyst from United Airlines, one of Caremark's customers. *(Courtesy Caremark International, Inc.)*

■ Distinguishing Characteristics of Service Organizations

Services produced cannot be inventoried for future sale. Therefore, cost accounting systems in most service organizations are not burdened with the financial reporting requirement of inventory valuation. Regulatory requirements for financial reporting, especially from the funding agencies of many for-profit and not-for-profit service organizations, have often restricted the structure of cost reports and limited their use for internal managerial purposes. Many service organizations, however, have developed and maintained alternative cost accounting systems that operate in parallel with the traditional financial reporting systems to facilitate managerial decision making. This has occurred because of decreased information processing costs and increased economic and fiscal pressure resulting from deregulation.

Another characteristic that often distinguishes service organizations from manufacturing plants reflects the previous discussion of measuring output/outcome in Chapter 2. It is difficult to measure the true output of a service organization because often it delivers a less tangible and measurable "product" than do manufacturing operations. For example, at Montex, one can quantify the number of satisfactorily produced pumps (output) and at Jim and Barrys', the same is true when evaluating the gallons of ice cream produced. But how do we measure the output of a hospital, of a school, of a savings and loan bank, or of a radio station? The answers are not straightforward or easy.

The difficulty in measuring output for service organizations raises special concerns about designing product costing systems and management control systems. Identifying direct material and direct labor costs also becomes difficult if the output remains ambiguous. As a result, many of the costs of service organizations are classified as indirect, and the concepts relating activity analysis and overhead costs become particularly salient as shown in the following example.

■ Riverside General Hospital: An Illustration for a Service Organization

Consider Riverside General Hospital, located on the banks of the Mississippi River in Minneapolis, Minnesota. Exhibit 3–6 displays information on 18 account names and expenses for the fiscal year 1994 collected from the hospital's financial ledgers.

Holly Ward, Riverside's controller, identifies three principal uses for the cost accounting system at Riverside:

1. Determine the costs of resources used during a patient's stay. This information is used to bill the patient. More recently, hospital management has been comparing patient care costs with predetermined reimbursement rates to assess the hospital's profitability in treating patients in different diagnosis-related groups (DRGs).

2. Provide the planning basis for operating expenditures. If cost rates are known accurately, the hospital may be able to plan better for its staffing and other resource requirements.

3. Provide the basis for comparing the hospital's costs to those of other hospitals and for determining the best opportunities for reducing expenses.

These expectations for the role of the hospital's cost accounting system are similar to those for many manufacturing establishments. In each case, it is important to obtain a good understanding of cost behavior.

Holly does not find the distinction between direct and indirect costs very useful for her organization. Direct materials include pharmaceutical pre-scriptions and supplies such as saline transfusions. Direct labor could include the actual hours of nursing service provided to the patient, but recording nurse hours individually by patient treated would be cumbersome and not likely to be informative. Therefore, virtually all of the costs in the hospital are classified as indirect costs. In contrast to our use of the term *indirect costs* to mean manufacturing overhead earlier in this chapter, *indirect costs* for Riverside and for service organizations are often referred to as **operating overhead**.

Operating overhead
Indirect costs of produc-ing services in a service organization.

Several activities are performed to make patient care possible. Refer next to Exhibit 3–7, which presents the cost drivers identified by Holly Ward for the activities corresponding to the cost accounts appearing in Exhibit 3–6. Activity overhead rates are determined as ratios of the cost of the activity to the level of the activity capacity made available. For instance, the cost driver for linen and laundry is pounds of laundry. The activity cost (from Exhibit 3–6, account number 106) is $358,736, and these resources make it possible to process 840,749 pounds of laundry (Exhibit 3–7). The activity overhead rate, therefore, is $0.4267 ($358,736/840,749) per pound of laundry. These activity rates are summarized in Exhibit 3–7.

EXHIBIT 3–6
Riverside General Hospital: Operating Costs for Fiscal Year 1994

ACCOUNT NUMBER	ACCOUNT NAME	COST
101	Nursing services	$2,973,154
102	Nursing administration	1,269,762
103	Pharmacy	496,629
104	Laboratory	312,347
105	Medical supplies	482,165
106	Linen and laundry	358,736
107	Dietary	813,148
108	Employee cafeteria	167,239
109	Housekeeping	706,308
110	Medical records and library	250,345
111	Social services	199,026
112	Patient scheduling and administration	60,238
113	Billing and collection	112,280
114	Plant operations	301,238
115	Plant maintenance	386,622
116	Medical equipment operations	496,275
117	Property insurance	38,350
118	Depreciation	960,573
	Total operating costs	$10,384,435

EXHIBIT 3–7
Riverside General Hospital: Activity Overhead Rates for Fiscal Year 1994

NUMBER	ACTIVITY	COST DRIVER	ACTIVITY LEVEL	OVERHEAD RATE
101	Nursing services	Nursing hours	280,621	$10.5949
102	Nursing administration	Nursing hours	280,621	4.5248
103	Pharmacy	Direct	—	—
104	Laboratory	Number of tests	80,224	3.8934
105	Medical supplies	Number of patient-days	45,606	10.5724
106	Linen and laundry	Pounds of laundry	840,749	0.4267
107	Dietary	Number of meals	88,673	9.1702
108	Employee cafeteria	Number of nurse-days	35,078	4.7676
109	Housekeeping	Square feet of space	23,798	29.6793
110	Medical records	Number of patients	8,367	29.6793
111	Social services	Number of patients	8,367	23.7870
112	Patient scheduling	Number of patients	8,367	7.1995
113	Billing and collection	Number of patients	8,367	13.4194
114	Plant operations	Square feet of space	23,798	12.6581
115	Plant maintenance	Square feet of space	23,798	1.6115
116	Equipment operation	Number of procedures	62,179	7.9814
117	Property insurance	Value of property	$21,567,322	0.1778%
118	Depreciation	Value of property	$21,557,322	4.4538%

Such activity overhead rates are often used to estimate the activity costs when the level of activity changes. For instance, if the number of pounds of laundry is expected to decrease to 803,250, the linen and laundry costs are estimated to be $342,747 (= $0.4267 * 803,250). One must be cautious, however, in using such rates as the activity levels change because, as you will recall from our previous discussion, the amount of expenditure for an activity depends on the *capacity made available* rather than on the *actual consumption* of the activity resources. It may not be possible to reduce costs as indicated if the capacity of resources made available cannot be reduced proportionally with the reduction in the demand placed on it.

Holly decided to develop a simple cost equation to estimate costs as a part of the hospital's annual budgeting process. She began by classifying the activities listed in Exhibit 3–7 into three distinct categories:

> ➤ The first category comprises activities related to the number of patient-days. Holly decided that the number of patient-days is the best measure of the "production volume" at the hospital, and activities related to it could be thought of as *unit-related* activities.

> ➤ The second category comprises activities related to the number of patients admitted to the hospital. Activities that are related to the number of patients, such as medical record keeping and patient billing, are analogous to *batch-related* activities in a manufacturing establishment in the sense that the demand for them is related to the number of patients, regardless of how many days they are actually hospitalized.

> ➤ The third category includes *facility-sustaining* activities, such as plant operations and maintenance. See these classifications of activities in Parts A, B, and C, respectively, of Exhibit 3–8.

Holly developed the following equation to represent the 1994 costs:

$$\text{Costs} = \$2,393,091 + \$161.59 * \text{Patient-days} + \$74.33 * \text{Patients}$$

The first term represents the total facility-sustaining costs (see Part C, Exhibit 3–8). Because Holly did not expect any significant changes in the plant and equipment, she believed that these costs would remain at the same level for the next year. In any case, these costs are independent of the number of patients and the number of patient-days. The last two terms in the equation, from Parts A and B, respectively, of Exhibit 3–8, reflect the expectation that these costs will change as the number of patients or the number of patient-days change.

Holly used the activity overhead rates obtained from the 1994 data to estimate costs for 1995 because the wage rates were frozen for 1995 at the

---

EXHIBIT 3–8
Riverside General Hospital: Activity Classification

NUMBER	ACTIVITY	COST
A. UNIT-RELATED ACTIVITIES		
101	Nursing services	$2,973,154
102	Nursing administration	1,269,762
103	Pharmacy	496,629
104	Laboratory	312,347
105	Medical supplies	482,165
106	Linen and laundry	358,736
107	Dietary	813,148
108	Cafeteria	167,239
116	Equipment operation	496,275
	Total unit-related costs	$7,369,455
	Number of patient-days	45,606
	Cost per patient-day	$161.59
B. BATCH-RELATED ACTIVITIES		
110	Medical records	$250,345
111	Social services	199,026
112	Patient scheduling	60,238
113	Billing and collection	112,280
	Total batch-related costs	$621,889
	Number of patients	8,367
	Cost per patient	$74.33
C. FACILITY-SUSTAINING ACTIVITIES		
109	Housekeeping	$ 706,308
114	Plant operations	301,238
115	Plant maintenance	386,622
117	Property insurance	38,350
118	Depreciation	960,573
	Total facility-sustaining costs	$2,393,091

1994 level. She expected *43,000 patient-days* and *8,200 patients* for 1995. Inserting these values into the cost equation, she now estimates the total costs for 1995 as follows:

$$Costs = \$2,393,091 + \$161.59 * 43,000 + \$74.33 * 8,200$$
$$= \$2,393,091 + \$6,948,370 + \$609,506$$
$$= \$9,950,967.$$

OBJECTIVE 3.8
How standard costs are determined

Standard costs
Efficient and attainable benchmarks established in advance for the costs of activity resources that should be consumed by each product.

STANDARD COST ACCOUNTING SYSTEMS

Cost accounting systems are often required not only to measure the actual costs incurred by the organization in the past period but also to project or estimate what the costs will be in the future. **Standard costs** are benchmarks based on standards established in advance for the *quantity* of activity resources that *should be consumed* by each product or other unit of output and the *price* of these resources. It is possible to estimate costs for different production and activity levels based on standards established for quantities and prices.

Most manufacturing organizations use some form of a standard cost accounting system. Eighty-seven percent of the firms participating in a 1990 survey indicated that they used a standard cost system.[3] Most of these systems involve measuring standard costs and actual costs and comparing them.

Why do the vast majority of firms use a standard cost system? There are three principal uses of such systems:

1. *Estimate product costs.* Standards are developed for the consumption of direct materials, direct labor, and overhead activity resources per unit of each product. Multiplying these quantity standards by the *standard prices* for the resources and adding to all the resources consumed by a product yields standard costs for individual products. These standard product costs are used to bid for customer orders and to evaluate product profitability.

2. *Budget for costs and expenditures.* Total costs representing the consumption of each activity can be estimated based on the *standard amount of consumption* of an activity required to manufacture different products and the *planned production levels* for those products. Some organizations use these estimated costs to plan expenditures for a forthcoming period. Such use can be misleading in some cases because of the time lag that is often observed between costs (representing consumption of activity resources) and expenditures for the acquisition of activity resources, as we shall see in Chapter 4.

3. *Control costs relative to standards.* Actual costs are compared with the standards, with the expectation that the actual costs will be kept in line with the standards. The differences between actual and standard costs are called **cost variances**. They are analyzed further into those caused by *quantity variations* and those caused by *price variations*. By associating these variations with managers responsible for the activities contributing to them, organizations can motivate managers to attain the targets embodied in the standards.

[3] Bruce R. Gaumnitz and Felix P. Kollaritsch, "Manufacturing Variances: Current Practice and Trends," *Journal of Cost Management* (Spring 1991), pp. 58–64.

■ Choosing the Level of Standards

One important question concerning standards pertains to the appropriate level to establish for them. Should we set standards for the consumption of materials and labor based on the technical specifications for the process under *ideal conditions*? Or should we set the standards at the level that reflects the most likely occurrence, given the known inefficiencies in the consumption of labor and materials, so that plans based on such standards will be most accurate?

Most experts recommend setting standards that fall somewhere between the two extremes described. Standards should be *efficient and attainable*, depending on how standards influence the behavior of workers and managers whose performance is evaluated relative to the standards. (See Chapters 2 and 14 for related discussions on the behavioral implications of organizational decisions.) A standard set at an average level that is easy to achieve will not motivate workers to exert more effort to eliminate existing inefficiencies and achieve a higher level of performance. On the other hand, if the standard is set too high and is difficult to attain even with considerable effort, workers will soon become frustrated and quit working hard to achieve what they perceive to be an impossible target. An efficient and attainable standard motivates higher levels of effort to eliminate inefficiencies and rewards performance sufficiently frequently to reinforce the worker's or manager's decisions to exert that extra effort.

Cost variances
Differences between actual and standard costs.

Motivated to reduce the cost of damaged work in process, which was higher than they deemed acceptable, these employees at Bausch & Lomb Incorporated developed methods to reduce damage to work in process, thereby significantly reducing costs and creating a new standard for performance. These employees, who receive extensive training in measuring, analytical, and presentation methods, are empowered to make decisions relating to process improvement and share in the resulting cost savings through a plantwide bonus system. *(Ted Kawalerski/Bausch & Lomb)*

■ Determination of Standards

To illustrate the idea of standard setting, consider the manufacture of Jim and Barry's ice cream. Each gallon of ice cream requires, on average, 0.19 pounds of pulverized sugar. These estimates are developed based on product engineering specifications and a careful analysis of past experience in making ice cream. Consultations with the purchasing department reveal that the price of sugar, inclusive of freight to Jim and Barry's plant, is $0.13 per pound. These 2 numbers represent quantity and price standards for sugar in the manufacture of ice cream at Jim and Barry's plant. Based on the quantity and price standards, the standard cost of sugar in a gallon of ice cream is $0.0247 (= 0.19 * $0.13). See Exhibit 3–9.

Direct labor standards are established in a similar manner. Industrial engineering studies of work, time, and motion are often used to determine the amount of direct labor effort required for each operation. Ice cream is manufactured at Jim and Barry's Springfield plant in standard batches of 1,000 gallons. For each batch produced, two loaders are required to work for 45 minutes (0.75 hours) each, and one operator works the machine for 3 hours. These represent quantity standards for the direct labor input. Price standards are obtained using payroll information. The average wage of loaders is $10.40 per hour, and benefits add another $5.40 per hour in costs borne

Consider this . . .

Trane Company's New Cost Accounting Systems

Trane Co. is a subsidiary of American Standard, a leading worldwide producer of air conditioning systems, and bathroom and kitchen fixtures and fittings, and a major European manufacturer of commercial vehicle braking systems. The Trane Co. plant in Pueblo, Colorado, produces water chillers for commercial and industrial building air-conditioning applications.

A new cost accounting system has been designed and implemented at the Pueblo plant. The guiding principle in the design of the cost accounting system is that it should be *simple*, its operation should be *low cost*, and it should *eliminate* unnecessary reporting procedures.

The new system is designed as a standard cost accounting system to monitor cost changes. It has no detailed labor reporting because direct labor is less than 5% of product cost, and past experience indicated that the cost (people and computers) required to track actual labor would not pay for itself in the form of savings resulting from better monitoring management of the labor resource. The new system also *excludes* from material costs all low-cost items (nuts, bolts, screws, labels, and the like), which represent 76% of the part

numbers but only 3% of the total production costs. The costs of these items are included instead in manufacturing overhead. As a result, the direct material records focus on only the 24% of the parts that comprise about 67% of the total production costs and present a greater opportunity for cost savings with better monitoring and management of the materials.

Source: Ronald B. Clements and Charlene W. Spoede, "Trane's Soup Accounting: It's a System of Utter Practicality," *Management Accounting* (June 1992), pp. 46–52.

Trane's production and cost management uses no computerized shop-floor control or labor reporting system.

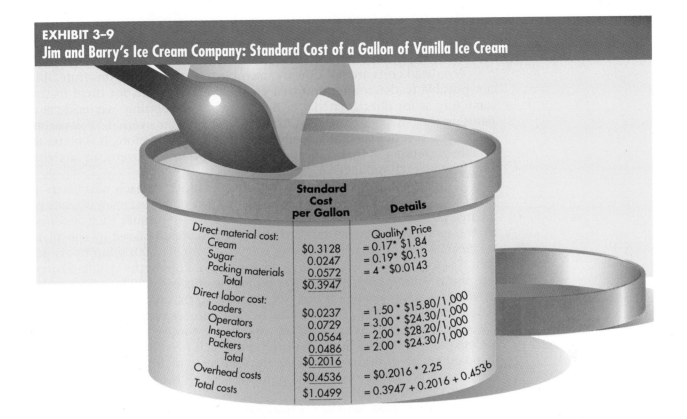

	Standard Cost per Gallon	Details
Direct material cost:		Quality* Price
Cream	$0.3128	= 0.17* $1.84
Sugar	0.0247	= 0.19* $0.13
Packing materials	0.0572	= 4 * $0.0143
Total	$0.3947	
Direct labor cost:		
Loaders	$0.0237	= 1.50 * $15.80/1,000
Operators	0.0729	= 3.00 * $24.30/1,000
Inspectors	0.0564	= 2.00 * $28.20/1,000
Packers	0.0486	= 2.00 * $24.30/1,000
Total	$0.2016	
Overhead costs	$0.4536	= $0.2016 * 2.25
Total costs	$1.0499	= 0.3947 + 0.2016 + 0.4536

by the employer. Therefore, the price standard for loaders is set at $15.80 per hour. The price standard for operators is set at $24.30 per hour, comprising $15.90 in wages and $8.40 in benefits. The standard cost of loader labor is $0.0237 (2 * 0.75 * $15.80/1,000) per gallon and the standard cost of operator labor is $0.0729 (3 * $24.30/1,000) per gallon of ice cream (batches include 1,000 gallons). Other direct labor per batch requires 1 inspector for 2 hours at $28.20 per hour, including benefits, and 1 packer for 2 hours at $24.30 per hour (see Exhibit 3–9).

Establishing, updating, and maintaining the information on direct materials and direct labor standards in a standard cost accounting system requires an enormous amount of time and effort. Setting up standards for overhead costs has usually received far less attention in many organizations. Jim and Barry's, for instance, uses a standard overhead rate of 225% of direct labor cost. The rate is based on the estimate of $936,000 of annual overhead costs, which is 2.25 times the estimate of $416,000 for the direct labor costs for the year. The total standard direct labor cost (inclusive of loader, operator, inspector, and packer labor, is $0.2016 per gallon. Therefore, the standard overhead cost is set at $0.4536 ($0.2016 * 2.25) per gallon.

Such overhead rates based on direct labor alone can often distort the estimates of overhead costs. The standard cost per gallon of ice cream at Jim and Barry's plant is determined as the sum of the standards for direct material, direct labor, and overhead costs, as shown in Exhibit 3–9. Direct material costs are based on standards for cream (given), sugar (shown in detail in the text), and packing materials (given); direct labor includes standard costs for loaders and operators (shown in detail in the text), as well as inspectors and packers (given). In contrast, overhead standards are based on only direct labor cost.

Overhead costs are not directly traceable to the products; therefore, it is not possible to determine industrial engineering standards for them in the same way as for direct material or direct labor costs. Setting overhead standards on the basis of direct labor, however, ignores how overhead costs arise, that is, the cost drivers that actually cause overhead. Therefore, it is better to establish standards that reflect the consumption of overhead activity resources by each product.

Consider the activity of setting up the machines for each new batch of ice cream at Jim and Barry's Worcester plant. Chocolate ice cream is made in a batch size of 1,000 gallons; each setup requires 30 minutes each (0.5 hrs) from 2 setup workers. The standard rate for the demand placed by chocolate ice cream on setup activity resources is 0.001 (2 * 0.5/1,000) setup hours per gallon of ice cream, based on the given assumptions about the standard batch size and effort required. Because wages plus benefits cost \$22.60 per hour, on average, for setup workers at the Worcester plant, the standard cost for setup is \$0.0226 (0.001 * \$22.60) per gallon of chocolate ice cream.

In contrast, raisins and nuts ice cream is produced in a batch size of 500 gallons and requires 45 minutes (0.75 hours) each from 2 setup workers. The standard rate for the consumption of the setup activity is 0.003 (2 * 0.75/500) setup hours per gallon of raisins and nuts ice cream; the setup cost is \$0.0678 (0.003 * \$22.60) per gallon.

Note that these *standard activity rates* represent only the rate of consumption of activity resources and that the corresponding standard costs represent the costs of the activity resources *consumed*. This should be distinguished from the amount expended on setup activity resources at the Worcester plant because the actual expenditure depends on the amount of activity resources *made available* (such as the number of setup workers employed) rather than *consumed*.

The Worcester plant employs 2 setup workers. Each setup worker works 36 hours a week. Therefore, 72 hours' worth of resources *are made available for the setup activity each week*, which costs a total of \$1,627.20 (72 * \$22.60). In the first week of August, the plant produced 35 batches of chocolate ice cream and 20 batches of raisins and nuts ice cream. To set up these 55 batches, it required 65 hours (35 * 0.5 * 2 + 20 * 0.75 * 2) of setup activity resources. The

Part of setting up a piece of equipment, and therefore an element in the standard setup cost, is to check the initial units of production from the equipment to ensure that they meet specification. These employees at the Colgate-Palmolive plant in Guayama, Puerto Rico, are ensuring that production from this packaging line meets specifications.
(Courtesy Colgate-Palmolive)

standard cost of these consumed resources is $1,469.00 (65 * $22.60), which differs from the amount of $1,627.20 *actually spent* for the setup personnel.

It is important to recognize that standard activity costs reflect the demand placed on different activity resources and are useful for long-term planning and deployment of resources for various activities. It would not be correct to use the standard costs for short-term (daily, weekly, or monthly) planning of expenditures on various activities.

OBJECTIVE 3.9
Uses and limitations of standard cost systems

■ Limitations of Standard Cost Systems

Many organizations use standard cost accounting systems, but an important caveat is in order. The usefulness of these systems is restricted largely to settings in which the production technology is stable and there are relatively few business changes taking place. If there is much volatility in the products or the manufacturing processes, the standards need to be changed frequently and much organizational effort is required to maintain current information on standards. Standards for product costs do not remain reliable for long in such settings, and standards for the consumption of direct labor, materials, and other activity resources are not very useful as benchmarks to evaluate current production.

More important, however, is the fact that overreliance on managing with a standard cost accounting system creates a mind-set of simply "meeting the standards." It diverts attention from the organization's strategic need, as discussed in Chapter 2, to remain a step ahead of its present and potential competitors by being able to respond to a changing environment. In a stable environment, when the product and process innovations are not frequent or critical, containing costs is a strategic necessity for many organizations. The use of standards to control costs is often effective in such settings. But when the strategic need is to focus the attention of the organization on constant innovation that anticipates customer requirements, then preoccupation with meeting current or past standards can, in fact, be detrimental to organizational performance.

A SUMMARY EXAMPLE

The following worked-out problem focuses on many of the chapter's important points. Grazioli Company in Milan, Italy, manufactures brakes for motor vehicles. At present, its overhead costs (OHCOST) are estimated as 75,000 lira per direct labor hour (DLH), as described in the following equation (amounts in thousand lira):

$$OHCOST = 75 * DLH$$

(One U.S. dollar equaled approximately 1,500 lira in early 1994.)

The company's new controller, Paula Penzoli, had noticed differences between the actual and estimated overhead costs when reviewing the monthly overhead cost reports. She believed that the present cost equation was not reflecting several activities performed in the plant. These activities were not driven by direct labor and included activities such as materials handling, machine setup, quality inspection, production supervision, and production scheduling, as well as lubricating oils and power.

After conducting a detailed investigation, Paula decided to employ two additional cost drivers in specifying the overhead cost equation: (1) the number of quality inspections (INSP) and (2) the number of batches manufactured (BATCH). Although different products require different numbers of inspections, each inspection takes the same amount of time. Direct labor required per unit manufactured also differs for different products. Further, products manufactured in small batch sizes require as much material handling and machine setup activities as products made in large batch sizes. To better estimate the overhead cost, Paula developed the following equation (amounts in thousand lira):

$$\text{OHCOST} = 37.5 * \text{DLH} + 150 * \text{INSP} + 750 * \text{BATCH}$$

Planned activity levels for the next two months and the average levels for the next year, are as follows:

Month	DLH	INSP	BATCH
1	4,000	180	150
2	4,200	200	160
Average 1995	4,000	200	160

1. List unit-related and batch-related activities performed at Grazioli's plant.
2. Estimate overhead costs using the current estimation procedure for each of the two months.
3. Estimate overhead costs using the alternative equation developed by Paula for each of the two months.
4. Explain why there is a difference between the two sets of estimates.
5. Repeat (2) and (3) using the averages for the year. Explain why the difference between the two estimation procedures is small in this case.

SOLUTION **[All amounts are in thousand lira (KL)]:**
1. Unit-related activities: Quality inspection, production supervision, lubricating oils and power

   Batch-related activities: Materials handling, machine setup, and production scheduling

2. Estimated overhead costs based on direct labor hour only:

   Month 1: 300,000 KL (= 75 * 4,000)
   Month 2: 315,000 KL (= 75 * 4,200)

3. Estimated overhead costs based on the new cost equation:

   Month 1: 289,500 KL (= 37.5 * 4,000 + 150 * 180 + 750 * 150)
   Month 2: 307,500 KL (= 37.5 * 4,200 + 150 * 200 + 750 * 160)

4. The two sets of estimates differ because the cost equation OHCOST = 75 * DLH omits two important cost drivers that are not proportional to direct labor hours.

5. Estimated overhead costs based on the present equation:

$$\text{Average} = 300{,}000 \text{ KL} \ (= 75 * 4{,}000)$$

Estimated overhead costs based on the new equation:

$$\text{Average} = 300{,}000 \text{ KL} \ (= 37.5 * 4{,}000 + 150 * 200 + 750 * 160)$$

The two cost equations provide the same estimates because the equations have been designed to fit the same cost data on average. But there can be large discrepancies in individual months as the three cost driver proportions each month may differ from those on average.

SUMMARY

It is common to classify costs according to their *function*. Direct material and labor costs are costs that can be traced easily to the products manufactured or services rendered. Indirect or overhead costs are not easily traced to products and services. The proportion of indirect costs in the overall cost structure has increased considerably in recent years.

To understand why organizations find it necessary to incur overhead costs, we must analyze the activities performed in the organization. Cost drivers are direct or surrogate measures for the level of activity. Activity costs depend on the level of capacity made available for the activity rather than the actual use of that capacity. Overhead rate for an activity is determined as the ratio of the cost of the activity to the level of capacity made available for the activity.

These basic cost concepts extend directly to service organizations. It is often more difficult to define outputs for a service organization, but the analysis of activity costs for a service organization resembles that for a manufacturing organization.

Many organizations use standard cost accounting systems. These systems estimate costs of products, jobs, and production processes by developing standards for the consumption of materials, labor, and other activities. These standards are usually set at efficient and attainable levels. Updating standards is a costly operation, and, therefore, the use of a standard cost accounting system is very difficult in fast-changing environments.

KEY TERM LIST

Activity cost driver, p. 102

Activity overhead rate, p. 106

Batch-related activities, p. 100

Cost variances, p. 117

Direct costs, p. 95

Facility-sustaining activities, p. 101

Indirect costs, p. 96

Manufacturing costs, p. 94

Manufacturing overhead costs, p. 100

Nonmanufacturing costs, p. 94

Operating overhead, p. 113

Period costs, p. 94

Product costs, p. 94

Product-sustaining activities, p. 101

Production volume, p. 92

Standard costs, p. 116

Unit-related activities, p. 100

ASSIGNMENT MATERIAL

QUESTIONS

3-1 Why do different types of cost information need to be reported to support different managerial decisions?

3-2 What are some different uses of cost information?

3-3 What is the difference between *costs* and *expenses*?

3-4 What categories of costs are classified by function?

3-5 Why do traditional cost accounting systems tend to analyze manufacturing costs in greater detail than other functional categories of costs?

3-6 How are direct costs distinguished from indirect costs?

3-7 What are the 3 principal categories into which manufacturing costs are classified?

3-8 How has the composition of manufacturing costs changed in recent years? How has this change affected the design of cost accounting systems?

3-9 What are the 4 categories of production activities? Explain the differences between them.

3-10 What do the terms *activity cost driver* and *activity overhead rates* mean? What is the activity cost equation?

3-11 What is the consequence of a cost accounting system omitting a significant cost driver?

3-12 What 5 steps must be performed to determine the activity overhead rates?

3-13 What are some special considerations in the design of cost accounting systems for service organizations?

3-14 What is the difference between *actual costs* and *standard costs*?

3-15 What are 3 benefits from using a standard cost accounting system?

3-16 Why should standards be *efficient* and *attainable*?

3-17 Why do estimates of overhead costs based on activity standards often differ from the actual costs?

3-18 What are some caveats for organizations using standard cost accounting systems?

3-19 When would you prefer to use the number of setups instead of the number of setup hours as the cost driver measure for the setup activity?

EXERCISES

3-20 Classify each of the following costs based on function:

(a) Direct labor

(b) Sales commissions

(c) Depreciation on delivery trucks

(d) Salary and bonus for the chief executive officer

(e) Direct materials

(f) Product design staff salaries

(g) Advertising

(h) Property taxes

(i) Accounting office staff salaries

(j) Customer credit evaluation staff salaries

3–21 Classify each of the following manufacturing costs as direct materials, direct labor, or overhead costs.

(a) Insurance on manufacturing equipment

(b) Steel plates used in making an automobile body

(c) Wages of assembly workers

(d) Salaries of plant security personnel

(e) Rubber used in making tires

(f) Overtime premiums paid to assembly workers

(g) Depreciation on the factory building

(h) Cost of electric power to operate machines

(i) Production workers' holiday and vacation pay benefits

(j) Wages of material-handling workers

(k) Grapes used to manufacture wine

(l) Quality inspection costs

3–22 Classify the following costs as unit-related, batch-related, product-sustaining, or facility-sustaining activity costs.

(a) Direct materials

(b) Setup labor wages

(c) Salaries of plant engineers responsible for executing engineering change orders

(d) Building depreciation

(e) Direct labor wages

(f) Purchase order clerk wages

(g) Product design engineer salaries

(h) Rent for plant building

3–23 Classify the following costs as unit-related, batch-related, product-sustaining, or facility-sustaining activity costs.

(a) Packing labor wages

(b) Material-handling labor wages

(c) Part administrators' salaries

(d) Plant management salaries

(e) Production scheduling staff salaries

(f) Equipment maintenance

(g) Property taxes

(h) Production expediters' salaries

(i) Insurance for plant facility

3–24 Classify the following activities as unit-related, batch-related, product-sustaining, or facility-sustaining activities.

(a) Supervision of direct labor

(b) Supervision of setup labor

(c) Setup of machines for a new batch

(d) Making product engineering changes

(e) Quality inspection

(f) Moving materials from one machine to the next

(g) Production scheduling

(h) Accounting

(i) Sales support for individual product lines

3–25 Classify each of the following activities as unit-related, batch-related, product-sustaining, or facility-sustaining activities.

(a) Plant security

(b) Purchase ordering

(c) Direct materials consumption

(d) Workers' training

(e) Product development

(f) Electricity usage

(g) Factory depreciation

(h) Engineering change

(i) Quality inspection

(j) Direct labor

3–26 The overhead costs of the machining department at Beatres Company's plant in Weston, Virginia, are represented by the equation

$$OHCOST = \$238 * SETUP + \$10.4 * DLH + \$8.7 * MHCAP$$

where

$$OHCOST = \text{overhead cost}$$
$$SETUP = \text{the number of setups}$$
$$DLH = \text{direct labor hours}$$
$$MHCAP = \text{the machine-hour capacity available}$$

The planned levels of the cost drivers for June and July are

	Setup	DLH	MHCAP
June	100	600	1,500
July	150	800	2,500

What is the expected level of overhead costs for June and July?

3–27 Creathon Company's plant in Columbus, Ohio, manufactures 2 products: BR12 and BR15. Product BR15 has a more complex design and requires more setup time than BR12.

Setups for BR12 require 2 hours, on average; setups for BR15 require 3 hours. Creathon's setup department employs 10 workers; their average wage is $10 per hour; fringe benefits cost 38% of the wages. Other costs for setup activities amount to $25 per setup. Creathon plans to hire all 10 workers for 40 hours each of the first three weeks of the winter quarter. The amount of work for these 3 weeks is

Week	Number of Setups for Product BR12	Number of Setups for Product BR15
1	85	75
2	90	70
3	80	80

(a) Determine the actual setup activity overhead rate based (1) on number of setups and (2) on number of setup hours.

(b) Is either of the 2 activity overhead rates, or some other rate, appropriate in this case? Why?

3–28 Cuomo Company uses the following equation to estimate monthly overhead costs:

$$Overhead = \$15 * DLH + \$250 * SETUP + \$180 * INSP$$

where

DLH = direct labor hours
$SETUP$ = the number of setups
$INSP$ = the number of inspections

The estimated levels of these three activities for January, February, and March are

	DLH	SETUP	INSP
January	1,400	250	100
February	1,100	200	80
March	1,200	210	85

Calculate the expected *total overhead costs* for the months of January, February, and March.

PROBLEMS

3–29 The customer billing department at U.S. West Telecommunication, Inc., currently employs 25 billing clerks on annual contract. Each clerk works 160 hours per month. The average monthly wages of billing clerks, including benefits, amount to $2,800. Other billing-related costs, including stationery and supplies, are $0.50 per billing.

The two types of customers are business and residential. For residential customers, billing takes, on average, 10 minutes to prepare; each business customer billing requires 15 minutes.

The following information pertains to the estimated number of customer billings for the months of June and July 1994:

Month	Number of Billings	
	Business Customers	Residential Customers
June	8,000	12,000
July	6,000	15,000

(a) Determine the billing activity overhead rate based on expected number of billings.

(b) Determine the billing activity overhead rate based on expected number of billing labor hours.

(c) Compare the overhead rates in (a) and (b) above. Which rate do you recommend? Why?

(d) Is there a better way to estimate the costs of this activity than using a single overhead rate?

3–30 Nestec Company estimated its manufacturing overhead costs (*MFGOH*) as 168% of its direct labor cost (*DLCOST*):

$$MFGOH = 1.68 * DLCOST$$

Alan DeLeon recently joined the company as an assistant plant controller. He analyzed in detail the activities performed at the plant and recognized that overhead costs were incurred to perform activities related to setting up the machines (*SETUPS*, number of setups); handling customer orders (*ORDERS*, number of customer orders), and inspecting and shipping finished products (*SHPMNTS*, number of shipments) and supervising direct labor. Therefore, he developed the following equation to estimate manufacturing overhead costs:

$$MFGOH = \$0.80 * DLCOST + \$180 * SETUPS + \$60 * ORDERS + \$80 * SHPMNTS$$

Planned activities for May and June are as follows:

	DLCOST	SETUPS	ORDERS	SHPMNTS
May	$85,000	212	132	386
June	91,000	208	104	312
Average for 12 months	$80,000	200	120	340

(a) Estimate the expected amount of manufacturing overhead costs for May and June using the old equation based on only direct labor cost.

(b) Estimate the expected manufacturing overhead costs for May and June using the equation developed by Alan DeLeon.

(c) Why is there a difference between the two sets of estimates? Which set of estimates is likely to be more accurate? Why?

(d) Repeat parts (a) and (b) using the averages for the year. Why are your comparisons different in this case?

3–31 Eagan Electrical Instruments Company estimates manufacturing overhead costs (*MFGOH*) as 950% of direct labor costs (*DLCOST*):

$$MFGOH = 9.50 * \$DLCOST$$

Eagan's controller, Jim Becker, is concerned that the actual manufacturing overhead costs have differed substantially from the estimates in recent months. He suspects that the problem is related to the use of only 1 overhead cost driver. Jim identified the following 3 additional cost drivers that reflect overhead activities: number of material moves (*MOVE*), number of setups (*SETUP*), and number of machine hours (*MACH*). He developed the following alternative equation to estimate manufacturing overhead costs:

$$MFGOH = \$1 * DLCOST + \$200 * MOVE + \$300 * SETUP + \$20 * MACH$$

Information for 2 recent months includes the following:

	May	June
Direct labor cost	$3,000	$4,200
Number of material moves	50	70
Number of setups	30	40
Number of machine hours	1,000	1,200

(a) Estimate manufacturing overhead costs using both equations.

(b) Why do the two sets of estimates differ?

(c) Why will both methods fail to predict accurately the manufacturing overhead costs? Is one of the two methods likely to be more useful than the other? Explain.

3–32 Belinda Smith, the controller of Jackson Company, is considering changing the company's current overhead cost (OHCOST) estimation procedures, which are based on direct labor hours (DLH) as described by the following equation:

$$OHCOST = \$25 * DLH$$

Her preliminary investigations revealed that the number of setups (SETUP) and the number of quality inspections (INSP) are important cost drivers in addition to the number of direct labor hours. She developed the following alternative equation to estimate overhead costs:

$$OHCOST = \$15 * DLH + \$250 * SETUP + \$34 * INSP$$

Activity levels for May and June are as follows:

Month	DLH	SETUP	INSP
May	20,000	480	2,400
June	18,000	430	2,150

(a) Estimate overhead costs for May and June using the current overhead cost estimation method based on DLH.

(b) Estimate overhead costs for May and June using Belinda's new equation.

(c) Explain why there is only a small difference between the two numbers.

(d) Do you agree with Belinda that the new method provides the more accurate estimates? Why?

3–33 Mankato Company is developing an activity-based cost system. The following information on overhead costs and activities has been compiled:

Activity	Estimated Costs	Activity Cost Drivers	Planned Activity Level
Purchase ordering	$ 20,000	Number of orders	400
Maintenance	44,000	Machine hours	2,000
Power	36,000	Kilowatt hours	30,000
Setups	62,500	Number of setups	500
Supervision	48,000	Direct labor hours	4,000
Total	$210,500		

Express the overhead cost as a *linear equation* in terms of the 5 activity cost drivers.

3–34 Poker's is a small hamburger shop catering mainly to students at a nearby university. It is open for business from 11 A.M. until 11 P.M., Monday through Friday. The owner, Chip Poker, employs two cooks, one server, and a part-time janitor. Because there is no space for dining inside the shop, all orders are take-out orders.

Poker's sold 10,000 hamburgers last month. The average hamburger requires 1 hamburger bun, 8 ounces of meat, 4 ounces of cheese, half a head of lettuce, and $0.07 worth of other ingredients. Costs incurred during the last month include the following:

Meat	$5,000
Cheese	1,000
Bread	800
Lettuce	600
Other ingredients	700
Cook's wages	5,000
Server's wages	1,500
Janitor's wages	600
Utilities	500
Depreciation on equipment	300
Paper supplies (napkins and bags)	200
Rent	600
Advertisement in local newspaper	300

(a) Classify these costs into one of the following categories: direct materials, direct labor, manufacturing overhead, selling overhead, and administrative overhead. What is the total cost for each category?

(b) Classify the costs as unit-related, batch-related, product-sustaining, or facility-sustaining costs. What is the total cost for each category?

3–35 PQR Company manufactures and sells Products P, Q, and R. The company uses the following equation to estimate overhead costs:

$$\text{Total overhead costs} = \$100,000 + \$12 \; LABHR + \$5 \; MACHR$$

where *LABHR* is direct labor hours and *MACHR* is machine-hours.

Estimated production levels and requirements for Products P, Q, and R for next month are

	Product P	Product Q	Product R
Number of units	4,000	5,000	8,000
Direct labor hours per unit	2	3	4
Machine hours per unit	3	5	2

Estimate the total overhead costs for the next month.

3–36 Dallas Devices Company has accumulated this information about its operations:

Overhead Activity	Activity Cost	Cost Driver	Committed Cost Driver Capacity
Power	$100,000	Kilowatt hours	200,000
Setups	400,000	Number of setups	10,000
Engineering	250,000	Engineering hours	2,500
Rent	200,000	Number of square feet	5,000

(a) Classify the overhead activities as unit-related, batch-related, product-sustaining, or facility-sustaining activities.

(b) Determine the activity overhead rate for each activity.

(c) Express total overhead costs in the form of a linear equation.

CASES

3–37 First Cherokee Bank uses standards to estimate the workload of its teller clerks. The standard amount of time for processing each withdrawal (*WTHDR*) is 4.0 minutes, for each deposit (*DEPST*) 2.2 minutes, and for each transfer (*TRNSF*) of funds between accounts 1.9 minutes. Total workload (in minutes) is estimated based on the following equation:

$$WORKLOAD = 4.0 * WTHDR + 2.2 * DEPST + 1.9 * TRNSF$$

First Cherokee uses these workload estimates to plan its staffing levels. Past experience indicates that it needs to provide for about 40% more time than the workload estimate to ensure that customers do not have to wait in line to be served for an unacceptably long time. The bank can hire either full-time tellers working 40 hours a week, or part-time tellers, working 20 hours a week. Estimates for the number of various teller transactions for the first 5 weeks of the fall quarter follow:

WEEK	WITHDR	DEPST	TRNSF
1	1,450	1,900	650
2	1,600	2,000	700
3	1,550	1,800	650
4	1,650	1,900	650
5	1,500	2,100	700

Determine the number of teller clerks that will be hired in each of these 5 weeks.

3–38 (See Case 3–37.) First Cherokee Bank compares the productivity of the teller labor across its 10 branches and determines productivity measure for each branch as a ratio of the standard workload hours to actual teller hours. An overall productivity measure for the bank also is determined as a benchmark on the basis of averages across all branches. The following data are compiled for Week 11 operations for the 10 branches:

Branch	Productivity Ratio	Full-Time Equivalent Tellers[a]	Standard Work Load (in minutes)	Number of Withdrawals	Number of Deposits	Number of Transfers	Number of Customer Transactions
1	0.628	6	9,040	1,000	1,600	800	2,840
2	0.581	12	16,720	2,400	2,200	1,200	3,400
3	0.632	8	12,130	1,600	2,000	700	3,440
4	?	9	?	1,700	1,800	900	3,350
5	?	6	?	900	1,200	600	2,250
6	?	5	?	800	1,000	500	1,900
7	?	10	?	2,100	2,000	1,100	3,710
8	?	12	?	2,300	3,000	1,400	3,820
9	?	11	?	2,100	2,900	1,100	3,700
10	?	11	?	2,300	3,100	1,200	3,880
Average	?	9	13,261	1,720	2,080	950	3,229

[a]Full-time equivalent tellers = total teller hours/40.

Standard workload (in number of minutes) is determined based on the following equation:

$$WORKLOAD = 4.0 * WTHDR + 2.2 * DEPST + 1.9 * TRNSF$$

(a) Determine the *productivity ratios* for all 10 branches.

On reviewing these productivity measures, Nick Chow, First Cherokee Bank's new controller, realized that the productivity ratios were highest for the 3 city branches (branches 8, 9, and 10). All 7 suburban branches were rated lower. On further inquiry, Nick determined that much of the teller's time was required for the initial interaction with each customer requiring service. This time was the same whether the customer had multiple transactions (several different deposits, or both a withdrawal and a deposit) or just one transaction to conduct. Recognizing this to be a batch-related cost, Nick altered the equation for workload as follows to explicitly include the number of customer transactions (*CSTRN*) as a cost driver to reflect the time spent interacting initially with the customer:

$$WORKLOAD = 1.6 * CSTRN + 4.0 * WTHDR + 2.2 * DEPST + 1.9 * TRNSF$$

(b) Determine the standard workload and the productivity ratio for each of the 10 branches with the new workload equation. Rank the branches and compare the new rankings with the previous rankings. Why do the rankings change? Which productivity measure is likely to be more useful?

3–39 McGourmet, Inc., a chain of fast-food stores, estimates the standard workload at its restaurants in terms of the time required for the operations of order receiving (*ORDER*), cooking (*COOK*), and packing (*PACK*). On average, each order receipt takes 1.9 minutes, each cooking operation requires 3.6 minutes, and each packing operation (for take-out orders) needs 0.5 minutes. Therefore, the estimation of standard workload (*WORKLOAD*) in number of minutes is represented by the following equation:

$$WORKLOAD = 1.9 * ORDER + 3.6 * COOK + 0.5 * PACK$$

McGourmet adds 30% to the standard workload estimate to determine its staffing requirements. Past experience has shown that customers do not need to wait very long because of this higher level of staffing. McGourmet hires only part-time workers for 20 hours per week and pays them $4.60 per hour, including benefits. The following information pertains to the estimated levels for various activities for the 4 weeks in February 1994.

Week	ORDER	COOK	PACK
1	5,600	7,200	1,150
2	5,800	7,900	1,200
3	6,000	8,600	1,400
4	5,800	7,600	1,100

Determine the number of workers hired for each of the 4 weeks and the total labor cost for February.

3–40 (See Case 3–39.) McGourmet, Inc., uses a productivity measure, defined as the ratio of the standard workload hours to the actual worker hours, to evaluate the performance of the managers in its 5 stores in Pittsburgh, Pennsylvania. The standard workload (in minutes) is estimated based on the following equation:

$$WORKLOAD = 1.9 * ORDER + 3.6 * COOK + 0.5 * PACK$$

The number of workers hired and the actual amount of work for the first week of March are

Store Location	Number of Workers	Number of Order Receipts	Number of Cooking Operations	Number of Packing Operations	Number of Products Offered
Oakland	134	20,000	25,000	2,600	9
Northside	45	6,000	8,400	720	11
Shadyside	88	11,000	13,000	800	16
Downtown	160	23,000	28,000	2,000	9
Southside	65	8,000	12,000	1,400	14

(a) Determine the standard workload hours. Rank the store managers' performance based on the productivity ratio.

Upon receiving the performance report, 2 managers who were ranked at the bottom argued that the number of products offered in the store also should be considered in estimating workload because more products add more complexity to the operations.

(b) How should McGourmet's controller address this concern?

COST BEHAVIOR

LEARNING OBJECTIVES

This chapter will introduce you to:

1. the difference between fixed and variable costs
2. the ways in which the commitment and consumption of activity resources influence cost variability
3. the normal costs of an activity
4. the reasons that activity costs tend to be variable in the long run
5. the ways to estimate overhead costs for multiple activities supporting the production of multiple products
6. the difference between the cost equation and the consumption equation for an activity
7. breakeven analysis
8. the way to sketch a planning model that captures the relationship between revenues, costs, and production volumes

■ Breaking Even at Riverside General Hospital: The Dilemma

"Look at how much our costs have increased compared to last year. In 1991 our costs were $206.50 per patient-day, but this year it costs us $227.70 to care for one patient for one day. Doesn't this indicate serious inefficiencies in our operations?" asked Eric Nelson, executive director of Riverside General Hospital. "What can we do to bring our costs back in line with those for 1991?" he questioned his controller, Holly Ward.

"Our problem is the change in demographics in our region that has resulted in a more than 5% reduction in the number of our patients. About 23% of our costs are *fixed costs*—costs that do not vary with the changes in the number of patients or patient-days. As a result, our costs have not decreased proportionally with the decrease in our output," replied Ward. "If we can't stimulate an increase in the demand for our services, then we must make some hard decisions to reduce our capacity and cut our fixed costs."

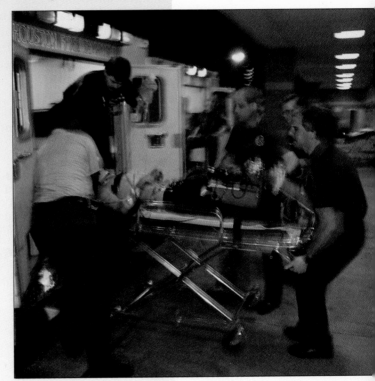

"With the present demographics, I don't believe we'll be able to increase the number of our patient-days. We must bring our costs down in line with our revenues. How much do we need to reduce our fixed costs in order to break even?" asked Nelson. [Riverside General Hospital would break even if its total revenues were exactly equal to its total costs.]

"Well, if we continue to have 8,367 patients and 45,606 patient-days of service, as we had in 1992, and if our present average reimbursement rate does not change, we must reduce our fixed costs by almost 15% to break even," answered Ward, after performing some quick calculations on the back of an envelope.

(© Greg Smith/SABA)

This scenario has significant implications. Before deciding *which* costs to reduce, Holly and others must understand how costs behave relative to variations in the level of activities at Riverside.

COST BEHAVIOR AND PRODUCTION VOLUME

Concerns about how *costs behave* in response to changes in production volume are the focus of decision makers in almost all industries. For example, erosion in customer demand resulted in an increase of sales force compensation costs by almost 0.5% to more than 6% of sales at Sears Roebuck and Company, prompting managerial action to control these costs. Similarly, the drastic reduction in capacity announced in late 1992 by General Motors translated into a reduction of 30% in its **breakeven point** (the production level at which sales volume would result in zero profits), reassuring investors about its financial viability even with a lower market share.

Cost behavior is also important for the airline industry. Airline executives monitor closely an operating statistic called *load factor,* the proportion of the airline's flying capacity (number of seats) that is filled with paying passengers. Airlines work hard at cost control to bring their *breakeven load factor down below 60%* because most airlines have difficulty sustaining load factors above that level. That is, they attempt to ensure that a load factor of only 60% of capacity is sufficient for revenues to be adequate to cover expenses.

Understanding the behavior of costs in response to changes in production and sales activity levels is clearly critical for the management of many organizations.

In this chapter, we introduce the basic concepts that will help you understand the relationship between costs and activity levels. First, let's turn to the fixed versus variable behavior of costs relative to production levels.

Breakeven point
The level at which profits from 2 alternative options are equal.

Almost all the cost associated with the flight that this aircraft is beginning is unrelated to the number of passengers on board. Airlines try to set their fares so that, on average, they will cover their costs if the aircraft is 60% full. If the average occupancy, or load factor, is above this target level, the airline expects to be profitable. (© *Bill Sallaz/Liaison International*)

Fixed Versus Variable Costs

Costs are related to the levels of multiple activity cost drivers, as described in Chapter 3. But managers are often interested in how costs change with a change in the level of one important cost driver, the volume of production, because many marketing, production, and investment decisions affect production volume. To supply this information to managers, organizations traditionally classify costs into fixed costs and variable costs based on their behavior in response to changes in production volume. These terms are defined as follows:

> **Fixed costs** (FC) do not change with changes in the level of production over short periods of time. Rent and insurance for plant facility, for instance, do not change if production is cut by 2%.

> **Variable costs** (VC) change in proportion to changes in the level of production. Direct material costs, for instance, may be expected to increase by 20% when production is increased by 20%.

Fixed costs
Costs that are independent of the level of production.

Variable costs
Costs that change proportionally with production volume. They represent resources whose consumption can be adjusted to match the demand placed for them.

If sales personnel are paid a flat salary, selling costs are fixed, but if, instead, they are paid a commission for every unit sold, these costs are variable.

Recall the discussion about Jim and Barry's Ice Cream Company in Chapter 3. Consider some of the distribution costs for Jim and Barry's. They lease 5 refrigerated trucks, for a quarterly lease payment of $2,000 per truck, to distribute ice cream to vendors all over New England. The company also incurs costs for gas and maintenance to operate the trucks. These costs increase with the number of trips, varying at the rate of $0.48 cents per mile traveled. As the production of ice cream increases in the summer months, the number of trips increases for the 5 trucks. Let us consider how costs change with production.

Truck rental cost is a fixed cost because it remains the same for different production volumes (see Exhibit 4–1). At either 400,000 or 800,000 gallons of production, total rental costs remain at $10,000 for the 5 trucks. Exhibit 4–2 shows the graph of these fixed costs (FC) plotted for different levels of pro-

---

EXHIBIT 4–1
Jim and Barry's Ice Cream Company: Quarterly Truck Rental Cost

QUARTERLY PRODUCTION (GALLONS)	MILES TRAVELED	TOTAL RENTAL COST	COST PER GALLON[a]	COST PER MILE[b]
400,000	32,000	$10,000	$0.0250	$0.3125
500,000	40,000	10,000	0.0200	0.2500
600,000	48,000	10,000	0.0167	0.2083
700,000	56,000	10,000	0.0143	0.1786
800,000	64,000	10,000	0.0125	0.1563

[a] Cost per gallon = (Rental cost)/(Number of gallons)
[b] Cost per mile = (Rental cost)/(Miles traveled)

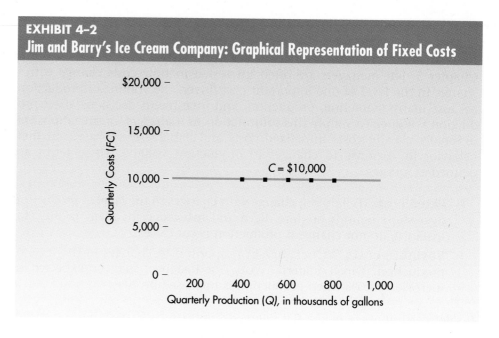

EXHIBIT 4–2
Jim and Barry's Ice Cream Company: Graphical Representation of Fixed Costs

duction (Q). It reveals a horizontal straight line, which signifies the same level of cost for different levels of production.

Now consider the behavior of fixed cost per unit volume by referring to the data in Exhibit 4–1 and the related graph presented in Exhibit 4–3. Notice that the fixed *cost per unit volume* (per gallon) *declines* when production

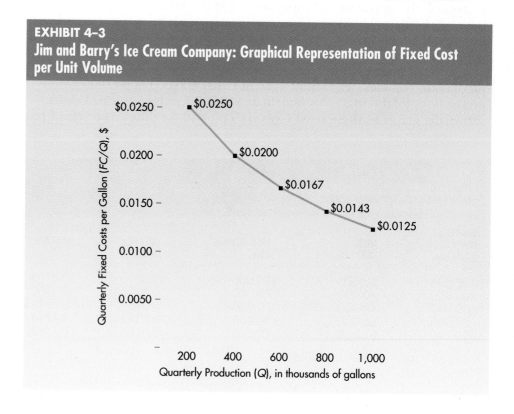

EXHIBIT 4–3
Jim and Barry's Ice Cream Company: Graphical Representation of Fixed Cost per Unit Volume

increases because the same amount of fixed costs is spread over more units. Although fixed costs *per unit volume* (FC/Q) decrease as the amount of production (Q) increases, do *not* jump to the conclusion that fixed costs depend on the volume of production.

In contrast, total variable costs (VC) change proportionally with production changes, yet variable costs *per unit volume*(VC/Q) remain the same at all levels of production (Q). See Exhibit 4–4, which shows the cost per gallon at $.0384 regardless of production volume. The graph in Exhibit 4–5 displays

---

EXHIBIT 4–4
Jim and Barry's Ice Cream Company:
Quarterly Gas and Maintenance Costs

QUARTERLY PRODUCTION (GALLONS)	MILES TRAVELED	TOTAL GAS AND MAINTENANCE COSTS	COST PER GALLON[a]	COST PER MIL[b]
400,000	32,000	$15,360	$0.0384	$0.4800
500,000	40,000	19,200	0.0384	0.4800
600,000	48,000	23,040	0.0384	0.4800
700,000	56,000	26,880	0.0384	0.4800
800,000	64,000	30,720	0.0384	0.4800

[a] Cost per gallon = (Total gas and maintenance costs)/(Number of gallons)
[b] Cost per mile = (Total gas and maintenance costs)/(Miles traveled)

EXHIBIT 4–5
Jim and Barry's Ice Cream Company: Graphical Representation of Variable Cost per Unit Volume

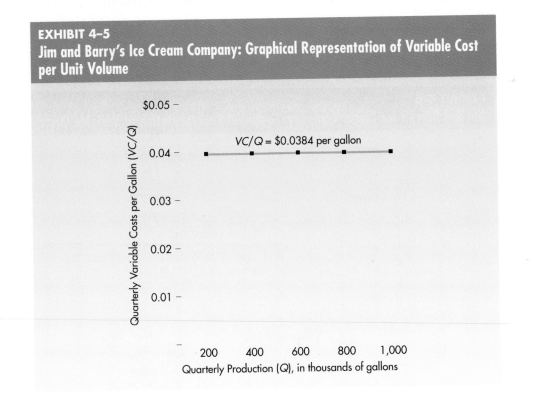

VC/Q = $0.0384 per gallon

a horizontal straight line, signifying that the variable costs per unit volume do not change with production volume.

Gas and maintenance costs are variable costs with respect to miles traveled for Jim and Barry's because they increase with increases in the production and sale of ice cream. The activity cost driver for these costs is the number of miles traveled. Notice that this is a *unit-related measure*. In fact, for this example, the number of miles traveled is *perfectly correlated* with the number of gallons produced. The sale of *every* additional 100,000 gallons of ice cream requires the trucks to travel an additional 8,000 miles for their distribution trips. Although we may not find such a perfect relationship in practice, all unit-related cost drivers will closely relate to the number of units produced. Therefore, activity costs that vary proportionally with a unit-related cost driver are usually *variable costs*.

Exhibit 4–6 presents the plot of these variable costs. It reveals a straight line, passing through the origin, whose slope equals the variable cost rate of $0.0384 ($0.48 * 8,000/100,000) per gallon of ice cream. That is, the variable cost rate of $0.0384 is obtained by multiplying $0.48, the cost per mile, by the rate of 8,000 miles required for every additional 100,000 gallons of ice cream produced.

■ Mixed Costs

In contrast, the activity cost driver for the truck rental costs is the number of trucks, which is a facility-sustaining activity measure. This measure is independent of the number of gallons produced; therefore, we classify truck rental costs as fixed costs.

The total truck operating cost is the sum of 2 components: (1) truck rental cost and (2) gas and maintenance costs. Exhibit 4–7 shows the tabulations of these costs, which appear as a straight line when graphed (see Exhibit

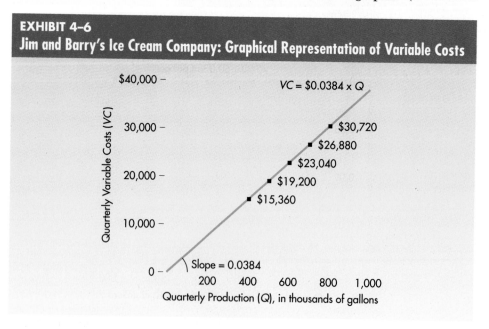

EXHIBIT 4–6
Jim and Barry's Ice Cream Company: Graphical Representation of Variable Costs

$40,000 –

$VC = \$0.0384 \times Q$

Quarterly Variable Costs (VC)

30,000 –   ■ $30,720
      ■ $26,880
      ■ $23,040

20,000 –   ■ $19,200
      ■ $15,360

10,000 –

0 –   Slope = 0.0384
    200   400   600   800 1,000
Quarterly Production (Q), in thousands of gallons

EXHIBIT 4–7
Jim and Barry's Ice Cream Company: Total Truck Operating Costs

QUARTERLY PRODUCTION (GALLONS)	FIXED COSTS COMPONENT	VARIABLE COST COMPONENT	TOTAL COSTS	COST PER GALLON[a]
400,000	$10,000	$15,360	$25,360	$0.0634
500,000	10,000	19,200	29,200	0.0584
600,000	10,000	23,040	33,040	0.0551
700,000	10,000	26,880	36,880	0.0527
800,000	10,000	30,720	40,720	0.0509

[a] Cost per gallon = (Total costs)/(Number of gallons)

4–8). The intercept on the vertical axis is $10,000, which corresponds to the amount of fixed truck rental costs depicted in Exhibit 4–2. Its slope is equal to the variable cost rate of $0.0384 per gallon of ice cream, as depicted in Exhibit 4–6.

The total truck operating cost is an example of a mixed cost. A **mixed cost** includes both fixed and variable cost components. We can write the cost equation for the total truck operating cost as follows:

Mixed costs
Costs comprising both fixed and variable cost components.

$$\text{Truck operating costs} = \$10,000 + 0.0384 * \text{Production in gallons}$$

The cost of using this furnace to make steel is mixed. There is a large fixed cost associated with the equipment and a large variable component relating to the fuel and raw materials used to make the steel. (© *The Telegraph Colour Library/FPG International*)

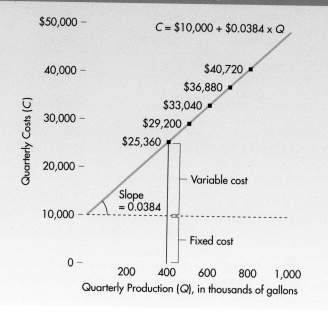

EXHIBIT 4–8
Jim and Barry's Ice Cream Company: Graphical Representation of Mixed Costs

This example focuses on a specific type of distribution cost, but we can apply a similar fixed and variable cost analysis to *all* manufacturing, selling and other costs incurred by an organization. Then we can represent total costs in terms of the following linear equation:

$$\text{(Total costs)} = \text{(Fixed costs)} + \text{(Variable cost rate)} * \text{(Quantity of production)} \quad (4.1)$$

or

$$C = F + VQ$$

Representing Activity Costs as Fixed or Variable Costs

Now compare equation (4.1) with our earlier representation of total costs as the sum of all activity costs, which appeared in equation (3.5) in Chapter 3.

$$C = R_1X_1 + R_2X_2 + R_3X_3 + R_4X_4 + R_5X_5$$

where R_1, R_2, R_3, R_4 and R_5 are the overhead rates for five activities. As we have observed, many of the activity cost drivers, (X_1, X_2, X_3, X_4, X_5), especially those that are unit-related measures, are closely related to the production volume, Q. When examined over a sufficiently long period of time in which managers have the flexibility to adjust *the level* of resources performing batch-related activities, some of the batch-related measures also vary with the production volume.

For example, let X_1, X_2, and X_3 be the 3 activity cost drivers that are highly correlated with production volume, Q, and let X_4 and X_5 be the remaining 2 activity cost drivers that are independent of Q. That is, the first 3 activity cost drivers vary with production volume, but the last 2 activity cost drivers remain fixed when the production level changes. In the Jim and Barry's example, recall that the activity cost driver, *miles traveled*, was perfectly correlated with production volume (*number of gallons*), but the activity cost driver, number of trucks, was independent of the production volume. Then, we can express *total* variable costs as $R_1X_1 + R_2X_2 + R_3X_3$. The variable cost rate, V, would be

$$V = \frac{R_1X_1 + R_2X_2 + R_3X_3}{Q} \qquad (4.2)$$

The total fixed costs, F, in this case, are

$$F = R_4X_4 + R_5X_5 \qquad (4.3)$$

The representation of the costs in terms of variable and fixed costs has the advantage of providing a quick perspective of the *behavior of costs* with respect to changes in production volume. But it is evident that this representation suppresses considerable detail about how costs arise when activities are performed. A detailed representation of an organization's costs in terms of activity costs is necessary to obtain a good understanding of its cost structure and to manage its activities efficiently. The simple representation of costs as

CONSIDER THIS . . .

Seagate Is Sluggard

Seagate Technology is the world's largest manufacturer of computer hard disk drives, commanding about one-fourth of the world's market. Over the past several years, however, it has appeared to be a sluggard giant in its industry when compared to fast-growing innovative competitors such as Conner Peripherals, Quantrin, and Maxtor.

Seagate owns and operates its own plants. This strategy differs from that of its competitors, who design their own products but rely on outside suppliers for the production of hard disk drives in accordance with their design specifications.

During the recent recessionary period, Seagate has been hampered by its massive facility-sustaining fixed overhead costs. Its profits declined more than those of its competitors, who have a much lower proportion of fixed costs. When demand fell, the other companies could cut costs quickly by simply reducing the orders placed with their suppliers. Seagate could not avoid its facility-sustaining costs. In addition, its competitors have been more flexible, switching faster from $5^1/4$-inch to $3^1/2$-inch drives by taking advantage of technological advances made in combination with external suppliers.

Seagate is making changes. It now relies on external suppliers for 40% of its disks, about twice the percentage of two years ago.

Source: R. E. Drtina, "The Outsourcing Decision," *Management Accounting,* March 1994, pp. 56–62; K. Yamada, "Once-Battered Seagate Gains in Computer Price War," *Wall Street Journal,* June 1, 1992, p. B3; G. P. Zachary, "High-Tech Firms Find It's Good to Line Up Outside Contractors," *Wall Street Journal,* July 29, 1992, pp. A1, A5.

fixed and variable is appropriate when the activity cost drivers are either (almost) perfectly correlated with production volume or (almost) fixed with respect to production volume.

■ Costs in an Economic Framework

If you have already had a course in economics, you will wonder how this accounting representation of costs can be interpreted in an economics framework. In many introductory economics textbooks, costs are represented by *an inverted S-shaped curve,* as displayed in Exhibit 4–9. For low production levels, *costs increase at only a decreasing rate* (the **cost curve** is *concave* in this region) because organizations are assumed to *avail themselves of* **economies of scale** that reduce average product costs. These economies of scale, or decreasing average costs with increases in production volume, typically arise from being able to produce more output without having to increase fixed costs. Once the production level reaches **capacity constraints** imposed by fixed resources, costs are assumed to increase at an increasing rate as **diseconomies of scale,** or increasing average costs with increases in production volume, prevail.[1]

This is a useful theoretical representation of cost opportunities available to any firm in a particular industry over the entire range of possible production levels. For most managerial decisions, however, accountants need to generate cost estimates that are applicable over a much smaller range of

Cost curve
Graph of costs plotted against activity cost driver or production volume.

Economies of scale
Decreasing average costs with increases in production volume.

Capacity constraints
Limitations on the quantity that can be produced because the capacity committed for some activity resources (such as plant space or number of machines) cannot be changed in the short run.

Diseconomies of scale
Increasing average costs with increases in production volume.

[1] The representation of *total costs* as an inverted S-shaped curve corresponds to *marginal costs* decreasing with production volume at first as economies of scale are realized and marginal costs increasing with production volume as capacity constraints begin to impose diseconomies of scale. (Marginal costs are the costs of producing an additional unit of the output).

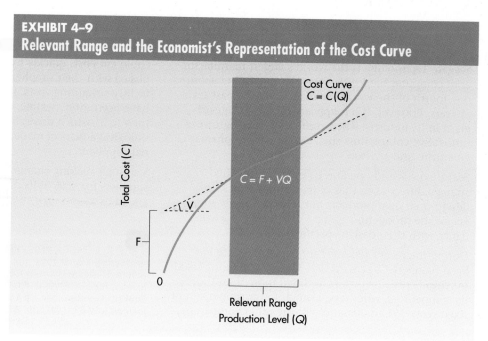

EXHIBIT 4–9
Relevant Range and the Economist's Representation of the Cost Curve

Cost Curve $C = C(Q)$

$C = F + VQ$

Total Cost (C)

V

F

0

Relevant Range
Production Level (Q)

production levels that a specific firm normally contemplates in its regular operations. This smaller range of relevant production levels is called the **relevant range,** or the range of production levels over which the classification of costs as fixed or variable is appropriate. The linear equations described earlier often provide good approximations of the behavior of costs for that firm. For instance, consider the shaded region in Exhibit 4–9 that defines the relevant range. The linear equation $C = F + VQ$ fits the part of the cost curve that falls within this relevant range. That is, when we extend in a straight line the segment of the cost curve falling within the relevant range (see dotted line), it begins to resemble the diagram in Exhibit 4–8, with the extended line displaying an intercept equal to F on the vertical axis and a slope equal to V.

Relevant range
The range of production levels over which the classification of a cost as fixed or variable is appropriate.

This representation of the cost curve as a straight line over the relevant range is only an approximation that we use to simplify our analysis. In individual cases that we encounter in practice, we must be careful to examine whether our assumption about the cost equation is valid.

■ The Step Function Cost Curve

A common departure from the assumption about cost equation applying over the relevant range is a *step function* cost curve. In our example of Jim and Barry's Ice Cream Company, if the production level is very high, the 5 trucks will not be adequate to distribute the product, and an additional truck may need to be rented to meet the workload. The addition of a new truck would "step up" the truck rental cost from $10,000 to $12,000 per quarter. Exhibit 4–10 depicts such a step function cost curve. The relevant range in this case is restricted to be within a step. If, however, decision makers contemplate production levels beyond a single step, they must consider different levels of fixed costs explicitly. In the Jim and Barry's example, the different levels are expressed as

$$C = \$10,000 + 0.0384 * Q \text{ if } Q \leq Q^{MAX}$$
$$C = \$12,000 + 0.0384 * Q \text{ if } Q > Q^{MAX}$$

where Q^{MAX} is the maximum volume that can be handled with only 5 trucks.

This customer service representative, who works for Paul Revere, a large insurance company, helps policy holders locate information about their policies and make any coverage changes the customers want. The cost of customer service is a step function since a customer service representative can handle only a certain number of customers. As the demand for customer information exceeds the capacity of the existing customer service representatives, another customer service representative is hired. (© Eric Myer Photography)

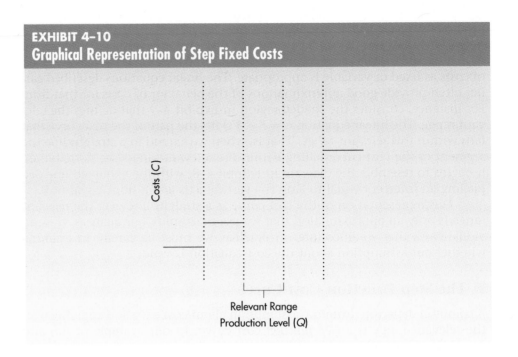

EXHIBIT 4–10
Graphical Representation of Step Fixed Costs

Costs (C)

Relevant Range
Production Level (Q)

Step fixed costs
Costs that increase in relatively wide discrete steps.

Step variable costs
Costs that increase in relatively narrow discrete steps.

If the steps in the cost function are relatively wide (that is, the costs remain the same over a wide range of production volumes), the costs are referred to as **step fixed costs.** If instead, the steps are relatively narrow, which is true, for example, when materials can be purchased only in whole units, not in fractions, such costs are referred to as **step variable costs** because the cost curve is approximated closely by a single straight line. Exhibit 4–11 displays an example of step variable costs graphically.

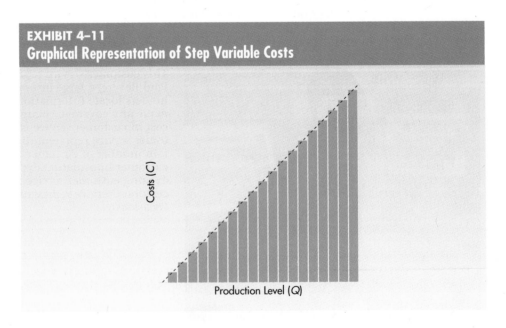

EXHIBIT 4–11
Graphical Representation of Step Variable Costs

Costs (C)

Production Level (Q)

COMMITMENT VERSUS CONSUMPTION OF ACTIVITY RESOURCES

Understanding the *behavior of costs* needs considerable care because it is contingent on time frame, range of activity levels, and a variety of other factors. For instance, the cost driver for direct materials is the number of units produced. Direct labor hours, the cost driver for direct labor cost, is also a unit-related measure. Therefore, it is commonly assumed that both direct material and direct labor costs are variable. This assumption is not always correct.

A more precise way to think of *variable costs* is that they represent resources whose consumption can be adjusted to match the demand placed for them. If only 100 automobile chassis are manufactured instead of a planned 110, steel for 100 chassis will be consumed, and the steel for the remaining 10 chassis will be inventoried and used later. Therefore, direct material costs are usually variable even in the short term. In contrast, the consumption of direct labor resources often cannot be changed readily in response to short-term fluctuations in production levels. This is true because workers usually are paid a fixed amount of wages for a day or a week, whether they are occupied productively for the entire period or not. The resulting inflexibility causes idle time for workers in some time periods and overtime in other periods, so that direct labor costs do not vary exactly in proportion with production volume.

Consider the Carex Muffler Company that specializes in same-day service. Cars brought in by 8:00 a.m. are guaranteed to be serviced before 6:15 p.m. The shop has 8 service blocks. As many as 8 mechanics are hired on a 8:00 a.m. to 4:00 p.m. daily shift to service the automobiles. Each muffler replacement takes a mechanic 45 minutes (0.75 hours). In a day's work, therefore, allowing for a 30-minute break for lunch, a mechanic is expected to service 10 cars (7.5 hours ÷ .75 hours/car).

The number of customers fluctuates daily. If the number of jobs is less than 10 times the number of mechanics on any day, some mechanics are idle for a period of time. If the number of jobs exceeds the available capacity, some mechanics are asked to work overtime to ensure that all cars are serviced before 6:15 p.m. the same day. Regular wages, including benefits, average $30 per hour. Overtime wages include a 50% premium in addition to the regular wages. Exhibit 4–12 summarizes the daily direct labor costs for different numbers of customer orders (jobs).

The *cost driver* for the muffler replacement activity is the number of mechanic hours. By hiring 8 mechanics, Carex is committed to paying regular wages for at least 64 mechanic hours (8 mechanics × 8 hours/day). The committed cost, therefore, is $1,920 ($30/hour * 64 hours). These committed resources make available a capacity of 60 hours (7.5 hours/day/mechanic * 8 mechanics), which is sufficient to service 80 jobs (10 jobs/mechanic * 8 mechanics). Additional resources are required *if and only if* the actual demand exceeds 80 jobs. When the demand is for 80 or fewer jobs (see columns for 50, 60, and 70 orders in Exhibit 4–12), some of the available 60 hours of mechanic labor are not utilized. In these cases, the mechanics are paid for the entire period, resulting in idle time. When the demand is for more than 80 jobs (see the 90- and 100-order columns), overtime is required.

EXHIBIT 4–12
Carex Muffler Company: Daily Direct Labor Costs

	NUMBER OF DAILY CUSTOMER ORDERS					
	50	60	70	80	90	100
Number of mechanics	8	8	8	8	8	8
Total demand for labor hours (= Number of orders * 0.75 hour/order)	37.5	45	52.5	60	67.5	75
Available regular time labor hours (= 7.5 hours/day * Number of mechanics)	60	60	60	60	60	60
Idle time (hours)	22.5	15	7.5	–0–	–0–	–0–
Overtime (hours)	–0–	–0–	–0–	–0–	7.5	15
Total regular wages (= 8 mechanics * $30/hour * 8 hours)	$1,920	$1,920	$1,920	$1,920	$1,920	$1,920
Total overtime wages	–0–	–0–	–0–	–0–	337.50	675
Total direct labor cost	$1,920	$1,920	$1,920	$1,920	$2,257.50	$2,595
Direct labor cost per job (= Total direct labor cost ÷ Number of orders)	$38.40	$32.00	$27.43	$24.00	$25.08	$25.95

If the actual demand is Q jobs, with Q > 80, then

$$0.75 * (Q - 80) = (0.75Q - 60)$$

hours of overtime are required.[2] The regular wages for overtime are

$$\$30 * (0.75Q - 60),$$

and the 50% overtime premium amounts to

$$.50 * \$30 * (0.75Q - 60)$$

---

[2] Overtime equals the number of jobs exceeding the capacity for 80 jobs with regular time (that is, Q – 80 jobs) multiplied by the 0.75 hours required to service each job. Alternatively, you can view overtime as the difference between the time required to service Q jobs, that is, 0.75 Q hours, less the 60 hours of capacity made available by hiring 8 mechanics.

The total overtime wages amount to

$$1.50 * \$30 * (0.75Q - 60)$$

The cost equation, therefore, takes two forms. The *committed resources* represent a fixed cost, and the cost for the overtime hours is added on when the required consumption of this activity resource exceeds the available capacity (80 jobs). We can write the cost equation for Carex Muffler Company as follows:

$$C = \$1,920, \text{ when } Q \leq 80$$

and

$$C = \$1,920 + 1.50 * \$30 * (0.75Q - 60), \text{ when } Q > 80$$

The graph in Exhibit 4–13 plots the total direct labor costs for different numbers of daily customer orders (jobs). We see that total costs remain fixed at $1,920 until all available resource capacity (80 jobs) is fully used. Then total costs increase with the number of jobs ($2,257.50 for 90 orders and $2,595.00 for 100 orders) because overtime is required to meet the additional demand for mechanic time.

■ Normal Costs

OBJECTIVE 4.3
The normal costs of an activity

Exhibit 4–14 displays the graph of the average labor cost per job plotted against the number of daily jobs. We see that the average or unit costs depend on the number of daily customer orders. They are lowest when the demand for direct labor exactly matches the available capacity (at 80 jobs). We define

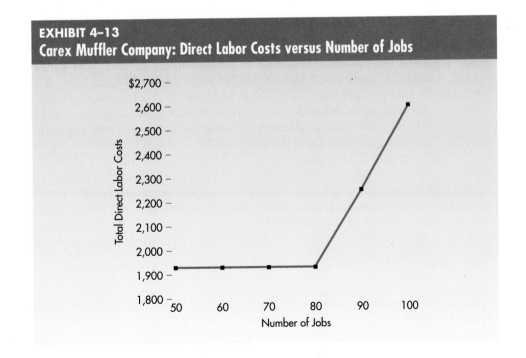

EXHIBIT 4–13
Carex Muffler Company: Direct Labor Costs versus Number of Jobs

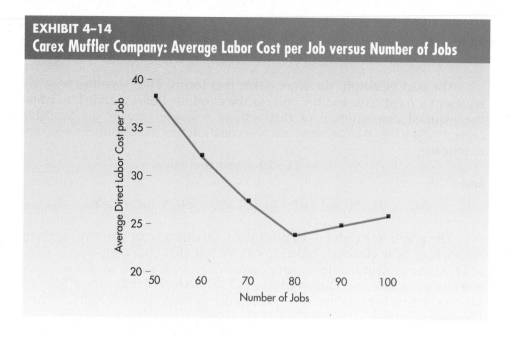

EXHIBIT 4–14
Carex Muffler Company: Average Labor Cost per Job versus Number of Jobs

**Normal unit cost
of an activity**
Average cost at the point
where activity demand
equals available capacity;
regular cost of providing
the resource capacity
made available for an
activity.

the **normal unit cost of an activity** to be the cost per unit capacity at the point where the demand for the activity exactly equals the available capacity:

$$\text{Normal unit cost} = \frac{\text{Regular cost of providing capacity}}{\text{Capacity made available}}$$

$$= \frac{\$1,920}{80 \text{ jobs}} \tag{4.4}$$

$$= \$24 \text{ per job}$$

If Carex management did not have to commit to hiring mechanics before knowing the customer demand, or had complete flexibility in adjusting the number of mechanic hours at regular wage rate of $32 per hour ($30 * 8/7.5), the cost per job would be $24 ($32 per hour * 0.75 hours per job). Thus, normal unit costs measure the average or unit costs *as if* the activity were perfectly variable. This cost information is useful for determining product prices used as benchmarks in the long run.[3]

When demand is less than the available capacity, actual unit costs are higher than normal unit costs because of idle time. The actual unit costs are also higher than the normal unit cost when demand exceeds available capacity because an overtime premium must be paid. Notice that the definition of the normal unit cost of an activity *extends and formalizes* the definition of activity overhead rates from Chapter 3 in the present context of the commitment and consumption of activity resources.

[3] The use of normal costs in product prices will be discussed in detail in Chapter 8. See also R. D. Banker and J.S. Hughes, "Product Costing and Pricing," The Accounting Review (July 1994), pp. 479–494.

We previously defined activity overhead rate as activity costs divided by the number of units of the activity cost driver. The precise definition presented here requires that (1) the activity costs in the numerator be the regular cost only (excluding additional costs, such as overtime) to provide just the capacity of activity resources, and (2) the number of units of the activity cost driver in the denominator measure the capacity made available by the resources committed to the activity.

RESOURCE FLEXIBILITY AND COST VARIABILITY

OBJECTIVE 4.4
The reasons that activity costs tend to be variable in the long run

Managers try to operate at a low unit cost level by maintaining flexibility in the use of resources. For example, concession obtained from labor unions in recent years by U.S. automobile and steel manufacturing firms involves elimination or reduction of worker job categories so that potentially idle workers can be deployed to different tasks. Many plants provide incentives to workers to acquire multiple skills so that they can be deployed on different tasks as required. Managers also try to plan production well in advance to smooth out demand for direct labor and other manufacturing resources. Smoothing is often attained, however, at the cost of increasing the levels of inventory or increasing the lead time for meeting customer orders.

If direct workers are paid on a piece-rate basis for units produced and shipped, direct labor costs vary in proportion to volume. More commonly, however, plants hire workers on a daily, weekly, monthly, or some other time basis. In such cases, we have seen that because of idle time and overtime, direct labor costs measured on a daily basis do not usually vary directly with the corresponding production volume. When considering direct labor costs over a longer duration, however, these costs are more likely to vary with production. This occurs because managers have more flexibility over the longer term to adjust staffing levels to meet anticipated seasonal or long-term changes in production volume. Managers at the Carex Muffler Company have the flexibility to temporarily add extra mechanics on some days.

Carex managers adjust the number of mechanics daily depending on the expected demand on each day. Demand on Friday is high because people repair their cars in anticipation of weekend driving needs. Demand on Monday is also high because repair shops are closed over the weekend. Generally, the demand on Fridays and Mondays varies from 76 to 92 jobs and averages 84 jobs. Demand on Tuesdays and Thursdays averages 75 jobs, and on Wednesdays it averages only 66. Therefore, 8 mechanics work on Mondays and Fridays, 7 on Tuesdays and Thursdays, and 6 on Wednesdays.

Exhibit 4–15 lists the actual demand for 20 days in August 1994. The direct labor cost each day comprises both the fixed cost of the committed resources and the additional cost for the overtime hours. The cost equation that applies here is as described before, except that we now have different equations, depending on whether there are 8, 7, or 6 mechanics.

If there are N mechanics, the number of hours available is $(7.5 * N)$ hours. A demand of Q jobs requires $(0.75 * Q)$ hours because each job requires 0.75 hours to complete. No overtime is required as long as the demand for the activity resource $(0.75 * Q)$ is no more than the amount of committed

DAY	DATE	NUMBER OF MECHANICS	NUMBER OF JOBS	IDLE TIME (HOURS)	OVERTIME (HOURS)	DIRECT LABOR COST	AVERAGE COST PER JOB
Mon	8/1	8	89	0.00	6.75	$2,223.75	$24.99
Tue	8/2	7	73	0.00	2.25	1,781.25	24.40
Wed	8/3	6	70	0.00	7.50	1,777.50	25.39
Thu	8/4	7	81	0.00	8.25	2,051.25	25.32
Fri	8/5	8	86	0.00	4.50	2,122.50	24.68
Mon	8/8	8	87	0.00	5.25	2,156.25	24.78
Tue	8/9	7	82	0.00	9.00	2,085.00	25.43
Wed	8/10	6	71	0.00	8.25	1,811.25	25.51
Thu	8/11	7	78	0.00	6.00	1,950.00	25.00
Fri	8/12	8	79	0.75	0.00	1,920.00	24.30
Mon	8/15	8	84	0.00	3.00	2,055.00	24.46
Tue	8/16	7	77	0.00	5.25	1,916.25	24.89
Wed	8/17	6	60	0.00	0.00	1,440.00	24.00
Thu	8/18	7	75	0.00	3.75	1,848.75	24.65
Fri	8/19	8	85	0.00	3.75	2,088.75	24.57
Mon	8/22	8	80	0.00	0.00	1,920.00	24.00
Tue	8/23	7	76	0.00	4.50	1,882.50	24.77
Wed	8/24	6	63	0.00	2.25	1,541.25	24.46
Thu	8/25	7	67	2.25	0.00	1,680.00	25.07
Fri	8/26	8	83	0.00	2.25	2,021.25	24.35
						Average	$24.75

resources (7.5 * N); that is, when $Q \leq 10 * N$.[4] This cost equation can be written as

$$C = \$30 * 8 * N, \text{ when } Q \leq 10 * N$$
$$C = \$30 * 8 * N + 1.5 * \$30 * (0.75 * Q - 7.5 * N), \text{ when } Q > 10 * N$$

For instance, on Tuesday, August 2, 7 mechanics were employed and 73 jobs were ordered. Thus, the need was for 2.25 hours of overtime (0.75 hours/job * 73 jobs) − (7.5 hours/mechanic * 7 mechanics), and total direct labor costs were $1,781.25 [($30 * 8 hours * 7 mechanics) + (1.5 * $30 * 2.25)]. Unit costs were $24.40 ($1,781.25/73).

Exhibit 4–16 shows actual costs plotted against the production volume for the 20 days in August. You can now see that the costs vary more or less in proportion to the number of jobs. This is in contrast to the cost curve shown in Exhibit 4–13, which describes the relationship between costs and production if the number of mechanics is fixed at 8. This variability of the costs when examined over a longer period arises because of the flexibility that management has to adjust the amount of resources (number of mechanics) made available in anticipation of the expected demand for them.

[4] If $0.75 * Q \leq 7.5 * N$, then $Q \leq 7.5/0.75 * N = 10 * N$.

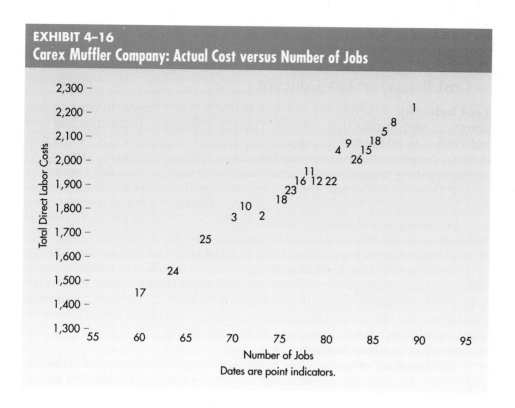

EXHIBIT 4–16
Carex Muffler Company: Actual Cost versus Number of Jobs

Exhibit 4–17 displays the unit costs plotted against the production volume (number of jobs). Notice that, unlike the corresponding graph in Exhibit 4–14, the unit costs are aligned around a horizontal straight line. This is consistent with the notion that the *variable cost rate* is independent of the production level. You will also notice that the *average cost of $24.75* (see the last

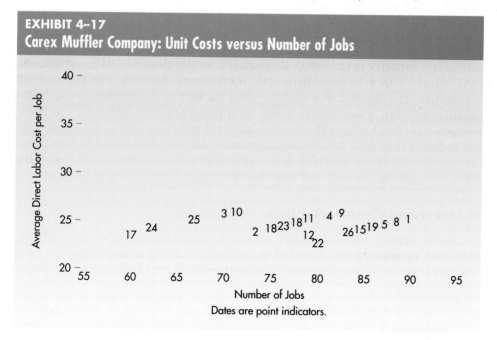

EXHIBIT 4–17
Carex Muffler Company: Unit Costs versus Number of Jobs

line in Exhibit 4–15) per job is higher than the normal cost of $24.00 per job because both overtime and idle time costs are incurred in actual operations.

■ Cost Behavior: Key Concept

Cost behavior describes the way costs change with changes in activity cost drivers or with production volume. The key concept in understanding cost behavior is to realize that managers must commit to providing for some production resources before knowing the actual demand for them. The cost of supplying these resources is incurred whether or not they are fully used. The cost of these resources will appear to be *fixed* with respect to actual production volume as long as the capacity of these resources is not exceeded.

Consumption of some resources, such as materials or power to operate machines, can be adjusted easily to match precisely the demand placed for them. The cost of such resources is said to be *variable* with production activity.

Resources such as direct labor usually cannot be adjusted precisely in the very short run. Such costs are fixed over the short-term horizon, but, in the longer run, managers can make adjustments by adding, retrenching, or redeploying workers to match the anticipated demand for direct labor. Therefore, the cost of direct labor appears to vary with production volume over this somewhat longer-term horizon.

The behavior of many other manufacturing costs is similar, with different degrees of commitment required for different types of costs. For manufacturing overhead costs associated with materials handling, management can adjust the number of workers and, hence, these total costs with relative ease. In contrast, management has much less flexibility in changing the plant capacity and, therefore, in adjusting the overhead costs associated with rent and insurance. Costs related to materials handling are, therefore, relatively more variable, but rent and insurance costs are relatively more fixed with respect to the production level.[5]

Variability of costs also depends on the time frame considered. In the Carex Muffler Company example, there was no flexibility to adjust the number of mechanics on any given day; therefore, the direct labor costs are fixed unless the capacity is exceeded. But when a longer time period is considered over which Carex management can increase or decrease the number of mechanics, the direct labor costs appear to vary with production volume (number of jobs). Over a sufficiently long period of time, almost all activity resources are flexible, and their costs vary with production volume when considered over that long time frame. Typically, activity resources that are flexible in the short to medium term are classified as *variable,* and activity resources that can be adjusted only in the long run are classified as *fixed.*

■ Overhead Cost Variability

Overhead activity resources may be flexible, discretionary, or committed. **Flexible resources** are acquired as needed; their costs vary with the production activity. Examples include materials and power to operate machines.

---

[5] R.D. Banker and H. Chang, "Flexibility of Activity Resources and Behavior of Activity Costs," *Chinese Accounting Review,* 1994.

This recently completed cracking unit at a Shell Oil Refinery cost many millions of dollars to build but reduced the company's need to purchase gasoline from other refiners. By building this unit, Shell has substituted a cost that was committed when the resource was acquired (the depreciation on this unit) for cost that was created when resources were used (the cost paid to suppliers for refined oil products). *(© Don Teiwes/Shell Oil)*

The use of discretionary resources is not directly related to the production volume. Such **discretionary costs** result from strategic and tactical decisions of managers and include expenditures made for advertising, publicity, and research and development, for example. In these cases, the expenditure for the activity resource influences the production level in the long run instead of the production level influencing the consumption of the activity resource. Costs of discretionary activities, therefore, are usually considered to be fixed with respect to production volume.

Committed resources are made available before their demand is known precisely. These resources cannot be reduced in case the demand is actually less than the capacity made available by committed resources. Commitment for some resources may be for the short run, and, for some other resources, it may extend over a longer term. The use of committed resources depends on the actual production levels, and the capacity of such resources made available may be inadequate or surplus to support actual production.

In this section, we focus on the analysis of committed overhead costs and examine the relationship between commitment to supply resources and the usage of the supplied resources by activities supporting production output.

Our examination of the variation in direct material and direct labor costs relative to production volume is meaningful because these costs can be traced

Discretionary costs
Costs that result from managers' strategic and tactical decisions, such that the expenditure levels chosen influence the production volume instead of production volume influencing the consumption of activity resources.

Committed resources
Resources made available for an activity prior to knowing the demand for it. These resources cannot be reduced in case the demand turns out to be less than the capacity made available by the com mitted resources.

directly to each product manufactured and sold. By definition, overhead costs cannot be traced to products in this fashion. Therefore, an important first step in the analysis of overhead costs is to identify each activity's cost driver.

Recall that overhead costs arise because of the performance of a number of different activities to support production or sales. Each activity may be associated with a direct or surrogate measure, referred to as its *cost driver*. For instance, the number of purchase orders is a driver for purchase department costs, and the numbers of setups and batches produced are drivers for setup and materials handling personnel costs. The number of active parts maintained and the number of engineering change orders (ECOs) are drivers for the engineering support activity costs.

We saw in the case of direct labor that managers first determine the level of resources to make available for production and, then, the actual production volume determines the demand for available resources. This structure for the commitment and use of resources applies to many activities that compose manufacturing overhead. Managers commit to incurring the expense for support activities when they hire personnel and provide them with the tools and facilities to perform their activities. The expense levels are influenced by the managers' expectations about the requirement for each activity. The actual demand for each activity and the consumption of its resources are related, in turn, to the actual production volume and mix.

Consider this example. If it takes 2 hours to set up a machine for each new batch, and 36 hours are available for setup work per week for each worker, the employment of 10 setup workers provides the capacity for 180 setups per week (10 workers * 36 hours ÷ 2 hours per setup). If the weekly wages (including benefits) average $720 per worker, the total expense for setup labor is $7,200. We also can measure the cost per unit of the activity capacity made available for production. In this case, for each setup that *can* be done with the available capacity, the labor cost averages $40 ($7,200/180 setups). The normal unit cost of the setup labor activity is thus $40 per setup.

The demand for setups depends on the number of batches of products manufactured. If 2,000,000 units are manufactured in the first week of April in batches of average size of 12,500, then 160 setups (2,000,000 ÷ 12,500) are required. There is, however, capacity for 180 setups, as described above. Therefore, the *unused capacity* for the first week of April is 20 setups (180 − 160), or, equivalently, idle time for setup labor is 40 hours (2 * 20 = (10 * 36) − 2 * 160) hours. The expenditure for setup labor remains, therefore, at $7,200 for the 10 workers employed at the plant. The setup workers, however, come to work each day prepared to do as many setups as they can. The *actual* average cost per setup is $45 ($7,200/160), which exceeds the normal cost of $40 per setup because of the unused capacity.

■ Multiple-Products and Activity Costs

An additional consideration is the relative mix of products. Different customers may require products to be manufactured in different-size batches. A product manufactured in batches of 10,000 units requires twice as many setups for the same volume of production as a product manufactured in batches of 20,000 units. The relative proportions of activity resources required

This flexible manufacturing cell, manufactured by Cincinnati Milacron, allows manufacturers to produce a wide variety of products on a single machine. The machine's flexibility allows fast, low-cost setups, as the machine is converted from making one part to making another part. *(Courtesy Cincinnati Milicron)*

by 2 products may be very different for different support activities. As a result, when the product mix changes, the demand for different activities may change by different amounts.

Consider Global Glass Company's plant that manufactures glass bottles of 3 different sizes: 2 ounces, 4 ounces, and 6 ounces. Indirect labor costs include setup of the glass extrusion machines and quality inspection of every finished bottle.

Proper setup is important because improper settings lead to higher defect and rejection rates. Setup workers, therefore, have specialized skills and many years of experience in working with the glass extrusion machine. The plant employs 10 setup workers. Each worker can work up to 36 hours a week setting up the machines. The average weekly wages, including benefits, are $720 per worker. Because the smaller bottles are more difficult to manufacture, a job order for the 2-ounce bottles requires more time per setup than the larger bottles do. Even if bottles with the same dimensions are to be manufactured in successive jobs, a new setup is required for each job because each customer has a different and distinctive design for its bottles. Thus, the demand for setup labor varies with both the number and types of jobs.

Quality inspection is not so specialized as setup work at Global Glass. The plant maintains some flexibility in adjusting the number of inspection workers with changes in the expected customer orders. In the past 2 years, however, the plant has maintained 52 inspectors in its payroll. They are paid $630, including benefits, per week, on average, and work 36 hours each week. Plant operations include 3 shifts a day around the clock and does not use overtime. If resource capacity committed at the outset is not adequate, the company delays the execution and delivery of customer orders, which results in the loss of goodwill and potential sales. The demand for quality inspection varies approximately with the number of bottles manufactured. Exhibit 4–18 presents detailed data for support activity requirements.

Exhibit 4–19 shows actual production data for 3 weeks. In week 1, the 2-ounce bottles required 80 setups (800,000 bottles produced/10,000 batch size). These setups took 176 hours (2.2 hours per setup [Exhibit 4–18] * 80 setups). In addition, 4-ounce bottles required 100 setup hours (2 * 1,000,000/20,000), and 6-ounce bottles required 64 setup hours (2 * 400,000/12,500). In comparison with the total of 340 setup hours (176 + 100 + 64) required for the production in week 1, the company had a potential of 360 hours (10 workers * 36 hours/worker) of setup work capacity available. As a result, 20 hours of setup work resources remained unused.

In week 3, 800 hours (1,000,000/1,250) of quality inspection were required for 2-ounce bottles, 720 hours (900,000/1,250) for 4-ounce bottles, and 400 hours (400,000/1,000) for 6-ounce bottles. In comparison with the

---

EXHIBIT 4–18
Global Glass Company: Support Activity Requirements

BOTTLE SIZE	HOURS PER SETUP	BATCH SIZE	BOTTLES INSPECTED PER HOUR
2 ounces	2.2	10,000	1,250
4 ounces	2.0	20,000	1,250
6 ounces	2.0	12,500	1,000

EXHIBIT 4–19
Global Glass Company

BOTTLE SIZE	WEEK 1	WEEK 2	WEEK 3
PANEL A: ACTUAL PRODUCTION QUANTITIES IN NUMBER OF BOTTLES			
2 ounces	800,000	900,000	1,000,000
4 ounces	1,000,000	900,000	900,000
6 ounces	400,000	500,000	400,000
PANEL B: NUMBER OF SETUP HOURS REQUIRED[a]			
2 ounces	176	198	220
4 ounces	100	90	90
6 ounces	64	80	64
Total	340	368	374
PANEL C: NUMBER OF QUALITY INSPECTION HOURS REQUIRED[b]			
2 ounces	640	720	800
4 ounces	800	720	720
6 ounces	400	500	400
Total	1,840	1,940	1,920

[a] Hours per setup * Number of bottles ÷ Batch size.
[b] Number of bottles ÷ Bottles inspected per hour.

total requirement of 1,920 hours (800 + 720 + 400) of quality inspection, only 1,872 hours (52 inspectors * 36 hours) of inspection worker time were available. Because of this resource shortage, some jobs were delayed, and the plant shop floor became congested with work in progress.

The costs of lost sales or goodwill because of delays or the costs of expediting delayed jobs in a congested plant do not show up as a setup or inspection expenses in a conventional income statement. Nonetheless, these are important costs for managers to track and control to make the right decisions about the number of support activity workers to employ and of customer jobs to accept.[6]

Expenditure Versus Consumption of Activity Resources

OBJECTIVE 4.6
The difference between cost equation and the consumption equation for an activity

Exhibit 4–20 summarizes the resource commitment and usage levels for both setup and quality inspection activities at Global Glass. The expenditure for setup and inspection labor ($7,200 + $32,760) that shows up on the financial accounting statements does not change each week, because it depends only on the managerial decision about the number of workers to employ for any time period. The actual use of the resources that are made available, however, depends on the production volume. Therefore, we find that the amount of idle time each week changes because of unused resource capacity or due to production delays attributable to resource shortages.

Even when a permanent change in the production levels results in a repeated occurrence of either unused capacity or excess capacity for an activity, we find that a delay occurs before the level of resources committed to the activity is adjusted to match the new consumption demands placed on it. When the production level goes down, committed activity resources often remain in place for several more months before the managers find an alternative use for the excess resources or make the politically difficult decision to permanently eliminate the surplus resources. When production increases place a demand on an activity that exceeds the present available capacity, people often work longer or faster in the short run, or they can delay production. Eventually, of course, excess demand adversely affects performance, and managers must make more resource capacity available for the activity to relieve the overload. Therefore, there is often a lag between the production demands to consume activity resources and expenditures for the resource capacity committed for the activities.

Although total expenditure levels are monitored in conventional financial accounting statements, the measurement of the specific demands placed on activity resources is sometimes ignored by cost accounting systems. A well-designed cost system seeks to measure the activity resources required to manufacture a product. It recognizes that changes in the consumption of activity resources must be followed by corresponding changes in the expenditure for the activities.

---

[6] R.D. Banker, S.M. Datar, and S. Kekre, "Relevant Costs, Congestion, and Stochasticity in Production," *Journal of Accounting and Economics* (Fall 1988), pp. 171–198.

EXHIBIT 4–20
Global Glass Company: Setup and Quality Inspection Expenses

	SETUP ACTIVITY			QUALITY INSPECTION		
	WEEK 1	WEEK 2	WEEK 3	WEEK 1	WEEK 2	WEEK 3
Number of workers employed	10	10	10	52	52	52
Total number of hours available per week (Number of workers * 36)	360	360	360	1,872	1,872	1,872
Total number of hours required (see Exhibit 4–19, panels A, B, and C)	340	368	374	1,840	1,940	1,920
Idle time hours (Hours available − Hours required, if positive; otherwise zero)	20	–0–	–0–	32	–0–	–0–
Resource shortage hours (Hours required − Hours available, if positive; otherwise zero)	–0–	8	14	–0–	68	48
Expenditure (10 setup workers * 720 weekly wages, and 52 inspectors * 630 weekly wages)	$7,200	$7,200	$7,200	$32,760	$32,760	$32,760

Recall our previous definition of normal unit cost as the average cost at the point where activity demand equals available capacity. In other words, the *normal activity cost* of a product measures the demand placed by the product for the consumption of resources for an activity charged at the normal unit cost rate for that activity. Exhibit 4–21 presents the normal unit costs for the activity resources (setup and quality inspection) required by the sizes of bottles that Global Glass produces. Because wages of $720 are paid weekly for a capacity of 36 hours for setups, the normal cost per setup hour is $20 ($720/36). To manufacture 100,000 2-ounce bottles in batch sizes of 10,000, we need 10 (100,000/10,000) batches. Each batch setup requires 2.2 hours (see Exhibit 4–18). Therefore, the normal cost of setup activity for 100,000 2-ounce bottles is $440 (2.2 hours/setup * 10 batches * $20 setup cost/hour). We determine the normal costs for the quality inspection activity in a similar manner. Each hour of quality inspection costs $17.50 ($630/36 hours available). Because 2-ounce bottles are inspected at the rate of 1,250 each hour (see Exhibit 4–18) we require 80 hours ($100,000/1,250) to inspect 100,000

EXHIBIT 4–21
Global Glass Company: Normal Activity Costs

| | NORMAL COSTS PER 100,000 BOTTLES FOR | |
BOTTLE SIZE	SETUP ACTIVITY	QUALITY INSPECTION
2 ounces	$440	$1,400
	(2.2 * 10 * $720/36)	(80 * $630/36)
4 ounces	$200	$1,400
	(2 * 5 * $720/36)	(80 * $630/36)
6 ounces	$320	$1,750
	(2 * 8 * $720/36)	(100 * $630/36)

2-ounce bottles. Therefore, the normal cost of the quality inspection activity for 100,000, 2-ounce bottles is $1,400 (80 hours * $17.50 per hour).

Chapter 7 extends this discussion by showing that activity-based costing systems determine product costs by aggregating normal costs over *all* the activities required to support the production of each product.

BREAKEVEN ANALYSIS

OBJECTIVE 4.7
Breakeven analysis

An analysis that management accountants commonly perform involves determining the level of production at which the profit resulting from 1 option is at least as large as the profit resulting from an alternative option. As mentioned previously, the level at which the profits under the 2 options are equal is called the *breakeven point*.

To illustrate, consider Carex Muffler Company, which is evaluating whether to employ 7 or 8 mechanics. What is the number of daily jobs above which employing 8 mechanics costs less and below which employing 7 mechanics costs less?[7]

To answer this question, let Q denote the number of daily jobs. Recall that each mechanic can service 10 jobs in a day. If there are fewer than 70 jobs in a day, evidently no more than 7 mechanics need be employed. If there are more than 80 jobs in a day, 8 mechanics must be employed to minimize overtime work. We shall consider, therefore, Q between 70 and 80 ($70 < Q < 80$) to find the value Q^0 at which the costs under the 2 alternatives (employing 7 or 8 mechanics) are equal. (Note that revenues from Q jobs are the same whether 7 or 8 mechanics are employed.)

If 8 mechanics are employed and Q is less than 80, there will be idle time, and the direct labor cost will be only the committed regular wages for the 8 mechanics. Costs, or C, would be

$$C = \text{\$30 per hour} * 8 \text{ hours} * 8 \text{ workers}$$
$$= \text{\$1,920 when } N = 8. \qquad (4.5)$$

---

[7] The output (number of jobs), and therefore, the revenues under both options are the same. Consequently, the comparison of profits to determine the breakeven point reduces to a comparison of only the costs in this case.

If 7 mechanics are employed and Q is greater than 70,

$$[(0.75 \text{ hours/job} * Q) - (7.5 \text{ hours/day} * 7 \text{ mechanics})]$$

hours of overtime will be required. Following our earlier analysis, we can write the direct labor cost as

$$
\begin{aligned}
C &= \$30 * 8 * 7 + 1.5 * \$30 * (0.75 * Q - 7.5 * 7) \\
&= \$1,680 + 33.75 * Q - \$2,362.50 \\
&= \$33.75 * Q - \$682.50 \text{ when } N = 7.
\end{aligned}
\tag{4.6}
$$

At the breakeven point, Q^0, the 2 cost expressions are equal. Therefore:

$$
\begin{aligned}
\$33.75 * Q^0 - \$682.50 &= \$1,920 \\
\$33.75 * Q^0 &= \$1,920 + \$682.50 \\
&= \$2,602.50 \\
Q^0 &= \$2,602.50 \div \$33.75 \\
&= 77.11
\end{aligned}
$$

The 2 cost expressions are graphed in Exhibit 4–22, which also depicts the breakeven point as the point of intersection of the two graphs.

The breakeven analysis indicates that if 77 or fewer orders are expected on any particular day, only 7 (or fewer) mechanics should be employed; if 78 or more orders are expected, 8 (or more) mechanics should be employed.

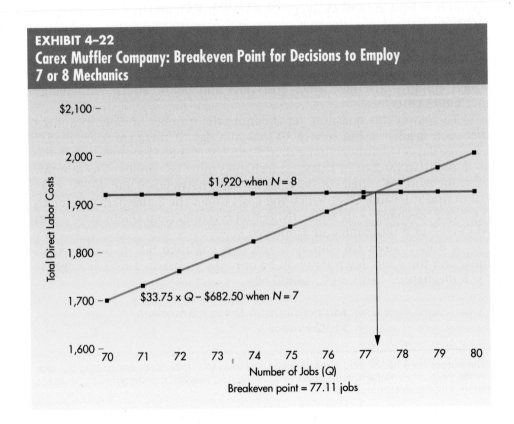

EXHIBIT 4–22
Carex Muffler Company: Breakeven Point for Decisions to Employ 7 or 8 Mechanics

$1,920 when N = 8

$33.75 x Q – $682.50 when N = 7

Total Direct Labor Costs

Number of Jobs (Q)
Breakeven point = 77.11 jobs

Evaluating a Business Venture

Of special interest is the case in which managers must evaluate whether investment in a business venture will be profitable. Breakeven analysis in this case determines the output volume at which the profit from the business venture equals zero—the profit when there is no investment in the business. The traditional breakeven analysis here relies on the decomposition of costs into fixed and variable costs. Recall that the cost equation can be written as follows:

$$C = F + V * Q$$

where C = total cost
F = fixed cost
V = variable cost rate per unit
Q = production level in units

If the production of Q units is sold at a price of $\$P$ per unit, sales revenue totals $\$P * Q$.[8] The profit for the firm from this operation is given by the following equation:

$$\begin{aligned}
\text{Profit} &= \text{Revenues} - \text{Costs} \\
&= (P * Q) - (F + V * Q) \\
&= (P - V) * Q - F \quad\quad (4.7)
\end{aligned}$$

The difference $(P - V)$ between the price and the variable cost per unit is defined to be the **contribution margin per unit.** If we increase production and sales by 1 unit, the sales revenue would increase by the amount of the sales price (P), and the total costs would increase by the amount of variable cost per unit (V). Therefore, the contribution margin per unit is the net increase $(P - V)$ in the profit when we increase production and sales by 1 unit. It is the amount that each unit produced and sold contributes to covering the fixed costs and earning profit. The above profit equation can now be written:

> **Contribution margin per unit**
> Difference between the price and variable cost per unit.

Profit = (Contribution margin per unit) * (Production in units)
           − (Fixed costs)   (4.8)

To determine the breakeven point, $Q^{0,}$ we set profit equal to zero to obtain

$$0 = (P - V) * Q^0 - F$$

$$Q^0 = \frac{F}{P - V}$$

Thus the breakeven point is obtained in this case by dividing the fixed cost by the contribution margin per unit of output:

$$\text{Breakeven point (in units)} = \frac{\text{Fixed costs}}{\text{Contribution margin per unit}} \quad (4.9)$$

---

[8] For most breakeven analysis problems, sales and production levels are assumed to be equal.

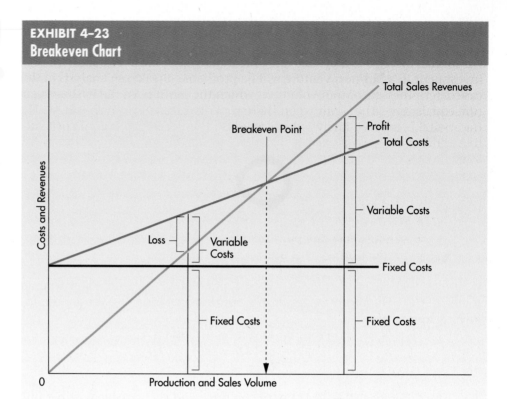

EXHIBIT 4–23
Breakeven Chart

Total Sales Revenues

Breakeven Point

Profit

Total Costs

Costs and Revenues

Variable Costs

Loss — Variable Costs

Fixed Costs

Fixed Costs

Fixed Costs

0   Production and Sales Volume

Breakeven chart
A set of graphs depicting the sales revenues and fixed, variable, and total costs. The breakeven point is the point of intersection of the sales revenue curve and the total cost curve.

We can illustrate this breakeven analysis by means of the graphs in Exhibit 4–23. Such a set of graphs is often referred to as a **breakeven chart**, which depicts sales revenues, and fixed, variable, and total costs, with a breakeven point at the intersection of the sales revenue and total cost curves. To construct a breakeven chart, we first draw a horizontal line to represent the fixed costs and then add on the variable costs to the fixed costs for different levels of production (and sales), as in Exhibit 4–8, to obtain the total cost curve. Next we draw a line through the origin to represent the total sales revenues increasing proportionally with the production (and sales) volume. The breakeven point is indicated by the point at which the total cost curve intersects the total sales revenue curve, because profit equals zero when total costs equal total sales revenues.

■ Target Profit

Breakeven analysis can be extended easily to address the case in which we need to determine the production volume necessary to obtain a target profit level, T. We set the profit equation as

$$T = (P - V) * Q^T - F$$
$$(P - V) * Q^T = F + T$$
$$Q^T = \frac{F + T}{P - V} \tag{4.10}$$

or

$$= \frac{\text{Fixed cost} + \text{Target profit}}{\text{Contribution margin per unit}}$$

At times, the profitability target is expressed in terms of the profit to sales ratio (Profit/Sales) instead of dollars of profit. The volume at which the target profit to sales ratio is attained can be determined by adjusting the approach we used above.

We begin, as before, with the expression for profit:

$$(P - V) * Q - F$$

The profit-to-sales ratio is obtained by dividing the above expression for profit by the expression $P * Q$ for sales. The resulting fraction is then equated to the target profit-to-sales ratio, Z, to determine the production volume Q^Z at which the target profit-to-sales ratio is attained:

$$\frac{(P - V)Q^Z - F}{PQ_Z} = Z \tag{4.11}$$

$$(P - V) Q^Z - F = ZPQ^Z$$
$$(P - V - ZP) Q^Z = F$$

$$Q^Z = \frac{F}{P - V - ZP}$$

You may choose to commit these formulas to memory. You will find it more convenient, however, to proceed from basic principles by writing down the profit equation and equating it to the target as required.

■ Breakeven Point in Dollars

Breakeven analysis applies also when production level is expressed in monetary units. To illustrate, consider Martha Jacobs' decision to rent a stall at the local fair to sell Jim and Barry's ice cream in 8 different flavors. She plans to set the price of the ice cream by adding 25% to its variable cost. Fixed costs comprise rent for the stall and cold-storage facility, amounting to $800. How many dollars of sales must Martha make to break even on this enterprise? If

$$\text{Sales} = 1.25 * (\text{variable cost})$$

then

$$\text{Variable cost} = \frac{\text{Sales}}{1.25} = 0.80 * \text{Sales because } 0.80 = 1 \div 1.25.$$

That is, for $1.00 of sales variable costs are $0.80. In other words, contribution margin is 20 percent ($1.00 − $0.80)/$1.00 of sales.

The contribution margin *expressed as a percentage of sales* is also referred to as the **contribution margin ratio.** To determine the breakeven point,

Contribution margin ratio
Contribution margin expressed as a percentage of sales.

CONSIDER THIS . . .

Pittsburgh's Pirates May Sail Away

In 1988, Pittsburgh's city government and corporate leaders together bought the Pirates, the city's baseball team, to keep major league baseball in Pittsburgh. Operating in a small metropolitan area with a population of about 2 million, the Pirates have faced financial problems in the 1980s and 1990s. The 1988 buyout contract provides for the ownership to revert to the city if the team amasses operating losses of $10 million or more in any consecutive three-year period. The city is expected to sell the team in this case.

In 1988, the Pirates had a breakeven point of 1.4 million tickets. With a steep increase in the team's payroll, the Pirates had to sell more than 2 million tickets in 1990 to break even. How were the breakeven points estimated?

The team's payroll in 1988 was $6.2 million. Administrative and other fixed operating costs amounted to $4.1 million. Revenues from television and radio broadcast rights and from concessions were $1.9 million. The contribution margin was $6 per ticket. The Pirates break even if the total revenues from ticket sales and broadcast rights equal the total payroll and administrative costs:

Breakeven point =

$$\frac{\text{Paroll costs} + \text{Administrative cost} - \text{Broadcast revenues}}{\text{Contribution margin per ticket}}$$

$$= \frac{\$6.2 + \$4.1 - \$1.9}{\$6 \text{ per ticket}}$$

$$= 1.4 \text{ million tickets}$$

Can you now determine how the breakeven point will change if the Pirates add high-priced talented players to strengthen their roster and increase their payroll by 58%, to $9.8 million? (Answer: The breakeven point increases to 2 million tickets.) Can you determine how many tickets the Pirates (with the $9.8 million payroll) must sell to keep their annual operating losses under $3.333 million? (Answer: 1.445 million tickets.)

Source: "How Business Went to Bat for the Pirates," *Business Week,* July 18, 1988, p. 98; "Pittsburgh's Pirates May Have to Sail Away," *Business Week,* April 16, 1990, p. 78; W. Wucinich, "Profit Is the Name of the Game," *Management Accounting,* February 1991, pp. 58–59.

Nova Woodcraft Ltd. purchased this expensive panel saw, which uses a built-in computer to cut wood very precisely and software to estimate the amount of wood and sawcuts required for any job. Because of the saw's high price, the company had to ensure that it had work available that would allow the company to recover the saw's costs. (© Chris Reardon)

we employ our earlier formula, treating $1 as the unit of measurement for the production level Q. Therefore, contribution margin per dollar (one unit of measurement) of sales is $1.00 - 0.80$, and the breakeven point, Q^0, is given by

$$Q^0 = \text{Fixed cost/Contribution margin}$$
$$= \frac{\$800}{1.00 - 0.80}$$
$$= \frac{\$800}{0.20}$$
$$= \$4,000$$

The breakeven quantity is expressed in dollars because our unit of measurement is $1. Martha must earn sales revenues amounting to $4,000 to break even.

◼ Breaking Even: Riverside Hospital Revisited

Let us return to the Riverside Hospital example we discussed in Chapter 3 and at the beginning of this chapter. Holly Ward, the controller at Riverside, had developed the following cost equation:

$$\text{Costs} = \$2,393,091 + \$161.59 * \text{Patient-days} + \$74.33 \text{ Patients}$$

The average reimbursement rate is expected to remain at $220 per patient-day. The number of patients and patient-days for 1993 are expected to remain at the 1992 levels of 8,367 patients and 45,606 patient-days. How much must the fixed costs be reduced if Riverside Hospital is to break even?

Holly's "back-of-the-envelope" calculations indicated that fixed costs must be reduced by almost 15% to break even. How did she reach this conclusion?

Because the number of patients and of patient-days is expected to be 8,367 and 45,606, respectively, the costs varying with these 2 measures of output are estimated to be $621,889 ($74.33 * 8,367) and $7,369,455 ($161.59 * 45,606), respectively (see Exhibit 3–8). Our objective is to determine the reduction required in fixed costs, and, therefore, we shall denote the fixed costs by the symbol F, and write the costs as follows:

$$\text{Costs} = F + \$7,369,455 + \$621,889$$
$$= F + \$7,991,344$$

Revenues are $220 per day for 45,606 patient-days. Therefore,

$$\text{Revenues} = \$220 * 45,606$$
$$= \$10,033,320$$

To break even, we must have

$$0 = \text{Revenues} - \text{Costs}$$
$$= 10,033,320 - F - \$7,991,344$$
$$F = \$2,041,976.$$

Because the fixed costs are $2,393,091 at present, they must be reduced by 14.67% [($2,393,091 − $2,041,976)/$2,393,091], or nearly 15%, for Riverside to break even.

■ Breakeven Analysis and Capacity Utilization

You may wonder whether breakeven analysis is restricted only to the types of situations we have described so far. For a managerial application of this analytical method in a more complex setting, consider Regal Airlines, which is evaluating a proposal to introduce a daily Boeing 757 round-trip flight on the New York to Los Angeles route. The costs to consider include: (1) the airplane equipment rental and airport gate rental fees of $136,000 per week, (2) maintenance and other ground staff costs of $32,000 per week, (3) flying crew (pilots, flight attendants) salaries and benefits of $48,000 per week, (4) fuel costs of $6,500 per (one-way) flight—that is, $91,000 for the 14 one-way flights per week. Discretionary advertising expenditure of $40,000 per week is planned to support the new operation. Commissions paid to travel agents average 10% of sales. The aircraft can hold 80 passengers in its specially designed comfortable seating configuration, and the average one-way fare is $600 per passenger.

How many passengers must Regal Airlines have to break even on this new operation? All costs except sales commissions become fixed once the decisions to operate and advertise the route are made. Direct labor (flying crew) and direct materials (fuel) do not vary with the output (number of passengers) in this case. The fixed costs amount to $347,000 ($136,000 + $32,000 + $48,000 + $91,000 + $40,000) per week. Each one-way passenger ticket contributes $540 ($600 − 0.10 * $600). Regal Airlines must have at least 642.6 ($347,000/$540) passengers per week, or 45.9 (642.6/14) passengers per flight on average, to break even.

Airline executives monitor the load factor, or capacity utilization, for each route on a daily basis. Load factor is measured as the ratio of the number of passengers per flight to the number of seats available per flight. Regal can expect to break even on this route when its load factor is 57.4% (45.9/80).

■ Step Fixed Costs and Multiple Breakeven Points

We have seen that the breakeven point is determined by dividing the fixed costs by the contribution margin unit. When the cost curve is characterized by step fixed costs, however, we need to consider a different amount of fixed cost corresponding to each step. Therefore, in principle, we could compute a breakeven point for each level of fixed costs. Some of these computed breakeven points may not be feasible because they may violate the limits imposed by the relevant range corresponding to the level of fixed costs considered in their computation.

To illustrate, consider Regal Airlines once again. Regal is considering a truncated flight schedule involving only 10 or 12 one-way flights (instead of

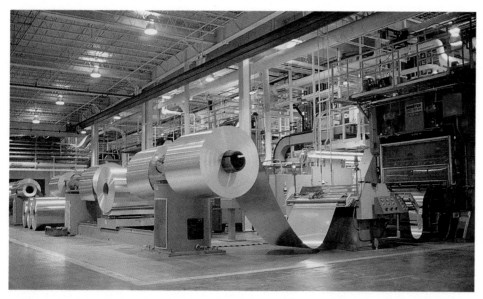

As demand for products increased, Ball Corporation added a fourth beverage can manufacturing line in this plant. The line can make 2,000 cans per minute. The fixed costs associated with the beverage can manufacturing lines are a good example of a step fixed cost. *(Courtesy Ball Corporation)*

14 flights) per week by not scheduling flights on Saturday and/or Sunday. Fixed costs will be only $306,000 if it schedules 10 flights, and $326,000 if it schedules 12 flights, instead of the $347,000 of fixed costs when it schedules 14 flights. Fixed costs will be lower because Regal can plan to reduce airport gate rental commitments, hire fewer ground staff and flying crew, and incur lower fuel costs. Thus, these costs behave as step fixed costs. How many passengers must Regal Airlines fly each week to break even?

If Regal decides to schedule only 10 flights per week, its breakeven point will be 566.7 ($306,000/$540) passengers per week, or 56.7 (566.7/10) passengers per flight on average, a 70.8% (56.7/80) load factor. If it decides to schedule 12 flights per week, instead, its breakeven point will be 605.6 ($327,000/$540) passengers per week, or 50.5 (605.6/12) passengers per flight on average, a 63.1% (50.5/80) load factor.

Notice that there are different breakeven points, depending on Regal management's decision concerning the level of capacity to make available. With the lower capacity level (10 flights), fewer passengers are required each week for the airline to break even. This decision also implies that the airline must achieve a higher load factor on its weekday flights to break even.

■ Cost Variability and Level of Analysis

Next consider the decision by National Airlines, Inc. regarding the number of flights to operate on the air shuttle route between New York and Boston. Its advertising, personnel, and other expenditures to support the operation in

New York and Boston amount to $150,000 per week. Flying crew, fuel, and other flight-related expenditures amount to $7,500 per flight. Aircraft rental and airport gate fees are $6,500 per week per flight. In addition, ground support personnel cost $4,000 per flight as company policy seeks to maintain service quality even when volume increases. National pays a commission of 8% to travel agents on a one-way fare of $160 per passenger. A full flight carries 100 passengers.

How many flights must National Airlines operate to break even if it expects the load factor to be 70% per flight? The analysis in Exhibit 4–24 indicates that National must operate 58 roundtrip flights each week to break even.

We see in the examples of Regal Airlines and National Airlines that the behavior of costs depends on the level of our analysis. When the number of flights is already decided, as in the Regal example, only a small portion of the costs varies with the number of passengers. When a decision about the number of flights is considered, as in the National example, we treat all flight-related costs as varying with volume (number of flights) in our analysis to determine the breakeven point.

OBJECTIVE 4.8
The way to sketch a planning model that captures the relationship between revenues, costs, and production volumes

■ A Planning Model

Understanding cost behavior also helps management to determine the level of operation that is likely to maximize profits. Suppose the load factor for National Airlines is not expected to be the same 70% for each flight. Instead,

---

EXHIBIT 4–24
National Airlines: Breakeven Point Analysis

DESCRIPTION	AMOUNT	CALCULATIONS
Revenue per passenger	$160.00	
Sales commission	$12.80	(8% * $160)
Contribution per passenger	$147.20	($160 − $12.80 sales commission)
Passengers per flight	70	(0.70 load factor * 100 capacity available)
Net revenue per round-trip flight	$20,608.00	(2 trips * 70 passengers * $147.20 contribution per passenger)
Cost per round-trip flight	$18,000.00	($7,500 crew salaries + 6,500 aircraft and gate rental + $4,000 support personnel)
Contribution per flight	$2,608.00	($20,608 − $18,000)
Costs not varying with flights	$150,000.00	(advertising, personnel, and the like)
Breakeven point	57.5 round-trip flights per week	($150,000/$2,608)

---

the load factor is expected to be 92% for the first flight scheduled in each direction. Each additional round-trip is expected to result in a decline in average load factor by 4% on all flights. How many round-trip flights should National Airlines operate?

It is possible to derive an algebraic expression to determine the number of flights that maximize profits, but the expression depends on the specific relationship between the expected demand (load factor) and the proposed supply (number of flights). The more general skill to be learned here is the ability to understand the basic equations that project profits as described in Exhibit 4–25.

The equations in Exhibit 4–25 specify the *behavior of costs* and revenues and enable us to determine the *best choice* using a spreadsheet model. Such articulation forms the basis for developing a *planning model* for the firm. Critical for this purpose is a thorough understanding of what drives costs and revenues and the way that each of them is related to factors that managers can control.

Exhibit 4–26 summarizes the cost and revenue implications of operating different numbers of flights. The numbers in this table are derived from the equations specified in the planning model in Exhibit 4–25. Exhibit 4–27 (on p. 174) displays the graph of profits plotted against the number of flights. Looking at the graph, we can see that the profits are the highest when National operates 11 round-trip flights.

EXHIBIT 4–25
National Airlines: A Planning Model Basis— Cost and Revenue Behavior

FACTOR	CALCULATION
(A) Net profit	Total revenues − Total expenses
(B) Total revenue	Average fare * Number of passengers
(C) Number of passengers	2 * Number of roundtrip flights per day * 7 days * Average load factor
(D) Average load factor	0.92 − 0.04 * (Number of round-trip flights per day − 1)
(E) Total expenses	Commission costs + Flying crew and fuel costs + Aircraft rental and gate fees + Ground support costs + Advertising and other costs
(F) Commission costs	0.08 * Total revenues
(G) Flying crew and fuel costs	$7,500 * Number of round-trip flights per day * 7
(H) Aircraft rental and gate fees	$6,500 * Number of round-trip flights per day * 7
(I) Ground support costs	$4,000 * Number of round-trip flights per day * 7
(J) Advertising and other costs	$150,000

Nursing Activity Resource Consumption Model at Braintree Hospital

Braintree Hospital is a private rehabilitation hospital providing in-patient and out-patient treatment. It is one of the largest rehabilitation network care providers in the United States with 168 beds on site.

Patients entering with physical disabilities due to neurological and orthopedic disease or injury and normally are diagnosed as having one of the following: stroke, spinal cord injury, congenital deformity, amputation, major multiple trauma, femur fracture, brain injury, polyarthritis and joint replacement, neurological disorders, burns, and neoplasms. The patient's average stay is approximately 21 days, during which time the individual progresses through a comprehensive program aimed at restoring and maintaining functional abilities.

Traditionally, the cost of nursing is factored into the daily room charge for a hospital. For example, a rate of $500 to $800 per day covers the 24-hour nursing availability for the patient. Nursing expenses, primarily labor costs, are part of the overhead rate included in the patient's daily bill. The same fixed charges are applied to all patients.

The problem with this typical convention is that not all patients use nursing services in equal amounts. As a result, fixed charges are not always related to the nursing services that individual patients utilize. Further, nursing services are available "on call" to handle possible patient emergencies, and their value is not readily identifiable with individual patients.

Typically, nursing services in the hospital comprise a varied skill mix: professional registered nurses (RNs), license practical nurses (LPNs), and ancillary nursing assistants (NAs). These professionals have different levels of education, training, and hospital experience.

Teams of nurses administer medication, maintain daily patient records, assist the physicians with medical care, monitor medical devices, conduct routine tests, and so on. They are responsible for the routine jobs of feeding and bathing the patients, ensuring their safety, and, most important, providing them personal care and comfort.

The professional RN is licensed to perform all of the many nursing functions in the hospital but concentrates on the more seriously ill or demanding patients. The other nursing team members normally work with the RNs to deliver care to their group of patients. Thus, a team with varying skill levels delivers the array of nursing services. There is a hierarchy of nursing from the RN to the NA with pay scales ranging from $26 per hour to $8 per hour, depending on specific position, skills, and education.

The amount of nursing services required by different patients varies widely, which the health care industry has now recognized. Third-party payers (including insurance companies and Medicare) are demanding that they pay only for the services actually used by the patient and at the lowest price.

EXHIBIT 4–26
National Airlines: Weekly Profits for Different Number of Flights

EQUATION IN EXHIBIT 4–25	NUMBER OF ROUND-TRIP FLIGHTS PER DAY						
	1	2	3	4	5	6	7
(D) Average load factor	92%	88%	84%	80%	76%	72%	68%
(C) No. of passengers	1,288	2,464	3,528	4,480	5,320	6,048	6,664
(B) Total revenue	206,080	394,240	564,480	716,800	851,200	967,680	1,066,240
(F) Commission costs	16,486	31,539	45,158	57,344	68,096	77,414	85,299
(G) Flying crew and fuel costs	7,500	15,000	22,500	30,000	37,500	45,000	52,500
(H) Aircraft rental and gate fees	6,500	13,000	19,500	26,000	32,500	39,000	45,500
(I) Ground support costs	4,000	8,000	12,000	16,000	20,000	24,000	28,000
(J) Advertising and other costs	150,000	150,000	150,000	150,000	150,000	150,000	150,000
(E) Total expenses	184,486	217,539	249,158	279,344	308,096	335,414	361,299
(A) Net profit	21,594	176,701	315,322	437,456	543,104	632,266	704,941

Mary-Jean Crockett, vice president of nursing, recognized that nursing service delivery needed to be understood better. She was determined to find an easy, reliable, and fair method to ascertain the amount, mix, and resulting cost of nursing services consumed by individual patients. She also wanted a more accurate approach to forecasting the skills mix required in the care of patients within particular diagnostic groups.

After conducting a detailed process analysis, Mary-Jean and her staff team determined that routine events such as performing vital sign tests, administering medication, and changing beds were easy to predict. The percentage of baseline routine nursing time could vary from 5% to 70%, depending on the medical problem and length of hospital stay. For example, a new brain-injury patient requires constant care, and routine nursing may account for just 5% of the total daily nursing services consumed. A burn patient about to be discharged, though, may be quite self-sufficient, and routine care may represent 70% of the total daily nursing services consumed. The staff team believed that nonroutine events were the drivers behind the varying levels of the nursing services consumed each day.

The team amassed detailed daily data over a period of several months on the amount and type of service provided by each nurse to individual patients classified by their diagnostic groups. A further analysis of these data demonstrated that the consumption of nursing services is a function of both patient diagnosis and the length of hospital stay. Most patients have a large consumption of nursing services during the initial period of their stay, and, over time, the consumption declines.

A matrix was built, and all the activities performed by various skill levels were determined for each category of patient illness and tracked over the length of hospital stay by patient category. The team had developed the *nursing activity resource consumption model* for the hospital—a model of the activities consumed by each patient by category detailing the amount of nursing services from each nursing skill level. Patient load and mix projections can be translated now into nursing resource consumption patterns. This information changes the economic focus of the managers from simply filling beds to seeking those patients who have a consumption pattern compatible with the available mix of nursing services. Managers now adjust the nursing mix for the forecasted consumption level. Armed with these new cost data, the hospital can also unbundle the previously fixed single nursing services charge and negotiate rate and fees with the third-party payers depending on actual circumstances.

Source: Lawrence P. Carr, "Unbundling the Cost of Hospitalization," *Management Accounting* (November 1993), pp. 43–48.

	NUMBER OF ROUND-TRIP FLIGHTS PER DAY							
	8	**9**	**10**	**11**	**12**	**13**	**14**	**15**
	64%	60%	56%	52%	48%	44%	40%	36%
	7,168	7,560	7,840	8,008	8,064	8,008	7,840	7,560
	1,146,880	1,209,600	1,254,400	1,281,280	1,290,240	1,281,280	1,254,400	1,209,600
	91,750	96,768	100,352	102,502	103,219	102,502	100,352	96,768
	60,000	67,500	75,000	82,500	90,000	97,500	105,000	112,500
	52,000	58,500	65,000	71,500	78,000	84,500	91,000	97,500
	32,000	36,000	40,000	44,000	48,000	52,000	56,000	60,000
	150,000	150,000	150,000	150,000	150,000	150,000	150,000	150,000
	385,750	408,768	430,352	450,502	469,219	486,502	502,352	516,768
	761,130	800,832	824,048	830,778	821,021	794,778	752,048	692,832

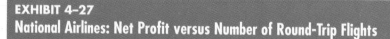

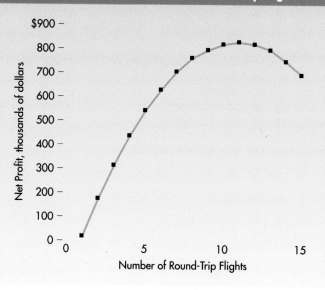

Number of Round-Trip Flights

A SUMMARY EXAMPLE

Let's consider some of this chapter's key points by working through 2 problems.

1. Bob's Barber Shop offers 2 types of haircuts, regular and special. Bob employs 10 full-time hairdressers who work 8 hours on Saturdays and Sundays and 6 hours on Tuesdays, Wednesdays, Thursdays, and Fridays. The shop is closed on Mondays. Average weekly wages, including fringe benefits, are $400 per week. If the workload on any day exceeds the available staff time, however, some hairdressers are asked to work overtime. Overtime wage rate is $15 per hour. Each regular haircut takes 30 minutes, and each special takes 60 minutes.

The following information pertains to the expected demand for the two types of haircuts:

Day	Regular	Special
Each weekday (except Monday)	44	25
Saturday	56	45
Sunday	60	59

(a) Determine the idle time (in terms of hairdresser labor hours) or overtime that is expected each day.
(b) Determine the total weekly hairdresser labor costs to service the expected demand with the present staffing levels.
(c) Determine the staffing levels that will minimize the labor cost for servicing the expected demand, assuming that the shop will remain

closed on Monday, but the number of full-time hairdressers (working 40 hours per week) can be changed, and the number of hours assigned to each day can also be changed (although it must add up to 40 hours per week per hairdresser).

2. Tony's Pizza delivers 12-inch pepperoni pizzas for phoned-in orders. Each pizza sells for $10. The manager, Tony Pena, has projected the following costs corresponding to sales of 10,000 and 12,000 pizzas for the next month's operation:

Cost Items	Sales Levels	
	10,000 Pizzas	12,000 Pizzas
Dough	$ 4,000	$ 4,800
Toppings	2,500	3,000
Cheese	4,500	5,400
Tomatoes	3,000	3,600
Energy	4,000	4,500
Kitchen personnel	3,000	3,000
Delivery personnel	2,200	2,640
Car expenses	3,500	3,800
Facilities	10,000	10,000
Advertisement	4,500	4,500
Total costs	$41,200	$45,240

(a) Classify these costs as variable, fixed, or mixed. Express each item in terms of a cost equation in the form $C = F + VQ$.
(b) Determine the contribution margin per pizza.
(c) Determine the breakeven sales level (in number of pizzas).
(d) Determine the sales level (in number of pizzas) that will generate a profit of $9,000 for the first month.

The following are the solutions to these 2 problems.

1. (a)

Day	Hours Available	Hours Required	Idle Hours	Overtime Hours
Each weekday (except Monday)	60 (10 * 6)	47 (44 * 0.5 + 25)	13	0
Saturday	80 (10 * 8)	73 (56 * 0.5 + 45)	7	0
Sunday	80 (10 * 8)	92 (66 * 0.5 + 59)	0	12

(b) Regular wages $4,000   ($400 * 10)
     Overtime costs   180   ($15 * 12)

     Total weekly labor costs $4,180

(c) Expected total demand: 353 (47 * 4 + 73 + 92) hours
     Full-time equivalents: 8.825 (353/40) hairdressers
     (Full-time equivalents are determined based on the regular work time of 40 hours per worker).

Overtime wages at $15/hour will exceed the weekly wages ($400) of an additional hairdresser if the number of overtime hours exceeds 26.667 ($400/$15), or equivalently overtime exceeds 0.667 ($26.67/$40) full-time equivalent hairdressers. Because 0.825 is larger than 0.667, Bob is better off hiring the additional 9th hairdresser. Therefore, he should hire 9 full-time hairdressers to minimize the labor cost to service the expected demand.

2. (a)

Item	Cost type	F	V
Dough	Variable	$-0-	$0.40
Toppings	Variable	-0-	0.25
Cheese	Variable	-0-	0.45
Tomatoes	Variable	-0-	0.30
Energy	Mixed	1,500[a]	0.25[b]
Kitchen personnel	Fixed	3,000	-0-
Delivery personnel	Variable	-0-	2.20
Car expenses	Mixed	2,000[c]	0.15[d]
Facilities	Fixed	10,000	-0-
Advertisement	Fixed	4,500	-0-
Total		$21,000	$4.00

[a] $4,500 − $0.25 * 12,000 = $1,500
[b] ($4,500 − 4,000)/(12,000 − 10,000) = $0.25
[c] $3,800 − $0.15 * 12,000 = $2,000
[d] ($3,800 − 3,500)/(12,000 − 10,000) = $0.15

(b) Contribution margin per pizza
= $10 − $4
= $6

(c) Let X be the number of pizzas to break even:
$6 * X − $21,000 = 0

$$X = \frac{21,000}{6} = 3,500 \text{ pizzas}$$

(d) Let X be the number of pizzas that will generate a profit of $9,000.
$9,000 = $6 * X − $21,000

$$X = \frac{21,000 + 9,000}{6} = 5,000 \text{ pizzas}$$

SUMMARY

Managers need to understand the behavior of costs so that they can estimate the impact of their decisions. A number of factors, including the range of activity levels and time frames, influence the way costs behave. The flexibility available to managers in adjusting the amount of activity resources to match the demand placed on them determines the variability of different types of costs.

In hiring personnel to work the machines or support production, managers commit to capacities for performing various production activities. These capacity decisions determine the expenditure for the activities. In contrast, the use of committed resources depends on the actual volume of production.

Understanding the relationships between production, activity use, and expenditure enables managers to develop planning models and perform breakeven analysis. The breakeven point is the production level at which sales revenue exactly equals the fixed and variable costs. Breakeven analysis is useful for evaluating company alternatives and the changes in profitability with changes in production and sales activity levels.

KEY TERM LIST

ASSIGNMENT MATERIAL

QUESTIONS

4–1 Why are a firm's profits more sensitive to demand fluctuations when a high proportion of its costs are fixed?

4–2 "Variable cost per unit remains the same for different levels of production, but fixed cost per unit decreases with increases in production." Do you agree with this statement? Explain.

4–3 How can you reconcile the economist's representation of costs as an inverted S-shaped curve with the accountant's representation of costs as a straight line?

4–4 What is the linear equation representing cost in terms of volume of production? What are each of the components of the equation?

4–5 What is the difference between discretionary and committed costs?

4–6 How does each of the following costs change with *increases* in the volume of production?

   (a) Total variable cost

   (b) Total fixed cost

   (c) Variable cost per unit produced

   (d) Fixed cost per unit produced

4–7 What does the term *relevant range* mean? Why is it important to consider what the relevant range is in individual applications?

4–8 What is the difference between each of these five cost terms: (a) fixed costs, (b) variable costs, (c) mixed costs, (d) step fixed costs, and (e) step variable costs. Illustrate your answer.

4–9 What does the term *contribution margin* per unit mean? How is contribution margin used in cost analysis to support managerial decisions?

4–10 What does the term *breakeven point* mean?

4–11 "Sales force compensation can be a fixed cost or a variable cost." Do you agree with this statement? Explain.

4–12 "Direct costs are always variable costs." Do you agree with this statement? Explain.

4–13 Why is unit-related overhead likely to be considered a variable cost?

4–14 Why is facility-sustaining overhead likely to be considered a fixed cost?

4–15 What is the difference between step fixed and step variable cost? Give an example of each type of costs.

4–16 "Presence of idle time and overtime indicates that direct labor is not a variable cost in the short run." Do you agree with this statement?

4–17 Activity resources are committed in advance, leading to idle time or overtime when the demand placed on activity resources is *realized*. When is the average cost of the activity the lowest in these circumstances?

4–18 Why are activity costs more likely to be variable when managers have greater flexibility in adjusting the level of resources committed for the activity?

4–19 Why is there often a delay before activity resources are adjusted downward in response to a permanent decline in the demand placed on them?

4–20 "Activity-based costs measuring the demand placed on activity resources are not good measures to help when budgeting for related activity expenses." Do you agree with this statement? Explain.

EXERCISES

4–21 Classify each of the following as a variable, fixed, or mixed cost.
   (a) Salaries of production supervisors
   (b) Salaries of production workers
   (c) Salary of the chief executive officer
   (d) Charges for janitorial services
   (e) Commissions paid to sales personnel
   (f) Advertising expenses
   (g) Salaries of billing clerks
   (h) Electricity used to operate machines
   (i) Lubricants for machines
   (j) Maintenance for machines

4–22 Classify each of the following as a variable, fixed, or mixed cost.
   (a) Paper used in newspaper production

(b) Steel used in automobile production

(c) Wood used in furniture production

(d) Glue used in furniture production

(e) Depreciation of factory equipment

(f) Depreciation of shipping truck

(g) Gasoline used to deliver products

(h) Boxes used for packing products

(i) Rent for factory building

(j) Factory insurance

4–23 The Metropolitan Museum of Art in New York is organizing a special 5-week exhibition of a collection of Henri Matisse's work. Insurance, security, utilities, and other facility-related costs total $20,000 per day. Costs of setting up the exhibit and transporting the works of art are $350,000. The museum expects an average of 6,000 visitors a day to view this exhibit. Determine the amount the museum must charge each patron to break even.

4–24 Packer Parkas Company budgets sales revenues at $900,000, variable costs at $585,000, and fixed costs at $140,000 for the year 1995.

REQUIRED:

(a) What is Packer's contribution margin *ratio*?

(b) Determine the sales revenue it must generate to break even.

(c) Determine the sales revenue required to earn (pre-tax) income equal to 20% revenue.

(d) Packer is considering increasing its advertising expenses by $38,500. How much of an increase in sales is necessary from expanded advertising to justify this expenditure?

4–25 Omega Corporation uses the following overhead equation based only on direct labor hours (*DLH*):

$$\text{Overhead} = \$800{,}000 + \$40 * DLH$$

A consultant has developed the following alternative overhead equation that recognizes machine-hours (*MH*) also as a cost driver:

$$\text{Overhead} = \$500{,}000 + \$35 * DLH + \$60 * MH$$

Data for 2 recent months include the following:

	February	April
Direct labor hours	7,500	6,000
Machine-hours	5,000	5,500

REQUIRED:

(a) Determine the total overhead costs for the 2 months using the equation based on *DLH*.

(b) Determine the total overhead costs for the 2 months using the new equation.

(c) How did the fixed overhead change in the new equation? Why?

(d) Compare the 2 overhead equations to explain the *direction* of the difference in the estimated costs with these equations.

4–26 The activity costs for Parker's Pizza Shop in March 1995 include the following:

	Cost Driver Quantity	Rate	Total Cost
Dough	1,200 lbs.	$ 0.25	$ 300
Other Ingredients	600 lbs.	0.60	360
Energy	120 kwh.	0.20	24
Kitchen personnel	240 hours	8.00	1,920
Delivery personnel	360 hours	6.00	2,160
Car expenses	2 cars	2,000.00	4,000
Facility expenses	300 sq. ft.	12.00	3,600
Total			$12,364

Parker's Pizza sold 1,200 pizzas in March 1995 at the average price of $11 per pizza.

REQUIRED:

(a) Classify the preceding costs as fixed or variable costs.

(b) Based on your classification of the costs, determine the values for F and V in the following cost equation:

$$\text{Total costs} = F + V * \text{Number of pizzas}$$

4–27 Hiawatha Company manufactures 3 products: HW1, HW2, and HW3. Overhead activities include setting up the machines and packing the finished product. The plant employs 5 setup workers and 10 packing workers. Each worker can work up to 40 hours a week. However, overtime work is performed, if necessary, to meet actual work load demand.

The average hourly wages are $20, including fringe benefits. Overtime premium is 50% of regular wages. Demand for setup and packing labor varies by the type of product produced. Detailed data for each product include the following:

Product	Hours per Setup	Batch Size	Units Packed per Hour
HW1	2	5,000	2,000
HW2	3	20,000	5,000
HW3	4	25,000	2,000

The actual production data for the first two weeks of January 1995 follow:

	Units Manufactured	
Product	Week 1	Week 2
HW1	100,000	120,000
HW2	600,000	400,000
HW3	500,000	500,000

REQUIRED:

(a) Prepare a schedule of actual costs of the 2 support activities for the first 2 weeks of January 1995.

(b) Compare the actual average costs of the support activities with their normal costs.

4–28 Jeren Company is considering replacing its existing cutting machine with a new machine that will help reduce its defect rate. Relevant information for the two machines includes the following:

	Existing Machine	New Machine
Monthly fixed costs	$32,000	$40,000
Variable cost per unit	44	40
Sales price per unit	55	55

REQUIRED:

(a) Determine the sales level, in number of units, at which the costs are the same for both machines.

(b) Determine the sales level in dollars at which the use of the new machine results in a 10% profit on sales (Profit/Sales) ratio.

(c) Determine the sales level in dollars at which the profit on sales ratio is the same with either machine.

4–29 Second City Airlines operates 35 scheduled round-trip flights between New York and Chicago each week. It charges a fixed one-way fare of $140 per passenger. Second City Airlines can carry 150 passengers per flight. Fuel and other flight-related costs are $5,000 per flight. On-flight meal costs are $5 per passenger. Sales commission averaging 5% of sales is paid to travel agents. Flying crew, ground crew, advertising, and other administrative expenditures for the New York–Chicago route amount to $400,000 each week.

REQUIRED:

(a) How many passengers must each of the 70 one-way flights have, on average, to make a total profit of $180,000?

(b) If the load factor is 60% on all flights, how many flights must Second City Airlines operate on this route to earn a total profit of $80,000?

(c) Are fuel costs variable or fixed?

4–30 Extel Corporation's Wedmark, California, plant manufactures chips used in PC486 computers. Its installed capacity is 2,000 chips per week. The selling price is $100 per chip. Production this quarter is 1,600 chips per week. Total costs of production this week (at 80% of capacity level) comprise $75,000 of fixed costs and $80,000 of variable costs.

REQUIRED:

(a) At what level of activity will the plant break even?

(b) What will the plant's profit be if it operates at capacity?

(c) If the plant's accounting system reports fixed cost per unit using its installed capacity level as the base, what is the reported cost per unit?

(d) Suppose that a new customer offers $80 per chip for an order of 200 chips per week for delivery beginning this quarter. If this order is accepted, production will increase from 1,600 chips at present to 1,800 chips per week. Should the company accept the order?

4–31 Seattle Sonic Company has recently developed a new product, SUPER79. It is debating whether to (1) establish its own distribution network or (2) engage independent sales agents to market the new product.

The information pertaining to the two options includes the following:

	Establish Own Network	Engage Sales Agents
Sales commission	5%	20%
Annual fixed selling expenses	$300,000	–0–

The selling price of SUPER79 is targeted to be $20 per unit. Unit variable manufacturing cost is $9 and fixed manufacturing cost will be $900,000.

REQUIRED:

(a) Determine Seattle Sonic Company's estimated breakeven point for its SUPER79 operations under each of the 2 options for marketing the product.

(b) Which of the 2 options should Seattle Sonic Company adopt to market SUPER79? Why?

PROBLEMS

4–32 Magnolia Medical Institute operates a 100-bed hospital and offers a number of specialized medical services. Because of the reputation Magnolia has developed over the years, demand for these services is strong. Magnolia's hospital facility and equipment are leased on a long-term basis.

The hospital charges $100 per patient-day. During November 1994, the total service volume at the hospital was measured as 2,000 patient-days. During December 1994, the service volume was 2,200 patient-days. Costs for November and December follow:

Month	November	December
Number of Patient-Days	2,000	2,200
Costs		
Wages, nurses	$ 29,400	$ 32,340
Wages, aides	11,400	12,240
Laboratory	17,600	18,860
Pharmacy	25,000	27,500
Laundry	17,000	18,700
Administration	22,000	22,000
Facility and equipment	60,000	60,000
Total costs	$182,400	$191,640

Magnolia Medical Clinic estimates the cost of each of these activities by using a linear equation of this form: Cost = $F + V *$ Number of patient-days.

REQUIRED:

(a) Classify each cost as fixed, variable, or mixed.

(b) Determine the values of the parameters F and V for each of the 7 activities.

(c) The hospital's administrator has estimated that the hospital will average 2,200 patient-days per month. How much will the hospital need to charge per patient-day to break even at this level of activity?

4–33 Premier Products, Inc., is considering replacing its existing machine with a new faster machine that will produce a more reliable product and will turn around customer orders in a shorter period. This change is expected to increase the sales price and fixed costs but not the variable costs.

	Old Machine	New Machine
Monthly fixed costs	$120,000	$250,000
Variable cost per unit	14	14
Sales price per unit	18	20

REQUIRED:

(a) Determine the breakeven point *in units* for the 2 machines.

(b) Determine the sales level (in units) at which the use of the *new* machine will achieve a 10% target profit on sales ratio (Profit/Sales).

(c) Determine the sales level (in units) at which profits will be the same for either the old of the new machine.

(d) Which machine represents a lower risk of incurring a loss? Explain why.

(e) Determine the sales level (in units) at which the profit on sales ratio will be equal with either machine.

4–34 Alpha Corporation and Beta Corporation compete directly against each other, selling the same product of identical quality but employing different manufacturing processes and selling methods. The estimated costs and prices for the 2 firms follow:

	Alpha Corporation	Beta Corporation
Sales price per unit	$9.00	$8.00
Direct materials per unit	$1.90	$2.25
Direct labor per unit	$1.25	$2.40
Variable manufacturing overhead per unit	$1.10	$1.15
Fixed manufacturing overhead	$675,000	$450,000
Advertising and fixed selling costs	$350,000	$400,000
Sales commission	4% of price	——
Sales units, number	350,000	$400,000
Capacity units, number	500,000	$400,000

REQUIRED:

(a) Determine the estimated breakeven points in annual sales units for the 2 firms.

(b) Determine the annual sales volume at which the 2 firms have the same manufacturing costs. Explain the circumstances under which 1 of the 2 firms enjoys a competitive cost advantage.

(c) How long can Alpha Corporation price its product and still break even, assuming that its sales volume stays at its existing level?

(d) Recommend a coherent competitive strategy for Alpha Corporation. Explain your answer, critically evaluating Alpha's current strategy.

4–35 In September 1994, Capetini Capacitor Company sold capacitors to its distributors for $250 per capacitor. The sales level of 3,000 capacitors per month was less than the *single-shift* capacity of 4,400 capacitors at its plant located in San Diego, California. Variable production costs were $100 per capacitor, and fixed production costs were $200,000 per month. In addition, variable selling and distribution overhead costs are $20 per capacitor and fixed selling and distribution overhead are $62,500 per month.

At the suggestion of the marketing department, Capetini reduced the sales price to $200 in October 1994 and increased the monthly advertising budget by $17,500. Sales are expected to increase to 6,800 capacitors per month. If the demand exceeds the single-shift capacity of 4,400 capacitors, the plant needs to be operated for 2 shifts. Two-shift operation will increase monthly fixed production costs to $310,000.

REQUIRED:

(a) Determine the contribution margin per capacitor in September 1994.

(b) Determine the sales level, in number of capacitors, at which the profit on sales ratio (Profit/Sales) would be 10%.

(c) Determine the 2 breakeven points for October 1994.

(d) Determine the sales level, in number of capacitors, at which the *profit on sales* ratio in October is the same as the actual *profit on sales* ratio in September. Is there more than 1 possible sales level at which this equality would occur?

4–36 The billing department of Union Credit Card Company in Wilmington, Delaware, employs 20 workers on a weekly basis. They are each paid $600 for 40 hours per week. Each worker can handle 12 billings per hour, on average. If the number of billings requires more than the available number of labor hours, overtime work is scheduled. A 50% overtime premium is paid in addition to regular wage. Workload information for the first 8 weeks of 1995 follows:

Week	Number of Billings
1	10,080
2	9,060
3	11,240
4	8,320
5	12,720
6	10,220
7	9,880
8	8,790

REQUIRED:

(a) Determine the normal unit cost per billing.

(b) Graph the total billing costs as a function of the number of billings for the first 8 weeks of operation in 1995.

(c) Graph the average cost per billing as a function of the number of billings for the first 8 weeks of operation in 1995.

4–37 Crown Cable Company provides cable television service in the Richfield metropolitan area. The company hires only full-time service persons working 40 hours a week at $18 per hour, including fringe benefits. Service persons handle additional service demand by working overtime, at the rate of $24 per hour. The service manager uses standards for estimating the work load and staffing requirements. Each service person can handle an average of 6 calls in an 8-hour work day. The estimated number of service calls for the first 3 weeks of October 1994 follow:

Week	Service Calls
1	1,280
2	1,340
3	1,200

(a) Determine the number of service persons that will be hired in each of these 3 weeks to minimize costs.

(b) Estimate the service labor cost for each of the 3 weeks.

(c) Suppose that the company cannot change the staffing level from week to week. Estimate the service labor costs assuming that the same number (38, 39, 40, 41, 42, 43, 44, or 45) of workers is hired for all 3 weeks. How much do costs increase under this restriction?

4–38 Tenneco, Inc., produces 3 models of tennis rackets: standard, deluxe, and pro. Sales and cost information for 1994 follows:

	Standard	Deluxe	Pro
Sales (units)	100,000	50,000	50,000
Sales price per unit	$30	$40	$50
Variable manufacturing cost per unit	$17	$20	$25

Fixed factory overhead is $800,000, and fixed selling and administrative costs are $400,000. In addition, the company pays its sales representatives a commission equal to 10% of the price of each racket sold.

REQUIRED:

(a) If the sales price of deluxe rackets decreases by 10%, its sales are expected to increase 30%, but sales of standard rackets are expected to decrease by 5% as some potential buyers of standard rackets will upgrade to deluxe rackets. What will be the impact of this decision on Tenneco's profits?

(b) Suppose that Tenneco decides to increase its advertising by $50,000 instead of cutting the price of standard rackets. This is expected to increase sales of all 3 models by 2% each. Is this decision advisable?

(c) The incentive created by sales commissions has led Tenneco's sales force to push the higher-priced rackets more than the lower-priced ones. Is this in the best interest of the company?

4–39 The following information pertains to Torasic Company's budgeted income statement for the month of June 1995:

Sales (1,200 units @ $200)	$240,000
Variable cost	120,000
Contribution margin	$120,000
Fixed cost	140,000
Net loss	($20,000)

REQUIRED:

(a) Determine the company's breakeven point in both units and dollars.

(b) The sales manager believes that a $20,000 increase in the monthly advertising expenses will result in a considerable increase in sales. How much of an increase in sales must result from increased advertising to justify this expenditure?

(c) The sales manager believes that an advertising expenditure increase of $20,000, coupled with a 10% reduction in the selling price, will double the sales quantity. Determine the net income (or loss) if these proposed changes are adopted.

4–40 Classic Containers Company specializes in making high-quality customized containers to order. Its agreement with the labor union ensures employment for all its employees and a fixed payroll of $80,000 per month, including fringe benefits. This payroll makes available 4,000 labor hours each month to work on orders the firm receives. The monthly wages must be paid even if the workers remain idle due to lack of work. If additional labor hours are required to complete jobs, overtime costs $30 per labor hour.

Each job requires 4 labor hours for machine setup and 0.05 labor hours per container. Variable costs comprise $1.60 per container for materials and $8.00 per labor hour for support expenses (energy, maintenance, and so forth). In addition, the firm must pay $20,000 per month for selling, general, and administrative expenses and $36,000 per month lease payments for machinery and physical facilities.

In April 1995, the firm won 90 orders, of which 60 were for 800 containers each and 30 were for 1,600 containers each. Determine the total costs for April.

4-41 Rochester Medical Clinic is a county-owned facility that provides outpatient services to the residents of Rochester county 5 days a week. It formerly employed 8 full-time nurses and 15 full-time aides in annual contracts. Average wages have remained at $500 and $300 per week in the past 2 years for nurses and aides, respectively. Because of recent budget cuts, clinic management has cut back 2 nurse and 3 aide positions. It employs temporary workers in months when higher work loads are anticipated.

Each patient must be serviced by both a nurse and an aide. On average, a regular nurse can service 20 outpatients *in a day*. Each outpatient visit also requires aides' service time. Each regular aide can service on average 10 outpatients *in a day*. Temporary workers are paid the same average daily wages as regular nurses and aides, but they are not as efficient. They can service on average 20% fewer outpatients than regular workers.

The following information pertains to the first 3 months of 1995:

| Month | Regular Personnel | | Temporary Personnel | | Average Patient Visits Per Day |
	Nurses	Aides	Nurses	Aides	
January	6	12	1	2	130
February	6	12	–0–	–0–	120
March	6	12	2	4	145

Determine the normal and actual cost per patient visit for each month.

4-42 Air Peanut Company manufactures and sells roasted peanut packets to commercial airlines. Price and cost data regarding Air Peanut's operations follow:

Costs per 100 packets
Selling price $35.00
Variable cost
  Raw materials $16.00
  Direct labor   7.00
  Manufacturing overhead   4.00
  Selling expenses   1.60
  Total variable costs per unit $28.60

Annual fixed costs	
Manufacturing overhead	$192,000
Selling and administrative	276,000
Total fixed costs	$468,000
Estimated annual sales volume	985,000 packets

REQUIRED:

(a) Determine Air Peanut's breakeven point.

(b) How many packets does Air Peanut have to sell to earn $156,000 before taxes?

(c) Air Peanut expects its direct labor costs to increase by 5% next year. How many units will it have to sell next year to break even if the selling price remains unchanged?

(d) If Air Peanut's direct labor costs increase by 5%, what selling price must it charge to maintain the same contribution margin to sales ratio?

CASES

4–43 Dr. Barbara Barker is the head of the pathology laboratory at Barrington Medical Center in Mobile, Alabama. Dr. Barker estimates the amount of work for her laboratory staff by classifying the pathology tests into 3 categories: simple-routine, simple-nonroutine, and complex. She expects a simple-routine test to require 2 hours, a simple-nonroutine test to require 2.5 hours, and a complex test to require 4 hours of staff time. She estimates the demand for each of the 3 types of tests for June through August to be the following:

	Simple-Routine	Simple-Nonroutine	Complex
June	800	250	450
July	600	200	400
August	750	225	450

Laboratory staff salaries, including fringe benefits, average $3,600 per month. Each worker works 150 hours per month. If the hospital work load exceeds the available staff time, Dr. Barker has the tests performed at a neighboring private pathology laboratory that charges $80 for a simple-routine test, $100 for a simple-nonroutine test, and $160 for a complex test.

Dr. Barker is thinking of employing 20 to 27 workers. Because of the difficulty in hiring reliable workers, Barrington's chief administrator has instructed her to employ laboratory staff for at least 1 quarter.

REQUIRED:

(a) Determine how many workers Dr. Barker should employ to minimize the costs of performing the tests. What is the minimum cost?

(b) Suppose the easy availability of experienced laboratory staff allows Barrington Medical Center to change staffing loads each month.

Determine the number of workers Dr. Barker should hire each month in these circumstances. What is the minimum cost?

4–44 Steelmax, Inc., sells office furniture in the Chicago metropolitan area. To better serve its business customers, Steelmax recently introduced a new same-day service. Any order placed before 2 p.m. is delivered the same day.

Steelmax hires 5 workers on an 8-hour daily shift to deliver the office furniture. Each delivery takes 30 minutes on average. If the number of customer orders exceeds the available capacity on some days, workers are asked to work overtime to ensure that all customer orders are delivered the same day. Regular wages are $12 per hour. Overtime wages include a 50% premium in addition to the regular wages.

The Steelmax management has noticed considerable fluctuation in the number of customer orders from day to day over the last 3 months, as shown here:

Day of the Week	Average Number of Orders
Monday	65
Tuesday	70
Wednesday	80
Thursday	85
Friday	95

Steelmax has now decided to pursue a more flexible hiring policy. It will reduce the number of delivery workers to 4 on Mondays and Tuesdays and increase the number to 6 on Fridays.

REQUIRED:

(a) Determine the total and unit delivery cost when the number of daily customer orders is 70, 80, or 90.

(b) Determine the expected total delivery cost per day and the expected delivery cost per customer order based on both the old and the new hiring policy. What is the expected value per week of the new flexible hiring policy?

4–45 Over the past 15 years, Anthony's Autoshop has developed a reputation for reliable repairs and has grown from a 1-man operation to having a manager and 8 skilled auto mechanics. In recent years, however, competition from mass merchandisers has eroded business volume and profits, leading the owner, Anthony Axle, to ask his manager to take a closer look at the cost structure of the autoshop.

The manager determined that direct materials (parts and components) are identified with individual jobs and charged directly to the customer. Direct labor (mechanics) also is identified with individual jobs and charged at a prespecified rate to the customers. The salary and benefits for a senior mechanic are $65,000 per year; for a junior mechanic, they are $45,000 per year. Each mechanic can work up to 1,750 hours in a year on customer jobs, but if there are not enough jobs to keep each of them busy, the cost of their compensation still will have to be incurred. The manager's salary and benefits amount to $75,000 per year. In addition, the following fixed costs are also incurred each year:

Rent	$36,000
Insurance	6,000
Utilities	6,000
Supplies	9,000
Machine maintenance	18,000
Machine depreciation	21,800
	$96,800

Because material costs are recovered directly from the customers, the profitability of the operation depends on the volume of business and the hourly rate charged for labor. At present, Anthony's Autoshop charges $51.06 per hour for all its jobs. Mr. Axle said he would not consider firing any of the 4 senior mechanics because he believes it is difficult to get workers with their skills and loyalty to the firm, but he is willing to consider releasing 1 or 2 of the junior mechanics.

REQUIRED:

(a) Determine the total fixed costs, including personnel costs, for each of the following 3 staffing levels:

	Senior Mechanics	Junior Mechanics
Option X	4	4
Option Y	4	3
Option Z	4	2

(b) What is the contribution margin per hour worked on customer jobs?

(c) Determine the *minimum* number of hours that must be charged to customer jobs for the autoshop to earn an annual profit of $50,000.

(d) Determine the *minimum* number of hours that must be charged to customer jobs for the autoshop to earn an annual profit equal to 10% of labor billing revenues (excluding charges for parts).

(e) Business is expected to increase if 1 more senior mechanic is hired. How much new business (in terms of hours charged to customer jobs) must be generated to justify adding a fifth senior mechanic?

BUDGETING FOR OPERATIONS

LEARNING OBJECTIVES

This chapter will introduce you to:

1. the role of budgets and budgeting in organizations
2. the elements of the budgeting process and the importance of each
3. the different types of operating budgets and financial budgets, their interrelationships, and their components
4. the way organizations use and interpret budgets
5. what-if and sensitivity analysis—2 important budgeting tools
6. the types of analyses used by budget planners
7. the role of budgets in service and not-for-profit organizations

CHAPTER 5

Fred Powell and the Legal Services Department: The Dilemma

Fred Powell, the manager of the Legal Services Department, was in trouble and he knew it. The Legal Services Department, a government department, provides legal advice to other government departments and agencies. The government, facing increasing pressures to reduce its deficit and unable to increase taxes, was engaging in continuing rounds of budget cuts. Last year all departments had their allocations cut by 7%; this year it was 5%, and Fred expected the trend to continue.

In the face of these funding cuts, the Legal Services Department was experiencing continuous increases in the demand for legal services. The funding cuts, combined with the increasing pressure on the remaining resources, were creating enormous pressures in the Legal Services Department. These pressures were now prompting resignations within the department and, because of the job stress created by chronic underfunding, Fred was starting to lose long-term employees whom he valued. He knew he had to do something but wondered if he was powerless in a world in which he controlled neither the allocations of funds nor the rate of demand on his department.

Like most managers, Fred Powers found himself in a position that required a systematic and comprehensive approach to planning, which is the topic of this chapter.

(© Bob Daemmrich/Stock Boston, Inc.)

Recall that in Chapter 2 we introduced the concept of the organization as a sequence of activities or value chain. We saw that the requirements of the organization's customers define the focus of the organization's value chain and that the requirements of the organization's other stakeholders define the characteristics, or constraints, that the design of the sequence of activities that the organization uses to make its products must meet. We also saw that cost is one of the important elements that characterize the performance of a sequence of activities.[1]

In Chapters 3 and 4, we began our study of costs by considering basic cost concepts and describing cost variability by discussing some fundamental cost behavior patterns. In this chapter, we use these definitions of cost and ideas about cost behavior to develop and summarize organization plans that management accountants call *budgets*.

There are actually two types of budgets: (1) operating budgets, which summarize broad activities such as sales, purchasing, and production and (2) financial budgets, such as a balance sheet, income statement, and cash flow statement, which identify the expected financial consequences of the activities summarized in the operating budgets.

This chapter also considers the way organization planners can use budgets to plan, coordinate, and finance activities and the way they can use budgets, once they have been prepared, to estimate the impact of different information or decisions on the operating and financial budgets.

[1] From the customer's perspective, we argued that the other two important facets are service and quality. Other important facets that are reflected in the design of the sequence of activities are employee considerations, such as job safety and income security; partner and owner considerations, such as profitability; and community considerations, such as social responsibility.

These employees at Bethelehem Steel's Sparrows Point Plant are part of the teams responsible for making many of Bethlehem Steel's important products, including coated sheet steel, tin plate, and steel plate. Producing many products under one roof requires planning and budgeting systems to organize and coordinate all the activities associated with making these products.
(*Courtesy Bethlehem Steel*)

BUDGETS AND BUDGETING

This chapter talks about budgets. **Budgets** are summaries of the expected consequences of the organization's short-term operating activities. For example, an organization might prepare a cash budget to predict its cash inflows and outflows, or it might prepare a production budget to plan its production levels. Budgets reflect many of the organization's important operating facets. Therefore, budgets are a *quantitative*[2] representation or a **model** of the organization.

Budgeting is the process of preparing budgets and requires several important skills, including forecasting, a knowledge of how activities affect costs, and the ability to see how the organization's different activities fit together.

■ The Role of Budgets and Budgeting

Budgets and budgeting serve many purposes. The most important purposes relate, however, to organization planning and control. This chapter focuses on the use of budgets in planning. Organization control includes coordination, problem signaling, and problem-solving activities, which we will discuss in subsequent chapters. Exhibit 5–1 shows the relationship between planning and control and the central role played by budgets. Note that there are dis-

___

[2] Financial budgets are denominated in currency amounts and operating budgets are denominated in unit amounts.

Budgets
A quantitative model, or summary of the expected consequences of the organization's short-term operating activities.

Model
A representation.

Budgeting
The process of preparing budgets.

OBJECTIVE 5.1
The role of budgets and budgeting in organizations

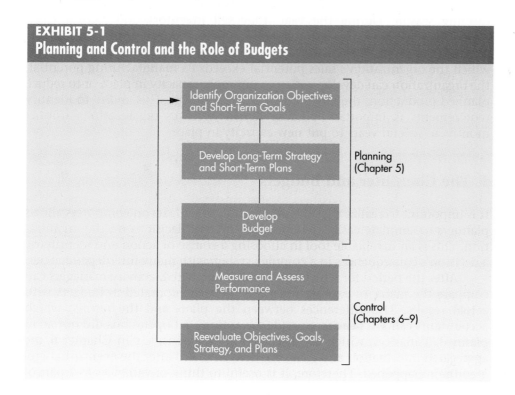

EXHIBIT 5-1
Planning and Control and the Role of Budgets

Identify Organization Objectives and Short-Term Goals

Develop Long-Term Strategy and Short-Term Plans

Develop Budget

Planning (Chapter 5)

Measure and Assess Performance

Reevaluate Objectives, Goals, Strategy, and Plans

Control (Chapters 6–9)

tinct, but linked, steps for each function—3 for planning and 2 for control (which are discussed in Chapters 6 through 9).

Budgets provide a means to *communicate* the organization's short-term goals to its members. By focusing on setting specific and measurable results, budgeting forces the organization to set specific goals. The budgeting activities of organization units provide insights into how well the unit managers understand the organization's goals as well as an opportunity for the organization's senior planners to correct misperceptions about the organization's goals. For example, suppose that an organization recognized quality as a critical success factor and wanted to promote quality awareness. If a department prepared a budget that reflected no expenditures on employee training to enhance quality awareness, a senior planner would recognize that the importance of quality training had not been communicated properly.

Budgeting supports the management functions of planning and coordination by tying the organization's activities together. For example, budgets show the effect of sales levels on acquisition, production, selling, and administrative activities or on the number of employees that have to be hired to serve customers. Therefore, budgeting is a tool that forces coordination of the organization's activities and serves as a means to identify coordination problems. Suppose that, for example, in reacting to market opportunities, the sales force plans to significantly expand sales. By comparing selling plans with manufacturing capacity, planners might discover that the manufacturing operations would be unable to support the planned level of sales.

By considering operating issues and their interrelationships, budgeting provides a means to anticipate problems. In turn, steps can be taken to avoid the problems. For example, organizations that engage in seasonal production, such as canners, must invest large amounts of cash in inventory during the canning season. During the year, they sell inventory and recover cash. Budgeting anticipates this cycle and allows the organization to plan the borrowing needed to finance this cycle. If planning identifies a situation in which the organization's sales potential exceeds its manufacturing potential, the organization can develop a plan to put more capacity in place or to reduce planned production, thereby correcting the problem. This ability to identify requirements is important because it usually takes organizations from 3 months to several years to put new capacity in place.

■ The Computer and Budgets

It is important to realize that the preparation of budgets on computers allows planners to simulate easily the effect of different decisions on the organization. This is an invaluable tool in choosing a course of action and identifying a decision's consequences in a complex system with many interdependencies.

After the period for which the budget is prepared, activity managers can compare the plans, or expectations, that were incorporated in budgets with actual results. The differences between the plans and the results, which accountants call **variances**, provide a warning that operations did not go as planned. Variances, which are discussed more extensively in Chapter 6, are aggregated information and often are delivered well after the events that created them happened. Therefore, it is useful to think of variances as a part of

Variance
The difference between a plan, or target, and a result. Variances provide a warning that operations did not go as planned.

a larger system that monitors results. Other more timely systems, such as rate of production, number of defects, or types of problems being experienced, provide information that helps employees detect and correct problems as they arise.

Because variances are not timely and reflect aggregated information, supervisory staff, often use them as an overall check on how well the people who are managing the day-to-day operations are discharging their responsibilities, the effectiveness of the control systems that operations people are using, and the organization's effectiveness relative to other organizations. We will develop these ideas in more detail in Chapter 11.

THE BUDGETING PROCESS

Exhibit 5–2 summarizes the elements of the budgeting process. The arrow from the projected financial statements (box 12) and statement of expected cash flows (box 11) back to the organization goals (box 1) reflects the evaluation of the *financial consequences*[3] of the organization's tentative budgets. This

---

[3] Operating decisions have many nonfinancial consequences, such as quality and service to customers, that budgets ignore (other than in their effects on sales and costs).

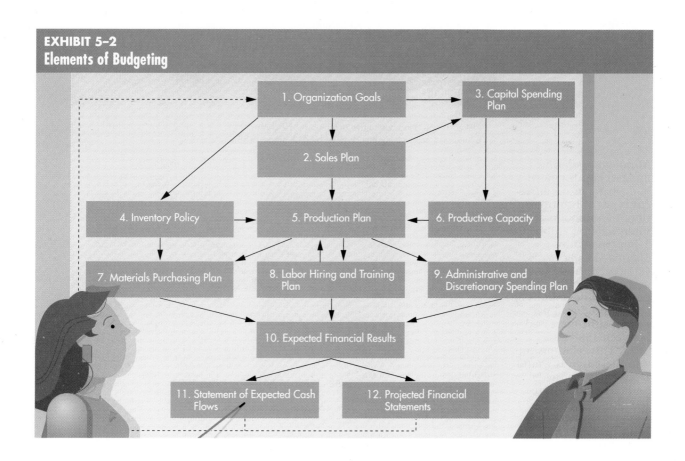

EXHIBIT 5–2
Elements of Budgeting

1. Organization Goals
2. Sales Plan
3. Capital Spending Plan
4. Inventory Policy
5. Production Plan
6. Productive Capacity
7. Materials Purchasing Plan
8. Labor Hiring and Training Plan
9. Administrative and Discretionary Spending Plan
10. Expected Financial Results
11. Statement of Expected Cash Flows
12. Projected Financial Statements

arrow shows that planners compare the projected financial results with the organization's financial goals and reflects the *recursive nature* of the budgeting process. If initial budgets prove infeasible or unacceptable, planners repeat the budgeting cycle with a new set of decisions until they find results that are feasible and financially acceptable.

The budgeting process describes the broad activities performed during the budget period. Planners can choose any budget period, but they usually choose 1 year, which we will assume in the following discussion.

MASTER BUDGET OUTPUTS

OBJECTIVE 5.2
The elements of the budgeting process and the importance of each

The master budget, the budget step 1 (box 3) in Exhibit 5–1, includes two sets of outputs that make up Exhibit 5–2 and summarize the organization's planned activities during the budget period: (1) the plans, or operating budgets, that operating personnel use to guide operations (see boxes 2, 3, 5, 6, 7, 8, and 9 in Exhibit 5–2) and the expected or projected financial results (see boxes 10, 11, and 12 in Exhibit 5–2).[4] Planners usually present the projected financial results, or **financial budgets**, in three forms: (1) a statement of cash inflows (box 11), (2) the projected balance sheet (box 12), and (3) the projected income statement (box 12). Items (2) and (3) are generally called the *projected*, or **pro forma**, financial statements.

Financial budget
A budget that summarizes the expected financial results from the chosen operating plans.

Pro forma statement
A forecasted or estimated statement.

[4] Boxes 1 and 4 in Exhibit 5–2 are derived from the organization's goals and plans, which are shown as the first two boxes in Exhibit 5–1.

Although operating budgets and financial budgets focus on different types of information, the numbers are interrelated. Exhibit 5–3, prepared by Magma Copper Company, shows how cost per pound of copper fell while pounds of copper produced per person-shift increased between 1988 and 1992. This relationship and these trends would be reflected in the labor and cost budgets prepared by Magma Copper planners. *Source: Magma Copper Company Promotional Brochure.*

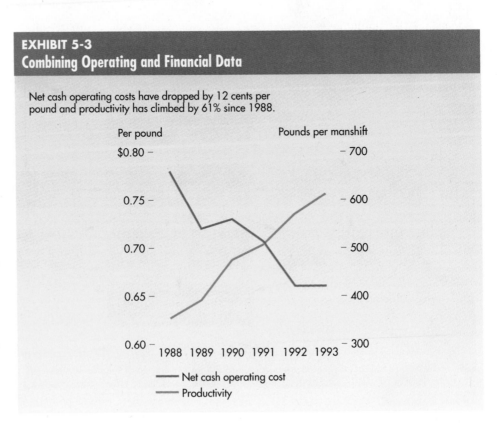

EXHIBIT 5-3
Combining Operating and Financial Data

Net cash operating costs have dropped by 12 cents per pound and productivity has climbed by 61% since 1988.

—— Net cash operating cost
—— Productivity

■ Operating Budgets

The operating budgets, or operating plans, include the following:

1. The **sales plan** (box 2 in Exhibit 5–2), which identifies the planned level of sales for each product
2. The **capital spending plan** (box 3 in Exhibit 5–2), which specifies when long-term capital investments such as buildings and equipment must be made to meet activity objectives
3. The **production plan** (box 5 in Exhibit 5–2), which schedules all required production[5]
4. The **materials purchasing plan** (box 7 in Exhibit 5–2), which schedules all required purchasing activities
5. The **labor hiring and training plan** (box 8 in Exhibit 5–2), which schedules the number, hiring, and training of people that the organization must hire, or release, to achieve its activity objectives
6. The **administrative and discretionary spending plan** (box 9 in Exhibit 5–2), which includes staffing, research and development, and advertising plans

Operating budgets specify the expected outcomes of any selling, capital spending, manufacturing, purchasing, labor management, and administrative activities during the planning period. Operations personnel use these plans to guide and coordinate activities during the planning period. (See Exhibit 5–3.)

■ Financial Budgets

Planners use the projected balance sheet and income statement to evaluate the financial consequences of proposed decisions. Financial analysts use the statement of projected cash flows to plan when excess cash will be generated so that they can undertake short-term investments or can organize to meet their cash shortages in the least expensive way.

The budgeting process can be both frustrating and time consuming. Some organizations invest thousands of person-hours over many months to prepare the master budget documents just described. (See Exhibit 5–4.)

THE BUDGETING PROCESS ILLUSTRATED

The following budgeting exercise covers many budgeting elements and illustrates the budgeting process.[6] You should read this section carefully since most of the discussion in this chapter is based on it.

[5] Box 6 indicates the productive capacity, which reflects capacity at the start of the period, plus or minus any additions or deletions made during the period.

[6] To understand the budgeting process, you must go through a budgeting exercise. The example that follows is a compromise between what people really face in practice and what is reasonable for you to consider as you study budgeting for the first time. This example considers most budgeting elements. The additional challenge in practice is to estimate and assimilate much more information into the budgeting process.

OBJECTIVE 5.3
The different types of operating budgets and financial budgets, their interrelationships, and their components

Sales plan
A document that summarizes planned sales for each product.

Capital spending plan
An operating plan that specifies when long-term capital expenditures such as acquisitions for buildings and special-purpose equipment must be made to meet activity objectives.

Production plan
An operating plan that identifies all required production.

Materials purchasing plan
An operating plan that schedules purchasing activities.

Labor hiring and training plan
An operating plan that schedules the hiring, releasing, and training of people that the organization must have to achieve its activity objectives.

Administrative and discretionary spending plan
An operating plan that summarizes administrative and discretionary expenditures.

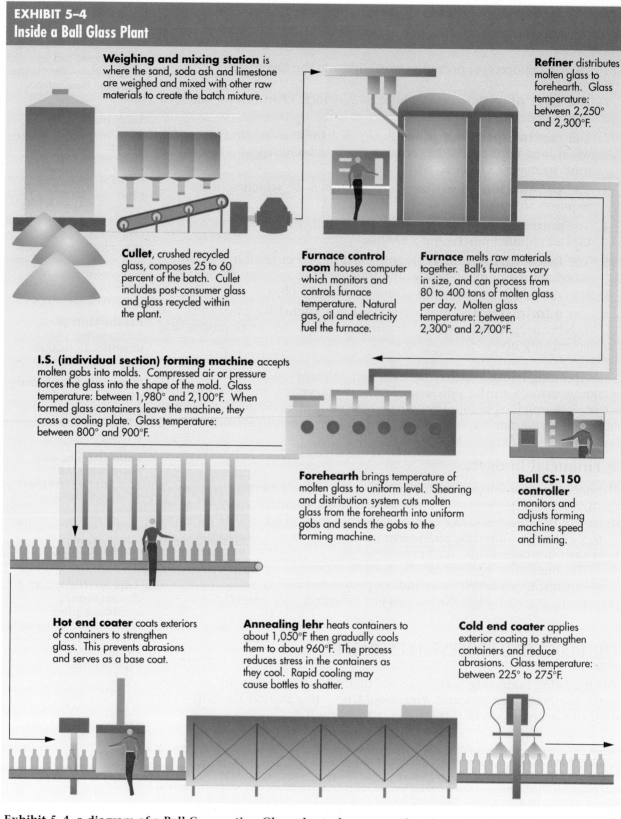

EXHIBIT 5–4
Inside a Ball Glass Plant

Weighing and mixing station is where the sand, soda ash and limestone are weighed and mixed with other raw materials to create the batch mixture.

Refiner distributes molten glass to forehearth. Glass temperature: between 2,250° and 2,300°F.

Cullet, crushed recycled glass, composes 25 to 60 percent of the batch. Cullet includes post-consumer glass and glass recycled within the plant.

Furnace control room houses computer which monitors and controls furnace temperature. Natural gas, oil and electricity fuel the furnace.

Furnace melts raw materials together. Ball's furnaces vary in size, and can process from 80 to 400 tons of molten glass per day. Molten glass temperature: between 2,300° and 2,700°F.

I.S. (individual section) forming machine accepts molten gobs into molds. Compressed air or pressure forces the glass into the shape of the mold. Glass temperature: between 1,980° and 2,100°F. When formed glass containers leave the machine, they cross a cooling plate. Glass temperature: between 800° and 900°F.

Forehearth brings temperature of molten glass to uniform level. Shearing and distribution system cuts molten glass from the forehearth into uniform gobs and sends the gobs to the forming machine.

Ball CS-150 controller monitors and adjusts forming machine speed and timing.

Hot end coater coats exteriors of containers to strengthen glass. This prevents abrasions and serves as a base coat.

Annealing lehr heats containers to about 1,050°F then gradually cools them to about 960°F. The process reduces stress in the containers as they cool. Rapid cooling may cause bottles to shatter.

Cold end coater applies exterior coating to strengthen containers and reduce abrasions. Glass temperature: between 225° to 275°F.

Exhibit 5–4, a diagram of a Ball Corporation Glass plant, shows a product layout designed to produce high volumes of high-quality, low-cost glass bottles. Although this product layout appears straightforward, planners need operating and financial budgets to estimate the operating and financial consequences of their operating plans and to evaluate the implications, both operating and financial, of changing plans. *(The above illustration has been reprinted by permission of Ball Corporation.)*

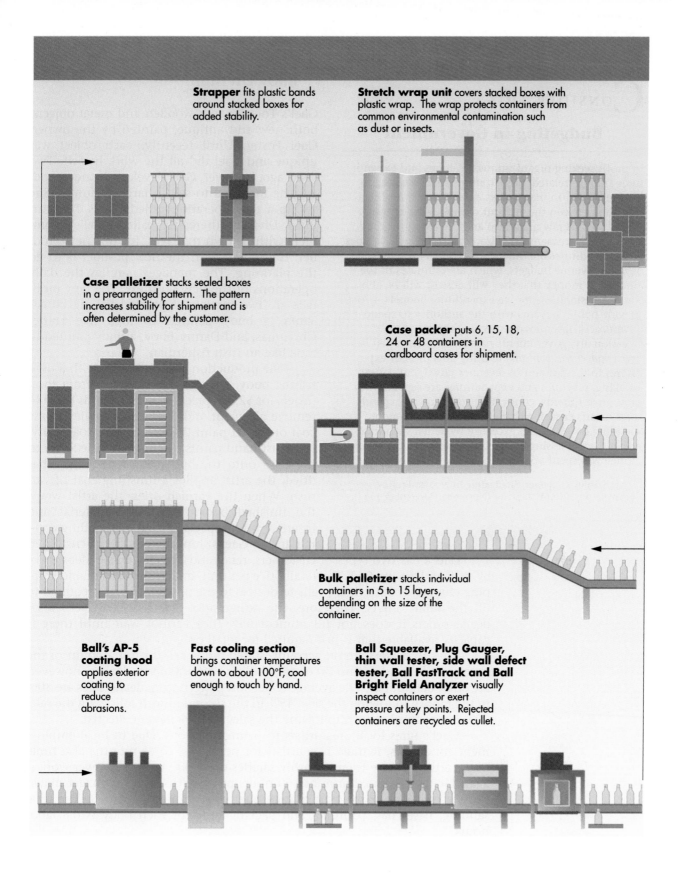

Strapper fits plastic bands around stacked boxes for added stability.

Stretch wrap unit covers stacked boxes with plastic wrap. The wrap protects containers from common environmental contamination such as dust or insects.

Case palletizer stacks sealed boxes in a prearranged pattern. The pattern increases stability for shipment and is often determined by the customer.

Case packer puts 6, 15, 18, 24 or 48 containers in cardboard cases for shipment.

Bulk palletizer stacks individual containers in 5 to 15 layers, depending on the size of the container.

Ball's AP-5 coating hood applies exterior coating to reduce abrasions.

Fast cooling section brings container temperatures down to about 100°F, cool enough to touch by hand.

Ball Squeezer, Plug Gauger, thin wall tester, side wall defect tester, Ball FastTrack and Ball Bright Field Analyzer visually inspect containers or exert pressure at key points. Rejected containers are recycled as cullet.

CONSIDER THIS . . .

Budgeting in Government

In profit-seeking organizations, revenues and expenditures are interrelated; organizations spend money to earn revenues. In many cases, there is a physical relationship between the amount of money spent (on things such as raw materials) and the amount of revenue. In government organizations, however, revenues and expenditures are independent. Governments develop revenue budgets, which are estimates of the amount of money that they will raise or will be allocated. Legislatures approve expenditure budgets, which provide public servants with the authority to spend government revenues on specific projects.

Occasionally, governments pass laws (often called *balanced budget requirements*) limiting government expenditures to the amount of revenues raised, but, strictly speaking, revenues and expenditures are separate. For most governments, controlling government expenditures means ensuring that authorized government spending has not been exceeded by actual spending rather than assessing whether the programs on which money was spent accomplished their objectives.

Source: Stanley C. Beiner, "Budgeting in Not-for-Profit Organizations," *CMA Magazine* (November–December 1987), pp. 20–27.

■ Gael's Tole Art, Buoy Division

Gael's Tole Art sells wooden and metal objects, both new and antique, painted by the owner, Gael Foster. Until recently, each object was unique and Gael did all the work herself. Two years ago, however, Gael developed a new product she intended to sell in larger volumes. She set up a new operation called Gael's Tole Art, Buoy Division (hereafter called Gael's), complete with its own manager, for this new product. Gael's role with the new product is to do the planning. The manager handles the daily operations of the new business. The new products are two models of painted fishing buoys, Santa, a buoy painted to look like Father Christmas, and Danny Buoy, a buoy painted to look like an Irish fisherman.

The production process begins with a used fishing buoy, which Gael purchases from local fishers for $2.25 apiece. The artist sands them to remove old paint and debris and applies a base coat of primer paint. When the base coat is dry, the artist hand paints the image of the Santa or the man onto the buoy. Once the image has dried, the artist applies a finishing coat of varnish. When the varnish dries, the artist wraps the finished buoy in packing material and inserts it into a specially designed mailing container that Gael's ships directly to the customer.

Gael's has two types of customers, retail and dealer. Retail orders arrive by mail and are prepaid. The retail price per unit, including packing and shipping charges, is $80. Gael's sells to dealers to use up capacity not required to fill the retail orders. Therefore, the dealer price is only $55. Gael's loses dealer orders it does not fill immediately; they cannot wait until there is capacity available that is not required for retail orders.

Sales to dealers are on account; stated terms call for full amount of the invoice to be paid within 30 days of billing. Receipts from dealers, however, are often delinquent. The average collection pattern from dealer sales are 30% in the month following the sale, 45% in the second month following the sale, 20% in the third month following the sale, and 5% never collected.

Gael's hires local area artists to paint the buoys. Due to local employment conditions, it must hire artists for periods of three months at a time. These artists receive their monthly salaries of $2,000 to do whatever work is available up to a maximum of 160 hours per month. Gael's manager makes staffing decisions at the start of each quarter beginning January 1. The total sanding, base coat, painting, and packing time for each buoy is 0.8 labor hours.

(Courtesy Anthony Atkinson)

Paint costs $3.15 for each buoy. Other manufacturing costs, including sandpaper, brushes, varnish, and other shop supplies, amounts to $2.75 per buoy. Packing materials cost $1.95 per buoy and shipping by courier costs $7.50 per buoy.

Gael's rents a unit in a local industrial mall where the employees work on the buoys. The lease is for a year and stipulates that rent is to be paid quarterly, in advance. The alternative sizes of available rental units provide the following monthly capacities in buoys: 600, 800, 1,000, and 1,200 and the quarterly rents for each of these units are $3,600, $4,800, $6,000, and $7,200, respectively. All production takes place to order, and Gael's acquires supplies only as needed.

Insurance, heating, lighting, and business taxes cost $20,000 per year; advertising expenses amount to $40,000 per year. Gael pays a manager $30,000 per year to supervise the operation, manage the raw materials acquisitions, handle all the order taking and billing, and do the accounting. All these expenses are incurred, and paid, in equal monthly installments.

Realized sales for October, November, and December of 1995 and forecasted demand for 1996 appear in Exhibit 5–5. Based on this demand forecast,[7] Gael and her manager have decided to rent an 800-capacity unit for 1996 and to hire 2 painters in the 1st quarter, 2 painters in the 2nd quarter, 1 painter in the 3rd quarter, and 3 painters in the 4th quarter.

Gael plans to withdraw $20,000 from the company at the start of each 6-month period to compensate her for her time. She maintains all the firm's

[7] We distinguish between a demand forecast, which is an estimate of the sales potential in a given market, and a sales plan, which is a forecast of the sales sought and planned in that market. Clearly, the numbers in the sales plan cannot exceed the numbers in the demand forecast.

EXHIBIT 5–5
Gael's Tole Art: Forecasted Unit Demand, 1995–1996

MONTH	TYPE OF DEMAND		
	RETAIL	DEALER	TOTAL
October (1995–actual)	275	510	785
November (1995–actual)	420	425	845
December (1995–actual)	675	175	850
January 1996	100	375	475
February	105	400	505
March	95	425	520
April	115	350	465
May	75	300	375
June	60	250	310
July	50	300	350
August	55	325	380
September	75	300	375
October	150	300	450
November	290	350	640
December	350	400	750

cash in a bank account. She wants to maintain a minimum cash balance of $5,000 (see Exhibit 5–6) in her business and has arranged a $50,000 line of credit with her bank to provide her with short-term funds for the company. At the start of each month, the bank charges interest at the rate of 1% on the balance of the line of credit at the end of the previous month. The bank pays interest at the rate of 0.6% on any cash in excess of $5,000 held in the account. The bank pays interest on the first day of each month based on the balance in the account at the end of the previous month.

■ Demand Forecast: Budget's Beginning

The organization's goals (see box 1 in Exhibit 5–2) provide the starting point for, and the basis for evaluation of, the budgeting process. The projected financial results of a tentative operating plan are compared to the organization's financial goals to assess the plan's acceptability.

The budgeting process is driven by the **demand forecast**, which is an estimate of demand given a product price. Organizations develop demand forecasts in many ways. Some use sophisticated market surveys conducted either by outside experts or their own sales staff. Other organizations use statistical models that base demand forecasts on trends and forecasts of eco-

Demand forecast
An estimate of the market demand, or sales potential, for a product under specified conditions.

✳ paper!

EXHIBIT 5–6
Gael's Tole Art: Projected Balance Sheet, January 1, 1996

Cash	$5,000	Owner's Equity	$34,948
Accounts receivable	29,948		
Total assets	$34,948	Total liabilities and owner's equity	$34,948

nomic activity in the economy and their past sales patterns. Others simply assume that demand will either grow or decline by some estimated rate over previous demand levels.

Regardless of the approach used to develop the demand forecast, the organization must prepare a sales plan for each key line of goods or services. The sales plans are used to develop plans to acquire the required factors of production, which include labor, materials, capacity, and cash. Production plans are sensitive to the sales plan; therefore, most organizations develop budgets on computers so that planners can explore the effects of changes in the sales plan on production plans.

Choosing the amount of detail to present in the budget involves making trade-offs. On the one hand, a greater level of detail in the forecast improves the ability of the budgeting process to identify potential bottlenecks and problems by specifying the exact timing of production flows in the organization. On the other hand, forecasting and planning in great detail, such as by each unique item of production, is prohibitively expensive and overwhelming to compute in most organizations. Therefore, most organizations strike a balance that reflects the judgment of production planners between the need for detail and the cost and practicality of detailed scheduling. Planners do this by grouping products into pools of products so that each product in a given pool places roughly equivalent demands on the organization's resources.

Because Gael's has only one product, its budget will be comprehensive. Organizations with many products and services may choose, however, to budget at a more aggregated level, such as by product line.

■ The Production Plan

Planners match the completed sales plan with the inventory policy and capacity levels to determine a production plan (box 5 in Exhibit 5–2). This plan identifies the intended production during each subperiod of the annual budget. Budget subperiods may be daily, weekly, or monthly.

Planners use the inventory policy (box 4 in Exhibit 5–2) with the sales plan to develop the production plan. Therefore, the inventory policy is critical and has a unique role in shaping the production plan. Some organizations use a policy of producing for inventory and attempt to keep a predetermined, or *target*, number of units in inventory. This inventory policy often reflects a *level* production strategy that is characteristic of an organization with highly skilled employees or equipment dedicated to producing a single product.[8] In

---

[8] A level production strategy reflects a lack of flexibility. Highly skilled production workers cannot be used to do various jobs in the organization. Therefore, they must be kept busy at one job. Similarly, dedicated equipment that can be used for only one job must be kept busy to justify its expense.

these organizations, monthly sales draw down the inventory levels, and the production plan for each month attempts to restore inventory levels to their target levels.

Other organizations have an inventory policy of producing for the planned sales in the next budget subperiod. Organizations moving toward just-in-time inventory policy, described in Chapter 2, often use the production policy of producing for the next subperiod's demand as an intermediate step on the path to moving to a full just-in-time inventory system. Each subperiod becomes shorter and shorter until the organization achieves just-in-time production. In this setting, the inventory target is the next week or next month's planned sales, and the scheduled production is the amount required to meet the inventory target.

The inventory policy of producing for demand is called a **chase demand strategy**. Implementing a chase demand inventory policy requires flexibility among employees, equipment, and suppliers and a well-designed production process. In organizations using this strategy, demand drives the production plan directly: the production in each period equals the next period's planned sales. This is the inventory policy that Gael's uses and is an example of box 4 in Exhibit 5–2.

■ Aggregate Planning

Throughout the production planning process, planners or computers with planning software compare the production plan implied jointly by the sales plan and the inventory policy to the productive capacity. This comparison assesses the feasibility of the proposed production plan. Planners call this **aggregate**, or rough-cut, **planning**.

Aggregate planning does not attempt to develop a detailed production schedule that people use to guide daily production in the organization. Rather, aggregate planning determines whether the proposed production plan can be achieved by the production capacity the organization either has in place or can put in place during the planning period. Even planning at this aggregate level can be complicated because planners may need to consider many adjustments to facilities that would otherwise constrain planned procedures.

■ Developing the Spending Plans

Once planners have identified a feasible production plan, they can make tentative resource commitments. The purchasing group prepares a materials purchasing plan (box 7 in Exhibit 5–2) to acquire the raw materials, supplies, and overhead items that the production plan requires. Materials purchasing plans are driven by the cycle of both the organization's and the suppliers' production plans. This plan notifies suppliers of the demands to be placed on them and the timing of those demands. Because most purchasing plans change, both the organization and its suppliers should be able to adjust their plans. At some point, however, the budget planning subinterval production and purchasing plans are committed for that subperiod. For most organizations, this commitment point occurs anywhere from 1 day to 1 quarter before the anticipated production date.

The personnel and production groups prepare the labor hiring and training plan (box 8 in Exhibit 5–2). This plan works backward from the date when personnel are required to develop the hiring and training schedules that will ensure the availability of needed personnel. This plan can include both expansion and contraction activities. In the case of contraction, the organization uses retraining plans to redeploy employees to other parts of the organization or develops plans to discharge employees from the organization. In the case of employees who lose their employment, discharge plans may include retraining and other activities to help them find new jobs. Because retraining and discharging employees reflect moral, ethical, and legal issues, and usually have high costs, most organizations plan these activities carefully.

Staff and other groups prepare an administrative and discretionary spending plan (box 9 in Exhibit 5–2), which summarizes the proposed expenditures on activities such as those for research and development, advertising, and training. Discretionary expenditures provide the infrastructure required by the emerging production and sales plan; the term *discretionary* is used because there is no direct relationship between the level of spending on these activities and actual production levels. Once determined, however, the spending on discretionary activities becomes fixed for the period, because the amount spent is independent of product volume and mix.

For example, if a fast-food restaurant plans to make 3,000 hamburgers during some planning interval, it knows the quantity of materials that it will use because there is a physical, or engineered, relationship between ingredients such as meat, buns, condiments, and packages and the number of hamburgers made.[9] However, there is no direct physical, or engineered, relationship between the number of hamburgers sold and the amount spent on advertising or employee training.

Finally, the appropriate authority in the organization approves the capital spending plan (box 3 in Exhibit 5–2) for putting new productive capacity in place. Because capital spending projects usually involve time horizons longer than the period of the operating budgets, the capital spending plan is driven by a long-term planning process rather than the 1-year cycle of the operating budget.

The spending plans for material, labor, and support resources are based on a forecast of the activities the organization must complete to achieve the

Engineered expenditure
An expenditure whose short-term cost is directly determined by the proposed level of activity. Engineered expenditures reflect product design and process design (e.g., materials costs and the cost of casual labor).

[9] Examples of **engineered expenditures** are raw materials costs in a manufacturing operation, extraction or acquisition costs in a natural resource company, and staff costs in a service company.

Most paper products companies are actively engaged in reforestation activities. This Potlatch Corporation employee is evaluating the growth of trees on a tree plantation. Reforestation activities are generally treated and budgeted as discretionary cost items. In some jurisdictions, however, governments are considering or have passed laws that would require companies to replace any trees cut. This type of law would convert a reforestation cost from a discretionary cost to an engineered cost. *(Courtesy Potlach Corporation)*

production targets identified in its production plan. As the planning period unfolds and time reveals the actual production requirements, production planners make commitments to detailed production schedules and purchasing requirements.

■ Choosing the Capacity Levels

At Gael's Tole Art, three types of resources, each reflecting a unique time perspective, determine the monthly production capacity:

1. *Flexible resources that the organization can acquire in the short-term*, such as paint and packing supplies. If suppliers either do not deliver these resources, or if they deliver unacceptable products, production may be disrupted. This problem was not identified as an issue for Gael's, but it is a practical concern for many organizations. As noted in the just-in-time discussion in Chapter 2, organizations spend a lot of time and money developing supply chains that can deliver reliable inputs when needed.

2. *Committed resources that the organization must acquire for the intermediate term*, in this case, labor. For example, between July 1 and September 30, Gael's plans to employ 1 painter. Because each painter works 160 hours per month and each buoy requires 0.8 hours to complete, the monthly capacity provided by intermediate-term activity decisions between July 1 and September 30 is 200 (160/0.8) units.

3. *Committed resources that the organization must acquire for the long term*, in this case, the shop. (This is an example of box 6 in Exhibit 5–2.) Gael plans to rent a shop that provides a monthly capacity of 800 units. This is a very simple setting with a relatively short commitment period.

Some organizations may take several years to acquire long-term capacity that may last for 10 years or more and whose cost is justified only if it is used that long. Consider the amount of time an oil company takes to build an oil refinery or the time that a municipality needs to build a hospital. Committed resources are expensive and are called *committed* because (a) the cost is the same whether the facility is used or not and (b) the level of capacity and capacity-related costs are very difficult to change in the short term. Therefore, committed resources impose risk on the organization.

Note that, as summarized in Exhibit 5–7, the nature of the resources defines whether they are short term, intermediate term, or long term. Many organizations develop sophisticated approaches for choosing a production plan that balances the use of short-term, intermediate-term, and long-term capacity to minimize the waste of resources.

For example, the size and the number of service areas in a bank represent the capacity provided by long-term building decisions. This long-term capacity provides the upper limit of capacity that can be used during any period. The level of long-term capacity chosen reflects the organization's assessment of its long-term growth trend. The cycle time for long-term capacity decisions reflects the longer of (1) the time needed to put long-term capacity in place or (2) the contracting period for long-term capacity. For Gael's, which is renting capacity, the cycle time for long-term capacity is defined by the lease stipulations, which is 1 year. If Gael's were building this capacity, the cycle time for long-term capacity would be defined by the time needed to plan and build the facility.

The number of full-time staff employed by a bank determines the amount of long-term capacity that can be used during the intermediate term. For example, if the long-term capacity plan were to acquire capacity that the organization would use increasingly as sales grew, the intermediate-term capacity decisions would put other elements that require intermediate-term commitments in place, such as people and banking equipment, that allow the bank to use its long-term capacity. These decisions allow for increasing the use of long-term capacity as the organization grows. The cycle time for intermediate-term capacity decisions reflects the longer of (1) the time needed to put intermediate-term capacity in place or (2) the contracting period contract for intermediate-term capacity. For Gael's this is the contracting period for artists, which is 3 months.

Finally, the number of part-time, or temporary staff, employed by a bank determines its capacity on a day-to-day basis. Short-term capacity decisions

EXHIBIT 5-7
Summary of Capacity Types and Commitment Time

TERM	TYPE OF CAPACITY ACQUIRED	EXAMPLES
Short (less than several weeks)	Provides the ability to use existing capacity	Raw materials, supplies, casual labor
Intermediate (several weeks to six months)	General-purpose capacity that is transferrable between organizations, given time	People, general-purpose equipment, specialty raw materials
Long (more than six months)	Special-purpose capacity that is customized for the organization's use	Buildings, special-purpose equipment

reflect the cyclical demands that the bank may face daily (staff to handle daily peaks), weekly (staff to handle the Friday increases in demand), monthly (staff to handle mid-month and end-of-month demands), or annually (staff to handle holiday demands and demands created by sales promotions such as retirement plan sales just before tax time). The cycle time for short-term capacity decisions reflects the time needed to put short-term capacity in place. For Gael's, this is the time period that suppliers require for delivery, which is unspecified in the problem description but is assumed to be virtually instantaneous. However, if Gael's had to order these supplies and wait for

This clean room facility at LSI Logic Corporation has many types of costs. The room itself reflects a cost of capacity acquired for the long term. The cost of hiring and training the people who work in the room reflects a cost of capacity acquired for the intermediate term. The cost of the power used is a short-term cost acquired only when the power is required. (*Courtesy LSI Logic*)

them, it would become very important to plan their acquisition so that, in the very short term, Gael's would not have to stop production while it waited for these supplies to arrive. In this sense, supplies provide the short-run capacity to use longer-term capacity.

This discussion raises the question of how production planners choose capacity levels. Organizations use many different approaches to plan capacity. The process Gael's used was (1) to choose a level of shop capacity (one of 600, 800, 1,000, or 1,200) and then (2) to hire the number of painters in each quarter that, given the forecasted demand and chosen shop capacity, provides the highest level of expected profits.

We can classify the resource-consuming activities for Gael's into three groups, which are typical of all organizations:

1. Activities that create the need for resources and, therefore, resource expenditures in the *short term*. For Gael's these short-term activities include the acquisition, preparation, painting, packing, and shipping of buoys. These short-term activities create expenditures that vary directly with the production levels because the inventory policy is to produce only to order.

2. Activities undertaken to acquire capacity for the *intermediate term*. For Gael's this is the quarterly acquisition of painting capacity, that is, hiring the painters to paint the buoys.

3. Activities undertaken to acquire capacity that must be acquired for the *long term*. For Gael's this includes the annual choice of the level of shop capacity, level of advertising, manager's salary, and expenditures for other items such as insurance and heat.

Planners classify activities by type because they plan, budget, and control short-, intermediate-, and long-term expenditures differently. Analysts evaluate short-term activities using efficiency and effectiveness considerations and ask questions such as the following:

1. Is this expenditure necessary to add value, from the customer's perspective, to the product?

2. Can the organization improve the execution of this activity?

3. Would changing how this activity is done provide more customer satisfaction?

Analysts evaluate intermediate- and long-term activities by using efficiency and effectiveness considerations and ask questions such as these:

1. Are alternative forms of capacity available that are less expensive?

2. Is this the best approach to achieve our goals?

3. How could we improve the capacity selection decision to make capacity less expensive?

Choosing the capacity plan, that is, making the commitments to acquire intermediate-term and long-term capacity, fixes or commits the intermediate-term and long-term expenditures. Choosing the production plan, that is, choosing the level of the short-term activities, fixes the short-term expenditures that the master budget summarizes.

Handling Infeasible Production Plans

Although the relationships between planning and production at Gael's are simple, the company's planning process reflects how planners use forecasted demand to plan activity levels and provide required capacity. If the planners find the tentative production plan infeasible because of resource or capacity constraints, they make provisions to acquire more capacity or reduce the planned level of production. For example, if the labor market is tight and Gael's can hire only 2 artists between January and June, Gael would have to revise her capacity plan and production plan to reflect this constraint.

Interpreting the Production Plan

3 elements drive planning

Exhibit 5–8 summarizes the production plan that Gael's has developed for 1996. The three elements that drive planning are: demand, which is what people are willing to buy at the stated price; the capacity levels chosen; and production output. Gael's makes nothing until it receives an order for that item. Therefore, *production is the minimum of demand and capacity*. In equation form, we might write

Production = Minimum (production capacity, total demand)

where, at Gael's,

Production capacity =
Minimum (shop capacity, painting capacity, supplies capacity)

and

Total demand = Retail demand + Dealer demand

In Gael's case, the production capacity is the minimum of the long-term capacity (the productive capacity of the shop), the intermediate-term capacity (the painting capacity provided by hiring artists), and the short-term

EXHIBIT 5–8
Gael's Tole Art: Demand and Sales Data, Number of Units, 1996

	JAN.	FEB.	MARCH	APRIL	MAY	JUNE	JULY	AUG.	SEPT.	OCT.	NOV.	DEC.
Retail demand	100	105	95	115	75	60	50	55	75	150	290	350
Dealer demand	375	400	425	350	300	250	300	325	300	300	350	400
Total demand	475	505	520	465	375	310	350	380	375	450	640	750
Shop capacity	800	800	800	800	800	800	800	800	800	800	800	800
Painting capacity	400	400	400	400	400	400	200	200	200	600	600	600
Production capacity	400	400	400	400	375	310	200	200	200	450	600	600
Retail units made and sold	100	105	95	115	75	60	50	55	75	150	290	350
Dealer units made and sold	300	295	305	285	300	250	150	145	125	300	310	250
Total units made and sold	400	400	400	400	375	310	200	200	200	450	600	600

capacity (the capacity provided by the short-term acquisition of materials that are assumed to be in instantaneous supply; therefore, in this situation, short-term capacity is equal to intermediate-term capacity). For example, in August the retail demand is 55 units and the dealer demand is 325 units, totaling 380 units. The shop capacity is 800 units and the painting capacity is 200 units. Therefore, production capacity, which is the minimum of the shop capacity and painting capacity, is 200 units. Planned production and sales of 200 units constitute the minimum of total demand (380 units) and production capacity (200 units).

■ The Financial Plans

Once the planners have developed the production, staffing, and capacity plans, they can prepare a financial summary of the tentative operating plans. The financial results implied by the production plan developed in Exhibit 5–8 for Gael's appear in the following exhibits. Exhibit 5–9 presents the cash flows expected from the production and sales plan. Exhibit 5–10 and Exhibit 5–11 summarize the projected balance sheet and income statement, respectively, expected as a result of the production and sales plans. (These are examples of the elements of boxes 11 and 12 in Exhibit 5–2.) Planners use the projected income statement as an overall test of the profitability of their proposed activities and the projected balance sheet as an overall evaluation of the net effect of operating and financing decisions during the budget period.

■ Understanding the Cash Flow Statement

If you study the cash flow statement in Exhibit 5–9, you will see that it is organized into three sections:

1. Cash inflows from sales and collections of receivables
2. Cash outflows for flexible resources that are acquired and consumed in the short term (buoys, paint, other supplies, packing, and shipping) and cash outflows for committed resources that are acquired and consumed in the intermediate term and long term (painters, shop rent, manager's salary, other shop costs, interest paid, and advertising costs)
3. Results of financing operations

Note that in each month, the format of the cash flow statement is

$$\text{Cash inflows} - \text{Cash outflows} = \text{Net cash flow}$$

and, in January, for example,

$$\text{Net cash flows} + \text{Opening cash} + \text{Effects of financing operations} = \text{Ending cash}$$

$$(3,676) + (5,000) + (-20,000 + 16,324) = (5,000)$$

To help you to understand where the numbers in the cash flow statement prepared for Gael's came from, let's look closely at the numbers for July.

EXHIBIT 5-9
Gael's Tole Art: Cash Flow and Financing Data—1996

CASH INFLOWS	JAN.	FEB.	MARCH	APRIL	MAY	JUNE	JULY	AUG.	SEPT.	OCT.	NOV.	DEC.
Retail sales	$ 8,000	$ 8,400	$ 7,600	$ 9,200	$ 6,000	$ 4,800	$ 4,000	$ 4,400	$ 6,000	$12,000	$23,200	$28,000
Dealer collections—1 Month	2,887	4,950	4,868	5,033	4,703	4,950	4,125	2,475	2,392	2,062	4,950	5,115
Dealer collections—2 Months	10,519	4,331	7,425	7,301	7,549	7,054	7,425	6,188	3,713	3,589	3,094	7,425
Dealer collections—3 Months	5,610	4,675	1,925	3,300	3,245	3,355	3,135	3,300	2,750	1,650	1,595	1,375
Total	$27,016	$22,356	$21,818	$24,834	$21,496	$20,159	$18,685	$16,363	$14,855	$19,301	$32,839	$41,915

CASH OUTFLOWS
For Flexible Resources

	JAN.	FEB.	MARCH	APRIL	MAY	JUNE	JULY	AUG.	SEPT.	OCT.	NOV.	DEC.
Buoys	$ 900	$ 900	$ 900	$ 900	$ 844	$ 698	$ 450	$ 450	$ 450	$ 1,013	$ 1,350	$ 1,350
Paint costs	1,260	1,260	1,260	1,260	1,181	977	630	630	630	1,418	1,890	1,890
Other supplies costs	1,100	1,100	1,100	1,100	1,031	853	550	550	550	1,238	1,650	1,650
Packing costs	780	780	780	780	731	605	390	390	390	878	1,170	1,170
Shipping costs	3,000	3,000	3,000	3,000	2,813	2,325	1,500	1,500	1,500	3,375	4,500	4,500

For committed resources

	JAN.	FEB.	MARCH	APRIL	MAY	JUNE	JULY	AUG.	SEPT.	OCT.	NOV.	DEC.
Painters' salaries	$ 4,000	$ 4,000	$ 4,000	$ 4,000	$ 4,000	$ 4,000	$ 2,000	$ 2,000	$ 2,000	$ 6,000	$ 6,000	$ 6,000
Shop rent	4,800	0	0	4,800	0	0	4,800	0	0	4,800	0	0
Manager's salary	2,500	2,500	2,500	2,500	2,500	2,500	2,500	2,500	2,500	2,500	2,500	2,500
Other shop costs	1,667	1,667	1,667	1,667	1,667	1,667	1,667	1,667	1,667	1,667	1,667	1,667
Interest paid (received)	0	163	127	95	81	48	17	208	177	160	231	145
Advertising costs	3,333	3,333	3,333	3,333	3,333	3,333	3,333	3,333	3,333	3,333	3,333	3,333
Total	$23,340	$18,703	$18,667	$23,435	$18,181	$17,004	$17,837	$13,228	$13,197	$26,380	$24,291	$24,205
Net cash flow this month	$ 3,676	$ 3,653	$ 3,151	$ 1,399	$ 3,315	$ 3,155	$ 848	$ 3,134	$ 1,658	-$7,079	$ 8,548	$17,710

FINANCING OPERATIONS

	JAN.	FEB.	MARCH	APRIL	MAY	JUNE	JULY	AUG.	SEPT.	OCT.	NOV.	DEC.
Opening cash	5,000	5,000	5,000	5,000	5,000	5,000	5,000	5,000	5,000	5,000	5,000	5,000
Cash invested (withdrawn)	-20,000	0	0	0	0	0	-20,000	0	0	0	0	0
Cash available	-11,324	8,653	8,151	6,399	8,315	8,155	-14,152	8,134	6,658	-2,079	13,548	22,710
Opening loan	0	16,324	12,671	9,520	8,121	4,806	1,652	20,803	17,669	16,010	23,089	14,541
Borrowing made	16,324	0	0	0	0	0	19,152	0	0	7,079	0	0
Borrowing repaid	0	3,653	3,151	1,399	3,315	3,155	0	3,134	1,658	0	8,548	14,541
Ending loan	16,324	12,671	9,520	8,121	4,806	1,652	20,803	17,669	16,010	23,089	14,541	0
Ending cash	5,000	5,000	5,000	5,000	5,000	5,000	5,000	5,000	5,000	5,000	5,000	8,168

EXHIBIT 5-10
Gael's Tole Art: Projected Balance Sheet, December 31, 1996

Cash	$ 8,168	Owner's equity	$35,613
Accounts receivable	27,445		
Total assets	$35,613	Total liabilities and owner's equity	$35,613

EXHIBIT 5-11
Gael's Tole Art: Projected Income Statement for the Year Ended December 31, 1996

Revenue		$279,134
Flexible resource expenses		
Buoys	$10,204	
Paint	14,285	
Other supplies	12,471	
Packing	8,843	
Shipping	34,013	79,816
Contribution margin		$199,318
Committed resource expenses		
Painter's salaries	$48,000	
Shop rent	19,200	
Other shop costs	20,000	
Manager's salary	30,000	117,200
Other expenses		
Advertising	$40,000	
Interest paid	1,452	41,452
Net income		$ 40,666

CASH INFLOWS SECTION OF THE CASH FLOW STATEMENT   Recall that the pattern of collections at Gael's is as follows: (1) retail orders are prepaid and the retail price per unit is $80 and (2) sales to dealers for $55 per unit are on account and the average collection pattern is 30% in the month following the sale, 45% in the second month following the sale, 20% in the third month following the sale, and 5% never collected.

Therefore, in July, Gael will collect (1) all the retail sales for July, (2) 30% of the dealer sales from June, (3) 45% of the dealer sales from May, and (4) 20% of the dealer sales from April. Exhibit 5–12 summarizes these July collections.

EXHIBIT 5-12
Gael's Tole Art: Summary of Cash Collections in July

ITEM	CALCULATION
Retail sales from July	$4,000
30% of June dealer sales[a]	30% * 250 * $55 = $4,125
45% of May dealer sales	45% * 300 * $55 = $7,425
20% of April dealer sales	20% * 285 * $55 = $3,135
Total	$18,685

[a] Sales equals units sold multiplied by the selling price of $55 per unit.

CASH OUTFLOWS SECTION OF THE CASH FLOW STATEMENT   Exhibit 5–13 summarizes the cash outflow numbers for July. Note that for expenditures on flexible resources that are acquired in the short-term.

$$\text{Cash outflow} = \text{Units purchased} * \text{Price per unit}$$

For expenditures on committed resources, that is, resources acquired in the intermediate term or long term

$$\text{Cash outflow} = \text{Committed cost}$$

THE FINANCING SECTION OF THE CASH FLOW STATEMENT   The financing section of the cash flow statement summarizes the effects on cash of transactions that are not a part of the normal operating activities on cash. This section includes the effects on cash of issuing or retiring stock or debt and buying or selling capital assets. Exhibit 5–14 shows a common format used in the financing section of the cash flow statement with the corresponding numbers for July. Note that the format of the financing section of the cash flow statement is

$$\text{Cash flow this period} + \text{Opening balance} \pm \text{Changes} = \text{Closing balance}$$

The major sources and uses of cash in most organizations are operations, investments or withdrawals by the owner in an unincorporated organization, long-term financing activities related to issuing or retiring stock or debt, and short-term financing activities.

Short-term financing is usually undertaken using a **line of credit** established with a financial institution. The line of credit may be secured or unsecured.[10] There is a limit on the line of credit and interest is usually paid periodically, such as monthly, on the outstanding balance. See the ending loan row in Exhibit 5–9 and note that Gael's line of credit balance varies

Line of credit
A short-term financing arrangement, with a prespecified limit, between an organization and a financial institution.

[10] The line of credit is secured if the organization has pledged an asset as collateral that the financial institution can seize if the borrower defaults on the line of credit provisions.

EXHIBIT 5–13
Gael's Tole Art: Cash Outflow Calculations for July

ITEM	AMOUNT	FORMULA	CALCULATIONS
Buoy cost	$ 450	July production * Price per buoy	200 * $2.25
Paint cost	630	July production * Paint cost per buoy	200 * $3.15
Other supplies cost	550	July production * Other supplies cost per buoy	200 * $2.75
Packing costs	390	July sales * Packing cost per buoy	200 * $1.95
Shipping costs	1,500	July sales * Shipping cost per buoy	200 * $7.50
Painters' salaries	2,000	Number of painters in July * Monthly salary	1 * $2000
Shop rent	4,800	Units of capacity * Capacity cost per unit	800 * $6
Manager's salary	2,500	Annual salary/12	$30000 /12
Other shop costs	1,667	Annual other costs/12	$20000 /12
Interest paid	17	June ending loan balance * 1%	$1652 * 1%
Advertising costs	3,333	Annual advertising/12	$40000/12

EXHIBIT 5–14
Format of Financing Section of Cash Flow Statement

	Net cash flow from operations	848
+	Opening cash	+ 5,000
±	Cash invested or withdrawn°	–20,000
±	Cash provided or used in issuing or retiring stock or debt	–0–
=	Cash available before short-term financing	–14,152
±	Cash used or provided by short-term financing	19,152
=	Ending cash	5,000

° In the case of a private business such as Gael's, this refers to the capital transactions by the owner.

between zero and $23,089 during the year, well within the limit of $50,000 that she negotiated with the bank.

Note that the format of the financing section of the cash flow statement for Gael's does not follow the format used in Exhibit 5–14. The financing section of Gael's cash flow statement provides information about the line of credit balance. Many organizations include line of credit information in the cash flow statement because most line of credit agreements have limits that can potentially constrain operations. Therefore, including the line of credit balance in the cash flow statement signals a warning when limits that might constrain operations are being approached.

■ Using the Financial Plans

OBJECTIVE 5.4
The way organizations use and interpret budgets

Gael's cash flow statement, Exhibit 5–9, provides several types of useful information. First, it contains a short-term financing plan that suggests that, if events unfold as expected, Gael's will increase its cash balances only modestly during the year because of the $40,000 withdrawal that Gael will make from the business. The company will rely heavily on its line of credit agreement, which will have a nonzero balance during 11 months of the year.

Organizations can raise money from outsiders by borrowing from banks, issuing debt, or selling shares. A cash flow forecast helps an organization identify if and when it will require external financing. It also shows whether the shortage will be temporary or cyclical, which can be met by a line of credit arrangement, or whether it will be permanent, which would require a long-term loan from a bank, further investment by the current owners, or investment by new owners. Based on the information provided by the cash flow forecast, organizations can plan the acquisition of needed external financing with minimum costs.

The projected income statement and balance sheet provide a general assessment of the operating efficiencies at Gael's. If Gael believes that these projected results are unacceptable, she must take steps to change the organization processes that create the unacceptable results. For example, if the employees consistently use more quantities of any factor of production than competitors use, such as paint, labor, or capacity, this excess use must be eliminated so that the company can compete profitably with its competitors.

Suppose that Gael's manager has studied the projected financial results in the initial budget plans and has decided that the 14.6% profit margin on sales ($40,666/$279,134 from Exhibit 5–11) is too low. The manager has reached this conclusion because Gael's business is in the craft industry in which competitors often duplicate attractive products quickly, resulting in short periods of product profitability. After determining that this profit margin on sales is too low, the manager might develop a program to improve the cost/revenue performance in Gael's.

■ Using the Projected Results

The operating budgets, like the production plan, hiring plan, capital spending plan, and purchasing plan for materials and supplies, provide a framework for developing expectations about activity levels in the upcoming period. Planners also use the operating budgets to test the feasibility of production plans. As the period unfolds, production and operations schedulers will make more accurate forecasts on which firm production commitments will be made. Then the budget information will be used to accomplish the following:

1. *Identify broad resource requirements* so that plans can be developed to put needed resources in place. For example, Gael's manager can use the activity forecast to plan when the organization will have to hire and train temporary help.

2. *Identify potential problems* so that plans can be developed to avoid those problems or deal with them systematically. For example, Gael's manager can use the statement of operating cash flows to identify when the business will need short-term financing from its bank. This will help plan for a line of credit that is both competitive and responsive to Gael's needs. The forecasted cash flows also will identify when the buoy business will generate cash that Gael can invest in other business opportunities.

3. *Compare projected operating and financial results* with those of competitors as a general test of the efficiency of the organization's operating processes. For example, the differences between planned and actual costs at Gael's will focus the manager's attention on understanding whether the plans were unrealistic or whether the execution of a sound business plan was flawed. This signals the need for improved planning, execution, or both.

OBJECTIVE 5.5
What-if and sensitivity analysis—2 important budgeting tools

WHAT-IF ANALYSIS

The budgeting process also allows management to consider alternative strategies. If planners use the computer for the budgeting process, they can use the budgeting framework to explore the effects of alternative marketing, production, and selling strategies.[11] Gael's manager might consider raising prices,

---

[11] This task, which is prohibitively time consuming without using a calculator, becomes routine with a computer.

opening a retail outlet, or using different employment strategies. Alternate proposals take the form of "what if"[12] questions in a process called **what-if analysis**.

Gael's manager might ask: What if I decrease prices on my retail products by 5% and sales increase by 10%? Is that desirable? The answer is that Gael's profits will fall from $40,666 to $37,695.[13] Therefore, this proposed price adjustment would be undesirable.

Gael's manager might also wonder: What if I opened a retail outlet? Suppose that Gael's opened a retail outlet, which cost $40,000 per year to operate (including all costs). Retail sales would increase by 50%. The retail outlet orders would be shipped by courier to the customer's address. Would that change be desirable? If Gael's follows that strategy, profit would increase to $46,586, which seems to be an improvement. However, Gael's manager might not want to put up with the problems associated with operating a retail store for an incremental return of only $5,920 ($46,586 – $40,666).

The structure and information required to prepare the master budget can be used very easily to provide the basis for what-if analysis. (It took only several seconds to answer the manager's questions using the spreadsheet developed to prepare the Gale's Tole Art cash flow forecast.)

What-if analysis
A strategy that uses a model to predict the results of varying a model's key parameters or estimates.

■ Evaluating Decision-Making Alternatives: A Detailed Example

Suppose that the manager at Gael's is considering renting a machine to automatically sand the buoys and apply the primer coat. The capacity of the machine is 1,300 buoys per month. This machine will increase annual shop costs from $20,000 to $35,000, and it will reduce the painting time per buoy from 0.8 hours to 0.5 hours. Therefore, the machine will reduce the number of painters needed for any level of scheduled production.

[12] What-if analysis is undertaken using computer spreadsheet software. Your instructor may have the spreadsheet that was used to prepare the cash flow budget in this chapter and to undertake the what-if analysis reported in the text. If so, you might use it to do your own what-if analysis.

[13] This revised profit number was found by inserting the revised price and demand in the spreadsheet that was used to prepare the original budget figures. Therefore, the detailed calculations used to develop these numbers are laborious and are not repeated here. If you wish, you can obtain the spreadsheet that was used to develop these numbers and verify that they are correct and also experiment with other numbers.

Exhibit 5–15 shows the revised pro forma income statement reflecting the rental of the sanding and priming machine.[14] Renting this machine will increase projected net income from the original level of $40,666 to $45,484, an increase of $4,818.

OBJECTIVE 5.6
The types of analyses used by budget planners

■ Sensitivity Analysis

What-if analysis is only as good as the model it uses. The model must be complete, it must reflect relationships accurately, and it must use reasonable estimates. If the model is complete and reflects capacity, cost, and revenue relationships accurately, the remaining issue is the accuracy of the data used. For this reason, planners test planning models by varying key estimates.

For example, if one machine or labor group is responsible for the bottleneck of a key resource in a manufacturing operation, that machine's productivity or output per hour is a key estimate used in developing the production plan. The production planner could test the effect of errors in this estimate on the production plan by varying the productivity number by 10 or 20% above and below the estimate used in the planning budget.

If forecasting errors have a dramatic effect on the production plan, planners say that the model is *sensitive* to that estimate. Depending on the consequences of a bad estimate, planners might want to invest time to improve the accuracy of their estimates. Planners call selectively varying a plan's or a budget's key estimates **sensitivity analysis**. If the model is reasonably accurate, sensitivity analysis allows planners to identify the estimates that have critical effects on decisions based on that model.

Sensitivity analysis
An analytical tool that involves selectively varying key estimates of a plan or budget. Sensitivity analysis allows planners to identify the effect of changes in estimates on decisions. If small changes in plan parameters (estimates and relationships) produce large changes in decisions or results, the plan is said to be sensitive to the estimates.

[14] Again, these numbers were found by inserting the change in the spreadsheet used to develop Gael's budget; the calculations are too laborious to reproduce here.

For example, the labor that Gael's needs to make each product is an important parameter in its planning budget. Small changes in this parameter, which is the key productive resource, produce large changes in the profit figure. If a study developed a process or product redesign that could reduce the labor time needed to make a buoy by 10% from 0.8 to 0.72 hours per buoy, projected profit rises from $40,666 to $53,255, a 31% increase.[15] This is a signal to Gael's manager that designing and running the manufacturing process so that the artists can work as efficiently as possible are keys to the success of the business.

COMPARING PLANNED AND ACTUAL RESULTS

Organizations often find it useful, for purposes of understanding results, to compare the results expected, or projected, in the master budget with actual results. In Chapter 6 you will see how organizations can use differences, or variances, between the planned and actual level of costs as a warning signal to trigger a more detailed investigation of the circumstances that caused the variances.

THE ROLE OF BUDGETING IN SERVICE AND NONPROFIT ORGANIZATIONS

OBJECTIVE 5.7
The role of budgets in service and not-for-profit organizations

To this point we have discussed the role of budgeting in manufacturing organizations. Budgeting serves a slightly different, but equally relevant, role in natural resource companies, service organizations, and nonprofit organizations such as government agencies. As in manufacturing organizations, budgeting in nonmanufacturing organizations supports the roles of planning, whose major activities are coordinating, formalizing responsibilities and relationships, and communicating. Exhibit 5–16 summarizes the main focus of the budgeting process in manufacturing, natural resource, service, and nonprofit organizations.

In the natural resources sector, the key focus is on balancing demand with the availability of natural resources, such as minerals, fish, or wood. Because the natural resource supply often constrains sales,[16] success requires managing the resource base effectively.

[15] Again, these numbers were developed by making the appropriate changes in the spreadsheet used to develop the original budget numbers for Gael's.

[16] That is, demand exceeds supply.

EXHIBIT 5–16
Focus of Budgeting in Different Organizations

ORGANIZATION TYPE	MAIN FOCUS OF BUDGETING PROCESS
Manufacturing	Sales and manufacturing activities
Natural resource	Sales, resource availability, and acquisition
Service	Sales activities and staffing requirements
Nonprofit	Raising revenues and controlling expenditures

In the service sector, the key focus is on balancing demand and the organization's ability to provide services, which is determined by the number and mix of skills in the organization. Although the service sector frequently uses machines to deliver products to customers, most machines are labor paced. That is, they operate at a pace dictated by their human operators. Therefore, people, rather than machines, usually represent the capacity constraint in the service sector. A key issue in planning in the service sector is to consider the time needed to put new people in place as sales increase. Planning is critical in high-skill organizations, such as a consulting business, because people capacity is expensive and services cannot be inventoried when demand falls below capacity.

In nonprofit organizations, such as government agencies and charities, the traditional focus of budgeting has been to balance revenues, raised by taxes or donations, with spending demands. Government agencies call planned cash outflows, or spending plans, **appropriations**. Appropriations set limits on a government agency's spending. Governments worldwide are facing increased pressures to eliminate deficits without raising tax revenues. Therefore, many governments are looking for ways to eliminate unnecessary expenditures and to make necessary expenditures more efficient rather than just ensuring that government agencies do not spend more than they have been authorized to do. Thus, they must prioritize expenditures as part of this process.

Appropriation
An authorized spending limit in a government department.

Organizations use many different approaches to planning and control. In some organizations, one staff group develops plans and another staff group verifies that employees have executed the plans as required. Other organizations ask the people who will be doing the work to develop the plans and to control their own work. This group of Stanley employees manages production and determines work schedules. The plant has no line supervisors, inspectors, or coordinators. *(Al Ferreira/The Stanley Works)*

THE SOURCE OF BUDGET INFORMATION

So far we have talked about the details of the master budget without being specific about the source of the data that planners use to prepare it. In many organizations, planners use information provided by the people who know the process best when developing the budget. For example, we might ask the sales staff what sales they expect for the upcoming period. On the surface, this may seem to make sense, but problems may arise when results are compared to the plan and people are held accountable for variances. For example, someone might say to a machine operator, "You said that this machine could make 50 pieces per hour but it only averaged 40 pieces per hour. What did you do wrong?" Therefore, when planning estimates are used to evaluate performance, they can affect what people say. This is a behavioral issue that has attracted much research and is considered further in Chapter 14.

CONSIDER THIS . . .

Ethics in Budgeting

Ivan Kilpatrick, a former vice president of Bombardier, Inc., a large Canadian manufacturer of specialty vehicles, has a complaint. He claims that many management accountants, under pressure from senior executives, knowingly prepare budgets that overstate revenues and understate expenses. As evidence to support his assertion, Mr. Kilpatrick observed that variances are invariably unfavorable, rather than being unfavorable, about 50% of the time, which is what would be expected if the estimates were unbiased. Mr. Kilpatrick observed, "Accountants must remember that we are members of a profession, and we should speak out against the nonsense of fantasy forecasts."

Source: Ivan Kilpatrick, "It's Time to Face the Music on Budgets," Management Perspectives, *CMA Magazine* (March 1994), p. 6.

PERIODIC AND CONTINUOUS BUDGETING

Many variations on the basic budgeting process described in the chapter are possible, such as periodicity of the budget process, the basic budget spending assumptions, and the degree of top-management control.

The budget process described for Gael's is an annual or **periodic budget** cycle. Gael's manager prepares budgets periodically for each planning period. Although planners update or revise the budgets during the period, periodic budgeting has little carryover from one budget period to the next.

In **continuous budgeting**, the organization budgets continuously. As one budget period, usually a month or a quarter, passes, planners delete that budget period from the master budget and add another one. Therefore, if Gael's used continuous budgeting with a 1-year cycle, the manager would drop 1 month from the beginning of the budget period and add 1 month to the end of the budget period as each month passes. For example, at the end of February 1996, the manager would drop that month from the budget and add February 1997.

The length of the budget period used in continuous budgeting reflects the competitive forces, skill requirements, and technology changes that the organization faces. The budget period must be long enough for the organization to anticipate important environmental changes and adapt to them, yet short enough so that estimates are not unrealistic.

Advocates of periodic budgeting argue that continuous budgeting takes too much time and effort and that periodic budgeting provides virtually the

Periodic budget
A budget that is prepared for a specified period of time, usually 1 year. As each budget period ends, the organization prepares a new budget for the next one.

Continuous budgeting
A budgeting process that plans for a specified period of time, usually 1 year, and organized into budget subintervals, usually a month or a quarter. As each budget subinterval ends, the organization drops the completed subinterval from the budget and adds the next budget subinterval.

same benefits at a smaller cost. Advocates of continuous budgeting argue that it keeps the organization planning and thinking strategically year-round rather than just at budget time.

CONTROLLING DISCRETIONARY EXPENDITURES

Organizations use three general approaches to budget discretionary expenditures: zero-based budgeting, incremental budgeting, and project funding. Each of these approaches has important differences, which explains why all three are used in practice.

■ Zero-Based Budgeting

Zero-based budgeting
An approach to developing appropriations for discretionary expenditures that assumes that the starting point for each discretionary expenditure item is zero.

Zero-based budgeting requires that proponents of discretionary expenditures continuously justify those expenditures because, for each planning period, the starting point for each budgetary item is zero. Planners allocate the organization's scarce resources to the spending proposals they think will best achieve the organization's goals. Practical considerations require justification for program spending every two or three planning periods because it is prohibitively expensive to justify an expenditure each planning period.

Using a zero-based approach to planning discretionary expenditures is controversial. This approach can be used to assess most government expenditures, but in profit-seeking organizations, it applies only to discretionary expenditures such as research and development, advertising, and employee training.

Zero-based budgeting ideas do not apply to engineered costs, which are short-term costs that have an identifiable relationship with some activity level. Engineered costs are controlled by measuring and using reports of the amounts of resources consumed by operating activities and by the cost variances that we described earlier.

■ Incremental Budgeting

Incremental budgeting
An approach to developing appropriations for discretionary expenditures that assumes that the starting point for each discretionary expenditure item is the amount spent on it in the previous budget.

Incremental budgeting bases a period's expenditure level for a discretionary item on the amount spent on that item during the previous period. For example, if the total budget for discretionary items increases by 10%, each discretionary item is allowed to increase 10%. This basic model has variations, for example, if the total spending on all discretionary items is allowed to increase by 10%, all discretionary spending might experience an across-the-board increase of 5%, and the remaining 5% increase in total spending might be allocated to discretionary items based on merit or need.

Some people have criticized incremental budgeting because it does not require justifications reflecting the organization's goals for discretionary expenditures. Incremental budgeting includes no provision to reduce or eliminate expenditures as the organization changes, nor does it have a mechanism to provide disproportionate support to discretionary items that have potential or are growing quickly.

■ Project Funding

Critics of zero-based budgeting have observed that it is very expensive because it requires so much employee time to prepare. These critics have proposed an intermediate solution between the two extremes of zero-based budgeting and incremental budgeting to mitigate the disadvantages of each. The intermediate solution is to develop sunset provisions for all discretionary expenditures.

Sunset provisions are a form of **project funding**.[17] People proposing discretionary expenditures state their request in terms of a project proposal that includes how long the project will last and how much money will be required each period during the project's life. Planners approve no discretionary spending for projects that have indeterminate lengths or spending amounts. If the planners approve the project, they agree to provide the level of support requested in the plan. Requests to extend, or modify, the project must be approved separately. The advantage of providing sunset provisions is that they strike an intermediate balance between the high cost resulting from the need for the close control and continuous justification provided by zero-based budgeting and the much lower cost of incremental budgeting.

Project funding
An approach to developing appropriations for discretionary expenditures that organizes appropriations into a package that focuses on achieving some defined output. For example, an organization might fund a project designed to identify and evaluate its practiced organization ethics.

MANAGING THE BUDGETING PROCESS

A critical facet of the budgeting process is its management. The budget team, headed by the organization's budget director, who is sometimes the controller, coordinates the budget-making process. The budget team usually

[17] Projects with indefinite lives are sometimes called *programs*.

After Hurricane Andrew hit the south Florida and Louisiana coasts in 1992, Shell Oil company established this aid center in Homestead, Florida, Shell funded this discretionary spending as a project. *(Courtesy Shell Oil Company)*

reports to a budget committee, which generally includes the chief executive officer, the chief operating officer, and the vice presidents. The composition of the budget committee reflects the role of the budget as a key planning document that should reflect and relate to the organization's goals. The danger of using a budget committee is that it may, and often does, signal to other employees that budgeting is senior management's tool. Senior management must take steps to ensure that the organization members do not perceive the master budget and the budgeting process as something that is beyond their control or responsibility.

FRED POWELL AND THE LEGAL SERVICES DEPARTMENT REVISITED

Faced with the certainty that funding matters would get worse, not better, Fred Powell identified the need for, and developed, a budgeting system. He took the funding allocations as given and was able to get planners who develop government spending allocations to commit to provide funding estimates for 2 or 3 years in advance. With this information, Fred identified the range of legal services that his department was offering and the approximate cost to perform each service. Then he organized services into three groups: those that were required by law, those that were critical, and those that were not critical. He was then able to identify the number and cost of each of the three groups of services and to compare them with estimates of the expected funding.

During this process, Fred discovered two things. First, the cost of some of the activities that his staff was undertaking seemed to be higher than comparable costs quoted for similar work by outsiders. On investigation, he discovered that most of these services occurred in court situations in which his staff was relatively inexperienced and required much longer preparation times than outsiders who specialized in these matters. Second, most of the growth in demand for services was coming from services that were required by law and were the result of changes in legislation.

Fred and his supervisor approached a government committee with this information and explained to them the consequences, in terms of work and cost, of the changes in the legislation. They reached an agreement allowing Fred to contract with outside organizations that could provide specialty legal services more efficiently and to divide Fred's budget into 2 components, the committed component and the discretionary component. The committee agreed to provide ongoing support in prioritizing services so that Fred, given the budget allocation and the committed amount of work, could identify which requests for discretionary services would be met and which would be rejected on the grounds of lack of funding.

SUMMARY

Budgeting is the set of activities that planners use to prepare budgets that are quantitative, often financial, models of the expected results of the organization's short-term operating and financing activities. Budgets support the management roles of planning and control by providing the means to express plans and the foundation for control activities.

The process of budgeting itself forces the organization to (1) identify its long-term objectives and short-term goals and to be specific in setting goals and evaluating its performance relative to those goals, (2) recognize the need to view the organization as a system of interacting components that must be coordinated, (3) communicate the organization's goals to all organization members and involve them in the budgeting process, and (4) anticipate problems, thereby handling them proactively rather than reactively.

The master budget is the set of operating and financial plans that summarize the organization's activities for the upcoming budget period, which is usually 1 year. The financial plans developed in the master budget include a projected or pro forma cash flow statement, balance sheet, and income statement. Planners use the projected balance sheet and income statement to evaluate the financial consequences of a proposed short-term business plan. Planners use the statement of projected cash flows to plan when excess cash will be generated so that they can plan short-term investments or plan to meet their cash shortages in the least expensive way.

The chapter presented a detailed master budgeting exercise and developed the financial plans for a set of given operating plans. Organizations make financial commitments when they acquire special-purpose facilities or capacity in the long term and general-purpose facilities or capacity in the intermediate term. In the short term, organizations acquire other resources, such as materials and casual labor, as needed, allowing them to use longer term capacity to produce products.

The chapter discussed the insights of what-if analysis, which is a modeling exercise that explores the operating and financial consequences of varying a proposed plan and the insights of sensitivity analysis, which explores the sensitivity of operating decisions and financial results to the estimates used in the planning model.

Some organizations compare planned and actual results to support the process of organization control. Chapters 5, 6, and 11 develop the role and calculation of variances, which are the differences between plans and results, in more detail.

The source of information used in budgeting models is important in two ways. First, the information source should be credible and reliable. Second, because of the potential use of planning information for control, a potential behavioral conflict was identified and will be explored in more detail in Chapter 14.

The insights and focus of budgeting in nonmanufacturing environments, such as the natural resource sector, the service sector, and the nonprofit sector, were discussed.

The chapter described the perspective of zero-base budgeting and compared it with incremental budgeting, which bases the appropriations in the current budget on those in the previous budget.

KEY TERM LIST

Administrative and discretionary spending plan, p. 197

Aggregate planning, p. 204

Appropriation, p. 220

Budgeting, p. 193

Budgets, p. 193

Assignment Material

Questions

5-1 What is a budget?

5-2 A student develops a spending plan for a school semester. Is that budgeting? Why?

5-3 What is a demand forecast and why is it relevant in budgeting?

5-4 Is employee training an example of a discretionary expenditure? Why?

5-5 What is a line of credit? How is it useful to a small organization?

5-6 Using the notion of aggregate planning, what problems would be faced by municipal authorities planning transportation for people attending a rock concert in the city's core?

5-7 What is an appropriation? Give an example of one in a university.

5-8 What does a capital spending plan do?

5-9 What is an example of a committed expenditure?

5-10 Are food costs in a university residence cafeteria an engineered cost or a committed cost? Briefly explain.

5-11 What is an example of a model? Why do you think people use models?

5-12 What is a production plan? Give an example of one in a courier company.

5-13 What is a variance? How is a warning light in a car that indicates that the oil pressure is low like a variance?

5-14 What do you think is the most significant committed resource, in terms of dollar expenditures, in a university?

5-15 What is what-if analysis?

5–16 Are materials always a flexible resource? Why?

5–17 You are planning your expenses for the upcoming school semester. You assume that this year's expenditures will equal last year's plus 2%. What approach to budgeting are you using?

5–18 You are willing to donate to worthy organizations. However, you believe strongly that each request for a donation should be evaluated based on its own merits. You would not feel bad in any year if you donated nothing. What approach to budgeting are you using?

5–19 What is the relationship between a demand forecast and a sales plan?

5–20 Would a labor hiring and training plan be more important in a university or a municipal government office that hires casual workers to do unskilled work? Why?

5–21 What is a periodic budget?

EXERCISES

5–22 The text mentioned that budgeting is often a recursive process. If the results of a plan are unacceptable, it is changed to find better results. Does this suggest anything to you about the process of planning?

5–23 Consider a company that sells prescription drugs. It has salespeople who visit doctors and hospitals to encourage physicians to prescribe its drugs. The company sells to drug stores. Each salesperson is evaluated based on the sales in her territory. The salesperson's income is a salary plus a bonus if actual sales exceed planned sales. To plan operations, this company needs to develop estimates of total sales. Where should it get this information?

5–24 Some people say that "budgets are great for planning but not for control." What do you think they mean by that? Do you agree with this sentiment?

5–25 For a university, identify a cost that you think is controllable in the short term and explain why you think it is. Identify a cost that you think is controllable in the intermediate term and explain why you think it is. Identify a cost that you think is controllable in the long term and explain why you think it is. What does this cost structure imply about the university's flexibility in responding to changing student demands?

5–26 Many managers consider the pro forma financial statements to be the most important product of the master budgeting process. Why do you think they believe this?

5–27 Cash budgets, which forecast monthly (usually) inflows and outflows, are an important part of the budgeting process in most organizations. In the course of preparing a cash budget, the organization must estimate its cash inflows from credit sales. Suppose that, in response to projected cash shortfalls, the organization decides to speed up its collections of credit sales. What effect might this have on the organization?

5–28 The text claims that budgeting allows the organization to identify broad resource requirements so that it can develop plans to put needed resources in place. Use an example to illustrate why this might be valuable in a consulting company that provides advice to clients.

5–29 The text claims that budgeting allows the organization to identify potential problems so that plans can be developed to avoid these problems or to deal with them systematically. Give an example of how budgeting might serve this role in a company that buys vegetables and cans them.

5–30 The text claims that budgeting allows the organization to compare its projected operating and financial results with those of competitors as a general test of the efficiency of the organization's operating processes. Explain how this might be valuable for a machine shop that does custom machining work for its customers.

5–31 The text identifies sensitivity analysis as an important component of any budgeting exercise. Which estimates do you think will be most crucial in developing a master budget. Why?

5–32 A university faced with a deficit reacts by cutting resource allocations to all faculties and departments by 8%. Do you think this is a good approach to budgeting? Why?

PROBLEMS

5–33 Elmira Manufacturing is developing a sales and production plan as part of its master budgeting process. Monthly sales, which occur uniformly during each month, for the upcoming year follow.

ELMIRA MANUFACTURING
MONTHLY SALES

Month	Unit Sales
January	9,343
February	9,022
March	7,120
April	8,181
May	7,942
June	9,681
July	2,217
August	2,768
September	2,768
October	2,283
November	1,140
December	2,408
January	8,725

Production for each month equals one-half of the current month's sales plus one-half of the next month's projected sales. Develop the production plan for Elmira Manufacturing for the upcoming year.

5–34 Spokane Planters provides reforestation services to large paper products companies. It must hire one planter for every 10,000 trees that it has contracted to plant each month. An employee must receive 1 week of evaluation and training before being profitably employed. For every 5 prospective employees who enter training, 3 are deemed suitable for employment. When cutbacks occur, employees are laid off on the first day of the month. Every employee laid off receives severance pay equal to 1 week's salary, which is approximately $400, regardless of how long the layoff will last. Laid-off employees inevitably drift away and new hires must be trained.

The company has been offered the following contracts for the upcoming year. Each monthly contract is offered on an accept or reject basis. That is, if a monthly contract is accepted, it must be completed in full. Partial completion is not acceptable. The revenue per tree planted is $0.20.

SPOKANE PLANTERS
MONTHLY TREE PLANTING CONTRACTS

Month	Trees
January	8,692
February	5,765
March	8,134
April	34,400
May	558,729
June	832,251
July	1,286,700
August	895,449
September	733,094
October	203,525
November	29,410
December	9,827

Prepare a labor plan for the upcoming year, indicating the following for each month:

(a) Whether you feel the company should accept or reject the proposed planting contract.

(b) How many people will be hired for training (recall that the employee is not available for planting during the week of training and that only 3 of the 5 employees accepted for training can be hired).

(c) How many people will be laid off. The organization will have 2 trained employees on January 1.

5–35 Greenville Chemical Company manufactures a wide range of chemical compounds. One of the most difficult compounds is a cleaning solvent made from an expensive and volatile raw material, *tetrax*, that is often in short supply. The company uses one liter of tetrax for every 100 liters of cleaning solvent that it makes.

Tetrax costs $560 per liter and must be stored in space leased in a special warehouse. The storage cost, including all related costs, is $2 per liter per day stored. The chemical is unstable and, on average, the loss is 1% of the volume stored per day. The cleaning compound can also be made from *monax*, which costs $1,000 per liter. Because of the prohibitive cost of monax, however, Greenville avoids using it unless it is absolutely necessary.

The 3 existing tetrax suppliers have been unreliable. For this reason, Greenville has refused to begin production of the cleaning compound. Recently, a new supplier joined the field and guarantees the supply of tetrax (it will replace any undelivered tetrax with monax) under 3 conditions. Customers must be prepared to take weekly deliveries of tetrax, the weekly order must be for precisely the same quantity each week, and the contract must cover 1 year.

Because the cleaning compound itself is also volatile, users demand the product when they are ready for it and no sooner. Suppliers carefully estimate the amount of cleaner that they require and will not accept less than the ordered amount.

The contracted cleaning compound sales for next year follow.

GREENVILLE CHEMICAL COMPANY CLEANING SOLVENT PRODUCT

Month	Unit Sales	Month	Unit Sales
January	41,203	July	41,889
February	48,077	August	42,107
March	53,646	September	47,488
April	60,038	October	49,638
May	46,332	November	49,942
June	50,508	December	37,593

REQUIRED:

(a) Set up a spreadsheet for this problem. The spreadsheet should allow you to compute the total cost of a contract with the new supplier. This total cost includes purchase price, storage cost, and the cost, if necessary, of any monax that would be purchased. The spreadsheet should be set up to allow you to vary the purchase quantity of tetrax easily

To simplify the problem, make the following assumptions:

(i) The loss each month is 1% times the number of days times the sum of (1) the average of the opening and ending inventory (before the loss) and (2) one-half the batch size.

(ii) The cost of carrying inventory each month is 2 times the number of days times the sum of (1) the average of opening and closing inventory (after the loss) and (2) one-half the batch size.

(iii) Production takes place 7 days per week.

(iv) January, March, July, and November have 5 weeks; the rest of the months of the year have 4 weeks.

(b) What is the best weekly quantity to contract for purchase from the new supplier?

5–36 Davenport Company makes cash (20% of total sales), credit card (50% of total sales), and account sales (30% of total sales). Credit card sales are collected in the month following the sale, net of a 3% credit card fee. That is, if the sale is $100, the credit card company's fee is $3, and Davenport receives $97. Account sales are collected as follows: 40% in the first month following the sale, 50% in the second month following the sale, 8% in the third month following the sale, and 2% never collected.

The following table identifies the projected sales for the next year.

DAVENPORT COMPANY PROJECTED SALES

Month	Sales	Month	Sales
January	12,369,348	July	21,747,839
February	15,936,293	August	14,908,534
March	13,294,309	September	11,984,398
April	19,373,689	October	18,894,535
May	20,957,566	November	21,983,545
June	18,874,717	December	20,408,367

If the collections from these sales are the only cash inflows in Davenport Company, prepare a statement showing the cash expected each month.

5–37 Brookhaven Dairy is preparing a third-quarter budget (July, August, and September) for its ice cream products. It produces 5 brands of ice cream, and each uses a different mix of ingredients. Brookhaven's suppliers supply ingredients just in time provided that they are given 2 months' notice. The following table indicates the units of each type of ingredient required per unit of each product.

BROOKHAVEN DAIRY REQUIRED INGREDIENTS

	Products				
Ingredients	Product A	Product B	Product C	Product D	Product E
Ice cream	1	1	1	1	1
Ingredient 1	2	–0–	3	1	2
Ingredient 2	–0–	1	2	3	–0–
Ingredient 3	1	3	–0–	2	3
Ingredient 4	–0–	2	1	–0–	1
Ingredient 5	3	1	2	–0–	1

The following table summarizes the estimated unit sales for each product in each of the months in the third quarter.

BROOKHAVEN DAIRY ESTIMATED UNIT SALES

	MONTH		
Product	July	August	September
Product A	194,875	164,033	129,857
Product B	104,856	98,375	76,495
Product C	209,855	194,575	174,654
Product D	96,576	75,766	55,966
Product E	47,867	29,575	10,958

Prepare a monthly purchases budget for the ice cream ingredients.

5–38 Livonia Motel is planning its operations for the upcoming tourist season. The motel has 60 units and the following table presents the average number of daily rentals expected for each of the 12 weeks of the tourist season.

LIVONIA MOTEL AVERAGE NUMBER OF DAILY RENTALS

Week	Average Units Rented	Week	Average Units Rented
1	46	7	55
2	48	8	55
3	54	9	50
4	60	10	45
5	60	11	37
6	60	12	30

The motel hires housekeeping staff on a weekly basis. Each person can clean 15 rooms per day. Employees must be hired for the entire week at a wage of $400 per employee per week. Because the motel is located in a small rural area, there are always trained people available to work on short notice.

The motel does not own its linen and towels but rents them from a rental agency in a nearby city. The rental contract must be signed for a 4-week period and for a fixed amount of linen and towels. Therefore, the motel must sign 3 contracts for the 12-week tourist season. The contract provides the linen required for each room for $3 per night.

Prepare a weekly budget for the hotel showing

(a) The number of housekeeping staff to employ

(b) The number of linen and towel units to contract

5-39 During the school year, the Brevard School band arranges concert dates in many communities. Because only part of the school's travel expenses are covered by the concert admission fees, the band raises money in the local community through events such as car washes to help defray its operating expenses.

To estimate its expenses for the upcoming year, the band's manager has estimated the number of concert dates for each of the school months, September through May. For each concert, the manager estimates hotel costs of $900, food costs of $480, bus rental costs of $600, and other costs of $200.

The following table presents the number of planned concerts during the upcoming year.

BREVARD SCHOOL BAND SCHEDULED CONCERTS

Month	Scheduled Concerts	Month	Scheduled Concerts
September	2	February	4
October	4	March	5
November	5	April	6
December	6	May	6
January	3		

Prepare a monthly schedule estimating the band's travel expenses.

5-40 Grand Junction Motor Shop does major repair work on automobile engines. The major cost in the shop is the wages of the mechanics. The shop employs 9 mechanics who are paid $750 for working a 40-hour week. The work week consists of 5 days of 8 hours. Employees actually work 7 hours each day, because they are given 1 hour of breaks each day. They are highly skilled and valued by their employer, so these mechanics are paid whether or not there is work available for them to do. They are also paid $30 for every overtime hour, or partial hour, that they work.

The machine shop industry estimates that for every mechanic hour actually worked in a shop like this, the employee consumes about $25 of variable overhead items, such as lubricants, tool parts, and electricity.

The motor shop has estimated that the following work will be available each week during the next 10 weeks.

GRAND JUNCTION MOTOR SHOP ESTIMATED WORK

Week	Hours of Work	Week	Hours of Work
1	285	6	295
2	330	7	260
3	300	8	300
4	255	9	325
5	325	10	355

Develop a weekly budget of mechanic wages and variable overhead costs.

5–41 Allentown Nurseries grows and sells garden plants. The nursery is active between January and October each year. During January, the potting tables and equipment are prepared. The potting and seeding are done in February. In March and April, the plants are cultivated, watered, and fertilized. May and June are the peak selling months. July, August, and September are the peak months for visiting customers in their homes to provide them with advice and to solve their problems. During October, the equipment and buildings are secured for the winter months, and in November and December, full-time employees take their paid holidays and the business is closed.

The nursery employs 15 full-time staff and, depending on the season, up to 20 part-time staff. The full-time staff are paid an average wage of $2,700 per month and work 160 hours per month.

The part-time staff are paid $10 per hour. Because the nursery relies on local students for part-time work, there is no shortage of trained people willing to work the hours that are available. The ratio of full-time employee hours worked to part-time employee hours worked is January, 5:1; February, 5:1; March, 3:1; April, 3:1; May, 1:1; June, 1:1; July, 1:1; August, 1:1; September, 2:1; and October, 4:1. Because part-time students are mainly used for moving and selling activities, their work creates very little incremental overhead costs.

Fixed costs, other than wages, associated with this operation are about $55,000 per month. The cost drivers in this operation are the activities that the full-time employees undertake. These cost drivers are proportional to the hours worked by the full-time employees. The variable costs depend on the season and reflect the common employee activities during that season. Average variable costs per employee hour worked are January, $15; February, $15; March, $15; April, $15; May, $5; June, $5; July, $20; August, $20; September, $20; and October, $10. These variable costs include both overhead items, such as power and water, and direct items such as soil and pots. Assume that all expenses are paid in the month that they are incurred.

Based on the information provided, prepare a cash outflow statement for the upcoming year.

5–42 Plattsburgh Insurance Company manages a medical insurance program for its clients. Employees of client firms submit claims for reimbursement of medical expenses. Plattsburgh processes these claims, checks them to ensure that they are covered by the claimant's policy, notes whether the claimant has reached any limit on coverage, computes any deductible, and issues a check for the claimant's refund.

Three types of clerks work in the claims processing department: supervisors, senior clerks, and junior clerks. The supervisors are paid $42,000 per year, the senior clerks are paid $37,000 per year, and the junior clerks are paid $32,000 per year. For every 150,000 claims processed per year, Plattsburgh plans to use 1 supervisor, 6 junior clerks, and 2 senior clerks.

In 1994 the company processed 2,000,000 medical claims and employed 14 supervisors, 30 senior clerks, and 83 junior clerks.

REQUIRED:

(a) Compute the excess costs or cost savings relating to the claims processing staff.

(b) How would you interpret these results? What additional information would you ask for if you were making a determination of the clerical group's processing efficiencies?

5–43 Island Pond Electronics manufactures and sells electronic components to electronics stores. The controller is preparing her annual budget and has asked the sales group to prepare sales estimates. All members of the sales force have been asked to estimate sales in their territory for each of the organization's 10 major products.

The marketing group is paid a salary and a commission based on sales in excess of some target level. You have discovered that the sales manager uses the sales estimates to develop the target levels at which commissions begin. Specifically, the sales manager takes the sales estimate, adds 10%, and the result becomes the sales hurdle level. If sales are less than the hurdle level, no commissions are paid. If sales are above the hurdle level, commissions are paid at varying rates.

REQUIRED:

(a) What is the motivation of the sales force if they know the relationship between their estimate and the target level of sales?

(b) What is the likely consequence of basing the organization's budgets on these estimates?

(c) If you were the controller in this situation and were responsible for both the reward system and the budgeting system, what would you do?

CASES

5–44 John Aqua is the dean of a business school. The university is under strong financial pressures, and the university president has asked all the deans to cut costs. John is wondering how he should respond to this request.

The university receives its operating funds from three sources: (1) tuitions (60%), (2) government grants (25%), and (3) gifts and endowment income (15%). The money flows into the university's general operating fund. A management committee consisting of the university president, the 3 vice presidents, and the 9 deans allocate funds to the individual schools. The university's charter requires that it operate with a balanced budget.

The initial allocation of funds reflects (1) committed costs that cannot be avoided, primarily the employment costs of tenured faculty and (2) committed costs relating to overhead items, such as staff, building maintenance, and other operations costs. The balance of funds is allocated to discretionary activities, such as scholarships, program changes or additions, and sports.

The various deans compare their respective funding levels. The basis of comparison is to divide total university expenditures by the number of full-time student equivalents to get an average cost per student. Then the average cost per student is multiplied by the number of full-time student equivalents to get the target funding for each school. On average, the actual funding for the business school has been about 70% of the target funding, which is the second lowest (the arts faculty is lowest) in the university.

Because of the rapid growth of committed and administrative costs, the amount of funds allocated to discretionary activities has been declining from a historic level of about 10%. This year, the projected revenues will not even cover the projected committed costs. In response to this development, the president has called on all deans to "do your best to reduce the level of expenditures."

The president's request has been met with scepticism by many deans, who are notorious for digging in their heels, ignoring requests for spending cuts, and then being bailed out by funds that were released from other activities or raised to meet the budget shortfall. Many deans believe that the departments that sacrificed and reduced their budgets would only create funds that would be used by the university to support other schools that had made little or no effort to reduce their budgets. Then these schools would be asked to make even more cuts to make up for the lack of cuts in schools that made little progress in cost reduction. On the other hand, the deans also believe that if there were no reaction to the president's initial request for cost reductions, arbitrary cutbacks would be imposed on the individual schools.

In response to this situation, John is wondering what to do. He knows that by increasing class sizes slightly, using some part-time instructors, and eliminating some optional courses that seldom attract many students, he can trim about $800,000 from his operating budget of $11,000,000. However, making these changes would create hardships for both the students and faculty in the business school and, given the historic relationship of the school's average funding to its target funding, John is wondering whether the business school should be asked to make additional sacrifices.

John knows that he has several alternatives:

(a) Do nothing, arguing that the business school is already cost effective relative to others and it is the time for them to reduce their cost structures.

(b) Make the cuts that he has identified but stretch them out over a number of years and stop making them if other schools are not doing their share in cutting costs.

(c) Make the cuts unilaterally and advise the administration that the business school budget can be reduced by about $800,000.

Explain what you would do if you were John and why. Your explanation should include your analysis of the motivation of all schools to cut costs in an environment that traditionally has taken advantage of those that cooperate.

5–45 Fred's Reproductions makes reproductions of antique tables and chairs and sells them through 3 sales outlets. The product line consists of 2 styles of tables, 3 styles of cabinets, and 2 styles of chairs. Although customers often ask Fred Molinari, the owner/manager of Fred's Reproductions, to make other products, he does not intend to expand the product line.

The planning group at Fred's Reproductions prepares a master budget for each fiscal year, which corresponds to the calendar year. It is December 1993, and the planners are completing the master budget for 1994.

Unit prices are $200, $900, and $1,800, respectively, for the chairs, tables, and cabinets. Customers pay (1) by cash and receive a 5% discount, (2) by credit card (the credit card company takes 3% of the revenue as its fee and remits the balance in the month following the month of sale), or (3) on account (only exporters buy on account). The distribution of cash, credit card, and exporter sales is 25%, 35%, and 40%. Of the credit sales to exporters, Fred's Reproductions collects 30% in the month following the sale, 50% in the second month following the sale, 17% in the third month following the sale, and 3% go uncollected. Fred's Reproductions recognizes the expense of cash discounts, credit card fees, and bad debts in the month of the sale.

Fred's employs 40 people who work in the following areas: 15 in administration, sales, and shipping; 2 in manufacturing supervision (director and a scheduler); 9 in manufacturing fabrication and assembly (carpenters); and 14 in manufacturing, finishing, and other (helpers, cleaners, and maintenance crew).

The carpenter-hours required to make the parts for and assemble a chair, table, or cabinet are 0.4, 2.5, and 6, respectively. Production personnel have organized the work so that each carpenter-hour worked requires 1.5 helper-hours. Therefore, production planners maintain a ratio of at least 1.5 helpers for every carpenter. The company pays carpenters and helpers $24 and $14 per hour, respectively (including all benefits).

Fred's Reproductions guarantees all employees their pay regardless of the hours of work available. When the employees are not doing their regular jobs, they undertake maintenance, training, community service, and customer relations activities. Fred's pays each employee weekly for that week's work. If an employee works 172 hours or less during the month, Fred's pays the employee the product of his hourly rate and 172. The company pays 150% of the normal hourly rate for every hour over 172 that the employee works during the month. Planners add new carpenters if the projected total monthly overtime is more than 5% of the total regular carpenter hours available. Fred's has a policy of no employee layoffs. Any required hiring is done on the first day of each month.

Fred's Reproductions rents a converted warehouse as a factory; it costs $600,000 per year. The company pays rent quarterly beginning January 1 of each year. Fred's pays other fixed manufacturing costs, which include manufacturing supervision salaries and which amount to $480,000, in equal monthly amounts.

The capital investment policy is to purchase, each January and July, $5,000 of machinery and equipment per carpenter employed during that month. Fred's recognizes depreciation at the rate of 10% of the year-end balance of the Machinery and Equipment account. Statistical studies of cost behavior have determined that supplies, variable overhead, and maintenance costs vary with the number of carpenter-hours worked and are $5, $20, and $15, per hour, respectively.

The units of wood required for chairs, tables, and cabinets are 1, 8, and 15, respectively. Each unit of wood costs $30. The inventory policy is to make products in the month they will be sold. Two suppliers deliver raw materials and supplies as required just as Fred's Reproductions requires them. The company pays for all materials, supplies, variable overhead, and maintenance items on receipt.

Annual administration salaries, fixed selling costs, and planned advertising expenditures are $300,000, $360,000, and $600,000, respectively. Fred's Reproductions makes these expenditures in equal monthly amounts. Packaging and shipping costs for chairs, tables, and cabinets are $15, $65, and $135, respectively. Variable selling costs are 6% for each product's list price. Fred's Reproductions pays packaging, shipping, and variable selling costs as incurred.

Using its line of credit, Fred's Reproductions maintains a minimum balance of $50,000. All line of credit transactions occur on the first day of each month. The bank charges interest on the line of credit account balance at the rate of 10% per year. Fred's pays interest on the first day of each month on the line of credit balance outstanding at the end of the previous month. On the first of each month, the bank pays interest at the rate of 3% per year on funds exceeding $50,000 in the company's Cash account at the end of the previous month.

Realized sales for October, November, and December 1993 appear in the following table.

FRED'S REPRODUCTIONS
UNIT SALES 1995

Item	October	November	December
Chairs	900	975	950
Tables	175	188	201
Cabinets	90	102	95

Sales staff estimates the unit demand for 1996 as follows: chairs, 1,000 plus a random number uniformly distributed between 0 and 50 plus 15% of the previous month's sales of chairs; tables, 200 plus a random number uniformly distributed between 0 and 20 plus 15% of the previous month's sales; and cabinets, 100 plus a random number uniformly distributed between 0 and 10 plus 15% of the previous month's sales of cabinets. This estimation process resulted in the demand forecasts and the sales plan found in the following table.

FRED'S REPRODUCTIONS
PROJECTED UNIT SALES 1996

Month	Chairs	Tables	Cabinets
January	1,020	200	109
February	1,191	237	120
March	1,179	243	119
April	1,195	250	126
May	1,200	252	122
June	1,204	255	125
July	1,194	242	123
August	1,199	253	121
September	1,222	243	127
October	1,219	248	126
November	1,207	244	126
December	1,192	255	119

Planners project Fred's Reproductions' balance sheet, at January 1, 1996, to be as follows:

FRED'S REPRODUCTIONS—
BALANCE SHEET, JANUARY 1, 1996

Cash	$ 50,000	Bank loan	$ –0–
Accounts receivable	575,008		
Machinery (net book value)	360,000	Shareholder's equity	985,008
Total	$985,008	Total	$985,008

REQUIRED:

(a) Prepare a sales forecast, staffing plan, production plan, cash flow statement, pro forma income statement, and pro forma balance sheet for 1996.

(b) The level of bad debts concerns Fred's Reproductions' controller. If Fred's insists on cash payments from exporters who would be given the cash discount, the sales staff expects that total sales to exporters in 1996 will fall by 5% (sales in 1995 will not be affected). Based on the effect of this change on profitability, is it desirable? (Round sales forecasts to the nearest unit.)

(c) Ignore the changes described in question 2 and return to the data in the original example. The sales staff is considering increasing the advertising budget from $600,000 to $900,000 and cutting prices by 5%. This should increase sales by 30% in 1996 (sales in 1995 will not be affected). Based on the effect of this change on profitability, is it desirable? (Round sales forecasts to the nearest unit.)

(d) Is there a criterion other than profitability that might be used to evaluate the desirability of the changes proposed in (b) and (c)? If yes, what is that criterion and why is it important? If no, why is profitability the sole relevant criterion?

5–46 On-Time Courier Company provides package courier services. Each afternoon its couriers pick up packages; they drive trucks operating out of local terminals. Packages are returned to the terminal and are transported to the central hub that evening. In the hub, packages are sorted during the late evening and are sent to the destination terminal overnight. The next morning couriers from the destination terminal deliver packages to the addressees.

Most of the routes that the couriers follow are fixed. Each day the couriers have both scheduled and unscheduled pickup and drop-off stops. However, studies have shown that adding an unscheduled stop to a route or picking up an additional shipment at a scheduled stop creates negligible additional costs. The key costs in terms of the courier's time, the vehicle, and the fuel costs are determined by the route itself. Therefore, most of the costs at On-Time Courier result from decisions that reflect the planned level of activity rather than decisions that reflect the actual volume of activity. The major exception is the sorting cost in the hubs and terminals. Because sorting labor is hired on a part-time basis as required, the sorting cost varies with the number of shipments handled.

Ellen Carter, the manager of the Houlton terminal, is preparing an expense budget for the upcoming year. She plans to base this year's budget on the trends from the previous years. The following table shows the level of costs in the previous 2 years.

ON-TIME COURIER COMPANY
ACTIVITY COST LEVELS

Item	1994	1995	1996
Shipments handled	8,500,000	10,300,000	11,100,000
Administrative costs	$ 300,000	$ 315,000	$ 320,000
Truck depreciation and maintenance	$ 750,000	$ 830,000	$ 850,000
Courier fuel costs	$ 600,000	$ 660,000	$ 670,000
Courier wages	$1,750,000	$1,810,000	$1,850,000
Terminal overhead costs	$ 240,000	$ 280,000	$ 260,000
Labor costs in terminal	$ 120,000	$ 150,000	$ 170,000

REQUIRED:

(a) Identify what you think are the cost drivers for each of the items in this table.

(b) Given the information provided, prepare an expense budget for the upcoming year, assuming that the volume of shipments handled is expected to be 14,000,000 units.

BASIC PRODUCT COSTING SYSTEMS

LEARNING OBJECTIVES

This chapter will introduce you to:

1. the use of job bid sheets to estimate product costs in a job order costing system
2. the use of overhead rates to apply overhead to products
3. the reasons that cost systems with multiple labor and overhead rates give different estimates of product costs than cost systems with a single rate
4. the evaluation of a cost system to understand whether it is likely to distort product costs
5. the relevance of recording actual costs and comparing them with estimated costs
6. the analysis of variances between actual and estimated costs, including first- and second-level variances
7. the importance of conversion costs and the measurement of costs in multistage, continuous-processing industries
8. the differences between job order costing and multistage process costing systems

CHAPTER 6

Archie's Auto Service: The Dilemma

Archibald Austin started Archie's Auto Service Company in 1974. Over a period of two decades, he built it into a business with more than $1 million in billings each year and a strong reputation for high-quality auto repair work. In the past three years, however, Archie had lost a considerable amount of business to quick service operations such as Carex Muffler Company for simple jobs including exhaust system replacements. Increased competition from companies such as Carex had cut into his sales volume and profit margins, and his take-home income from the business had declined precipitously.

Archie expanded his auto shop over this period. The shop has 5 service bays and employs 5 mechanics, 2 of whom were highly skilled and trained in doing complex repair jobs. The salary and benefits of $60,000 for each expert mechanic exceeded the average compensation of the other three mechanics by almost $25,000. The three junior mechanics primarily worked on routine repairs such as brake relinings and muffler replacements.

Archie met with his accountant, Ace Acton, who asked Archie to explain the problem that led to poor financial performance over the last 2 years. "Archie, your net income numbers look terrible," he said. "What has happened to your business?"

"Operators like Carex Muffler Company have taken away most of my simple repair business with their low prices. How can they price their jobs so low and still make a profit?"

"Let me take a look at your job order costing system," Ace said. "I may be able to find the answer to that question."

(© Blair Seitz/Photo Researchers)

As the case of Archie's Auto Service shows, management accountants today face interesting challenges in the area of product costing. What costs should be included as part of product costs, and why? How should such costs be calculated, accumulated, and reported to decision makers to help them in their planning and operations decisions? This chapter builds on the ideas of the previous chapters, which focused on cost classification (Chapter 3), cost behavior and variability (Chapter 4), and budgeting for operations (Chapter 5). Let's examine some of the systems for estimating and presenting costs to management and to other decision makers by first turning to the subject of job order costing systems.

CONSIDER THIS . . .

Costing Bicycles

Paramount Cycles, based in Dayton, Ohio, is a manufacturer of high-quality bicycles for children and adults. Paramount cycles are sold primarily through specialty bicycle shops.

Paramount uses a standard cost accounting system to estimate the cost per bicycle for each model it manufactures. Engineering standards are developed for material quantity and labor hours for each part and for each operation. The industrial engineering department also provides lists for parts and component materials for each bicycle. By multiplying material quantity by estimated cost obtained from the purchasing manager, the finance department is able to calculate direct material cost. Manufacturing records of direct labor hours required for each job are used with labor costs per hour, estimated by the personnel department, to calculate direct labor cost for bicycle. An overhead rate is determined by dividing the annual budgeted overhead by the budgeted direct labor dollars to obtain an overhead cost per direct labor dollar. The total of direct material, direct labor, and overhead is used as the cost of a bicycle for both inventory valuation and for product pricing.

Source: "Paramount Cycle Company," Harvard Business School, Case 180–069.

OBJECTIVE 6.1
The use of job bid sheets to estimate product costs in a job order costing system

Job order costing system
System for estimating costs of manufacturing products for a job.

Job bid sheet
Format for estimating job costs.

JOB ORDER COSTING SYSTEMS

A **job order costing system** is a common method for estimating product costs in firms that have several distinct products. Specifically, a job order costing system estimates costs of manufacturing products for different jobs required for customer orders.

Products may differ in their materials content and the hours of labor required to manufacture them. Products also may differ in the demand they place on support activity resources or in response to special customer needs that may lead to customized production, with different product characteristics targeted for different markets. Therefore, it becomes important for firms to assess the costs of individual products to adequately evaluate their profitability.

Many firms are required to bid on jobs before customers decide to place an order with them. Costs need to be estimated for each job so that a bid can be prepared, and job order costing systems provide the means to measure these costs.

■ Components of a Job Bid Sheet

Exhibit 6–1 displays a **job bid sheet**, a format for estimating job costs, prepared by Vernon Valve Company, which manufactures a variety of special valves for several customers. The bid sheet has five distinct panels. Panel 1 identifies the customer, the product, and the quantity required. Panel 2 lists all the materials required to complete the job. For each item of material, the quantity required is estimated based on *standard engineering specifications*. For instance, each unit of valve L181 requires 2.4 pounds of bar steel stock. Therefore, the order for 1,500 units of L181 requires 3,600 pounds of bar steel stock. The current price of $11.30 per pound is obtained from current records maintained and updated by the purchasing department. Therefore, the cost of bar steel stock required for this job is $40,680 ($11.30 [price per pound] * 3,600 [pounds]).

The 3rd panel lists the amount of direct labor required for the job. These estimates are obtained from *industrial engineering specifications* developed on the basis of *work and motion* studies or by *analogy with comparable standard products*. For instance, engineering staff at a major steel company studies how workers perform each task necessary to make steel to customer specifications and measures how much time each task requires. Project managers at a software system development firm compare new project specifications with projects they have managed before to estimate the amount of programmer time required to develop the new software system.

EXHIBIT 6–1
Vernon Valve Company: Job Bid Sheet

Panel 1

Bid Number: J4369   Date: July 6, 1995
Customer: Michigan Motors
Product: Automobile engine valves (Valve #L181)
Engineering Design Number: JDR-103   Number of Units: 1,500

Panel 2

Materials	Quantity	Price	Amount
Bar steel stock 3"	3,600 lbs.	$11.30	$40,680
Subassembly	1,500 units	39.00	58,500
Total direct materials			$99,180

Panel 3

Labor	Hours	Rate	Amount
Lathe operators	480	$26.00	$12,480
Assembly workers	900	18.00	16,200
Total direct labor	1,380		$28,680

Panel 4

Overhead	Amount
600 machine-hours @ $40 per hour	$24,000
1380 direct labor hours @ $36 per hour	49,680
Total overhead	$73,680

Panel 5

Total costs	$201,540
Add 25% margin	50,385
Bid price	$251,925
Unit cost	$134.36
Unit price	$167.95

After estimating the direct labor hours required for a job, Vernon Valve must determine a separate wage rate for each grade of labor required for the operations performed to manufacture the valves. The wage rate for assembly workers is $18 per hour, and 0.6 assembly hours are required per valve. Therefore, 900 assembly hours (1500 [units] * 0.6 [hours/unit]) are required for 1,500 valves. The cost is estimated to be $16,200 (900 [hours] * $18.00 [wage rate/hour]).

The 4th panel of the bid sheet contains estimates for overhead costs. Vernon assigns overhead to jobs based on the number of machine-hours and direct labor hours expected for the job. For this purpose, Vernon uses two overhead rates based on the assumption that all indirect manufacturing costs are related either to machines or direct labor. The company classifies them into 2 cost pools based on whether the cost drivers are machine-hours or direct labor hours and computes a separate overhead rate for the 2 cost pools. Subsequent sections describe the procedure for calculating overhead rates in detail. To obtain the total amount of overhead costs allocated to the job, it is necessary to multiply the number of machine hours (600) and the number of direct labor hours required for the job (1,380) by their respective overhead rates ($40 per machine hour and $36 per direct labor hour). Then Vernon Valve must add the two estimates to obtain a total of $73,680 (600 [hours] * $40 [overhead rate] + 1,380 [hours] * $36 [overhead rate]).

Panel 5 of the job bid sheet shows the total costs estimated for the job, which requires adding the total direct materials, total direct labor, and total overhead costs ($99,180 + $28,680 + $73,680) to obtain $201,540.

■ Job Costs and Markup

Job costs
Total of direct material, direct labor, and overhead costs estimated for or identified with a job.

Markup or margin
Amount of profit added to estimated job costs to arrive at bid price.

Markup rate
Ratio of the markup amount to the estimated costs for a job.

Rate of return
Ratio of net income to investment (also called *return on investment*).

The total of direct material, direct labor, and overhead costs for the job is referred to as the **job cost**. Most firms **mark up** the job costs by adding an additional amount, or *margin*, to create a profit on the job. The total job costs plus the margin equal the bid price. At Vernon Valve, the **markup rate**, or the percentage by which job costs are marked up, is 25%. Markup rate depends on a variety of factors, including the amount of overhead costs excluded from the *overhead rate*, for example, corporate-level costs; the target **rate of return** (ratio of net income to investment) desired by the corporation; competitive intensity; past bidding strategies adopted by key competitors; demand conditions; and overall product-market strategies.

The markup rate may differ for different product groups and for different market segments, depending on local conditions. It also may change over time as conditions change. For instance, managers may decide to decrease profit margins when demand is weak and when unused capacity is likely to be available but may use higher markups to create higher profits when demand is expected to be high and little unused capacity exists. [Chapter 8 presents the issue of how costs are related to prices in greater detail.]

OBJECTIVE 6.2
The use of overhead rates to apply overhead to products

■ Determination of Overhead Rates

Overhead cost pools
Identified categories of overhead costs; each category has a separate rate, that is used.

Overhead rate
The rate at which overhead costs are applied to individual jobs. It is the ratio of the normal cost for a support activity accumulated in a cost pool to the normal level of the cost driver for the activity.

As discussed previously, determining realistic overhead rates has become increasingly important in recent years because overhead now comprises a large portion of the total costs in many industries. Notice that allocated overhead costs in the Vernon Valve example are more than twice the direct labor costs and almost as much as direct material costs. In addition, many firms now recognize that overhead costs are not related to just one factor, such as direct labor hours, but that several different factors may be driving costs. As a result, greater care should be taken in analyzing overhead costs and identifying what part of costs relate to what cost driver. For instance, costs identified with the activity of setting up machines are related to the cost driver, setup hours. All costs associated with a cost driver, such as setup hours, are accumulated separately. Each such portion of total overhead costs associated with a distinct cost driver is referred to as an **overhead cost pool**.

Each cost pool has a separate overhead rate. The **overhead rate** is the ratio of the normal cost (as defined in Chapter 4) for a support activity accumulated in the cost pool to the normal level of the cost driver for the activity. That is,

$$\text{Overhead rate} = \frac{\text{Normal cost of support activity}}{\text{Normal level of cost driver}} \qquad (6.1)$$

Recall that the normal cost of the support activity is the cost of the resources committed to the particular activity. The normal level of cost driver is the long-term capacity made available by the amount of resources committed to a support activity. For example, if 10 setup workers are hired at weekly wages (including benefits) of $810 each, and if each worker has the time to complete 15 setups in a week, then the normal cost for the setup activity is $8,100 per week ($810 * 10 workers), which makes available a capacity for performing 150 setups in a week (15 setups * 10 workers). Then the overhead rate is $54 per setup ($8,100 normal cost ÷ 150 setup capacity). Normal cost of a support activity, therefore, excludes fluctuations in costs caused by short-term adjustments, such as overtime payments. Normal level of the support activity also excludes short-term variations in demand, as reflected in overtime or idle time. Because the ratio in (6.1) is based on normal costs and normal cost driver levels, the rate remains stable over time and does not fluctuate as activity levels change in the short run. As a result, this overhead rate does not change simply because of short-run changes in exogenous (external) factors that do not affect the efficiency or price of the activity resources.

■ Problems with Using Fluctuating Overhead Rates

OBJECTIVE 6.3
The reasons that cost systems with multiple labor and overhead rates give different estimates of product costs than cost systems with a single rate

Consider the overhead rate based on machine hours at Vernon Valve Company. The cost pool includes machine depreciation, maintenance, power, and other machine-related costs. The normal machine-related costs amount to $900,000 per year, the normal capacity made available is 20,000 machine-hours per year, or 5,000 machine-hours (20,000/4) per quarter. Therefore, the machine-related overhead rate is $45 per machine-hour ($900,000/20,000 hours).

The *actual* machine usage varies each quarter because of fluctuations in demand. Machine-hours used are 5,400 in the spring quarter, 4,500 in the summer, 5,000 in the fall, and 3,600 in the winter. The normal level of the cost driver is the capacity of 5,000 machine-hours made available each quarter by the installed machines in the plant. This capacity is exceeded in the spring quarter by operating the machines overtime beyond regular shift hours.

Machine-related costs each quarter are $225,000. If the overhead rate is based on quarterly *cost driver levels* instead of the normal levels, the rate increases as the demand for the machine activity falls, and the rate decreases as the demand increases. For example, as the number of machine-hours decreases from 5,400 in the spring to 4,500 in the summer, the overhead rate increases from $41.67 per machine-hour for spring to $50 per machine-hour for summer (see Exhibit 6–2). In contrast, the overhead rate based on normal costs and normal activity levels remains fixed at $45 per machine-hour ($225,000/5,000 hours) throughout the year because costs depend on the machine capacity made available, and not on the season.

Determination of overhead rates based on planned or actual short-term usage results in higher rates in periods of lower demand. In such job costing

EXHIBIT 6–2
Overhead Rate and Quarterly Cost Driver Levels

QUARTER	DETAILS[a]	Overhead Rate
Spring	$\dfrac{\$225,000}{5,400}$	= $41.67 per machine-hour
Summer	$\dfrac{\$225,000}{4,500}$	= $50.00 per machine-hour
Fall	$\dfrac{\$225,000}{5,000}$	= $45.00 per machine-hour
Winter	$\dfrac{\$225,000}{3,600}$	= $62.50 per machine-hour

[a] Overhead Rate = $\dfrac{\text{Quarterly actual costs}}{\text{Quarterly actual machine hours}}$

systems, job costs appear to be higher in time periods when demand is lower. If bid prices are based on estimated job costs, the firm is likely to end up bidding higher prices during periods of low demand when, in fact, it could have been considering lowering prices. The higher bid price can further decrease demand, which, in turn, leads to higher overhead rates and even higher prices. Thus, the firm could enter an unnecessary death spiral, with successively higher overhead cost estimates and bid prices and lower demand for its products. Conversely, overhead rates appear low in such a cost system when demand is high and capacity is short. This leads to attracting additional business just when the company should be raising prices to ration demand.

Support activity costs are caused by the *level of capacity of each activity that is made available rather than the level of actual usage of these committed resources*. Therefore, the correct method for determining the overhead rate is to *estimate the normal cost per unit of the activity level committed*. Determining the overhead rate as the budgeted (or actual) cost per unit of the budgeted (or actual) use of that activity results in misleading product costs.

ARCHIE'S AUTO REVISITED—EVALUATING A COST SYSTEM

OBJECTIVE 6.4
The evaluation of a cost system to understand whether it is likely to distort product costs

Let us return to the case of Archie's Auto Service Company that we considered at the beginning of this chapter. Ace Acton prepared the description of the cost accounting system used to prepare bids for Archie's customers' jobs (see Exhibit 6–3).

■ System Description

A cost estimate is prepared for each customer job, as shown in Exhibit 6–3. After initially checking the customer's car, Archie prepares a list of replacement parts required (see [a]). He consults his authorized dealer price book to

Estimate Number: 1732				Date: August 9, 1995

Customer Name: Mr. Brandon Briggs

Address: 43, Bridget Blvd.
          Bournemouth

				Amount
Direct labor, overhead, and markup	Replacement of exhaust system—2 hours[c] @ $61.20[d] per hour			$122.40

Direct material	Parts:[a]	Quantity	List Price[b]	Amount	
	Muffler	1	$38.00	$38.00	
	Tailpipe	1	$15.00	$15.00	

Total parts	$ 53.00
Total cost	$175.40[e]

Prepared by: Archie Austin

obtain list prices for the parts (see [b]). He also consults his "blue book" to obtain the number of standard labor hours for the work required to service the car (see [c]). Then he multiplies standard hours by the combined labor, overhead, and markup rate of $61.20 per hour (see [d]). The combined overhead rate includes the following:

1. The mechanic's wages and benefits
2. Shop overhead, including tools and machine depreciation
3. Markup of 20% to provide a reasonable profit for Archie

The total cost estimate, or bid price, is the sum of the replacement parts cost and the labor cost charged at the combined labor, overhead, and markup rate (see [e]).

Ace Acton investigated further how the combined labor, overhead, and markup rate of $61.20 per hour was determined. He examined the accounting and operating records in detail to prepare the following summary of costs budgeted for 1992:

Salaries of 2 expert mechanics ($60,000 each; total of 3,600 billable hours)	$120,000
Salaries of 3 other mechanics ($35,000 each; total of 5,400 billable hours)	105,000
Fringe benefits	90,000
General and administrative costs	26,000

Depreciation and maintenance on physical facilities, bays, equipment, etc.	64,000
Depreciation and maintenance on special tools and machines (3,600 machine-hours)	54,000
Total costs	$459,000

The combined labor and overhead rate in dollars is determined by dividing the total costs by the total billable hours and then multiplying by 1.20 to represent a markup of 20%.

$$\text{Present overhead rate} = \left[\frac{\$459,000}{3,600 + 5,400} \right] * 1.20$$

$$= \$61.20 \text{ per labor hour}$$

Ace Acton determined that Archie's had lost considerable business for simple jobs, such as exhaust system replacement and brake relining, that did not require expert mechanics or specialized tools and machines. The present job costing system was deficient in not distinguishing between the expert and other types of labor and in not recognizing that *some of the overhead costs ($54,000) resulted from the need to use special tools and machines.* Costs of different types of labor and costs related to special tools and machines were all included in a single overhead rate of $61.20 per labor hour without identifying whether a job required expert or other labor and/or whether a job required the use of special tools and machines.

■ Recommended System Changes

Ace recommended the following changes in the cost system. He suggested that instead of using a single overhead rate, Archie's should use the following four different rates:

➤ Expert labor wage rate
➤ Other labor wage rate
➤ Depreciation and maintenance on physical plant
➤ Depreciation and maintenance on special tools

While this ship is in this dry dock, many different types of materials, people, and equipment will be used to make the required repairs or alterations. Because the amount and type of specialized employees and equipment used in each job are highly variable, the cost accountants in this dry dock must use multiple cost pools to accumulate costs. Multiple cost pools will allow the dry dock to price competitively, but at the same time ensure that prices reflect cost. *(Dana Downie/Impact Images)*

The labor and overhead costs should be separated, therefore, into the 4 cost pools depicted in Exhibit 6–4. To do this, it is necessary first to apportion fringe benefits between the 2 types of labor costs (expert and other mechanics) in the ratio of their respective costs. Then, labor rates should be determined by dividing the total costs for wages and apportioned fringe benefits by the respective billable hours in each labor category and then adding a 20% markup (see Exhibit 6–5). Notice that both overhead and markup are included in the *labor rate* here. In contrast, Vernon Valve added markup after determining *all* product costs (materials, labor, and overhead—Exhibit 6–1, Panel 5). Both methods are common in practice. Archie's method is used more in service organizations; Vernon's method is common in manufacturing and trading establishments.

The new overhead rate for special tools and machines is $18 per machine-hour (1.20 [markup] * $54,000 [costs /3,600 [hours]). The remaining overhead comprising general and administrative costs and depreciation and maintenance on physical facilities, bays, and equipment, is expected to be related to total labor hours of both types of mechanics. Therefore, to determine the remaining overhead rate, we use the following formula:

Other overhead rate =

$$\frac{1.20 \text{ (markup)* [\$26,000 (G\&A) + \$64,000 (depreciation)]}}{3{,}600 \text{ (expert mechanics' billable hours) + 5{,}400 (other mechanics' billable hours)}}$$

$$= \$12 \text{ per labor hour}$$

■ New Cost Accounting System Illustrated

To illustrate how the new cost accounting system provides better information about job costs, Ace picked two representative jobs. Details of the work requirement for these two jobs appear in Exhibit 6–6. The first job involved

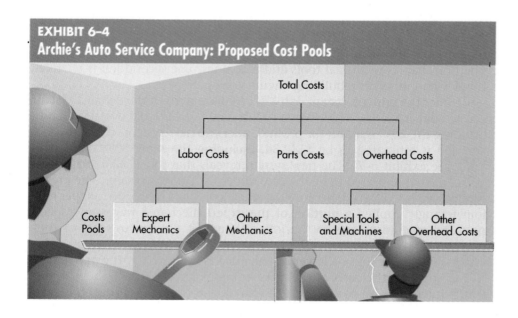

EXHIBIT 6–4
Archie's Auto Service Company: Proposed Cost Pools

EXHIBIT 6–5
Archie's Auto Service Company: Labor Rates

ELEMENTS	EXPERT MECHANICS	OTHER MECHANICS
Wages	$120,000	$105,000
Fringe benefits	48,000[a]	42,000[b]
Total cost	$168,000	$147,000
Markup	20%	20%
Total cost plus markup	$201,600	$176,400
Total billable hours	3,600	5,400
Labor rate	$56.00 per hour	$32.67 per hour

[a]$\dfrac{\$90,000 \text{ Benefits} * \$120,000}{\$120,000 (\text{salaries of expert mechanics}) 1 \$105,000 (\text{salaries of other mechanics})}$

$\dfrac{\$90,000 \text{ Benefits} * \$105,000}{\$120,000 (\text{salaries of expert mechanics}) 1 \$105,000 (\text{salaries of other mechanics})}$

EXHIBIT 6–6
Archie's Auto Service Company: Two Representative Jobs

WORK DESCRIPTION	JOB 1732 REPLACEMENT OF EXHAUST SYSTEM	JOB 2326 REBUILDING ENGINE VALVES
Parts cost	$53	$412
Expert mechanic hours	–0–	4
Other mechanic hours	2	2
Total labor hours	2	6
Special tools and machine-hours	–0–	4

the replacement of an exhaust system, a simple job that does not require expert mechanics or special tools and machines. The second job is relatively complex and involves rebuilding engine valves.

Under the present system, job 1732 (replacement of the exhaust system) is costed out at $175.40 ($53 (parts) + [2 (hours) * $61.20 (old overhead rate)]), including the 20% markup for profit. Under the new system, the cost of the same job is estimated to be $142.34, including the same 20% markup for profit (see Exhibit 6–7). The new system reveals that job 1732 actually costs less than what appeared to be the case under the present system. The present system overcosted the job because the single overhead rate of $61.20 per labor hour wrongly applied a portion of the expert mechanic wages and special tools and machines costs to the job, although it did not use any of these resources. Thus, Archie's may be in a position to win back some of its lost business for simple jobs by lowering the price as indicated by the new system.

In contrast, the costs of the more complex job 2326 (rebuilding engine valves) increase from $779.20 ($412 (parts) + [6 (hours) * $61.20 (old over-

CONSIDER THIS . . .

Sentry Group

Sentry Group, based in Rochester, New York, manufactures fireproof and insulated metal products, including safes, containers, and files for home and office use. Production of steel parts for metal safes starts in the Press Department, where cold-rolled steel is cut to the proper length and width on shear presses. Door jambs and frames are spot-welded to add strength and create a smoother appearance, and door hinges are welded to add durability. When all welding is finished, the safe frame and door are filled with vermiculite insulation (a mixture of water, chemicals, and cement) and set aside to cure for 24 hours. When the insulation is dry, safe pieces are cleaned and painted. When the pieces are dry, the safe frame, door, and lock are assembled to form a completed safe, which is then packed for shipment.

Sentry Group uses a standard cost accounting system. Material and labor standards are reviewed annually and updated as necessary. There are six production departments (Press, Spot Welding, Mig Welding, Insulation, Clean and Paint, and Final Assembly) for metal products. Labor costs for each production department are divided into direct labor and indirect labor (such as materials handling). The direct labor cost of each product is calculated by summing the standard hours per unit for each production department and multiplying the result by the company's average labor rate. Standard materials costs are calculated by multiplying the material content of each product by the standard price per unit of each item of materials used in its production.

Overhead costs include five major elements: indirect labor in production departments, other production department costs, general plant costs, shipping and receiving costs, and maintenance costs. The overhead rate is determined annually by dividing the total overhead of the previous year by the total direct labor costs. The resulting overhead rate is multiplied by the direct labor content of each product to obtain the overhead cost per unit of that product. All other manufacturing costs, including engineering, quality control, and materials management—along with selling and general and administrative expenses—are considered period costs and not included in product costs.

Sentry Group is considering changing to an activity-based costing system to obtain more accurate estimates of its product costs.

Source: "Sentry Group," Harvard Business School, Case 190–124.

EXHIBIT 6–7
Archie's Auto Service Company: Costs Under the New Job Costing System

	JOB 1732	JOB 2326
Parts cost	$53.00	$412.00
Expert mechanics	–0–	$224.00 (4 hours * $56 wage rate)
Other mechanics	$65.34 (2 hours * $32.67 wage rate)	$65.34 (2 hours * 32.67)
Special tools overhead	–0–	$72.00 (4 hours * $18 overhead rate)
Other overhead	$24.00 (2 hours * $12 overhead rate)	$72.00 (6 hours * $12 overhead rate)
Total cost	$142.34	$845.34

head rate)]) to $845.34 when the new system is used and the higher costs of expert labor and special tools are recognized (see Exhibit 6–7). Thus, the correct assignment of costs reveals that Archie currently may be underpricing the services of his expert mechanics using special tools. Although this underpricing means that he is getting these more complex jobs, he is making much less profit (perhaps, even taking a loss) on these jobs than the present costing system leads him to believe.

The difference between the old and the new product costing systems results from the difference in the structure of the cost pools. The new system recognizes 2 types of labor and overhead costs that include costs of special tools and machines that are not required for all jobs.

■ Number of Cost Pools

You will ask the question: How many cost pools should there be? Cost accounting systems in many German firms use more than 100 cost pools. The general principle to use in determining the number of pools is that separate cost pools should be used if the cost or productivity of resources is different, and if the pattern of demand varies across resources. The increase in measurement costs required by a more detailed cost system, however, must be traded off against the benefit of increased accuracy in estimating product costs. If cost and productivity differences between resources are small, more cost pools will not make much of a difference.

OBJECTIVE 6.5
The relevance of recording actual costs and comparing them with estimated costs

RECORDING ACTUAL JOB COSTS

So far we have discussed systems for estimating job costs to prepare bids. The design of job order cost accounting systems allows the systems to record the costs actually incurred on individual jobs as they occur. This process allows comparison of actual costs with the estimated costs to determine whether unexpected variations in the quantity (efficiency) of the use of various resources exist.

Consider once again job J4369 of the Vernon Valve Company (p. 243). Once Vernon has received the customer order and scheduled production, the company prepares a **materials requisition note** that lists the materials required to commence production. The materials requisition note M47624 (Exhibit 6–8) lists the bar steel stock required for the initial machining work. Vernon obtains the steel requirements from engineering specifications for part design JDR-103 identified in the customer order. On receipt of the materials requisition note, the stores department issues the bar steel stock and moves the materials to the machining department.

Materials requisition note
A note instructing the stores department to issue materials to the shop floor in order to commence production.

The 720 pounds of materials issued are for only 20% of the total customer order. The customer requires that the delivery of the product be spread over several months, and Vernon Valve schedules production as needed for meeting delivery schedules. Such a production system is often called a *pull system*. The present production order is for 300, L181 valves (20% of the total customer order for 1,500 L181 valves; see Exhibit 6–1). Each valve requires 2.4

EXHIBIT 6–8
Vernon Valve Company: Materials Requisition Note

Materials Requisition Note Number: __M47624__   Date: _August 2, 1995_
From: Machining Department

Approved by: __Mike Machina__   (Machining Supervisor)
                __Steve Stuart__   (Stores Supervisor)
Job Number: __J4369__

Engineering design: __JDR-103__

Identification Number	Description	Quantity	Rate	Amount
24203	Bar steel stock 3"	720 lbs	$11.50	$8,280.00

pounds of materials, and, therefore 720 pounds (300 [valves] * 2.4 [pounds per valve]) of bar steel stock has been requisitioned.

Once the machining department receives the materials, lathe operators are assigned to the job. A record of the time they spend working on a job is recorded on **worker time cards**, such as the one shown in Exhibit 6–9 for machinist William Wiley (employee number M16).

After the completion of machining work, the machined bars are either stored as work in process or are moved to the assembly department if they are scheduled for assembly. The just-in-time pull system that Vernon Valve uses moves the materials almost immediately to the next department. The assembly department then prepares an additional materials requisition note to have the stores department issue the appropriate subassemblies. Time cards are also prepared to record the time that assembly workers spend on job J4369.

Copies of all materials requisition notes and worker time cards are forwarded to the accounting department, which then posts them on a **job cost**

Worker time card
Record of hours spent by each worker each day or week on different jobs.

Job cost sheet
Format for recording actual job costs.

EXHIBIT 6–9
Vernon Valve Company: Worker Time Card

TIME CARD

Employee Number: __M16__   Name: __William Wiley__

Date: _August 2, 1995_   Department: __Machining__

Checked by: __Mike Machina__ (Machining Supervisor)

Job Number	Start Time	Stop Time	Total Hours	Wage Rate	Amount
J4369	6:00	10:00	4	$28.00	$112.00
J4362	10:00	1:00	3	28.00	84.00
J4371	1:00	2:00	1	28.00	28.00
Total			8		$224.00

sheet, described in Exhibit 6–10. Even if time cards are recorded in an integrated computerized information system instead of a manual accounting system, job cost sheets are prepared using data obtained from actual materials requisition and time card records.

Then, it is necessary to determine total costs for the portion of the job completed and to compare them with costs projected on the job bid sheet. The structure of the job cost sheet is similar to that of the job bid sheet, except that the direct material and direct labor costs on the job cost sheet represent *actual* costs incurred on the job. Direct material costs include $11,020 for sub-

---

EXHIBIT 6–10
Vernon Valve Company: Job Cost Sheet

Panel 1

Job number: J4369   Date: August 12, 1995
Customer: Michigan Motors
Product: Automobile engine valves
Engineering design number: JDR-103
Total number of units ordered: 1500

Panel 2

Materials Requisition Number	Description	Quantity	Price	Amount
M47624	Bar Steel Stock 3"	720 lbs.	$11.50	$ 8,280.00
A35161	Subassemblies	290 units	38.00	11,020.00
Total direct materials cost				$19,300.00

Panel 3

Dates	Employee Number	Hours	Rate	Amount
8/2, 8/3, 8/4, 8/5	M16	24	$28.00	$ 672.00
8/2, 8/3, 8/4, 8/5	M18, M19	64	26.00	1,664.00
8/6, 8/7, 8/8, 8/9, 8/10	A25, A26, A27	120	18.00	2,160.00
8/6, 8/7, 8/8, 8/9, 8/10	A32, A34, A35	60	17.00	1,020.00
Total direct labor cost		268		$5,516.00

Panel 4

Overhead	Amount
117 Machine hours @ $40 per hour	$ 4,680.00
268 Direct labor hours @ $36 per hour	9,648.00
Total overhead:	$14,328.00

Panel 5

Total cost	$39,144.00
Number of units produced	290
Cost per unit	$ 134.98
Projected unit cost	$ 134.36

---

assemblies, in addition to $8,280 for 720 pounds of bar steel stock recorded in materials requisition note M47624 (Exhibit 6–8). Referring to Exhibit 6–10, we see that direct labor costs comprise the hours charged by 3 machinists (M16, 18, 19—lathe operators) and 6 assembly workers (A25, A26, A27, A32, A34, A35) for this job. (This includes the 4 hours charged for employee number M16 on August 2 as recorded in the time card described in Exhibit 6–9.) Overhead is applied to the job based on actual direct labor hours (268 hours) and machine-hours (117 hours). The same predetermined overhead rates ($36 per direct labor hour and $40 per machine-hour) as in the job bid sheet (Exhibit 6–1, panel 4) are used because actual total overhead costs for the plant are not known until the end of the fiscal period.

Total costs are determined as before by adding together the direct material, direct labor, and overhead costs applied to the job to date. Notice that the actual unit costs of $134.98 ($39,144 [total costs]/290 [number of units produced]) for the portion of the job completed through August 12, 1992 (Exhibit 6–10, panel 5) are higher than the unit costs of $134.36 ($201,540 [total cost]/1,500 [number of units]) estimated on the job bid sheet (Exhibit 6–1, panel 5). The next section presents variance reports that analyze the reasons for the variations.

BASIC VARIANCE ANALYSIS

Analysis of the factors causing the differences (variances) between the actual and the estimated costs is called **variance analysis**. It can help managers in several ways. If managers find that the actions they took on some jobs helped lower their actual costs, then it is possible to obtain further cost savings if managers repeat those actions on other jobs. If the company can identify the factors causing actual costs to be higher, then managers may be able to take the necessary actions to eliminate or control those factors. And if cost changes are likely to be permanent, the company can use the revised cost information in bidding for jobs.

Because Vernon Valve has completed only a part of job J4369, we need to prorate the estimated costs in the job bid sheet. Exhibit 6–11 shows these prorated calculations. For instance, each valve requires 2.4 pounds of bar steel stock (3,600 [pounds of bar steel stock]/1,500 [valves]); therefore, 696 pounds (2.4 [pounds per valve] * 290 [valves]) are required for the 290 valves manufactured. At the price of $11.30 per pound of steel (Exhibit 6–1), the estimated cost of bar steel required is $7,864.80.

▪ First-Level Variances

Column 3 in Exhibit 6–12 displays the **first-level variances** for different cost items. The *first-level variance* for a cost item is the *difference between the actual and estimated costs for that cost item*. Variances are "favorable," or "F," if *the actual costs are less than estimated costs*. "Unfavorable," or "U," variances arise when actual costs exceed estimated costs. A variance is favorable when it indicates that actual profits are higher than those estimated (and, therefore, that actual costs are lower than those estimated), and unfavorable when it

OBJECTIVE 6.6
The analysis of variances between actual and estimated costs, including first- and second-level variances

Variance analysis
Decomposition of differences between actual and estimated costs into amounts related to specific factors causing the variance between actual and estimated costs.

First-level variance
Difference between actual and estimated costs for a cost item.

EXHIBIT 6–11
Vernon Valve Company: Prorated Cost Estimates for 290 Valves

	ESTIMATED QUANTITY REQUIRED FOR 290 VALVES	ESTIMATED RATE	ESTIMATED COST
Direct material			
Bar steel stock 3″	2.4 * 290 = 696 pounds	$11.30	$ 7,864.80
Subassemblies	1 * 290 = 290 units	39.00	11,310.00
			$19,174.80
Direct labor			
Lathe operators	0.32 * 290 = 92.8 hours	$26.00	$2,412.80
Assembly workers	0.60 * 290 = 174 hours	18.00	3,132.00
			$5,544.80
Overhead			
Based on machine-hours	0.40 * 290 = 116 hours	$40.00	$4,640.00
Based on direct labor hours	0.92 * 290 = 266.8 hours	36.00	9,604.80
			$14,244.80

EXHIBIT 6–12
Vernon Valve Company: First-Level Analysis of Variances

	(1) ESTIMATED COST FROM EXHIBIT 6–11	(2) ACTUAL COST FROM EXHIBIT 6–10	(3) FIRST LEVEL VARIANCE [(a) - (b)]	(4) VARIANCE PER VALVE [(c) ÷ 290]
Direct material				
Bar steel stock 3″	$ 7,864.80	$ 8,280.00	$415.20 U	$1.43 U
Subassemblies	11,310.00	11,020.00	290.00 F	1.00 F
	$19,174.80	$19,300.00	$125.20 U	$0.43 U
Direct labor				
Lathe operators	$ 2,412.80	$ 2,336.00ᵃ	$ 76.80 F	$0.26 F
Assembly workers	3,132.00	3,180.00ᵃ	48.00 U	0.16 U
	$5,544.80	$5,516.00	$ 28.80 F	$0.10 F
Overhead				
Based on machine-hours	$ 4,640.00	$ 4,680.00	$ 40.00 U	$0.14 U
Based on direct labor hours	9,604.80	9,648.00	$ 43.20 U	0.15 U
	$14,244.80	$14,328.00	$ 83.20 U	$0.29 U
Total costs	$38,964.40	$39,144.00	$179.60 U	$0.62 U

ᵃ From panel 3 in Exhibit 6–10: ($2,336 = $672 + $1,664 and $3,180 = $2,160 + $1,020).

indicates that the actual profits are less than those estimated (and, therefore, that actual costs are higher than those estimated). Thus, the cost variance for bar steel is $415.20 unfavorable ($8,280 actual bar steel cost − $7,864.80 estimated cost of bar steel required).

■ Second-Level Variances

First-level direct material and direct labor variances are analyzed further into efficiency (use) and price variances, which are referred to as **second-level variances**. See Exhibit 6–13. To illustrate this analysis, consider the decomposition of the bar steel cost variance.

Second-level variance analysis
Analysis of a first-level variance into efficiency and price variances.

MATERIAL USAGE AND PRICE VARIANCES   Material usage variance is determined by using the following formula:

$$\text{Usage variance} = (AQ - SQ) * SP \qquad (6.2)$$
$$= (720 - 696) * \$11.30$$
$$= \$271.20 \text{ U}$$

where

AQ = actual quantity of materials used
SQ = estimated or standard quantity of materials required
SP = estimated or standard price of materials

Cost variances are unfavorable when positive, because a positive cost variance means that actual costs exceed estimated costs. Variances are favorable when negative because actual costs are less than estimated costs. In this case, the positive variance ($271.20) indicates that more bar steel was used than estimated at the time of bidding for the job. This inefficient use contributed to

---

EXHIBIT 6–13
Vernon Valve Company: Second-Level Analysis of Variances

		AMOUNT	TOTAL
Direct material			
Bar steel stock 3"			
Usage variance	(720 − 696) * $11.30 =	$271.20U	
Price variance	($11.50 − $11.30) * 720 =	144.00U	$415.20U
Subassemblies			
Usage variance	(290 − 290) * $39 =	$ 0.00	
Price variance	($38 − $39) * 290 =	290.00F	290.00F
Total direct material variance			$125.20U

		AMOUNT	TOTAL
Direct labor			
Lathe operators			
Efficiency variance	(88 − 92.8) * $26 =	$124.80F	
Rate variance	($28 − $26) * 24 + ($26 − $26) * 64 =	48.00U	$ 76.80F
Assembly workers			
Efficiency variance	(180 − 174) * $18 =	$108.00U	
Rate variance	($18 − $18) * 120 + ($17 − $18) * 60 =	60.00F	48.00U
Total direct labor variance			$ 28.80F

In this operation at J & L Specialty Products Corporation, a continuous steel strip that has just been rinsed in water is put in an acid tank to remove surface impurities. The material use variance for acid in the acid tank operation was unfavorable because water from the rinsing operation was traveling with the steel strip into the acid tank and diluting the acid. This employee installed the rubber strip shown in this picture to remove water from the steel strip as it emerged from the rinsing operation. This strip prevents the water from entering the acid tank and reduces acid use, saving the company about $18,000 every month this line is operated. *(Dave Rentz, CPP/Visual Perceptions, Inc.)*

increasing the actual costs by an additional $271.20 from the amount estimated.

Material price variance for bar steel stock is calculated using the following formula:

$$\text{Price variance} = (AP - SP) * AQ \qquad (6.3)$$
$$= (\$11.50 - \$11.30) * 720$$
$$= \$144.00 \text{ U}$$

where

AP = actual price of materials
SP = estimated or standard price of materials
AQ = actual quantity of materials used

Thus, we have decomposed the total variance for bar steel stock into material usage and material price variances. When we add these 2 second-level variances together ($271.20 U + $144.00 U), we obtain the first-level variance (shown in Exhibit 6–13) for bar steel stock ($415.20 U).

The general result relating first- and second-level variances is verified easily by adding together the algebraic formulas for material usage and price variances. The sum of the second-level variances is

$$= \text{Usage variance} + \text{Price variance} \qquad (6.4)$$
$$= (AQ - SQ) * SP + (AP - SP) * AQ$$
$$= (AQ * SP) - (SQ * SP) + (AP * AQ) - (SP * AQ)$$
$$= (AP * AQ) - (SQ * SP)$$
$$= \text{Actual cost} - \text{Estimated cost}$$
$$= \text{Total (first-level) variance}$$

MATERIAL PRICE VARIANCE IDENTIFIED WITH PURCHASING FUNCTION Vernon Valve purchases materials as required for individual jobs. Because material purchases are identified directly with jobs, it makes sense to determine material price variance separately for each job. More commonly, however, materials used in several jobs are purchased in larger quantities and stored until requisitioned for individual jobs. In these situations, it is common to separate out the material price variance *at the time of the purchase* and to charge jobs for materials only at their standard prices. Thus, material price variances are identified in the aggregate for the purchasing function instead of at the level of individual jobs described previously. In other words, the actual material cost recorded in a job cost sheet equals *standard* price times actual quantity ($SP * AQ$) instead of *actual* price times actual quantity ($AP * AQ$) mentioned in Exhibit 6–10, panel 2, for Vernon Valve. The first-level variance is the difference between actual and estimated costs, which, in this case, is

$$
\begin{aligned}
\text{First-level variance} &= \text{Actual costs} - \text{Estimated costs} \qquad (6.5)\\
&= (SP * AQ) - (SP * SQ)\\
&= SP * (AQ - SQ)
\end{aligned}
$$

which is the same as the material usage variance calculated in the second-level variance analysis in (6.2). Thus, only the material usage variance is identified with individual jobs, and material price variance is associated, in the aggregate, directly with the purchasing function.

EFFICIENCY AND WAGE RATE VARIANCES FOR DIRECT LABOR COSTS

These variances are determined in a manner very similar to that described for material usage and price variances. The formulas follow:

$$
\begin{aligned}
\text{Efficiency variance} &= (AH - SH) * SR \qquad (6.6)\\
\text{Rate variance} &= (AR - SR) * AH \qquad (6.7)
\end{aligned}
$$

where

AH = actual number of direct labor hours
AR = actual wage rate
SH = estimated or standard number of direct labor hours
SR = estimated or standard wage rate

And, as before, total cost variance is computed:

Efficiency variance + Rate variance
$$
\begin{aligned}
&= (AH - SH) * SR + (AR - SR) * AH\\
&= (AH * SR) - (SH * SR) + (AR * AH) - (SR * AH)\\
&= (AR * AH) - (SR * SH)\\
&= \text{Actual cost} - \text{Estimated cost}\\
&= \text{Total cost variance}
\end{aligned}
$$

SECOND-LEVEL ANALYSIS OF OVERHEAD VARIANCES   Second-level overhead variance analysis is not necessary because, you will recall, the same predetermined overhead rates are used for actually charging overhead costs to specific jobs. All variation between actual and estimated overhead costs for a job, therefore, arises from differences in the number of units of the basis on which overhead costs are applied to jobs (direct labor hours and machine-hours in the case of Vernon Valve).

■ Managerial Use of Job Cost Variance Information

How can the managers at Vernon Valve use the information provided by the first- and second-level variance analysis reports in Exhibits 6–12 and 6–13? They would find it reassuring to know that the actual costs exceed the estimated costs by only $0.62 per valve, an amount that is less than .05% of the bid price. However, many interesting details appear when analyzing this small overall variance for the completed part of the job into its components.

As we had noted earlier, inefficiency in the use of bar steel stock is indicated by the second-level variance analysis, and the reasons for the excess usage need to be investigated. Further inquiry revealed that the higher than estimated waste in the use of bar steel stock was caused by a breakdown of the lathe machine after it produced several defective pieces that had to be rejected. This problem had since been corrected; therefore, bar steel consumption was not expected to exhibit unfavorable usage variance for the rest of the job. Furthermore, although bar steel prices were higher than estimated, the material price variance indicated that the purchasing manager had been successful in saving $1 per valve in the price of subassemblies.

Inquiries pursuant to labor cost variance analysis revealed that more experienced lathe operators worked on this job. The unfavorable rate variance because of their higher wages was more than offset by the favorable variance resulting from their increased efficiency. In contrast, less-experienced assembly (lower wage) workers were assigned to this job. The resulting favorable

Some organizations use technology to correct chronic unfavorable material usage variances. Pentair Inc. uses this electronic measuring system to ensure that sheet metal parts are cut to exact specifications. By reducing waste and rework, this machine reduces material and labor use. *(Courtesy Pentair, Inc.)*

wage rate variance, however, was not adequate to compensate for the unfavorable efficiency variance. In both cases, therefore, the variance information suggests that the use of the more experienced workers should result in lower costs for the rest of this job.

Vernon analyzes and reports the direct cost variances for each job. In companies that work on a large number of small jobs, these variances are aggregated for all jobs completed in a month, and only the total variances for the month are reported to managers. This procedure avoids presenting a lot of potentially confusing detail in the variance analysis reports. The principles for analyzing these variances, however, remain the same as those employed at Vernon.

MULTISTAGE PROCESS COSTING SYSTEMS

OBJECTIVE 6.7
The importance of conversion costs and the measurement of costs in multistage, continuous-processing industries

For many plants engaged in continuous processing—such as those in the chemicals, basic metals, pharmaceuticals, grain milling and processing, and electric utilities industries—first it is necessary to determine costs for each stage of the process and, then, to assign the costs to individual products. In contrast to a job shop manufacturing establishment, in continuous processing, production flows continuously, semicontinuously (that is, continuously, but with a few interruptions), or in large batches from one process stage to the next. At each successive process stage, there is further progress toward converting the raw materials into the finished product.

The design of product costing systems in such process-oriented plants enables measurement of the costs of converting the raw materials during a time period separately for each process stage. Then, these conversion costs are applied to products as they pass through successive process stages. This type of system for determining product costs, known as a **multistage process costing system**, is common in process-oriented industries. We find multi-

Multistage process costing system
System for determining product costs in multistage processing industries.

This packing area is the end of a multistage system used in a Colgate-Palmolive plant in Puerto Rico to make fabric softener. The costs associated with this batch of production would be accumulated at each stage (blending, filling, and packaging) and allocated to the batch of production to determine the cost per unit for blending, filling, and packaging. (*Courtesy Richard Alcorn/Colgate-Palmolive*)

stage process costing systems also in some discrete parts manufacturing plants such as those producing automobile components and small appliances.

The common feature in all these settings is that the products manufactured are all relatively homogeneous. Few and relatively small differences occur in the production requirements for different products. As a result, it is not necessary to maintain separate cost records for individual jobs. Instead, costs are measured only for process stages, and cost variances are determined only at the level of the process stages instead of at the level of individual jobs.

OBJECTIVE 6.8
The differences between job order costing and multistage process costing systems

■ Comparison with Job Order Costing

Multistage process costing systems have the same objective as job order costing systems. Both types of systems assign material, labor, and manufacturing overhead costs to products. However, some important differences exist between the two systems that we summarize in Exhibit 6–14. Note that the factors in the exhibit (column 1) highlight the major points for consideration.

■ Process Costing Illustrated

Next, consider the product costing system at Calcut Chemical Company's plant that processes organic chemical products through 3 stages: (1) mixing and blending, (2) reaction chamber, and (3) pulverizing and packing (see Exhibit 6–15). First, Calcut Chemical estimates costs for these three stages, as shown in Exhibit 6–16. These costs include production labor assigned to each stage, support labor performing tasks such as materials handling and setup, and laboratory testing. We refer to the total cost of all the activities performed at each stage of the process as the **conversion costs** for that stage. That is, conversion costs are the costs to convert the materials or product at each stage. The total estimated conversion costs for each stage are divided by the corresponding total number of process hours to obtain the estimated conversion cost rate per process hour for that stage.

Conversion costs
Costs of production labor and support activities to convert the materials or product at each process stage.

EXHIBIT 6–14
Differences between Job Order and Multistage Process Costing Systems

FACTORS	JOB ORDER COSTING SYSTEM	MULTISTAGE PROCESS COSTING SYSTEM
Production	(a) Carried out in many different jobs	(a) Carried out continuously, semi-continuously, or in large batches
Production requirements	(b) Different for different jobs	(b) Homogeneous across products or jobs
Costs	(c) Measured for individual jobs	(c) Measured for individual process stages
Variances	(d) Between actual and estimated direct material and direct labor costs are determined for individual jobs	(d) Between actual and estimated costs are determined for individual process stages

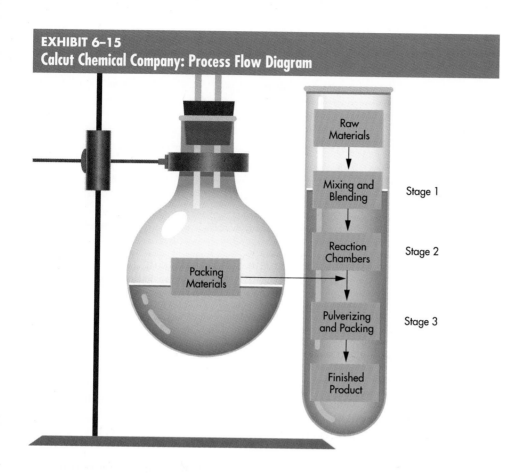

EXHIBIT 6–15
Calcut Chemical Company: Process Flow Diagram

Raw Materials

Mixing and Blending — Stage 1

Reaction Chambers — Stage 2

Packing Materials

Pulverizing and Packing — Stage 3

Finished Product

EXHIBIT 6–16
Calcut Chemical Company: Estimated Process Costs for 1994

	MIXING AND BLENDING	REACTION CHAMBERS	PULVERIZING AND PACKING
Production labor	$230,000	$1,040,000	$360,000
Engineering support	20,000	46,000	22,000
Materials handling	18,000	18,000	27,000
Equipment maintenance	10,000	32,000	8,000
Laboratory expenses	20,000	20,000	4,000
Depreciation	40,000	160,000	48,000
Power	32,000	78,000	24,000
General and administrative	16,000	16,000	16,000
Total conversion costs	$386,000	$1,410,000	$509,000
Total number of process hours	8,760	35,040	8,760
Conversion cost per process hour	$44.06	$40.24	$58.11

Consider 2 representative products, G307 and G309, manufactured and sold by Calcut Chemical (see Exhibit 6–17). Both products are derivatives of ethyl oleate and require the same basic raw materials, which cost $1,240 per ton of finished product. The product G309 requires $234 of packing materi-

EXHIBIT 6-17
Calcut Chemical Company: Product Costs per Ton

COSTS	G307	G309
Materials		
Raw materials	$1,240.00	$1,240.00
Packing materials	146.00	234.00
	$1,386.00	$1,474.00
Conversion costs		
Mixing and blending	$ 264.36 (6 hours)	$ 264.36 (6 hours)
Reaction chamber	965.76 (24 hours)	965.76 (24 hours)
Pulverizing and packing	232.44 (4 hours)	464.88 (8 hours)
Total conversion costs	$1,462.56	$1,695.00
Total cost	$2,848.56	$3,169.00

als per ton, almost 60% more than the $146 of packing materials per ton required for G307. The first product, G307, requires the following:

> 6 hours per ton for mixing and blending

> 24 hours of reaction time

> 4 hours for pulverizing and packing

The second product, G309, requires the same processing time for the mixing and blending and for the reaction chamber stages. But because of the special requirements of the customers, it needs twice as much processing time for pulverizing and packing (8 versus 4 hours). Exhibit 6–17 presents the costs per ton of the 2 products.

To determine individual product costs, it is necessary to (1) identify the costs of the material input required at various stages and (2) add the estimated conversion costs for all the process stages to the material costs. For example, as Exhibit 6–17 shows, material costs per ton of product G307 comprise $1,240 of raw materials required initially for the mixing and blending stage and $146 of packing materials used at the final pulverizing and packing stage.

The conversion costs for a product for a process stage are estimated by multiplying the number of process hours for that stage by the corresponding conversion cost rate per process hour. For instance, the conversion costs per ton of product G307 are $264.36 (6 hours * $44.06 conversion cost rate in Exhibit 6–16) for the mixing and blending stage, $965.76 (24 hours * $40.24 conversion cost rate in Exhibit 6–16) for the reaction chamber stage, and $232.44 (4 hours * $58.11 conversion cost rate in Exhibit 6–16) for the pulverizing and packing stage. The conversion costs per ton of product G309 are the same for the first 2 stages but are higher at $464.88 (8 hours * $58.11) for the pulverizing and packing stage, as noted before.

■ Variance Analysis in Process Costing Systems

Multistage process costing systems accumulate actual costs for individual process stages. Then, it is important to determine variances between actual and estimated costs for individual process stages.

Actual conversion costs for the mixing and blending process stage are presented in Exhibit 6–18. As in the case of our previous job order costing example, first-level variances are the difference between actual costs and estimated costs. In this case, the variances for production labor, engineering support, materials handling, and laboratory costs are unfavorable because actual costs exceed the estimated costs. Variances for equipment maintenance and power are favorable because actual costs are less than estimated costs.

A SUMMARY EXAMPLE

We turn now to a problem that reviews some of this chapter's most important points. Blegen Company manufactures a variety of electronic components. In June 1994, the company received an invitation from Precision Electronics, Inc., to bid on an order of 1,000 units of component ICB371 that must be delivered by August 15, 1994. The following are the standard requirements and prices for 1,000 units of ICB371:

	Quantity	Price
Direct material	2,000 units	$10 per unit
Direct labor	1,000 hours	$10 per hour

Overhead is assigned to jobs based on direct labor hours. The estimated overhead cost and direct labor hours for 1994 are $300,000 and 50,000 hours, respectively.

Blegen has a policy to add a 20% markup to estimated job costs to arrive at the bid price.

a. Prepare a job bid sheet to determine the bid price for this job.

Assume next that Precision Electronics, Inc., accepted Blegen's bid. On

EXHIBIT 6–18
Calcut Chemical Company: First-Level Variance Analysis for Mixing and Blending Process Stage

	ACTUAL COSTS	ESTIMATED COSTS	FIRST-LEVEL VARIANCE
Production labor	$236,000	$230,000	$6,000 U
Engineering support	20,400	20,000	400 U
Materials handling	19,000	18,000	1,000 U
Equipment maintenance	9,800	10,000	200 F
Laboratory expenses	20,800	20,000	800 U
Depreciation	40,000	40,000	–0–
Power	31,600	32,000	400 F
General and administrative	16,000	16,000	–0–
Total conversion costs	$393,600	$386,000	$7,600
Total number of process hours	8,760	8,760	–0–
Conversion costs per process hour	$44.93	$44.06	$0.87 U

delivering the 1,000 units of ICB371 to Precision, the following information was compiled by Blegen for this job:

	Quantity	Price
Direct material	2,100 units	$ 9.75 per unit
Direct labor	1,000 hours	$11.00 per hour

b. What were the total direct material and direct labor cost variances?
c. What was the direct material purchase price variance?
d. What was the direct material quantity variance?
e. What was the direct labor rate variance?
f. What was the direct labor efficiency variance?

The following are solutions to (a) through (f).
a. Blegen Electronics, Inc.: Job bid sheet ICB-PR1
   Date: June 18, 1994
   Customer: Precision Electronics, Inc.
   Product: ICB371

   Number of units: 1,000 units

	Quantity	Price	Amount
Direct material	2,000 units	$10/unit	$20,000
Direct labor	1,000 hours	$10/hour	10,000
Overhead	1,000 hours	$6/hour	6,000
Total estimated costs			$36,000
Markup (20%)			7,200
Bid price			$43,200

b. Total direct material cost variance
   = Actual direct material cost − Standard direct material cost
   = ($9.75 * 2,100) − $20,000
   = $475 U

   Total direct labor cost variance:
   = Actual direct labor cost − Standard direct labor cost
   = $11,000 − $10,000
   = 1,000 U

c. Direct material purchase price variance:
   = $AP − SP$) * AQ = ($9.75 − $10) * 2,100
   = $525

d. Direct material quantity variance:
   = ($AQ − SQ$) * SP = (2,100 − 2,000) * $10
   = $1,000 U

Because they comprise such a large portion of the total cost of bread, the amount of raw materials and power used in the production of bread is monitored closely by bakeries. The required cooking time, and therefore the energy used to cook the bread, will vary with the bread recipe—and different recipes can be used to make the same product. Therefore, raw materials and energy usage variances are highly interrelated and cannot be interpreted separately. *(Courtesy Flowers Industries, Inc.)*

e. Direct labor rate variance:
$$= (AR - SR) * AH$$
$$= (\$11 - \$10) * 1,000$$
$$= \$1,000 \text{ U}$$

f. Direct labor efficiency variance:
$$= (AH - SH) * SR$$
$$= (1,000 - 1,000) * \$10$$
$$= \$0$$

SUMMARY

This chapter describes the basic principles underlying product costing systems used to estimate costs of discrete job orders and to estimate product costs in continuous process industries. Although these systems are described here as 2 different costing systems, many costing systems observed in practice exhibit elements of both systems. Both types of cost systems identify materials and labor costs directly with jobs or products. Both systems also assign the remainder of costs to jobs or products on the basis of predetermined overhead rates.

The overhead rate should be determined as the normal cost per unit of capacity of support activity that is made available. If the overhead rate is based instead on actual or budgeted activity levels that fluctuate over time, then overhead costs will be understated in periods of high demand and will be overstated in periods of low demand. If product costing systems do not adequately reflect the systematic differences in prices and productivity of materials and labor resources and of factors driving overhead costs, the resultant job or product costs are likely to be distorted. In particular, if there are several grades of labor with widely differing productivity levels and wage rates, but only a single common rate is used for all labor, then product costs are likely to be distorted for products that require different grades of labor in different proportions. Similarly, if overhead costs are caused by multiple cost drivers, but only a single overhead rate is employed to assign all overhead costs, then product costs are likely to be distorted for products that require different proportions of the multiple cost drivers.

Most companies need to estimate product costs before actually manufacturing the products so that they can bid on jobs or price the products. Job bid sheets are prepared to calculate the estimated costs for a job. If the bid based on these estimated costs is accepted, then a job cost sheet is prepared to record the actual costs of production for the job. Recording actual costs enables companies to compare actual costs with the estimated costs. Variances between actual and estimated costs are analyzed into components such as materials price, materials usage, labor rate, and labor efficiency variances so companies can understand the factors contributing to the difference between actual and estimated costs. Based on this variance analysis, companies can revise their product costs or take corrective action to improve its operations by eliminating unfavorable variances.

KEY TERM LIST

Conversion costs, p. 262

First-level variance, p. 255

Job bid sheet, p. 242

Job costs, p. 244

Job cost sheet, p. 253

Job order costing system, p. 242

Markup or margin, p. 244

Markup rate, p. 244

Materials requisition note, p. 252

Multistage process costing system, p. 261

Overhead cost pools, p. 244

Overhead rate, p. 244

Rate of return, p. 244

Second-level variance analysis, p. 257

Variance analysis, p. 255

Worker time card, p. 253

ASSIGNMENT MATERIAL

QUESTIONS

6–1 Why do costs need to be estimated for individual jobs?

6–2 What information is presented in a typical job bid sheet?

6–3 What is the source of the information to estimate the cost of materials?

6–4 What is the source of the information to estimate the direct labor cost?

6–5 How are overhead rates determined?

6–6 How is overhead cost estimated for individual jobs?

6–7 What is the *markup* rate? On what factors does it depend?

6–8 What is an *overhead cost pool*? Why are multiple overhead cost pools required?

6–9 What problem arises when overhead rates are based on planned or actual short-term usage instead of normal usage? Why?

6–10 What is the *normal cost* of a support activity? What is the *normal usage level* of a cost driver?

6–11 "Use of a single overhead rate when there are multiple cost drivers leads to distortions in job costs." Do you agree with this statement? Explain.

6–12 What is the managerial use of tracking actual costs of individual jobs?

6–13 What documents initiate the recording of actual direct materials and direct labor costs for individual jobs?

6–14 Why are *predetermined* overhead rates used when recording actual job costs?

6–15 How does analysis of reasons for variances between actual and estimated job costs help managers?

6–16 What is the difference between the first and the second levels of variance analysis?

6–17 "If more experienced workers work on the job than planned in developing the labor standards, the labor efficiency variance is likely to be favorable but the labor wage variance is likely to be unfavorable." Do you agree with this statement? Explain.

6–18 What is the possible benefit from analyzing variances into a price variance and a quantity variance?

6–19 What effect is the purchase and use of cheaper, lower-quality materials likely to have on price and quantity components of both materials and labor variances?

6–20 What does the term *conversion costs* mean?

6–21 What considerations are important in estimating product costs in continuous processing plants?

6–22 Why do variations in yield rates across products introduce additional complexity in estimating product costs?

EXERCISES

6–23 Wright Wood Products has two production departments: cutting and assembly. The company has been using a single predetermined overhead rate based on plantwide direct labor hours. The estimates for 1995 follow:

	Cutting	Assembly	Total
Manufacturing overhead	$25,000	$35,000	$60,000
Direct labor hours	1,000	3,000	4,000
Machine-hours	4,000	2,000	6,000

(a) What was the single predetermined overhead rate for 1995?

(b) Determine departmental overhead rates based on direct labor hours for assembly and machine-hours for cutting.

6–24 The following information is available for job KL37 for Burjor Company:

- Actual:
  - Materials used: 10,500 pounds purchased at $2.50 per pound
  - Direct labor: 1,800 hours at $12.00 per hour
  - Units produced: 500
- Standard:
  - Materials: 20 pounds per unit at a price of $2.20 per pound
  - Direct labor: 4 hours per unit at a wage rate of $10.00 per hour

(a) Determine the material price variance and quantity variance.

(b) Determine the direct labor rate variance and efficiency variance.

6–25 Phiroze Company employs a standard cost system. Job 8822 is for the manufacture of 500 units of the product P521. The company's standards for 1 unit of the product P521 are as follows:

	Quantity	Price
Direct material	5 ounces	$2/ounce
Direct labor	2 hours	$10/hour

The job requires 2,800 ounces of raw material costing $5,880. An unfavorable labor rate variance of $250 and a favorable labor efficiency variance of $100 also were determined for this job.

(a) What was the direct material purchase price variance?

(b) What was the direct material quantity variance?

(c) Determine the actual quantity of direct labor hours used on job 8822.

(d) Determine the actual direct labor costs incurred for job 8822.

6–26 Each unit of product Y7023 has standard requirements of 5 pounds of raw material at a price of $100 per pound and 0.5 hours of direct labor at $12 per hour. To produce 9,000 units of this product, job Y7023 actually required 40,000 pounds of the raw material costing $97 per pound. The job used a total of 5,000 direct labor hours costing a total of $60,000.

(a) Determine the material price and quantity variances.

(b) Assume that the materials used on this job were purchased from a new supplier. Would you recommend continuing with this new supplier? Why or why not?

(c) Determine the direct labor rate and efficiency variances.

6–27 Assembly of the product P13 requires 1 unit of component X, 2 units of component Y, and 3 units of component Z. Job J1372 produced 220 units of P13. The following information pertains to material variances for this job, analyzed by component:

	X	Y	Z
Price variance	160U	120F	192U
Usage variance	168U	100U	84F

The actual prices were $0.30 more, $0.20 less, and $0.50 more per unit for components X, Y, and Z, respectively, than their standard prices.

(a) Determine the number of units consumed of each component.

(b) Determine the standard price per unit of each component.

6–28 Health Foods Company produces and sells canned vegetable juice. The ingredients are first combined in the blending department and then packed in gallon cans in the canning department. The following information pertains to the blending department for January 1995.

	Price per Gallon	Gallons
Ingredient A	$0.40	10,000
Ingredient B	$0.60	20,000
Vegetable juice		27,000
Materials loss		3,000

Conversion costs for the blending department are $0.55 per gallon for January 1995.

(a) Determine the yield rate.

(b) Determine the cost per gallon of blended vegetable juice before canning.

6–29 Washington Chemical Company manufactures and sells Goody, a product that sells for $10 per pound. The manufacturing process also yields 1 pound of a waste product called Bady in the production of every 10 pounds of Goody. Disposal of the waste product costs $1 per pound. During March 1995, the company manufactured 220,000 pounds of Goody. Total manufacturing costs were as follows:

Direct materials	$200,000
Direct labor	120,000
Overhead costs	60,000
Total costs	$380,000

Determine the cost per pound of Goody.

PROBLEMS

6–30 Portland Electronics, Inc., delivered 1,000 custom-designed computer monitors on February 10 to its customer Video Shack; they had been ordered on January 1. The following cost information was compiled in connection with this order:

- Direct materials used:
    Part A327; 1 unit costing $50 per monitor
    Part B149; 1 unit costing $100 per monitor

- Direct labor used:
    Assembly; 5 hours per monitor at the rate of $10 per hour
    Inspection; 1 hour per monitor at the rate of $12 per hour

In addition, manufacturing overhead is applied to the job at the rate of $5 per direct labor hour. The selling price for each monitor is $350.

(a) Prepare a job cost sheet for this job.

(b) Determine the cost per monitor.

6–31 The following costs pertain to job 379 at Baker Auto Shop.

	Quantity	Price
Direct materials:		
Engine oil	12 ounces	$ 2/ounce
Lubricant	2 ounces	$ 3/ounce
Direct labor	2 hours	$15/hour
Overhead (based on direct labor hours):	2 hours	$10/hour

Prepare a job cost sheet for Baker Auto Shop.

6–32 Airporter Service Company operates scheduled coach service from Boston's Logan Airport to downtown Boston and to Cambridge. A common scheduling service center at the airport is responsible for ticketing and customer service for both routes. The service center is regularly staffed to service traffic of 2,400 passengers per week, two-thirds for downtown Boston passengers and the balance for Cambridge passengers. The costs of this service center are $7,200 per week normally, but they are higher in weeks when additional help is required to service higher traffic levels. The service center costs and number of passengers serviced during the five weeks of August follow:

Week	Cost	Boston Passengers	Cambridge Passengers
1	$7,200	1,600	800
2	7,200	1,500	900
3	7,600	1,650	800
4	7,800	1,700	850
5	7,200	1,700	700

How much of the service center costs should be charged to the Boston service, and how much to the Cambridge service? Explain why your method should be preferred over the other alternatives.

6-33 Bravo Steel Company supplies structural steel products to the construction industry. Its plant has 3 production departments: cutting, grinding, and drilling. The estimated overhead cost and activity levels for each department for June 1995 follow:

	Cutting	Grinding	Drilling
Overhead cost	$36,000	$200,000	$240,000
Direct labor hours	5,000	8,000	12,000
Machine-hours	80,000	40,000	30,000

The direct labor and machine-hours consumed by job ST101 are as follows:

	Cutting	Grinding	Drilling
Direct labor hours	2,000	2,500	3,000
Machine-hours	8,000	3,000	2,000

(a) Assume that a single, plantwide predetermined overhead rate is used on the basis of direct labor hours. Determine overhead cost applied to job ST101.

(b) Determine the departmental overhead rate and overhead costs applied to job ST101, assuming that machine-hours are used as the overhead application base in the cutting department and that direct labor hours are used for the grinding and drilling departments.

6-34 Duluth Metalworks Company has 2 departments, milling and assembly. The company uses a job costing system that employs a single, plantwide overhead rate to apply cost to jobs on the basis of direct labor hours. The following estimates are for May 1995:

	Milling	Assembly
Overhead costs	$120,000	$160,000
Direct labor hours	8,000	12,000
Machine-hours	12,000	6,000

The following information pertains to job 691, which was started and completed during May 1995:

	Milling	Assembly
Direct labor hours	10	40
Machine-hours	18	8
Direct materials costs	$800	$50
Direct labor costs	$100	$600

(a) Prepare a job cost sheet for job 691.

(b) Assume next that instead of using a single, plantwide overhead rate, the company uses machine-hours and direct labor costs as allocation bases for the application of overhead costs in milling and assembly departments, respectively. Prepare a job cost sheet for job 691.

6–35 For each of the following 2 jobs manufacturing 2 different products, determine the missing amounts for items (a) through (h).

	Job 321	Job 322
Units produced	200	(e)
Standards per unit:		
Material quantity	5 lbs.	(f)
Material price	$2/lb.	$3/lb.
Labor hours	2 hours	3 hours
Labor rate	$15/hour	$12/hour
Actual consumption:		
Material quantity	(a)	1,000 lbs.
Material cost	$2,000	(g)
Labor hours	(b)	(h)
Labor cost	(c)	$5,800
Variances:		
Material quantity	(d)	$100 F
Material price	$50 U	$500 F
Labor hour	$100 F	$50 U
Labor rate	$60 U	$200 F

CASES

6–36 Refer to the facts presented in Case 4.45 about the operations of Anthony's Autoshop. The following additional information is available:

The present job costing system uses a single rate for all jobs. The overhead rate is determined currently by dividing estimated overhead costs by expected hours charged to customers. The 8 mechanics are expected to be busy on customer jobs for 95% of the total available time. The price of $51.06 per hour is determined by adding a markup of x% to the overhead rate, that is $51.06 = [1 + (x/100)] * Overhead Rate. Note that all personnel costs are included in overhead costs at present.

The manager is considering switching to the use of 2 rates; 1 for class A repairs and another for class B repairs. Class A repairs require careful measurements and adjustments with equipment such as an oscilloscope or infrared gas analyzers. Electronic ignition system repairs or internal carburetor repairs are examples of Class A repairs. Class B repairs are simple repairs such as shock absorber replacements or exhaust part replacements. Class A repairs can be done only by senior mechanics; class B repairs are done mainly by junior mechanics. Half of the hours charged to customers are expected to be for class A repairs and the other half for class B repairs. Because class A repairs are expected to account for all of the senior mechanic time and most of the machine usage, 60% of the total costs (including personnel costs) are attributable to class A repairs and the remaining 40% to class B repairs.

(a) Determine the markup of x% currently used.

(b) Determine the two new rates, one for class A repairs and another for class B repairs, using the same markup of x% that you determined in (a) above.

(c) The following are expected labor hours anticipated for 2 customer jobs:

Job No.	Description	Class A Repairs	Class B Repairs
101	Carburetor repairs	4.5 hours	1.5 hours
102	Exhaust replacement	none	2.0 hours

Determine the price to be charged for each of the 2 jobs:

(i)   Under the present accounting system

(ii) Under the proposed accounting system

(d) What change in service mix is likely to result from the proposed price change?

TWO-STAGE ALLOCATIONS AND ACTIVITY-BASED COSTING SYSTEMS

LEARNING OBJECTIVES

This chapter will introduce you to:

1. the difference between production departments and service departments
2. the process of allocating service department costs to production departments
3. the two stages of cost allocations and the differences between them
4. the reason that conventional two-stage allocation methods often distort production costs
5. the use of activity-based costing systems to estimate product costs
6. the method for assigning selling and distribution costs to products

CHAPTER 7

Medequip: The Challenge

"We have been very successful with our new product line over the last 2 years. Sales reports from every market indicate sales growth of 25% or better for the new line. You report a gross margin of 80% for all of our new products, yet our operating profits have gone down almost 20%," said Charles Eager to his controller, Kendra Rivers. "Please explain to me why our financial performance does not reflect the excellent sales performance."

Charles Eager had assumed the post of the chief executive officer of Medequip, Inc., in 1994. Medequip is a Minneapolis-based manufacturer of equipment for bacteriological analysis with about $32 million in annual sales. Soon after taking over the helm at Medequip, Eager introduced a new line of equipment for special hematological (blood) analysis to beef up the old product line, whose growth rate had begun to slow down. The Medequip sales force can sell the old products several units at a time to medium and large hospitals, but the new products need to be sold one unit at a time to special pathology laboratories. The sales force had adapted well to the need to service this new group of customers, and sales of the new product line had indicated a good response to its efforts.

The present product costing system reports only a 25% gross margin on average for the old products, in contrast to the 80% gross margin on average for the new products. Medequip found sales of its old product line declining in a market that was growing slowly. In contrast, its new product line had captured more than 30% of the market share despite its apparently high gross margins. The new line now accounted for approximately 33% of Medequip's sales revenues. Although overall sales had grown, *costs had increased more than expected,* and Kendra Rivers found that Medequip profits had declined in each of the last 2 years.

As Kendra thought more about the possible factors that might explain declining profitability, she decided to take a closer look at the cost accounting system. First, she needed to understand why the actual costs were higher than those projected based on the product costs determined using Medequip's existing product costing system.

TWO-STAGE COST ALLOCATION METHOD

It is important to understand the conventional method that cost accounting systems have used to allocate costs among departments. Let's begin by discussing how departmental structure has affected allocation and then move to examples of the use of specific allocation methods.

■ The Effect of Departmental Structure on Allocation

Many plants are organized into departments responsible for performing designated activities. Cost accounting systems often are designed for this type of departmental structure. Departments directly responsible for some of the work of converting raw materials into finished products are called **production departments.** In a manufacturing plant such as Medequip, casting, machining, assembly, and packing are production departments. Departments performing activities that support production, such as machine maintenance, machine setup, production engineering, and production scheduling, are **service departments.** All service department costs are indirect (or overhead) costs because they do not arise from direct production activities.

Conventional product costing systems assign indirect costs to jobs or products in 2 stages. In the first stage, the system identifies indirect costs with various pro-

Ball Corporation, which manufactures metal and glass containers, uses Computer-Aided-Design to develop containers that meet customer requirements while providing for ease in manufacturability. The cost of this product designer and the equipment he is using must be assigned to the product lines that benefit from the design work. The challenge facing the management accountant in this operation would be to choose the appropriate cost driver(s) to use to allocate the product design costs. *(Courtesy Ball Corporation)*

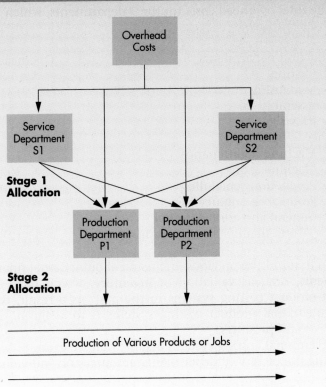

duction and service departments, and then all of the service department costs are allocated to production departments. In the second stage, the system assigns the accumulated indirect costs for the production departments to individual jobs or products based on predetermined departmental overhead rates. See Exhibit 7–1.

The 9 departments at the Medequip plant include 4 production departments—casting, machining, assembly, and packing—and 5 service departments—machine maintenance, machine setup, production scheduling, production engineering, and general and administrative. The cost accounting system accumulates overhead costs separately for each of the 9 departments.

Overhead costs for the 4 production departments (casting, machining, assembly, and packing) include supervision, supplies, and machine depreciation costs. Costs for the machine maintenance, machine setup, production scheduling, and production engineering service departments include the salaries, wages, and benefits for the engineers and workers responsible for these activities, in addition to the costs of the tools and materials they use. Costs for the general and administrative service department include the salaries and benefits for plant managerial staff, rent, heating and lighting, and janitorial services.

■ Stage 1 Cost Allocations

The first step in Stage 1 of the cost allocation procedure involves estimation of the normal overhead costs for each department. The following summary reflects the total overhead costs for the 9 departments, which are depicted in Exhibit 7–2:

Production departments	Overhead Costs
Casting	$ 65,600
Machining	131,600
Assembly	51,000
Packing	29,600
Service departments	
Machine maintenance	160,000
Machine setup	300,000
Production scheduling	120,000
Production engineering	180,000
General and administrative	90,000
Total manufacturing overhead costs	$1,127,800

Keep in mind the previous discussion about external financial reporting requirements, such as valuation of inventory, which have influenced the design of product costing systems in the past. As a result, the objective of most conventional product costing systems is to assign *all* manufacturing costs to jobs and products.

Conventional costing systems assume that we cannot obtain *direct* measures of the use of service departments' resources on individual jobs as con-

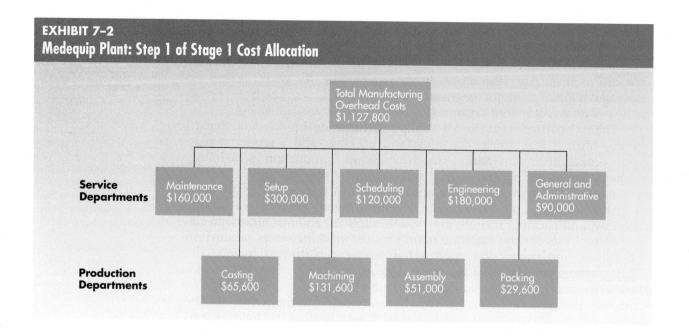

EXHIBIT 7–2
Medequip Plant: Step 1 of Stage 1 Cost Allocation

Data processing costs are significant in most large organizations. This employee in Upjohn's Administrative Computer Center, a service department, has developed a system that administrators can use to mail reports to customers and that customers can use to retrieve reports electronically. This system improves the report delivery cycle time and reduces the amount of paper used by Upjohn by about 2.5 million pages each month. This new system means that the costs in this department can no longer be allocated based on report pages printed, a common method of allocating computer center costs. *(Courtesy The Upjohn Company)*

veniently as we can of production departments' resources because jobs are worked on only in production departments. Therefore, conventional costing systems allocate the service department overhead costs first to the production departments before assigning them to individual jobs. This assignment of costs from the service departments to production departments is the second step in Stage 1 of the cost allocation procedure. Several different methods are used to allocate service department costs. We shall consider only the basic principles of **Stage 1 allocation** with reference to a specific method.

■ Direct Allocation Method

The **direct allocation method** is a simple method that allocates the service department costs directly to the production departments, ignoring the possibility that some of the activities of a service department may benefit other service departments in addition to the production departments. Other allocation methods are designed for situations in which considerable interaction occurs between service departments. The **sequential allocation method** allocates service department costs to 1 service department at a time in sequential order. The **reciprocal allocation method** determines service department cost allocations simultaneously. Appendix 7–1 discusses these 2 methods in detail. Here we describe only the direct allocation method.

■ Allocation Bases at Medequip

Allocation of costs requires the identification of a basis, or cost driver, for each service department that best reflects and measures the activity performed by that department. The Medequip plant uses the following bases to allocate service department costs by the direct allocation method.

Stage 1 allocations
Identification of costs with individual production and service departments (step 1), followed by allocation of service department costs to production departments (step 2).

Direct allocation method
A simple method to allocate service department costs to production departments that ignores interdependencies between service departments.

Sequential allocation method
A method that recognizes interdependencies between service departments and allocates service departments costs, 1 service department at a time, in a sequential order.

Reciprocal allocation method
A method to determine service department cost allocations simultaneously, recognizing the reciprocity between pairs of service departments.

Service Department	Allocation Basis
Machine maintenance	Book value of machines in each production department
Machine setup	Number of setups in each production department
Production scheduling	Number of machine-hours in each production department
Production engineering	Number of direct labor hours in each production department
General and administrative	Number of square feet occupied by each production department

The allocation bases do not always perfectly reflect the activities that generate service department costs. For example, the number of hours of setup work in each production department is a better basis than the number of setups for allocating setup department costs if the time required per setup differs across production departments. Similarly, expected maintenance hours for each department is a better measure for allocating machine maintenance costs than the book value of machines. However, the additional cost of collecting such information must be traded off against the potential benefits of the greater accuracy that its use may provide. For instance, the costs of obtaining information about maintenance hours in each department at Medequip were not believed to be justified by the benefit from the greater accuracy they might provide. So Medequip uses the book value of machines to allocate maintenance costs, because this measure is easily available.

It is often difficult to obtain any reasonable measures to allocate the costs of product-sustaining or facility-sustaining activities to production departments. Production scheduling, engineering, and plant administration activities do not benefit specific production departments, although their use may differ across different products. Medequip uses machine-hours and direct labor hours as the bases to allocate these costs to the production departments.

EXHIBIT 7–3
Medequip, Inc.: Allocation Bases Values for Production Departments

	Allocation Bases	Production Department				Total
		Casting	Machining	Assembly	Packing	
1.	Book value of machines	$300,000	$600,000	$180,000	$120,000	$1,200,000
2.	Number of setups	200	400	200	200	1,000
3.	Machine-hours	6,000	22,000	9,000	3,000	40,000
4.	Direct labor hours	2,000	11,000	6,000	6,000	25,000
5.	Square feet	6,000	9,000	9,000	6,000	30,000

EXHIBIT 7–4
Medequip, Inc.: Allocation Ratios

	SERVICE DEPARTMENT	ALLOCATION BASIS	CASTING	PRODUCTION DEPARTMENT MACHINING	ASSEMBLY	PACKING	TOTAL
1.	Machine maintenance	Book value of machines	0.250	0.500	0.150	0.100	1.000
2.	Machine setup	Number of setups	0.200	0.400	0.200	0.200	1.000
3.	Production scheduling	Machine-hours	0.150	0.550	0.225	0.075	1.000
4.	Production engineering	Direct labor hours	0.080	0.440	0.240	0.240	1.000
5.	General & administrative	Square feet	0.200	0.300	0.300	0.200	1.000

Exhibit 7–3 presents the allocation bases and their values for the production departments at Medequip. The normal costs of the service departments are allocated to the production departments in proportion to their *respective allocation basis values*. Exhibit 7–4 shows the allocation ratios that represent these proportions. To obtain the ratio of 0.250 for the allocation of machine maintenance service department costs to the casting department, use the ratio of $300,000, the book value of machines in the casting department (Exhibit 7–3), to $1,200,000, the total book value of machines in the 4 production departments to obtain 0.250 ($300,000/$1,200,000).

Then determine the amount of service department costs allocated to the production department by multiplying the allocation ratio by the corresponding service department costs (see Exhibit 7–5). For instance, the casting department receives $40,000 of machine maintenance service department costs, which is obtained by multiplying the allocation ratio 0.250 (Exhibit 7–4) by the total overhead costs of $160,000 (Exhibit 7–2) for the machine maintenance service department.

EXHIBIT 7–5
Medequip, Inc.: Allocation of Service Department Costs to Production Departments

	CASTING	PRODUCTION DEPARTMENT MACHINING	ASSEMBLY	PACKING
Overhead costs identified directly in step 1 of stage 1 allocations	$ 65,600	$131,600	$ 51,000	$ 29,600
Allocated from service department in step 2 of stage 1				
1. Machine maintenance	40,000	80,000	24,000	16,000
2. Machine setup	60,000	120,000	60,000	60,000
3. Production scheduling	18,000	66,000	27,000	9,000
4. Production engineering	14,400	79,200	43,200	43,200
5. General and administrative	18,000	27,000	27,000	18,000
Total overhead costs for the production department	$216,000	$503,800	$232,200	$175,800

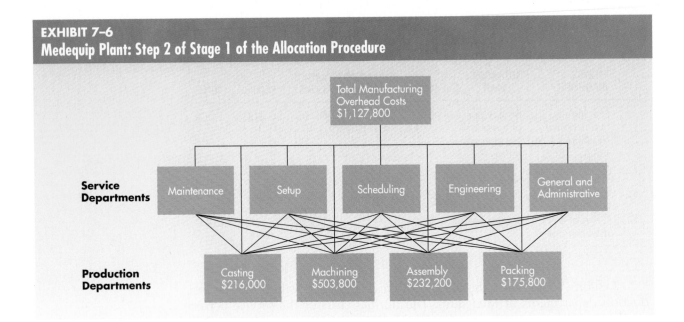

The allocated costs from the service departments are then added to the overhead costs originally identified directly with the production departments. The total of $216,000 (Exhibit 7–5) for the casting department is the sum of the original $65,600 (Exhibit 7–2) and $150,400 ($40,000 + $60,000 + $18,000 + $14,400 + $18,000) allocated from the 5 service departments. This completes Stage 1 of the cost allocation procedure. The $1,127,800 of overhead costs for the Medequip plant (Exhibit 7–2) now are allocated $216,000 to casting, $503,800 to machining, $232,200 to assembly, and $175,800 to the packing department (see Exhibit 7–6). Next, these amounts are used in Stage 2 of the allocation procedure to determine the departmental overhead rates for assignment of these costs to the jobs worked on in each production department.

■ Stage 2 Cost Allocations

Stage 2 allocations
Assignment of production department costs to jobs and products when they are worked on in the departments.

Stage 2 allocations require the identification of appropriate allocation bases for each production department. These are often unit-related measures, such as the number of units made, the number of direct labor hours (or cost), and the number of machine-hours. Medequip uses machine-hours as the allocation basis for the casting and machining departments because of the high reliance on machines for the operations performed in these departments. The assembly and packing operations are more labor intensive; therefore, Medequip uses direct labor hours as the allocation basis in these 2 departments (see Exhibit 7–7).

Overhead allocation rates are determined for these 4 production departments by dividing the indirect (overhead) costs accumulated in each production department by the total number of units of the corresponding allocation basis. To illustrate, the total indirect (overhead) costs from Stage 1 are

	CASTING	PRODUCTION DEPARTMENT MACHINING	ASSEMBLY	PACKING
Total overhead costs (from step 2 of stage 1)	$216,000	$503,800	$232,200	$175,800
Allocation basis	Machine-hours	Machine-hours	Direct labor hours	Direct labor hours
Total machine-hours	6,000	22,000	9,000	3,000
Total direct labor hours	2,000	11,000	6,000	6,000
Allocation rate	$36.00	$22.90	$38.70	$29.30

$216,000 for the casting department, with total machine-hours estimated to be 6,000. Therefore, the overhead rate for the casting department is $36 per machine-hour ($216,000/6,000).

Overhead is applied to each job as it is worked on in the production departments. Exhibit 7–8 presents data on the number of machine and direct

This maintenance department employee at a Wheeling-Pittsburgh steel mill designed an effective way to balance the cost associated with premature parts replacement and the cost of equipment failure to determine the best time to undertake preventative maintenance on equipment. The number of hours worked might be a way of allocating the cost of this employee's activities to the production department so that product costs will reflect the cost of his contribution. *(Courtesy Wheeling Pittsburgh Steel)*

EXHIBIT 7–8

Medequip, Inc.: Machine and Labor Hours for Two Representative Jobs

	JOB J189-4 (OLD PRODUCT LINE)	JOB J273-2 (NEW PRODUCT LINE)
Machine-hours		
Casting	40	16
Machining	140	56
Assembly	60	24
Packing	20	18
Direct labor hours		
Casting	18	7
Machining	70	28
Assembly	40	16
Packing	40	16

labor hours incurred on 2 representative jobs, J189-4 and J273-2, in each production department. Job J189-4 involves the production of a batch of 12 units of E189, bacterial analysis equipment in the old product line. Job J273-2 is for the production of a batch of 5 units of E273, 1 of the new products whose sales have been increasing rapidly.

Exhibits 7–9 and 7–10 present the costs for direct materials, direct labor, and overhead applied to these 2 jobs. Recall from Chapter 6 that direct material costs are identified with the jobs based on requisition notes issued for materials required in the casting department, subassemblies required in the assembly department, and packing materials required in the packing department. Direct labor costs are determined by multiplying the number of direct labor hours (Exhibit 7–8) by the labor wage rate applicable to each department. The wage rate is higher in the machining department than in the packing department because more skilled workers are required for machining operations.

To obtain overhead costs for the jobs J189-4 (Exhibit 7–9) and J273-2 (Exhibit 7–10), multiply the number of machine-hours by the overhead rate for the casting and machining departments, and the number of direct labor hours by the overhead rate for the assembly and packing departments (Exhibit 7–7). Notice that the machine-hours and direct labor hours used for these calculations correspond to the amount of time spent on the job in a particular department rather than on the *totals* for the job in the entire plant. The total manufacturing costs for each job are the sum of the direct material, direct labor, and overhead costs. Obtain the (manufacturing) cost per unit by dividing total manufacturing costs for the job by the number of units produced in the job.

OBJECTIVE 7.4
The reason that conventional two-stage allocation methods often distort production costs

DISTORTIONS CAUSED BY TWO-STAGE ALLOCATIONS   Product costing systems installed in many plants employ the 2-stage allocation method just described. The structure of these systems, however, can actually distort product costs. Consider the following example.

Assume that Minnetka, a company that makes steel valves, has a plant that is organized into 3 departments: machine setups, which is a service department, and machining and assembly, which are both production

EXHIBIT 7–9
Medequip, Inc.: Application of Overhead to Job J189-4

ITEM	COSTS	CALCULATION DETAILS
Direct materials costs		
Casting	$ 2,658.40	
Assembly	1,446.60	(All amounts up to *Overhead* Costs are given.)
Packing	632.80	
Total materials	$ 4,737.80	
Direct labor costs		
Casting	$ 331.20	= 18 * $18.40 Given
Machining	1,666.00	= 70 * $23.80 Given
Assembly	632.00	= 40 * $15.80 Given
Packing	528.00	= 40 * $13.20 Given
Total direct labor costs	$ 3,157.20	
Overhead costs		
Casting	$ 1,440.00	= 40 * $36.00 (Exhibit 7–7)
Machining	3,206.00	= 140 * $22.90 (Exhibit 7–7)
Assembly	1,548.00	= 40 * $38.70 (Exhibit 7–7)
Packing	1,172.00	= 40 * $29.30 (Exhibit 7–7)
Total overheads	$ 7,366.00	
Total manufacturing costs	$15,261.00	
Number of units	12	
Cost per unit	$ 1,271.75	

EXHIBIT 7–10
Medequip, Inc.: Application of Overhead to Job J273-2

	COSTS	CALCULATION DETAILS
Direct materials costs		
Casting	$1,186.00	(All amounts up to *Overhead* Costs are given.)
Assembly	788.80	
Packing	491.40	
Total materials	$2,466.20	
Direct labor costs		
Casting	$ 128.80	= 7 * $18.40 (Given)
Machining	666.40	= 28 * $23.80 (Given)
Assembly	252.80	= 16 * $15.80 (Given)
Packing	211.20	= 16 * $13.20 (Given)
Total direct labor costs	$1,259.20	
Overhead costs		
Casting	$ 576.00	= 16 * $36.00 (Exhibit 7–7)
Machining	1,282.40	= 56 * $22.90 (Exhibit 7–7)
Assembly	619.20	= 16 * $38.70 (Exhibit 7–7)
Packing	468.80	= 16 * $29.30 (Exhibit 7–7)
Total overhead	$2,946.40	
Total manufacturing costs	$6,672.40	
Number of units	5	
Cost per unit	$1,334.48	

This newsprint roll, which is sitting on a computer-guided vehicle, is being loaded into a press. The setting-up operation is costly because it involves the use of skilled workers and expensive equipment. Because costs associated with this setup would include the cost of the workers and the equipment, the management accountant would have to use several cost drivers to allocate setup costs to production runs. *(Courtesy Media General)*

departments. Total setup costs of $200,000 are allocated, $120,000 to the machining and $80,000 to the assembly departments in proportion to the respective setup hours of 480 and 320 in the 2 production departments.

The plant manufactures 2 products. Exhibit 7–11 shows the information for Products A and B. From the prior information regarding setup costs, the setup activity cost is $250 per hour ($200,000/(480 + 320 setup hours)). Intuitively, it would seem logical to charge product A $1.5625 per unit ($250 * 5 hours setup/800 units) for setup costs and product B $6.2500 per unit ($250 * 5 hours setup/200 units) for setup costs.

Let us see now how the 2-stage allocation method actually charges setup

7–11
Minnetka Production Factors: Products A and B

| | PRODUCTS | |
RELEVANT FACTORS	A	B
Batch size, number of units	800	200
Setup hours required		
Machining	3	3
Assembly	2	2
Normal production, number of units	64,000	16,000
Normal production, number of batches	80	80

costs to the 2 products. The second stage of allocations assigns overhead costs to products based on machine-hours for both production departments at Minnetka. Both products require 0.1 machine-hours per unit in each department, machining and assembly. Therefore, each department has a total of 8,000 machine-hours (0.1 * (64,000 + 16,000 units of normal production)). The overhead rates are $15 per machine-hour ($120,000 setup costs/8,000 machine hours) for the machining and $10 per machine-hour ($80,000 setup costs/8,000 machine-hours) for the assembly department. Both products A and B are charged $2.50 ((0.1 * $15) + (0.1 * $10)) per unit for the setup costs.

Product A is overcosted because it is charged more than its fair share of setup costs. In contrast, product B is undercosted because it is charged less than its fair share of setup costs. Why does the 2-stage allocation method distort product costs in this manner?

REASON FOR 2-STAGE ALLOCATION DISTORTION The reason for the distortion is the break in the link between the cause for the overhead costs (setup hours) and the basis for assignment of the costs to the individual products (machine-hours). Two related factors contribute to these cost distortions: (1) allocations based on unit-related measures and (2) differences in relative consumption ratios.

Both products A and B have the same number of machine-hours per unit; therefore, both are assigned the same amount of setup costs ($2.50 per unit). In reality, however, the demand for setup activity is less for product A because it is produced in larger batches. It is charged the same rate as for product B because of the use of machine-hours as the basis in the second stage of allocations. Conventional 2-stage allocation methods use unit-related measures to allocate overhead costs in the second stage, but the demand for overhead activities is driven, in fact, by batch-related and product-sustaining measures such as setups and engineering changes.

Cost distortions are greater when the difference between the relative proportion of the cost driver for the activity (setup hours) and the relative proportion of the basis for second-stage assignment of overhead costs (machine-hours) is greater. Product A needs 0.00625 setup hours per unit (5/800), on average, but product B needs more—0.02500 setup hours per unit (5/200). Both products need the same number of machine-hours per unit. The *actual* consumption ratio of product A to product B for setup activity is 1:4 (0.00625/0.02500) based on the ratio of the actual cost driver, setup hours. But the *apparent* consumption ratio used to allocate setup costs is 1:1 based on machine-hours (0.1/0.1). This difference in the actual cost driver consumption ratio and the allocation basis ratio results in overcosting product A and undercosting product B.

Such distortions could be eliminated if we designed a costing system that used the actual cost driver for *each* overhead activity to assign costs directly to the products. This is the logic underlying the development of activity-based costing systems.

ACTIVITY-BASED COSTING SYSTEMS

OBJECTIVE 7.5
The use of activity-based costing systems to estimate product costs

The fundamental assumption on which the 2-stage allocation method is founded is the absence of a strong direct link between the support activities and the products manufactured. For this reason, service department overhead costs are first allocated to production departments in the conventional 2-stage allocation method.

CONSIDER THIS . . .

Activity-Based Costing Helps AT&T

Throughout its history, the telephone business has been regulated in North America. Regulators have determined pricing formulas under a mandate established by political processes. The Federal Communications Commission developed its methods for establishing prices on the basis of cost plus an allowable profit. Regulatory requirements detailed cost allocation procedures that were followed by AT&T.

AT&T's breakup into smaller, more focused business units combined with gradual relaxation of price regulation has made understanding and managing, rather than simply allocating, costs critical. As a result, AT&T managers decided to implement an activity-based costing (ABC) system to understand the activities driving their business.

The business billing center was selected for an ABC pilot project. Billing activities included monitoring billing records; editing checks; validating data; correcting errors; and printing, sorting, and dispatching invoices to business customers. A cross-functional team prepared a schematic flowchart of the business and operational relationships to identify how resources and activities related to each other and to trace outputs from the activities to services provided to each customer.

The cost of service provided to different types of customers was determined by identifying activity and cost driver consumption characteristics. Deciding on activity cost drivers was relatively straightforward because team members from the various business functions were familiar with the operations. Some of the drivers selected were number of customer accounts tested, change requests, service orders, customer locations, printer hours, and pages printed.

AT&T managers find the pilot ABC model to be an innovative tool for managing costs and an education in enhancing the operation of their business. It has led to improvements in internal operating processes, supplier relationships, and customer satisfaction.

Source: T. Hobdy, J. Thomson, and P. Sharman, "Activity-Based Management at AT&T," *Management Accounting,* April 1994, pp. 35–39.

CONVENTIONAL 2-STAGE ALLOCATION SYSTEM	ACTIVITY-BASED COSTING SYSTEM
Stage 1 *Step 1* Trace all overhead costs to production and service department cost pools. *Step 2* Allocate service department costs to production departments.	Stage 1 Trace all overhead costs to activity cost pools associated with distinct activity cost drivers.
Stage 2 Assign costs to jobs or products based on production department overhead rates computed as ratios of overhead costs accumulated in each production department to the corresponding level of a (unit-related) measure of production volume in the department.	Stage 2 Assign costs to jobs or products based on activity overhead cost rates computed as ratios of overhead costs accumulated in each activity cost pool to the corresponding level of the activity cost driver.

■ The Basis of Activity-Based Costing

Activity-based costing rejects this assumption and, instead, develops cost drivers that *directly link the activities performed to the products manufactured.* These cost drivers measure the average demand placed on each activity by the various products. Then activity costs are assigned to products in proportion to the demand that the products place, on average, on the activities. This eliminates the need for the second step in Stage-1 allocations that allocates service department costs to production departments before assigning them to individual jobs and products. Exhibit 7–12 summarizes and compares the various stages and steps in the conventional and activity-based costing systems.

Activity-based costing systems
Costing systems based on cost drivers that link activities performed to products and allocate overhead activity costs directly to products using these cost drivers.

■ Activity-Based Costing at the Medequip Plant

Let us consider once again the allocation of overhead costs at the Medequip plant. Stage 1 of the activity-based cost allocation procedure involves identifying activities, their cost drivers, and the corresponding costs incurred to perform the activities. Exhibit 7–13 lists the activities and their costs at Medequip. The total overhead costs of $1,127,800 are distributed over 13

EXHIBIT 7–13
Medequip, Inc.: Activities, Cost Drivers, and Overhead Rates

NO.	ACTIVITY	TOTAL COSTS	COST DRIVER	TOTAL COST DRIVER LEVELS	OVERHEAD RATES
1.	Supervision: Casting	$ 26,000	Casting setup hours	500	$52.00
2.	Supervision: Machining	39,600	Machining setup hours	600	66.00
3.	Supervision: Assembly	42,000	Assembly direct labor hours	6,000	7.00
4.	Supervision: Packing	23,600	Packing direct labor hours	6,000	3.93
5.	Depreciation: Casting	39,600	Casting machine-hours	6,000	6.60
6.	Depreciation: Machining	92,000	Machining machine-hours	22,000	4.18
7.	Depreciation: Assembly	9,000	Assembly machine-hours	9,000	1.00
8.	Depreciation: Packing	6,000	Packing machine-hours	3,000	2.00
9.	Machine maintenance	160,000	Total machine-hours	40,000	4.00
10.	Machine setup	300,000	Total setup hours	300	1,000.00
11.	Production scheduling	120,000	Number of batches	500	240.00
12.	Production engineering	180,000	Engineering change orders	200	900.00
13.	General and administrative	90,000	Total machine hours	40,000	2.25
	Total	$1,127,800			

activities. In some cases, such as with machine maintenance at the Medequip plant, an activity may correspond exactly to a service department, but such 1-to-1 correspondence is not necessary. For example, activities such as materials handling and materials movement may be performed by workers in several different departments.

Referring to Exhibit 7–13, we can see that overhead costs for each of the 4 production departments at the Medequip plant are traced to 1 of the 2 activities, supervision or machine depreciation. Supervision in casting and machining departments (numbers 1 and 2) at the Medequip plant is required at the beginning of each batch to ensure that it is set up right. Therefore, setup hours in the casting and machining departments are used as the cost drivers for the supervision activity in the 2 departments. In contrast, supervision in the assembly and the packing departments (numbers 3 and 4) extends over the entire time of a job. Therefore, departmental direct labor hours are used as the cost drivers in these departments. Depreciation costs (numbers 5–8) are associated with the use of machines in all 4 departments, and, accordingly, departmental machine-hours are used as the cost drivers. Total machine hours, total setup hours, number of batches, and engineering change orders are the cost drivers for machine maintenance, machine setup, production scheduling, and production engineering activities (numbers 9–12, respectively). The general and administrative costs (number 13) arise from a facility-sustaining activity represented by the capacity made available at the plant. Therefore, these costs are allocated to jobs on the basis of their total machine-hours.

Stage 2 allocations to assign overhead costs to jobs and products are based on separate overhead rates for the activities. The estimated total cost for an activity shown in Exhibit 7–13 (column 3) is divided by the corresponding estimated total amount for its cost driver (column 5) to obtain the activity

CONSIDER THIS . . .

Activity-Based Costing at a Hewlett-Packard Plant

In 1989, Hewlett-Packard (HP) implemented an ABC system at its Boise Surface Mount Center (BSMC) plant in Idaho. The plant manufactures about 50 different electronic circuit boards for internal customers within HP. With surface-mount technology, patches of a semiliquid solder are placed on the surface of a circuit board, and electronic components are placed on the solder patches. Then the board goes through an oven to melt the solder to form a strong mechanical board and a reliable electronic circuit. The process is highly automated, with computer-controlled machines that can select more than 100 different components each minute from the correct reel and place each one on the surface of the board within a tolerance of four-thousandths of an inch. Production volumes for each board fluctuate from a few hundred to several thousand per month.

Prior to adopting ABC, the BSMC plant applied *all* overhead as a percent of direct material cost. The ABC system uses 10 different cost pools and drivers, as shown below:

Cost Pools	Activity Cost Drivers
1. Panel operations	Percent of a whole panel; if one panel contains four individual boards, then each board is charged 25% of the panel rate.
2. Small component placement	Number of "small" components placed on the board's surface.
3. Medium component placement	Number of "medium" size components placed on the board's surface.
4. Large component placement	Number of "large" components placed on the board's surface.
5. Through-hole component insertion	Number of components with wires that are inserted through holes on the board.
6. Hand load component placement	Minutes required to place all components that must be hand loaded rather than automatically placed on the board.

Cost Pools	Activity Cost Drivers
7. Material procurement & handling	Number of unique parts in the board.
8. Scheduling	Number of scheduling hours.
9. Assembly setup	Number of minutes of setup time.
10. Test & rework	Number of minutes of test and rework time for each board.

The BSMC plant compared the costs of its 57 products under the old and the new costing systems to evaluate the extent of cost distortion caused by the old system. Their findings follow:

Distortion Caused by the Old System, Expressed as a Percent Difference from ABC Cost	Number of Products
Under-costed:	
More than 100%	1
Between 50% and 100%	5
Between 20% and 50%	6
Between 5% and 20%	23
Little Change:	
Less than 5% under or over-costed	13
Over-costed:	
Between 5% and 20%	9
Total	57

Under the old costing system, products with low material costs had low amounts of overhead assigned to them. The ABC system indicated that several of these products were undercosted by the old system. It also indicated that 9 large volume products that had high material costs were over-costed by the old system.

Source: C.M. Merz and A. Hardy, "ABC Puts Accountants on Design Team at HP," *Management Accounting,* September 1993, pp. 22–27.

The McDonnell Douglas employee on the right in this picture is a carpenter employed in the Maintenance Department in a McDonnell Douglas aircraft assembly plant. This employee designed the container shown in this picture to move parts around the plant. The container reduced the costs associated with moving, lost parts, and damage. Because this service department activity was labor intensive, its costs would be appropriately allocated to the production process using the number of hours worked. *(Courtesy McDonnell Douglas)*

overhead rates (column 6). For instance, the overhead rate of $900 per engineering change order for activity 12, production engineering, is obtained as the ratio of the total cost, $180,000, to the total cost driver level, 200.

Overhead is assigned to individual jobs on the basis of their respective cost driver levels. Exhibit 7–14 presents this information for jobs J189-4 and J273-2. Exhibit 7–15 displays the costs assigned to the 2 jobs.

EXHIBIT 7–14
Medequip, Inc.: Activity Cost Driver Values for 2 Representative Jobs

ACTIVITY	COST DRIVER	JOB J189-4	JOB J273-2
1	Casting setup hours	1.0	1.0
2	Machining setup hours	1.2	1.2
3	Assembly direct labor hours	40.0	16.0
4	Packing direct labor hours	40.0	16.0
5	Casting machine-hours	40.0	16.0
6	Machining machine-hours	140.0	56.0
7	Assembly machine-hours	60.0	24.0
8	Packing machine-hours	20.0	18.0
9	Total machine-hours	260.0	114.0
10	Total setup hours	2.2	2.2
11	Number of batches	1.0	1.0
12	Engineering change orders	0.4	0.3
13	Total machine-hours	260.0	114.0

EXHIBIT 7–15
Medequip, Inc.: Activity-Based Costs for 2 Representative Jobs

ITEM	JOB J189-4 COSTS	JOB J189-4 DETAILS	JOB J273-2 COSTS	JOB J273-2 DETAILS
Direct material costs	$4,737.80	(Exhibit 7–9)	$2,466.80	(Exhibit 7–10)
Direct labor costs	3,157.20	(Exhibit 7–9)	1,259.20	(Exhibit 7–10)
Overhead costs				
Supervision				
1. Casting	52.00	= 1.0 * $52.00	52.00	= 1.0 * $52.00
2. Machining	79.20	= 1.2 * $66.00	79.20	= 1.2 * $66.00
3. Assembly	280.00	= 40.0 * $7.00	112.00	= 16.0 * $7.00
4. Packing	157.20	= 40.0 * $3.93	62.88	= 16.0 * $3.93
Depreciation				
5. Casting	264.00	= 40.0 * $6.60	105.60	= 16.0 * $6.60
6. Machining	585.20	= 140.0 * $4.18	234.08	= 56.0 * $4.18
7. Assembly	60.00	= 60.0 * $1.00	24.00	= 24.0 * $1.00
8. Packing	40.00	= 20.0 * $2.00	36.00	= 18.0 * $2.00
9. Machine maintenance	1,040.00	= 260.0 * $4.00	456.00	= 114.0 * $4.00
10. Machine setup	2,200.00	= 2.2 * $1,000	2,200.00	= 2.2 * $1,000
11. Production scheduling	240.00	= 1.0 * $240	240.00	= 1.0 * $240
12. Production engineering	360.00	= 0.4 * $900	270.00	= 0.3 * $900
13. General and administrative	585.00	= 260.0 * $2.25	256.50	= 114.0 * $2.25
Total overhead costs	$5,942.60		$4,128.26	
Total manufacturing costs	$13,837.60		$7,854.26	
Number of units	12	(Exhibit 7–9)	5	(Exhibit 7–10)
Cost per unit	$1,153.13	= 13,837.60 ÷ 12	$1,570.85	= 7,853.26 ÷ 5

Notice that the costs assigned to job J273-2 under activity-based costing ($1570.85) are much higher than those assigned under the conventional method ($1334.48, Exhibit 7–10). Job J273-2 is smaller than job J189-4; therefore, the conventional method assigns fewer costs to job J273-2. This occurs because Stage 2 allocations are in proportion to the unit-related machine-hour and direct labor hour measures instead of the true activity cost drivers for the job.

This distortion is corrected in activity-based costing because setup and other batch-related activity costs are assigned to the jobs on the basis of batch-related cost drivers, and product engineering and other product-sustaining activity costs are assigned to the jobs on the basis of product-sustaining cost drivers.

SELLING AND DISTRIBUTION ACTIVITIES

You will have noticed so far that all of the product costing systems described in this and the previous chapter considered only manufacturing costs but not selling and distribution costs. This focus on manufacturing costs is typical of conventional cost accounting systems because, as we mentioned previously, only manufacturing costs can be considered in valuing inventories for external financial reporting purposes. External financial reporting requires accountants to design cost accounting systems that track manufacturing costs and allocate them between costs of goods sold and inventories on hand.

OBJECTIVE 7.6
The method for assigning selling and distribution costs to products

In the first 3 quarters of the 20th century, without the help of inexpensive electronic data-processing facilities, accountants did not want to be burdened with the responsibility for maintaining multiple accounting systems. Therefore, external reporting requirements also dictated the structure of the product cost systems for internal managerial decision making.

Conventional product costing systems either completely excluded selling and distribution and other nonmanufacturing costs or assigned them to products on a rather arbitrary basis, such as relative sales value, manufacturing cost, conversion cost, or gross margin. Neither of these methods reflected the demand for the selling and distribution activities placed by different products sold to different types of customers through different distribution channels.

When costs for selling and distribution, corporate, administrative, research and development, and other nonmanufacturing activities were small relative to manufacturing costs, excluding these costs from the product costing system did not have a significant impact on the validity of managerial decisions. Recently, however, with the increasing emphasis on customer orientation and technological innovation to obtain a competitive edge, it has become necessary to examine whether some products demand more of selling and distribution or other nonmanufacturing activities, and to determine whether to incorporate their different consumption patterns in the determination of product costs.

■ Selling and Distribution Costs at Medequip, Inc.

Let us return to our discussion of product costs at the Medequip plant. Kendra Rivers, Medequip's controller, assigned 2 of her brightest young accountants and 1 experienced sales manager to a task force responsible for analyzing selling and distribution costs.

The task force determined that there were 7 selling and distribution activities performed at Medequip (see Exhibit 7–16). These activities include *order-getting* activities, such as marketing management and travel, distributing sales catalogs, and providing customer service, and *order-filling* activities such as order execution, warehousing, and shipping.

The task force also identified costs directly with the 7 activities based on the personnel, facilities, equipment, and services required for each activity (see Exhibit 7–17). Based on the responsibility of the personnel performing the different activities, costs for each activity are further identified with 1 of the 2 major product lines, bacterial analysis or hematology equipment. More customer service and order execution costs are assigned to the new hematology equipment line because it has more demanding and fewer customers than the bacterial analysis line. Customers of the new line also purchase fewer units than do the customers for the bacterial analysis line.

Exhibit 7–18 displays the cost drivers and overhead rates for the 7 selling and distribution activities. The amount of time and effort spent on customer service (number 4), for instance, depends largely on the number of units installed. As in the case of manufacturing support activities, the overhead rate is determined by dividing the activity costs by the cost driver lev-

EXHIBIT 7–16
Medequip, Inc.: Selling and Distribution Activities

TYPE OF ACTIVITY	DESCRIPTION OF ACTIVITY
Order getting	1. *Marketing Management:* Salaries and benefits of marketing managers, depreciation and maintenance on facilities and equipment used by them, power, telephone charges, and supplies. Allocated to product groups based on estimated proportion of time spent on each group.
	2. *Marketing Travel:* Travel and entertainment expenditures. The new hematological equipment products business required much more travel to build up a network of new customers because each customer ordered only 1 unit. Allocated to product groups based on business purpose.
	3. *Sales Catalog:* Costs of developing, printing, and mailing sales catalog to current and potential customers. Allocated to product groups based on number of mailings.
	4. *Customer Service:* Salaries and benefits of customer service representatives and costs of equipment and supplies used by them. Hematological equipment product group required more customer service hours because the product designs were new and product installations were dispersed. Allocated to product groups based on estimated proportion of time spent on each group.
Order filling	5. *Order Execution:* Salaries and benefits of staff responsible for contacting customers before receiving and after filling orders, coordinating production to schedule deliveries, invoicing, and collection. Allocated to product groups based on estimated proportion of time spent on each group.
	6. *Warehousing:* Costs of storing finished goods inventory in the warehouse awaiting shipment to customers. Allocated to product groups based on their inventory levels.
	7. *Shipping:* Costs of shipping finished goods to customers. Directly identified with product groups based on shipping records.

EXHIBIT 7–17
Medequip, Inc.: Selling and Distribution Activity Costs

ACTIVITY	ACTIVITY COSTS AND ALLOCATION TO PRODUCT GROUPS		
	TOTAL	BACTERIAL ANALYSIS EQUIPMENT	HEMATOLOGY EQUIPMENT
1. Marketing management	$ 97,800	$ 52,800	$ 45,000
2. Marketing travel	49,800	12,000	37,800
3. Sales catalog	48,000	18,000	30,000
4. Customer service	76,800	26,400	50,400
5. Order execution	146,000	56,000	90,000
6. Warehousing	46,800	28,800	18,000
7. Shipping	99,000	54,000	45,000
Total	$564,200	$248,000	$316,200

EXHIBIT 7-18
Medequip, Inc.: Selling and Distribution Overhead Costs

ACTIVITY	COST DRIVER	BACTERIAL ANALYSIS EQUIPMENT			HEMATOLOGICAL EQUIPMENT		
		ALLOCATED ACTIVITY COST	COST DRIVER LEVEL	OVERHEAD RATE	ALLOCATED ACTIVITY COST	COST DRIVER LEVEL	OVERHEAD RATE
1. Marketing management	Dollars of sales	$52,800	$528,000	10.00%	$45,000	$300,000	15.00%
2. Marketing travel	Number of orders	12,000	80	$150.00	37,800	120	$315.00
3. Sales catalog	Number of orders	18,000	80	$225.00	30,000	120	$250.00
4. Customer service	Number of units	26,400	240	$110.00	50,400	120	$420.00
5. Order execution	Number of orders	56,000	80	$700.00	90,000	120	$750.00
6. Warehousing	Average inventory volume (c. ft.)	28,800	5,760	$5.00	18,000	3,600	$5.00
7. Shipping	Units * miles	54,000	72,000	$0.75	45,000	60,000	$0.75

CONSIDER THIS . . .

Activity Costs at Fireman's Fund

Fireman's Fund is among the top 20 U.S. property/casualty insurance companies. It sells its products through a network of 50 major field offices using a sales force of 6,000 independent insurance agents and brokers. Approximately 20% of its business is in personal lines (homeowners and private passenger automobile insurance), with the balance being commercial lines insurance.

In 1991 the company had revenues of $3.3 billion, assets of $9.1 billion, and approximately 10,000 employees nationwide. Its earnings had been squeezed because of declining revenues due to severe price competition accompanied by increases in costs of claims and other operating expenses.

As part of efforts to restore profitability, Fireman's Fund implemented a sophisticated new on-line reporting system that provided detailed revenue and cost information to each product manager and each local branch manager. The company discovered, however, that it was particularly weak in measuring internal operating expenses because a large portion of them was allocated somewhat arbitrarily to the various product lines.

Implementing activity-based costing is difficult for a service company such as Fireman's Fund. More than 75% of its internal operating expenses are staff driven, comprising salaries and benefits, so it is critical to understand the use of staff resources. Because each employee works on multiple activities and performs a variety of tasks for more than one product line, it is difficult to isolate employee time devoted to specific activities. Also, the activity times vary greatly by product line and customer segment so that using a simple average to estimate product costs leads to cost distortions, subsidizing the more complex products at the expense of the simpler products.

Consider a typical claims adjuster whose basic responsibility is to settle claims fairly while protecting the company's interests. In practice, this responsibility for an individual claim translates to many different tasks that may be spread over a period from a few days to several years, depending on the complexity of the claim. Tasks include investigating the facts of the claim; evaluating the amount of damages by gathering information from appraisers, employers, body shops, and attorneys; managing outside resources such as accident experts, attorneys, and medical authorities; documenting the facts and the damages; negotiating settlement with the claimant; making court appearances; processing payments; and

els. Thus, separate overhead rates are determined for the 2 product lines because of the large differences in the nature of the sales support activities required for each of them. For instance, the customer service activity overhead rate for the older bacterial analysis equipment product line is $110 per unit, which is obtained by dividing the cost of $26,400 (Exhibit 7–17) by the number of units, 240. The overhead rate for the hematological equipment product line is $420 per unit ($50,400/120) and reflects the higher intensity of demand for the customer service activity for the new product line.

Differences in the consumption of sales support activities by the 2 representative jobs J189-4 and J273-2 also are reflected in the cost driver data collected by the task force for these two jobs (see Exhibit 7–19). The impact of these differences in activity consumption rates on the product costs is apparent in the data in Exhibit 7–20. Activity costs are assigned to jobs, as before, based on overhead rates and cost driver information. For instance, customer service activity cost of $1,320 is assigned to job J189-4, which had 12 units (Exhibit 7–19), at the rate of $110 per unit (Exhibit 7–18). Job J273-2 is charged $2,100 for customer service activity for its 5 units (Exhibit 7–19) because of the higher overhead rate of $420 per unit (Exhibit 7–18) for the new product line.

The mechanics of assigning the selling and distribution costs are very

estimating the resources needed to cover future payments. The amount of effort varies significantly by type of loss, by legal jurisdiction, and by size of loss. Each adjuster is responsible for many different claims at any one time. Thus, the challenge of understanding the real costs of doing business is indeed considerable in such a complex environment.

At first, the reporting system used expense allocation information based primarily on the judgment of local managers who supplied estimates as to how the employee resources were spent on various products. The company now supplements this information by periodically sampling employee work activity. Each employee is sampled twice during a one-month period to record the nature of the work and the product being supported at the instant. By selecting arbitrary but representative points in time, and by taking a snapshot of employee work activity, the company now develops estimates of the percentage of time devoted to various products, activities, and tasks.

The activity and product costs estimated using the cost sampling method have several important implications for management:

1. *Pricing:* Activity cost analysis revealed that small accounts consume disproportionately more staff resources than large accounts. The company is adjusting its price (policy premium) structure to reflect better the differences in the costs of processing different policies.

2. *Reengineer process:* The company is implementing new, more streamlined methods to reduce the staff resources required for processing small, routine accounts.

3. *Benchmarking:* With the detailed activity analysis, the company is better able to determine the appropriate level of staff resources required for activities such as claims processing at local branch offices, especially as the mix of business changes over time.

4. *Leveraging human resources:* Activity analysis enabled the company to estimate, for instance, how much time an underwriter spends on certain processing tasks that could be delegated to (lower wage) clerical employees, or the cost savings from better automated support for certain information-processing tasks.

5. *Business segment evaluation:* By determining the amount of staff effort devoted to new business quoting and insuring, marketing new programs, managing agency production, and the like, the company was able to assess the full costs of developing new business and to decide how to spend its limited resources knowing the value of retaining existing business.

Source: Michael Crane and John Meyer, "Focusing on True Costs in a Service Organization," *Management Accounting* (February 1993), pp. 41–45. Copyright by Institute of Management Accountants, Montvale, N.J.

similar to those described earlier for manufacturing service activities. However, the additional analysis of sales support activities can provide useful insight about differences in the cost of the activity resources consumed by different product lines, types of customers, or market segments.

EXHIBIT 7-19
Medequip, Inc.: Selling and Distribution Cost Drivers for 2 Representative Jobs

ACTIVITY	COST DRIVER	JOB J189-4	JOB J273-2
1	Dollars of sales	$26,400	$12,500
2	Number of orders	4	5
3	Number of orders	4	5
4	Number of units	12	5
5	Number of orders	4	5
6	Average inventory volume (c. ft.)	864	540
7	Units * miles	3,600	2,500

EXHIBIT 7-20
Medequip, Inc.: Selling and Distribution Costs for 2 Representative Jobs

ACTIVITY	JOB J189-4 COSTS	DETAILS[a]	JOB J273-2 COSTS	DETAILS[a]
1. Marketing management	$ 2,640.00	= 0.10 * $26,400	$ 1,875.00	= 0.15 * $12,500
2. Marketing travel	600.00	= 4 * $150	1,575.00	= 5 * $315
3. Sales catalog	900.00	= 4 * $225	1,250.00	= 5 * $250
4. Customer service	1,320.00	= 12 * $110	2,100.00	= 5 * $420
5. Order execution	2,800.00	= 4 * $700	3,750.00	= 5 * $750
6. Warehousing	4,320.00	= 864 * $5	2,700.00	= 540 * $5
7. Shipping	2,700.00	= 3,600 * $0.75	1,875.00	= 2,500 * $0.75
Total selling and distribution cost	$15,280.00		$15,125.00	
Number of units	12		5	
Selling and distribution cost per unit	$ 1,273.33	= $15,280 ÷ 12	$ 3,025.00	= $15,125 ÷ 5
Manufacturing cost per unit	1,153.13	(Exhibit 7-15)	1,570.85	(Exhibit 7-15)
Total cost per unit	$ 2,426.46		$ 4,595.85	

[a] Refer to Exhibits 7-18 and 7-19 for the source of these numbers.

A SUMMARY EXAMPLE

The following problem reviews some key aspects of this chapter.

The Winona plant of Minnehaha Electronic Company manufactures 2 products: CD 107 and CD 635. The company has established the following 3 cost pools for its manufacturing overhead:

Cost Pool	Manufacturing Overhead
S	$640,000
P1	400,000
P2	200,000
Total	$1,240,000

Pool S includes all support activity costs at the plant. Pools P1 and P2 include overhead costs traced directly to the 2 production departments, fabrication (P1) and assembly (P2), respectively. The current cost accounting system at the plant employs a 2-stage cost allocation method that first allocates overhead costs in pool S to the pools P1 and P2 on the basis of machine-hours and then assigns the accumulated overhead costs in the pools P1 and P2 to the 2 products on the basis of direct labor hours. A separate overhead rate is computed for each of the 2 production departments. The direct labor wage rate (including benefits) is $15 per hour.

The following information was collected from plant records for June 1995:

Department	Direct Labor Hours (DLH)		
	CD 107	CD 635	Total
Fabrication (P1)	20,000	20,000	40,000
Assembly (P2)	25,000	15,000	40,000
Total	45,000	35,000	80,000

Department	Machine-Hours (MH)		
	CD 107	CD 635	Total
Fabrication (P1)	27,000	18,000	45,000
Assembly (P2)	20,000	15,000	35,000
Total	47,000	33,000	80,000

	CD 107	CD 635
Sales price per unit	$260	$220
Direct material cost per unit	$80	$40
Units produced and sold	8,000	6,000

The plant is considering implementing an activity-based costing system. The controller has compiled the following information to reassign the overhead costs for June 1995 from the existing overhead cost pools (S, P1, P2) to 5 new activity cost pools:

Activity Cost Drivers	Existing Overhead Cost Pool			Total
	S	P1	P2	
P1—DLH	$ 40,000	$ 40,000	—	$ 80,000
P2—DLH	150,000	—	$ 80,000	230,000
P1—MH	50,000	110,000	—	160,000
P2—MH	60,000	—	40,000	100,000
Setup hours	340,000	250,000	80,000	670,000
Total	$640,000	$400,000	$200,000	$1,240,000

The number of setups in June 1995 was 1,000 for each of the 2 products, but each setup for CD 107 takes twice as long as a setup for CD 635.

1. Determine the product cost per unit for both CD 107 and CD 635 using the existing cost accounting system.

2. Determine the product cost per unit for the 2 products using the proposed activity-based costing system.

3. Explain why the product costs are different under the 2 cost accounting systems.

The solutions follow.

1. Stage 1 allocation:

	Department P1	Department P2
Directly identified overhead	$400,000	$200,000
Allocated from S	360,000[a]	280,000[b]
Total overhead	760,000	480,000
DLH	40,000	40,000
Overhead rate	$19 per DLH	$12 per DLH

[a] $640,000 * (45,000/80,000) = $360,000.
[b] $640,000 * (35,000/80,000) = $280,000.

Stage 2 allocation:

Allocated from	CD 107		CD 635
Department P1 ($19.00 * 20,000 =)	$380,000	($19.00 * 20,000 =)	$380,000
Department P2 ($12.00 * 25,000 =)	300,000	($12.00 * 15,000 =)	180,000
Total overhead	$680,000		$560,000

		CD 107		CD 635
Direct material	($80 * 8,000 =)	$640,000	($40 * 6,000 =)	$240,000
Direct labor	($15 * 45,000 =)	675,000	($15 * 35,000 =)	525,000
Overhead	(from Stage 2)	680,000	(from Stage 2)	$1,560,000
Total cost		$1,995,000		$1,325,000

		CD 107		CD 635
Number of units		8,000		6,000
Unit cost	($1,995,000 ÷ 8,000 =)	$249.38	($1,325,000 ÷ 6,000 =)	$220.83
Sales price		$260.00		$220.00
Gross margin	($260.00 − $249.38 =)	$10.62	($220.00 − $220.83 =)	($0.83)

2. Activity-based cost analysis:

Cost driver		CD 107		CD 635
P1—DLH	($80,000 * (20,000/40,000) =)	$40,000	($80,000 * (20,000/40,000) =)	$40,000
P2—DLH	($230,000 * (25,000/40,000) =)	143,750	($230,000 * (15,000/40,000) =)	86,250
P1—MH	($160,000 * (27,000/45,000) =)	96,000	($160,000 * (18,000/45,000) =)	64,000
P2—MH	($100,000 * (20,000/35,000) =)	57,143	($100,000 * (15,000/35,000) =)	42,857
Setup hours	($670,000 * (2,000/(2,000 + 1,000)) =)	$446,667	($670,000 * (1,000/(2,000 + 1,000)) =)	$223,333
Total		$783,560		$456,440

Product costing:

		CD 107		CD 635
Direct material	($80 * 8,000 =)	$640,000	($40 * 6,000 =)	$240,000
Direct labor	($15 * 45,000 =)	675,000	($15 * 35,000 =)	525,000
Overhead	(from activity cost analysis)	783,560	(from activity cost analysis)	456,440
Total cost		$2,098,560		$1,221,440
Number of units		8,000		6,000
Unit cost	($2,098,560 ÷ 8,000 =)	$262.32	($1,221,440 ÷ 6,000 =)	$203.57
Sales price		$260.00		$220.00
Gross margin	($260.00 − $262.32 =)	($2.32)	($220.00 − $203.57 =)	$16.43

3. Product CD 107 was undercosted and CD 635 was overcosted under the existing system because the existing system ignored the fact that more than half of overhead costs are caused by the setup activity and that a unit of CD 107 requires twice as much setup activity resources as a unit of CD 635.

SUMMARY

This chapter describes the 2 stages of allocations in conventional product costing procedures. The first stage traces all overhead costs, including those pertaining to support services, to the production departments in 2 steps. The second stage assigns the overhead costs accumulated in the production departments to individual products based on unit-related measures such as direct labor hours or machine-hours. As a result, products manufactured in small batches or in small annual volumes are undercosted because batch-related and product-sustaining costs are assigned only in proportion to the number of units.

Activity-based costing corrects these distortions because it employs separate cost drivers for different activities and assigns costs to products based on unit-related, batch-related, product-sustaining, or facility-sustaining cost drivers, as appropriate. Activity-based costing principles apply also to non-manufacturing costs, such as selling and distribution, as well as to service industries.

KEY TERM LIST

Activity-based costing systems, p. 291

Direct allocation method, p. 281

Production departments, p. 278

Reciprocal allocation method, p. 281

Sequential allocation method, p. 281

Service departments, p. 278

Stage 1 allocations, p. 281

Stage 2 allocations, p. 284

Appendix 7-1

Sequential and Reciprocal Allocation Methods

Several different methods are used to allocate service department costs to production departments. Sequential and reciprocal allocation methods are used when service departments consume services provided by other service departments.

SEQUENTIAL ALLOCATION METHOD

The sequential method is used if there is no pair of service departments with each service department consuming a significant proportion of the services produced by the other department. To illustrate this method, consider a plant with 2 production departments, machining and assembly, and 2 service departments, power and engineering. Service department costs are allocated on the basis of kilowatt-hours and engineering-hours, respectively. Exhibit 7A–1 displays the directly attributable costs of the 4-departments and their consumption of the 2 services.

In the sequential allocation method, first the service departments are arranged in order so that a service department can receive costs allocated from another service department only *before* its own costs are allocated to other departments. Once a service department's costs are allocated, no costs of other departments can be allocated back to it.

In this example, the power department does not receive engineering services, but the engineering department uses power. Therefore, in the sequen-

	SERVICE DEPARTMENTS		PRODUCTION DEPARTMENTS		
EXHIBIT 7A–1	**POWER**	**ENGINEERING**	**MACHINING**	**ASSEMBLY**	**TOTAL**
Directly Identified Costs and Service Consumption Levels					
Directly identified costs	$320,000	$180,000	$120,000	$ 80,000	$700,000
Consumption of service					
Power (Kilowatt-hours)	—	100,000	480,000	220,000	800,000
Engineering (Engineering-hours)	—	—	2,000	2,000	4,000
Allocation ratios					
Power	—	0.125	0.600	0.275	1.000
Engineering	—	—	0.500	0.500	1.000

EXHIBIT 7A-2
Sequentially Allocated Costs

| | SERVICE DEPARTMENTS | | PRODUCTION DEPARTMENTS | |
	POWER	ENGINEERING	MACHINING	ASSEMBLY
Directly identified costs	$ 320,000	$ 180,000	$120,000	$ 80,000
Allocation of power department costs	(320,000)	40,000	192,000	88,000
Allocation of engineering department costs	—	(220,000)	110,000	110,000
	$–0–	$–0–	$422,000	$278,000

tial method, the power department costs are allocated first, followed by allocation of the engineering department costs.

The total cost of a service department allocated to other departments equals the amount directly identified with the service department *plus* the amount allocated earlier to the service department from other service departments. That is,

$$
\begin{array}{c}
\text{Total} \\
\text{costs} \\
\text{allocated}
\end{array}
=
\begin{array}{c}
\text{Directly} \\
\text{identified} \\
\text{costs}
\end{array}
+
\begin{array}{c}
\text{Costs} \\
\text{allocated} \\
\text{to it}
\end{array}
$$

These costs are allocated to the other service and production departments in proportion to their consumption of the service, as detailed in Exhibit 7A–1. Therefore, for the allocation of the costs of the power department, the allocation ratios in Exhibit 7A–1 are based on the consumption of power by the engineering, machining, and assembly departments. The allocation ratios for the engineering service are based on the consumption by the machining and the assembly departments. Exhibit 7A–2 shows the resulting allocations.

Power department costs are allocated first because it does not consume any other service. Engineering department costs are allocated next. Allocated costs of $220,000 for engineering are the directly identified costs of $180,000 plus the costs allocated to the engineering department from the power department of $40,000. Notice that no costs are allocated back to the power department.

If both the service departments in this example consumed each other's services, the reciprocal allocation method is appropriate. The sequential method ignores or suppresses such reciprocal relations.

RECIPROCAL ALLOCATION METHOD

This method recognizes reciprocal interactions between different service departments. We shall alter the consumption data in Exhibit 7A–1 to illustrate this method. Notice that the information in Exhibit 7A–3 is the same as that in Exhibit 7A–1, except that the power department also consumes 1,000 hours of engineering service.

EXHIBIT 7A-3
Directly Identified Costs and Service Consumption Levels

| | SERVICE DEPARTMENTS | | PRODUCTION DEPARTMENTS | | |
	POWER	ENGINEERING	MACHINING	ASSEMBLY	TOTAL
Directly identified costs	$320,000	$180,000	$120,000	$ 80,000	$700,000
Consumption of service					
Power (Kilowatt-hours)	—	100,000	480,000	220,000	800,000
Engineering (Engineering-hours)	1,000	—	2,000	2,000	5,000
Allocation ratios					
Power	—	0.125	0.600	0.275	1.000
Engineering	0.200	—	0.400	0.400	1.000

The sequential method does not work in this situation because when the engineering department's costs are allocated, 20% must be allocated back to the power department, whose costs already were allocated. This would leave us with unallocated costs in the power department. If we were to allocate this new balance in the power department on the basis of the same allocation ratios as before, we would be left with unallocated costs in the engineering department. In principle, of course, we could repeat these sequential allocations until the unallocated balance of costs became negligible. The same result, however, can be obtained by using the algebraic approach of the reciprocal allocation method.

We shall denote the total costs to be allocated for the power department as P and those for the engineering department as E. As before,

$$\begin{array}{ccc} \text{Total} & & \text{Directly} & & \text{Costs} \\ \text{costs} & = & \text{identified} & + & \text{allocated} \\ \text{allocated} & & \text{costs} & & \text{to it} \end{array}$$

Because the power department consumes 20% of the engineering services, we have

$$P = \$320{,}000 + 0.20E \qquad (7A.1)$$

Also, because the engineering department uses 12.5% of the power consumed in the plant, we have

$$E = \$180{,}000 + 0.125P \qquad (7A.2)$$

Equations (7A.1) and (7A.2) thus recognize that the power department's total costs include a 20% share of the engineering department's total costs, and the engineering department's total costs include a 12.5% share of the power department's costs. We can now solve these 2 equations simultaneously. For this purpose, we shall substitute the expression for E into the first equation for P. Thus,

$$P = \$320,000 + 0.20\,(\$180,000 + 0.125P)$$
$$P = \$320,000 + \$36,000 + 0.025P$$
$$0.975P = \$356,000$$
$$P = \$365,128$$

We also can solve for E by substituting this value of P in the second equation.

$$E = \$180,000 + 0.125\,(\$365,128)$$
$$= \$180,000 + \$45,641$$
$$= \$225,641$$

Now that we have determined the total costs for the 2 service departments, we can calculate the amounts to be allocated to the 2 production departments using the allocation ratios in Exhibit 7A–3. These cost allocations appear in Exhibit 7A–4. Notice that the allocations are different from those obtained in the earlier illustration for the sequential method because we began with different data. The power department's total costs were higher because it also consumed some engineering services. Because the machining department consumed a relatively larger amount of power, we find that, in this case, the costs allocated to it are also higher.

EXHIBIT 7A–4
Sequentially Allocated Costs

| | SERVICE DEPARTMENTS | | PRODUCTION DEPARTMENTS | |
	POWER	ENGINEERING	MACHINING	ASSEMBLY
Directly identified costs	$ 320,000	$ 180,000	$120,000	$ 80,000
Allocation of power department costs	(365,128)	45,641	219,077	100,410
Allocation of engineering department costs	45,128	(225,641)	90,256	90,256
	$–0–	$–0–	$429,333	$270,666

ASSIGNMENT MATERIAL

QUESTIONS

7–1   What is the difference between *production departments* and *service departments*?

7–2   What are the 2 stages of cost allocations in conventional product costing systems?

7–3   Why do conventional product costing systems allocate service department overhead costs first to the production departments before assigning them to individual jobs?

7–4   What are the different situations for which direct, sequential, and reciprocal allocation methods are designed?

7–5   What is the difference between the allocation bases used in the first stage and those used in the second stage of conventional product costing systems?

7–6   Why are conventional 2-stage cost allocation systems likely to systematically distort product costs?

7–7   What are 2 factors that contribute to cost distortions resulting from the use of conventional, 2-stage cost allocation systems?

7–8   What fundamental assumption implicit in conventional 2-stage cost allocation systems is rejected in activity-based costing systems?

7–9   How do activity-based costing systems avoid distortions in allocations of batch-related costs?

7–10 Why do conventional product costing systems often exclude selling and distribution costs?

7–11 What recent changes have made it more important to have nonmanufacturing costs assigned to products, product lines, or market segments?

7–12 Why are conventional product costing systems more likely to distort product costs in highly automated plants? How do activity-based costing systems deal with such a situation?

7–13 "Conventional product costing systems are likely to overcost high-volume products." Do you agree with this statement? Explain.

7–14 How are allocation bases selected in the 2 stages of conventional product costing systems?

7–15 How are allocation bases selected in activity-based costing systems?

7–16 "Activity-based costing systems yield more accurate product costs than conventional systems because they use more cost drivers as allocation bases." Do you agree with this statement? Explain.

7–17 What are *cost pools*? How is the appropriate number of cost pools selected?

EXERCISES

7–18 Identify a cost driver for each of the following activities:
(a) Machine maintenance
(b) Machine setups

(c) Utilities

(d) Quality control

(e) Material ordering

(f) Production scheduling

(g) Factory depreciation

(h) Warehouse expense

(i) Production supervision

(j) Payroll accounting

(k) Custodial service

(l) General and administration

7–19 Potter Corporation has gained considerable market share in recent years for its specialty, low-volume, and complex line of products, but the gain has been offset by a loss in market share for its high-volume simple line of products. This has resulted in a net decline in its overall profitability. Advise management about specific changes that may be required in its cost accounting system and explain why the existing system may be inadequate.

7–20 San Miguel Company has 2 production departments, assembly and finishing, and 2 service departments, machine setup and inspection. Machine setup costs are allocated on the basis of number of setups while inspection costs are allocated on the basis of number of direct labor hours. Selected information on the 4 departments follows:

	Direct Costs	Number of Setups	Direct Labor Hours
Machine setup	$40,000	–	–
Inspection	15,000	–	–
Assembly	25,000	300	200
Finishing	20,000	100	500

REQUIRED:

(a) Using the direct method, determine the amount of machine setup costs allocated to the 2 production departments.

(b) Using the direct method, determine the amount of inspection costs allocated to the 2 production departments.

7–21 Dance Division of Nitterhouse Video Company markets 2 dance videos: jazz and rap. To motivate the sales of the rap video, the company offers its marketing personnel a sales commission of 10% sales price for each copy of rap they sell. Selected data for the two videos for the last month follow:

	Jazz	Rap
Unit price	$20	$30
Manufacturing costs		
Material	6	12
Labor	4	6
Overhead	2	3
Number of copies sold	5,000	8,000

The monthly fixed selling expenses of $80,000 are allocated equally to the 2 videos. Although the demand for the jazz videos is still very strong, the company has been experiencing losses on its sales over the last 6 months. The owner of Nitterhouse Video Company has asked your opinion on whether the jazz video should be discontinued. What course of action do you recommend? Explain.

7–22 VG Company has identified the following overhead cost pools and cost drivers:

Cost Pool	Activity Costs	Cost Drivers
Machine setups	$360,000	6,000 setup hours
Material handling	100,000	50,000 pounds of material
Electric power	40,000	80,000 kilowatt-hours

The following cost information pertains to the production of Product V203 and G179:

	V203	G179
Number of units produced	5,000	15,000
Direct material cost	$25,000	$33,000
Direct labor cost	$14,000	$16,000
Number of setup hours	120	150
Pounds of material used	5,000	10,000
Kilowatt-hours	2,000	3,000

Determine the unit cost for each of the 2 products using activity-based costing.

7–23 (Appendix) Cooper Company has 2 service departments and 2 production departments. Information on annual overhead costs and allocation bases follows:

	Service Department		Production Department	
	S1	S2	P1	P2
Overhead cost	$65,000	$55,000	$160,000	$240,000
Direct labor hours	2,000	1,500	2,000	3,000
Number of square feet	800	1,200	2,400	2,600

The company allocates service department costs using the sequential method. First, S1 department costs are allocated on direct labor hours. Next, S2 department costs are allocated based on square footage. The square footage for S1 department is assumed to be zero for this purpose. Determine the total overhead costs allocated to each of the 2 production departments.

PROBLEMS

7–24 Normal manufacturing overhead costs of McInnes Company for September 1995 are as follows:

Cost Pool	Normal Costs
Power	$40,000
Material handling	80,000
Setups	60,000
Quality inspections	20,000

The present cost accounting system allocates overhead costs to final products based on machine-hours. Estimated machine-hours for September 1995 are 50,000. After losing several bids recently, McInnes' president has asked the controller to implement an activity-based costing system because he was told that activity-based costing can provide more accurate product cost estimates. The controller has collected the following data:

Activities	Cost Drivers	Available Capacity	Costs
Electric power	Kilowatt hours	20,000 kwh	$24,000
Material handling	Material moves	5,000 moves	60,000
Setups	Machine setups	1,000 setups	80,000
Quality inspections	Number of inspections	3,000 inspections	36,000

The company recently received a request for a bid to supply 1,000 units of its product M5. The following estimates were prepared for the production of 1,000 units of M5:

Direct materials costs	$20,000
Direct labor cost	$50,000
Machine-hours	1,800
Direct labor hours	2,000
Kilowatt-hours of electricity	2,000
Number of material moves	40
Number of machine setups	5
Number of quality inspections	20

REQUIRED:

(a) What is the estimated cost per unit of M5 under the present cost accounting system?

(b) What is the estimated cost per unit of M5 if activity-based costing is used?

7–25 Ferreira Company has established the following overhead cost pools for 1995:

Cost Pool	Committed Costs	Cost Drivers	Committed Level
Maintenance	$20,000	Machine-hours	10,000
Material handling	10,000	Number of moves	250
Machine setup	30,000	Setup hours	1,000
Inspection	40,000	Number of inspections	500
Total	$100,000		

The following information pertains to 2 representative jobs completed during January 1995:

	J101	J102
Direct material cost	$10,000	$7,500
Direct labor cost	$8,000	$5,500
Number of units	2,000	1,500
Direct labor hours	640	400
Machine-hours	700	650
Number of material moves	40	15
Number of setup hours	80	40
Number of inspections	35	15

REQUIRED:

(a) Determine the unit cost of each job using machine-hours to allocate all overhead costs.

(b) Determine the unit cost of each job using activity-based costing.

(c) Which of the 2 methods produces more accurate estimates of job costs? Explain.

7–26 Ittner Company manufactures 2 models of electronic valves for automobile engines. The design of valve IO23 is simpler than that for valve IO29. Ittner Company's plant has 2 service (S1, S2) and 2 production departments (P1, P2). Total overhead costs for 1994 were $600,000. Of this total, $100,000 was traced to S1, $160,000 traced to S2, $200,000 traced to P1, and $140,000 traced to P2. The existing cost accounting system allocates overhead costs in the following 2 stages. In Stage 1, overhead costs of service department S1 are allocated to the production departments based on the proportion of their respective machine-hours, and S2 overhead costs are allocated in the proportion of their total direct labor hours. In Stage 2, separate overhead rates are determined for the 2 production departments on the basis of direct labor hours (DLH) to assign overhead costs to 2 products. The direct labor wage rate is $10 per hour in both production departments.

Total Direct Labor Hours

Product	P1	P2	Total
IO23	1,500	2,000	3,500
IO29	1,500	3,000	4,500
Total	3,000	5,000	8,000

	P1	P2
Machine-hours	400	600

An activity-based costing system has been proposed; it traces production overhead to 4 cost pools, each identified with a unique cost driver as presented in the following table:

Activity	Activity Costs	Cost Driver Levels Total	IO23	IO29
P1, DLH	$ 90,000	3,000	1,500	1,500
P2, DLH	100,000	5,000	2,000	3,000
Setup hours	200,000	200	50	150
Number of inspections	210,000	500	150	350
Total overhead costs	$600,000			

Other relevant information follows:

	IO23	IO29
Sales price per unit	$120	$150
Materials cost per unit	60	80
Number of units sold	5,000	6,000

REQUIRED:

(a) Determine unit product costs using the existing accounting system.

(b) Determine unit product costs using the proposed ABC method.

(c) Explain the principal reason that the existing 2-stage cost allocation system may be distorting product costs.

(d) Analyze the profitability of the 2 products. What should Ittner do to improve its profitability?

7–27 Anderson Company uses a conventional 2-stage cost allocation system. In the first stage, all manufacturing overhead costs are assigned to 2 production departments, P1 and P2, based on machine-hours. In the second stage, direct labor hours are used to allocate overhead to individual products.

Anderson Company manufactures 2 products, X and Y, for which the following information is available:

	Product X	Product Y
Units sold	1,000	3,000
Direct material cost per unit	$60	$50
Direct labor wage rate per hour	$25	$15
Direct labor hours in P1 per unit	2	1
Direct labor hours in P2 per unit	1	1

During 1995 manufacturing overhead costs totaled $200,000. Machine-hours in production departments P1 and P2 were 5,000 and 15,000 hours, respectively. Direct labor hours in production departments P1 and P2 were 5,000 and 10,000, respectively.

Anderson Company is considering implementing an activity-based costing system. Its controller has compiled the following information for activity cost analysis:

Activity	Activity Costs	Activity Driver	Activity Overhead Rate	Cost Driver Demanded X	Y
Material movement	$ 30,000	Number of production runs	$15/run	200	800
Machine setups	150,000	Number of setups	$500/setup	40	150
Quality inspections	50,000	Number of units	$2/unit	1,000	3,000
Shipment	20,000	Number of shipments	$10/shipment	50	300
Total overhead costs	$250,000				

REQUIRED:

(a) Determine the unit costs for each of the 2 products under the existing cost accounting system.

(b) Determine the unit costs for each of the 2 products if the proposed ABC system is adopted.

7–28 Kallapur Company manufactures 2 products: SK33 and SK77. Manufacturing overhead costs are estimated to be $2,000,000 for the current year. Estimated unit cost and production data follow:

	SK33	SK77
Direct material cost	$30	$45
Direct labor cost (rate: $12/hour)	$24	$60
Estimated production in units	25,000	15,000

REQUIRED:

(a) Estimate the manufacturing cost per unit of each product if overhead costs are assigned to products on the basis of number of units produced.

(b) How does your answer change if overhead costs are assigned to products on the basis of direct labor hours?

Assume next that the company's manufacturing overhead costs can be traced to 4 activities as follows:

Activity Cost Driver	Activity Costs	Cost Driver	Cost Driver Units Demanded by SK33	SK77
Machine setups	$ 400,000	Number of setups	100	400
Purchase ordering	600,000	Number of orders	200	100
Machine-hours	500,000	Number of machine-hours	2,000	6,000
Inspection and shipments	500,000	Number of shipments	200	300
Total	$2,000,000			

(c) Estimate the manufacturing cost per unit of each product if activity-based costing approach is used.

7–29 (Appendix) Stephens Company has 2 service departments (S1 and S2) and 2 production departments (P1 and P2). In July 1995, directly identified overhead costs were $200,000 for S1 and $300,000 for S2. Information on the consumption of their services follows:

Supplying Department	User Department			
	S1	S2	P1	P2
S1	—	40%	30%	30%
S2	20%	—	20%	60%

REQUIRED:

(a) Determine the service department costs allocated to the 2 production departments using the direct method.

(b) Determine the service department costs allocated to the 2 production departments using the sequential method, beginning with the allocation of S1 department costs.

(c) Determine the service department costs allocated to the 2 production departments using the reciprocal method.

7–30 (Appendix) Sherman Company manufactures and sells small pumps made to customer specifications. It has 2 service departments and 2 production departments. Information on March 1995 operations follows:

	Service Department		Production Department	
	Maintenance	Power	Casting	Assembly
Overhead costs	$750,000	$450,000	$150,000	$110,000
Machine-hours	—	80,000	80,000	40,000
Kilowatt-hours	40,000	—	200,000	160,000
Direct labor hours	—	—	100,000	60,000

An overhead rate is determined on the basis of machine-hours for the casting department and on the basis of direct labor hours for the assembly department. It takes 1 machine-hour to manufacture a pump in the casting department and 0.5 labor hours to assemble a pump in the assembly department. Direct labor and material costs amount to $32 per pump.

A prospective customer has requested a bid on a 2-year contract to purchase 1,000 pumps every month. Sherman Company has a policy of adding a 25% markup to the full manufacturing cost to determine the bid.

REQUIRED:

(a) What is the bid price when the direct method is used?

(b) What is the bid price when the sequential method that begins by allocating maintenance department costs is used?

(c) What is the bid price when the reciprocal method is used?

CASES

7–31 The Redwood City plant of Crimson Components Company makes 2 types of rotators, R361 and R572, for automobile engines. The old cost accounting system at the plant traced overhead costs to 4 cost pools:

Cost Pool	Overhead	Allocation Basis
S1	$1,176,000	Direct labor cost
S2	1,120,000	Machine-hours
P1	480,000	—
P2	780,000	—
	$3,556,000	

Pool S1 included service activity costs related to setups, production scheduling, plant administration, janitorial services, materials handling, and shipping. Pool S2 included overhead costs related to machine maintenance and repair, rent, insurance, power, and utilities. Pools P1 and P2 included supervisors' wages, idle time, and indirect materials for the 2 production departments, casting and machining, respectively.

The old accounting system allocated overhead costs in Pools S1 and S2 to the 2 production departments using *direct labor cost* and *machine-hours*, respectively, as the bases. Then the accumulated overhead costs in pools P1 and P2 were applied to the products on the basis of direct labor hours. A separate rate was determined for each of the 2 production departments. The direct labor wage rate is $15 per hour in casting and $18 per hour in machining.

Department	Direct Labor Hours (DLH)			Direct Labor Cost
	R361	R572	Total	
Casting (P1)	60,000	20,000	80,000	$1,200,000
Machining (P2)	72,000	48,000	120,000	2,160,000
	132,000	68,000	200,000	$3,360,000

Department	Machine-Hours (MH)		
	R361	R572	Total
Casting (P1)	30,000	10,000	40,000
Machining (P2)	72,000	48,000	120,000
	102,000	58,000	160,000

	R361	R572
Sales price per unit	$ 19	$ 20
Sales units	500,000	400,000
Number of orders	1,000	1,000
Number of setups	2,000	4,000
Materials cost per unit	$ 8	$ 10

Now the plant has implemented an activity-based costing system. The following table presents the amounts from the old cost pools that are traced to each of the new activity cost pools.

| Activity | | Old Cost Pools | | | |
Cost Drivers	S1	S2	P1	P2	Total
P1—DLH	$ 120,000	—	$120,000	—	$ 240,000
P2—DLH	240,000	—	—	$120,000	360,000
Setup hours	816,000	$ 80,000	240,000	540,000	1,676,000
P1—MH	—	260,000	120,000	—	380,000
P2—MH	—	780,000	—	120,000	900,000
	$1,176,000	$1,120,000	$480,000	$780,000	$3,556,000

Setups for R572 are 50% more complex than those for R361, that is, each R572 setup takes 1.5 times as long as one R361 setup.

REQUIRED:

(a) Determine the product costs (per unit) using the old system. Show all intermediate steps for both Stage 1 and Stage 2 allocations, including departmental overhead rates and a breakdown of product costs into each of their components.

(b) Determine the product costs (per unit) using the new system.

(c) Explain the intuitive reason that the product costs differ under the 2 accounting systems.

(d) What should Crimson Components do to improve the profitability of its Redwood City plant?

(e) Describe how experienced production and sales managers are likely to react to the new product costs.

7–32 The Fishburn plant of Hibeem Electronics Corporation makes 2 types of wafers, W101 and W202, for electronic instruments. The old cost accounting system at the plant traced overhead costs to 3 *cost pools*.

Cost Pool	Overhead	Allocation Basis
S	$1,740,000	Machine-hours
P1	680,000	—
P2	240,000	—
	$2,660,000	

Pool S included all service activity costs at the plant. Pools P1 and P2 included overhead costs traced directly to the 2 production departments, photolithography and assembly, respectively.

The old cost accounting system allocated overhead costs in pool S to the 2 production departments on the basis of *machine-hours*. Then the accumulated overhead costs in P1 and P2 were applied to the products on the basis of direct labor hours. A separate rate was computed for each of the 2 production departments. The direct labor wage rate is $20 per hour. The following data were compiled from plant records for January:

| Department | Direct Labor Hours (DLH) | | |
	W101	W202	Total
Photolithography (P1)	80,000	20,000	100,000
Assembly (P2)	40,000	20,000	60,000
	120,000	40,000	160,000

Department	Machine-Hours (MH)		
	W101	W202	Total
Photolithography (P1)	80,000	30,000	110,000
Assembly (P2)	20,000	15,000	35,000
	100,000	45,000	145,000

	W101	W202
Sales price per unit	$11.50	$12.25
Sales units	600,000	300,000
Number of orders	1,000	1,000
Number of setups	2,000	4,000
Materials cost per unit	$ 4.00	$ 5.00

Now the plant has implemented an activity-based costing system. The following table presents the amounts from the old cost pools that are traced to each of the new activity cost pools.

	Old Cost Pools			
Activity Cost Drivers	S	P1	P2	Total
P1—DLH	$ 180,000	$140,000	—	$ 320,000
P2—DLH	120,000	—	$ 60,000	180,000
Setup hours	900,000	390,000	145,000	1,435,000
P1—MH	400,000	150,000	—	550,000
P2—MH	140,000	—	35,000	175,000
	$1,740,000	$680,000	$240,000	$2,660,000

Each W202 setup takes 1.25 times as long as a W101 setup.

REQUIRED:

(a) Determine the product costs (per unit) using the old system. Show all intermediate steps for both Stage 1 and Stage 2 allocations, including departmental overhead rates and a breakdown of product costs into each of their components.

(b) Determine the product costs (per unit) using the new system.

(c) Explain the intuitive reason that the product costs are different under the 2 accounting systems.

(d) What should Hibeem Electronics Corporation do to improve the profitability of its Fishburn plant?

7–33 Sandra Saldana, senior vice president for sales for Showman Shoes, Inc., noticed that the company had substantially increased its market share for the high-quality boomer boots (BB) and lost market share for the lower-quality lazy loafers (LL). Sandra found that Showman's prices were lower than the competitors' for BB but higher for LL. She did not understand the reasons for these price differences because all companies used the same production technology and were equally efficient.

The manufacturing process is relatively simple. Showman's manufacturing facility has a cutting department and an assembly department. The high-quality BB is produced in small batches (1,000 pairs of shoes each), and the lower-quality LL is produced in large batches (3,000 pairs each). Sandra has asked you, the company's new controller, to analyze the product costing method to see if the product prices should be changed.

The company currently uses a plantwide overhead rate based on direct labor hours. The rate is computed at the beginning of the year using the following budgeted data:

Total manufacturing overhead	$1,200,000
Total direct labor hours	49,000
Total machine-hours	49,400
Total setup hours	520

Your assistant has provided you with the following additional information about the production of batches of BB and LL:

EACH BATCH OF (BB): 1,000 PAIRS

	Cutting	Assembly	Total
Direct labor hours	80	120	200
Machine-hours	160	120	280
Setup hours	3	1	4
Direct costs	$7,500	$6,000	$13,500

EACH BATCH OF (LL): 3,000 PAIRS

	Cutting	Assembly	Total
Direct labor hours	150	180	330
Machine-hours	150	120	270
Setup hours	1	1	2
Direct costs	$9,000	$7,200	$16,200

On further inquiry, your assistant has been able to trace the overhead costs to the 2 service departments and the 2 production departments and to identify the following details for potential allocation bases for the service departments.

	Maintenance	Setup	Cutting	Assembly	Total
Overhead costs	$160,000	$400,000	$440,000	$200,000	$1,200,000
Direct labor hours	—	—	21,400	27,600	49,000
Machine-hours	—	—	27,800	21,600	49,400
Setup hours	—	—	340	180	520

Your assistant has also collected the following information on activities and their cost drivers:

Overhead Activities	Cost	Activity Category	Cost Driver
Maintenance	$160,000	Product sustaining	Machine-hours
Setups	400,000	Batch related	Setup hours
Cutting supervision	280,000	Batch related	Setup hours
Cutting depreciation	160,000	Facility sustaining	Machine-hours
Assembly supervision	160,000	Unit related	Direct labor hours
Assembly depreciation	40,000	Facility sustaining	Machine-hours

REQUIRED:

(a) Using a single, plantwide overhead rate based on direct labor hours, determine the costs per pair of BB and LL.

(b) Determine the costs per pair of BB and LL using departmental overhead rates based on machine-hours for the cutting department and direct labor hours for the assembly department. Allocate service department costs using the direct method.

(c) Determine the costs per pair of BB and LL using activity-based costing.

(d) Explain why unit costs for product BB are higher when departmental overhead rates are used than when a single plantwide rate is used.

(e) Explain why activity-based costs for product LL are lower than the corresponding costs based on a single plantwide rate.

7–34 Petersen Pneumatic Company makes 3 products. Its manufacturing plant in Petersburg has 3 production departments and 3 service departments.

Department	Overhead
Machining (MC)	$ 40,000
Plating (PL)	50,000
Assembly (AS)	15,000
Purchasing and inventory (PI)	50,000
Setup and scheduling (SS)	120,000
Quality control (QC)	70,000

Overhead costs are first traced to the 6 departments. The old cost accounting system allocated the service department overhead costs to the production departments using the following allocation bases:

Department	Allocation Basis
PI	Materials cost (MAT)
SS	Direct labor hours (DLH)
QC	Machine-hours (MCH)

The old cost accounting system applied overhead costs to the 3 products on the basis of direct labor hours. A different overhead application rate was determined for each department. The direct labor wage rate at the plant is $10 per hour.

Department	Direct Labor Hours (DLH) GT101	GT102	GT103	Machine-Hours (MCH)
MC	7,000	2,800	2,200	5,200
PL	3,500	1,700	1,800	1,900
AS	2,500	1,000	1,000	2,900

Product	Price	Product Sales Sales Units	Batch-Related Drivers Orders	Setups	Materials Cost per Unit MC	PL
GT101	$1.25	500,000	25	110	$0.30	$0.10
GT102	1.20	200,000	10	43	0.25	0.10
GT103	1.30	200,000	40	166	0.28	0.10

The profitability of the Petersburg plant has been declining for the past 3 years despite the successful introduction of the new product GT103, which has now captured more than a 60% share of its segment of the industry. In an attempt to understand the reasons for its declining profitability, the company has appointed a special task force.

The task force is considering a new cost accounting system based on activity analysis. This system employs 5 cost drivers: 3 departmental DLH, setups (SET), and orders (ORD). Each departmental overhead cost pool is divided into homogeneous cost pools identified with a unique driver. The following table presents the percentages of the departmental overhead costs that are put in each of the homogeneous cost pools. The total amounts in the 5 cost pools are allocated to the 3 products based on their respective cost drivers.

Department	DLH	SET	ORD
MC	30%	70%	—
PL	70%	30%	—
AS	60%	40%	—
PI	—	40%	60%
SS	???	???	???
QC	—	70%	30%

Peter Gamble is the leader of the task force responsible for activity-based overhead cost analysis. He interviewed Nola Morris, who was responsible for the setup and scheduling department, to determine the cost drivers for the departmental overhead.

PG: How many people work in the setup and scheduling department?

NM: I have 12 people who work on setups. Three more are responsible for production scheduling. I spend most of my time supervising them.

PG: How do you assign setup workers to production jobs?

NM: Almost all of the time they set up machines in the machining department. The effort depends only on the number of setups.

PG: On what does the time spent on scheduling depend?

NM: It depends on the number of orders.

PG: So a large batch or order will require the same amount of setup and scheduling time as a small batch or order.

NM: Yes, that's right.

REQUIRED:

(a) List the reasons that the old cost accounting system at Petersen Pneumatic may be distorting its product costs.

(b) Determine the product costs (per unit) using both the old and new cost accounting systems. Show all the intermediate steps including the overhead application rates, amounts in the 3 new cost pools, and a breakdown of product costs into each of their components.

(c) Analyze the profitability of the 3 products. What insight is provided by the new profitability analysis? What should Petersen Pneumatic do to improve the profitability of its Petersburg plant?

(d) Mike Meservy is a veteran production manager and Shannon Corinth is a marketing manager with considerable experience as a salesperson. Discuss how each of them is likely to react to your analysis and recommendations. Explain how their expected reactions may affect the way you will present your recommendations.

7–35 Pharaoh Phawcetts, Inc., manufactures 2 models of faucets, a regular and a deluxe model. The deluxe model, introduced just 2 years ago, has been very successful. It now accounts for more than half of the firm's profits as evidenced by the following income statement for 1994:

	Total	Regular	Deluxe
Sales	$2,400,000	$1,200,000	$1,200,000
Cost of goods sold	1,540,000	771,000	769,000
Gross margin	$ 860,000	$ 429,000	$ 431,000
Selling & administrative expenses	500,000	250,000	250,000
Net income	$ 360,000	$ 179,000	$ 181,000
Number of units	500,000	300,000	200,000

Its manufacturing plant in Phoenix, Arizona, has 2 production departments, a machining department and an assembly department. The cost of goods sold included $720,000 in production overhead. The plant accountant traced $192,000 of the production overhead to the machining department and $168,000 to the assembly department. The balance of $360,000 was attributed to the various service departments, and in Stage 1 of the existing overhead cost allocation system, it was allocated to the machining and the assembly departments in the proportion of their respective machine-hours. In Stage 2, separate overhead rates were determined for the 2 production departments based on their respective direct labor hours to assign the overhead to the two products.

Total Direct Labor and Machine-Hours

Product	Machining Department	Assembly Department	Total
Regular	15,000DLH	3,000DLH	18,000DLH
Deluxe	13,000DLH	5,000DLH	18,000DLH
Total DLH	28,000DLH	8,000DLH	36,000DLH
Total machine-hours	52,000MH	8,000MH	60,000MH

The direct labor wage rate is $10.00 per hour. Direct materials cost is $0.80 per unit of the regular model and for the deluxe model is $1.10 per unit. An average customer order for the regular model is for 5,000 faucets, but for the deluxe model, each order is for 2,000 units. The machines required a setup for each order. Three hours are required per machine setup for the regular model; the more complex deluxe model requires 5 hours per setup.

Pharaoh Phawcetts' profitability has been declining for the past 2 years despite the successful introduction of the deluxe model, which has now captured over 65% share of its segment of the industry. Market share for the regular model has decreased to 12%. In an attempt to understand the reasons for its declining profitability, the company has appointed a special task force.

The task force is considering a new cost accounting system based on activity analysis. This system employs 4 cost drivers: 2 departmental direct labor hours, setup hours, and number of orders. Production overhead is traced to 4 homogeneous cost pools, each identified with a unique driver as presented in the following table.

Activity Cost Driver	Traceable Costs	Number of Units of Cost Driver		
		Total	Regular	Deluxe
Machining dept. DLH	$112,000	?	?	?
Assembly dept. DLH	96,000	?	?	?
Setup hours	272,000	?	?	?
Number of orders	240,000	?	?	?
Total production overhead	$720,000			

The task force also analyzed selling and administrative expenses. These costs included 5% sales commission on regular models and 10% on deluxe models. Advertising and promotion expenses were $50,000 for the regular model and $90,000 for the deluxe model. The remaining $180,000 of selling and administrative expenses as attributed equally to the 2 products.

REQUIRED:

(a) Determine the product costs (per unit) using the existing cost accounting system. Show all the intermediate steps including the overhead application rates and a breakdown of product costs into each of their components.

(b) Determine the product costs and profits (per unit) using the new activity-based costing system. Show all the intermediate steps including the overhead rates and components of product costs.

(c) Explain the principal reasons that the old cost accounting system at Pharaoh Phawcetts may be distorting its product costs and profitability. Support your answer with numbers when necessary.

(d) Analyze the profitability of the 2 products. What insight does the new profitability analysis provide? What should Pharaoh Phawcetts do to improve its profitability? What options may be available?

(e) Ryan O'Reilley is a marketing manager with considerable experience as a salesperson. Discuss how he is likely to react to your analysis and recommendations.

7–36 Sweditrak Corporation manufactures 2 models of its exercise equipment: regular (REG) and deluxe (DLX). Its plant has 2 production departments, fabrication (FAB) and assembly (ASM), and 2 service departments, maintenance (MNT) and quality control (QLC). The parts for each model are manufactured in the fabrication department and put together in the assembly department. The maintenance department supports both production departments, and QLC performs all inspections for both production departments. Each unit of both products needs 1 inspection in each production department. Each inspection takes 30 and 60 minutes for REG and DLX models, respectively. The two production departments have set the following standards for direct material cost, direct labor cost, and machine-hours for each unit of product.

	Fabrication		Assembly	
	REG	DLX	REG	DLX
Direct material cost	$40.00	$80.00	$10.00	$20.00
Direct labor cost	20.00	40.00	20.00	30.00
Machine-hours	2.0	3.0	1.0	2.0

The average wage rate for direct labor is $10 per hour. The following table gives the production volume and overhead cost for the past 2 weeks:

Week	Production Volume REG	DLX	Costs MNT	QLC
45	450	430	$35,000	$63,100
46	450	450	$35,400	$63,500

The present cost accounting system allocates overhead costs in MNT to the production departments on the basis of machine-hours and assigned QLC cost to the 2 production departments based on the number of inspections. The accumulated overhead costs in FAB and ASM are applied to products using direct labor hours as the basis.

The company is considering implementing an activity-based costing system using machine-hours as the cost driver for MNT cost and inspection hours as the cost driver for QLC cost.

REQUIRED:

(a) Using the present cost accounting system, determine the product costs (per unit) for each product for the 2 weeks.

(b) Using the proposed ABC system, determine the unit product costs for each product for the 2 weeks.

PRICING AND PRODUCT MIX DECISIONS

LEARNING OBJECTIVES

This chapter will introduce you to:

1. the way a firm chooses its product mix in the short-term in response to prices set in the market for its products
2. the way a firm adjusts its prices in the short-term depending on whether capacity is limited
3. the way a firm determines a long-term benchmark price to guide its pricing strategy
4. the way a firm evaluates the long-term profitability of its products and market segments

CHAPTER 8

Precision Springs, Inc.: Should We Slash Prices?

"We cannot possibly make a profit if we sell at a price below costs. The quarterly product cost reports from the accounting department indicate a cost of $2.79 per pound for our 0.25 inch steel springs. I do not see any benefit in your proposal, Mike, to accept Genair's offer to buy 120,000 pounds of our 0.25 inch springs at only $2.48 per pound. How can we survive in this business if we keep slashing our prices?" asked Robert Smith.

Bob is the owner and president of Precision Springs, Inc., a manufacturer of high-precision steel springs for industrial customers. He was meeting with Michael Gaston, his marketing manager, and Alex Reed, his controller, to evaluate an offer from Genair Corporation to purchase a large quantity of 0.25 inch springs at sharply reduced prices. His outburst followed Alex Reed's comments about the costs and price of this product.

"Our accounting records show that the full cost of the 0.25 inch springs is $2.79 per pound, comprising $1.38 of direct materials, $0.76 of direct labor, and $0.65 of overhead costs. We usually mark up our products 30% over costs, which implies a mark up of $0.84 and a price of $3.63 per pound for the 0.25 inch springs. This means that Genair is demanding a discount of $1.15 per pound, which is almost 32% off our normal price," Alex had observed earlier.

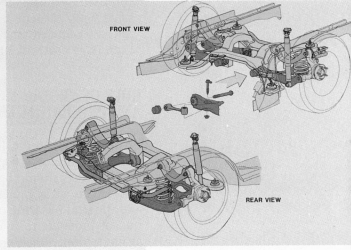

(Courtesy Ford Motor Company)

Mike realized that Alex's comments about the product costs and Bob's reaction to it meant that he could not justify his proposal simply by appealing to the value of developing a reputable firm such as Genair Corporation as a large customer. He had to make a case for accepting a lower price by comparing it with the *incremental costs (or revenues)* of producing the springs. *Incremental cost per unit* of a product is the amount by which the total costs of production and sale increase when 1 additional unit of that product is produced and sold.

"It is true that the full cost of the 0.25 inch springs is $2.79, but that includes $0.65 of overhead. We know that overhead costs comprise rent, depreciation, insurance, heating and lighting, janitorial services, and so on. These overhead are fixed costs and will not increase if we accept

Genair's order. So, the only costs we need to consider are materials and labor, which add up to only $2.14. Even at a price of $2.48, we can earn a margin of $0.34 per pound," Mike explained.

"Mike is right about overhead such as rent, depreciation, and insurance being fixed costs," replied Alex. "But such fixed costs are only 60 percent of our overhead at present. Overhead also includes costs such as supervision, setups, and inspection, which will increase if we accept the Genair order. Variable manufacturing costs for the 0.25 inch springs are $1.38 direct materials, $0.76 direct labor, as mentioned, plus $0.26 variable overhead costs. This adds up to $2.40 of variable costs, so it seems we would have a contribution margin of $0.08 per pound. But that is before we consider selling and distribution costs, which will, I believe, add another $0.23 to the variable costs of the 0.25 inch springs. I figure the total variable costs to be $2.63 per pound, which is more than the offer of only $2.48 per pound."

"Well, should we counter Genair's offer by suggesting that we would accept it for a $2.70 price? That would earn us a contribution of $0.07 per pound by your calculations," asked Mike.

Before Alex could respond, Bob interrupted this discussion. "I am very confused by all this talk about only variable costs. Costs are costs," he said. "I pay for rent and insurance just as I pay our workers and our suppliers. If our customers do not pay me a price that covers all our costs—both fixed and variable—I cannot possibly make money in this business."

ROLE OF PRODUCT COSTS IN PRICING AND PRODUCT MIX DECISIONS

As in the situation at Precision Springs, most firms need to make decisions about offering or accepting a price for their products. Understanding how product costs should be analyzed is important for making such pricing decisions. Even when prices are set by overall market supply and demand forces and the firm has little or no influence on product prices, it has to decide the mix of products to manufacture and sell, given their market prices. Once again, a proper analysis of product costs is important when determining the most profitable mix of products and, in a related vein, when deciding how best to deploy marketing and promotion resources, including how much commission (or how many other incentives) to provide the sales force for different products.

An important function of the management accountant, therefore, is to supply the cost information that helps to support these types of decisions. Accounting departments in many organizations supply product cost reports periodically to the marketing departments to help them make pricing and product mix decisions. In addition, they also prepare special analyses and reports to facilitate the evaluation of specific offers or bids. To design such cost reports properly, it is necessary to understand how cost information is used in making these decisions.

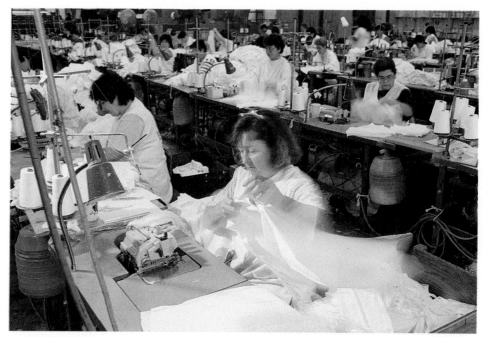

The relationship between the cost of the clothes made in this factory and their price depends on the nature of the market for the clothes. If the market is competitive, planners will use cost information to identify whether or not the company is making or losing money on each product line. If the product market is noncompetitive, then the company will use the cost information to set a market price that reflects its competitive strategy. For example, the mark-up over cost might be high enough to provide a reasonable return on investment but low enough to discourage other competitors from entering the market.
(© Michael Grecco/Sygma)

■ Short- and Long-Term Pricing Considerations

The decisions we refer to here are classified as *short-term* or *long-term* decisions. Recall from Chapter 4 that the costs of many resources committed to activities are likely to be fixed costs in the short term because capacities made available for many production and support activities cannot be altered easily. Consequently, for short-term decisions, we need to pay special attention to whether surplus capacity is available for additional production or whether the available capacity limits additional production alternatives. Of special concern here is the time period of the contract over which capacity must be committed to the particular order being evaluated by the firm. The time period is relevant because such capacity commitments may prevent the firm from deploying the capacity for more profitable products or orders if demand for such products arises in the future.

In the case in which production is constrained by inadequate capacity, we need to consider whether overtime production or the use of subcontractors can help augment capacity in the short term. In the long term, managers have considerably more flexibility in adjusting the capacities of activity

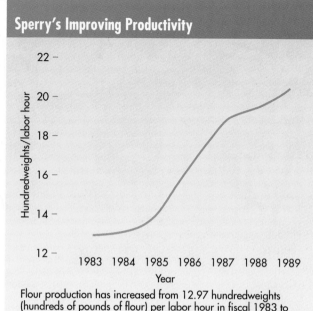

Sperry's Improving Productivity

Flour production has increased from 12.97 hundredweights (hundreds of pounds of flour) per labor hour in fiscal 1983 to 20.49 hundredweights per labor hour in fiscal 1989.

The key controllable costs for organizations selling commodity food products are raw materials and labor. Because General Mills is a price-taker in the highly competitive flour market, it continuously searches for opportunities to reduce its labor costs. These improvements in labor use are reflected in labor productivity. (© Ed Lallo/General Mills)

resources to match the demand for these resources resulting from the actual production of different products. Decisions to introduce new products or eliminate existing products have long-term consequences, and our emphasis in analyzing such decisions will be on the demand placed on activity resources by each product.

We also shall classify decisions based on whether the firm can influence the price of its products. If the firm is one of a large number of firms in an industry and if there is little to distinguish the products of different firms from each other, economic theory tells us that the prices are set by overall market forces of supply and demand and that no one firm can influence the prices significantly by its own decisions. For instance, in commodity businesses such as grains, meat, and sugar, prices are set by traders in the commodity markets based on industry supply and demand. Similarly, if prices are set by one or more large firms leading an industry, a small firm on the fringe must match the prices set by the industry leaders. In such a situation, a small firm is a **price taker**, choosing its product mix given the prices set for its products.

In contrast, firms in an industry with relatively few competing firms, and firms enjoying large market shares and exercising leadership in an industry must decide what prices to set for their products. Firms in industries in which products are highly customized or otherwise differentiated from each other because of special features, characteristics, or customer service also need

Price taker
A firm that has little or no influence on the industry supply and demand forces, and, consequently, on the prices of its products.

SAID &HSC

to set the prices for their differentiated products. Such firms are **price set-ters**. In such cases, production follows the pricing decision as customer orders are received in response to the announced prices.

We shall consider four different situations in this chapter. As shown in Exhibit 8–1, we begin the next section by considering the short-term product mix decision of a price-taker firm (quadrant 1). Then we analyze short-term pricing decisions for a price-setter firm (quadrant 2) and follow with an examination of long-term benchmark prices for a price-setter firm (quadrant 3). Finally, we return to the price-taker firm and consider the long-term evaluation of product and customer profitability for that type of firm (quadrant 4).

Price setter
A firm that sets or bids the prices of its products because it enjoys a significant market share in its industry segment.

SHORT-TERM PRODUCT MIX DECISIONS

Production decisions by a firm with a very small market share in its industry have little impact on the overall industry supply and demand and, therefore, on the prices of its products. Examples are industries manufacturing auto parts (such as mufflers and brakes), steel, generic chemicals and pharmaceuticals, gypsum wallboard, low-end copier machines, and so on, in which the products are standardized and there is little to differentiate the products of one firm from those of another. Prices are determined by the aggregate of the production decisions of all the firms in such industries. Or, if there are a few dominating firms, their decisions influence the prices.

A small firm, or a firm with a negligible market share in this industry, behaves as a *price-taker* firm because it takes the industry prices for its products as given and then decides how many units of each product it should produce and sell. If it demands a higher price for any of its products, it risks losing its customers to other competing firms in the industry, unless it can successfully differentiate its products by offering special features or services. Also, if it seeks to increase its market share by asking a price lower than the industry prices, it risks a retaliatory reduction in prices from its competitors.

OBJECTIVE 8.1
The way a firm chooses its product mix in the short term in response to prices set in the market for its products

---

EXHIBIT 8–1
Classification of Pricing and Product Mix Decisions

	Firms	
Decision Type	Price-Taker	Price-Setter
Short-Term Decisions	1	2
Long-Term Decisions	4	3

The price that regulated utilities, such as power and cable companies, can charge their customers is set by regulatory agencies. Although there are many approaches to setting regulated prices, many regulators base prices on the average costs in the industry and provide incentives to the regulated company to monitor and improve cost performance. In this setting, regulated companies behave like price-taking firms—they focus on customer service and product quality and on keeping costs as low as possible.
(© Guy Gilette/Photo Researchers, Inc.)

Such an action might result in a price war that would make the firm (and the entire industry) worse off than it would have been if it complied with industry prices.

Given industry prices, it makes economic sense for a price-taker firm to produce and sell as much as it can of all products whose costs are less than their prices. This may appear to be a simple decision rule, but there are two considerations of importance to cost accounting which complicate matters. First, it is important to decide what costs are relevant to the short-term product mix decision. Should all of the product costs considered in Chapter 3 or Chapter 6 be included, or should we consider only those costs that vary in the short-term? Second, we need to recognize that in the short term, managers may not have the flexibility to alter the capacities of some of their activity resources. For instance, the available plant capacity may limit the ability of a firm to produce and sell more of products whose costs are less than their prices.

■ An Illustration of Short-Term Product Mix Decisions

To illustrate, consider Texcel Company, which sells ready-made garments to discount stores, such as KMart and Caldor. It has located its manufacturing plant in Jamaica, a Caribbean island country, to take advantage of lower wages.

The plant manufactures five types of garments; Exhibit 8–2 presents budgeted production for the third quarter of 1995. The exhibit also displays the minimum sales quantities of each type of garment that must be supplied under long-term contracts with various retail stores. The sales manager has estimated the maximum sales quantities based on assessment of the number of orders that can be obtained for delivery in the third quarter of 1995.

Exhibit 8–3 shows unit costs for the five products. Direct material costs are based on estimated materials requirements and their estimated prices. Cutting, stitching, and packing workers are paid on a piece-rate basis. For instance, column 2 (shirts) shows that workers are paid $1.00 for cutting,

EXHIBIT 8–2
Texcel Company:
Budgeted Production in Quantities for 1995, Quarter 3

GARMENT TYPE	BUDGETED PRODUCTION	MINIMUM SALES	MAXIMUM SALES
Shirts	12,000	6,000	14,000
Dresses	5,000	2,000	8,000
Skirts	10,000	6,000	16,000
Blouses	15,000	5,000	15,000
Trousers	8,000	4,000	9,000
Total Units	50,000	23,000	62,000

EXHIBIT 8–3
Texcel Company: Product Costs per Unit

	SHIRTS	DRESSES	SKIRTS	BLOUSES	TROUSERS
Direct materials:					
Textile	$1.80	$6.00	$4.00	$2.00	$4.50
Supplies	0.20	0.90	0.60	0.40	0.60
Direct labor:					
Cutting	1.00	1.50	1.00	1.00	1.00
Stitching	0.80	1.80	1.00	0.80	1.00
Inspection	0.15	0.15	0.15	0.15	0.15
Packing	0.05	0.05	0.05	0.05	0.05
Overhead:					
Utilities	0.03	0.03	0.03	0.03	0.03
Plant administration	0.04	0.04	0.04	0.04	0.04
Machine maintenance	0.02	0.02	0.02	0.02	0.02
Machine depreciation	0.04	0.04	0.04	0.04	0.04
Facility maintenance	0.04	0.04	0.04	0.04	0.04
Facility depreciation	0.03	0.03	0.03	0.03	0.03
Total	$4.20	$10.60	$7.00	$4.60	$7.50

Organizations use two broad approaches to improve the contribution per hour of the constraining factor of production. One approach is to produce the product with the highest contribution margin per unit of time in the bottleneck resource. The other approach is to increase the productivity of the bottleneck resource. For Magma Copper, the bottleneck was its costing machines. By using a casting wheel and a simple flow-regulating device, Magma Copper has doubled the productivity of its casting operation. The company can now cast copper in two molds simultaneously. (© Arthur Meyerson)

$0.80 for stitching, and $0.05 for packing one shirt. Inspection labor costs total $7,500 per quarter and are assigned to products at the rate of $0.15 per garment. Overhead costs total $10,000 each quarter and are assigned to the 50,000 units budgeted for production at the rate of $0.20 per unit.

Production is limited by the capacity of the garment manufacturing machines, which is 23,800 machine-hours. Exhibit 8–4 displays the number of machine-hours required to manufacture each garment. There are considerable differences in the required machine time, ranging from 0.4 hours for one shirt or blouse to 0.8 hours for one dress. The planned production for the third quarter of 1995 seeks to utilize all of the 23,800 machine-hours available at present.

Our objective is to evaluate the profitability of the different products and to decide the production levels for the five products that will maximize the profits for the Texcel Company for the third quarter of 1995. Here, Texcel is considering short-term adjustments in its product mix. Therefore, first we must determine what costs will vary with production levels in this period and, then, what costs will remain fixed when the production mix is changed.

You will recognize immediately that the costs of direct materials and direct labor compensated on a piece-rate basis vary with the quantity of each garment that is produced. Inspectors are paid a monthly fixed salary, but they are employed as required to support the production of different garments. If production increases, it is necessary to employ more inspectors. Therefore, inspection labor costs also vary with the quantity of production of different garments. This situation occurs because of the flexibility that management has in adjusting the level of this activity resource during the period for which the product mix decision is made.

In contrast, the costs of utilities, plant administration, maintenance, and depreciation for the machinery and plant facility will not change when the product mix is changed, because the plant is being operated at its full capacity. All of these overhead costs will be considered to be fixed in our analysis.

The contribution from each of the garments to the firm's profits is determined by subtracting the variable costs from the price of the product. Exhibit 8–5 displays the contribution per unit for the five products. All five products have a positive contribution margin. Therefore, if the capacity were unlimited, Texcel could produce garments to fill the maximum demand for them. Here we consider a situation, however, in which the capacity is constrained, and Texcel must decide how best to deploy this limited resource.

EXHIBIT 8–4
Texcel Company: Machine-Hour Requirements

GARMENT TYPE	MACHINE-HOURS PER UNIT	PRODUCTION IN UNITS	TOTAL MACHINE-HOURS REQUIRED
Shirts	0.4	12,000	4,800
Dresses	0.8	5,000	4,000
Skirts	0.5	10,000	5,000
Blouses	0.4	15,000	6,000
Trousers	0.5	8,000	4,000
Total		50,000	23,800

EXHIBIT 8–5
Texcel Company: Contribution from Each Product

GARMENT TYPE	SHIRTS	DRESSES	SKIRTS	BLOUSES	TROUSERS
Price per unit:	$5.00	$15.20	$9.00	$8.00	$11.00
Variable costs per unit:					
Textiles	$1.80	$6.00	$4.00	$2.00	$4.50
Supplies	0.20	0.90	0.60	0.40	0.60
Cutting labor	1.00	1.50	1.00	1.00	1.00
Stitching labor	0.80	1.80	1.00	0.80	1.00
Inspection labor	0.15	0.15	0.15	0.15	0.15
Packing labor	0.05	0.05	0.05	0.05	0.05
Total	$4.00	$10.40	$6.80	$4.40	$7.30
Contribution per unit	$1.00	$4.80	$2.20	$3.60	$3.70
Machine-hours per unit	0.4	0.8	0.5	0.4	0.5
Contribution per machine-hour	$2.50	$6.00	$4.40	$9.00	$7.40
Budgeted production	12,000	5,000	10,000	15,000	8,000

The total contribution of $141,600 ($12,000 + $24,000 + $22,000 + $54,000 + $29,600—last line, Exhibit 8–5) for the budgeted production is obtained by multiplying the contribution per unit and the budgeted production quantity for each product and adding them together. The budgeted profit is $131,600, which is obtained after subtracting the fixed overhead costs of $10,000 (previously given) from the total contribution of $141,600.

Notice that the *contribution per unit* is the highest for dresses ($4.80). Does that mean that dresses are the most profitable product and that Texcel should produce as many dresses as it can sell?

The answer is *no*, because, in this case, *production is limited by the available machine capacity*. The capacity is fixed in the short term, so Texcel must plan production to maximize the contribution to profit for every available machine-hour. Therefore, the products should be rank ordered, not by their contribution per unit, but by their *contribution per machine-hour*.

Contribution per machine-hour is obtained by dividing the contribution per unit by the number of machine-hours per unit. Notice in Exhibit 8–5 that blouses have the highest contribution per machine-hour ($9.00); therefore, Texcel should produce a total of 15,000 blouses (see Exhibit 8–2), the maximum it can sell in the third quarter of 1995. Trousers have the next highest contribution per machine-hour ($7.40), so Texcel should produce a total of 9,000 trousers, the maximum it can sell in this quarter. Texcel must proceed to develop this rank order to decide which products to make until the entire available machine capacity (after reserving capacity for the minimum sales levels) is exhausted.

Exhibit 8–6 displays the production quantities that maximize profits in the short term. The minimum production for the 5 products required under existing sales contracts requires a total of 11,000 machine-hours (Exhibit 8–6, column 3). This leaves a balance of 12,800 machine-hours of capacity (23,800 − 11,000), which is sufficient to produce the maximum quantities of blouses, trousers, and dresses it is possible to sell. These three products rank

Bidding on Business Forms

FMI Forms Manufacturers, a medium-sized printing company that produces business forms, was operating at full capacity, but it was continually "in the red." Until the late 1980s, FMI bid on jobs without a reliable analysis of its cost structure. The direct costs considered for a job were the material or paper used in the printing process. Overhead costs were assigned to jobs in proportion to their direct costs.

FMI is a machine-intensive operation. Nine presses are available to print the forms. Six collators are used to combine parts of forms, glueing, crimping, and punching holes. The resources demanded by a job depend on the type and amount of paper used and the composition and the construction of the form. All jobs are constrained by the time necessary on a press and on a collator capable of producing forms at the required size.

Now, FMI determines a separate overhead rate for each machine. Costs of machine operator, support personnel, and supplies are identified directly with presses and collators. Other overhead costs—including supervision, office salaries, and insurance—are allocated to machines based on their processing capacity (number of feet of form per minute) weighted by the maximum paper width and complexity

(number of colors and stations) that they are capable of handling. This allocation is made at the beginning of each fiscal year, with the previous year used as a base from which to project current year costs. Once the yearly costs are allocated to each machine, cost per hour is determined for each press and collator assuming normal operations at 80% of full capacity.

When FMI receives a request for a bid on a particular job, the company turns to a computerized estimating software. It determines direct costs based on the type and quantity of paper. Then it identifies the least expensive press and collator that are mechanically capable of handling the specifications for the business form ordered. The estimated time to complete the job is multiplied by the cost per hour for the machines identified. The bid is completed by adding a standard markup to the total press, collator, and direct material costs. A higher markup is used for rush jobs and jobs requiring special features, such as nonstandard perforations, to cover the additional costs of errors and remakes.

Source: Jacci L. Rodgers, S. Mark Comstock and Karl Pritz, "Customize Your Costing System," *Management Accounting,* May 1993, pp. 31–32.

the highest in terms of their contribution per machine-hour. The remaining capacity of 1,500 machine-hours (12,800 − (4,000 + 2,500 + 4,800)) is not adequate to produce the maximum possible quantity of skirts, the next high-

EXHIBIT 8–6
Texcel Company: Production Quantities Required to Maximize Profits

GARMENT TYPE	MINIMUM QUANTITY	MACHINE-HOURS REQUIRED	ADDITIONAL QUANTITY	MACHINE-HOURS REQUIRED
Blouses	5,000	2,000 (5,000 * .4)	10,000	4,000
Trousers	4,000	2,000 (4,000 * .5)	5,000	2,500
Dresses	2,000	1,600 (2,000 * .8)	6,000	4,800
Skirts	6,000	3,000 (6,000 * .5)	3,000	1,500
Shirts	6,000	2,400 (6,000 * .4)	—	—
Total	23,000	11,000		12,800

est ranked product. This remainder capacity is sufficient for the production of only 3,000 (1,500/0.5) additional skirts. Then no machine capacity remains for the production of any additional shirts, the product with the lowest contribution per machine-hour.

To summarize, the available machine capacity should be allocated to the 5 garments as shown in Exhibit 8–7. This production plan would result in a profit of $141,500, which is $9,900 more than the $131,600 ($141,600 – $10,000) profit possible with the original production plan.

This example illustrates the basic principle that you should use when making such decisions: the contribution margin *per unit of the constrained resource* (machine-hours, in this example) as the criterion to decide which products are the most profitable to produce and sell at the prevailing prices.

■ The Impact of Opportunity Costs

Consider next a variation of the problem we have analyzed so far. Suppose that a new customer needs to place an order for 2,000 shirts, which was not included in earlier sales forecasts, and is willing to pay a higher price for this order. How high must this price be to make it profitable for Texcel to accept this order?

If Texcel produces more shirts, its costs will increase in the short term by the amount of variable costs. But a simple comparison of the price with the variable costs shown in Exhibit 8–5 is not adequate for this decision. Because the production capacity is limited, Texcel must cut back the production of some other garment to enable it to produce more shirts. Giving up the production of some profitable product results in an **opportunity cost**, which is the sacrificed potential benefit when, in selecting 1 alternative, another alternative is given up.

Each shirt requires 0.4 machine-hours (Exhibit 8–4) hours, so the new order for 2,000 shirts requires a total of 800 machine-hours. To find the capacity of 800 machine-hours required to produce the additional shirts, Texcel

Opportunity cost
The potential benefit sacrificed when, in selecting one alternative, another alternative is given up.

EXHIBIT 8–7
Texcel Company: Final Production Plan

GARMENT TYPE	PRODUCTION QUANTITY (EXHIBIT 8–6, MINIMUM & ADDITIONAL QUANTITIES)	TOTAL MACHINE HOURS (EXHIBIT 8–4)	TOTAL CONTRIBUTION (EXHIBIT 8–5, CONTRIBUTION/UNIT)
Blouses	15,000	6,000 (15,000 * .4)	$ 54,000 (15,000 * $3.60)
Trousers	9,000	4,500 (9,000 * .5)	33,300 (9,000 * $3.70)
Dresses	8,000	6,400 (8,000 * .8)	38,400 (8,000 * $4.80)
Skirts	9,000	4,500 (9,000 * .5)	19,800 (9,000 * $2.20)
Shirts	6,000	2,400 (6,000 * .4)	6,000 (6,000 * $1.00)
Total	47,000	23,800	$151,500
Less: Fixed costs			10,000
Profits			$141,500

must forgo a part of the production of some other garment. How should Texcel decide what garment's production to sacrifice? Clearly, it should make the decision that minimizes the opportunity cost. Therefore, the product that has the *lowest* contribution margin per unit of the constrained resources should be sacrificed.

We know from our earlier ranking of the products that of all the products whose production exceeds the minimum required, skirts have the lowest contribution per machine-hour (Exhibit 8–5). Texcel must sacrifice 800 machine-hours' worth of production of skirts. Because each skirt requires 0.5 machine-hours, Texcel must give up producing 1,600 skirts. Each skirt contributes $2.20, so cutting back the production of 1,600 skirts will result in a sacrifice of $3,520 in profits ($2.20 * 1,600).

There is an alternative way to check that the opportunity cost is $3,520. The contribution margin per machine-hour is $4.40 for skirts, and a cutback of 800 machine-hours' worth of production of skirts results in a sacrifice of $3,520 of profits ($4.40 * 800).

The cost implications of producing an additional order of 2,000 shirts are now clear.

	Total	Per Unit
Variable cost	$8,000	$4.00
Opportunity cost	3,520	1.76
	$11,520	$5.76

Therefore, if Texcel does not charge a price of at least $5.76 per shirt, the incremental costs will exceed the incremental revenues from this order, and Texcel would be worse off as a result. The lowest price that should be acceptable to Texcel is $11,520 for the order or $5.76 per shirt.

Also notice that if the price of a shirt is $5.76, the contribution margin per machine-hour is $4.40 ([$5.76 − $4.00]/0.4), the same as that for skirts, whose production is cut back. The basic principle to realize here is that Texcel must earn at least as much *contribution margin per machine-hour* on the new order as it must sacrifice on the alternative that it must give up.

SHORT-TERM PRICING DECISIONS

OBJECTIVE 8.2
The way a firm adjusts its prices in the short term depending on whether capacity is limited

So far, we have examined the way managers should adjust their product mix in the short term when the prices for their products have already been determined in the marketplace. In many businesses, however, potential customers request that suppliers bid a price for an order before they decide on the supplier with whom they will place the order. In this section, we examine the relationship between costs and prices bid by a supplier for special orders that do not involve long-term relationships with the customer.

Consider Chaney Tools and Dies Company in Cleveland, Ohio. Chaney manufactures customized steel tools and dies for a wide variety of manufacturing businesses. A new customer, Hamilton Industries of Ontario, has asked for a bid for a set of customized tools.

Chapter 6 showed the way to prepare and use the information on a job bid sheet. Based on the tool design, production engineers determine the routing through different production departments and estimate the quantity of different materials required for the order and the number of labor hours required in each department. This information, along with materials prices and labor wage rates, is used to estimate the direct materials and direct labor costs displayed in Exhibit 8–8. Overhead costs are assigned to the job based on activity drivers and the corresponding activity overhead rates, as described in Chapter 7.

The **full costs** for the job, that is, the sum of all costs (direct materials, direct labor, and overhead), are estimated to be $28,500, comprising $8,400 of direct material, $9,900 of direct labor, and $10,200 of overhead costs. The bid price for regular customers usually is determined at Chaney Tools by marking up 40% over the full costs. If Hamilton Industries were a regular customer, the bid price would have been $39,900 (1.40 * $28,500). But for this special order from a new customer, what is the minimum acceptable price?

We now consider two distinct cases. First, we examine Chaney's pricing decision when there is surplus machine capacity available in the short term to complete the production for the job. Then we shall examine the decision when the existing demand for Chaney's services is sufficient to fill all available capacity and the only way to manufacture the customized tools for Hamilton Industries is by working overtime or an extra shift.

Full costs
Sum of all costs (direct materials, direct labor and overhead) assigned to a product.

Available Surplus Capacity

Chaney must incur direct material costs of $8,400 to produce customized tools for Hamilton Industries. Direct production labor is paid on an hourly basis; therefore, these costs will increase by $9,900 if Chaney accepts the Hamilton order. In addition, batch-related costs will *increase by $3,700* as a new production batch is needed for the customized tools. The costs of supervision and facility-sustaining overhead, however, will not increase if additional capacity of these resources is available to meet the production needs of the Hamilton Industries order.

Incremental costs (or revenues) are defined as the amount by which costs (or revenues) increase if one particular decision is made instead of

Incremental costs (or revenues)
The amount by which costs (or revenues) change if one particular decision is made instead of another.

EXHIBIT 8–8
Chaney Tools and Dies Company: Job Cost Estimate

Direct materials		
Steel		$8,400
Direct labor		
Lathe	$2,600	
Grinding	3,200	
Machining	4,100	
		9,900
Overhead		
Supervision	$3,400	
Batch-related	3,700	
Facility-sustaining	3,100	
		10,200
Total costs		$28,500
Markup (40%)		11,400
Bid price		$39,900

Product Costing and Pricing at Kenco Engineering

Kenco Engineering Inc. is a family-owned firm with about $5 million in sales per year. It enjoys a reputation as a producer of high-quality cutting-edge tools made of steel impregnated with tungsten. These tools are used in construction, road building, and mining power equipment. The firm's key proprietary process is merging tungsten carbide chips with a steel plate. When the company's profit margins were good, management felt little need to collect much cost data and to control costs. However, when the company experienced its first losses, it was time to implement detailed and accurate cost standards. The new costing system divides the production process into three stages: tungsten crushing, steel cutting, and conversion processing (merging tungsten and steel).

Because crushed tungsten may be purchased on the open market, it is a candidate for outsourcing. Costs assigned to the tungsten-crushing process are based on the long-term costs of operation that can be avoided if crushed tungsten is purchased from outside. This costing method yields the relevant cost of the process, which management needs in deciding whether or not to outsource.

In the past, the steel-cutting operation required an overhead crane, a cutting machine, and storage areas because steel was ordered in huge sheets and cut in-house. Kenco now has pre-cut steel delivered on a just-in-time basis by a preferred supplier, and most internal costs for this operation have been eliminated.

Conversion processing has five distinct steps: bevelling, bolt-hole cutting, tungsten impregnating, straightening, and drilling. The critical, capacity-limiting step is the proprietary tungsten impregnating. Purposely, the other four steps have greater capacity and do not limit this expensive activity. The tung-

sten process is expected to run 80% of the available time under normal efficient operating circumstances.

There exists only one common cost pool for all five steps of conversion processing. This pool includes costs for all overhead and all labor, and they are assigned to the products in the proportion of the time spent on the tungsten-impregnating process based on its normal capacity. Only the time spent on this one step is considered for assigning costs. The other four steps are ignored because tungsten impregnating is the critical process that cannot be outsourced, and so it limits capacity. For example, reducing setup time in the bevelling step would not reduce production cycle time or generate any cost savings.

The bid sheet at Kenco Engineering breaks the cost of each product into setup, tungsten crushing, steel cutting, conversion processing, and so on. Bid prices also reflect prevailing market forces. Therefore, profit margins vary widely from one product to the next. Products with low gross-profit percentages receive priority attention from Kenco managers.

Most Kenco products are customized orders, but all products have several attributes in common. Therefore, knowledge from past jobs helps improve efficiency and future bidding. For example, one job required that numerous tungsten strips make several passes through a tungsten-impregnating machine. Analysis of actual job costs revealed a negative gross profit. After engineering consultation, the product was redesigned to use a smaller number of critically placed tungsten strips, and the product became profitable.

Source: James T. Mackey and Vernon H. Hughes, "Decision Focused Costing at Kenco," *Management Accounting,* May 1993, pp. 22–26.

another. For our present example, the decision under consideration is whether to accept the Hamilton Industries order; the alternative is not accepting it. The incremental costs in this case include $8,400 of direct material, $9,900 of direct labor, and $3,700 of batch-related overhead costs, which total $22,000.

The price charged Hamilton Industries must cover these incremental costs for the order to be profitable for Chaney. In other words, the **minimum** acceptable price is $22,000 *when surplus production capacity is available.* This is

Significant overcapacity in the industry caused major price reductions in steel during the 1980s. Intense competition forced mill closings as the industry eliminated underused and inefficient facilities and caused significant upgrading to improve the cost performance of the remaining mills. This steel strip mill at Weirton Steel eliminated several steps in the old process of converting a steel slab into strip steel. The reduction in the industry's excess capacity and improvements in processing have lowered the industry's cost structure and improved its profit performance. *(Courtesy Barton Denmarsh Esteban, Inc.)*

the price at which Chaney will break even on the Hamilton Industries order. In practice, Chaney will add a profit margin to mark up incremental costs, and the bid price will be set above $22,000, depending on competitive and demand conditions.

■ No Available Surplus Capacity

If surplus machine capacity is not available, Chaney will have to incur additional costs to acquire the necessary capacity. Chaney often meets such short-term capacity requirements by operating its plant overtime. When this occurs, Chaney pays supervisors overtime wages and incurs additional expenditures for heating, lighting, cleaning, and security. In addition, it is necessary to perform more machine maintenance and plant engineering activities as past experience has shown that the incidence of machine breakdowns increases during the overtime shift. Under its machinery leasing contract, Chaney also incurs additional rental costs for the extra use of machines when an overtime shift is worked.

The incremental supervision costs (including overtime premium) for the Hamilton Industries order are estimated to be $5,100, and the incremental facility-sustaining costs are estimated to be $5,400, to total $10,500 ($5,100 + $5,400), if overtime is required to manufacture customized tools for Hamilton Industries. Therefore, the minimum acceptable price in this case is $32,500 ($22,000 + $10,500). The actual price will depend on the amount of markup over the incremental costs charged by the Chaney Tools and Dies Company.

RELEVANT COSTS   **Relevant costs (or revenues)** are defined as the costs (or revenues) that must be considered in deciding which alternative is the best. In deciding whether to accept the Hamilton Industries order or what price to charge for the special order, Chaney must consider the appropriate incremental costs depending on whether surplus production capacity is available. The incremental costs are the relevant costs for such short-run decisions.

Relevant costs (or revenues)
The costs (revenues) that differ across alternatives and, therefore, must be considered in deciding which alternative is the best.

Most of the cost of providing guest accommodations in a hotel are fixed—a hotel's incremental costs are tied mainly to linen services. Therefore, during off-peak periods like weekends in large cities, or the low season in resort areas, hotels often cut their prices significantly to attract customers. Even at these lower prices, a hotel can cover its incremental costs and provide a contribution toward covering fixed costs. Hotels that have peak and off-peak periods plan to recover most of their fixed costs through the prices they charge peak-use customers. *(Spencer Grant/Photo Researchers, Inc.)*

LONG-TERM PRICING DECISIONS

You may have noticed that the relevant costs for the short-term special order pricing decision differ from the full costs of the job reported in Exhibit 8–8. Is there any benefit to reporting this full cost information to managers who are responsible for the firm's pricing decisions?

In fact, most firms rely on full cost information reports when setting prices.[1] Typically, the accounting department provides cost reports to the marketing department, which then adds appropriate markups to the costs to determine benchmark or target prices for all products normally sold by the firm.

This reliance on full costs for pricing decisions can be economically justified in 3 types of circumstances:

1. Many contracts for the development and production of customized products and many contracts with governmental agencies specify prices as full costs plus a markup. Prices set in regulated industries such as electric utilities also are based on full costs.

[1] Lawrence Gordon, Robert Cooper, Haim Falk, and Danny Miller, *The Pricing Decision* (New York: National Association of Accountants, 1981), p. 23; Rajiv D. Banker and John S. Hughes, "Product Costing and Pricing," *The Accounting Review*, (July 1994), pp. 479–494.

When oil companies lease or buy off-shore drilling platforms, like this one operated by Oryx Energy Company, the decision reflects planners' beliefs about the long-term trend of the prices of petroleum products and the trend in the cost of alternative sources of crude oil. Oryx Energy Company believed that the average long-term price of oil products could support the recovery of the cost of its commitment to this drilling platform, or it would not be operating it. *(Courtesy Onyx Energy Co.)*

2. When a firm enters into a long-term contractual relationship with a customer to supply a product, it has great flexibility in adjusting the level of commitment for all activity resources. Therefore, most activity costs will depend on the production decisions under the long-term contract, and full costs are relevant for the long-term pricing decision.

3. The third situation is representative of many industries. Most firms make short-term adjustments in prices instead of rigidly employing a fixed price based on full costs. When demand for their products is low, they recognize the greater likelihood of a surplus capacity in the short term. Accordingly, they adjust the prices of their products downward to acquire additional business, based on the lower incremental costs when surplus capacity is available. Conversely, when demand for their products is high, they recognize the greater likelihood that the existing capacity of activity resources is inadequate to satisfy all of the demand. Accordingly, they adjust the prices upward based on the higher incremental costs when capacity is fully utilized.

Because demand conditions fluctuate over time, prices also fluctuate over time with the demand conditions. For instance, demand is low on weekends in the hotel industry compared to weekdays. Therefore, most hotels offer special weekend rates that are considerably lower than their weekday rates. Many amusement parks offer lower prices on weekdays when demand is expected to be low. Airfares between New York and London are higher in summer when the demand is higher than in winter when the demand is lower. Also, long distance telephone rates are lower in the evenings and on the weekends when the demand is lower.

Although the fluctuating short term prices are based on the appropriate incremental costs, over the long term, their average tends to equal the price based on full costs that may be set in a long-term contract.[2] See Exhibit 8–9. In other words, the price determined by adding on a markup to the full costs of a product serves as a benchmark or target price from which the prices are adjusted up or down, depending on demand conditions. Most firms use full cost-based prices as target prices, giving sales managers limited authority to modify prices as required by the prevailing competitive conditions.

not in a regulated industry ←

We have not discussed the way to determine the amount of markup. We have already seen that prices depend on demand conditions. Markups increase with the *strength of demand*. If more customers demand more of a product, the firm is able to command a higher markup for the product. Markups also depend on the **elasticity of demand.** Demand is said to be elastic if customers are very sensitive to the price, that is, when a small increase in the price results in a large decrease in the demand. Markups are lower when demand is more elastic. Markups also decrease with increases in the *intensity of competition*. If competition is intense, it is more difficult for a firm to sustain a price much higher than its incremental costs.[3] See Appendix 8–1 for an economic analysis of the pricing decision.

Elasticity of demand
Demand is elastic if a small increase in price results in a large decrease in demand.

markups
↑ strength of demand ↑
↓ elasticity of demand ↑
↓ intensity of competition ↑

To see how demand elasticity affects the pricing decision, consider the decision by Jim and Barry's Ice Cream Company, mentioned in previous chapters, to increase ice cream prices from $2.40 per gallon to $2.50 per gallon. When prices increase, they expect the demand to decline from 80,000 gallons to 75,000 gallons. The incremental cost is $1.60 per gallon of ice cream. How much will the profits increase because of this price increase?

[2] Rajiv D. Banker, John S. Hughes, and Inder S. Khosla, "Product Costing and Short-Run Pricing Heuristics," University of Minnesota, Working Paper, 1994.

[3] For achieving a targeted return on investment, a firm may use higher markups for the more capital-intensive production processes.

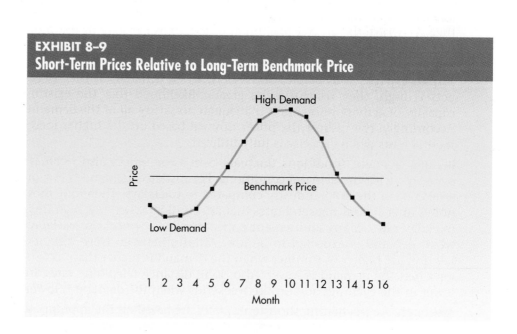

EXHIBIT 8–9
Short-Term Prices Relative to Long-Term Benchmark Price

High Demand

Price

Benchmark Price

Low Demand

1 2 3 4 5 6 7 8 9 10 11 12 13 14 15 16
Month

Pricing in Pharmaceutical Companies

President Bill Clinton's health-care reform proposal makes the accounting for and pricing of pharmaceutical products more critical than ever. An error in judgment or a miscalculation when initial prices are set could have a strong impact on the company producing the pharmaceuticals for many years.

The pharmaceutical company's goals for its pricing strategy are to recoup its research and development investment, earn money for future projects, and earn a fair return for its investors. For a pharmaceutical company, research and development of new products will keep the company a going concern. Without it, the company would cease to exist.

It can cost a company, on average, $275 million to develop a new drug, and that process can take 10 to 15 years. The odds of a company's laboratory developing a breakthrough drug are 1 in 1,000. In addition, only 3 of every 10 drugs that get to market recover the investment a company has made in them. With these statistics, the importance of pricing strategy cannot be overemphasized.

So how does the company determine the price of a drug? Before any project starts, the company produces a projected cash flow analysis. This analysis is repeated with updated data when the product is ready to be introduced to the market. Included in the calculations are the costs to manufacture and distribute the product. In addition, the company's strategy probably includes a markup objective for its products to cover the other costs of operation, such as general selling and administration, and additional funds for research projects.

Pricing is affected by the nature of the product and market conditions. A patented breakthrough product will be priced at a premium. This strategy enables the company to recoup the higher research costs. Once the patent expires (after 17 years, which includes the time spent in R&D) and open competition and substitution of generic drugs evolve, prices will decrease in response to basic supply and demand economics.

Improvements that give a drug a therapeutic advantage may create market conditions that allow for the product to be priced above the competition. Careful analysis of the competition and current market conditions will be critical to setting the price. A price too high could discourage consumers from purchasing the product. A price too low could hinder the recovery of the investment it took to bring the product to market. New and improved products such as Merck's Vasotec will be priced in the middle of the range. Originally approved as an antihypertensive, Vasotec is now used for treating congestive heart failure. A new and improved product, such as a new dosage amount in the form of sustained release tablets, can also be priced above the competition.

At the other end of the scale are the "me, too" products and the products that have generic competition. Open market conditions will force lower prices and lead to even pricing among the competition. A high price will not generate the sales when a lower-priced product with equal qualities is available. Lower prices can be charged because there are no extensive outlays for basic research to discover new compounds that will lead to new products.

Source: Marjorie E. Holmes, "Research RX: Is Health Care Reform a Bitter Pill for the Pharmaceutical Industry?" *Management Accounting* (November 1993), pp. 40–42. Reprinted from *Management Accounting.* Copyright by Institute of Management Accountants, Montvale, NJ.

Contribution to profits from each gallon of ice cream increases from $0.80 ($2.40 − $1.60) to $0.90 ($2.50 − $1.60) with the increase in the price. The price increase has 2 effects on profits: (1) It increases the contribution for the units sold but (2) it also decreases the number of units sold, and, therefore, the contribution from these units is lost. In this case, the increase in contribution is $0.10 per gallon ($0.90 − $0.80), or $7,500 ($0.10 * 75,000) for the 75,000 gallons of expected sales after the price increase. The decrease in contribution is $4,000 ($0.80 * 5,000) because of the 5,000 gallon decline in sales (80,000 − 75,000) of ice cream on which a contribution margin of $0.80 per gallon was earned prior to the price increase. Therefore, the net impact of the price increase on profits is an increase of $3,500 ($7,500 − $4,000).

If the demand were more elastic and sales were expected to decline by 10,000 gallons (to 70,000 gallons instead of 75,000 gallons), the higher price markup would not be advisable. The increase in contribution of $7,000 ($0.10 * 70,000) would be more than offset by the decline of $8,000 ($0.80 * 10,000) due to the sharp decrease in sales. The price increase, therefore, would result in a net decrease of $1,000 ($7,000 − $8,000) in profits.

This example illustrates the important point that, when demand is less elastic, profits can be higher due to a higher price markup. When demand is more elastic, there are usually lower price markups and, therefore, lower profits.

Markups often are lowered for strategic reasons. A firm may choose a low markup for a new product to penetrate the market and win over market share from an established product of a competing firm. In contrast to this **penetration pricing strategy,** a **skimming pricing strategy** may be employed, as in the audio and video equipment industry, to charge a higher price initially from customers willing to pay more for the privilege of possessing the latest technological innovations.

Penetration pricing strategy
Charging a lower price initially to win over market share from an established product of a competing firm.

Skimming pricing strategy
Charging a higher price initially from customers willing to pay more for the privilege of possessing a new product.

OBJECTIVE 8.3
The way a firm determines a long-term benchmark price to guide its pricing strategy

OBJECTIVE 8.4
The way a firm evaluates the long-term profitability of its products and market segments

LONG-TERM PRODUCT MIX DECISIONS

We return once again to the case of a price-taker firm that is now making long-term product mix decisions. Decisions to add a new product or to drop an existing product from the portfolio of products usually have long-term implications on the cost structure of a firm. Product-sustaining costs, such as product design and engineering, part maintenance, and dedicated sales force costs, are relevant costs for such decisions. Batch-related costs, such as setups, materials handling, and first-item inspection (where only the first few items in each batch are inspected), also are likely to change if the product mix is changed in favor of, or against, products manufactured in large batches. Bear in mind, however, that resources committed for many product-sustaining and several batch-related activities cannot be changed easily in the short run. Introduction of a new product and the deletion of an existing product cannot be done suddenly, because both decisions require careful implementation plans stretching over several periods. Normal costs of products are determined as described in this chapter based on the consumption of various activity resources by the product manufactured. In the long term, the firm is able to adjust the capacity of activity resources, such as the number of setup staff or the number of quality inspectors, to match the resource levels demanded by the production quantities.

A comparison of the costs with the market prices reveals which products are not profitable in the long term when activity resource capacities have been adjusted to match production requirements. If some products have full costs that exceed the market prices, the firm must consider several options. While dropping these products is a prominent option, it may be important to maintain a full product line to make it attractive for customers to have a one-stop shopping for their orders. But a comparison of the prices with costs is

Companies such as Aluminum Company of America produce thousands of specialty products for their customers. Most multiproduct companies try to understand which products are making money and which are losing money so they can decide whether a product's long-term price can sustain the costs of making that product. In deciding to drop a product because its price cannot cover its costs, a company must consider whether it can eliminate the unit, batch, product, and facility costs associated with the product. *(© Steve Krongard for Alcoa)*

useful because it indicates the *net* cost of the strategy to offer a full product line.

Managers also may consider other options such as reengineering or redesigning the products to eliminate or reduce costly activities and bring their costs in line with market prices. For example, they could improve the production processes to reduce setup times and streamline material and product flows. They also may want to explore the market conditions more carefully to differentiate their products further to raise the prices and bring them in line with the costs. Customers could be offered incentives, such as quantity discounts, to increase order sizes as that would reduce total batch-related costs. If these steps fail, and if the marketing strategy of offering such a full product line cannot justify the high net cost of such products, managers must consider a plan to phase out the products from their line, and to shift customers, instead, to substitute products retained in the company's product line.

A caveat is in order, however. Dropping products will help improve profitability *only* if the managers eliminate the activity resources not required any longer to support the discontinued product or redeploy these resources for the profitable products that are continued. Costs result from activity resource commitments, and, therefore, they do not disappear automatically with the dropping of unprofitable products.

PRECISION SPRINGS, INC., REVISITED

Should Precision Springs slash the price of its 0.25 inch springs from $3.63 per pound to $2.48 per pound to obtain business from a reputable customer, the Genair Corporation? Should it make a counteroffer of $2.70, instead, to cover all of its variable manufacturing and selling costs although full costs amount to $2.79 per pound? How would the fixed costs be covered if the selling price covers only the variable costs? These were some of the problems contemplated by Bob Smith as he questioned his controller and his marketing manager.

The concepts discussed in this chapter help us to answer these questions. Variable costs alone are relevant, and fixed costs, such as facility-sustaining costs, are ignored in the analysis for a pricing decision only if it is in a short-term context over a period that is too short to adjust facility resources. If the pricing decision is for the long run, all of these costs are relevant as most resources can be adjusted over the long run. If prices are set to cover only short term variable costs, the firm cannot survive in the long term because the existence of fixed costs will result in losses over the long term.

A case for a lower price for Genair could be made as a part of a penetration pricing strategy. However, Precision Springs also must consider the reaction of its existing customers, who may demand a lower price themselves when they learn that Precision Springs discounts its regular prices for some customers.

A SUMMARY EXAMPLE

We turn now to a worked-out problem that emphasizes some important points discussed in this chapter. Faxtronics, Inc., is a Minnesota-based company that manufactures and sells 2 models (FM101 and FM102) of high-quality fax modem machines, for which the following information is available:

Cost per unit	FM101	FM102
Direct material	$120	$160
Direct labor ($20 per hour)	50	80
Variable overhead ($5 per machine-hour)	20	40
Fixed overhead	20	20
Total cost per unit	$210	$300
Price per unit	$260	$400

Demand for the 2 models of fax modem machines has grown rapidly in recent years, and Faxtronics can no longer meet the demand with its current production capacity. At present, the monthly demand is 8,000 units for FM101 and 5,000 units for FM102. Monthly capacity is limited to 60,000 machine-hours.

(a) Determine the contribution margin per unit for each of the 2 products.

(b) Determine the product mix that will maximize profits.

(c) Suppose Faxtronics has received a special order from a new customer willing to buy 2,000 units of FM101 at $300 each. What is the opportunity cost associated with this order?

(d) Should Faxtronics accept this order?

The solution to the review problem follows:

(a)

	FM101	FM102
Selling price per unit	$260	$400
Variable cost per unit		
Direct material	$120	$160
Direct labor	50	80
Variable overhead	20	40
Total variable cost per unit	190	280
Contribution margin per unit	$70	$120

(b) Contribution margin per unit of the scarce resource:

	FM101	FM102
Contribution margin per unit of product	$70	$120
Number of machine-hours per unit	4 (20/5)	8 (40/5)
Contribution margin per machine-hour	$17.50	$15.00

Because FM101 has a higher contribution margin per unit of the scarce resource (machine-hours) than FM102, it is more profitable to fill first all the demand for FM101 and then use the remaining machine-hours to manufacture FM102. Therefore, the optimal production plan is as follows:

➤ 8,000 units of FM101

➤ 3,500 units of FM102 [{60,000 − (8,000 * 4)}/8]

(c) Faxtronics has no surplus capacity available for the production of an additional 2,000 units of FM101, which requires 8,000 (2,000 * 4) machine-hours. Because FM102 has the lowest contribution margin per machine-hour, Faxtronics can best make the capacity (8,000 machine-hours) necessary for the special order available by reducing the production of FM102 by 1,000 units (8,000/8). The contribution margin for FM102 is $120 per unit. Therefore, the opportunity cost is $120 * 1,000 = $120,000.

(d)

Variable cost for the special order	$380,000	($190 * 2,000)
Opportunity cost for the special order	120,000	
Relevant cost for the special order	$500,000	
Relevant cost per unit	$ 250	($500,000/2,000)

Therefore, Faxtronics should accept this order because the price of $300 is higher than the relevant cost of $250 per unit. It will increase profits by $100,000 ($(300 − 250) * 2,000).

SUMMARY

An important function of management accountants is to provide appropriate cost information to managers to assist in their pricing and product mix decisions. The manner in which cost information is used in these decisions depends on whether the firm is a major player in its industry influencing the setting of prices or whether it is a minor player taking the industry prices as given and adjusting its product mix in response to the prices. The role of cost information also depends on the time frame involved in the decision: different costs are more relevant for short-term decisions than they are for long term decisions.

Short-term prices are based on incremental costs that depend on the availability of activity resource capacity. If the capacity is likely to be fully utilized, then the incremental costs of overtime and other means to obtain the additional required capacity are also relevant for the pricing decision. If the firm commits to a price under a long-term contract, the normal costs of all activity resources consumed in the manufacture and selling of a product are relevant. Interestingly, such a long-term price also serves as a benchmark price around which actual prices fluctuate when the firm can make short term price adjustments, depending on the demand conditions prevailing at that point in time.

Short-term product mix decisions also require information on incremental costs that vary in the short term. If the capacity is limited for the short term, the contribution per unit of the limited capacity is used as the criterion to rank order the products in the production plan. For long-term product mix decisions, managers rely on the normal costs of the products that reflect the consumption of different activity resources for the manufacture and sale of different products.

The nature of the cost information required for pricing and product mix decisions depends on the time frame considered but is similar whether the firm is a *price setter* or a *price taker*.

KEY TERM LIST

APPENDIX 8-1

Economic Analysis of the Pricing Decision

In this chapter, we considered a firm's decision about product *prices* to maximize its profits or, more broadly, whether to pursue a strategic goal such as market penetration that would maximize its long-term profits. In contrast, introductory textbooks in economics usually analyze the profit maximization decision by a firm in terms of the choice of a *quantity* to produce. In turn, the quantity choice determines the price of the product in the marketplace.

■ Quantity Decision

We first briefly discuss this economic analysis of the quantity choice before examining the pricing decision. The quantity choice is presented in terms of equating marginal revenue and marginal cost. **Marginal revenue** is defined as the increase in revenue corresponding to a unit increase in the quantity produced and sold. **Marginal cost** is defined as the increase in cost for a unit increase in the quantity produced and sold. If marginal revenue is greater than marginal cost, then increasing the quantity by 1 unit will increase profit. If marginal revenue is less than the marginal cost, profit can be increased by decreasing production. Therefore, if profit is maximized, marginal revenue must equal marginal cost.

Exhibit 8A–1 depicts marginal analysis. The marginal revenue curve is decreasing because additional sales quantity is generated only with a lower price. The average revenue curve represents the price itself because average revenue equals total revenue divided by the quantity, and total revenue is obtained by multiplying the price by the quantity. Marginal cost is depicted by a horizontal line because total cost is assumed to increase at a constant rate and to the variable cost per unit. The profit-maximizing quantity is determined by the intersection of the marginal revenue and marginal cost curves because marginal revenue equals marginal cost at the point of intersection.

Marginal revenues (costs)
The increase in revenues (or costs) for a unit increase in the quantity produced and sold.

EXHIBIT 8A–1
Marginal Analysis of Profit-Maximizing Quantity Choice

Q^* = Profit-maximizing quantity choice
P^* = Profit-maximizing price
V = Variable cost per unit

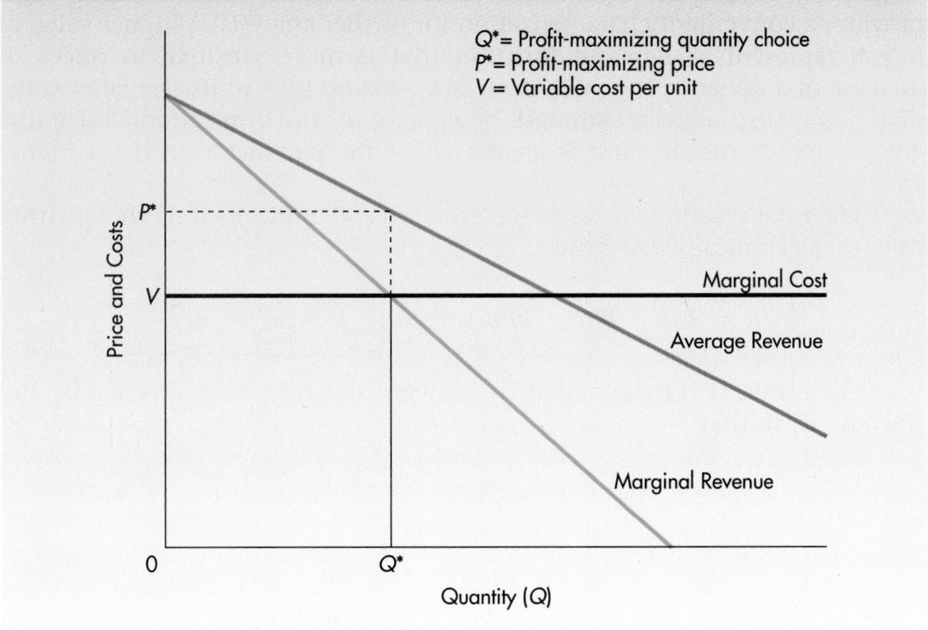

The profit-maximizing price is determined by reading off the average revenue curve corresponding to the profit-maximizing quantity.

In this analysis, the firm chooses the quantity level, and the market demand forces determine the corresponding price. Consider next a firm that must choose a price, not a quantity, to announce to its customers. Customers then react to the price announced and determine the quantity that they demand. The analysis of the firm's pricing decision cannot be represented graphically as conveniently as the analysis of the quantity decision we discussed earlier. Therefore, we shall use instead differential calculus to analyze the firm's pricing decision.

■ Pricing Decision

As in Chapter 4, we express the total costs, C, in terms of its fixed and variable cost components:

$$C = f + vQ$$

where f is the fixed cost, v is the variable cost per unit, and Q is the quantity produced in units. Quantity produced is assumed to be the same as quantity demanded. The demand, Q, is represented as a decreasing linear function of the price P:

$$Q = a - bP$$

In general, we may have nonlinear demand functions, but the linear form provides a convenient characterization for further analysis. A higher value of $b > 0$ represents a demand function that is more sensitive to price; an increase of a dollar in the price decreases demand by b units. A higher value of $a > 0$ reflects a greater strength of demand for the firm's product. For any given price, P, the demand is greater when the parameter, a, has a higher value.

The total revenue, R, is given by the price, P, multiplied by the quantity sold, Q. Algebraically, we write

$$R = PQ = P(a - bP). \text{ Therefore, } R = aP - bP^2.$$

The profit, Π is measured as the difference between the revenue, R, and the cost, C, so that

$$
\begin{aligned}
\Pi &= R - C \\
&= PQ - (f + vQ) \\
&= P(a - bP) - f - v(a - bP) \\
&= aP - bP^2 - f - va + vbP
\end{aligned}
$$

To find the profit-maximizing price, P^*, we set the first derivative of profit Π with respect to P equal to zero.

$$d\Pi/dP = a - 2bP + vb = 0 \text{ implies}$$

$$P^* = \frac{a + vb}{2b} = \frac{a}{2b} + \frac{v}{2}$$

■ Long-Term Benchmark Prices

This simple economic analysis suggests that the price depends only on the variable cost per unit; fixed costs are not relevant for the pricing decision. A more complex analysis (not described here) that considers simultaneously the pricing decision with the long-term decisions of the firm to commit resources to facility-sustaining, product-sustaining, and other activity capacities indicates that the costs of these committed resources do play a role in the pricing decision.[4] The costs of these committed activity resources appear to be fixed costs in the short term, but they can be changed in the long term. The prices that a firm sets and adjusts in the short term based on changing demand conditions fluctuate around a long-term benchmark price, P^L, that reflects the unit costs of the activity resource capacities:

$$P^L = \frac{a}{2b} + \frac{v + m}{2}$$

where $m = f/X$ is the cost per unit of normal capacity, X, of facility-sustaining activities.[5] In this case, the degree of price fluctuations around the benchmark price increases with the proportion of fixed costs. As a result, prices appear more volatile in capital intensive industries.

■ Competitive Analysis

How does the pricing decision change when other firms compete in the same industry with products that are similar but not identical to each other? In such a situation, some customers may switch their demand to a competing supplier firm if the competitor reduces its price. Therefore, a firm's pricing decision must consider the prices that may be set by its competitors.

We consider two firms, A and B, and represent the demand, Q_A, for firm A's product as a function of its own price, P_A, and the price, P_B, set by its competitor:

$$Q_A = a - bP_A + eP_B$$

The demand for firm A's product falls by b units for each dollar increase in its own price, but increases by e units for each dollar increase in the competitor's price because firm A gains some of the market demand that firm B loses.

[4] Rajiv D. Banker, and John S. Hughes, "Product Costing and Pricing," *The Accounting Review*, July 1994, pp. 479–494.

[5] Rajiv D. Banker, John S. Hughes, and Inder S. Khosla, "Product Costing and Short-Run Pricing Heuristics," University of Minnesota Working Paper, 1994.

The profit, Π_A, for firm A is represented by:

$$\Pi_A = P_A Q_A - (f + vQ_A)$$
$$= P_A (a - bP_A + eP_B) - f - v(a - bP_A + eP_B)$$

Profit maximization requires

$$d\Pi_A/dP_A = a - 2bP_A + eP_B + vb = 0$$

Therefore, the profit-maximizing price P_A^0 given the other firm's price P_B is:

$$P_A^0 = (a + vb + eP_B)/2b$$

The pricing decision thus depends on what the competitor's price is expected to be. If the firm expects its competitor to behave as it does and expects it to choose the same price as its own, then we set $P_A = P_B = P^*$ in the equation $a - 2bP_A + eP_B + vb = 0$ to obtain

$$a - 2bP^* + eP^* + vb = 0$$

$$P^* = \frac{a + vb}{2b - e}$$

We refer to this price as the equilibrium price because no firm can increase its profits by choosing a different price, provided the other firm maintains the same price P^*.

ASSIGNMENT MATERIAL

QUESTIONS

8–1 "Prices must cover both variable and fixed costs of production." Do you agree with this statement? Explain.

8–2 Why is the evaluation of *short term* pricing and product mix decisions different from the evaluation of *long term* decisions?

8–3 What distinguishes a *commodity-type business* from other businesses?

8–4 What 2 considerations complicate short-term product mix decisions?

8–5 What firms are likely to behave as *price-taker* firms?

8–6 What firms are likely to behave as *price-setter* firms?

8–7 "When production capacity is constrained, determine what products to make by ranking them in order of their *contribution per unit*." Do you agree with this statement? Explain.

8–8 "When production capacity is limited, and it is possible to obtain additional customer orders, then *opportunity costs* must be considered to evaluate the profitability of these new orders." Do you agree with this statement? What are the opportunity costs in this context?

8–9 What additional costs must be considered in making a short-term pricing decision when surplus production capacity is not available, and overtime, extra shift, subcontracting, or other means must be employed to augment the limited capacity?

8–10 Should facility-sustaining costs be considered in making a short-run pricing decision? Give two examples to illustrate your answer.

8–11 Describe three situations in which the use of full costs for pricing decisions can be justified economically.

8–12 How do price markups over costs relate to the strength of demand, the elasticity of demand, and the intensity of competition?

8–13 Why do short-run prices fluctuate over time?

8–14 What strategic reasons may influence the level of markups?

8–15 What options may be considered when long-run market prices are below full costs?

8–16 Why is full cost information useful for long-run product mix decisions?

EXERCISES

8–17 Bibi Company manufactures and sells a single product, Beta. Because of an economic recession, Bibi is experiencing idle capacity sufficient to manufacture an additional 10,000 units of Beta. Variable costs are $70 per unit, and fixed costs total $200,000 per month. A Swedish manufacturer has offered $75 per unit for 8,000 units of Beta. This special order will not require any additional selling expenses. Should Bibi accept this special order? What will the impact on Bibi's operating income be if it accepts this special order?

8–18 Shorewood Shoes Company makes and sells a variety of leather shoes for children. For its current mix of different models and sizes, the average selling price and costs per pair of shoes are as follows:

Price		$20
Direct materials	$6	
Direct labor	4	
Variable manufacturing overhead	2	
Variable selling overhead	1	
Fixed overhead	3	$16

Shoes are manufactured in batch size of 100 pairs. Each batch requires 5 machine-hours to manufacture. The plant has a total capacity of 4,000 machine-hours per month, but current month production consumes only about 80% of the capacity.

A discount store has approached Shorewood to buy 10,000 pairs of shoes. It has requested that the shoes bear its own private label. Embossing the private label will cost Shorewood an additional $0.50 per pair. However, there will be no variable selling cost for this special order.

Determine the minimum price that Shorewood Shoes should charge for this order.

8–19 Charlotte Company produces two types of floppy disks: standard and high density. The selling price and variable costs per box (of 10 disks) of each product are as follows:

	Standard	High Density
Selling price per box	$7.00	$10.00
Variable costs:		
Direct materials	$2.00	$3.00
Direct labor	1.50	2.50
Overhead	0.50	0.50

Because of a strike in the plant of 1 of its principal competitors, the demand for Charlotte's disks exceeds its capacity at present. The direct labor rate is $10 per hour, and only 4,000 hours of labor time are available each week.

REQUIRED:

(a) Determine the contribution margin per direct labor hour for each product.

(b) Which product should Charlotte's sales force promote?

8-20 Boyd Wood Company makes a regular and a deluxe grade of wood floors. Regular grade is sold at $16 per square yard, and the deluxe grade is sold at $25 per square yard. The variable cost of making the regular grade is $10 per square yard; it costs an extra $5 per square yard to make the deluxe grade. It takes 15 labor hours to make 100 square yards of the regular grade and 20 labor hours to make 100 square yards of the deluxe grade. There are 4,600 hours of labor time available for production each week. The maximum weekly sales for the regular and the deluxe model are 30,000 and 8,000 square yards, respectively. Fixed production costs total $600,000 per year. All selling costs are fixed. What is the optimal production level (in number of square yards) for each product?

8-21 Berry Company produces and sells 30,000 cases of fruit preserves each year. The following is a breakdown of its costs:

	Costs per Case	Total Costs
Variable production costs	$16	$480,000
Fixed production costs	8	240,000
Variable selling costs	5	150,000
Fixed selling and administrative costs	3	90,000
	$32	$960,000

Berry marks up its prices 40 percent over full costs. It has surplus capacity to produce 15,000 more cases. A French supermarket company has offered to purchase 10,000 cases of the product at a special price of $40 per case. Berry will incur additional shipping and selling costs of $3 per case to complete this order. What will be the effect on Berry's operating income if it accepts this order?

8-22 The manufacturing capacity of Ritter Rotator Company's plant facility is 60,000 rotators per quarter. Operating results for the first quarter of 1994 are as follows:

Sales (36,000 units @ $10)	$360,000
Variable manufacturing and selling costs	198,000
Contribution margin	162,000
Fixed costs	99,000
Operating income	63,000

A foreign distributor has offered to buy 30,000 units at $9 per unit during the second quarter of 1994. Domestic demand is expected to remain the same as in the first quarter.

(a) Determine the impact on operating income if Ritter accepts this order.

(b) Assume that Ritter decides to run an extra shift so that it can accept the foreign order without forgoing sales to its regular domestic customers. The proposed extra shift would increase capacity by 25% and increase fixed costs by $25,000. Determine the impact on operating income if Ritter operates the extra shift and accepts the export order.

8–23 Delta Screens Corporation is currently operating at 60% of capacity and producing 6,000 screens annually. Delta recently received an offer from a company in Germany to purchase 2,000 screens at $500 per unit. Delta has not previously sold products in Germany. Budgeted production costs for 6,000 and 8,000 screens follow:

Units Produced	6,000	8,000
Direct materials cost	$750,000	$1,000,000
Direct labor cost	750,000	1,000,000
Overhead cost	2,100,000	2,400,000
Total cost	$3,600,000	$4,400,000
Full cost per unit	$600	$550

Delta has been selling its product at a markup of 10% above full cost. Delta's marketing manager believes that although the price offered by the German customer is lower than current prices, the order should be accepted to gain a foothold in the German market. The production manager, however, believes that the order should be rejected because the unit cost is higher than the price offered.

REQUIRED:

(a) Explain what caused the apparent decrease in cost from $600 per unit to $550 per unit when production increased from 6,000 to 8,000 units.

(b) If the president of Delta Screens Corporation calls on you to resolve the difference in opinions, what will you recommend?

8–24 Columbia Bicycle Company manufactures and sells 12 different models of bicycles. Columbia is contemplating a 5% price cut across the board for all 12 models. It expects the price cut to result in an 8% increase in the number of units sold of models M124, M126, M128, W124, W126, and W128. The other 6 models (B112, B116, B120, and G112, G116, G120) are expected to experience a 4% increase in the number of units sold.

The following are the sales prices, variable costs, and sales volume (units) at present. You are required to assess the impact of the price cut on Columbia's profits.

Model	Sales Price	Variable Costs	Sales Volume
B112	$60	$30	3,000
B116	70	33	4,500
B120	80	36	5,000
G112	60	30	4,000
G116	70	33	4,000
G120	80	36	4,000
M124	100	42	5,000
M126	120	46	5,000
M128	140	50	10,000
W124	100	42	6,000
W126	120	46	7,000
W128	140	40	6,000

8–25 Andrea Kimball has recently acquired a franchise of a well-known fast-food restaurant chain. She is considering a special promotion for a week during which hamburger prices would be reduced to $0.69 from the regular price of $1.09. Local advertising expenses for this special promotion will amount to $4,500. Andrea expects the promotion to increase sales of hamburgers by 20% and french fries by 12%, but she expects the sales of chicken sandwiches to decline by 8% because some customers, who may have otherwise ordered a chicken sandwich, now will order a hamburger because of its attractive low price. The following data have been compiled for sales prices, variable costs, and weekly sales volumes:

Product	Sales Price	Variable Costs	Sales Volume
Hamburgers	$1.09	0.51	20,000
Chicken sandwiches	1.29	0.63	10,000
French fries	0.89	0.37	20,000

Evaluate the expected impact of the special promotion on sales and profits. Should Andrea go ahead with this special promotion? What other considerations are relevant in this decision?

PROBLEMS

8–26 (Appendix) Carver Company has a demand function given by

$$Q = 400 - 5 * P$$

and a cost function given by

$$C = 2,000 + 20 * Q$$

where

P = price

Q = quantity produced and sold

Determine the optimal price and the corresponding demand quantity and product's unit cost.

8–27 Excel Corporation manufactures 3 products at its plant. The plant capacity is limited to 120,000 machine-hours per year on a single shift basis. Direct material and direct labor costs are variable. The following data are available for planning purposes:

Product	Demand for Next Year (Total Units)	Sales Price	Direct Materials	Direct Labor	Variable Overhead	Machine-Hours
XL1	200,000	$10.00	$4.00	$2.00	$2.00	0.20
XL2	200,000	14.00	4.50	3.00	3.00	0.35
XL3	200,000	12.00	5.00	2.50	2.50	0.25

REQUIRED:

(a) Given the capacity constraint, determine the production levels for the 3 products that will maximize profits.

(b) If the plant is worked overtime, direct labor cost per unit will be higher by 50% due to overtime premium. Materials cost and variable overhead per unit will be the same for overtime production as regular production. Is it worthwhile operating overtime?

8–28 Prime Printer, Inc., is a corporation based in Eagan, Minnesota, that sells high-quality printers in the Midwest regional market. It manufactures 2 products, L8011 and L8033, for which the following information is available:

Costs per Unit	L8011	L8033
Direct materials	$ 300	$ 375
Direct labor	400	500
Variable overhead	500	625
Fixed overhead	400	500
Total cost per unit	$1,600	$2,000
Price	$2,000	$2,500
Units sold	400 units	200 units

The average wage rate (including fringe benefits) is $20 per hour. The plant has a capacity of 14,000 direct labor hours, but current production uses only 13,000 direct labor hours of capacity.

REQUIRED:

(a) A new customer has offered to buy 40 units of L8033 if its price is lowered to $2,000 per unit. How many direct labor *hours* will be required to produce 40 units of L8033? How much will Prime Printer's profit increase (or decrease) if it accepts this proposal? All other prices will remain as before.

(b) Suppose the customer has offered instead to buy 60 units of L8033 at $2,000 per unit. How much will the profits increase (or decrease) if this proposal is accepted? Assume that the company cannot increase its production capacity to meet the extra demand.

(c) Answer the question in (b) above, assuming instead that the plant can work overtime. Direct labor costs for the *overtime* production increase to only $30 per hour. Variable overhead costs for overtime production are 50% more than for normal production.

8–29 The Emerson Electric Company estimates the following variable manufacturing overhead costs for 1994 for its plant in Minnetonka, Minnesota.

Cost Pool	Amount	Activity-Based Cost Drivers		Rate
Machine operations and maintenance	$ 48,000	12,000	Machine-hours	$ 4.00
Supervision	45,000	225,000	Direct labor dollars	0.20
Materials handling	75,000	100,000	Pounds	0.75
Quality control	66,000	550	Number of inspections	120.00
Machine setups	75,000	250	Production runs	300.00
Total	$309,000			

Emerson's Minnetonka plant manufactures 3 products at present. Cost and production data (per unit) are as follows:

	Product A	Product B	Product C
Direct materials	$12.00	$15.00	$18.00
Direct labor	$9.00	$15.00	$20.00
Machine-hours	0.4	0.7	0.9
Pounds	4.0	5.0	7.0
Number of inspections	0.02	0.02	0.05
Number of production runs	0.01	0.01	0.02
Sales price	$40.00	$57.00	$78.00
Maximum demand	12,000 units	12,000 units	6,000 units
Actual production in 1991	10,000 units	5,000 units	5,000 units

     (a) Determine the product costs using an activity-based costing system.

     (b) At present, production capacity is limited to 12,000 machine-hours and capacity can not be expanded in the next 2 years. Determine the optimal production levels for 1994 that will maximize profits. Present your reasoning with detailed steps. List the specific assumptions that you need to make about fixed manufacturing, fixed selling, and variable selling costs.

     (c) Suppose Emerson can work its plant overtime for no more than 4,000 additional machine-hours. Overtime premium will add 50% to direct labor costs and 30% to variable manufacturing overhead costs. Determine the optimal production levels for 1994 under overtime. How many machine hours of overtime should Emerson work?

8–30 Barney Toy Company manufactures 2 different sizes (large and small) of stuffed animals. It has a long-term contract with a large chain of discount stores to sell 3,000 large and 6,000 small stuffed animals each month. The following cost information is available for large and small stuffed animals:

	Large	Small
Price per unit	$30	$20
Variable cost per unit:		
Direct material	$12	$10
Direct labor	6	2
Overhead	2	1
Fixed cost per unit	3	3
Total unit cost	$23	$16
Estimated demand (inclusive of long-term contract)	15,000	25,000

Production occurs in batches of 100 large or 200 small stuffed animals. Each batch takes a total of 10 machine-hours to manufacture. The total machine-hour capacity of 3,000 machine-hours cannot be increased for at least a year.

REQUIRED:

     (a) Determine the contribution margin per unit for each of the 2 sizes of stuffed animals.

     (b) Determine which size is more profitable to produce. How many units should Barney produce of each size?

Because of an unexpected high demand for stuffed dinosaurs, the discount store chain has requested an additional order of 5,000 large stuffed dinosaurs. It is willing to pay $35 for this special order.

     (c) Determine the opportunity cost associated with this order.

     (d) Should Barney Toy Company accept this order? Explain.

Suppose that the company can subcontract the production of up to 10,000 small stuffed animals to an outside supplier at a cost of $21 per animal.

     (e) How many units of each size should Barney produce, subcontract, and sell? What other qualitative factors should be considered?

8–31 Chang Company makes 2 types of wood doors: standard and deluxe. The doors are manufactured in a plant consisting of 3 departments: cutting, assembly, and finishing. Both labor and machine time are spent on the 2 products as they are worked on in each department.

In planning the production schedule for the next month, management is confronted with the fact that there is a labor shortage and some machines must be shut down for major maintenance and repair. The following information pertains to the estimated levels of capacity of direct labor hours and machine-hours available next month in the 3 departments:

Capacity Available	Cutting	Assembly	Finishing
Machine-hours	40,000	40,000	15,000
Labor hours	8,000	17,500	8,000

Direct labor and machine-hours required per unit of each product are as follows:

Product	Cutting	Assembly	Finishing
Standard			
Direct labor hours	0.5	1	0.5
Machine-hours	2	2	1
Deluxe			
Direct labor hours	1	1.5	0.5
Machine-hours	3	3	1.5

The estimated demand for the next month is 10,000 units of standard doors and 5,000 units of deluxe doors. Unit cost and price information are as follows:

	Standard Doors	Deluxe Doors
Unit selling price	$150	$200
Unit cost:		
Direct materials	$60	$80
Direct labor	40	60
Variable overhead	10	15
Fixed overhead	10	5

Average wage rate is $20 per hour. Direct labor and machine availability in individual departments cannot be switched from one department to another.

REQUIRED:

(a) Determine whether the direct labor hour and machine-hour capacities are adequate to meet the next month's demand.

(b) How many units of each product should the company produce to maximize its profits?

(c) Suggest alternatives the company might consider to satisfy all of its customers' demand.

8–32 Anticipating a shortage of raw material supplies for the next month, Alphonso Company has to make a product mix decision. The following unit cost information is available for products A1 and A2:

	A1	A2
Selling price	$25.00	$30.00
Direct materials cost (rate: $4/lb)	$12.00	$8.00
Direct labor cost (rate: $10/hr)	5.00	10.00
Variable overhead cost	2.50	5.00

The maximum sales for A1 and A2 are estimated to be 4,000 and 8,000 units, respectively. Only 25,000 pounds of the raw material will be available next month. Determine the optimal product mix.

8–33 Alphabet Company manufactures 2 products, A and B. Information on the 2 products is given below:

	Product A	Product B
Selling price	$150	$110
Variable costs:		
Materials	20	15
Labor (rate: $10/hr)	30	20
Overhead	10	5

Total demand is 400 units for Product A and 600 units for Product B. Total capacity is 2,100 direct labor hours.

REQUIRED:

(a) What product mix should Alphabet Company choose?

(b) Suppose Alphabet Company can increase capacity by paying an additional 50% overtime premium to its workers. What are the optimal production levels for the 2 products?

8–34 Refer to the data for Crimson Components Company presented in problem 7–31. The following additional information is available:

➤ The company believes that it cannot change its selling prices.

➤ All manufacturing overhead described in problem 7–31 are variable costs.

➤ All nonmanufacturing costs are fixed.

➤ The plant has a capacity of 80,000 casting department *machine-hours* and 120,000 machining department *machine-hours* on a single-shift basis.

➤ Estimated demand for the next year is 600,000 units of R361 and 800,000 units of R572.

REQUIRED:

(a) Determine the total casting department machine-hours and machining department machine-hours required to produce all of the estimated demand for the next year. In which department is the capacity inadequate to meet estimated demand?

(b) Determine the contribution margins for the 2 products based on your analysis for requirement (b) in problem 7–31.

(c) Determine the contribution per machine-hour for the department(s) in which capacity is inadequate. Given the capacity constraint(s), determine the production levels for the 2 products that will maximize profits.

(d) Either or both of the casting and machining departments can be worked overtime. Direct labor cost per unit would be higher by 50% due to overtime premium. Manufacturing overhead per unit would be the same for overtime production as normal production. Is it worthwhile operating either department overtime? Explain.

8–35 Orion Outdoors Company produces a standard model and a high-quality deluxe model lightweight tents. Orion's workforce is organized into production teams responsible for cutting, stitching, and inspection activities. Orion has determined that its labor and overhead costs depend on direct labor hours (cutting, stitching, and inspection), number of batches, and number of shipments. Production information is as follows:

	Standard Model	Deluxe Model
Direct labor time (cutting and stitching)		
per tent	10 minutes	15 minutes
Average batch size	60 tents	30 tents
Direct labor inspection time per batch	2 hour	2.5 hour
Average size per shipment	60 tents	10 tents
Selling price per tent	$10	$20
Materials costs per tent	$5	$11

Demand for standard and deluxe models is expected to be 6,000 and 3,000 tents, respectively. Direct labor time available for cutting, stitching, and inspection activities is 2,000 hours. The labor cost is $12 per hour (including fringe benefits) and shipping cost is $15 per shipment. Orion produces to demand and maintains no inventory on hand.

REQUIRED:

(a) Determine the production quantities for the 2 models that will maximize profits. Assume in this case that the available labor hours cannot be changed.

Suppose next that labor time available for cutting, stitching, and inspection can be increased as needed. The sales manager has received an offer from Northlands Retail Company for 2,000 deluxe model tents at a price of $18.50 each. This order will be produced and shipped in batch sizes of 50 tents. Inspections for this order of deluxe model batches will take 2.5 hours per batch.

(b) Should this order be accepted? What other qualitative factors must also be considered?

8–36 (Appendix 8–1) Colway Company estimates the relation between the demand for its products and the price it sets, in terms of the equation

$$Q = a - bP$$

where

Q = the quantity demanded
P = the price of the product

The marketing manager, Trisha Colway, conducted a market research study in fall 1994 that indicated that $b = 500$ and $a = 8,400$, on average, for the first quarter of 1995.

Capacity costs are $m = \$3.00$ per unit, and variable costs are $v = \$8.10$ per unit, but if committed capacity is exceeded, the variable costs increase to $w = \$12.70$ per unit.

Trisha determined that the long-term benchmark price is given by

$$P^L = \frac{a}{2b} + \frac{v + m}{2}$$

$$= \frac{8,400}{2 * 500} + \frac{8.10 + 3.00}{2}$$

$$= \$13.95$$

Trisha also set the capacity level at $X = 2,150$ units.

Colway Company keeps track of demand conditions throughout the quarter.

It announces a new price for each week in the Sunday morning newspaper based on the most current information it has on demand conditions. The following are the estimates of the demand parameter for each of the 13 weeks in the first quarter of 1995.

Week t	Current estimate of a_t	Weekly Price P_t
1	8,200	$12.25
2	8,350	?
3	8,600	?
4	8,500	?
5	8,400	?
6	8,850	?
7	8,300	?
8	8,050	?
9	8,200	?
10	8,800	?
11	8,350	?
12	7,950	?
13	8,650	?

The estimate of b remained at $b = 500$ for all 13 weeks. The short-term (weekly) price is set at

$$P_t^* = \frac{a_t}{2b} + \frac{v}{2}$$

if the capacity is *not* exceeded by the realized demand, and at

$$P_t^* = \frac{a_t}{2b} + \frac{w}{2}$$

if the capacity *is* exceeded.

Note that if the price is set at $P_t = \frac{a_t}{2b} + \frac{v}{2}$, the resultant demand will not exceed the capacity $X = 2,150$ only if

$$Q = a_t - b\,P_t = a_t - 500\left[\frac{a_t}{1000} + \frac{8.10}{2}\right] = \frac{a_t}{2} - 2,025$$

is less than $X = 2,150$, that is, if $a_t < 8,350$.

Similarly, if the price is set at $P_t = \frac{a_t}{2b} + \frac{w}{2}$, the resultant demand will exceed the capacity $X = 2,150$ only if $a_t > 10,650$.

REQUIRED:

(a) You are required to determine these weekly prices, plot them on a graph for each of the 13 weeks, and compare them with the long-term benchmark price. What is the average of the weekly prices?

(b) Determine the total profit over the 13-week period. Repeat the same exercise after setting the capacity (X) at different levels ($X = 1750, 1950, 2350, 2550$). Plot the total profit on a graph against different levels of capacity that you select.

CASES

8–37 Aramis Aromatics Company produces and sells its product AA 100 to well-known cosmetics companies for $940 per ton. The marketing manager is considering the possibility of refining AA 100 further into finer perfumes before selling them to the cosmetics companies. Product AA 101 is expected to command a price of $1,500 per ton, and AA 102 a price of $1,700 per ton. The maximum expected demand is 400 tons for AA 101 and 100 tons for AA 102.

The annual plant capacity of 2,400 hours is fully utilized *at present* to manufacture 600 tons of AA 100. The marketing manager proposed that Aramis sell 300 tons of AA 100, 100 tons of AA 101, and 75 tons of AA 102 in the next year. It requires 4 hours of capacity to make a ton of AA 100, 2 hours to refine AA 100 further into AA 101, and 4 hours to refine AA 100 into AA 102 instead. The plant accountant has prepared the following cost sheet for the 3 products:

| | Costs per Ton | | |
	AA 100	AA 101	AA 102
Direct materials:			
Chemicals and fragrance	$560	$400	$470
AA 100	—	800	800
Direct labor	60	30	60
Manufacturing overhead:			
Variable	60	30	60
Fixed	120	60	120
Total manufacturing cost	$800	$1,320	$1,510
Selling overhead:			
Variable	20	30	30
Fixed	10	10	10
	$830	$1,360	$1,550
Proposed sales level	300 tons	100 tons	75 tons
Maximum demand	600 tons	400 tons	100 tons

REQUIRED:

(a) Determine the contribution margin for each product.

(b) Determine the production levels for the 3 products (under the present constraint on plant capacity) that will maximize total contribution.

(c) Suppose a customer, Cosmos Cosmetics Company, is very interested in the new product AA 101. It has offered to sign a long-term contract for 400 tons of AA 101. It is also willing to pay a higher price if the entire plant capacity is dedicated to the production of AA 101. What is the minimum price for AA 101 at which it becomes worthwhile for Aramis to dedicate its entire capacity to the production of AA 101?

(d) Suppose instead that the price of AA 101 is $1,500 per ton and that the capacity can be increased temporarily by 600 hours if the plant is operated overtime. Overtime premium payments to workers and supervisors will increase direct labor and variable manufacturing overhead costs by 50% for all products. All other costs will remain unchanged. Is it worthwhile operating the plant overtime? If the plan is operated overtime for 600 hours, what are the optimal production levels for the 3 products?

8–38 Refer to the data for Sweditrak Corporation presented in case 7–36. The following additional information is now available.

The production volume budgeted for each product in weeks 47 to 52 is the same as the volume level in week 46. In early December, the company is considering contracting with a French company to *produce* 400 units of the deluxe model, on a 4-week trial basis, for $200 per unit. Accepting this offer would restrict Sweditrak's own deluxe production to 50 units per week.

REQUIRED:

(a) Is it profitable for Sweditrak to accept this offer? What other qualitative factors should also be considered in evaluating this offer?

Suppose that Sweditrak is pleased with the quality of the trial shipment and the French company is willing to commit to produce 400 units of the deluxe model each week for the next 3 years and charge $200 per unit. Sweditrak expects the domestic demand for its 2 models to remain stable at 450 units per week for the next 3 years. During this 3-year time period, Sweditrak can adjust the capacity of each department to any desired levels. Capacity changes will result in proportional changes in fixed costs.

(b) What are the relevant costs for this long-term decision?

(c) Will it be profitable for Sweditrak to accept the long-term offer?

8–39 Pricing Experiment (Rajiv D. Banker and P. Jane Saly)

In this pricing experiment, you will work in a team using cost accounting information in pricing decisions. Each team represents one firm in a market. Each market is completely independent of other markets. Your market has four firms that use similar production technology to produce two types of hiking boots—a lightweight model (LT) and a mountaineering model (MT). Each firm faces the same demand curves:

Demand (lightweight) $= 19919 - 500 * P + 84 * (P1 + P2 + P3)$
Demand (mountaineering) $= 6632 - 109 * P + 18 * (P1 + P2 + P3)$

where P is your price and P1, P2, and P3 are the other three firms' prices. Notice that if you increase your price, your demand will fall. If, however, your competitors raise their prices, you will gain some of the market share that they lose.

Your instructor will provide you a confidential cost report that you should use in your pricing decisions. No cost data should be shared with other teams.

There will be five periods in this pricing experiment. For each period, your firm must submit the prices at which you are prepared to sell each type of boot. Your firm operates on a just-in-time basis and produces to order. Hence, there are no inventory or production-quantity decisions to be made.

The market share you obtain or the profit you make in any one period will *not* in any form affect your performance in subsequent periods. Your parent company has committed to remain in this market for all 5 periods. However, your parent company expects you to maximize profits in each period.

You should come to the experiment session with your first set of prices. The prices should be specified in whole dollars only (no cents). Once you have

PRICING SHEET					
FIRM:_____				MARKET:_____	
	Period 1	Period 2	Period 3	Period 4	Period 5
LT—Price					
MT—Price					

decided on prices, enter the prices on the pricing sheet above and submit it to the instructor. The instructor will determine the quantities sold for each firm and return the pricing sheet to you with a market report (shown below) containing the following information: what each firm sold, what prices each firm charged, and what the actual net income was for each firm. Then, you will need to decide on prices for the next period.

	MARKET REPORT				
MARKET:_____			PRICE:_____		
	Lightweight Boots		Mountaineering Boots		
Firm	Price	Quantity	Price	Quantity	Net Income

Prior to the experiment session, your team should spend 2 to 3 hours understanding the cost and demand structure and thinking about how to set prices. You should also devise a strategy to adjust prices, if necessary, based on what you observe about your competitors' decisions and about your own and your competitors's performance in each period. Remember the purpose of this experiment is to learn about pricing in a competitive setting.

After participating in the experiment you are required to prepare a report of no more than 4 double-spaced pages that describes how you determined your costs and pricing rules and how competition affected your pricing. Your report must also include the Statement of Budget versus Actual in the format shown below, together with detailed calculations of the costs of your two products.

STATEMENT OF BUDGET VERSUS ACTUAL						
FIRM:_____	MARKET:_____					
	Period 1	Period 2	Period 3	Period 4	Period 5	Total
Number of LT sold						
Price—LT						
Revenues—LT						
Number of MT sold						
Price—MT						
Revenues—MT						
Total revenues						
Estimated costs—LT						
Estimated costs—MT						
Total costs						
Estimated net income						
Actual net income						
Variance between actual and estimated net income						

PROCESS AND ACTIVITY DECISIONS

LEARNING OBJECTIVES

This chapter will introduce you to:

1. the reasons that sunk costs are not relevant costs
2. the analysis required to decide whether to make or buy components for a product
3. the way in which qualitative factors influence the quantitative analysis of such decisions
4. the reasons that reductions in inventories, especially work-in-process inventories, and reduction in production cycle time result in cost savings
5. the way that improvements in production yields and reductions in rework and defect rates result in cost savings

CHAPTER 9

■ Jorgenson Jewelry Products

"We spent almost $300,000 last year to train our workers to improve production yields and to provide shop floor performance information to them so that they could learn what actions would result in higher yields. But I have yet to see how much this expenditure has improved our bottom line," said Diane Jorgenson, owner and chief executive officer of Jorgenson Jewelry Products Company. "Paul, I would like you to prepare a report quantifying the benefits from our *continuous quality improvement program*," she told Paul Peterson, who had joined Jorgenson Jewelry Products Company 2 months earlier as its controller. The continuous quality improvement program at Jorgenson involved worker training in statistical quality control procedures and investing in a shop floor performance reporting system to help workers identify opportunities to improve the production processes.

Jorgenson Jewelry Products was a relatively new entrant in the market for college and high school commemorative rings. Because of the high quality of its product, it had captured a 5% market share and held it despite increasing competition in the industry. To maintain the high level of quality required by its customers, Jorgenson had instituted strict inspection procedures.

Because of the high level of seasonality in demand and production orders, there was a high turnover in Jorgenson's work force, which resulted in production of many defective rings that were rejected when inspected. Rework—production activities required to bring defective units up to minimum quality standards—was necessary to correct the defects in the rings to meet the high quality standards maintained for all Jorgenson products.

The company had a continuous quality improvement program with the objective of reducing the need for rework. Accomplishing this goal required training the workers to exercise greater accuracy in the mold-making, casting, coloring, polishing, and stone-setting operations.

(Courtesy Jostens)

Paul checked the weekly rework reports prepared by the plant production manager. Rework was classified as major or minor. Major rework required scrapping the ring. The material content of the ring, however, was almost fully recovered as the scrapped ring was melted along with purchased metal and cast as a new ring. Minor repairs were performed in a separate rework area to correct minor defects in coloring, polishing, or stone setting.

Paul plotted a graph of major and minor rework rates over time. (See Exhibit 9–1.) It was evident that the major rework rate had declined by almost 1% (from 5.8% down to 4.9%) over the past 2 years, while the minor rework rate had shown a more dramatic decrease of about 3%, down from 13.6% to 10.4% within the last year.

Paul had read several articles recently that argued that an improvement in production yield rates also should improve production cycle time and, consequently, decrease the amount of work-in-process inventory. (**Production cycle time** is the time elapsed between the receipt of raw materials and the shipment of finished product.) On checking the weekly production and inventory reports, he found that average production cycle time had, indeed, decreased from 16.4 days to 11.9 days, and the work-in-process inventory also had declined correspondingly from an average of $1,774,000 down to $1,218,000 in the current year. Paul was not sure, however, what impact all these improvements in production had on the company's profits. He decided to check recent issues of professional journals in accounting to see if they could provide any guidance in translating the production gains into their monetary equivalents.

Production cycle time
Time elapsed beginning with the receipt of raw materials and ending with the shipment of the final product.

EVALUATION OF MONETARY IMPLICATIONS

Management accountants are often called on to make such evaluations of the monetary implications of decisions so that managers can make the appropriate tradeoffs between the costs and benefits resulting from different alterna-

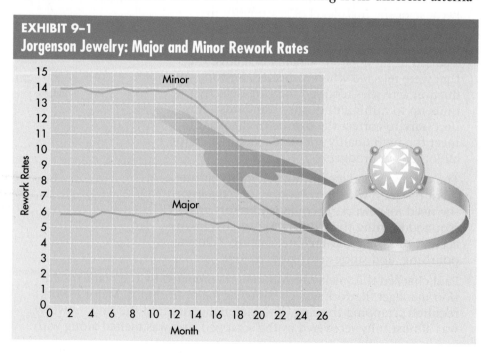

EXHIBIT 9–1
Jorgenson Jewelry: Major and Minor Rework Rates

tives. Such information is required for decisions ranging from buying product components from outside subcontractors instead of making them in-house, to reconfiguring the plant layout to improve production flows. Information on the benefits of inventory reduction, for instance, is useful for the evaluation of continuous quality improvement and just-in-time programs, which result in cutbacks in the levels of work-in-process and other inventory. Different types of cost and other financial information are required to assist in the evaluation of different decisions affecting an organization's activities and processes. In this chapter, we discuss how to develop the information necessary to evaluate these managerial decisions.

SUNK COSTS ARE NOT RELEVANT

In evaluating different alternatives, it is useful to concentrate on only those costs and revenues that differ across different alternatives. If some costs remain the same regardless of what alternative is chosen, then those costs are not relevant for the decision because they are not affected by the outcome of the decision. Therefore, instead of diverting attention with irrelevant facts, accounting reports evaluating the decision alternatives focus only on costs and revenues that are *relevant*.

OBJECTIVE 9.1
The reasons that sunk costs are not relevant costs

The costs and revenues that are relevant depend on the decision context and the alternatives available. There is one principle, however, that is applicable in all situations: *sunk costs are not relevant costs.*

Sunk costs are costs of resources that already have been committed, and, regardless of the decision, these costs cannot be avoided. Because sunk costs cannot be influenced by whatever alternative the manager chooses, these costs are not relevant for evaluation of the alternatives.

Sunk costs
Costs of resources that have already been committed, and, regardless of what decision managers make, that cannot be avoided.

■ Relevant Costs for the Replacement of a Machine

Consider the following situation. Milanca Company purchased a new drilling machine from Syntech Corporation on July 1, 1994, paying $30,000 in cash and financing the remaining $150,000 of the price with a bank loan. The loan requires a monthly payment of $5,200 for the next 36 months.

On July 27, 1994, a sales representative of another supplier of drilling machines approached Milanca Company with a newly designed machine that only recently had been introduced into the market. Oxtrim Machinery Company, the supplier of this new machine, offered special financing arrangements. It agreed to pay $50,000 for the old Syntech machine. The trade-in of the old machine would serve as the down payment of $50,000 required for the new Oxtrim machine. In addition, Oxtrim would require monthly payments of $6,000 for the next 35 months.

The new Oxtrim design relied on an innovative use of computer chips that would reduce the amount of labor required to operate the machine. Milanca estimated that direct labor costs would decrease by $4,400 per month, on the average. In addition, the new machine would decrease maintenance costs by $800 per month because it had fewer moving parts. The greater reliability of the machine also would allow Milanca to reduce materials scrap cost by $1,000 per month.

OBJECTIVE 9.2
The analysis required to decide whether to make or buy components for a product

■ Analysis of Relevant Costs

Should Milanca dispose of the Syntech machine it had just purchased on July 1 and buy the new machine from Oxtrim Corporation? What costs are relevant for this decision?

If Milanca buys the new machine from Oxtrim, it would still be responsible for the monthly payments of $5,200 it committed to when it purchased the Syntech machine on July 1. Therefore, the $30,000 that Milanca paid in cash for the Syntech machine and the $5,200 it has committed to pay each month for the next 36 months are all sunk costs. Milanca already has committed these resources, and, whether it decides to buy the new machine from Oxtrim or not, it cannot avoid any of these costs. *All of these sunk costs are not relevant for the decision.*

What costs, then, are relevant for the evaluation of the decision to purchase the new Oxtrim machine? The 35 monthly payments of $6,000 and the down payment of $50,000 are relevant costs because they depend on Milanca's decision. In addition, labor, materials, and machine maintenance costs are expected to be affected if Milanca acquires the new Oxtrim machine. The expected monthly savings of $4,400 in labor costs, $1,000 in materials costs, and $800 in machine maintenance costs are all relevant. The revenues of $50,000 expected on the trade-in of the old machine are also relevant because the old machine will be disposed of only if Milanca decides to acquire the Oxtrim machine.

Exhibit 9–2 summarizes the relevant costs and revenues of this decision. When comparing the cost increases/cash outflows to cost savings/cash inflows, notice that the down payment required for the new Oxtrim machine is matched by the expected trade-in value of the Syntech machine acquired just a month earlier. Furthermore, the expected savings in labor, materials, and machine maintenance costs each month are higher than the monthly lease payments for the new Oxtrim machine. Thus, it is apparent that Milanca Company will be better off trading in the Syntech machine it acquired just a month earlier and replacing it with the new Oxtrim machine.

EXHIBIT 9–2
Milanca Company: Relevant Costs and Revenues

COST INCREASES AND CASH OUTFLOWS		COST SAVINGS AND CASH INFLOWS	
1. Down payment on the new Oxtrim machine	$50,000	1. Disposal of the old Syntech machine	$50,000

2. Monthly lease payments on the Oxtrim machine	$6,000	2. Monthly cost savings
		    Labor
		    Materials
		    Maintenance
			$4,400
			1,000
			800
			$6,200

■ Comparisons of Cash Flows at Different Points in Time

How would we evaluate this decision if the comparisons of both the immediate cash flows (Exhibit 9–2: down payment versus *disposal value*) and the recurrent cash flows (monthly lease payments versus monthly cost savings) were *not* in the same direction, as at present, favoring the same alternative to purchase the Oxtrim machine?

Cash flows at different points in time cannot be compared directly because of the time value of money that requires interest to be paid on bank deposits or borrowings from financial institutions. The problem of evaluating and aggregating multiperiod implications of managerial decisions will be addressed in the next chapter.

■ Summary of Relevant Costs

The ability to identify the costs and revenues that are relevant for the evaluation of alternatives is important at this stage. Equally important is the ability to recognize that some costs and revenues are not relevant in such evaluations. For the decision problem that Milanca faces, notice that the payments that Milanca already has made on the Syntech machine and the remaining monthly payments that it committed to make when it purchased the Syntech machine are both not relevant for this evaluation because they are sunk costs. None of the alternatives available to Milanca can change what it already has committed to do.

■ Ethical Considerations

The correct decision for Milanca Company on a technical level is to dispose of the machine it had purchased just a month earlier and replace it with a new machine, but not all managers actually would make this "correct" decision when confronted by similar alternatives. Many managers are concerned about their reputations within their organizations for making good decisions. Reversing a major decision made just a month earlier might make it apparent to the organization that the earlier decision was made in error. By persisting with the original course of action, there is hope that the error will never be revealed to others in the organization. On the other side of this ethical dilemma, however, is the respect that the manager would earn for showing the moral courage to admit his or her mistake.

MAKE-OR-BUY DECISIONS

Management accountants are often called on to supply information on relevant costs and relevant revenues to help managers make special one-time decisions. One such decision that many managers have had to make in recent years as they have attempted to reduce costs and increase the competitiveness

PRODUCT LINE	STANDARD FRONT HALOGEN LAMP	STANDARD REAR LAMP	MULTICOLORED REAR LAMP	CURVED SIDE AND REAR LAMP
Dimensions	20" × 6"	14" × 4"	14" × 4"	18" × 4"
Product number	SF120	SR214	MR314	CS418
Product costs per unit:				
Direct materials	$49	$36	$56	$58
Direct labor	25	22	24	28
Unit-related overhead	16	14	18	20
Batch-related overhead	16	10	19	22
Product-sustaining overhead	12	6	14	19
Facility-sustaining overhead	10	8	11	14
Total manufacturing costs	$128	$96	$142	$161
Bids from outside suppliers:				
Lowest	$109	$82	$140	$156
Second-lowest	$116	$88	$147	$164
Annual production (units)	48,500	36,000	6,800	8,700

Make-or-buy decision
Decision either to make a part or component in-house or to purchase it from an outside supplier.

of their products is a *make-or-buy decision*—whether they should manufacture some parts and components for their products in-house, at their own plant, or whether they should subcontract with another company to supply these parts and components. Such **make-or-buy decisions** illustrate how to identify relevant costs and revenues.

Consider the decision faced by Tom O'Brien, production manager at Michigan Motors, Inc. The company manufactures about 15% of the lamps required for its automobiles in its own plant near Dayton, Ohio. As a part of overall corporate efforts to reduce costs, Tom wanted to evaluate the possibility of **outsourcing** all of the lamps, that is, buying them from an outside supplier instead of manufacturing some of them in-house. He obtained firm quotes from several suppliers for the 4 types of lamps now manufactured in-house.

Outsourcing
Purchasing a product, part, or component from an outside supplier instead of manufacturing it in-house.

Exhibit 9–3 displays details of the two lowest quotes from outside suppliers for a representative lamp for each of the four product lines manufactured in-house. Apparently, the best outside bids for all 4 products are lower than the total manufacturing costs. Should Tom accept the outside bids and terminate the in-house production of these products?

■ Avoidable Costs

Avoidable costs
Costs that are eliminated when a part, a product, a product line, or a business segment is discontinued.

To answer this question, we need first to identify what costs are relevant for the decision. The concept of avoidable costs is useful for this purpose. **Avoidable costs** are the costs eliminated when a part, a product, a product line, or a business segment is discontinued.

CONSIDER THIS . . .

Target Costing for Make-or-Buy Decisions at Teijin Seiki Co., Ltd.

Teijin Seiki Co., Ltd., is a diversified manufacturer of machines and machine components for industries such as heavy equipment, textile, aerospace, robotics, and printing. It has plants in several locations around Japan. Its textile machinery division introduced a flexible manufacturing system (FMS) in its main factory with the expectation that it would achieve high quality, low costs, and quick delivery. However, unexpected confusions arose from the product cost calculations.

Consider a part that was shifted to in-house production to take advantage of the FMS. This work takes outside suppliers 20 hours to process but only 10 hours in-house. With an $80 per direct labor hour in-house conversion cost (direct labor plus manufacturing overhead) rate, in-house production cost was estimated as $800 ($80 * 10 hours). But outside suppliers charged only $35 per hour for conversion costs, and therefore, outside costs worked out to $700 ($35 * 20 hours). Production people who introduced FMS were frustrated by this cost analysis that showed that farming the work out was more economical than doing it in-house even though FMS

processing time was one-half that of outside suppliers.

Management considered an alternative—to include only variable costs in the in-house conversion cost rate. However, this proposal was rejected because management felt that in the long term all fixed costs should be recovered in product costs. Makoto Kawada, the general manager in charge of the Office of Technology Development for Teijin Seiki Co., Ltd., and his colleagues worked out an ingenious solution based on target costs: When outside suppliers can make a part at a conversion cost rate of $35 per hour, Teijin Seiki must do in-house work at the same rate to stay competitive. The $35 hourly rate is the *target cost* representing the baseline to be achieved through a cost-reduction program. The conversion cost under this target costing method is $350 ($35 * 10 hours), and the $450 residual ($800 − $350) is a "competitive variance," viewed as nothing less than waste to be eliminated.

Source: Makoto Kawada and Daniel Johnson, "Strategic Management Accounting—Why and How," *Management Accounting* (August 1993), pp. 22–38. Reprinted with permission of Management Accounting.

Here, the alternatives being evaluated are whether each product should be manufactured in-house or whether it should be outsourced. If Tom O'Brien decides to outsource a product, Michigan Motors can avoid certain costs associated with its production. If the standard rear lamp SR214 is purchased directly from the lowest bidder, Michigan Motors would pay $2,952,000 ($82 * 36,000). But it will avoid $1,296,000 of direct material costs ($36 * 36,000). It would also be able to adjust downward its direct labor and supervisory and other resources contributing to unit-related overhead costs. As a result, the company can avoid $792,000 of direct labor costs ($22 * 36,000) and $504,000 of unit-related overhead costs ($14 * 36,000). In addition, with a suitable contraction or redeployment of resources, Michigan Motors also should be able to avoid $360,000 of batch-related ($10 * 36,000) overhead costs and $216,000 of product-sustaining ($6 * 36,000) overhead costs if it decides to outsource product SR214.

To decide whether facility-sustaining overhead costs also are avoidable requires further consideration. Michigan Motors cannot dispose of the part of the plant facility that is used to support the production of SR214 because most of the facility-sustaining overhead costs represent prorated costs of common facilities used to support SR214 production only part of the time. These

Outsourcing Fleet Maintenance

Many companies are now finding it economical to outsource their sales distribution activities. Distribution activities are rarely central to a firm's core competence, and, unlike a proprietary manufacturing process, distribution activities do not need to be controlled in-house. Also, several suppliers are now capable of delivering distribution sources at a world-class standard of performance for such critical success factors as availability, timeliness, flexibility, customer satisfaction, and efficiency.

After a careful study, Home Depot decided to contract with Ryder for its fleet maintenance activities. As a result, Home Depot eliminated all of its fleet department employees. Relevant costs connected to these employees include their salaries, benefits, and training expenses, as well as supplies, parts, and the like required to maintain the vehicles. The only cost Home Depot will continue to incur is depreciation on the maintenance facility, which will be rented out. Rental revenues represent the opportunity costs of the idled facility and are a deduction to the cost of outsourcing. Utilities, maintenance, and other facility costs will be born directly by the new tenant.

The decision to outsource its fleet maintenance activities is a multiyear commitment for Home Depot. Having eliminated its maintenance employees and rented out the facility, Home Depot will find it difficult and costly to reverse its outsourcing decision in case economic conditions change significantly, and outsourcing becomes less attractive.

Source: Ralph Drtina, "The Outsourcing Decision," *Management Accounting,* March 1994, pp. 56–62.

represent indivisible resources, such as those pertaining to building space and machines that cannot be disposed of in parts less than the whole. Therefore, facility-sustaining overhead costs are unavoidable, or fixed, with respect to a decision to outsource the product SR214.

It is sometimes possible to find an alternative use for the part of the facilities made available because of the elimination of a product. Tom considered the possibility of shifting the production of another product line to the Dayton plant. Presently, this product line is manufactured in a rented facility. By transferring its production to the Dayton plant, Michigan Motors could save the facility-sustaining costs for the rental facility by terminating its lease. Such indirect savings in facility-sustaining costs for the organization, therefore, are relevant for the decision to outsource the product SR214 because the cost savings can arise only if SR214 is outsourced. On further inquiry, however, Tom determined that it would be technically infeasible to transfer the manufacture of the other product line to the Dayton plant. For our present example, therefore, we do not need to evaluate the amount of savings in facility-sustaining costs.

To summarize our analysis so far, we note that if the product SR214 is outsourced, $3,168,000 of manufacturing costs ($1,296,000 + $792,000 + $504,000 + $360,000 + $216,000) are avoidable. This is $216,000 more than the total price of $2,952,000 Michigan Motors will have to pay the outside supplier ($3,168,000 − $2,952,000). Therefore, Michigan Motors can expect to increase its profits by $216,000 by outsourcing SR214 instead of producing it in-house.

Alternatively, notice that avoidable costs average $88 per unit ($36 + $22 + $14 + $10 + $6) in comparison with the lowest bid of $82 per unit. Therefore, Michigan Motors stands to gain $6 per unit, or $216,000 overall, by outsourcing SR214 ($6 * 36,000).

■ Qualitative Factors

OBJECTIVE 9.3
The way in which qualitative factors influence the quantitative analysis of such decisions

Are these quantitative estimates of costs and revenues the only relevant considerations before Tom decides to outsource SR214? In fact, for most such decisions, several other more qualitative factors play an important role.

A question naturally arises about the permanence of the lower price. Has this supplier chosen to "low-ball" to get a "foot in the door" so that once Michigan Motors discontinues the production of SR214 at its Dayton plant, the supplier could raise the prices for subsequent orders? The reputation of the selected outside supplier is clearly important in this case. Even more important is the reliability of the supplier in meeting the required quality standards and in making deliveries on time. Poor performance on either of these dimensions can result in considerable cost downstream in the organization, especially if the component outsourced is critical for the final product. Lack of availability of the component or a high reject rate for the component can lead to idling of assembly lines and delays in meeting customer delivery schedules. Therefore, many companies have adopted the practice of certifying a small set of suppliers and providing the **certified suppliers** with incentives, such as quick payments and guaranteed total purchase volumes, to comply with strict quality and delivery schedules.

In many industries, technological innovation is an important determinant of competitive advantage. For example, Teijin Electronics Corporation has identified several different technologies as being critical for its businesses in the next 20 years. It relies on certified suppliers for many of the components for its products, but it has a corporate policy to produce in-house all components requiring a technology on its critical list. The purpose behind this policy is to provide an opportunity to its research and development staff to experiment, learn, innovate, and implement these technologies in-house and to ensure that it retains control over innovations that take place in these critical areas.

REDUCTION IN CYCLE TIME AND INVENTORY

Treadwell Electric Corporation is a leader in the manufacture of small electrical appliances for household and industrial use. It produces a variety of electrical valve controls at its plant in Monroeville, Pennsylvania. Until recently, the plant was organized into 5 production departments: casting, machining, assembly, inspection, and packing. Now the plant layout has been reorganized to streamline production flows and to enable cellular manufacturing. **Cellular manufacturing** refers to the organization of the plant into a number of cells so that within each cell, all machines required to manufacture a group of similar products are arranged sequentially in close proximity to each other.

The plant manufactures 128 different products that have been grouped into 8 product lines for accounting purposes based on common product features and production processes. The 128 products followed a similar sequence of steps in the manufacturing process under the old plant layout. See Exhibit 9–4.

Panels for valve controls were manufactured in large batches in the casting department and then stored in a large work-in-process storage area located near the machining department, where they remained until the lathes and drilling machines were free to work on them. The machined panels were stored until requisitioned for assembly. Switches and other components received from outside suppliers were assembled onto each panel. Another storage area located near the assembly department was used for work in

Cellular manufacturing
Organization of the plant into a number of cells so that within each cell, all machines required to manufacture a group of similar products are arranged sequentially in close proximity to each other.

OBJECTIVE 9.4
The reasons that reduction in inventories, especially work-in-process inventories, and reduction in production cycle time result in cost savings.

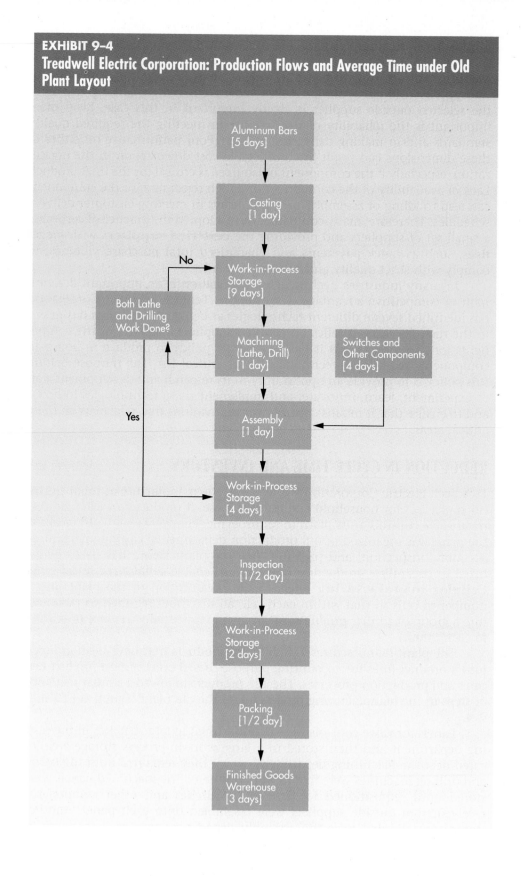

EXHIBIT 9–4
Treadwell Electric Corporation: Production Flows and Average Time under Old Plant Layout

Aluminum Bars
[5 days]

Casting
[1 day]

Work-in-Process Storage
[9 days]

Both Lathe and Drilling Work Done?

No

Machining (Lathe, Drill)
[1 day]

Switches and Other Components
[4 days]

Yes

Assembly
[1 day]

Work-in-Process Storage
[4 days]

Inspection
[1/2 day]

Work-in-Process Storage
[2 days]

Packing
[1/2 day]

Finished Goods Warehouse
[3 days]

process awaiting inspection or packing. All assembled valve control panels were inspected and then packed. Packed valve control panels were stored in the finished goods warehouse until they were shipped to distributors and other customers.

Notice that work-in-process inventory is stored for a long time and at several times in the production process awaiting the beginning of the next stage. As mentioned previously, *production cycle time* is measured as the time from the receipt of the raw materials from the supplier to the delivery of the finished goods to the distributors and customers. This required 27 days (5 + 1 + 9 + 1 + 1 + 4 + $^1/_2$ + 2 + $^1/_2$ + 3) under the old plant layout. The 4 days that switches and other components are kept as inventory are not added to the production cycle time because the time they spend in inventory represents parallel time with other production activities, such as work-in-process storage and machining, occurring at the same time. Therefore, it does not prolong the time for the total production activity in the plant.

You also will notice that of the 27 days required for the production cycle, only 4 days (1 + 1 + 1 + $^1/_2$ + $^1/_2$) are spent on actual manufacturing activity, and the amount of time materials spend in inventory can be as many as 23 days. These time requirements at the Treadwell plant are representative of many other plants that manufacture components and products from basic metals.

■ Cellular Manufacturing Reorganization

A primary objective of the reorganization of the plant layout was to reduce the production cycle time. Thus, the plant was reorganized into 8 manufacturing cells (corresponding to the 8 product lines), in addition to the casting department. Each cell focused on the manufacture of similar products belonging to the same product line.

Exhibit 9–5 depicts the production flows under the new plant layout. While the casting department remains a separate department, the other 4 operations—machining, assembly, inspection, and packing—are now located in close proximity of one another in manufacturing cells. Aluminum panels received from the casting department are lathe machined, drilled, and assembled in the manufacturing cells. Workers in the cells are also responsible for inspection and packing operations.

Concurrent with the change in the plant layout is a transition toward just-in-time production. No work-in-process inventories are required between the various stages of operations in the manufacturing cells because panel production flows immediately from lathe to drilling to assembly to inspection to packing operations. There is no waiting between operations because production is pulled from one stage to the next based on orders for the finished product.

On comparing Exhibits 9–4 and 9–5, notice that Treadwell Electric Corporation did not reduce the amount of time spent on actual manufacturing operations when it changed the plant layout. The time spent on manufacturing operations, 4 days (1 + 3) after the change is the same number (1 + 1 + 1 + $^1/_2$ + $^1/_2$) as before the change. The production cycle time, how-

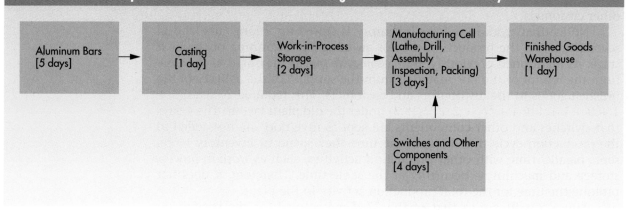

Aluminum Bars [5 days] → Casting [1 day] → Work-in-Process Storage [2 days] → Manufacturing Cell (Lathe, Drill, Assembly Inspection, Packing) [3 days] → Finished Goods Warehouse [1 day]

Switches and Other Components [4 days] →

ever, is reduced substantially from 27 days to only 12 days, a reduction of 56% $\left(\frac{27 - 12}{27} * 100\%\right)$ due to eliminating the need for work-in-process inventory between many of the manufacturing operations.

■ Analysis of Relevant Costs and Benefits: Treadwell Electric

Has this change helped improve the profitability of the Monroeville plant? Karen Leonard, the Monroeville plant controller, identified the following costs associated with the implementation of the changes in the plant layout:

Moving machines and reinstallation	$ 600,000
Training workers for cellular manufacturing	400,000
	$1,000,000

These employees are part of a manufacturing, or work, cell at McDonnell Douglas. The manufacturing cell groups together employees with different skills and the different types of equipment needed to make a specific group of products. These employees used to be separated by department lines. The cell employees—natural work group—undertake all the problem-solving and decision-making activities related to the parts they make. *(Courtesy McDonnell Douglas Helicopter)*

Karen also identified 2 types of benefits resulting from the plant reorganization: (1) increase in sales because of the decrease in production cycle time and (2) reduction in inventory-related costs because of the decrease in work-in-process inventory.

Karen interviewed several production and sales managers to assess the extent of these benefits. She began with Sam Nichols, a senior sales manager with 17 years of experience at Treadwell.

Karen Leonard: Has the reduction in production cycle time helped increase sales?

Sam Nichols: Yes, we have been able to win over many customers from our competitors because we can now quote a much shorter delivery lead time to them. In fact, I believe we also have been able to retain some of our own customers because we have cut our delivery lead time.

We commissioned a market research study to ascertain the impact that reduction in delivery lead time has had on our sales. Based on this study, our best estimate is that an increase of $880,000 in sales this year can be attributed to the change in our production cycle time. Details of estimated sales increases for individual products are provided in this study. I think you'll find it interesting.

Karen next turned to her assistant, Mark Lester, to collect the information necessary to assess the impact of the sales increase on the Treadwell profits. Karen asked Mark to determine the contribution margin for the Monroeville plant's products. Mark returned the next day with several detailed cost accounting reports.

Mark Lester: I've prepared a detailed analysis of the incremental costs for all our products. Here is a summary that gives the totals for all 128 products. [See Exhibit 9–6].

I began with the estimate of the increase in sales for each of the 128 products. Here is an example for Product TL32. [See Exhibit 9–7.] I multiplied the 800-unit sales increase by the direct materials cost of $7 per unit, direct labor cost of $4 per unit, and unit-related overhead of $3 per unit. I also deter-

EXHIBIT 9–6
Treadwell Electric Company
Impact of Increase in Sales on Profits

Increase in sales revenues		$880,000
Increase in costs		
Direct materials	$245,000	
Direct labor	140,000	
Unit-related overhead	108,000	
Batch-related overhead	86,000	$579,000
Net increase in profits		$301,000

mined that 8 additional batches are required for the increased production by using the fact that TL32 is manufactured in batch size of 100 units (8 = 800/100).

I decided that none of the product-sustaining or facility-sustaining overhead will increase because we haven't added any new products, and we haven't increased the plant area or added to plant machinery. The $10,000 increase in profit is obtained by calculating the difference between the increase in sales revenue ($23,200) and the increase in costs ($13,200). The summary [in Exhibit 9–6] displays the totals of similar revenue and cost numbers across all of our 128 products.

Karen Leonard: Thanks, Mark, for all your effort. I see that our best estimate is that the increase in sales because of the lower production cycle time has led to an overall increase of $301,000 in profit this year.

Karen next met with Peter Stone, production and inventory manager at the Monroeville plant, to find out how the reduction in the level of work-in-process inventory may have affected the consumption of support activity resources.

Karen Leonard: Has the change in the plant layout led to changes in the handling and storage of work-in-process inventory?

Peter Stone: Yes, there have been many changes. We do not need a materials handling crew to move work-in-process inventory from lathes to drilling machines to storage areas on the shop floor. Moreover, we do not need to move and store work-in-process inventory between the assembly, inspection, and packing stages either. We did not retrench these workers right away, but as work patterns stabilized a few weeks after the change in the plant layout, we reduced our materials handling crew from 14 to only 8 workers.

Karen Leonard: Were there any other changes in the work load of people performing these support activities?

Peter Stone: Well, with an almost 70% reduction in work-in-process inventory (from $2,270,000 down to $690,000), we also had a corresponding decrease in inventory-related transactions. We did not require as much recordkeeping for movement of materials in and out of storage. We expect to be able to reduce our shop floor stores staff also by about 70%, from 4 to only 1 worker. So far we have reassigned only 1 worker, but 2 more will be reassigned to other production-related tasks next week.

Karen Leonard: We have so far talked about personnel. Were any other resources freed up as a result of the reduction in work-in-process inventory?

Peter Stone: Yes, we need only one-third of the storage space we used earlier for work-in-process inventory. The extra space is idle at present, however, because we haven't yet found an alternative use for it. I don't believe there was any proposal to use that extra space in the 3-year facilities plan we prepared last month.

Karen Leonard: So you don't expect any benefit to arise from the availability of the extra storage space.

Peter Stone: Yes, that is right. But there is an additional item that you shouldn't forget. When some panels are produced in large batches and stored awaiting the next stage of processing, we always find that some of them get damaged in handling, and, at times, some of them become obsolete because the customer no longer requires them. The change to just-in-time production in the manufacturing cells and the elimination of much of our work-in-process inventory have resulted in a reduction in materials scrap and obsolescence cost from 0.32% of materials cost to only 0.12%.

Karen Leonard: Thank you. The information you have provided will be very useful to us in evaluating the impact of the change in the plant layout.

Karen and Mark sat down in Karen's office to analyze the information that they had collected so far. Facility-sustaining costs pertaining to plant space included building depreciation, insurance, heating, lighting, janitorial services, building upkeep, and maintenance. The overhead rate for this activity was $108 per square foot. However, Karen and Mark decided that the costs associated with the extra storage space was sunk cost and that no cost savings resulted when this space was freed up.

A check of the materials handling activity costs indicated that the annual wages of workers in this grade averaged $21,000, with 35% more, or $7,350 ($21,000 * 0.35), added to this for fringe benefits. The total materials handling cost savings, therefore, were $170,100 ($28,350 * 6), because the crew size was reduced by 6 workers. In a similar fashion, Mark determined that the annual wages of stores personnel averaged $26,400. With a 35% fringe benefit rate and an expected reduction of 3 workers, the total annual cost savings were $106,920 ($26,400 * 1.35 * 3).

An important cost is the cost to finance the funds tied up in inventories. Karen estimated the interest rate on bank loans to finance the investment in inventories to be 12% per year. Because the work-in-process inventory is reduced by $1,580,000 ($2,270,000 − $690,000), the cost of their financing is reduced correspondingly by $189,600 ($1,580,000 * 0.12).

Finally, Ken determined that the total annual materials cost was $31,000,000. If the rate of materials, scrap and obsolescence had remained at the earlier 0.32% of materials cost, this loss would have been $99,200 ($31,000,000 * 0.0032). But because of the reduction in the rate to 0.12%, the cost of materials scrap and obsolescence is reduced to only $37,200 ($31,000,000 * 0.0012), a cost saving of $62,000 ($99,200 − $37,200).

■ Summary of Costs and Benefits

Karen then summarized the information on cost savings resulting from the change in the plant layout (Exhibit 9–8).

She estimated annual benefits to be $829,620. In comparison, the one-time costs of implementing the change were only $1,000,000. If benefits from the changed layout continue to accrue at the same rate for at least the next 3 months, the total benefits ($1,037,025 = $829,620 * 15/12) will exceed the amount that Treadwell invested in this project. In other words, the investment will be paid off in only 1.25 years with the benefits resulting from the investment. We shall discuss the concept of payoff period in more detail in the next chapter.

The Treadwell case study introduced several important concepts. We have identified several different ways in which new manufacturing practices can improve a plant's profitability. In particular, we have seen that a principal inventory-related cost is that of financing the funds tied up in inventory. It is important to consider this cost, although financing costs are often not emphasized in many traditional cost accounting systems. Streamlining manufacturing processes also reduces the demand placed on many support activity resources. Activity analysis, therefore, is useful for assessing the potential cost savings.

Many of the new manufacturing practices are designed to promote continuous improvement in manufacturing performance by enabling workers to learn and innovate better methods. Change to a manufacturing cell layout often results in improvements in production yield rates and, consequently,

EXHIBIT 9–8
Treadwell Electric Corporation: Annual Benefits Resulting from the Change in Plant Layout

Contribution from increased sales			
Sales increase	(Exhibit 9–6)	$880,000	
Incremental manufacturing costs	(Exhibit 9–6)	(579,000)	$301,000
Cost savings from work-in-process inventory reduction			
Cost of financing investment in work-in-process inventory		$189,600	
Cost of materials handling labor		170,100	
Cost of stores labor		106,920	
Cost of materials scrap and obsolescence		62,000	$528,620
Total benefits			$829,620

CONSIDER THIS . . .

Quest for Quality: Working on Rework

Tennant Company, based in Golden Valley, Minnesota, is a worldwide leader in the manufacture of industrial sweeper and scrubber machines. It is also recognized as a leader in the quality improvement programs being adopted increasingly by U.S. manufacturers.

In planning its manufacturing capacity over a decade ago, Tennant management counted 20 rework mechanics in manufacturing, one rework person in sheet metal, and a rework station in welding, plus a touch-up paint booth in assembly. Rework tied up almost 10,000 square feet of manufacturing floor space. Why such a large amount? It was the custom for every assembled sweeper and scrubber machine to routinely go through rework. It was not uncommon to have 50 to 100 machines waiting in line to be checked and to have defective parts replaced. If this continued, the managers realized, they would soon need a football field for the waiting machines, and there would be no space left for manufacturing at current plants.

At about that time, the quality guru, Phil Cosby, famous for his claim that "quality is free," visited the Tennant Company. "Build the machines right *the first time*," he advised. "That will cut the need for

rework machines in half." Thus began Tennant Company's quest for quality.

Tom Peters, the well-known management consultant and author of *In Search of Excellence*, describes Tennant's success story as "one of passionate commitment, persistence, wholesale people involvement—and sound management systems and problem-solving techniques. The results so far . . . are compelling. Manufacturing rework dropped from 33,000 hours to 4,800 hours between 1980 and 1988." Rework mechanics were reassigned to assembly lines, the final test area, or engineering. Their experience was valuable in solving quality-related problems and in reducing first-pass defect rates by over 50%. Almost 8,000 square feet of floor space was freed for production. Also, production cycle time was reduced, with the number of orders shipped within 24 hours increasing from 47% to 75%.

The cost of quality, estimated at 17% of sales in 1980, dropped to 66% by 1988. Interestingly, prevention-related activities comprised only 15% of the cost of quality in 1980, but 44% in 1988.

Source: R. L. Hale, D. R. Hoelscher, and R. E. Kowak, Quest for Quality, Tennant Company, 1989.

improvements in overall plant productivity. Although the managers at Treadwell did not consider this possibility, it is often the most important benefit from the implementation of new manufacturing practices. We shall discuss in our next case study how we may evaluate the profit impact of gains in production yield.

JORGENSON JEWELRY REVISITED

At the beginning of this chapter, we described the way that Jorgenson Jewelry Products Company had succeeded in decreasing its major rework rate from 5.8% to 4.9%, and its minor rework rate from 13.6% to 10.4%. Major rework required scrapping the ring. Minor rework required correction of coloring, polishing, or stone-setting defects and was usually conducted in a specially designated rework area.

As a result of these improvements in the rework rates, average produc-

OBJECTIVE 9.5
The way that improvements in production yields and reductions in rework and defect rates result in cost savings

tion cycle time was reduced by 4.5 days from 16.4 days to 11.9 days, and average work-in-process inventory was reduced from $1,774,000 to $1,218,000. The task before Paul Peterson, Jorgenson Jewelry Products Company's controller, was to prepare a report for his chief executive officer detailing how these improvements had affected the company's profits.

■ Production Flows

Paul began by obtaining a production flow chart, presented in Exhibit 9–9. Based on customer order specifications, wax molds are prepared and covered in gypsum plaster casting. Sixty of these molds are arranged together on a

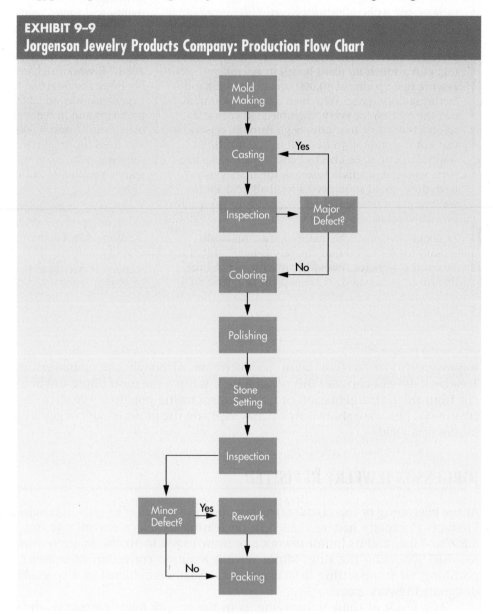

EXHIBIT 9–9
Jorgenson Jewelry Products Company: Production Flow Chart

The laser-beam cutting guide seen projected onto this steel plate in a Bethlehem Steel mill directs the operator of the shear that will cut the plate along its length. The cutting guide reduces rework by ensuring that the cut is made accurately the first time and improves production yield by minimizing the amount of steel waste. *(Courtesy Bethlehem Steel)*

frame that has the appearance of a tree with branches; therefore, production of rings occurs in batches of 60. Then each batch of 60 ring molds is placed in the furnace, and molten precious metal (gold, silver, or platinum) is poured into the casts.

On cooling, the molten metal takes the shape of the wax mold. All rings cast in this fashion are inspected by experienced workers to detect any major defect in casting. Defective rings are rejected and returned to the casting stage for the metal to be melted again for use in other rings. A new wax mold must also be made to fill the original customer order for which the ring casting was rejected.

A series of finishing operations is performed next. The metal casting is colored in appropriately engraved parts as required by the ring design; the ring is polished and semi-precious stones, such as rubies, emeralds, or sapphires, are set into the ring. Each ring is inspected again by experienced workers to detect any minor defects in coloring, polishing, or setting. A separate rework area is set aside for workers responsible for correcting these defects and inspecting the reworked rings to ensure that no defects remain. Rings that pass inspection, either before or after rework, are packed and then await shipment to customers.

■ Effects on Work-in-Process Inventory

Paul next turned his attention to records for work-in process inventory. He already had found that average work-in-process inventory had decreased by $556,000 after the implementation of the quality improvement program. He determined from meetings with production personnel that work-in-process inventory was maintained between each pair of successive process stages because each batch of rings had to await the completion of the work on the preceding batch of rings. Paul could not find any more detailed records to identify change in work-in-process inventory between specific stages of the production process. Work-in-process inventory, however, was known to be influenced directly by the number of major and minor defects. When defect rates were high, inventory of rejected rings would build up, awaiting rework or melting down to recover the metal content. More important, production supervisors in stages following the 2 inspection stages sought to accumulate large inventory of work in process from the preceding stages to enable them to keep busy, even when many rings were rejected. Therefore, production managers attributed the reduction in the work-in-process inventory entirely to improvements in the defect rates.

■ Impact on Production Costs

An important part of Paul's analysis was an assessment of the impact that the improvement in defect rates had on the production costs. Direct material costs included the cost of the metal content and the cost of the semiprecious stone set in the ring. The average cost of the metal in a ring is $168.30 with the current mix and prices of different metals used in rings. Past experience indicated that 0.6% of the metal content was lost, on average, in the melting and casting operations.

Paul also collected information on direct labor, unit-related overhead, and batch-related overhead costs for each stage of the production process. Exhibit 9–10 includes these costs presented on a per-unit (per ring) basis. Unit-related overhead costs include labor supervision, wax, gypsum plaster, coloring and polishing supplies, packing materials, and power costs. Batch-related costs are presented on per-unit basis, assuming that each batch comprises 60 rings. Batch-related costs include materials handling and setup of molds and furnace for casting operations.

Paul excluded product-sustaining and facility-sustaining costs from the analysis. There were no new product introductions or deletions as a consequence of the implementation of the quality improvement program. The installed plant machine capacity was already greater than its maximum use in recent years, and reductions in defect rates did not change the fact that there was surplus capacity at the Jorgenson plant.

EXHIBIT 9–10
Jorgenson Jewelry Products Company: Incremental Conversion Costs per Unit (Ring) by Production Stage

	MOLD MAKING AND CASTING	FIRST INSPECTION	COLORING, POLISHING, AND SETTING	SECOND INSPECTION	PACKING
Direct labor (including fringe benefits)	$14	$10	$20	$8	$6
Unit-related overhead	6	2	12	2	2
Batch-related overhead	8	1	2	1	8
	$28	$13	$34	$11	$16

This employee was part of an employee involvement group at a Ford Motor Corporation truck plant that discovered that paint marks and smudges were being caused by paint-booth gloves that were too large and cumbersome. This discovery led to the design and use of the less cumbersome gloves, which reduced the rework cost associated with repainting the damaged parts. *(Courtesy Ford Motor Corporation)*

■ Cost of Rework

What is the cost of a major defect detected during the first inspection following the casting stage? A ring with a major defect cannot be processed further. It is sent back to the casting stage to recover its metal content, and a new wax ring mold is required. Therefore, all of the incremental conversion costs already incurred on such a ring are wasted, and all operations must be repeated, therefore incurring the same incremental conversion costs again. There is also an additional cost corresponding to the 0.6% of the metal that is lost, on average, in the melting and casting operations. Therefore, Paul summarized the costs associated with the correction of a major defect, as displayed in Exhibit 9–11, and found that they cost $42 per ring.

EXHIBIT 9–11
Jorgenson Jewelry Products Company:
Cost per Unit (Ring) for the Correction of a Major Defect

	AMOUNT
Conversion costs for molds and casting	
Direct labor	$14
Unit-related overhead	6
Batch-related overhead	8
Costs of first inspection	
Direct labor	10
Unit-related overhead	2
Batch-related overhead	1
Cost of materials lost*	1
	$42

*Cost of materials lost = $168.30 * 0.006 = $1.0098.

Unit- and batch-related overhead costs are included for this estimation because more of these costs would be incurred when all of the mold-making, casting, and first inspection operations are repeated to rectify the major defect. But product- and facility-sustaining overhead costs would not increase simply because production operations are repeated. Therefore, they are not relevant for this analysis. If the plant and machine capacity already were fully utilized and there was no slack to accommodate these repeated operations, however, it would have been necessary to consider the incremental costs of acquiring the additional capacity.

Paul found it somewhat easier to assess the costs of correcting minor defects, which are detected at the second inspection but do not require the rejection of the entire ring. Instead, such minor defects require additional rework operations. Therefore, the incremental costs of correcting minor defects are the rework costs. Paul determined that the cost of rework per ring comprised the following:

Direct rework labor	$24
Unit-related overhead	12
	$36

Because each ring is reworked independently of the batch in which it was produced, Paul determined that there were no batch-related overhead costs. Product- and facility-sustaining overhead costs also were not relevant for reasons discussed earlier in the case of major defects.

Jorgenson manufactures and sells 180,000 rings each year. Before implementation of the quality improvement program, on average, 10,440 major defects (180,000 * 0.058) and 24,480 minor defects (180,000 * 0.136) occurred each year. Now, only 8,820 major defects (180,000 * 0.049) and 18,720 minor defects (180,000 * 0.104) occur, representing a reduction of 1,620 and 5,760 defects, respectively. Therefore, the savings in the cost of correcting major and minor defects because of the quality improvement are $68,040 for major rework ($42 * 1,620) and $207,360 for minor rework ($36 * 5,760).

■ Cost of Carrying Work-in-Process Inventory

Paul turned next to the problem of evaluating the cost savings resulting from the reduction in the work-in-process inventory. Interest rates on bank loans to finance the investment in inventories averages 12.5% per year. With a reduction of $556,000 in work-in-process inventory ($1,774,000 – $1,218,000), the cost of financing also decreases by $69,500 ($556,000 * 0.125).

In addition, Paul estimated that batch-related overhead costs for the various production stages included a total cost of $30 per batch (of 60 rings) that pertained to activities such as work-in-process, inventory handling and storage. With the 31.3% reduction in work-in-process inventory (100 * 556,000/1,774,000), Paul expected these related costs also to decrease by about 30%, or equivalently by about $9 per batch ($30 * 0.30). With an annual production of 180,000 rings in 3,000 batches (180,000/60), Paul expected a decrease of $27,000 in the costs of work-in-process inventory handling and storage costs ($9 * 3,000). As in the case of Treadwell Electric Corporation,

Customer complaints that paper rolls supplied by Consolidated Papers were breaking in their printing presses led a group of employees at Consolidated Papers to identify the cause. The employees discovered that the breakage occurred because of slight tears at the edges of the paper that were created when the paper was being trimmed to width during its production. The solution was to design a simple device that held the paper tightly while it was being slit. The cost of this investigation and the device designed to eliminate the problem was justified on the grounds that failing to solve the problem would have cost the company far more in lost sales. *(Courtesy Consolidated Papers, Inc.)*

however, Paul's estimate of $27,000 represents the reduction in the *demand* for these activities because of the reduction in work-in-process inventory. Over time, these costs *should* decrease by this amount. But for the reduction to actually occur, the plant management must identify the personnel and other resources it has committed presently to this activity and take action to eliminate the resources that are not required because of the reduction in the demand for them.

■ Benefits from Increased Sales

Paul finally decided to evaluate whether the reduction in the production cycle time had resulted in any gains in sales. For this purpose, he met with the marketing manager, Chris Yardley. Chris pointed out to Paul that annual sales had remained stable at around 180,000 rings for the past 3 years. However, he believed that the improvement in the production cycle time did have an impact on sales. Because of the increased competition in the athletic events' commemorative rings segment of the market, Chris had expected to

EXHIBIT 9-12
Jorgenson Jewel Products Company:
Incremental Costs of Production per Ring

	COST PER RING
Direct materials:	
Metal	$168
Stone	62
Incremental conversion costs:	
Molds, casting	28
First inspection	13
Coloring, polishing, setting	34
Second inspection	11
Packing	16
Prorated rework costs	
Major defects[a]	2
Minor defects[b]	4
Total incremental costs	$338
Average net sales price	$400
Contribution margin per ring	$62

$$^a\ \frac{4.9}{100 - 4.9} * \$42 = \$2.16.$$

$$^b\ \frac{10.4}{100 - 10.4} * \$36 = \$4.18.$$

lose about 2,000 rings' worth of sales. But the reduction of 4.5 days in the production cycle time had permitted him to respond more aggressively to market demand by manufacturing the rings with a much shorter lead time to be available in time for the athletic events. As a result, Jorgenson had not lost any market share in this market segment. Chris thus attributed the maintenance of the sale of about 2,000 rings to the reduction in the production cycle time.

Paul determined that the average net selling price (net of sales commission and shipping costs) for these 2,000 rings was $400. Exhibit 9–12 presents his list of the incremental costs for the production of these rings.

You will notice in Exhibit 9–12 that rework costs are prorated over the good production. For instance, incremental costs for major rework are $42 for each ring that requires rework. For every 1,000 rings, an average of 49 rings (1,000 * 4.9%) now requires major rework. Therefore, we obtain 951 good rings (1,000 − 49). The total incremental major rework cost for 49 rings is $2,058 ($42 * 49) which is borne by the 951 good rings at the rate of $2.16 ($2,058/951) per good ring.

The contribution margin is estimated to be $62 per ring, or $124,000 in total for the 2,000 rings ($62 * 2,000). Without the quality improvement program and the consequent reduction in cycle time, this contribution from sales would have been lost. This is a benefit attributable to the program being evaluated, like the contribution margin on the sales increase in our case study of the plant layout changes at Treadwell Electric Corporation.

■ Summary of Costs and Benefits

Exhibit 9–13 displays Paul's summary of the benefits from the quality improvement program. Total annual benefits of $495,900 are apparently much greater than the costs of $298,800 spent on worker training and shop floor reporting last year to support the program.

A SUMMARY EXAMPLE

Let's wrap up the chapter by working through a numerical problem. Telemark Corporation is a major producer of telephone products. The corporation is considering introducing a videophone that will be targeted for the business market. The proposed price is $1,000 per unit. The following cost information is based on the expected annual sales level of 60,000 units for the new product:

Direct material cost	$18,000,000
Direct labor costs	12,000,000
Variable manufacturing overhead	6,000,000
Fixed manufacturing overhead	10,000,000

The average inventory levels for the videophone are estimated to be as follows:

Direct material	2 months of production
Work-in-process (100% complete for materials and 50% for labor and variable manufacturing overhead)	2 months of production
Finished goods	1 month of production

Annual inventory carrying costs, not included in these variable costs, are estimated to be 10%. In addition, the marketing manager estimates that the total sales revenue of the existing products will be reduced by $12,000,000 once the videophone is on the market. The average contribution margin ratio for the existing products is 30%.

  (a) Compute the relevant costs (revenues) for the videophone.
  (b) Should Telemark introduce the new product?
  (c) Determine the breakeven point in units for the videophone.

The following is the solution to this problem.

  (a)

Selling price per unit		$1,000
Variable cost per unit		
Direct material	($18,000,000/60,000)	(300)
Direct labor	($12,000,000/60,000)	(200)
Overhead	($6,000,000/60,000)	(100)
		$400

Contribution margin per unit
Inventory carrying value
  Direct material: $300 * 60,000 * (2/12) = $3,000,000
  Work in process: [$300 + (200 + 100) * 50%] * 60,000 * (2/12)
  = $4,500,000
  Finished goods: [$300 + 200 + 100] * 60,000 * (1/12) = $3,000,000
Inventory carrying cost: ($3,000,000 + $4,500,000 + $3,000,000) * 10%
$1,050,000

Relevant costs
  Increase in contribution margin for the sale of the videophone: $400 * 60,000 = $24,000,000
  Decrease in contribution margin from cannibalization of existing sales: $12,000,000 * 30% = $3,600,000
  Additional inventory carrying costs: $1,050,000
  Increase in fixed manufacturing overhead: $10,000,000
  (b) Increase in Telemark's operating profit
    = $24,000,000 − 3,600,000 − 1,050,000 − 10,000,000
    = $9,350,000
    Therefore, Telemark should introduce the videophone.
  (c) Let X be the breakeven point in units

$$\$400 * X = \$10,000,000 + \$3,600,000$$
$$+ [\$300 * X * (2/12) + 450 * X * (2/12) + \$600 * X * (1/12)] * 0.1$$
$$\$382.5X = \$13,000,000$$
$$X = 35,556 \text{ units.}$$

SUMMARY

An important component of the management accountant's responsibility is to evaluate the impact of managerial decisions and actions that affect the organization's activities and processes. To support decision making, different alternatives available to managers must be identified, and the way that costs and revenues differ across alternative actions must be evaluated. Relevant costs (and revenues) are those costs (and revenues) that differ across the alternative choices available to managers. As a general rule, sunk costs are not relevant costs.

Management accountants also must evaluate the financial impact of activity and process decisions that already have been implemented. Such evaluations help managers decide whether to persist with the selected course of action or to chart a new path. Confirmation of the success or failure of such implemented actions also helps managers decide whether to take similar actions in other parts of the organization where they have not yet been implemented. Detailed evaluations of implemented actions also may shed light on ways to increase the benefits derived from them.

We have examined 2 implementations of new manufacturing practices in this chapter. The first was a change in the plant layout accompanied by a shift to cellular manufacturing and just-in-time production. The second was a quality improvement program that led to a reduction in the defect rate. In both cases, we saw that it was important to evaluate the cost of financing the investment in work-in-process inventory, the cost of support activities of handling and storing work-in-process inventory, the benefits from improvements in production yield rates, and the contribution margins on sales gains attributed to improvement in production cycle time.

KEY TERM LIST

Avoidable costs, p. 372

Cellular manufacturing, p. 375

Certified supplier, p. 375

Make-or-buy decision, p. 372

Outsourcing, p. 372

Production cycle time, p. 368

Sunk costs, p. 369

ASSIGNMENT MATERIAL

QUESTIONS

9–1 Why is it better to focus only on the relevant costs?

9–2 Are sunk costs relevant? Explain.

9–3 Are direct materials and direct labor costs always relevant? Explain with examples.

9–4 When are (1) product-sustaining and (2) facility-sustaining costs relevant? Given examples of each case.

9–5 Why can we not directly compare cash flows at different points in time?

9–6 What behavioral factors may influence some managers to consider sunk costs as being relevant in their decisions?

9–7 Are avoidable costs relevant? Explain.

9–8 What are two examples of costs and decision contexts in which the costs are not relevant for a short-term context but are relevant for a long-term context?

9–9 Why are facility-sustaining overhead costs often not relevant for make-or-buy decisions? Give an example when facility-sustaining overhead costs *are* relevant for a make-or-buy decision.

9–10 What qualitative considerations are relevant in a make-or-buy decision?

9–11 What are the opportunity costs that are relevant in a make-or-buy decision?

9–12 What is the difference between cellular manufacturing and just-in-time production?

9–13 What creates the need to maintain work-in-process inventory? Why is work-in-process inventory likely to decrease on the implementation of (a) cellular manufacturing, (b) just-in-time production, and (c) quality improvement programs?

9–14 Why are production cycle time and work-in-process inventory level positively related?

9–15 List 3 types of costs incurred when implementing a cellular manufacturing layout.

9–16 What are 4 types of financial benefits resulting from a shift to cellular manufacturing, just-in-time production, or continuous quality improvements?

9–17 What is the additional cost of replacing 1 unit of a product that is rejected at inspection and must be scrapped?

9–18 What is the additional cost if a unit rejected at inspection can be reworked to meet quality standards by performing some additional operations?

9–19 What costs and revenues are relevant in evaluating the profit impact of an increase in sales?

9–20 "Design an accounting system that routinely reports only relevant costs," advised a management consultant. Is this good advice? Explain.

EXERCISES

9–21 Chad Lundquist's 5-year-old Camaro requires repairs estimated at $4,200 to make it roadworthy again. His friend, Steve Snead, suggested that he should buy a 5-year-old used Chevette instead for $4,200 cash. Steve estimated the following costs for the 2 cars:

	Camaro	Chevette
Acquisition cost	$24,000	$4,200
Repairs	4,200	—
Annual operating costs		
(Gas, maintenance, insurance)	3,000	1,800

REQUIRED:

(a) What costs are relevant and what costs are not relevant for this decision?

(b) What should Chad do?

(c) What quantitative and qualitative factors are relevant for his decision?

9–22 Lumina Company has 10,000 obsolete lamps carried in inventory at a cost of $12 each. They can be sold as they are for $4 each. They can be reworked, however, at a total cost $40,000 and sold for $10 each. Determine whether it is worthwhile to rework these lamps.

9–23 Primosa Company's plant manager is considering buying a new grinding machine to replace an old grinding machine or overhauling the old one to ensure compliance with the plant's high quality standards. The following data are available:

Old grinding machine:	
Original cost	$50,000
Accumulated depreciation	40,000
Annual operating costs	18,000
Current salvage value	4,000
Salvage value at the end of 5 years	–0–
New grinding machine:	
Cost	$70,000
Annual operating costs	13,000
Salvage value at the end of 5 years	–0–
Overhaul of old grinding machine:	
Cost of overhaul	$25,000
Annual operating costs after overhaul	14,000
Salvage value at the end of 5 years	–0–

REQUIRED:

(a) What costs should be considered as sunk costs for this decision?

(b) List all relevant costs and the time at which they are incurred.

(c) What should the plant manager do?

9–24 The assembly division of Heidi Resolution, Inc., is bidding on an order of 1,000 TV sets. The division is very anxious to get this order since it has substantial unused capacity. The variable cost for each TV set is $500 in addition to the cost of the picture tube. The divisional purchasing manager has received 2 bids for the tube. One is from Heidi Resolution's picture tube division. This bid is for $55 per picture tube, although its variable cost is only $36 per tube. The other is from an outside vendor for $51 per unit. Heidi Resolution's picture tube division has sufficient unused capacity for this order.

REQUIRED:

(a) Determine the relevant costs for this order for the assembly division under both internal and external sourcing arrangements.

(b) Determine the relevant costs for this order for Heidi Resolution as a company under each of the sourcing arrangements.

9–25 Gemini Company is considering outsourcing a key component. A reliable supplier has quoted a price of $64.50 per unit. The following costs of the component when manufactured in-house are expressed on a per-unit basis.

Direct materials	$23.40
Direct labor	16.10
Unit-related overhead	14.70
Batch-related overhead	9.80
Product-sustaining overhead	2.20
Facility-sustaining overhead	6.90
	$73.10

REQUIRED:

(a) What assumptions need to be made about the behavior of overhead costs?

(b) Should Gemini Company outsource the component?

(c) What other factors are relevant for this decision?

9–26 Megalin Company is considering reorganizing its plant into manufacturing cells. The following estimates have been prepared to assess the benefits from the change.

	Before the Change	After the Change
Production cycle time	68 days	32 days
Work-in-process inventory	$160,000	$105,000
Total sales	$1,260,000	$1,690,000
Costs as percentage of sales:		
Direct materials	30%	26%
Direct labor	22%	21%
Variable overhead	28%	22%
Fixed overhead	12%	8%

Inventory financing cost is 12% per year. Estimate the total benefits likely to result from the switch to cellular manufacturing operations.

9–27 Vitalis Valves Company manufactures brass valves meeting precise specification standards. All finished valves are inspected before packing and shipping to customers. Rejected valves are returned to the initial production stage, to be melted and recast. As a result of a quality improvement program, the reject rate has decreased from 5.2% to 3.8%. The following unit cost data are available:

	Casting	Finishing	Inspection	Packing	Total
Direct materials	$225	$12	—	$8	$245
Direct labor	84	121	$24	16	245
Variable overhead	122	164	30	20	336
Fixed overhead	63	89	16	10	178
	$494	$386	$70	$54	$1,004

Improvements in reject rates have also led to a decrease in work-in-process inventory from $386,000 to $270,000. Inventory carrying costs are estimated to be 16% per year. Estimate the cost annual savings as a result of the quality improvement, assuming that 10,000 valves are sold each year.

9–28 Jandoe Company manufactures gear model G37 that is used in several of its farm equipment products. Annual production volume of G37 is 20,000 units. Unit costs for G37 follow:

Direct materials costs	$ 60
Direct labor costs	30
Variable overhead costs	25
Fixed overhead costs	15
	$130

Jandoe can also purchase the gear G37 from an outside supplier for $120 per unit. If G37 is outsourced, Jandoe can use the facility where G37 is currently manufactured for production of another gear, model G49. This would save Jandoe $113,000 in facility rental and other costs incurred at present. Should Jandoe make or buy G37?

9–29 Perfect Printers, Inc., is considering replacing its current printing machines with a newer, faster, and more efficient printing technology. The following data have been compiled:

	Existing Machines	New Machines
Original cost	$80,000	$120,000
Annual operating costs	$50,000	$30,000
Remaining useful life	5 years	5 years
Salvage value after 5 years	$5,000	$10,000

The existing machines can be disposed of now for $40,000. Keeping them will cost $20,000 for repair and upgrading. Should Perfect Printers keep the existing printing machines?

9–30 Michigan Motors has manufactured compressor parts at its plant in Pitcairn, Indiana, for the last 18 years. An outside supplier, Cotter Compressor Company, has offered to supply compressor model A238 at a price of $200 per unit. Unit manufacturing costs for A238 are as follows:

Direct materials	$80
Direct labor	55
Unit-related overhead	26
Batch-related overhead	22
Product-sustaining overhead	8
Facility-sustaining overhead	17
	$208

REQUIRED:

(a) Should Cotter Compressor's offer be accepted if the plant is presently operating below capacity?

(b) What is the maximum acceptable purchase price if the plant facilities are fully utilized at present and any additional available capacity can be deployed for the production of other compressors?

PROBLEMS

9–31 To facilitate a move toward JIT production, Manhattan Company is considering a change in its plant layout. The plant controller has been asked to evaluate the costs and benefits of the change in plant layout. After meeting with production and marketing managers, the plant controller has compiled the following estimates:

(1) Machine moving and reinstallation will cost $120,000.

(2) Total sales will increase by 20% to $1,200,000 because of a decrease in production cycle time under the new plant layout. Average contribution margin is 31% of sales.

(3) Inventory-related costs will decrease by 25% because of expected decrease in work-in-process inventory. The annual average carrying value of work-in-process inventory is $200,000 at present. The annual inventory financing cost is 15%.

Should the proposed change in plant layout be implemented? What are the total benefits associated with the change?

9–32 Atlantic Appliance Company manufactures 12,000 units of part AA77 annually. The part is used in the production of one if its principal products. The following unit cost information is available for part AA77.

Direct materials	$12
Direct labor	8
Unit-related overhead	4
Batch-related overhead	5
Product-sustaining overhead	2
Facility-sustaining overhead	2
Allocated corporate overhead	5
	$38

A potential supplier has offered to manufacture this part for Atlantic Appliance for $30 per unit. If Atlantic Appliance outsources the production of part AA77, 50% of batch-related and 80% of product-sustaining activity resources can be reduced, and costs corresponding to those resources will no longer be incurred. Furthermore, the production facility now being used to produce this part can be used for a fast-growing new product line that would otherwise require the use of a neighboring facility at a rental cost of $20,000 per year. Should Atlantic company purchase part AA77 from the outside supplier? What costs are relevant for this decision? What additional factors must be considered?

9–33 Iversen Instruments, Inc., is considering leasing new state-of-the-art machinery at an annual cost of $900,000. The new machinery has a 4-year expected life. It will displace existing machinery, leased 1 year earlier, at an annual lease cost of $490,000 committed for 5 years. Early termination of this lease contract will incur a $280,000 penalty. There are no other fixed costs.

The new machinery is expected to decrease variable product costs from $42 to $32 per unit because of improved materials yield, faster machine speed, and lower direct labor, supervision, materials handling, and quality inspection requirements. The sales price will remain at $56. Improvements in quality, production cycle time, and customer responsiveness are expected to increase annual sales from 36,000 units to 48,000 units.

The variable product costs stated earlier exclude the inventory carrying costs. Because the new machinery is expected to affect inventory levels, the following estimates also are provided. The enhanced speed and accuracy of the new machinery are expected to decrease production cycle time by half and consequently lead to a decrease in work-in-process inventory level from 3 months to just 1.5 months of production. Increased flexibility with these new machines is expected to allow a reduction in finished goods inventory from 2 months of production to just 1 month of production. Improved yield rates and greater machine reliability will enable a reduction in raw materials inventory from 4 months of production to just 1.5 months. Annual inventory carrying cost is 20% of inventory value.

	Old Machine	New Machine
Average per unit cost of raw materials inventory	$12	$11
Average per unit cost of work-in-process inventory	25	20
Average per unit cost of finished goods inventory	38	28
Selling cost per unit sold	4	4
Variable product cost per unit produced	42	32

REQUIRED:

(a) Determine the total value of annual benefits from the new machinery. Include changes in inventory carrying costs.

(b) Should Iversen replace its existing machinery with the new machinery? Present your reasoning with detailed steps identifying relevant costs and revenues.

(c) Discuss whether a manager evaluated on the basis of Iversen's net income will have the incentive to make the right decision as evaluated in (b) above.

9–34 Danson Department Stores is considering the replacement of the existing elevator system at its downtown store. A new system has been proposed that runs faster than the existing system, experiences few breakdowns and, as a result, promises considerable savings in operating costs. Information on the existing system and the proposed new system follow:

	Existing System	New System
Original cost	$300,000	$900,000
Remaining life	6 years	6 years
Annual cash operating costs	$150,000	$8,000
Salvage value at present	$100,000	—
Salvage value in 6 years	$30,000	$100,000

REQUIRED:

    (a) What costs are not relevant for this decision?

    (b) What are the relevant costs?

9-35 Jethrow Company manufactures and sells 3 models of electronic printers. Henry Thoreau, president of the company, is considering dropping model JT484 from its product line because the company has experienced losses for this product over the last 3 quarters. The following product-level operating data have been compiled for the most recent quarter:

	Total	JT284	JT384	JT484
Sales	$1,000,000	$500,000	$200,000	$300,000
Variable costs	600,000	300,000	100,000	200,000
Contribution margin	$400,000	$200,000	$100,000	$100,000
Fixed costs:				
Rent	50,000	25,000	10,000	15,000
Depreciation	60,000	30,000	12,000	18,000
Utilities	40,000	20,000	5,000	15,000
Supervision	50,000	15,000	5,000	30,000
Maintenance	30,000	15,000	6,000	9,000
Administrative	100,000	30,000	20,000	50,000
Total fixed costs	$330,000	$135,000	$58,000	$137,000
Operating income (loss)	$70,000	$65,000	$42,000	($37,000)

In addition, the following information is also available:

(i) Factory rent and depreciation will not be affected by a decision to drop Model JT484.

(ii) Quarterly utility bills will be reduced from $40,000 to $31,000 if JT484 is dropped.

(iii) Supervision costs for JT484 can be eliminated if it is dropped.

(iv) The maintenance department will be able to reduce quarterly costs by $7,000 if JT484 is dropped.

(v) Elimination of JT484 will make it possible to eliminate 2 administrative staff positions; their combined salaries total $30,000 per quarter.

REQUIRED:

    (a) Should JT484 be eliminated?

    (b) Jethrow's sales manager believes that it is important to continue to produce JT484 to maintain a full product line. He expects the elimination of JT484 to reduce sales of the remaining 2 products by 5% each. Will this information change your answer to (a)? Explain.

9-36 National Battery Company is considering accepting a special order for 50,000 batteries that it received from a discount retail store. The order specified a price of $4.00 per unit, which reflects a discount of $0.50 per unit relative to the company's regular price of $4.50 per unit. National's accounting department has prepared the following analysis to show that there will be cost savings resulting from additional sales:

	Cost per Unit Without the Additional Sales (100,000 units)	Cost per Unit with the Additional Sales (150,000 units)
Variable costs	$3.30	$3.30
Fixed costs	.90	.60
	$4.20	$3.90

No additional fixed costs will be incurred for this order because the company has surplus capacity. Because the average cost per unit will be reduced from $4.20 to $3.90, National's president believes that a reduction in the price to $4.00 is justified for this order.

REQUIRED:

(a) Should the order for the 50,000 units at a price of $4 be accepted? What will be the impact on National's operating income?

(b) Is the accounting department's analysis the best way to evaluate this decision? What alternative method would you suggest?

(c) What other considerations are important in this case?

9–37 Dakota Company is considering introducing a new model of personal compact disk players at a price of $105 per unit. Its controller has compiled the following incremental cost information based on an estimate of 120,000 units of sales annually for the new product.

Direct materials cost	$3,600,000
Direct labor cost	2,400,000
Variable manufacturing overhead	1,200,000
Sales commission	10% of sales
Fixed cost	$2,000,000

The average inventory levels for the new product are estimated as follows:

Raw materials	2 months of production
Work in progress (100% complete for materials and 50% complete for labor and variable manufacturing overhead)	1 month of production
Finished goods	2 months of production

Annual inventory carrying costs not included in the variable manufacturing overhead listed earlier are estimated to be 12% of inventory value.

In addition, the sales manager expects the introduction of the new model to result in a reduction in sales of the existing model from 300,000 to 240,000 units. The contribution margin for the old product is $20 per unit.

REQUIRED:

(a) Determine the total impact on Dakota's profit from the introduction of the new product.

(b) Should Dakota introduce the new product?

(c) Determine the breakeven point (in units) for the new product. Assume that sales of the old product decrease by 1 unit for every 2-unit increase in the sales of the new product.

9–38 Glenn Gould, the production manager at Steinway Company, purchased a cutting machine for the company last year. Six months after the purchase of the cutting machine, Glenn learned about a new cutting machine that is more reliable than the machine that he purchased.

The following information is available for the 2 machines:

	Old Machine	New Machine
Acquisition cost	$300,000	$360,000
Remaining life	4 years	4 years
Disposal value now	$100,000	—
Salvage value at the end of 4 years	$4,000	$5,000

Annual operating costs for the old machine are $140,000. The new machine will decrease annual operating costs by $60,000. These amounts do not include any charges for depreciation. Steinway Company uses the straight-line depreciation method. These estimates of operating costs exclude rework costs. The new machine will also result in a reduction in defect rate from the current 5% to 2.5%. All defective units are reworked at a cost of $1 per unit. The company produces on average 100,000 units annually.

REQUIRED:

(a) Should Glenn Gould replace the old machine with the new machine? Explain, listing all relevant costs.

(b) What costs should be considered as sunk costs for this decision?

(c) What other factors may affect Glenn's decision?

CASES

9–39 Amundsen Bicycle Company manufactures and sells bicycles nationwide through marketing channels ranging from sporting goods stores to specialty bicycle shops. Amundsen's average selling price to its distributors is $185 per bicycle. The bicycles are retailed to customers for $349.

After several years of high sales, Amundsen's sales have slumped to 160,000 bicycles per year in the last 3 years. This level is only 70% of its installed capacity. Amundsen expects the demand for its products to remain the same in the next few years.

Target Stores, a nationwide chain of discount retail stores, has recently approached Amundsen to manufacture bicycles under Target's own private label. Target has offered to purchase 40,000 bicycles annually for a 3-year period at $125 per bicycle. It is not willing to pay a higher price because it plans to retail the bicycles at only $200. Amundsen has not previously sold bicycles through any marketing channel other than specialty stores.

Amy Amundsen is the chief executive officer of Amundsen Bicycle. Although Target's offer is well below Amundsen's normal price, Amy is interested in the offer because Amundsen has considerable surplus capacity. She has been supplied with the following information:

Direct material costs	$50*
Direct labor costs	30
Variable manufacturing overhead costs	25
	$105

*Includes $2 for embossing Target's private label on the bicycle.

Fixed overhead costs total $2,000,000 annually. Amundsen also pays a 10% commission on sales to its sales staff but will not need to pay any salesperson for the special sale to Target. Average inventory levels for Target's offer are estimated to be as follows:

Raw materials	1 month of supply
Work in process	1.5 months of supply (100% complete for materials and 50% complete for other variable manufacturing costs)
Finished goods	0.5 month of supply

Annual inventory carrying cost is estimated to be 10% of the inventory carrying value. Target's offer requires Amundsen to deliver bicycles to Target's regional warehouse so that Target can have ready access to an inventory of bicycles to meet fluctuating market demand.

Amy estimated that about 5% of Amundsen's present sales will be lost if she accepts Target's offer because some customers will comparison shop and find the same quality bicycle available at a lower price in Target stores.

REQUIRED:

(a) Should Amy Amundsen accept Target's offer?

(b) What strategic and other factors should be considered before Amundsen makes a final decision?

CAPITAL BUDGETING

LEARNING OBJECTIVES

This chapter will introduce you to:

1. the importance of long-term assets
2. the nature of capital budgeting, investment and return, the time value of money, future value, effective and nominal rates of interest, present value, annuities, cost of capital, net present value, and return on investment
3. the effect of taxes on investment decisions
4. the role and nature of what-if and sensitivity analysis
5. the ways in which strategic considerations affect capital budgeting
6. the role of postimplementation audits in capital budgeting

CHAPTER 10

Teledesic Corporation: The Dilemma

Everyone expects telecommunications projects to be large and expensive. Experts in this area, used to ambitious proposals, have become somewhat jaded. Nevertheless, the proposal, announced in March 1994, to create Teledesic Corporation created considerable interest in the financial and information technology communities.

Conceived by Craig O. McCaw of McCaw Cellular Communications and William H. Gates of Microsoft Corporation, Teledesic Corporation proposed to spend about $9 billion to put between 800 and 900 satellites into low-level orbit by 2001. These satellites would provide low-cost, high-capacity, multimedia telecommunications services.

When the project was announced, observers questioned both the technical and financial feasibility of this proposal. They argued that the technology is not proved—the system would require complex and yet undeveloped software—and the project would mean launching more than twice the number of satellites currently in orbit around the earth. Also, Motorola Inc. was already working toward developing *Iridium*, a competing communication system.

Despite these doubts, Teledesic announced that it was looking for business partners to begin development of its system.

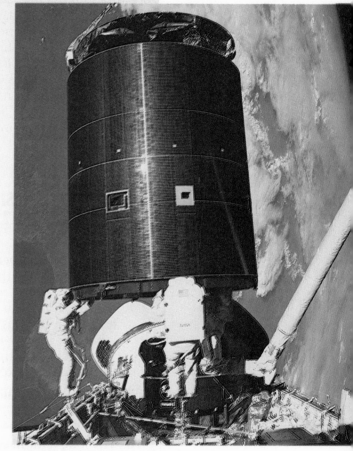

(Courtesy NASA)

THE IMPORTANCE OF LONG-TERM (CAPITAL) ASSETS

Long-term or capital assets
Equipment or facilities that provide productive services to the organization for more than 1 accounting period.

In considering the case of Teledesic Corporation, reflect back to Chapters 5 and 6, where we described the cost of resources (assets) that organizations contract for (purchase) in advance and then use for several years to make goods and provide services. These **long-term assets,** or **capital assets,** create the committed costs that we call batch-related, product-related, and process-sustaining costs. The investment proposal by Teledesic Corporation also illustrates issues that we will consider in this chapter, including the approach that planners[1] use to evaluate the acquisition of long-term assets that create these cost commitments.

We also discuss the nature of assets that organizations buy and use over extended periods of time and describe the ways that organizations evaluate the financial attributes of long-lived assets. We consider the relationship between investment and return, a fundamental investment criterion that organizations use to evaluate the desirability of long-term assets. We describe and develop the financial approach to evaluating investments. This approach uses the time value of money, present value and future value, the cost of capital, and net present value as basic ideas and tools. We complete our study of the process of making long-term financial commitments by considering the ways that organizations can test the sensitivity of long-term investment decisions to the estimates required to make those decisions. The issue faced by Teledesic Corporation, described at the beginning of the chapter, is a situation involving capital investment, which is a common example of a discretionary expenditure.

WHY IS THE ACQUISITION OF LONG-TERM ASSETS IMPORTANT?

Organizations have developed specific tools to control the acquisition and use of long-term assets for three reasons:

1. Unlike short-term assets whose acquisition rate can be modified quickly in response to changes in demand, organizations usually are *committed* to long-term assets for extended periods of time. This commitment creates the potential for either excess or scarce capacity that, in turn, creates excess costs or opportunity losses, respectively.

2. The amount of capital committed to the acquisition of capital assets is usually very *large*; therefore, acquiring long-term assets creates significant financial risks for organizations.

3. The long-term nature of capital assets creates *technological risk* for organizations.

---

[1] We should not assume that only managers develop capital spending proposals. We call anyone who develops and proposes a capital spending proposal a *planner.*

Capital budgeting is the collection of tools that planners use to evaluate the desirability of long-term assets.[2] Capital budgeting uses tools and ideas borrowed from finance, statistics, and engineering control theory—it is part theory and part art. In this text, we develop the fundamentals of capital budgeting. Other texts develop capital budgeting for more advanced applications.

INVESTMENT AND RETURN

By definition, a long-term asset is acquired and paid for before it generates benefits, which it must do for two or more years. The fundamental evaluation issue in dealing with a long-term asset is whether the future benefits associated with it justify its initial cost.

[2] Other financially based approaches are used to evaluate an investment proposal. The most popular approach is the payback method. The payback method computes the length of time, called the **payback period**, taken by a project's net cash flows to recover the initial investment made in the project. In the payback method, a project is accepted if its payback period is less than a critical value. Because the payback method does not formally consider the time value of money, financial theorists reject it. However, repeated surveys of practice have found that *the payback method is the most widely used approach to project selection.*

Capital budgeting
The collection of tools that planners use to evaluate the desirability of long-term assets.

OBJECTIVE 10.2
The nature of capital budgeting, investment and return, the time value of money, future value, effective and nominal rates of interest, present value, annuities, cost of capital, net present value, and return on investment

Payback period
The number of years taken for the cash inflows associated with a project to recover the initial investment.

This skilled technician is using a sophisticated temperature and vibration detector to assess the condition of a piece of equipment used by Southdown, Inc. On the basis of this information, maintenance personnel, if required, will work on the machine to prevent costly failures. Although financial reporting conventions do not consider the amount of money invested in training this employee an asset for reporting purposes, most employee training programs do provide benefits that extend over many periods. *(Courtesy Southdown, Inc.)*

Investment is the monetary value of the assets that the organization gives up to acquire a long-term asset. *Return* refers to the increased cash flows in the future attributable to the long-term asset acquired. The ideas of investment and return are the foundations of capital budgeting analysis.

Capital budgeting analysis focuses on whether the investment in a long-term asset is justified by the increased cash flows that the organization expects the asset to create. All the tools and methods used in capital budgeting focus on comparing investment and return.

TIME VALUE OF MONEY

The most important idea in capital budgeting is the concept of the **time value of money;** that is, because money can earn a return, its value depends on *when* it is received. Like all commodities, money has a cost. The cost of using money is not an out-of-pocket cost, like the cost of buying raw materials or paying a worker. Rather, the cost of using money is the opportunity lost from being unable to invest the money in another investment alternative. For example, if you spend money today, you forgo the opportunity to deposit it in a savings account and earn interest on it.

Because money has a time-dated value, the most fundamental and important thing to remember in capital budgeting is that amounts of *money received at different periods of time must be converted to their value on a common date to be compared.*

■ Future Value

Consider the difference between having $1.00 now and $1.00 a year from now. If you have $1.00 now, you could invest it in a savings account to earn 5% interest. After 1 year, you would have $1.05. We call this $1.05 the **future value** of $1.00 in 1 year when the opportunity rate of interest is 5%, that is, the amount to which an amount invested today will increase over a stated number of periods at a stated interest rate. The following equation provides the formula for future value.

Future value of investment in 1 year =

Investment * (1 + Annual rate of interest)

Because of the time value of money, it is always better to have money now, rather than in the future. Having $1.00 today is more valuable than receiving $1.00 in 1 year or 5 years because the $1.00 on hand today can be invested to grow to more than $1.00 in the future.

Suppose that Karl Nesarajah wants to borrow $10,000 to buy a used car. Karl has $6,000 in cash and wants to buy a car that costs $16,000, financing the $10,000 balance with a car loan. He plans to repay the loan in full after 1 year. If the rate of interest is 8% per year, Karl will have to repay $10,800 at the end of the year, as shown in the following equation.

Amount repaid = (1.08) * $10,000 = $10,800

Most people must take a loan to buy a new car. The lender and borrower negotiate a contract that provides for periodic payments that repay the loan with interest.
(Courtesy Mark Richards)

In summary, future value is the amount to which a present sum of money will accumulate given some specified rate of interest.

Multiple Periods

Because cash flows can take place over multiple periods, we must have a way to compute future value over several periods. Exhibit 10–1 shows how an initial amount of $1.00 accumulates to $1.2763 over 5 years when the money earns 5% interest per year. Note that the calculations shown assume that (1) any *interest earned is not withdrawn* until the end of the fifth year, and, therefore, interest is earned each year on both the initial investment and the interest earned in previous periods (called the **compounding effect of interest**) and (2) the annual rate of *interest is constant.*

We can use the equation for future value to compute the value of $1.2763 directly, as shown in the following equation:[3]

Future value of $1 in 5 years = $1 * $(1.05)^5$ = $1 * 1.2763 = $1.2763

More generally, the formula for future value, when the number of compounding periods is n and the periodic rate of return is r, is

Future value of investment in n periods = investment * $(1 + r)^n$ (10.1)

To illustrate, suppose that two parents have just won $100,000 in a lottery. They decide to place $20,000 of this money in a trust fund for

> **Compounding effect (of interest)**
> The phenomenon of earning interest on interest previously earned.

[3] The text assumes that you have a calculator that can evaluate an expression of the form $(1 + a)^b$. For example, $(1.07)^5$ equals 1.4026 rounded to 4 decimal places. The table in Appendix 10–2 provides values of the inverse of $(1 + a)^b$ for selected combinations of a and b where a is the periodic interest rate and b is the number of periods. If you look at the table in Appendix 10–2, you will find that the tabulated value for 5 periods at 7% is 0.712986. $1/0.712986 = 1.4026$ (rounded to 4 decimal places).

SPREADSHEET APPLICATION

The *Lotus 1-2-3* formula for this calculation is

20000 * (1.07) ^ 18

EXHIBIT 10–1
Compounded Growth of Initial Investment over Multiple Periods

YEAR	PRINCIPAL AT START OF YEAR	INTEREST EARNED THIS YEAR AT 5%	TOTAL PRINCIPAL AND INTEREST AT END OF YEAR
1	$1.0000	$0.0500	$1.0500
2	1.0500	0.0525	1.1025
3	1.1025	0.0551	1.1576
4	1.1576	0.0579	1.2155
5	1.2155	0.0608	1.2763

their newborn child's education. If the money is invested to earn 7% each year and interest is reinvested, we can use the equation for future value to determine the amount that it will have accumulated in the trust fund after 18 years.

$$\text{Future value of } \$20{,}000 \text{ in } 18 \text{ years} = \$20{,}000 * (1.07)^{18}$$

and, noting that $(1.07)^{18} = 3.3799$, we have

$$\text{Future value of } \$20{,}000 \text{ in } 18 \text{ years} = \$20{,}000 * 3.3799 = \$67{,}599$$

Returning to the automobile-purchasing example, suppose that Karl believes that it will take 3 years to accumulate enough money to repay his car loan. If the required interest is 8% per year, the loan repayment in 3 years would be

$$\text{Loan repayment amount} = 10{,}000 * (1.08)^{3} = 10{,}000 * 1.259712 =$$
$$\$12{,}597.12$$

■ Effective and Nominal Rates of Interest

To this point, we have assumed that the compounding period is 1 year. Flexibility requires, however, that we be able to make such calculations for any compounding period because an investment might provide cash flows monthly, quarterly, semiannually, or annually.

Financial institutions usually express the rate of interest they pay in annual terms. That is, if a financial institution promises a rate of return of 6% on investments, the 6% is the **nominal or stated** annual **rate of interest**.

Nominal or stated rate of interest
The stated annual rate of interest.

Consider what happens, however, if a financial institution pays interest quarterly when the nominal rate of interest is 6% per year. Interest is paid at the rate of 1.5% (6% ÷ 4) per quarter. Therefore, the effective quarterly rate of interest is 1.5%.

Exhibit 10–2 shows that, under these conditions, $1.00 invested at the beginning of the year accumulates to $1.0614 at the end of the year (4 quarters later). We can see that the effective annual rate of interest is 6.14%, not the nominal rate of interest of 6%. Why is this true? The answer is that periodic compounding has allowed the saver to earn interest on her interest earned during the year, yielding a higher return than the nominal rate of return. This is known as the **effective rate of interest**.

Effective rate of interest
The actual annual rate of interest earned on an investment.

QUARTER	PRINCIPAL AT START OF QUARTER	INTEREST EARNED THIS QUARTER AT 1.5%	TOTAL PRINCIPAL AND INTEREST AT END OF QUARTER
1	$1.0000	$0.0150	$1.0150
2	$1.0150	$0.0152	$1.0302
3	$1.0302	$0.0155	$1.0457
4	$1.0457	$0.0157	$1.0614

We can compute the effective annual rate of interest, r_e, where r_n is the stated, or nominal, annual rate of interest and n is the number of compounding periods per year, as follows:

$$r_e = \left(1 + \frac{r_n}{n}\right)^n - 1$$

Consider the interest that a credit card company charges on outstanding monthly balances. The nominal rate of interest is 18%. What is the effective annual rate of interest? Because interest is computed and charged monthly, the effective annual rate of interest is

$$\text{Effective annual rate of interest} = \left(1 + \frac{.18}{12}\right)^{12} - 1 = 19.56\%$$

You should consider this when you accumulate unpaid charges on your credit card! For example, suppose that a student uses a credit card in January to buy a $500 portable stereo system. The student plans to repay the amount on June 1 when he receives the first paycheck from his summer job. He receives the credit card bill on February 1 but makes no payment[4] until June 1. Therefore, the bill will accumulate interest for 4 months. If the stated interest rate on unpaid balances is 18% per year, or 1.5% per month, the amount that the $500 purchase will have accumulated to by June 1 is

Future value of $500 in 4 months = $500 * (1.015)⁴ = $500 * 1.0614 =
$530.70

which is a significant amount to consider.

■ Present Value

An investor may expect a proposed investment to generate benefits in the form of increased cash flows over many periods into the future. These cash flow benefits, or **inflows,** must be compared to the investment's costs, or **outflows**. Because of the time value of money, all cash flows associated with

Inflows
The incremental cash inflows associated with an asset.

Outflows
The incremental cash outflows associated with an asset.

---

[4] This example, which is being used to show how credit charges quickly accumulate, is unrealistic because most credit card companies require a minimum payment on any outstanding account balance.

This huge shovel improves productivity in coal mining at Kerr-McGee Corporation by reducing the number of passes needed to fill a haul truck. When deciding to make the investment in this shovel, planners at Kerr-McGee had to compare its purchase price with the cost savings resulting from the productivity improvements expected from using this equipment during its lifetime.
(Courtesy Kerr-McGee)

Time zero (or period zero)
The point in time when the investment is undertaken.

Present value
The current monetary worth of an amount to be paid in the future under stated conditions of interest and compounding.

Discounting
The process of computing present value.

an investment must be converted to their equivalent value at some common date to make comparisons.

Although any point in time could be chosen as the common date for comparing inflows and outflows, the conventional choice is the point when the investment is undertaken. Analysts call this point **time zero** or **period zero**. Therefore, conventional capital budgeting analysis converts all cash flows to their equivalent value at time zero.

Analysts call a future cash flow's value at time zero its **present value**, and the process of computing present value, **discounting**. The present value formula is the inverse of the future value formula (see Appendix 10A–2):

$$\text{Present value} = \frac{\text{Future amount received in period } n}{(1 + \text{Required periodic return})^n} \quad (10.2)$$

Return to the college tuition example. Suppose that two parents want to accumulate $70,000 over 18 years for their newborn child's education. These parents have idle cash available now to make this investment, which will earn 6% annually. What amount of money must they invest now? The present value of $70,000 received in 18 years, when the interest rate is 6%, is

$$\text{Present value} = \left[\frac{\$70,000}{(1.06)^{18}} \right] = \left[\frac{\$70,000}{2.85434} \right] = \$24,524$$

This means that $24,524 invested today at 6% annual interest will, if the interest is left untouched, accumulate to $70,000 in 18 years.

Present Value and Future Value of Annuities

Not all investments have cash outlays at time zero and provide a single benefit at some point in the future. Most investments provide a series, or stream, of benefits over some specified period in the future. We call the situation in which an investment promises a constant amount each period over n periods an *n-period* **annuity.** For example, a retiree may have $200,000 in accumulated savings upon her retirement. The retiree might use this $200,000 to purchase a contract that will pay her $18,000 each year for 20 years.

Formulas and financial tables that allow analysts to compute the present value of annuities directly were produced before the widespread availability of financial calculators and spreadsheets. Today, most present value calculations are performed on calculators or computer spreadsheets that can calculate present values directly, so that knowledge of the formulas and tables is less important.

Equation (10.3) presents the formula to compute the present value of an annuity, where r is the required return[5] per period and n is the number of periods (see Appendix 10A–3):[6]

Present value of an annuity =

$$\text{Periodic annuity amount} * \left[\frac{(1 + r)^n - 1}{r * (1 + r)^n} \right]. \quad (10.3)$$

Consider a bond with a face value of $1,000 that pays $50 in interest every 6 months for 20 years (that is, $50 per period for 40 six-month periods) and a lump sum of $1,000 at the end of the twentieth year. If an investor's required return is 8% per year, what would the investor be willing to pay for this bond?

Because this investment has 40 six-month periods, to begin this analysis, we must first convert the 8% annual required return into the equivalent 6-month return. That is, what 6-month return yields an effective return of 8% per year? Using the following equation, we find that the required 6-month rate of interest is 3.923%:

$$
\begin{aligned}
0.08 &= (1 + r_e)^2 - 1 \\
1.08 &= (1 + r_e)^2 \\
1.03923 &= 1 + r_e \\
0.03923 &= r_e
\end{aligned}
$$

Therefore, 3.923% is the required rate of interest that would be used to compute the present value of the periodic cash flows promised by the bond.

SPREADSHEET APPLICATION: PV

The *Lotus 1-2-3* formula for this calculation is

$$70000 \div (1.06) \, \wedge \, 18$$

Annuity
A contract that promises to pay a fixed amount each period for a stated number of periods.

---

[5] The required return is often called the **discount rate.**
[6] The table in Appendix 10–3 evaluates this formula for selected values of r, the periodic rate of interest, and n, the number of interest periods.

Discount rate
The interest rate used to compute present values.

In the equation for the present value of an annuity, we find that the present value of the 40 interest payments of $50, when the required rate of interest each interest period is 3.923%, equals $1,001.08:

$$\text{Present value of interest annuity} = \$50 * \left[\frac{(1.03923)^{40} - 1}{0.03923 * (1.03923)^{40}} \right]$$

$$= \$1,001.08$$

Using the present value equation, we find that the present value of the principal repayment of $1,000 at the end of the fortieth interest period, when the interest rate is 3.923% per period, is $214.55.

$$\text{Present value principal repayment} = \$1,000 * \left[\frac{1}{(1.03923)^{40}} \right] = \$214.55$$

Therefore, the investor would be willing to pay $1,215.63 ($1,001.08 + $214.55) for this bond.

We can reorganize the equation for the present value of an annuity, as shown in equation (10.4), to develop the formula for the periodic annuity amount, or payment, required to recover a given present value.

$$\text{Periodic annuity amount} = \text{Amount borrowed} * \left[\frac{r * (1 + r)^n}{(1 + r)^n - 1} \right] \quad (10.4)$$

In our car-purchasing example, suppose Karl discovers that no one will lend him $10,000 to be repaid at the end of 3 years because lending agencies reduce risk by requiring periodic loan repayments. Karl is told that the nominal rate is 8% for the loan and that he must make loan payments monthly. If loan payments are made every month for 3 years (36 months), the required monthly payment is $313.36, as shown in the following equation:

$$\text{Periodic annuity amount} = \$10,000 * \left[\frac{0.08/12 * (1 + 0.08/12)^{36}}{(1 + 0.08/12)^{36} - 1} \right] = \$313.36$$

(See Appendix 10A–1 for a summary of important formulas.)

Cost of capital
The minimum return that the organization must earn on its investments to meet its investors' return requirements.

▪ Cost of Capital

The **cost of capital** is the minimum return that the organization must earn on its investments to meet its investors' return requirements. From a financial perspective, when it expects to earn less than its cost of capital from a proposed investment, the organization would be better off returning the funds that otherwise would be committed to the proposed investment to its providers of capital. If the organization expects to earn more than its cost of capital from a proposed investment, the investment is desirable and the surplus increases the organization's wealth. The cost of capital becomes the benchmark that the organization uses to evaluate investment proposals.

Finance courses cover in depth the way that organizations determine their cost of capital. It is important to note here, however, that the organization's cost of capital reflects both the amount and cost of debt and equity in its financial structure and the financial market's perception of the financial risk of the organization's activities.

■ Net Present Value

Capital budgeting uses the idea of **net present value** to determine the desirability of an investment proposal. It is the sum of the present values of all cash inflows and outflows associated with a project and is computed as follows:

1. Choose the appropriate **period length** to evaluate the investment proposal. The period length is determined by the periodicity of the investment's cash flows. The most common period length used in practice is annual, although quarterly and semiannual period lengths also are used.
2. Identify the organization's *cost of capital* and convert it to an appropriate rate for the period length chosen in step (1).
3. Identify the **incremental cash flow** in each period of the project's life.
4. Compute the *present value* of each period's cash flow.
5. Sum all the present values of the periodic cash inflows and outflows to determine the investment project's *net present value*.
6. If the project's net present value (also known as *residual income, economic income,* or *economic value added*) is *positive*, the project is acceptable from an economic perspective.

Net present value
The sum of the present values of all the cash inflows and cash outflows associated with a project (also called *residual income, economic income,* and *economic value added*).

Period length
The time period over which interest is computed (e.g., monthly, quarterly, semiannually, or annually) in a capital budgeting analysis.

Incremental cash flow
Cash flows that change as a result of acquiring or disposing of a long-term asset.

■ Evaluating an Investment Proposal

Suppose that Wendy's Pizza Parlor is considering the purchase of a new automatic pizza oven. The new oven would cost $60,000 and would last for 4 years. It would expand capacity and allow Wendy's to increase profits by about $20,000 per year. Wendy's Pizza Parlor's cost of capital is 10%, and the new oven would be worth $5,000 at the end of the 4 years. Is this investment worthwhile?

In effect, the question is whether the 4-year annuity of $20,000, plus the single salvage payment of $5,000 after 4 years, is worth $60,000 to Wendy's Pizza Parlor. At first glance, this investment seems like a no-brainer. Wendy's Pizza Parlor will earn $80,000 ($20,000 * 4) over 4 years and will be able to get $5,000 for the used oven after 4 years. Thus, $85,000 of cash inflows are received in exchange for $60,000 of cash outflows. But the $60,000 is spent now and the $85,000 in cash flows are received in the future. Therefore, we must compute the present value of the future cash flows.

Let's follow the 6 steps just mentioned to determine the net present value of this investment.

STEP 1 The period length is 1 year because all cash flows are stated annually. The convention in capital budgeting is to assume, unless otherwise stated, that the cash flows occur at the end of each period.

STEP 2 Wendy's Pizza Parlor's stated cost of capital is 10% per year. Because the period chosen in step 1 is annual, we do not have to adjust this rate of return.

STEP 3 The incremental cash flows, as shown in Exhibit 10–3 are $60,000 immediately, $20,000 at the end of each year for 4 years, and $5,000 at the end of 4 years. It is very useful to organize the cash flows associated with a project on a time line like the one shown in Exhibit 10–3. This allows you to identify and consider all the project's cash flows systematically.

STEP 4 The present value of a 4-year annuity of $20,000 when the organization's cost of capital is 10% is $63,397, as shown in the following equation:

$$\text{Present value of benefits annuity} = \$20,000 * \left[\frac{(1.1)^4 - 1}{0.1 * (1.1)^4} \right] = \$63,397$$

The present value of the $5,000 salvage in 4 years when Wendy's Pizza Parlor's cost of capital is 10% equals $3,415:

$$\text{Present value of the salvage amount} = \$5,000 * \left[\frac{1}{(1.1)^4} \right] = \$3,415$$

STEP 5 The present value of the cash inflows attributable to this investment is $66,812 ($63,397 + $3,415). Because the investment of $60,000 takes place at time zero, the present value of the total outflows is $60,000. The net present value of this investment project is $6,812 ($66,812 − $60,000).

STEP 6 Because the project's net present value is positive, the oven is economically desirable and should be purchased.

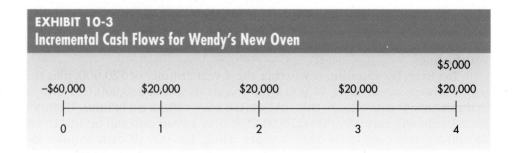

EXHIBIT 10-3
Incremental Cash Flows for Wendy's New Oven

■ Return on Investment

We briefly introduced the idea of return on investment (ROI) in Chapter 1. Now we present the concept in more detail. *Return on investment*, also called the *internal rate of return*, is the actual rate of return expected from an investment. ROI is the discount rate that makes the investment's net present value equal zero. If an investment's expected net present value is positive, its return on investment exceeds the required return. If an investment's net present value is negative, its return on investment is less than its required return. In the pizza parlor example, the ROI is 14.97%.[7] Because a 14.97% return on investment is greater than the required return of 10%, the project is desirable.

Because a project's net present value summarizes all of its financial elements, return on investment is not a criterion that we need to use when preparing capital budgets. Return on investment is pervasive in financial markets, however, and is widely used in capital budgeting (see Exhibit 10–4).

[7] Computer spreadsheets can compute the return on investment directly, or you can use trial and error. Vary the cost of capital until the project's net present value is zero. The cost of capital that makes the project's net present value zero is the return on investment.

EXHIBIT 10-4
Criteria Used for Investment Justification

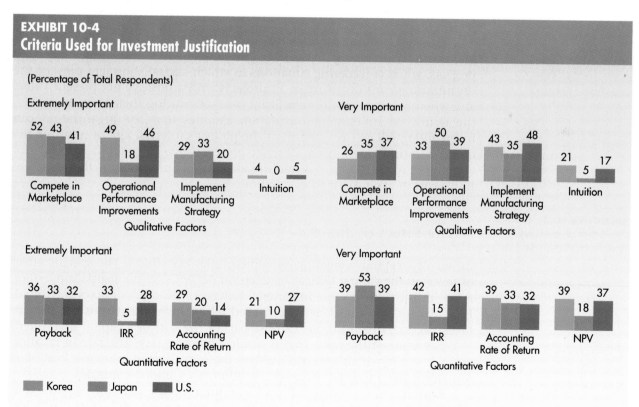

(Percentage of Total Respondents)

A survey of criteria used to justify capital investments found that organizations use a variety of both qualitative and quantitative factors. These preferences varied somewhat across different countries. (*Reprinted from* Management Accounting. *Copyright by Institute of Management Accountants, Montvale, N.J.*)

The planners of Coastal Corporation considered both financial factors such as return on investment from this huge gas-processing plant and nonfinancial benefits. The plant extracts liquid hydrocarbons from the gas byproducts of nearby refineries and reduces local air pollutants by more than 1 ton of sulfur a day, thereby helping the refineries comply with air-quality standards. Including nonfinancial considerations in an evaluation of an investment proposal raises complex questions of how to weight these nonfinancial benefits in the overall investment decision. *(Courtesy The Coastal Corporation)*

Using the return on investment criterion to evaluate proposed investments can create ambiguous results, particularly when evaluating competing projects, when considering situations in which capital shortages prevent the organization from investing in all projects with a positive net present value, and when projects require significant outflows during their lives. Moreover, the return on investment calculation assumes that the organization can invest intermediate cash returns at the project's internal rate of return, a frequently invalid assumption. The net present value calculation is a superior alternative requiring only 1 additional piece of information, the organization's cost of capital, for its calculation.

OBJECTIVE 10.3
The effect of taxes on investment decisions

■ The Effect of Taxes

In practice, capital budgeting should consider tax effects. The specific effect of taxes on the capital budgeting decision depends on tax legislation, which is tax-jurisdiction specific. In general, however, the effect of taxes is twofold. First, part of any net benefits provided by an investment must be paid in taxes. Second, organizations can use part of the cost of a capital investment to offset some of the taxes that it would otherwise pay. The rate of taxation and the way in which legislation allows the organization to use the cost of its long-term assets to offset taxes create differences among countries.

Let's return on Wendy's Pizza Parlor for a specific example. Suppose that Wendy's Pizza Parlor's income is taxed at the rate of 40%. Tax legislation allows it to claim straight-line depreciation of its investment in long-term assets to offset the benefits provided by the investment. If Wendy's Pizza Parlor's after-tax cost of capital is 6%, is the oven project desirable?

For this analysis, we must convert all pre-tax cash flows to after-tax cash flows. In turn, this requires that we know the amount of depreciation that will be claimed each year. Using straight-line depreciation, Wendy's Pizza Parlor will claim $13,750 of depreciation each year as shown in the following equations:

Depreciation =

$$\left[\frac{\text{Initial investment} - \text{Salvage value}}{\text{Project life}} \right]$$

$$\text{Depreciation} = \left[\frac{\$60,000 - \$5,000}{4} \right] = \$13,750$$

With this information, we can now compute the after-tax cash flows attributable to this investment. These calculations are shown in Exhibit 10-5.

We can see that the investment in the oven provides two after-tax benefits: (1) a 4-year annuity of $17,500 and (2) a lump-sum payment of $5,000 at the end of 4 years. Because the oven's book value at the end of 4 years is $5,000, there is no gain in selling it for $5,000, and its salvage value is treated as a return of capital and is not taxed. When the organization's cost of capital is 6%, the value of the 4-year annuity of $17,500 is $60,639, as shown in the following equation.

$$\text{Present value of benefits annuity} = \$17,500 * \left[\frac{(1.06)^4 - 1}{0.06 * (1.06)^4} \right] = \$60,639$$

The present value of the lump-sum payment of $5,000 is $3,960, as shown in the following equation:

$$\text{Present value salvage} = \left[\frac{\$5,000}{(1.06)^4} \right] = \$3,960$$

EXHIBIT 10–5
Calculating After-Tax Cash Flows
Wendy's Pizza Parlor

(1) YEAR	(2) BEFORE-TAX CASH FLOW	(3) DEPRECIATION	(4) TAXABLE CASH FLOW (2) − (3)	(5) TAX @40% (4) * 40%	(6) AFTER-TAX CASH FLOW (2) − (5)
1	$20,000	$13,750	$6,250	$2,500	$17,500
2	$20,000	$13,750	$6,250	$2,500	$17,500
3	$20,000	$13,750	$6,250	$2,500	$17,500
4	$20,000	$13,750	$6,250	$2,500	$17,500
4	$ 5,000	$–0–	$–0–	$–0–	$ 5,000

Because they must operate the equipment and because they have the most direct knowledge of the conditions under which it will be used, production-level employees are increasingly involved in capital investment decisions. These Mobil Corporation employees are discussing ways to improve the production process that makes wrapping film. *(© Cheryl Rossum/Mobil Corp.)*

Therefore, the present value of the incremental inflows attributable to this investment is $64,599 ($60,639 + $3,960). Because the $60,000 investment takes place at time zero, the present value of the total outflows is $60,000, and the net present value of this investment project is $4,599 ($64,599 − $60,000). Because the project's net present value is positive, it is economically desirable.

Let us return to the car-buying example. Suppose that Karl wants to use the car as a taxi. He expects the car to have a 3-year life and to generate revenues of $10,000 per month. This is fine with Karl, who plans to enroll in a university in 3 years. The operating expenses associated with using the car as a taxi, exclusive of the loan repayments, are $6,100 per month. Karl's tax rate is 25%. The car will have a $1,060 salvage value at the end of the 3 years. If Karl does not pursue the taxi option, he could place the $6,000 not invested in the taxi in a comparable investment that yields a nominal return of 8% per year. The interest on this investment would be paid monthly, and the principal would be repaid in full at the end of the 3 years. If Karl takes the investment option, he would continue in his current job, which pays $3,300 per month. Karl plans to use straight-line depreciation to depreciate the taxi.

Let's consider this investment opportunity in 2 steps. First, we consider its incremental cash flows. Second, we consider the effects of taxes on the incremental cash flows and the investment decisions. The cash flows will be as follows:

1. If Karl invests his $6,000 in the taxi, he will experience, relative to doing nothing, a cash outflow at time 0 of $6,000. (See Exhibit 10–6, column 2.)

2. The monthly revenues associated with the taxi venture are $10,000. The monthly operating expenses associated with the taxi venture are $6,100. Therefore, the incremental cash inflows that come from the taxi operations are $3,900 ($10,000 − $6,100) per month. (See Exhibit 10–6, column 3.)

3. The interest expense that Karl will have to pay is the interest portion of the $10,000 car loan amortization. The monthly rate of interest is 0.67%

(8%/12) and is applied on the outstanding balance of the car loan. At the end of each month, Karl will make a loan payment of $313.37.[8] In the first month, this loan payment will consist of interest amounting to $66.67 (0.6667% * $10,000) and a loan amortization of $246.70. Therefore, the incremental cash outflows in month 1 will be $66.67 for loan interest and $246.70 for the loan amortization. (See Exhibit 10–6, columns 4 and 5.)

[8] We calculated this loan repayment amount earlier. The actual amount of the monthly loan repayment is ($940.10/3), which is slightly less than $313.37. To compensate for this overstatement of the required amount, the payment in some months will be $313.36.

EXHIBIT 10–6
Karl's Taxi: Investment Example

(1)	(2)	(3)	(4)	(5)	(6)	(7)	(8)	(9)	(10)	(11)
MO	INVEST-MENT	TAXI PROFITS	INTEREST EXPENSE	LOAN AMORT	DEPN	SALARY LOST	TAXABLE INCOME	TAX INCREASE	NET	NPV
0	−6000	−0−	−0−	−0−	−0−	−0−	−0−	−0−	−6000	−6000
1	−0−	3900	66.67	246.70	415	2475	3418.33	854.58	227.05	255.35
2	−0−	3900	65.02	248.34	415	2475	3419.98	854.99	226.64	253.25
3	−0−	3900	63.37	250.00	415	2475	3421.63	855.41	226.23	251.17
4	−0−	3900	61.70	251.66	415	2475	3423.30	855.83	225.81	249.10
5	−0−	3900	60.02	253.34	415	2475	3424.98	856.24	225.39	247.05
6	−0−	3900	58.33	255.03	415	2475	3426.67	856.67	224.97	245.00
7	−0−	3900	56.63	256.73	415	2475	3428.37	857.09	224.54	242.98
8	−0−	3900	54.92	258.44	415	2475	3430.08	857.52	224.12	240.96
9	−0−	3900	53.20	260.17	415	2475	3431.80	857.95	223.69	238.96
10	−0−	3900	51.46	261.90	415	2475	3433.54	858.38	223.25	236.97
11	−0−	3900	49.72	263.65	415	2475	3435.28	858.82	222.82	235.00
12	−0−	3900	47.96	265.40	415	2475	3437.04	859.26	222.38	233.03
13	−0−	3900	46.19	267.17	415	2475	3438.81	859.70	221.93	231.09
14	−0−	3900	44.41	268.95	415	2475	3440.59	860.15	221.49	229.15
15	−0−	3900	42.62	270.75	415	2475	3442.38	860.60	221.04	227.23
16	−0−	3900	40.81	272.55	415	2475	3444.19	861.05	220.59	225.32
17	−0−	3900	38.99	274.37	415	2475	3446.01	861.50	220.14	223.42
18	−0−	3900	37.17	276.20	415	2475	3447.83	861.96	219.68	221.53
19	−0−	3900	35.32	278.04	415	2475	3449.68	862.42	219.22	219.66
20	−0−	3900	33.47	279.89	415	2475	3451.53	862.88	218.75	217.80
21	−0−	3900	31.60	281.76	415	2475	3453.40	863.35	218.29	215.95
22	−0−	3900	29.73	283.64	415	2475	3455.27	863.82	217.82	214.12
23	−0−	3900	27.84	285.53	415	2475	3457.16	864.29	217.35	212.29
24	−0−	3900	25.93	287.43	415	2475	3459.07	864.77	216.87	210.48
25	−0−	3900	24.02	289.35	415	2475	3460.98	865.25	216.39	208.68
26	−0−	3900	22.09	291.28	415	2475	3462.91	865.73	215.91	206.89
27	−0−	3900	20.14	293.22	415	2475	3464.86	866.21	215.42	205.12
28	−0−	3900	18.19	295.17	415	2475	3466.81	866.70	214.93	203.35
29	−0−	3900	16.22	297.14	415	2475	3468.78	867.19	214.44	201.60
30	−0−	3900	14.24	299.12	415	2475	3470.76	867.69	213.95	199.86
31	−0−	3900	12.25	301.12	415	2475	3472.75	868.19	213.45	198.13
32	−0−	3900	10.24	303.12	415	2475	3474.76	868.69	212.95	196.41
33	−0−	3900	8.22	305.14	415	2475	3476.78	869.20	212.44	194.71
34	−0−	3900	6.18	307.18	415	2475	3478.82	869.70	211.93	193.01
35	−0−	3900	4.14	309.23	415	2475	3480.86	870.22	211.42	191.33
36	1060	3900	2.08	311.29	415	2475	3482.92	870.73	210.91	1024.14
										2800.08

4. If Karl gives up his current job to drive a taxi, he immediately loses his monthly salary of $3,300. Since 25%, or $825, of this salary would be paid in taxes, the net effect on Karl's giving up his existing salary is a reduced inflow of $2,475 ($3,300 − $825). This is a cash outflow (opportunity cost) associated with the taxi venture. If you find this difficult to follow, think of the $2,475 as an after-tax salary that Karl must pay himself to be equally well off incomewise in the taxi venture as he would be under his status quo position. (See Exhibit 10–6, column 7.)

5. After month 36, Karl will receive the $1,060 salvage from the taxi. This is an incremental cash inflow. (See Exhibit 10–6, column 2, bottom.)

Now that we have summarized the before-tax effects of the taxi venture, we are ready to consider the tax effects. Taxes are paid on taxable income, which equals income less allowed expenses. In Karl's case, taxable income equals revenue, less operating expenses, less interest expense, less depreciation. We know that revenue less operating expenses is $3,900 per month, and we have computed the interest expense for month 1. The interest expense for each of the remaining months is computed as 0.67% of the balance of the loan outstanding that month. Depreciation is computed on a straight-line basis and equals $415 per month. (See Exhibit 10–6, column 6.)

$$\text{Monthly depreciation} = \frac{\text{Initial investment} - \text{Salvage}}{36} = \frac{16{,}000 - 1{,}060}{36}$$
$$= \$415$$

The tax payment will be 25% of taxable income. Exhibit 10-6, column 8, shows Karl's taxable income in each month.

The net incremental cash flow of the taxi venture relative to keeping Karl's current job equals the investment amount plus the taxi operating profits, less the loan payment (this is the sum of interest expense and the loan amortization from Exhibit 10–6, columns 4 and 5), less the salary lost, less taxes. This amount is shown in Exhibit 10–6, column 10. The net incremental cash flows are discounted at Karl's required rate of return, which is 0.67% per month. The present value of each month's incremental cash flow is shown in Exhibit 10–6, column 11.

The net present value of the incremental cash flows associated with the taxi investment relative to staying in the current job is $2,800.08. (See Exhibit 10–6, column 11, bottom.) This means that the taxi investment would allow Karl to increase his wealth. Karl must decide whether this amount is appropriate compensation for the increased burden of managing his own business.

WHAT-IF AND SENSITIVITY ANALYSIS

We have seen that capital budgeting analysis relies on estimates of future cash flows. Because estimates are not always realized, many decision makers like to know how the estimates affect the decision they are making. In the Wendy's Pizza Parlor example, Wendy might ask, "What must the cash flows be to make this project unattractive?" Fortunately, it is easy to answer this question.

Most planners today use personal computers and electronic spreadsheets for capital budgeting. The planner can easily set up the spreadsheet so that

Many uncertainties must be considered when evaluating a large investment, such as the investment Amerada Hess Corporation made in this drilling platform. The acquisition and operating costs of the platform, the amount of crude oil that it will recover, the cost of processing the crude oil, and the prices the company will receive for the products that it refines from the crude oil are all uncertain. Planners of large investments must consider these uncertainties and decide whether the probability that the project will be profitable is sufficiently high. *(Courtesy Amerada Hess Corporation)*

changes can be made to the estimates of the decision's key parameters. If the analysis explores the effect of a change in a parameter on a *result*, we call the investigation a *what-if analysis*. For example, the planner might ask, "What will my profits be if sales are only 90% of plan?" A planner's investigation of the effect of a change in a parameter on a *decision* is called a *sensitivity analysis*, as discussed in Chapter 5. For example, the planner might ask, "How low can sales fall before this investment is unattractive to me?"

As an example, in the situation in which Wendy's Pizza Parlor faced taxes, suppose that the expected cash flows from the operation were only 90% of what was planned. That is, suppose that they are $18,000 instead of $20,000. Would the oven still be an attractive investment? The answer is yes. The annual cash benefits would have to fall to $17,788 each year before the project is economically undesirable.[9] This is a drop of 11% from the estimated amount, which is not a big error. Therefore, the decision is relatively sensitive to the estimated benefits.

STRATEGIC CONSIDERATIONS

OBJECTIVE 10.5
The ways in which strategic considerations affect capital budgeting

So far, we have considered only the profits from incremental revenues or the expected cost savings offered by a long-term asset. These are the most common benefits associated with acquiring long-term assets, but the strategic benefits of a long-term asset are of increasing importance. Including these strategic benefits in a capital budgeting example is very controversial because, as many people argue, they are difficult to estimate and, therefore, are risky to include. Strategic benefits are likely to be no more difficult to estimate, however, than the profits from expected sales or expected cost savings.

Strategic benefits reflect the enhanced revenue and profit potential that derive from some attribute of a long-term asset. The following are the most common strategic benefits provided by a long-term asset:

[9] This was determined by setting up the problem on a computer spreadsheet and varying the annual cash benefits until the project net present value is zero.

1. *Being able to make goods or deliver a service that competitors cannot* (for example, developing a patented process to make a product that competitors cannot replicate).

2. *Improving the quality of the product* by reducing the potential to make mistakes (for example, improving machining tolerances or reducing reliance on operator settings).

3. *Shortening the cycle time* to make the product (for example, 1-hour photo developing or being able to make a custom-designed product, such as a suit or dress, on the spot).

For example, Wendy's Pizza Parlor might consider investing in a new oven that can sense when a pizza is cooked and then eject it automatically. This oven may offer a number of benefits. First, it might allow Wendy to hire less-skilled and lower-paid employees to work in the pizza parlor. Second, by compensating for ambient factors such as external temperature and humidity, the oven would improve the consistency of cooking and, therefore, the quality of the pizzas. As customers recognize the high pizza quality, they are likely to find Wendy's pizzas more desirable. Thus, the benefits from the automatic oven would include increased sales and lower operating expenses if the competitors did not have this oven. On the other hand, the automatic oven would prevent an erosion of sales if Wendy's competitors had also purchased it. In either situation, acquisition of the automatic oven would provide benefits to Wendy's Pizza Parlor that should be incorporated in the capital budgeting analysis.

POSTIMPLEMENTATION AUDITS AND CAPITAL BUDGETING

OBJECTIVE 10.6
The role of postimplementation audits in capital budgeting

As you might suspect, the decisions reached using capital budgeting models rest heavily on the estimates, particularly on the project's cash flows and its life, used in these models. These estimates come from many sources: past experience, judgment, or the experience of others, such as competitors.

When using estimates to plan recognizing the behavioral implications that lie behind them is important. For example, a production supervisor who is very anxious to have the latest production equipment might be very optimistic, to the point of being reckless, in forecasting the benefits in terms of cost reduction, quality improvement, and cycle time reduction offered by that machine to promote its purchase. This type of behavior is mitigated if people understand that, once equipment is acquired, the results will be compared to the claims that were made in support of its acquisition.

Many organizations fail to compare the estimates made in the capital budgeting process with the actual results. This is a mistake for three reasons:

1. By comparing estimates with results, the organization's planners can identify *where their estimates were wrong* and try to avoid making similar mistakes in the future.

2. By assessing the skill of planners, organizations can *identify and reward* those who are good at making capital budgeting decisions.

3. By not auditing projects, companies create an environment in which *planners may be tempted to inflate their estimates* of the cash benefits associated with the projects to get them approved.

After the fact audits therefore provide an important discipline to a subjective judgmental process. Revisiting the decision to purchase a long-lived asset is called a **postimplementation audit** of the capital budgeting decision and provides many valuable insights for decision makers.

Postimplementation audit
Reevaluating a past decision to purchase a long-lived asset by comparing expected and actual inflows and outflows.

BUDGETING OTHER SPENDING PROPOSALS

As discussed in Chapter 5, organizations develop spending proposals for discretionary items, such as research and development, advertising, and training, which are not capital expenditure items. Some discretionary expenditure items that are not related to capital (such as research and development, advertising, and training) provide benefits that may be realized for many periods into the future. However, financial accounting conventions relating to external reporting (GAAP) require that discretionary expenditure items that are not related to capital be expensed in the periods that they are made, even if they do provide future benefits.

Despite the financial accounting treatment of discretionary expenditures, their magnitude suggests that they should be evaluated like capital spending projects as much as possible. The approach to analyzing a discretionary expenditure is identical to that used when deciding whether to make a capital investment. Planners should estimate the discounted cash inflows (benefits) and discounted cash outflows (costs) associated with any discretionary spending project and accept the project if the net present value of the discounted cash flows is positive.

TELEDESIC CORPORATION REVISITED

Now that we have studied the issues in capital budgeting, we understand the problem that Teledesic Corporation faces, which we considered at the start of the chapter. Suppose that the actual investment outlays would be $1 billion per year in 1995, 1996, and 1997 and $2 billion per year in 1998, 1999, and 2000. Suppose that net cash inflow expected from this system is $3 billion per year, beginning in 2001, and that the system will last 15 years before the technology is obsolete and would be abandoned with no terminal value.

If Teledesic estimates its cost of capital as 20%, we can compute the present value of cost outflows and benefit inflows using the start of 1995 as time zero for the present value calculations. The present value, at the start of 1995, of the three-year $1 billion outflow annuity beginning in 1995 is $2,106,481,482, as shown in the following equation:

$$\text{Present value of cost annuity} = \$1,000,000,000 * \left[\frac{(1.20)^3 - 1}{0.20 * (1.20)^3} \right]$$

$$= \$2,106,481,482$$

The present value, at the start of 1998, of the 3-year $2 billion outflow annuity beginning in 1998 is $4,212,962,963, as shown in the following equation:

$$\text{Present value of cost annuity} = \$2,000,000,000 * \left[\frac{(1.20)^3 - 1}{0.20 * (1.20)^3} \right]$$

$$= \$4,212,962,963$$

The present value, at the start of 1995, of the 3-year $2 billion outflow annuity beginning in 1998 is $2,438,057,270, as shown in the following equation:

$$\text{Present value of outflow annuity} = \left[\frac{4,212,962,963}{(1.2)^3}\right] = \left[\frac{4,212,962,963}{1.728}\right]$$

$$= \$2,438,057,270$$

Therefore, the total present value, at the start of 1995, of the outflow costs between 1995 and the end of 2000 is $4,544,538,752 ($2,106,481,482 + $2,438,057,270).

The present value at the start of 2001 of the 15-year inflow annuity starting in 2001 is $14,026,417,927 as shown in the following equation:

$$\text{Value of benefits annuity at 2001} = \$3,000,000,000 * \left[\frac{(1.2)^{15} - 1}{0.2 * (1.2)^{15}}\right]$$

$$= \$14,026,417,927$$

This annuity begins in 2001, so the annuity equation gives the present value of the annuity at the *start* of year 2001. To compare the benefits with the cost, we must compute the present value of the benefit annuity at the start of 1995. The present value of this inflow annuity is $4,697,418,984:

$$\text{Present value of benefits annuity} = \left[\frac{14,026,417,927}{(1.2)^6}\right] = \left[\frac{14,026,417,927}{2.98598}\right]$$

$$= \$4,697,418,984$$

Therefore, the net present value of this project is $152,880,232 ($4,697,418,984 − $4,544,538,752), and it is economically attractive. Note that the net present value of this project is very small compared to the magnitude of the estimates. In fact, if the cost outflows in each period increase by about 3.5% or the cash inflows in each period decrease by about 3.5%, the project's net present value will be negative. Therefore, the decision to accept this project on economic grounds is very sensitive to the cost and benefit estimates.

Note that we have considered only the financial facets of this decision. There are important issues relating to technical risk, which are partially reflected in the cost of capital, and issues relating to the synergy between this business and the founders' original business. Managers must evaluate this project from many angles.

SUMMARY

In this chapter, we have introduced some of the basic capital budgeting concepts. Capital budgeting compares the costs and benefits of a long-term, or capital, asset. The acquisition of long-term assets requires organizations to plan carefully because such assets involve long-term commitments of large amounts of money. Therefore, this acquisition should receive careful attention.

To discuss capital budgeting, we introduced the concepts of investment and return, the present and future value of money, effective and nominal interest rates, annuities, cost of capital, net present value, and return on investment. You should be certain that you have a good grasp of these concepts because you will use them frequently whether you choose a career in business or another field.

Because the costs and benefits associated with a long-term asset invariably take place at different points in time, and because money has a time value, we use the concept of present value to convert all cash outflows and inflows to a common point in time so that they are comparable.

Taxes affect cash flows in two ways. First, taxing authorities define the income that is subject to taxes and the depreciation schedule, which includes both the pattern of depreciation and the period over which the depreciation can be recognized in computing taxable income. Second, taxing authorities set the tax rate that organizations apply to taxable income in determining taxes payable.

Capital budgeting involves uncertainties relating to estimating future cash flows, including estimates of cost savings that result from the acquisition of the asset and estimates of increased profits that result from the increased revenues associated with the acquisition of the asset. We discussed two tools, what-if analysis and sensitivity analysis, that planners can use to investigate the effects of forecasting uncertainties on the capital budgeting model.

Because capital budgeting compares the incremental cash inflows and incremental cash outflows attributable to the acquisition of a long-term asset, it is critical that the baseline, or status quo, position be carefully chosen. For example, if competitors are acquiring equipment to improve quality and to retain customers, the capital budgeting analysis associated with acquiring that equipment must reflect the revenue and profit losses if the existing equipment is kept while competitors upgrade their equipment.

KEY TERM LIST

annuity, p. 413

capital budgeting, p. 407

compounding effect (of interest), p. 409

cost of capital, p. 414

discount rate, p. 413

discounting, p. 412

effective rate of interest, p. 410

future value, p. 408

incremental cash flow, p. 415

inflows, p. 411

investment, p. 408

long-term or capital assets, p. 406

net present value, p. 415

nominal or stated rate of interest, p. 410

outflows, p. 411

payback period, p. 407

period length, p. 415

postimplementation audit, p. 425

present value, p. 412

time value of money, p. 408

time zero (or period zero), p. 412

EXHIBIT 10A–1
Summary of Capital Budgeting Formulas

NAME	EQUATION NUMBER	FORMULA	USE
Future value (FV)	10–1	$FV = \text{Investment} * (1 + r)^{n-1}$	To compute the future value of an investment when the rate of interest is r per period and the number of periods is n.
Present value (PV)	10–2	$PV = \left[\dfrac{\text{Future Amount}}{(1 + r)^n}\right]$	To compute the present value of a future amount when the rate of interest is r per period and the number of periods is n. Appendix 10–2 lists the values of this formula for a future amount of $1 and selected values of r and n.
Present value of an annuity (PVA)	10–3	$PVA = a * \left[\dfrac{(1 + r)^n - 1}{r * (1 + r)^n}\right]$	To compute the present value of an annuity that pays an annuity of $1 at the end of each of n periods when the interest rate per period is r. Appendix 10–3 lists the values of this formula for an annuity of $1 and selected values of r and n.
Annuity required to repay a loan (A)	10–4	$A = p * \left[\dfrac{r * (1 + r)^n}{(1 + r)^n - 1}\right]$	To compute the annuity A to be paid at the end of each of n periods to repay an amount borrowed p when the interest rate per period is r.

EXHIBIT 10A–2
Present Value of $1

PERIODS	2%	5%	7%	10%	12%	15%	20%	25%
1	0.980392	0.952381	0.934579	0.909091	0.892857	0.869565	0.833333	0.800000
2	0.961169	0.907029	0.873439	0.826446	0.797194	0.756144	0.694444	0.640000
3	0.942322	0.863838	0.816298	0.751315	0.711780	0.657516	0.578704	0.512000
4	0.923845	0.822702	0.762895	0.683013	0.635518	0.571753	0.482253	0.409600
5	0.905731	0.783526	0.712986	0.620921	0.567427	0.497177	0.401878	0.327680
6	0.887971	0.746215	0.666342	0.564474	0.506631	0.432328	0.334898	0.262144
7	0.870560	0.710681	0.622750	0.513158	0.452349	0.375937	0.279082	0.209715
8	0.853490	0.676839	0.582009	0.466507	0.403883	0.326902	0.232568	0.167772
9	0.836755	0.644609	0.543934	0.424098	0.360610	0.284262	0.193807	0.134218
10	0.820348	0.613913	0.508349	0.385543	0.321973	0.247185	0.161506	0.107374
11	0.804263	0.584679	0.475093	0.350494	0.287476	0.214943	0.134588	0.085899
12	0.788493	0.556837	0.444012	0.318631	0.256675	0.186907	0.112157	0.068719
13	0.773033	0.530321	0.414964	0.289664	0.229174	0.162528	0.093464	0.054976
14	0.757875	0.505068	0.387817	0.263331	0.204620	0.141329	0.077887	0.043980
15	0.743015	0.481017	0.362446	0.239392	0.182696	0.122894	0.064905	0.035184
16	0.728446	0.458112	0.338735	0.217629	0.163122	0.106865	0.054088	0.028147
17	0.714163	0.436297	0.316574	0.197845	0.145644	0.092926	0.045073	0.022518
18	0.700159	0.415521	0.295864	0.179859	0.130040	0.080805	0.037561	0.018014
19	0.686431	0.395734	0.276508	0.163508	0.116107	0.070265	0.031301	0.014412
20	0.672971	0.376889	0.258419	0.148644	0.103667	0.061100	0.026084	0.011529

EXHIBIT 10A–3
Present Value of an Annuity of $1 in Arrears

PERIODS	2%	5%	7%	10%	12%	15%	20%	25%
1	0.980392	0.952381	0.934579	0.909091	0.892857	0.869565	0.833333	0.800000
2	1.941561	1.859410	1.808018	1.735537	1.690051	1.625709	1.527778	1.440000
3	2.883883	2.723248	2.624316	2.486852	2.401831	2.283225	2.106481	1.952000
4	3.807729	3.545951	3.387211	3.169865	3.037349	2.854978	2.588735	2.361600
5	4.713460	4.329477	4.100197	3.790787	3.604776	3.352155	2.990612	2.689280
6	5.601431	5.075692	4.766540	4.355261	4.111407	3.784483	3.325510	2.951424
7	6.471991	5.786373	5.389289	4.868419	4.563757	4.160420	3.604592	3.161139
8	7.325481	6.463213	5.971299	5.334926	4.967640	4.487322	3.837160	3.328911
9	8.162237	7.107822	6.515232	5.759024	5.328250	4.771584	4.030967	3.463129
10	8.982585	7.721735	7.023582	6.144567	5.650223	5.018769	4.192472	3.570503
11	9.786848	8.306414	7.498674	6.495061	5.937699	5.233712	4.327060	3.656403
12	10.575341	8.863252	7.942686	6.813692	6.194374	5.420619	4.439217	3.725122
13	11.348374	9.393573	8.357651	7.103356	6.423548	5.583147	4.532681	3.780098
14	12.106249	9.898641	8.745468	7.366687	6.628168	5.724476	4.610567	3.824078
15	12.849264	10.379658	9.107914	7.606080	6.810864	5.847370	4.675473	3.859263
16	13.577709	10.837770	9.446649	7.823709	6.973986	5.954235	4.729561	3.887410
17	14.291872	11.274066	9.763223	8.021553	7.119630	6.047161	4.774634	3.909928
18	14.992031	11.689587	10.059087	8.201412	7.249670	6.127966	4.812195	3.927942
19	15.678462	12.085321	10.335595	8.364920	7.365777	6.198231	4.843496	3.942354
20	16.351433	12.462210	10.594014	8.513564	7.469444	6.259331	4.869580	3.953883

ASSIGNMENT MATERIAL

QUESTIONS

10–1 What is the cost of capital?

10–2 What does the time value of money mean?

10–3 What is discounting?

10–4 What are the significance and role of time zero in capital budgeting?

10–5 What is the defining feature of a long-term, or capital, asset?

10–6 What are inflows and outflows in capital budgeting?

10–7 What is an investment?

10–8 What is an example of an annuity?

10–9 What is the discount rate?

10–10 Why are incremental cash flows important in capital budgeting?

10–11 What does the compounding effect mean?

10–12 How is the idea of net present value used in capital budgeting?

10–13 What is the role of future value in capital budgeting?

10–14 What is the difference between the nominal and effective rate of interest?

10–15 What does payback period mean?

10–16 Why do planners compute the present value of a sum that will be received in the future?

10–17 How would you explain the idea of return on investment using nonfinancial terms?

10–18 What is capital budgeting?

10–19 Why are postimplementation audits useful?

10–20 What is an example of the use of sensitivity analysis?

EXERCISES

10–21 What are the attributes of long-term assets? Why do organizations use capital budgeting to evaluate the acquisition of long-term assets?

10–22 What are the major objectives in capital budgeting?

10–23 How would you describe capital budgeting to someone who is intelligent but knows nothing about the time value of money or the concept of return on investment?

10–24 Suppose that you work for a bank and are proposing a system that customers could access from their home computers to do their banking. Only about half of the estimated cost of this system would be covered by decreased clerical time in the banks. However, you believe that the balance of the cost will be more than made up by improved customer service that will attract more customers. How would you handle this situation in a capital budgeting exercise?

10–25 Is it always true that money now is worth more than the same amount of money received a year from now?

10–26 Which is a better deal, $1,000 at the end of one year or $500 at the end of 6 months and $500 at the end of 12 months? Why?

10–27 Explain the notion of compounding interest using an example.

10–28 You have won a lottery with an advertised prize of $1,000,000. The prize is to be paid in installments of $50,000 per year for the next 20 years. Is this prize really worth $1,000,000? Explain.

10–29 Suppose that a financial instrument promises to pay you, your heirs, or their heirs $1,000 a year forever. What is the current worth of this instrument? Make any assumption that you believe you need to answer this question.

10–30 Would you expect the cost of capital to be higher for a telephone utility or a clothing store? Explain.

10–31 Suppose that, in a capital budgeting exercise, you were considering the choice between 2 machines to do a job. However, 1 machine lasts 5 years and the other lasts only 4 years. How would you make a financial comparison between the 2 machines in this situation?

10–32 You have inherited a small convenience store. How would you compute the return on investment from this store if you decided to keep it?

10–33 Describe the effect of taxes in capital budgeting.

10–34 Suppose that you are advising someone who is using capital budgeting to evaluate the purchase of a sporting goods store. What role might sensitivity analysis play in this evaluation?

10–35 Suppose that you are using capital budgeting to evaluate two alternative business opportunities. Both require comparable investments and have comparable average cash flows. However, the cash flows of one business appear to be more volatile than those of the other, that is, the cash flows of this opportunity vary more about its average. Is this an important consideration in capital budgeting?

PROBLEMS

10–36 Compute the effective annual rate of interest in each of the following cases:

(a) A bank promises 6% interest compounded annually.

(b) A bank promises 6% interest compounded semiannually.

(c) A bank promises 6% interest compounded quarterly (every three months).

(d) A bank promises 6% interest compounded monthly.

(e) A bank promises 6% interest compounded daily.

(f) (Bonus question) A bank promises 6% interest compounded continuously.

10–37 A state lottery promises a prize of $25,000,000. However, the $25,000,000 prize is not paid immediately. The payment provision is $500,000 every 6 months for 25 years. What is the present value of the lottery prize if the current annual interest rate offered by a bank is 8% compounded semiannually?

10–38 A company issues a bond with the following characteristics:

(a) Semi-annual interest payments of $40 for 20 years

(b) A lump-sum repayment of the $1,000 face value of the bond after 20 years

If the bond market requires 7% interest, compounded semiannually for the debt issued by this company, what is the market price (present value) of this bond?

10–39 A government issues a savings bond that will pay the holder $500 in 20 years. If the bond market is now requiring 5% annual interest on government debt, what will be the issue price (present value) of this bond?

10–40 Review the data in 10–39. Suppose that you purchased the bond mentioned in that question. It is now 1 year later and the bond market requires 5.5% interest on government debt. What will you receive for this bond if you sell it today?

10–41 A bank issues a home mortgage that includes the following statement about mortgage payments and interest: "Mortgage payments are payable monthly to the bank. Mortgage interest is 9.25% per annum calculated half yearly, not in advance." If a $100,000 mortgage is repayable over 25 years, and if the monthly mortgage payment to the bank is $844.45, explain what the payment and interest provision mean.

10–42 Your credit card does not require that you pay off the monthly balance. The credit card company states that the annual interest is 18.5%. Your account is charged interest monthly on the outstanding balance. What is the effective annual rate of interest your credit card company is charging you?

10–43 Carolyn Martin, who is now 25, wants to retire at age 50 with $2,000,000 in an investment account. If funds can be invested to earn 12.5% compounded annually, what equal amount must she invest at the end of each year to accumulate $2,000,000 at the end of 25 years?

10–44 Review the data in 10–43. Suppose that Carolyn decides that it is unrealistic to invest an equal annual amount to her retirement fund and decides to invest increasing amounts each year in her retirement fund. If the amount that she invests each year is 5% more than the amount she invested in the previous year, what amount must she invest in the first year to accumulate $2,000,000 in 25 years?

10–45 Fred Samson is evaluating higher education as an investment. He is trying to decide between a career in business or as an electrician. Fred figures that tuition at a university will cost him $8,000 a year for the next 4 years and the tuition while he is becoming an electrician will be $2,500 a year for the next 4 years. Because he will be working as he is qualifying to become an electrician but will work only in the summer if he is going to the university, he figures that he will lose about $25,000 a year (before the effect of taxes) in wages for the next 4 years if he goes to the university. Because he will incur living expenses either way, Fred ignores them in his analysis.

In 4 years, Fred would either be a university graduate with a business degree or a fully certified electrician. Because he figures that he will be equally successful in business or as electrician, Fred figures that the permanent difference in his income would be about $10,000 in favor of the business degree. Fred is now 18 and plans to work until he is 60. Assume that Fred's required return is 6% after taxes and that his tax rate is 25%. Assume for the sake of convenience that Fred's retirement benefits will be the same following either career path.

(a) If Fred makes career choices purely based on economic considerations, which career should he choose?

(b) If you were advising Fred, what other facets of this decision would you suggest that he consider?

10–46 Ronnie's Welding uses welding equipment mounted in the bed of a pickup truck to provide on-site welding services. The expected life of his existing equipment is 5 more years, after which the equipment will be worthless and scrapped for zero salvage.

Ronnie is considering replacing the existing equipment with new equipment that will allow him to do jobs that he must now decline and to reduce the costs of his current jobs. The new equipment should last 5 years, reduce the operating costs associated with existing jobs by $4,000 per year, and attract new jobs with profits of about $2,000 per year. The purchase price of the new equipment would be $25,000, net of what Ronnie could get from selling his old equipment now. The salvage value of the new equipment would be $1,000 in 5 years. Assume that Ronnie can borrow money at 10%. (Ignore the effect of taxes when answering this question.)

(a) Is this investment desirable?

(b) Suppose that while he is considering this project, Ronnie discovers that the quality of the welds produced by the new machine far exceeds the quality of the welds provided by the old machine. Because weld quality is related to safety, Ronnie knows that this will be attractive to many of his customers. Suppose that Ronnie believes that if he buys the machine and his competitors do not, the increased profits associated with the new machine will be $5,000 instead of the original estimate of $2,000. Is this investment desirable?

(c) Ronnie knows that his competitors have access to the same trade information that he does and that he cannot restrict their access to the equipment that he is considering. What do you think would happen if all these competitors purchased the equipment? What do you think would happen if only one competitor purchased the equipment?

10–47 Jane Eby, the chief financial officer of Baden Discount Enterprises, is faced with choosing between two machines. They are required to replace an existing machine that makes plastic mop handles for one of the company's most popular products. Jane is not sure about the demand for these mops but estimates that it would not be less than 5,000 units per year or more than 10,000 units per year for the next 5 years.

The two machines are the semiautomatic and the automatic. Relative to the semiautomatic machine, the automatic machine makes the handles more quickly and makes fewer mistakes that require rework. Thus, the total cost per unit for materials and labor for mop handles made by the automatic and semiautomatic machines is not the same. The total costs for mop handles are $3 on the automatic machine and $5 on the semiautomatic machine.

The automatic and semiautomatic machines cost $150,000 and $100,000, respectively, and both would last 5 years. After 5 years of use, either machine could be scrapped for a salvage value that is 10% of its original cost. This organization has a cost of capital of 10%. (Ignore the effect of taxes when answering this question.)

How should Jane choose between the two machines in this situation? Be specific. You do not have to make a specific decision about one machine or the other, but your recommendation should tell her exactly how she should make the decision.

10–48 Many organizations use the payback period to evaluate investments in long-term assets. The payback period is the length of time the project takes to recover its initial investment. For example, the payback period for the example summarized in Exhibit 10–5 is 3.4 years (60,000/17,500).

The payback period is used as a broad measure of the organization's risk exposure. The further cash flows extend into the future, the more uncertain, and therefore risky, they become.

Consider the following 2 mutually exclusive projects, each of which requires an initial investment of $35,000. This organization, which has a required return of 12%, must choose one or the other.

Year	Project A Cash Flows	Project B Cash Flows
1	10,000	2,000
2	10,000	5,000
3	10,000	10,000
4	10,000	20,000
5	10,000	20,000

(a) Compute the payback period of these projects. Using the payback criterion, which project is more desirable?

(b) Compute the net present value of these two projects. Using the net present value criterion, which project is more desirable?

(c) What do you think about the idea of using the payback period to adjust for risk?

(d) How do you think conventional capital budgeting adjusts for a project's risk?

10–49 Some organizations use the accounting rate of return to evaluate investment proposals. The accounting rate of return is computed by dividing the average accounting income by the average level of investment.

For example, consider the example given in Exhibit 10–5. The average accounting income in this example is $6,250. (Because there are no accruals other than depreciation in this business, cash flow adjusted for depreciation equals net income.) The average investment level of $27,500 is given by

$$\text{Average investment} = \left[\frac{\text{Initial investment} - \text{Salvage value}}{2}\right]$$

$$= \left[\frac{\$60,000 - \$5,000}{2}\right] = \$27,500$$

Therefore, the accounting rate of return for the example in Exhibit 10–5 of the text is

$$\text{Average rate of return} = \left[\frac{\text{Average income}}{\text{Average investment}}\right] = \left[\frac{6,250}{27,500}\right] = 22.73\%$$

(a) Assuming that straight-line depreciation is used to compute income, compute the accounting rate of return for the two projects described in question 10–48.

(b) What do you think of the accounting rate of return criterion?

10–50 Inflation is a general increase in the price level. For example, if the annual cash flows and salvage value in Exhibit 10–5 were subject to inflation at the annual rate of 5%, the cash flows would be as follows. (Note that, under these conditions, the annual depreciation is now \$13,480.62 [(\$60,000 −\$6,077.53)/4].)

CALCULATING AFTER-TAX CASH FLOWS
WENDY'S PIZZA PARLOR,
INFLATION AT 5%

(1)	(2)	(3)	(4)	(5)	(6)
	Before-Tax		Taxable	Tax	After-Tax
Year	Cash Flow	Depreciation	Cash Flow	@ 40%	Cash Flow
			(2) − (3)	(4) * 40%	(2) − (5)
1	\$21,000.00	\$13,480.62	\$ 7,519.38	\$3,007.75	\$17,992.25
2	\$22,050.00	\$13,480.62	\$ 8,569.38	\$3,427.75	\$18,622.25
3	\$23,152.50	\$13,480.62	\$ 9,671.88	\$3,868.75	\$19,283.75
4	\$24,310.13	\$13,480.62	\$10,829.51	\$4,331.80	\$19,978.33
4	\$ 6,077.53	\$–0–	\$–0–	\$–0–	\$ 6,077.53

However, with inflation, the required rate of return must be increased so that it will provide for both the time value of money and the purchasing power loss due to inflation. In general, the required rate of return is

(1 + Required rate of return) = (1 + Real rate of interest) * (1 + Inflation rate)
Required rate of return = (1 + Real rate of interest) * (1 + Inflation rate) − 1
Required rate of return = Real rate of interest + Inflation rate + Real rate of interest * Inflation rate

where the real rate of interest is the return required in the absence of inflation.

(a) Using the appropriate required return, compute the project's net present value.

(b) Why is the net present value of the project lower under conditions of inflation than it was without inflation?

10–51 Magic Mountain Enterprises runs a ski center. Its 14 downhill runs vary in difficulty from beginner to expert. To attract more customers, Maria Jasper, the owner/manager, is considering developing cross-country skiing trails. The cross-country ski trails would take 2 years to build and would cost $500,000 *per year to* build. The trails would open for business in year 3 and would generate $250,000 per year in net cash flows. Maria has a required return of 15% on all investments.

The land on which the trails would be built is leased. The lease costs are included in the $250,000 annual net cash flow calculation. The lease will expire 10 years from now, that is, after the trails have been operated for 8 years. There will be no opportunity to renew the lease, and Maria will not be compensated for any of the work done building the ski trails.

(a) Compute the net present value of the decision to enter the cross-country ski business. Should the investment be made? Ignore taxes in your analysis.

(b) What is the minimum annual net cash flow from the cross-country ski business during the 8 years of operations that would make this investment desirable?

CASES

10–52 The U.S. government has enacted the MACRS (modified accelerated cost recovery system), which specifies how organizations must compute depreciation (recover costs in MACRS parlance) for tax purposes. Using the asset depreciation range (ADR), which identifies guidelines to determine an asset's depreciable life, MACRS assigns a capital asset to 1 of 8 pools. The pool determines the asset's allowed depreciation lifetime and method.

An organization can use either MACRS or straight-line depreciation based on the ADR specified for that asset. The straight-line rate for an asset equals one divided by the ADR estimated useful life for the asset. In the first year of the asset's life, only one-half of the depreciation otherwise allowable can be claimed.

The MACRS rate is multiple of the straight-line rate. For example, 200% declining balance means that the allowable annual depreciation rate equals twice the straight-line rate applied on the declining balance of the asset's value. The declining balance of the asset's value equals the asset's purchase price less all the depreciation claimed to date. This value is also known as the asset's *net book value.*

When computing depreciation for tax purposes, the asset's estimated salvage value is ignored. When the asset is sold, the organization deducts its salvage value from its net book value. If the result is less than zero, it is called a *gain on disposal* and is treated, and taxed, as income. If the result is greater than zero, it is called a *loss on disposal* and is treated, and taxed, as a loss. The following table summarizes the MACRS pools and some of their attributes.

ADR Life (Years)	MACRS Life	Depreciation Method	Important Pool Member(s)
0 ≤ life < 4	3	200% declining balance	Some tools
4 < life < 10	5	200% declining balance	Automobiles, office machines
10 ≤ life < 16	7	200% declining balance	Office furniture, machinery, and equipment
16 ≤ life < 20	10	200% declining balance	Railroad cars
20 ≤ life < 25	15	150% declining balance	Telecommunication switching equipment
25 ≤ life	20	150% declining balance	Farm buildings
Residential property	27.5	Straight-line	Rental accommodation
Nonresidential property	31.5	Straight-line	Buildings

The following table provides the factors that can be used to compute the maximum allowable depreciation in any year of any asset's depreciable life. These factors reflect the rule that only one-half of the otherwise allowable depreciation can be claimed in the first year of the asset's life. Moreover, because it is beneficial for organizations to claim depreciation for tax purposes at the maximum possible rate, the table incorporates the switch from MACRS depreciation to straight-line when the straight-line rate is higher. The factors in the table are used as follows:

Depreciation claimed in a year = Cost recovery factor for that year * Investment cost

MACRS MAXIMUM COST RECOVERY FACTORS

Year	3 Year	5 Year	7 Year	10 Year	15 Year	20 Year
1	0.333333	0.200000	0.142857	0.100000	0.050000	0.037500
2	0.444444	0.320000	0.244898	0.180000	0.095000	0.072188
3	0.148148	0.192000	0.174927	0.144000	0.085500	0.066773
4	0.074074	0.115200	0.124948	0.115200	0.076950	0.061765
5		0.115200	0.089249	0.092160	0.069255	0.057133
6		0.057600	0.089249	0.073728	0.062330	0.052848
7			0.089249	0.065536	0.059049	0.048884
8			0.044624	0.065536	0.059049	0.045218
9				0.065536	0.059049	0.044615
10				0.065536	0.059049	0.044615
11				0.032768	0.059049	0.044615
12					0.059049	0.044615
13					0.059049	0.044615
14					0.059049	0.044615
15					0.059049	0.044615
16					0.029525	0.044615
17						0.044615
18						0.044615
19						0.044615
20						0.044615
21						0.022308

(a) Using the MACRS factors, develop a depreciation schedule for the Wendy's Pizza Parlor example summarized in Exhibit 10–5 and compute the project's net present value. Assume that the oven is a MACRS 7-year asset.

(b) The following table of factors can be used to compute the tax savings associated with the cost recovery of a capital asset. The factors in the table are used as follows: the present value of the tax reductions caused by the cost recovery associated with the capital asset equals

Tax benefits = Table factor * Tax rate * Investment cost

For example, suppose that an organization acquires a piece of machinery (a 7-year class asset) costing $50,000.

If the organization's required after-tax return is 11%, and its tax rate is 30%, the present value of the tax savings associated with the depreciation is 0.700709 * 0.30 * 50,000 = $10,510.64. This calculation assumes that the asset's salvage value is zero.

Show how the 7-year factor for 11%, which was used in the preceding calculation, was derived.

MACRS PRESENT VALUE OF TAX SHIELD PROVIDED BY COST RECOVERY
(ASSUMING MAXIMUM COST RECOVERY CLAIMED)

Discount Rate	3 Year	5 Year	7 Year	10 Year	15 Year	20 Year
5%	0.909501	0.874602	0.842246	0.797468	0.698446	0.634888
6%	0.893081	0.852624	0.815533	0.764887	0.654907	0.586686
7%	0.877165	0.831548	0.790184	0.734432	0.615469	0.544067
8%	0.861733	0.811326	0.766106	0.705925	0.579659	0.506241
9%	0.846764	0.791911	0.743218	0.679207	0.547065	0.472546
10%	0.832239	0.773260	0.721443	0.654133	0.517331	0.442421
11%	0.818141	0.755335	0.700709	0.630571	0.490143	0.415394
12%	0.804452	0.738096	0.680951	0.608403	0.465228	0.391063
13%	0.791156	0.721510	0.662110	0.587523	0.442348	0.369086
14%	0.778237	0.705543	0.644128	0.567831	0.421290	0.349171
15%	0.765681	0.690165	0.626955	0.549239	0.401871	0.331068
16%	0.753474	0.675346	0.610542	0.531665	0.383927	0.314563
17%	0.741602	0.661059	0.594844	0.515037	0.367313	0.299470
18%	0.730053	0.647278	0.579821	0.499287	0.351901	0.285630
19%	0.718815	0.633980	0.565433	0.484353	0.337579	0.272905
20%	0.707876	0.621142	0.551645	0.470178	0.324244	0.261174
21%	0.697225	0.608742	0.538423	0.456711	0.311808	0.250332
22%	0.686853	0.596760	0.525737	0.443904	0.300190	0.240288
23%	0.676748	0.585177	0.513556	0.431714	0.289319	0.230962
24%	0.666901	0.573976	0.501854	0.420101	0.279130	0.222283
25%	0.657304	0.563138	0.490606	0.409027	0.269565	0.214189

10–53 Your instructor has a *Lotus 1-2-3* spreadsheet file for the Wendy's Pizza Parlor example used in the chapter. You will need it to answer this question. The file shows how easily capital budgeting calculations can be done on a computer. (Knowledge and judgment are required to perform capital budgeting analysis; however, the computer makes the necessary calculations easy.) This exercise shows you how quickly you can answer what-if or sensitivity analysis questions after you have set up the spreadsheet. Do not be misled by the simple nature of the problem. The procedure is the same for more complex problems.

After you retrieve this file into your computer, look at the layout of the spreadsheet. The key problem parameters are the initial investment amount in cell C3, the annual benefits in cell C4, the salvage value in cell C5, the required return in cell C6, and the tax rate in cell C7. The project's net present value is shown in cell F3.

(a) Move to cell C4 and change the annual benefits up or down until the amount in cell F3 is zero. (This will be about $17,788.). This is the annual benefit that just makes the project desirable. Note that $17,788 is about 89% of the estimated value of the benefit—if the annual benefit has been overestimated by as little as 12%, the project will be undesirable. This causes us to focus on our attention on the estimate of cost savings.

(b) Put the value of $20,000 in cell C4. The net present value shown in cell F3 should be $4,600. Now move to cell C6 and experiment with the rate of return amount until you force the net present value in cell F3 to zero. (This will be about 9.2%.). This is 52% more than the estimated required return of 6%, so we would consider the decision to invest in the oven relatively insensitive to the estimate of the required return.

(c) Put the value of 6% (0.06) in cell C6. Again, the net present value shown in cell F3 should be $4,600. Now let's look at the project life estimate. This simple spreadsheet is not set up in a way that allows us to vary the project life easily, although if you want to, that can be done fairly easily with spreadsheet macros.

(d) Suppose that you want to know if the pizza oven investment would be justified if the oven lasted only 3 years. Move to cell A15 and enter 3. Move to cell A16 and enter 3. This terminates the project after 3 years. Now move to cell B15 and enter 0. This indicates that there is no additional project cash flow. However, there is a cash flow related to depreciation, which amounts to $13,750. This is the correction for having understated depreciation in the first 3 years (all the depreciation should have been claimed in 3 years instead of 4). This is called a *loss on disposal* and provides a tax benefit equal to the amount of unclaimed depreciation multiplied by the tax rate. You can see that the project now has a present value of −$4,406, which means that the project is undesirable. Our decision to buy the oven is very sensitive to the estimate of the oven's life.

This simple example gives you the idea of how sensitivity analysis can be used to identify what estimates are critical to the project's acceptance or rejection and where you might want to spend more time or money improving the accuracy of estimates used in the analysis.

Suppose that the required return is 8%. If everything else in the problem remains the same, what is the minimum amount of the annual benefits that would make the project desirable?

10–54 Skeeter Rourke, general manager of the hapless Hogtown Flyers, is considering the acquisition of Bull Flanagan to bolster his team's sagging fortunes. Bull has played the last 2 seasons in Europe, so there would be no compensation to be paid to another team if he is hired. Bull, a prolific scorer and brawler, is holding out for a 10-year contract with contract demands of (1) an immediate and one-time payment of $200,000 as a signing bonus and (2) $1,000,000 in salary in the first year. Bull is demanding that his salary increase at the rate of 12% each year.

Skeeter figures that hiring Bull will increase ticket sales by 35,000 per year. Tickets sell for $20 per game, and total variable costs associated with each customer per game are about $5. In addition, Skeeter is certain that with Bull, the Flyers will get into the playoffs each year. Getting into the playoffs means sales of at least 50,000 playoff tickets, which sell for $30 each. The variable (unit-driven) cost associated with each playoff ticket is about $5. Because the Flyers have the highest ticket prices in the league and would operate at capacity if Bull were signed, Skeeter does not expect these numbers to change over the life of Bull's contract.

Skeeter's only concern is that Bull is demanding a guaranteed contract. That is, he will be paid whether he plays or not. Skeeter is virtually certain that Bull will play for 7 years. However, after that, he is not so certain of the possibilities, but he is certain that whenever Bull stops playing, ticket sales will revert to their current levels.

(a) Prepare a 10-year statement of cash flows associated with this opportunity.

(b) Assume that the Flyer's cost of capital is 10%. Compute the net present value of this deal if Bull plays for (a) 7 years, (b) 8 years, (c) 9 years, and (d) 10 years. Ignore the effect of income taxes in answering this question.

(c) What would you advise Skeeter to do?

10–55 National Courier Company picks up and delivers packages across the country and, through its relationships with couriers in other countries, provides international package delivery services. Each afternoon couriers pick up packages. In late afternoon, the packages are returned to the courier's terminal, where they are placed in bins and shipped by air to National Courier Company's hub . . . In the hub, these bins are emptied. The packages are sorted and put into different bins according to their destination terminal. Early the next morning, the bins arrive at the various destination terminals, where they are sorted by route, put onto trucks, and delivered.

An operations study determined that about $1,800,000 of employee time could be saved each year by using a scanning system. Each package's bill of lading would have a bar code that the courier would scan with a hand-held scanner when the package is picked up. The shipment would be scanned again as it reaches the terminal, when it leaves the terminal, when it reaches the hub, when it is placed into a bin at the hub, when it arrives at the destination terminal, when it is sorted onto a courier's truck for delivery, and when it is delivered to the customer. Each scanning would eliminate the manual, and less accurate, completion of a form, thereby providing courier time savings.

The total cost of the scanning system is estimated to be $7,000,000. It is thought to have a life of 5 years, when the equipment will be replaced with new technology. The salvage value of the equipment in 5 years is estimated to be $100,000.

At the end of each shift, the information from all the scanners will be loaded into National Courier Company's main computer, providing the exact location of each shipment. This tracking information provides for increased security, a lower mis-sort rate, and improved service in tracing shipments that have been mis-sorted. The reduced time spent tracing missing shipments accounts for the balance of the estimated employee time savings. The marketing manager believes that the increased security and service will result in an increased contribution margin of about $1,000,000 per year if competitors do not adopt this technology and National Courier Company does. If competitors buy this technology and National Courier Company does not, it will lose $1,000,000 in contribution margin. If everyone buys this technology each competitor will maintain its current sales level.

If National Courier Company's marginal tax rate is 30%, and it has an after-tax cost of capital of 7%, should it make this investment? Assume that National Courier Company will use straight-line depreciation to compute depreciation for tax purposes.

PLANNING AND CONTROL

This chapter will introduce you to:

1. the concept of an organization as an open system that must adapt to its environment to be successful and survive
2. the nature and interrelationship of organization planning and control
3. the ways that organizations develop goals to reflect the requirements of the stakeholders whom the organization is committed to serving
4. the different types and classifications of control systems
5. the critical role of performance measurement in control
6. the importance of self-regulating systems and employee involvement in control

■ "Struggling Dinosaurs": The Dilemma

The title of the cover story in the May 3, 1993, issue of *Fortune* magazine was "Dinosaurs." The story discussed three giants of capitalism, General Motors Corporation, Sears Roebuck, and International Business Machines Corporation. The article observed that, unlike dinosaurs, in 1993 the three companies were not "extinct, only painfully and wheezingly gasping for breath. Nonetheless, in capturing an image of broad and coincident decline among several species of onetime dominant creatures, the word works beautifully. It is truly amazing to see these legends struggling all at once, as if they had simultaneously suffered an industrial accident."

During the late 1980s and early 1990s, these three organizations experienced increasing difficulties. Each organization had suffered billions of dollars in losses and had declined from being the dominant force in its industry. Their costs of operations had increased, making them noncompetitive, and they had failed to identify what their customers preferred, although providing unique and valued customer services had made them successful in the past. These organizations failed to recognize compelling evidence showing that competitors were gaining ground. Their planning and control systems did not allow for effective responses to competitive threats and failed to exploit important emerging technologies that would prove vital to the success of their competitors.

(John M. Mantel/Sipa Press)

ORGANIZATIONS AS ADAPTIVE SYSTEMS

Successful organizations, whether they are profit seeking, such as a company that makes cars or sells insurance, or not for profit, such as a government agency or a charitable foundation, must learn how to adapt to their environments successfully. Thus, organizations are open systems because they must interact with their *environments*. The organization's *stakeholders* decide its success by actively helping it or by defining the environment within which the organization operates. Stakeholder requirements define and reflect the nature of the organization's relationship with its environment.

■ Problems Experienced by Organizations That Do Not Adapt

Unfortunately, many organizations act as if they are closed systems that are self-contained and have virtually no relationship with the surrounding world. There are very few examples of closed systems, and most of those are very artificial. For example, people with severe allergies or with no resistance to disease are sometimes put into sealed environments that protect them; prisons are operated as closed systems; secret societies operate as closed systems; and many monasteries are operated as closed systems. Such systems do not need to adapt, do not want to adapt, or avoid adapting to their environment. Organizations that act as closed systems quickly experience problems unless they are truly independent. As an example, consider the history of Ford Motor Corporation.

Henry Ford made the Ford Motor Corporation into a large successful company by developing extraordinarily efficient production systems. He refused to bow to pressures to provide variety, however, because variety was inconsistent with the low-cost, high-efficiency production systems he had designed. Mr. Ford was successful until General Motors developed a means to provide customers with the variety of products they wanted at the same cost as the Ford products. This increased General Motors' sales dramatically at Ford's expense. Henry Ford did not understand the benefit of managing the

This employee at Parrsboro Metal Fabricators is punching holes in a metal sheet. The sheet is positioned by a guide that allows the holes to be punched only in the proper locations. Preventive control, which involves using systems that prevent problems from happening, is one of the most effective approaches to control. *(Courtesy Parrsboro Metal Fabricators Limited)*

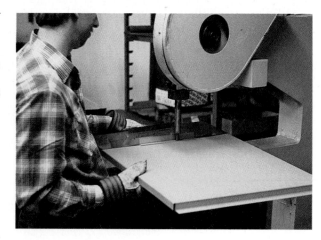

Ford Motor Corporation as an open system. This example shows how an organization's skill at dealing with the **threats** and **opportunities** in its environment helps to decide its success and, ultimately, its survival.

■ Adapting to the Environment Successfully

An organization needs to do two things to adapt to its environment. First, it must be able to *understand what is going on* in its environment and sense what is important for its future success. Management accountants, through the information systems they develop for organization members, play a crucial role in this step.

Commenting on the importance of information in helping organizations recognize and adapt to customer trends, a general manager at Mead Corporation, a paper products company, observed, *"When your customers change, you have two choices. You can change with them, or you can stand still and watch them become former customers."*

Second, the organization must be able to use the information that it gathers about its environment to *develop plans and strategies* that will allow it to adapt effectively and efficiently to that environment. For example, Dell Computer recognized that many customers already understood their computing requirements. These customers wanted high-quality computers at low prices. Dell Computer adapted to this knowledge by designing a mail-order computer selling business that eliminated the costs of personal selling, which most customers said they did not require. Dell Computer designed its order-taking, computer assembly, packaging, and shipping functions to deliver to customers the products and services they required at attractive prices.

THE NEED FOR PLANNING AND CONTROL

This chapter first considers how organizations set their goals and objectives, which is the *planning* part of this chapter. Then it considers how organizations keep themselves on track toward achieving those objectives, which is the *control* part of the chapter.

Planning and control work together. Without control, planning is meaningless because there is no followup to identify whether plans are being achieved and, if not, why they are not being achieved. Without planning, control is meaningless because there is no target, or plan, against which results are compared.

Think of planning and control as the elements of a road trip. **Planning** identifies where you are going. The strategies developed during planning identify the path or highways that you will follow to reach your destination. The short-term objectives (part of the organization's management accounting system) identify where you plan to spend each night during the trip. The maps and progress reports are the *controls* that you use and develop during your trip to ensure that you are on track toward achieving your objectives—that is, reaching your destination at the designed time.

Threat
A change in the organization's environment that diminishes its ability to achieve its goals. A new competitor is a threat.

Opportunity
A change in the organization's environment that enhances its ability to achieve its goals. A change in customer tastes is an opportunity.

OBJECTIVE 11.2
The nature and interrelationship of organization planning and control

Planning
The way that organizations set their goals and objectives.

CONSIDER THIS . . .

Strategic Planning at Harley-Davidson

In the early 1980s, Harley-Davidson, a motorcycle manufacturer, faced declining sales, losses, and customers who were unhappy with the poor quality of its motorcycles. After some executives became the company's owners, they decided to change things. A market segment, which demanded a high-powered American-made motorcycle, provided an *opportunity* for Harley-Davidson to exploit. The *threat* was from Japanese motorcycle manufacturers that produced high-quality motorcycles very efficiently and were about to overrun this segment as they had other segments of the motorcycle market.

Planners identified Harley-Davidson's *strengths* as the quality of its employees and its name and the major *weaknesses* as its horrible financial state, outmoded production practices, and rigid management style. The *corporate-level strategy* was to stabilize the organi-

zation, which was on the verge of financial collapse. The *business-level strategy* was to organize the administrative and processing systems to deliver a consistently high-quality motorcycle at low cost. Finally, Harley-Davidson put in place *functional-level strategies* consistent with its business strategies. Out of financial necessity the company adopted a just-in-time inventory strategy to trim inventory levels to the absolute minimum required, the idea being to free cash from the large work-in-process inventories. Production employees were trained to use statistical tools to measure and analyze their performance and were given the responsibility and authority to address quality and cost problems. After several lean years involving a lot of hard work, Harley-Davidson turned itself around.

STRATEGIC PLANNING

Strategic planning
The tools and processes an organization uses to identify its goals.

Goals
The long-term results sought by an organization.

Strength
A characteristic or resource that offers the organization an advantage in successfully pursuing its goals. Highly motivated employees are a strength.

Weakness
An organization characteristic or liability that inhibits the organization as it pursues its goals. A bad public image is a weakness.

Strategic planning is a set of tools, methods, and processes that organization members use to identify the organization's **goals**, which are the long-term results it wishes to achieve. Strategic planning begins with developing an understanding of what the organization's stakeholders expect from it.

The next step in strategic planning is to size up the organization's **strengths** and **weaknesses** and to identify which stakeholder objectives it intends to seek by examining the opportunities and threats that it faces. This evaluation process leads to the development of broad organization goals and a **corporate-level strategy** that specifies its chosen markets and the results that it expects from competing in those markets. The corporate strategy is translated into **business-level strategies** that define the approach that the organization will take to compete in its chosen markets, such as being a low-cost producer or an innovator, and **functional-level strategies** that define how the organization will organize its daily activities to meet its long-term goals—for example, adopting employee involvement systems to improve production performance. Then the organization defines its short-term targets, or *objectives*, for individual organization units to accomplish to support the organization in achieving its long-term goals.

KEY ELEMENTS IN AN ORGANIZATION'S ENVIRONMENT

As Chapter 2 discussed, the relevant stakeholder groups for most organizations are *customers*, who buy or use the organization's products; *employees*, whom the organization hires to make and deliver its products to its customers; *business partners* with whom the organization interacts to deliver the product to the final customer;[1] *shareholders* and other suppliers of capital (or sponsors in not-for-profit organizations), who provide the organization with resources used to achieve goals and objectives; and the *community*, whose interests may coincide or conflict with the organization's other stakeholders.

The organization must identify each stakeholder group and decide what goals it will seek for it. The goals that the organization commits itself to achieve for each stakeholder group become the organization's goals and provide the focus of the organization's planning and control activities.

THE BALANCED SCORECARD

The concept of the balanced scorecard formally recognizes that organizations must measure various facets of their performance that reflect the diverse needs or requirements of their different stakeholder groups. The **balanced scorecard** is a set of performance targets and results that reflect the organization's performance in meeting its objectives relating to its customers, employees, business partners, shareholders, and community.

The word *balanced* is used because, for many years, performance measurement systems in organizations focused only on financial or spending results, which reflected mainly the owners' perspective. During the late 1980s and early 1990s, attention shifted to customer issues, such as quality and service, but ignored the perspectives of other stakeholders. There are several organizations that have won quality awards and now find themselves in bankruptcy proceedings. An unbalanced focus, whatever it might be, is undesirable; successful organizations monitor all facets of relevant performance.

For example, McDonald's Corporation, the fast-food restaurant chain, was an early and enthusiastic user of customer-oriented performance measures. Ray Kroc, who built McDonald's Corporation into a major chain, argued that the organization should focus on quality, service, cleanliness, and

[1] Business partners include suppliers, who provide raw materials and components, and organizations, such as wholesalers, retailers, and carriers, who undertake key functions in the sequence of activities or *value chain* that connects the organization and the final consumer.

McDonnell Douglas is an enthusiastic supporter of employees working together to solve problems. Because they deal first-hand with problems, production-level employees often have useful suggestions to improve a process. These employees are part of a group that combined two steps in a product assembly process to make the assembly easier, save assembly time, and improve quality. (*Courtesy McDonnell Douglas*)

value (or QSCV) to the customer. This was one of the first systematic and comprehensive statements of customer requirements. What was exceptional was that most McDonald's employees had been taught, and understood, the importance of QSCV.

Although QSCV is a comprehensive statement of customer requirements, it is not a balanced scorecard because it considers only customers. McDonald's also was well known for expecting its managers and franchisees to be involved in local community activities and for working closely with suppliers to redesign how they prepared, packaged, and shipped food to the individual restaurants. McDonald's Corporation monitored each of these activities through an informal system that reported directly to Ray Kroc.

Recently, several organizations have formalized the notion of, and have begun to use, the balanced scorecard idea.[2] For example, the Bank of Montreal, one of Canada's largest banks, has developed a balanced scorecard system. The bank's balanced scorecard sets detailed goals and measures the performance in the areas of customer service, employee relations and development, return to owners, and community relations.

A valuable feature of the Bank of Montreal's system is that the scorecard is tailored to each level in the organization and reflects what the employees at that level can control and contribute. For example, at the upper level of the organization, the focus of measurement is on broad results, such as general levels of customer and employee satisfaction, profitability, and the bank's image in the community. Such results reflect the influence of corporate strategy developed by senior management. At lower levels of the organization, such as the level of the branch manager, the focus of measurement is on variables relating to customer service, employee relations, revenue generation and cost control, and community service activities in a particular branch. Note that the balanced scorecard at the Bank of Montreal is focused: Each level of the organization focuses on the same stakeholders so that all organization levels work together to support corporate strategy.

◼ Different Stakeholder Roles

Although all stakeholders affect the organization, the 5 stakeholder groups have different roles in deciding the organization's success. These roles can be divided into 2 groups: (1) stakeholders who have an active role in shaping the organization's success, such as employees and suppliers, and (2) stakeholders whose role is to define the environment in which the organization operates, such as customers, shareowners, and the community. (See Exhibit 11–1.)

Employees and suppliers are directly involved in managing the value chain that connects the raw materials with the final customer. Shareowners provide the resources that organizations need to supply customers with goods and services. The community defines the broad expectations about organization behavior relating to the environment, employees, customers, and the public. Customers are unique in that they define the focus for the organization's value chain.

---

[2]For examples, see Robert S. Kaplan and David P. Norton, "Putting the Balanced Scorecard to Work," *Harvard Business Review* (September–October 1993), pp. 134–142.

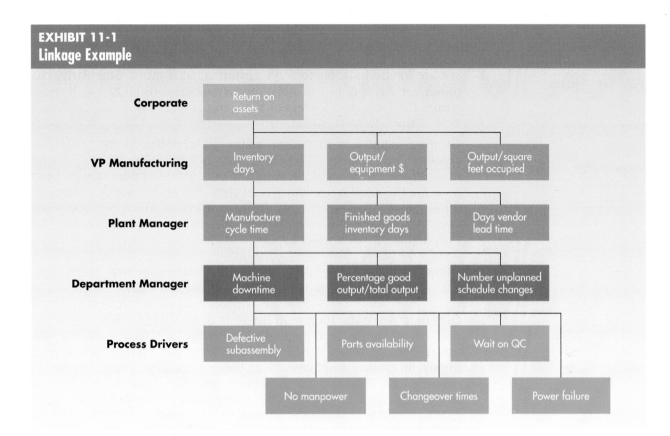

EXHIBIT 11-1
Linkage Example

Corporate	Return on assets		
VP Manufacturing	Inventory days	Output/equipment $	Output/square feet occupied
Plant Manager	Manufacture cycle time	Finished goods inventory days	Days vendor lead time
Department Manager	Machine downtime	Percentage good output/total output	Number unplanned schedule changes
Process Drivers	Defective subassembly	Parts availability	Wait on QC
	No manpower	Changeover times	Power failure

This exhibit shows how *improving one facet* of organization performance, shareholder return, can be linked to all levels of the organization reflecting each level's responsibility. This organization has identified better resource management as a corporate-level strategy to improve return on assets and shareholder return. The vice president for manufacturing and the plant manager develop the specific business-level and functional-level strategies, such as just-in-time production, employee training, improving raw material quality, and using new technologies to achieve the goal of better resource management. The department manager implements the chosen strategies. This diagram shows the key performance indicators that each level might use in this process to assess the degree of success in improving resource management. Note that the performance measures are tied together in two ways. First, all levels are focused on the same objective—improved resource management. Second, no level in the organization can improve its performance without the contribution of all levels below it. (*Management Accounting*, October 1991, published by Institute of Management Accountants,10 Paragon Drive, Montvale, NJ 07645.)

■ The Preeminence of the Customer

Of all the stakeholder groups, the most important is the customer.[3] Without customers, the organization loses its reason and ability to exist. Customers

[3]Clearly, all stakeholder groups are important. What is unique about customers is that they provide the means for the other stakeholder groups to achieve their objectives. Some people will object to this statement and argue that the organization was created by the owners to serve their purposes; therefore, the owners are the most important. But consider this: Can the owners achieve their objectives without first satisfying the customers' objectives?

provide the organization with its focus. Consider the following observations, which reflect this point of view:

> We are in the business to serve customers at a profit. Singularly, customer satisfaction is the most important responsibility we have to ensure the long-term success of the Company (Brunswick Corporation, 1990 Annual Report).

> Creating value is a matter of taking stakeholders' perspectives into account. A company's ability to create value for investors derives from its ability to create value, in turn, for the customers who buy its products, for the employees who put in time and effort, and for the many other constituencies which make it possible to run a business effectively (Rosabeth Moss Kanter in commentary appearing in NCR Corporation, 1986 Annual Report).

The following statement is interesting because it argues that the owners' interests are tied to the interests of all the organization's stakeholders:

> Olin must serve the long-term interests of its shareholders. We believe that by providing superior quality products and services to our customers, being a leader in our market segments, having outstanding, highly motivated employees, and being responsible members of our communities, Olin will grow, be more profitable, and deliver superior long-term shareholder value (Olin Corporation, 1991 Annual Report).

Many authors argue that owners create organizations to serve their needs and, therefore, that owners define the organization's goals. Although it is true that the organization's ultimate purpose may be to create value for its owners (or, for a not-for-profit organization, to meet the founding sponsors' goals), creating shareholder value is a result of doing other things well. More generally, the organization's ability to meet its other stakeholders' needs is decided by its success in meeting its customers' requirements.

■ Conflicting Stakeholder Goals

Sometimes the goals of different stakeholders conflict. For example, in 1990 and 1991, explosions at 3 chemical companies in the United States killed more than 40 people. These explosions and deaths led to charges that the companies were cutting safety-related expenditures and jeopardizing employee welfare to improve shareholder returns, an example of a conflict between employees and owners. Additional examples include those organizations cited for breaking environmental consumer laws to increase the return to shareholders (an example of a conflict between the community or customers and owners) and situations in which customers demand unusual products too expensive to make (an example of a conflict between customers and owners), too environmentally hazardous to make (an example of a conflict between customers and the community), or too dangerous to make (an example of a conflict between customers and employees).

Senior management's responsibility is to identify and resolve these conflicts by setting limits or constraints that reflect the stakeholders' goals it has committed itself to achieving. For example, organizations cannot abuse employees to achieve shareholders' return goals. Organizations cannot pollute the environment to make products that customers demand. Organizations cannot manufacture products that provide high returns but are dangerous to customers. Nor can organizations make unprofitable products, even if customers want them.

THE ORGANIZATION'S MISSION STATEMENT

Once the organization has identified which stakeholders it intends to serve and the level of its commitments to each stakeholder group, it expresses this commitment in its **mission statement**. Mission statements come in all sizes and forms and serve different purposes in different organizations. Some mission statements are very comprehensive and describe the organization's values, make specific commitments to stakeholders, and identify the major strategies the organization plans to use to meet its commitments. Other mission statements are little more than a general statement about the organization's main operating principles.

Mission statements should identify the following:

1. The organization's stakeholders. This specifies who matters to the organization.

2. What the organization believes matters to each stakeholder group that it has committed itself to satisfying. This identifies those factors important for the organization's success—its *critical success factors* (described in Chapter 2).

The organization's mission statement communicates to employees its guiding principles, beliefs, and values. It helps organization members identify what is important, thereby guiding employees as they formulate business strategies and make the decisions that help the organization achieve its stated purposes. Communicating to all employees what the organization stands for and what it needs to do to be successful provides the foundation for organization control.

Consider NCR Corporation's mission statement:

NCR is a successful, growing company dedicated to achieving superior results by assuring that its actions are aligned with stakeholder expectations. Stakeholders are all constituencies with a stake in the fortunes of the company. NCR's primary mission is to create value for our stakeholders.

➤ We believe in building mutually beneficial and enduring relationships with all of our stakeholders, based on conducting business activities with integrity and respect.

➤ We take customer satisfaction personally: we are committed to providing superior value in our products and services on a continuing basis.

> We respect the individuality of each employee and foster an environment in which employees' creativity and productivity are encouraged, recognized, valued, and rewarded.

> We think of our suppliers as partners who share our goal of achieving the highest quality standards and the most consistent level of service.

> We are committed to being caring and supportive corporate citizens within the worldwide communities in which we operate.

> We are dedicated to creating value for our shareholders and financial communities in a manner that will enhance returns on investments.[4]

Note what NCR Corporation's mission statement does:

1. It identifies customers, employees, suppliers, community, and shareholders as the organization's stakeholders. This provides a clear signal of what the organization stands for to people both inside and outside the organization.

2. It provides a general statement of what NCR believes matters to each stakeholder group. This provides a signal to each stakeholder group about how NCR Corporation plans to act toward them.

FROM PLANNING TO CONTROL

The mission statement is the result of the organization's planning process. It provides the basis for organization control. Exhibit 11–2 summarizes the relationship between planning and control. Note how planning and control are joined: planning feeds into control and control provides feedback to the planning activity.

As mentioned earlier, *control* represents the tools and methods that an organization uses to assess and improve its progress toward achieving its goals. The *focus of control* is on the organization's goals or process objectives identified during the planning stage. The *object of control* is the set of performance measures that suggest when the organization is not meeting its objectives and, whenever possible, identify the reasons for the failure.

All planning and control systems have 5 common steps:

STEP 1 Setting *goals*.

STEP 2 *Measuring* performance.

STEP 3 *Comparing* performance to goals and computing the differences, or variances, between the goals and performance.

STEP 4 *Analyzing* the causes of the variances.

STEP 5 Taking action and *correcting* the causes of the variances.

We can classify organization control systems in 2 ways: (1) to reflect the cycle, or timing, of measuring performance (step 2) and to compare performance to goals (step 3) and (2) to reflect how a goal is stated (step 1) and how results are measured (step 2).

[4]NCR Corporation, 1986 Annual Report.

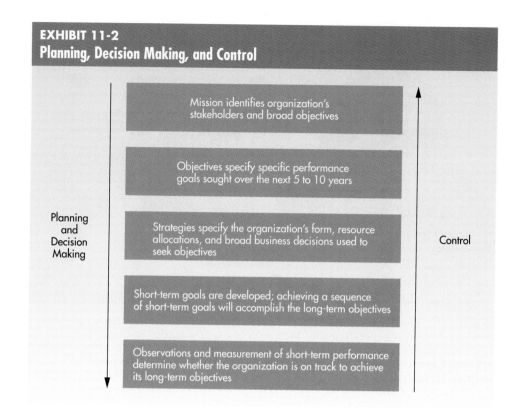

EXHIBIT 11-2
Planning, Decision Making, and Control

Planning and Decision Making

Mission identifies organization's stakeholders and broad objectives

Objectives specify specific performance goals sought over the next 5 to 10 years

Strategies specify the organization's form, resource allocations, and broad business decisions used to seek objectives

Short-term goals are developed; achieving a sequence of short-term goals will accomplish the long-term objectives

Observations and measurement of short-term performance determine whether the organization is on track to achieve its long-term objectives

Control

THE CYCLE, OR TIMING, OF CONTROL

We can classify control methods by their timing relative to the controlled event. Control methods can be feedforward, concurrent, or feedback.

Feedforward control (often called *preventive control*) happens before the good is made or service is delivered and is designed to prevent an unfavorable outcome. This fail-safing approach designs a product or service, or the process to make that product or service, so that the product cannot be made incorrectly. Fail-safing often is accomplished by developing jigs or patterns used to build the product that allow the pieces to be connected only in the proper way. Or, for services, training and educating employees provide feedforward control. This is a form of preventive control in the sense that it prevents mistakes from happening.

Preventive control can be very effective and efficient and is the objective of most quality systems. For example, inspectors in a shipyard that was building ships discovered that people had welded some huge plates forming part of the ship's hull backwards. If planners had designed these plates with simple notches so that they would fit together only when in the proper orientation, this mistake would have not happened. Preventive control is a particularly important approach to designing safety systems.

Consequently, people often think of preventive control only in the context of operational systems that control processing activities. However, preventive control can work at the administrative level. For example, an organization concerned with ethics might take steps to develop a code of

OBJECTIVE 11.4
The different types and classifications of control systems

Feedforward control
Often called *preventive control*, this approach to control focuses on preventing an undesired outcome and occurs before the activity is undertaken.

One form of preventive control is to work with suppliers so that they provide products that meet specification. Motorola is a world leader in developing relationships with suppliers and has invested millions of dollars in training suppliers to deliver what Motorola wants when it is needed. This Motorola employee is helping representatives of one of its suppliers develop methods to improve quality and cut cycle time in their operations. *(© Michael L. Abramson)*

Concurrent control
An approach to control that relies on detecting problems when they are happening so that the process can be adjusted to prevent further undesired outcomes.

ethics and ethics awareness seminars. Such an organization would then be using education as a form of preventive control to reduce incidents of ethical lapses in the organization.

Concurrent control happens while the good or service is being made and is used to detect unfavorable outcomes and correct the process. For instance, a dentist might pause while performing a procedure to ask the patient for feedback and then make the appropriate adjustments before proceeding. Consider, for example, the manufacturer of automobile engines that was experiencing a problem of premature engine failure. After a long investigation process, analysts traced the problem to the machine that bored the cylinder holes in the engine block. The analysts discovered that when the drill bits became blunt, they began to vibrate and drilled out-of-specification holes. The engine manufacturer corrected the problem by attaching a torque monitor to the drill. When the torque monitor sensed increased torque caused by dull drill bits, the machine operator replaced the drill bits, thereby avoiding the drilling of a defective hole. Concurrent control is usually quite effective because it allows limited, or no, production of defective items. Concurrent control is not as effective as preventive control, however, because it suggests that the organization has not yet dealt with the conditions that cause the system to go out of control. In the case of drilling the holes, the next step is to design a system that cannot go out of control by developing drill bits that do not get dull or by developing a different way to put holes in an engine block.

Feedback control
An approach to control that reports data on completed activities to decide whether they were completed as planned.

Feedback control reports data on completed activities to decide whether such activities were completed as planned. For example, a quality inspector might verify that a batch of completed products work properly by testing a sample, or perhaps all, of the completed units. Defective items would be tagged and sent back for rework. Or an auditor might ask a client whether he or she was satisfied with the work performed after completing the job.

Feedback control is the weakest and lowest order form of control. It is also more expensive because it is reactive and deals with problems, and their consequences, *after* they have happened rather than *before*. The following are examples:

1. Testing a batch of production after it is complete may reveal that most of the production is defective because a machine was set improperly. If the first few items had been tested as soon as they were produced (an example of concurrent control), the error would have been found and the remaining items would have been made correctly.

2. Telling a production supervisor several weeks after the fact that productivity was low and, therefore, that costs were excessive may be too late to suggest the cause of the problem if it is transitory.

3. Products found defective in the customer's hands are invariably more expensive to correct (both in terms of out-of-pocket cost and the loss of customer goodwill) than correcting the problem before it reaches the customer.

CONTROL METHODS

Organization goals can be stated, generally, in many ways and in different ways at different levels of the organization. Stating goals for an individual or, more broadly, for an administrative unit can be accomplished in 2 broad

These employees at an Eaton Corporation plant use a penetrating dye and visual inspection to test the welds in these diesel engine valves. This inspection, which takes place after production is completed, identifies defective production and, if done promptly, helps the organization identify the conditions that caused production problems.
(Courtesy Eaton Corporation)

ways, however. The administrative unit can be told what to do or it can be asked to use its discretion, knowledge, and skills to achieve specified results.

We call a method or a process designed to enforce a compliance with stated organization rules a **task control**[5] method or process—one that pertains to the situation in which members of the unit are told what to do. In contrast, we call a method or process designed to motivate compliance with stated organization goals or unit objectives a **results control**[6] method or process. The choice of using a task control or a results control approach reflects the nature of the organization, the nature of the decision, and the training of the person making the decision.

Choosing the appropriate approach to control is an important and continuing management decision in any organization.

■ Task Control

The most important determinant of whether a task or a results approach should be used for control is the nature of the organization's **environment**. If the organization's external environment is stable and well known, such as the environment facing an electrical utility or the

Task control
Systems or procedures designed to ensure that employees follow stated procedures or rules.

Results control
A system focused on results or outcomes that is designed to motivate decision-making behavior to achieve the organization's behavior.

Environment
Those elements outside the organization that affect the organization's ability to achieve its goals.

demand on a fast-food outlet for hamburgers, the organization can develop, test, and identify successful strategies and business plans.

Once they develop successful strategies and plans to deal with a stable process or environment, organizations communicate these plans to employees through training programs. Task control systems ensure that organization members follow specified rules. That is, organizations use task control systems in situations in which the process is both stable and understood and for which rules have been developed to promote the effective and efficient operation of the process. The attributes of task control systems are laid-down rules, a means to ensure that employees follow rules, and well-known consequences for failing to comply with the laid-down rules.

There are two broad approaches to task control. One is to develop a system that can be operated only the way it was intended. This is a *preventive approach* to control. The other approach to task control is to use training to ensure that people understand how the system is supposed to work and then

---

[5]Task control methods are also called *action control*, *input control*, and *pretransaction control* methods.
[6]Results control methods are also called *decision control*, *outcome control*, and *management control* methods.

use random audits to decide whether it is working as intended. This is the *audit approach* to task control.

Situations in which control system designers use task control systems to ensure that employees follow laid-down rules include these:

1. Those in which there are legal requirements to follow a specific process to provide for public safety to ensure that employees follow these legal stipulations. For example, companies manufacturing critical parts for aircraft must maintain detailed production control documents. If the product fails, investigators use these documents to identify the cause and extent of the problem. Electrical utilities operating nuclear generating facilities must follow documented and approved procedures designed to ensure that employees follow standard operating practices when dealing with equipment failure.

2. Those in which employees handle *liquid assets* to ensure that employees follow prescribed practices designed to eliminate the opportunity for fraud. For example, **internal control procedures** for retail counters specify that the clerk provide the customer with a receipt to ensure that the cash register records the receipt of cash. Banks use surprise audits to ensure that the daily operations in the branches follow the prescribed internal control procedures designed to protect the bank's assets and customers.

3. Those in which *quality* or *control considerations* demand compliance with procedures to ensure that employees follow the practice designed to improve quality or reduce costs. For example, corporate audit groups check the performance of individual hotels and restaurants, on a surprise and sometimes covert basis, to ensure that these operating units are following corporate practice designed to enhance and maintain the company's quality and cost performance.

4. Those for which *technology* has replaced skill to ensure that equipment operators follow the equipment operating rules developed. In this situation, organizations train employees to operate equipment in the prescribed manner to ensure that the equipment operates as planned and that it is not damaged.

Internal control procedures
Systems and rules used to enforce or promote task control.

Results Control

Task control systems are not useful for organizations in changing environments because as soon as the organization develops and programs a task, the environment changes and the programmed approach is no longer valid. In changing environments, or poorly understood environments (so that programmed approaches cannot be developed), organizations use results control systems that assign responsibility to individual employees and make them accountable for specific outcomes or results that reflect the organization's commitments to its stakeholders. The usefulness of results control systems depends, to a large degree, on how well organization members understand the factors leading to the organization's success. In such cases, when these factors are understood, it is possible to measure outcomes (as described in Chapter 2), and individual employees are directed to improve measured performance on those activities.[7]

When the organization is not clear about how its operations combine to create success, results control systems often use financial results (such as achieving a target return on investment), cost results (such as cost per unit or productivity), or, simply, inputs (such as number of hours worked).

The major benefits of a results control system are that (1) it takes advantage of employee knowledge and skills to develop new approaches to meeting the organization's goals and (2) it involves employees in decision making, which usually makes them more supportive of the organization's goals. The major disadvantages of results control are that (1) often uncontrollable factors can affect the results being assessed, making performance measurement problematic (this is often called the *controllability problem*); (2) in a group setting, a group goal can create a situation in which one employee benefits, or suffers, from the work done by others (this is often called the *public good* or *free rider problem*); and (3) sometimes the performance of one group can affect the results reported by another group (this is often called the *externality problem*). In settings in which such problems can exist, it is important either to develop and interpret results to avoid, or recognize, the confounding problems that these situations create or to use a task control system.

Exhibit 11–3 summarizes the conditions that favor the use of task and results control systems.

[7]For example, if the organization believes that cost, quality, and service of operations are critical to its success, it will develop measures of cost, quality, and service for each activity and direct individual employees to monitor and improve performance on those dimensions.

EXHIBIT 11–3
Task and Results Control Summary

ELEMENT	TASK CONTROL	RESULTS CONTROL
Organization environment	Stable	Changing
Control question	Were rules followed?	Were objectives achieved?
Locus of responsibility	Top down	Bottom up
Employee role	Follow rules	Achieve stated objectives
Risk level	High	Low

RESULTS CONTROL AND THE ORGANIZATION'S CRITICAL PERFORMANCE INDICATORS Once the organization members, usually senior management, have identified the organization's critical success factors, controllers must develop a means to monitor and assess the organization's performance on those critical success factors so that they can improve the organization's performance. Choosing the actual performance measures, or *critical performance indicators*, usually falls to the organization's management accountants and is a key management accounting contribution to the organization.

The critical performance indicators must be chosen carefully for each organization group, and they must reflect the role that the group plays in the organization. To be effective in helping a person manage her job, performance indicators must (1) be comprehensive in measuring all facets of the job, (2) reflect how the job contributes to the organization's success, and (3) reflect how the job's incumbent thinks about the job. For these reasons, different performance measures should be used at different levels of the organization.

CONSIDER THIS . . .

Results Control in Problematic Situations

The owner of a landscaping services company decided to reward employees based on customer satisfaction. Employees complained about the proposed system, however, pointing out that the appearance of a customer's lawns, trees, and bushes reflects the joint effect of employee care, weather, pollution, and pests. Therefore, a poor appearance may not necessarily reflect poor employee attention to the customer's property. Some employees argued that if their performance was to be based on group performance (the employees worked in teams of 3), they wanted the right to pick their own teams. No one wanted inexperienced or lazy employees on their team. Some employees pointed out that the pesticide unit (2 employees with a truck who did all the lawn spraying work and were not part of the landscaping group) was often careless and the pesticide drifted from the lawn onto bushes, killing them and ruining the work of the landscaping team.

OBJECTIVE 11.5
The critical role of performance measurement in control

RESULTS CONTROL AT THE LOWEST LEVELS OF THE ORGANIZATION

At lower levels[8] in the organization, people manage the daily activities that create the organization's products. Here, control and performance measurement focus on local activities and how well employees are managing existing systems. The focus of performance measurement reflects what these employees control, which is usually the process elements related meeting to customer requirements. These process elements include the rate of resource consumption (productivity and cost) and the quality of production and the rate of production (service and response time). At this level of the organization, the performance measurement system is really asking: How well are you using and managing the organization systems that you have in place?

RESULTS CONTROL AT THE MIDDLE LEVEL OF THE ORGANIZATION

At the middle level of the organization, people coordinate and improve the operation of the ongoing activities and redesign the organization's products and processes to meet the changing requirements of the organization's stakeholders. At this level, control and performance measurement focus on how well the organization is meeting its commitments to different stakeholder groups and how well the operating systems designed to meet these needs are working together.

---

[8]The organization's lowest level is often called the *touch level* of the organization because the employees touch the product or deal face-to-face with the customer.

The focus of performance measurement includes aggregate measures of operating performance that summarize how groups of activities work together. These measures include the ability to meet

➤ Customer delivery requirements
➤ Cycle time performance
➤ Cost performance, such as cost per unit
➤ Employee development performance, such as employee training hours or employee turnover
➤ Performance with business partners, such as number of suppliers, supplier returns, cost per unit supplied, logistics system cycle time
➤ Community-related performance, such as environmental incidents, community activities, and community perception of the organization

At this level of the organization, the performance measurement system really is asking

1. How well do the systems that the organization has put in place to meet customer requirements fit together?
2. Do the designs of these systems reflect appropriate consideration of the organization's different stakeholders?
3. How effective are these systems compared with what competitors are using?

RESULTS CONTROL AT THE UPPER LEVEL OF THE ORGANIZATION

At the upper level of the organization, people are concerned with long-term performance and aggregate results. At this level, performance measurement focuses on the aggregate performance of the organization, and the performance measurement system looks at trends in the organization's performance. Here, we are really asking these questions: Is this organization headed in the right direction? From the stakeholders' perspective, are things improving or getting worse? Exhibit 11–4 summarizes these ideas.

The fundamental idea of performance measurement is simple and twofold. First, the performance measurement system should focus all organization members on the *organization's objectives* and reflect how each individual or group *contributes to the organization's objectives*. Second, the performance measurement system *should change in orientation* to reflect each organization level's ability to affect results. At the lower level, the performance measurement system should assess how well people are managing what is now in place because the major role of these employees is to manage existing processes. This question is asked: Are we executing the tactics developed by middle level employees as intended? At the middle level, where the major responsibility is to design business strategies and coordinate the activities of existing systems, the performance measurement system should assess the design of the current systems, both in terms of how well they are working together to achieve the organization goals and in terms of how good they are compared with what competitors are doing. This question is asked: Are the tactics we are using the best ones to meet the strategy developed by senior

EXHIBIT 11–4
Organization Level and Measurement Focus

ORGANIZATION LEVEL	MAJOR RESPONSIBILITY	PERFORMANCE MEASUREMENT TYPE
Lower (for example, production workers, sales staff, customer relations staff)	Monitor and improve the operations of existing systems to meet short-term performance goals in cost containment, quality, and response time	Measures of short-term operating performance that include both output and outcome measures such as yield, productivity, and on-time delivery that reflect the operations of a single unit in the organization
Middle (for example, supervisors and managers)	Coordinate existing systems and develop new ones to achieve intermediate-term performance on critical success factors	A mix of operating measures that include both output and outcome measures and reflect how well units are working together to meet stakeholder requirements (system response time, system quality, and rate of new product introduction) and financial measures (cost per unit, productivity, or profit margin) that compare performance to competitors to evaluate the efficacy of the systems the organization has in place
Upper (for example, vice presidents, presidents)	Identify opportunities to develop new markets	Aggregated measures of outcome performance, such as return on investment, number of safety incidents, rate of new product introduction that reflects senior level employees' responsibility for meeting the organization's organization's commitment to its stakeholders

level employees? At the upper level, which is responsible for setting broad organization strategy, the performance measurement system should assess aggregate performance that is usually summarized by broad measures of performance for each important stakeholder group, for example, long-term sales growth for customers, employee turnover for employees, return on investment for owners, supplier turnover for suppliers, and the organization's image in the community. This question is asked: Have we chosen a good strategy to meet our objectives?

For example, suppose that senior level employees decide that a key strategy to achieve organization success is to improve product quality. The appropriate evaluation at this level is whether the resulting quality improvement affects organization performance as planned. This strategy initiative is passed along to middle level employees, who develop specific tactics to improve quality, for example, working with suppliers to improve the quality of raw materials, training employees to undertake quality improvement initiatives using statistical process control tools, and acquiring new equipment that reduces process variation. The appropriate evaluation at this level is the cost effectiveness of the different tactics. These tactics are passed along to the appropriate operations groups for implementation. For example, the group

EXHIBIT 11–5
Critical Success Factors and Critical Performance Indicators
at the Organization's Upper Level

CRITICAL SUCCESS FACTOR	MEANING	CRITICAL PERFORMANCE INDICATORS
Cost	General cost levels, which reflect the organization's broad production strategy	Cost as a percentage of sales, cost trends, costs relative to competitors
Quality	Product quality in customer's hands	The cost and number of warranty claims, quality rankings relative to competitors, quality image in the market
Service	Ability of systems to meet customer's delivery date requirements for products, requests, and complaints	Rate of new product introduction, percentage of sales provided by new products, customer satisfaction survey results

chosen to work with suppliers to improve incoming raw materials might assess changes in quality of incoming raw materials to evaluate whether the work done with suppliers has had its intended effect and, if not, what actions should be taken to secure the intended effect.

Exhibit 11–5 summarizes the critical success factors and some associated critical performance indicators that would apply, in one form or another, at the upper level in most organizations.

At all levels of the organization, the critical performance indicator must reflect not only the meaning of the critical success factor but also the degree of controllability of the person or organization unit to which the performance measure applies. In other words, the critical performance indicator used should capture the facets of relevant performance (the critical success factors) that the organization unit controls. Therefore, each organization unit could potentially use different performance indicators to assess its contribution to achieving the organization's critical success factors. In this setting, an important facet of a performance indicator is that it assess what the organization group controls and that it provide insights to the organization group about how it can improve its performance.

At the organization's middle level, attention focuses on coordination and system performance issues. Exhibit 11–6 summarizes the critical success factors and how they might be interpreted in a courier company at the middle level. Note that the critical performance indicators assess the performance of the business level strategies chosen by middle level employees to achieve the broad strategic goals chosen by upper level employees, which focus on cost, quality, and service and whether existing business level strategies need to be changed. These measures should direct middle level employees' attention to questions such as these: Are there better systems we might use to improve cost, quality, or service performance? Are the lower levels in the organization managing the existing systems well? How does our performance in each of these areas compare to that of our competitors?

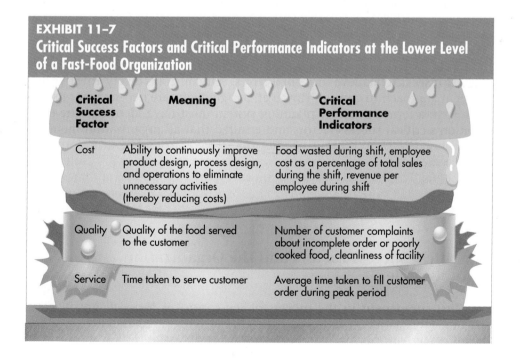

EXHIBIT 11-6
Critical Success Factors and Critical Performance Indicators at the Middle Level of a Courier Company

Critical Success Factor	Meaning	Critical Performance Indicators
Cost	Cost performance levels	Cost per shipment delivered, cost per route served, cost per customer served, total fuel costs, time spent by shipment in terminals, hubs, and in transit
Quality	Meeting service promises	Percentage of shipments that fail to meet service time commitments, number of customer complaints about damage or loss, missort rates, rate of billing errors
Service	Time to respond to customer requests	Time to develop new product, average time taken to locate lost shipment

Exhibit 11–7 summarizes how the critical success factors and their associated critical performance indicators might be applied and interpreted at the level of a shift manager in a fast-food restaurant. The list of critical performance indicators is intended to provide examples, not to be comprehensive. Note that operating personnel use these critical performance indicators to monitor their management of the existing systems, which includes asking questions such as these: Are we managing these systems to their full potential? Can we modify the existing system to improve our performance?

EXHIBIT 11-7
Critical Success Factors and Critical Performance Indicators at the Lower Level of a Fast-Food Organization

Critical Success Factor	Meaning	Critical Performance Indicators
Cost	Ability to continuously improve product design, process design, and operations to eliminate unnecessary activities (thereby reducing costs)	Food wasted during shift, employee cost as a percentage of total sales during the shift, revenue per employee during shift
Quality	Quality of the food served to the customer	Number of customer complaints about incomplete order or poorly cooked food, cleanliness of facility
Service	Time taken to serve customer	Average time taken to fill customer order during peak period

Team Hiring at R. R. Donnelley & Sons Company

One approach to control that the accounting literature virtually ignores is giving a group the responsibility for achieving objectives and leaving the discipline of individual members in the group to the group members. This approach to control is called *clan control* in the organization behavior literature.

R. R. Donnelley & Sons Company uses self-directed work teams to control quality, waste, budgets, production, and vacation scheduling and to undertake team hiring.

Team hiring means that the team hires its own employees. Teams also evaluate each member's performance and terminate the employment of members whose work does not meet the team's standards and who have been unable to improve performance after help and counseling from others on the team.

Team members say that they can do a better job

than the human resources department in choosing people to fill jobs because the team members understand the dimensions or traits it takes to do the job well. Moreover, because team members must accept responsibility for training new employees or helping team members who are not living up to expectations, they take the process of hiring people very seriously.

One supervisor commented: "In the past performance problems may have been hidden from the supervisor. . . Now that performance is reflected directly on the team, it's not the supervisor who monitors the team. The team is looking out for itself."

Source: R. R. Donnelley & Sons Company, *The Printer* (Winter 1993), pp. 16–19.

SELF-CONTROL

OBJECTIVE 11.6
The importance of self-regulating systems and employee involvement in control

Self-control
The ability of a system to accept objectives and regulate itself as it seeks to achieve those objectives.

As the histories of General Motors, Sears Roebuck, and International Business Machines suggest, one vital organization trait is its ability to delegate decision-making responsibilities within the organization so that it can identify and react quickly to environmental changes. (*Delegation* is also known as *decentralization, empowerment*, and *employee involvement*.) Organizations that delegate responsibility must meet the conditions of self-control.

Self-control describes a system that can accept objectives and regulate itself as it seeks to achieve those objectives. Self-control is a very effective and efficient approach to control. However, 3 ingredients are necessary for its success. First, a formal strategic planning system must have identified the organization's critical success factors and ensured that all organization members know them. Second, the organization must have an excellent performance measurement system that measures performance on each unit's critical success factors. Third, the organization must employ well-trained and motivated employees who have been given, and accept, the responsibility for identifying and making improvements.

■ Critical Success Factors and the Organization Unit's Role

The first component in the process of self-control is for each organization unit to understand the organization's critical success factors and its role in helping the organization achieve its objectives relating to each factor.

Individuals responsible for strategic planning should identify these critical success factors and goals and then communicate this information to all organization members. Then each organization unit can develop strategies for contributing to organization success.

For example, the Canadian Department of Veterans' Affairs is responsible for matters concerning the health and welfare of veterans of Canada's armed forces. During the early 1980s, veterans' groups complained that the department was ineffective and inefficient in meeting their needs. After some study, the department's minister announced a new mission statement and the following critical success factors: service, that is, treating veterans with dignity and respect and responding quickly and effectively to their requests for help or information and quality, by approving and paying benefit claims accurately. Planners communicated these critical success factors broadly both within the department to employees and outside the department to veterans and their advocacy groups. The minister made it clear that he took these critical success factors seriously and expected the department's employees to assess and improve their performance in these areas.

By making a public commitment to the organization's stated critical success factors and by communicating these critical success factors broadly, the minister made it clear to all employees what mattered and what they were to concentrate on improving. Each group within the department could identify how it contributed to service and quality and how it could improve its processes to enhance its performance on each of these two critical success factors.

■ Performance Measurement Relative to Objectives

The second component in the process of self-control is for each organization unit to measure its performance relative to its objectives. This requires that objectives be stated in precise and measurable ways, which ensures that each critical performance indicator focuses performance on what is critical for the organization's success. It also requires that objectives reflect the unit's contribution to the organization, which ensures that all relevant performance facets are considered.

■ Well-Trained Employees

The third component in the process of self-control is for each organization unit to have well-trained employees with the required skills to respond to performance measures to improve results. The prevailing trend in most organizations today is *employee involvement* or *empowerment*. Employee involvement asks individual employees to use their knowledge and skills to make independent decisions rather than following laid-down rules.

For example, the employees controlling the steel-making process in one of Steel Company of Canada's mills used a specific recipe, developed by engineers and chemists, to blend steel. These employees found that, for various reasons, the steel-making process consistently overused iron, a high-cost ingredient of steel. The employees developed a process control system, which

Using Employee Empowerment to Improve Results

When Ford Motor Company was planning the Ford Taurus automobile, it asked its production employees for suggestions that would enhance their ability to build the car quickly and without mistakes. The employees made many suggestions that helped to improve the quality of the cars and reduce their costs. For example, one employee suggested making all bolts the same size. This eliminated the need to search through bins of different bolts to find the right size and the need to constantly change wrenches. Another employee suggested that a hole in the car door, through which the employees had to insert a bolt, be widened. The larger hole made it easier to install the bolt (which reduced costs), easier to retrieve lost bolts (which reduced costs and improved quality since some employees, unable to retrieve lost bolts, simply left them to rattle in the car door). These suggestions reflect the knowledge and experience that people doing the work can bring to an employee empowerment program. These programs improve quality and productivity by using the knowledge and insights of all employees. Perhaps more important, productivity improves because attitudes change as these employees understand that they are valued partners in the process.

used quality control charts, to ensure that the amount of iron used was closer to what the recipe required. This innovation resulted in steel that consistently met customer specifications and lowered costs significantly. The employees could do this because they understood their jobs and that the 2 critical success factors relating to their jobs were cost and quality. This is a good example of supervisors extending decision-making responsibility to all organization members, with a results control system as the prevailing method of control.

Consider the following statement about employee involvement that appeared in the General Mills, Inc., 1992 annual report:

> We believe that every employee can and must take leadership at General Mills. After all, no one should have better knowledge of a particular job and how it can be made more productive than the person doing the job.
>
> When the power to lead is released, the results can be outstanding. We are working hard to eliminate bureaucracy and to re-educate supervisors who may hinder their fellow employees' efforts to take leadership. Leadership and feeling ownership for end results go hand in hand. With ownership go pride of accomplishment and the self-confidence to persist and succeed in the face of adversity. Self-confident employees will challenge the status quo and accept challenge from customers, subordinates and supervisors.

Employee involvement is important for 3 reasons:

1. Many observers of organization behavior believe that when supervisors delegate, and employees accept, real decision-making authority, employees' *commitment* to the organization and their motivation to pursue the organization's stated goals increases.

2. Delegating decision-making responsibility through the organization hierarchy puts decision making closer to the customer, which, in turn, generally leads to more *responsive* and more informed decision making.

3. Delegating decision-making responsibility through the organization taps the skills and knowledge of all organization members and provides the *motivation* for all organization members to develop their skills further and the knowledge to work continuously to improve the organization's processes.

This employee of R. R. Donnelley & Sons is teaching, training, and cajoling her subordinates to accept the responsibility for hiring, firing, and scheduling—the things that she does now. Once the team has accepted these responsibilities and becomes self-managed, she hopes to move on to another job in the company. She observed about this process, "I'd like to manage my way out of my current job in two years." (© Brian Smith/Outline Press)

To generate an effective environment of employee involvement, there must be a *real* delegation of decision-making responsibility. Many employee involvement programs have failed because employees believe that their superiors have delegated only trivial decision-making responsibilities.

CHALLENGES FOR MANAGEMENT ACCOUNTING IN SUPPORTING EMPLOYEE INVOLVEMENT SYSTEMS

The hallmarks of an effective system of employee involvement are decentralized decision-making authority and empowered decision makers who use critical performance indicators that reflect their contribution to the organization to fulfill their responsibilities in the organization. This environment creates 3 critical challenges for the management accountant.

1. The management accountant must ensure that the organization control system *conveys the organization's critical success factors* to all organization members. This can be done through information and training sessions and through the choice of the measures the organization uses to judge individual performance.

2. The management accountant must *study the critical performance indicators* chosen by each organization unit to ensure that they reflect the organization's critical success factors, that they are comprehensive, and that they reflect the organization unit's responsibilities in the organization. For example, consider the operations of a customer service unit responsible for tracing overdue or lost orders. This unit must be responsive and effective. Therefore, it would be inappropriate to measure the performance of this unit using the number of calls handled (a measure of output, not outcomes, as defined in Chapter 2) or the percentage of

It is imperative that employees monitor all, not a subset, of the critical performance indicators for their job. This worker can increase his productivity and reduce cycle time, thereby reducing labor and machine costs and improving quality and cycle time performance, by not aligning the cutters that form these cookies. However, this failure will increase the amount of dough used per cookie, thereby increasing raw material cost. Like most people, he must balance performance on different facets of his job. (© Charles Gupton/Uniphoto)

lost orders found (this only partially measures performance, which includes urgency as well.) A useful measure might be to use the percentage of orders reported lost that are found within 12 hours of notification. This measure includes both effectiveness and timeliness considerations.

3. The management accountant must study the critical performance indicators chosen by each organization unit to ensure that they can be *measured consistently and accurately*. The performance measures that organization units design and use to control their performance results reflect their understanding of what they contribute to the organization. An organization unit measuring only cost when quality and response time are also important in meeting customer requirements has misunderstood the elements of its performance that customers value.

MANAGEMENT BY OBJECTIVES

Organizations have developed many different approaches to focus employee attention on critical performance indicators in employee involvement systems. A widely known approach is management by objectives.

Management by objectives provides a systematic means for organizations to recognize and meet the 3 conditions required for self-control that we have just discussed. A management-by-objectives system requires that each organization unit act in a way that helps the organization achieve its stated goals by using employee involvement and a system of results control. This is accomplished through a process that decomposes

Management by objectives
A control system that uses the idea of self-control in an environment of employee involvement to promote results control.

the organization's goals and assigns them downward through the organization's hierarchy. The nature of management by objectives is independent of whether an organization group consists of many people or only 1 person.

Management by objectives works as follows:

1. Superiors *communicate the organization's mission*, critical success factors, and goals to all organization members.

2. Superiors ask each responsibility unit to *identify how it contributes to the organization's goals*. This identifies the role of each responsibility unit.

3. Precise and measurable *critical performance indicators assess the role or contribution of each responsibility unit*. The performance indicators are comprehensive and consider all relevant attributes of the responsibility unit's controllable performance.

4. Each responsibility unit develops, with its superior, *specific performance objectives* on each of its critical performance indicators.

5. During the reporting period, the manager of each responsibility unit *monitors performance* on the critical performance indicators.

6. During the reporting period, the manager of each responsibility unit *assesses its performance* on the critical performance indicators and identifies the cause of deviations and opportunities for improvement.

7. Each responsibility unit manager meets with the unit's supervisor to discuss the results, review the scope and adequacy of the performance indicators, and *set performance objectives for the following period*.

■ Martin's QuikPrint: An Example

To illustrate the process of management by objectives and show how it relates to the organization's system of planning and control, consider the application of management by objectives in Martin's QuikPrint, a custom printing shop that has 4 organization units: layout, printing, marketing, and administration. Rachel Martin, the owner, has developed the following mission statement:

> Our mission is to provide our customers with what they want quickly and at a fair price that reflects our position as an efficient supplier of custom printed products. Our customers, suppliers, employees, and our environment will be treated with respect.

Martin's QuikPrint has identified its critical success factors: (1) quality—meeting the customer's criteria of what is required and how it should look; (2) service—promising short delivery times and meeting them; and (3) cost—keeping costs low so that the prices charged will be equal to, or lower than, competitors' prices while keeping the company profitable. Within this framework, each of the four organization groups can develop specific plans.

Consider the operations of the layout group that designs and makes the plates used in the printing process. The critical performance indicators for layout, which reflect how the layout group contributes to Martin's QuikPrint's critical success factors, might be the following:

1. Cycle time (the average time taken to design and manufacture a printing plate)
2. Percentage of time that deliveries meet customer time requirements
3. Number of defects in plates that printers have returned to layout to be corrected
4. Cost of the layout group compared with the cost of the layout group in the competitor with the best practices
5. When appropriate, measures of customer satisfaction with the design creativity

Periodically, usually quarterly, the layout department manager meets with Rachel Martin for the following reasons:

➤ To set specific performance objectives for cycle time, with the goal of reducing it

➤ To increase the percentage of time that deliveries meet customer time requirements with the long-term goal of 100% and with short-term objectives reflecting continuous improvement toward that goal

➤ To reduce the number of defects, with the goal of zero defects and with short-term objectives reflecting decreasing levels of defects per 100 or 1,000 jobs

➤ To reduce cost, with the goal of being best in the industry with short-term objectives reflecting continuous improvement toward that goal

➤ To improve customer satisfaction, with the goal of carrying out every practical customer suggestion for improvement

Once specific performance objectives have been agreed to for each indicator, the manager of the layout department monitors performance on these indicators and compares the results to the plan. Causes of deviations are identified and corrected. Strategies, such as buying better machines, having more employee training, or designing a better manufacturing layout, are used to achieve continuous performance improvement on the critical performance indicators. At the end of the period, the manager meets again with Rachel Martin to discuss results, identify the improvements accomplished, and develop objectives for the following period.

■ U.S. Government Performance and Results Act: An Example

The objectives specified in the management-by-objectives process must support the organization's broad goals. The U.S. Senate's Government Performance and Results Act of 1993 shows how strategic planning and management by objectives complement each other and ties together most of the material covered in this chapter.

The act specifies the following:

No later than September 30, 1997, the head of each agency shall submit to the Director of the Office of Management and Budget and the Congress a strategic plan for program activities. Such a plan shall contain—(1) a comprehensive mission statement covering the major functions and operations of the agency; (2) general goals and objectives, including outcome-related goals and objectives, for the major functions and operations of the agency; (3) a description of how the general goals and objectives contained in the strategic plan are to be achieved, including a description of the operational processes, skills and technology, and the human, capital, information, and other resources required to meet those goals and objectives; (4) a description of how the performance goals included in the plan for the agency . . . shall be related to the general goals and objectives contained in the strategic plan.

Here, the strategic plan provides the basis for the agency's funding support and the basis to communicate the agency's goals to its employees. Annual activities will be guided by agency performance plans:

The Director of the Office of Management and Budget shall require each agency to prepare and submit to the Director an annual performance plan covering each program activity set forth in the budget of such agency. Such plan shall—(1) establish performance goals to define the level of performance to be achieved by a program activity; (2) express such goals in an objective, quantifiable, and measurable form unless authorized to be in an alternative form . . . ; (3) briefly describe the operational processes, skills, and technology and the human capital, information, or other resources required to meet the performance goals; (4) establish performance indicators to be used in measuring or assessing the relevant outputs, service levels, and outcomes of each program activity; (5) provide a basis for comparing actual program results with the established performance goals; and (6) describe the means to be used to verify and validate measured values.

The performance plans must link explicitly to each agency's strategy plans. Moreover, the performance plans must be specific, in the sense of including precise and measurable performance goals. This type of performance plan forces each organization unit to make its objectives clear to all members and to be precise about what it expects to accomplish with the resources that it consumes. Moreover, the performance plan provides the basis for accountability because deviations from the expected results must be explained.

Each report on program performance shall—(1) review the success of achieving the performance goals of the fiscal year covered by the report; (2) evaluate the performance plan for the current fiscal year relative to the performance achieved toward the performance goals in each fiscal year covered by the report; (3) explain and describe, where a performance goal has not been met—(a) why the goal was not met; (b) those plans and schedules for achieving the established performance goal; and (c) if the performance goal is impractical or infeasible, why that is the case and what action is recommended.

Clearly, the process of setting and evaluating performance under this program is subjective. Some degree of objectivity might be included in this evaluation if agency managers were required to benchmark their performance against comparable organizations, both inside and outside government, to provide a standard for comparison.

INTEGRATED SYSTEMS FOR CONTROL

Planning identifies the organization's goals; control provides the tools that organization uses to keep on the path to achieve its goals. Because planning is meaningless without control and control is meaningless without planning, organizations have developed approaches to tie the 2 together. We have seen already how the balanced scorecard idea has the potential to integrate planning and control activities. The balanced scorecard is a relatively new idea that has, however, been neither widely adopted nor tested.

Total quality management
Also known as *total quality control* and *TQM*, this is a results control system that is widely used, in various forms, to focus an organization on meeting customer requirements.

An important systematic and widely used model of planning and control is **total quality management** or, as it is sometimes called, *total quality control*. The following quotations, which reflect the sentiments of many organizations, suggest the importance of total quality management for many organizations.

> Our mission is to continuously improve the Company's long-term value to customers, employees, shareholders, and society. We will achieve our mission through the dedicated pursuit of Total Quality. We will follow a three-part strategy of efficiency, distinctive competence, and focused growth (Boise Cascade Corporation, 1990 Annual Report).

> Quality is the cornerstone of cost-effective management. Over the last five years, our quality efforts have resulted in savings of $2.2 billion (Motorola, Inc., 1991 Annual Report).

> By conforming to the requirements of our customers, both internal and external, and by doing the job right the first time, Heinz, I think, can expect $200 million in additional annual savings. This will flow from reductions in the price we pay for correcting our mistakes and failing to conform to requirements (A. J. O'Reilly, CEO, H. J. Heinz Company, Annual Shareholders' Meeting, 1990).

Despite these impressive testimonials to total quality management, (TQM) many organizations have tried it and abandoned it, arguing that it has not helped. In 1992 and 1993, many articles appeared in business periodicals announcing, "Total quality management is dead." Yet some organizations continue to insist that TQM has been their salvation. What is critical in deciding its value is the nature of the organization culture, how TQM is applied, how TQM is supported by a system of employee involvement, and whether each of TQM's critical elements was present.

THE ELEMENTS OF TOTAL QUALITY MANAGEMENT

Total quality management is an example of a systematic approach to planning and control and represents a comprehensive, organization-wide results control system rather than a specific quality tool. TQM means different things to different people. Organizations that have had a successful experience with TQM appear to have focused on it as a philosophy rather than as a set of tools. The successful experiences with TQM seem to have these common elements:

1. *Focus on the customer's needs* and wants. This focuses organization attention of the customer.

2. *Measurement of the organization's performance* from the customers' perspectives. This promotes effectiveness.

3. *Documentation of all activities* and viewing them as processes whose efficiency can be improved through continuous study and evolution.

4. *Involvement of everyone* in the organization. Senior management contributes the commitment that creates the culture needed to support TQM. From other employees, there is full participation in the TQM process. For example, Coca-Cola Enterprises, in its 1990 annual report, made the following statement about quality: "We believe in quality. We have made quality the responsibility of everyone who comes in contact with our products—not just those who produce them."

5. *Establishment of specific goals* and objectives to promote an understanding of the organization's goals, participation, accountability, and a commitment to improvement.

EFFECTIVE STRATEGIC PLANNING

Although many ideas in this chapter may seem more vague or even philosophical than those of the other chapters, effective strategic planning is important business as the decline of General Motors, Sears, and IBM suggests. The fundamental idea of strategic planning is quite simple: Continuously reassess what customers want, what competitors are doing, and other relevant environmental elements (such as emerging technology and trends in government legislation); size up these environmental changes; and use, or develop, available resources to turn these changes into advantages. Obviously, carrying out strategic planning successfully is a lot more difficult than understanding what it is.

Strategic planning requires the following:

1. Information
2. An organization that has learned how to, and can, adapt to information
3. Decision makers who are empowered to make decisions and know what is important for the organization's success

ROLE OF MANAGEMENT ACCOUNTING

Providing information and coordinating decision makers' activities as they use information are the most important roles of management accounting. The critical role of information and of management accounting in supporting the process of strategic planning and organization control is illustrated by a comment made by Roger Smith, chairman of General Motors, when asked to explain what had gone wrong and why General Motors had lost its dominance in the automobile industry and many billions of dollars. Mr. Smith said, "I don't know. It's a mysterious thing." Mr. Smith's comments reflected the failure of the design and operation of the management accounting and management control systems at General Motors. Having timely information about what is going on in the organization's environment and developing an effective reaction to that information are critical to the process of strategic planning and organization control and, therefore, proves to be vital to organization success.

DINOSAURS REVISITED

As a counterpoint to the discussion of General Motors Corporation, Sears Roebuck, and International Business Machines Corporation, the *Fortune* article described at the beginning of this chapter mentions General Electric, another large organization, but one that has sustained its success. The article attributes this success to General Electric's president, Jack Welch, whose approach to management has been to make General Electric adaptive. Mr. Welch uses intense face-to-face sessions between senior managers and employees, called *workout sessions*, in which groups of 50 employees challenge company practices with promises of no retribution and immediate action from senior management on the issues raised in these sessions. The intention is to break down boundaries between managers and employees, different departments, and the company and its customers. Mr. Welch plans to hold about 700 sessions per year and expects every employee, and important suppliers and customers, to attend at least one of them.

SUMMARY

This chapter considered planning and control and their interrelationship. Planning is the process of identifying the organization's stakeholders and, given the organization's strengths and weaknesses and the opportunities and threats that it faces in its environment, choosing the stakeholder requirements that it commits itself to achieving. Planning is critical to the organization's success because organizations, as open systems, must adapt to their environments so they can survive.

We have seen that an organization cannot commit itself to meeting all stakeholder requirements because some stakeholder requirements may be inconsistent with the organization's strengths and weaknesses, and other stakeholder requirements may conflict with the minimum commitments that the organization has made to another stakeholder group.

The organization expresses its commitments to stakeholders in terms of the critical success factors that it identifies in its mission statement. The mission statement and the critical success factors provide the basis for organization control—the tools and methods that the organization uses to monitor and assess its progress toward achieving its goals.

A critical element of control is identifying critical performance indicators—the performance measurement system the organization uses to assess its progress toward achieving its goals. The critical performance indicators become the organizing framework for the control system to compare performance to that planned and to identify ways to improve realized performance.

Because he was asked to contribute, this employee at Ford Motor Corporation helped to design a way to install lightbulbs in automobiles that reduced problems and warranty claims. *(Courtesy Ford Motor Company)*

Organizations use many different types of control systems, which differ by the timing of control and the object of control. Control systems can focus on preventing undesired behavior, reporting ongoing undesired behavior, or reporting undesired behavior that has already occurred. The object of control can be to decide whether employees followed rules or whether they achieved results consistent with the organization's objectives.

Each organization level or unit should be assessed using key performance indicators that reflect that unit's responsibilities and contribution to the organization's objectives. When people are asked to take the responsibility for decision making, the critical performance indicators should focus on the unit's outcomes.

Management by objectives is a system that organizations use to support the delegation of decision-making responsibility in a systematic way. Total quality management is one approach to organization control that emphasizes meeting customer requirements.

KEY TERM LIST

ASSIGNMENT MATERIAL

QUESTIONS

11–1 What is an open system?

11–2 What is a stakeholder?

11–3 What is an open system's environment?

11–4 What does *an open system adapting to its environment* mean?

11–5 What does *planning* mean?

11–6   What is the idea of control?

11–7   What are organization goals?

11–8   What are objectives?

11–9   What is a critical success factor?

11–10   What are organization strengths and weaknesses?

11–11   What are opportunities and threats?

11–12   What does a *balanced scorecard* mean?

11–13   What is a stakeholder requirement?

11–14   What is a mission statement?

11–15   What do *feedforward, concurrent,* and *feedback control* mean?

11–16   What is task control?

11–17   What is results control?

11–18   What is a critical performance indicator?

11–19   What is self-control?

11–20   What is employee involvement?

11–21   What does *management by objectives* mean?

11–22   What is total quality management?

EXERCISES

11–23   Why is strategic planning important for any organization?

11–24   Identify the critical success factors for your university.

11–25   Identify the critical performance indicators for the business school in your university.

11–26   Give an example of an open (adaptive) system. Explain why it is important for that system to be adaptive.

11–27   Give an example of a closed system. Explain how that system can survive while being closed.

11–28   Identify the stakeholders in your university. Explain why each group is important. What does each group expect from the university? Can you think of conflicts that might arise among the university's stakeholder groups?

11–29   Why are customers important to an organization?

11–30   Why is a mission statement useful?

11–31   Do you believe that an organization's mission statement should identify specific goals that it intends to pursue for each stakeholder group? Explain.

11–32   Give an example of feedforward control not mentioned in the text. The text claims that preventive control is more effective than concurrent or feedback control. Do you agree? Why?

11–33   Give an example of concurrent control that is not mentioned in the text. When do you think it is more appropriate to use concurrent control rather than feedforward or feedback control?

11–34   When should organizations use employee involvement?

11–35   Give an example of task control not mentioned in the text. Explain why the example is a proper use of task control.

11–36 Student evaluation based on grades is an example of results control. Would task control be more appropriate in a college or university setting? Explain.

11–37 Explain how management by objectives might work for the manager of a fast-food restaurant.

PROBLEMS

11–38 GenCorp's mission statement includes the following:

Our mission is to continuously improve the company's value to shareholders, customers, employees, and society (*The GenCorp Business Review*).

REQUIRED:

(a) Why do organizations need a mission statement?

(b) Interpret how each of GenCorp's stakeholder groups might interpret the *company's value* in GenCorp's mission statement and, given each group's interpretation, how would it be measured for that group?

(c) GenCorp has identified shareholders, customers, employees, and society as its stakeholders. Is any group missing? Why? Should any of these groups be dropped as part of GenCorp's stakeholder group? Why?

11–39 Harris Company, a manufacturer of electronic systems and equipment, has identified the following stakeholder goals in an annual report:

Customers   For customers, our goal is to achieve ever-increasing levels of satisfaction by providing quality products and services with distinctive benefits on a timely and continuing basis worldwide. Our relationships with customers will be forthright and ethical and will be conducted in a manner to build trust and confidence.

Shareholders   For shareholders, the owners of our company, our goal is to achieve sustained growth in earnings-per-share. The resulting stock-price appreciation combined with dividends should provide our shareholders with a total return on investment that is competitive with similar investment opportunities.

Employees   The people of Harris are our company's most valuable asset, and our goal is for every employee to be personally involved in and share the success of the business. The company is committed to providing an environment that encourages all employees to make full use of their creativity and unique talents, and to providing equitable compensation, good working conditions, and the opportunity for personal development and growth that is limited only by individual ability and desire.

Suppliers   Suppliers are a vital part of our resources. Our goal is to develop and maintain mutually beneficial partnerships with suppliers who share our commitment to achieving increasing levels of customer satisfaction through continuing improvements in quality, service, timeliness, and cost. Our relationships with suppliers will be sincere, ethical, and will embrace the highest principles of purchasing practice.

Communities   Our goal is to be a responsible corporate citizen. This includes support of appropriate civic, educational, and business activities, respect for the environment, and the encouragement of

Harris employees to practice good citizenship and support community programs. Our greatest contribution to our communities is to be successful so that we can maintain stable employment and create new jobs.

The role of the management accountant is to help management develop the control and measurement systems it needs to achieve the organization's goals. Identify a set of measures that will help Harris Corporation management to identify and track performance that it has specified is relevant for each stakeholder group.

11–40 Does your university have a mission statement? If so, find and study it. If not, try to compose one.

REQUIRED:

(a) What stakeholder groups does your university's mission statement specifically identify? Who do you think are the university's stakeholders?

(b) Who is the university's customer? Be careful, this is a tricky question. Legitimate arguments can be made for each of the following: students, students' parents or sponsors, high-school guidance counselors, and prospective employers.

(c) Some universities identify either alumni or faculty as the university's customer. Explain why you agree or disagree with specifying alumni or faculty as the university's customer.

(d) Has your university developed specific and measurable performance goals relating to each stakeholder group? If so, what do you think of them? If not, what should they be?

11–41 The text claims that cost, quality, and service are the critical success factors for most organizations.

REQUIRED:

(a) For any organization you choose, identify why cost, quality, and service are, or are not, critical success factors.

(b) Identify some critical performance indicators for each critical success factor that each organization might use.

11–42 The following is a statement of beliefs issued by The Gitano Group, Inc.

We believe that quality is a total commitment. Quality in people, performance and product. We believe we are leaders at what we do. And that leadership is based on innovation, creativity and teamwork. We believe that the team works best if we keep people informed by communicating in a consistent, comprehensive and direct manner. We believe in empowering people with increased authority at all levels, allowing decisions to be made and work to progress. Individuals and teams are rewarded and applauded for their successes and accomplishments. We believe in streamlining our business by simplifying systems, procedures and methods. Thrive on change and free yourself of limitations.

We believe in traditional business ethics, hard work and fair, respectful, and honest behavior in business and personal relationships. We believe in a work place that is productive, efficient, dynamic and exciting. A place where friendships develop. A home away from home. A place where all benefit from each other's backgrounds and experiences, ideas and opinions. We are a learning organization where everyone has a lot to teach and learn.

We believe the true measure of a successful company is a distinguished financial performance. We believe in setting goals and reaching them. We believe we have a social responsibility that extends into our community. We believe success should be measured by enrichment of our lives and the enhancement of relationships. Success is being satisfied after putting in a hard day's work. We believe in being who we are. The brightest and the best.

REQUIRED:

(a) What is this statement of beliefs?

(b) What purpose does this statement of beliefs serve?

11–43 The following appeared in the 1990 annual report of Varian Associates, Inc., a manufacturer of high-quality industrial electrical equipment:

During 1990 Varian began a sweeping change in corporate direction best exemplified by its drive to achieve Operational Excellence. Unlike previous strategies that lived largely on paper, the elements of Operational Excellence are dynamic, filtering through every level of the organization, and laying the critical base on which the Company will build its future. Operational excellence encompasses five key elements:

Commitment to quality— A deep-seated belief that the Company must deliver products and services that meet realistic, clearly defined customer requirements on time, every time. Employees work in ways that ensure that customer expectations are met.

Customer focus— An operating orientation in which the Company continually invests the time needed to understand customers and their needs and delivers the products or services that satisfy those needs.

Excellent time to market— A method of operation that combines teamwork and concurrent engineering to ensure that new products are consistently introduced to the market-place during the critical window of opportunity that allows maximum product life and optimum profit potential.

Flexible factories— Manufacturing operations designed to deliver a wide variety of products competitively. Such facilities are capable of responding quickly to changing demand, and still meeting customers' expected delivery dates.

Operational excellence— A company whose structure, actions, and work force are honed to deliver the best net comparative customer value. Implicitly customer oriented, the employees themselves are a competitive advantage, because they are better trained, equipped, and organized to meet customer needs, regardless of geographic or technological boundaries.

The people of Varian are committed to achieving world-class superiority in each of these elements, thus reaching true Operational Excellence.

Note: *Concurrent engineering* is an approach to product design that involves everyone affected by the new product (usually purchasing, design, manufacturing, marketing, and logistics) in a team that works together, rather than sequentially, to develop the product.

REQUIRED:

(a) What is this statement of operational excellence? What purpose does it serve? Do you think it will be effective at achieving its purpose?

(b) Given that Varian Associates is committed to its program of Operational Excellence, explain what critical performance indicators it might use to assess its performance on each of the defined elements of operational excellence.

11–44 The following exhibit appeared in Weirton Steel Corporation's 1990 annual report.

We are bound together in these common beliefs and values. We must . . .

For the Customer

➤ Have a total quality commitment to consistently meet the product, delivery and service expectations of all customers.

➤ Give customers increased value through processes that eliminate waste, minimize costs and enhance production efficiency.

For the Employee

➤ Reward teamwork, trust, honesty, openness and candor.

➤ Ensure a safe workplace.

➤ Recognize that people are the corporation and provide them with training and information that allows for continuous improvement.

➤ As employee-owners, obligate ourselves to provide a high level of performance and be accountable for our own actions.

➤ Respect the dignity, rights and contributions of others.

For the Company

➤ Continuously invest in new technology and equipment to ensure competitiveness and enhance stockholder value.

➤ Manage our financial and human resources for long-term profitability.

For the Community

➤ Commit to environmental responsibility.

➤ Fulfill our responsibility to enhance the quality of community life.

Develop a balanced scorecard that Weirton Steel Corporation might use to measure performance on each of these imperatives.

11–45 The following statement of basic corporate strategies appeared in the 1990 annual report of Allegheny Ludlum, producer of specialty metal products:

These strategies are at the core of all we do—and all that is reviewed in this Annual Report.

➤ To be a cost competitive producer of specialty materials.

➤ To make major quality improvements to meet changing customer requirements while remaining cost competitive.

➤ To find specialty niches less sensitive to competition.

➤ To exceed our customers' expectations for on-time deliveries and service.

➤ To seek opportunities to grow in the materials field horizontally and in related areas vertically.

➤ To expand a profitable export presence.

Suggest how Allegheny Ludlum can measure performance on each of the strategic elements that it has identified.

11–46 Many people believe that preventive control is more effective (that is, results in higher quality) and is more efficient (that is, costs less) than concurrent control which, in turn, is more effective and efficient than feedback control.

Consider the operations of any organization making any product or service. Identify three alternative systems to control the quality of some facet of that product or service, one involving feedforward control, one involving concurrent control, and one involving feedback control.

11–47 Consider the following statement that appeared in Boise Cascade's 1990 annual report.

At Boise Cascade, we define Total Quality as a way of managing characterized by:

➤ A focus on the customer in order to earn and retain the status of preferred supplier.

➤ A focus on involving people in quality improvement.

➤ A focus on continuous improvement of all of our processes.

REQUIRED:

(a) Indicate why each of these elements is a necessary or unnecessary part of total quality management.

(b) Is there anything that you believe that Boise Cascade should add to its definition of total quality?

11–48 A critical management system at Domino's Pizza Distribution, a subsidiary of Domino's Pizza, Inc., is Super Vision. As described in *The Domino Effect*, a text written by D. J. Vleck and J. P. Davidson, Super Vision consists of the following steps:

1. Identify your publics [stakeholders].

2. Investigate and take inventory of each of these groups' special needs.

3. Arrange those needs into major patterns [stakeholder needs].

4. Condense need patterns into a mission statement.

5. Transfer the patterns into numbers that can be used to measure performance and establish accountability.

6. Compare actual with desired performance.

7. Create an automatic reward and corrective action system based on measured performance. (© 1992. Reprinted with permission from Irwin Professional Publishing)

Assume that you are a planner working for Domino's Pizza Distribution. Based on your understanding of the fast food business, undertake the first 5 steps of Super Vision.

11–49 The Liquor Control Board of Ontario is a government agency charged with the acquisition, transportation, storage, and retailing of beverage alcohol in Ontario, Canada's largest province. The following was taken from the LCBO's strategic plan

Our Commitment

To succeed as a dynamic retailer and progressive organization, the LCBO must continue to foster a climate of trust and co-operation, where corporate values are clearly communicated and responsibilities readily accepted. To our employees, customers, suppliers, government, and communities, we commit the following:

Customers

To exceed our customers' expectations by providing them with service excellence. This will be demonstrated in the selection and quality of our products, the ambience and convenience of our stores, the professionalism of our employees, and our ongoing commitment to introduce new products and services.

To rigorously test all products sold to our customers to ensure that they exceed established health and quality standards.

To deliver quality customer services throughout our organization by ensuring that every employee's first priority is to serve the customer or to support someone who does.

Employees

To recognize employees' capabilities, empower them to made decisions, impart responsibility for results, and reward their achievements.

To challenge and encourage employees to reach their potential, and coach and support them in their professional development.

To treat employees as individuals, and to value and respect their diversity in experience and perspective.

To create and maintain a workplace environment free from harassment and discrimination.

To respect our employees' right to a healthy and safe working environment, where safe working conditions are promoted and achieved.

To establish a proactive dialogue and positive working relationship with our Union, and to work together with all employees to address the challenges which face the LCBO.

Suppliers

To ensure fairness in our relations with suppliers and trade associations, and to support an equitable system where suppliers can market and sell their products according to customer demand.

Government

To operate our business in a profitable manner on behalf of the people of Ontario, and to support government policies and programs.

Communities

To respond with sensitivity in all our business decisions to the concerns and changing societal values regarding the marketing, distribution, and consumption of beverage alcohol.

To continually consider and address the environmental implications of our business decisions.

To encourage employees to become involved in their communities by supporting charities and cultural programs, and voluntarily contributing their time and talent to community activities.

Recall that, as a government agency, the LCBO's sole shareholder is the government. The LCBO is organized into 5 operating groups, called *divisions*. These divisions and their charges are the retail division (operating the LCBO's 815 liquor outlets), merchandising division (acquiring the products that will be stocked in the retail outlets), distribution division (transporting products between suppliers and retail outlets), finance and administrative division (financial planning and organization control), human resources (providing services to employees), information technology division (implementing leading edge technology), and executive offices (reporting directly to the chief executive officer).

REQUIRED:

(a) What do you think about the commitment statement?

(b) Name the LCBO's stakeholder groups.

(c) Based on the contents of the commitment statement, identify the LCBO's critical success factors.

(d) For each of the organization's operating divisions, except the executive offices division, identify 3 critical performance indicators that would reflect that division's contribution to the LCBO's critical success factors.

11–50 Stuben Glass, the maker of glassware, is said to destroy every imperfect piece of crystal rather than to rework or sell that piece under another name as an inferior quality product. What might be the strategy at Stuben Glass that would explain this behavior?

11–51 The following appeared in the 1993 annual report of General Mills, Inc.:

Innovation, Speed, Commitment. These three central values are the keys to General Mills' superior growth record and prospects. Innovation is the principal driver of growth in established businesses and in new business development. Speed drives productivity gains. And the collective innovation, speed and commitment of General Mills people in every area of the company drives our ability to deliver financial performance that ranks at the top 10 percent of major U.S. corporations.

REQUIRED:

(a) What purpose does this statement serve?

(b) What do you think of this statement?

11–52 Mr. John F. Welch, Jr., the chairman and chief financial officer of General Electric, is engaged in a personal crusade against bureaucracy and layers of management at General Electric Corporation. The process that Mr. Welch uses is called *workout* and is a 3-day session of about 50 people that uses a format patterned after New England town meetings (events with minimal rules designed to evoke the maximum level of participation). These meetings, which include employees from all levels of the business and key customers and suppliers, are intended to promote self-confidence in questioning procedures at General Electric and developing new ways to do things. The vision is of an organization in which no functional or territorial boundaries promote parochialism and protect the status quo.

Mr. Welch made the following observation:

Layers [of management] insulate. They slow us down. They garble. Leaders in highly layered organizations are like people who wear several sweaters outside on a freezing winter day. They remain warm and comfortable but are blissfully ignorant of the realities of their environment. They couldn't be further from what is going on.

REQUIRED:

(a) Someone, sometime, must have thought that many layers of management, what Mr. Welch calls *insulation*, was a good idea. What structural or management reasons might have prompted General Electric to develop an administrative structure with many levels of management?

(b) Do you agree with what Mr. Welch says about the effect of many layers of management? Explain.

(c) The elements of a parochial organization are departments, which are usually organized on a functional basis, for example, marketing, engineering, and accounting. The problem that Mr. Welch is alluding to is that these departments tend, over time, to focus inward on their problems rather than outward on the problems of the organization. Why do you think this happens? What problems do you think this might cause?

(d) Think of a highly layered organization as a pyramid, and an organization with relatively few management layers as flat. Are there any circumstances when the pyramid style of organization is preferred? Under what conditions would the pyramid style of organization be a disaster?

11–53 Some people argue that the only relevant stakeholder to consider in a profit-seeking organization is the owner. These people argue that, in competitive markets, an organization that pursues social or other goals that increase costs is inappropriately diverting economic resources. These people argue that firms pursuing social objectives will be disciplined by the market; they will suffer losses because their prices can be no higher than the competition while their costs will be higher. Despite this, we see many organizations that pursue both social and economic goals. How can this observation be rationalized with the economic view, or does this phenomenon call the economic view into question?

CASES

11–54 Margaret Wilson and Martin Walters have just graduated from a culinary school and are thinking of starting a catering service, MW Catering, that will provide food to various social events including receptions and parties.

REQUIRED:

(a) What type of planning should Margaret and Martin do before they make a commitment to start this business?

(b) What type of on-going planning should this business do once it has started operations?

(c) Who are the major stakeholders in this business? Explain why each is important and what each would expect from the organization.

(d) What are this organization's critical success factors?

(e) What type of information does this business use on an ongoing basis to monitor its operations?

11–55 (Used with the permission of the Society of Management Accountants of Canada)

Richard Gogan, Ritchie to his friends, stood looking at his first, and flagship, store. He remembered that when he opened the store how he worked alone, often for 16 hours a day, to keep the business going. Life seemed easier then. Keep the store clean, provide a product the customer wanted, and deal with complaints promptly. He wondered how he was going to deal with the new challenges that now faced his organization.

HISTORY

Ritchie's Seafoods was founded in 1971 with the opening of a single store in River Hebert, Nova Scotia. The opening represented the realization of Ritchie's dream to manage his own business. The business was a fast-food restaurant, catering to both take-out and eat-in customers. To this day, the distribution of customers had remained about the same—70% take out and 30% eat in.

The restaurant had been established, and run, using 3 basic principles: quality, cost, and service. The restaurant provided a narrow line of foods: fried fish (2 types); fried clams; fried potatoes; fried onion rings; seafood salads (3 types); coleslaw; and drinks of various types. The restaurant used only high-quality ingredients to make the food. The facilities were spotlessly maintained. Any food not meeting Ritchie's rigid standards, relating to both preparation and appearance, was discarded. Over the years, by perfecting process and training methods, Ritchie had succeeded in raising the yield on food (ratio of the weight of food sold to the weight of food entered into preparation) from 85% to 98%. Since food costs traditionally represented about 75% of costs in the fast food business, this was a critical strategic advantage.

This improvement in food yield, while holding food quality at very high levels, had resulted in very efficient operations. Ritchie sold his food at very competitive prices. In fact, competitors chose not to compete with Ritchie directly since they were unable to operate profitably at his prices. Ritchie's interest in improving his relative cost advantage over his competitors was reflected in other areas. The store and cooking areas were laid out to provide the greatest functionality and the minimum amount of wasted space and employee effort. Long-run contracts had been established with a small number of food suppliers to provide high-quality food at very favorable prices. All supplies and wrapping materials for food were industry standard products to ensure the availability of high quality, low cost, supplies.

Service, the third element of Ritchie's focus, stressed promptness and courtesy. The focus of service was the promise that no customer would wait more than 5 minutes from the time she entered the store until delivery of the food. This promise was facilitated by 2 factors—the minimal product line and a very well-trained, and well-paid, sales staff who used food production techniques and specialized equipment that Ritchie himself had developed over the years. The staff training also emphasized courtesy. Not only were staff trained to be courteous, but they were also recruited from the local community to provide an atmosphere of cordiality and recognition. Many employees knew the customers who came into the store and addressed them on a first-name basis.

Once Ritchie had perfected the highly efficient operations providing high quality and service, he had begun to expand. The first outlet had been located in the downtown core of River Hebert. The first expansion had been to a plaza on the edge of town, beside a large shopping center. The success of that expansion had led to the opening of other outlets in other communities. By 1990, the chain comprised 32 outlets located in 19 communities in Nova Scotia, New Brunswick, and Prince Edward Island.

The operating rules were simple. Each outlet used the same menu, cooking and operating procedures, floor plan, and training. The chain featured total standardization. Innovations and improvements were developed in the original outlet and, when perfected, were rolled out to the others. For example, Ritchie had experimented with, and introduced, a computer-based ordering and scheduling system in 1988. This order system, by matching current demand with traditional volume patterns (based on season of year, day of week, and time of day), had improved scheduling and simultaneously improved service and yields. Over the past 2 years, 2 new products, lobster salad and onion rings, had been successfully introduced. However, new products were introduced very infrequently because of Ritchie's goal of maintaining simple and efficient operations and controlling quality and service through standardization. To this point in time, Ritchie's Seafoods continued to set the standards for quality, service, and cost in its fast-food market.

THE SITUATION

Over the years Ritchie had found that each outlet achieved its total sales potential in about 2 years. That is, for each outlet after 2 years and absent new product introductions, sales stabilized at their long-run potential. Increases in sales came mostly from opening new outlets since Ritchie rarely introduced new products.

Recently, however, Ritchie was feeling pressures. The elaborate customer suggestion and market intelligence system, both verbal and written, that he had established in each outlet was providing consistent advice that his traditional menu and focus might have to change. There were 2 elements of change evident: the need to broaden the menu and the change in mix of food being sold.

While there had always been pressures to introduce new products, in the past Ritchie had been satisfied with being successful with a limited product line. Ritchie believed that the success of his outlets had come through the maintenance of high and strict quality and service standards combined with highly efficient operations. The critical ingredient that facilitated this strategy was the limited product line. Ritchie was concerned that the complexity of an expanded product line could create quality, service, and cost problems. Ritchie had always resisted pressure to provide a menu with more variety.

However, a new dilemma had arisen. Increasing health consciousness was shifting customer preferences. Ritchie's market intelligence system, and the sales distribution system, were showing a distinct trend away from heavy fried foods, which had been, and were currently, the mainstay of his operations. If this trend continued, the financial success of operations would be severely affected. Ritchie was convinced that the time had come for change.

THE OPPORTUNITIES

There were many opportunities that presented themselves. For example, 1 opportunity was a seafood bar where the customers, for a fixed price, could eat as much of a variety of food as they desired. This could provide customers with a variety of baked, poached, or fresh seafood products, nutritionally more desirable than fried foods. However, Ritchie was concerned about quality and cost. He worried about quality because seafood products tended to degrade very quickly when exposed to room temperature, as they would be in a buffet style of operation. He worried about cost because a seafood bar represented a different way of doing business that might not be amenable to the systematization that, in the past, had driven his service, cost competitiveness, and quality advantages.

Another possibility was to act as a retailer of fresh seafood products such as fish fillets, lobsters, clams, and seafood salads. This provided the opportunity to expand markets while maintaining the traditional focus on quality food. While this complemented Ritchie's traditional purchasing strengths, selling fresh seafood was a new focus that would require new management and sales skills, and a considerable investment in new equipment and facilities.

Still another possibility was to refocus the organization away from the take-out business and become a family style restaurant with a broader menu.

Ritchie was sure that there were other possibilities but, above all, he wondered about his focus. He worried about a shift away from being a low-cost, low-variety, high-quality, and high-service provider of convenience food. All his systems, employee training, and success had been based on this focus. He wondered what path he should follow. How would he decide what to do? How could he refocus and retrain his employees? What skills would be required that were not currently available? Perhaps his major concern was that he did not have a strong feeling for the risk that he was taking as he thought about these new ideas.

REQUIRED:

(a) Address Ritchie's concerns that are mentioned in the last paragraph of the case.

FINANCIAL CONTROL

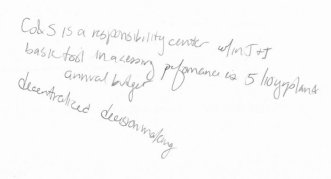

■ Ford Motor Corporation: The Dilemma

After several decades of success, by the mid-1940s, Ford Motor Corporation was in trouble. Fostered by Henry Ford's distrust of professional managers and conventional managerial tools that had been developed and were widely used at General Motors Corporation, decision making at the Ford Motor Corporation was highly centralized, budgets were virtually nonexistent, and Ford made no attempt to measure either production costs or divisional performance. As a result, Ford's share of the North American car market was about one-third of General Motor's, and Ford had barely covered its costs for over a decade.

Enter Charles "Tex" Thornton, who, during the war years, had taken a group of people, put them through a crash course at the Harvard Business School, and then created the Army Air Force's Statistical Control Command, which

transformed the Army Air Force from a shambles into a sleek machine (by) bringing order, rationality, and efficiency to an outfit that, till then, didn't know how many planes and pilots it had.

When the war ended, Thornton persuaded nine of the best to join him and use their statistical skill to conquer corporate America. He then talked Henry Ford II into hiring them in a package deal. Young Henry had just taken over the automaker from his senescent grandfather, and it was a godawful mess—its accounts in chaos, its business in peril, its executives ignorant louts. The ten brash go-getters didn't know anything about cars, but they knew their numbers—and used them to bring the company to heel. By 1955 the whiz kids headed Ford's three biggest divisions and its controller's office, with more to come. (Thomas A. Stewart, "Smart Guys, Salaries, and What We Buy," *Fortune*, October 18, 1993.)

(© Rene Burri/Magnum)

THE ROLE AND CONTRIBUTION OF FINANCIAL CONTROL

Ford Motor Corporation in the 1940s is a good example of an organization that was flying blind and following the whims of senior managers. With no financial control system, the company had no idea where it was making or losing money. With an authoritarian president and majority shareowner who preferred to concentrate decision making in his own hands and in those of trusted advisers, the organization was not using the knowledge and insights of its employees. Instead, it was relying on the impressions of people who were far removed from production facilities and customers. The result was predictable. The company had no focus and was unable to deal with the most fundamental business issue, identifying how and where the company should concentrate its efforts to improve its financial performance.

In Chapters 2 and 11, we talked about the organization's goals and control systems and described the way many organizations today are using employee empowerment systems to develop and use information critical to helping them achieve their goals. In this chapter, we talk about financial control, which involves using financial information in the process of organization control. We begin this chapter by identifying a phenomenon that prompted the original use of financial control in organizations—decentralization—in the early 1900s.

OBJECTIVE 12.1
The motives and issues underlying the design and use of responsibility centers in an organization

Centralization
Reserving decision-making power for senior management levels.

DECENTRALIZATION

Organizations in which most of the decision-making power is reserved for senior executives are called *centralized*. In Chapter 11, we saw that most highly centralized organizations are not able to respond effectively or quickly to their environments; therefore, **centralization** is most suited to entities whose environments are stable. In the past, people pointed to utilities and companies such as couriers, fast-food operations, financial institutions, or companies in the natural resource industries as examples of organizations facing stable environments.

In such organizations, technology and customer requirements were thought to be well understood, and the product line consisted mostly of commodity products for which the most important attributes were price and quality. When price is critical, controlling cost and quality becomes critical. When controlling cost and quality becomes critical, organizations often develop standard operating procedures to ensure that they are using the most efficient technologies and practices to promote both low cost and consistent quality and that there are no deviations from the preferred way of doing things.

McDonald's Corporation raised the use of standard operating procedures to a science. Its restaurant layout, product design, form of the raw materials, and prescribed operating procedures are all intended to keep costs low and quality high. McDonald's Corporation is not looking for a chef who wants to be creative when it hires someone for a cooking crew in one of its restaurants. Rather, it wants someone who can follow standardized procedures that have been developed to promote consistent quality and low costs.

Today, in response to increasing competitive pressures, many organizations—even utilities, couriers, and financial institutions that were once thought to face stable environments—are changing the way that they are organized and the way that they do business. These organizations have found that they need to be willing and able to change quickly in a world in which technology, customer tastes, and competitors' strategies are constantly changing.

For example, in the past, financial institutions developed rigid and authoritarian management systems to protect their assets and to meet regulatory requirements. Although these rigid, highly centralized systems helped these financial institutions to protect their assets, in many cases, they have not served financial institutions very well in dealing with their customers. Financial institutions have found that they must adapt to customer requirements. This includes remaining open in the evenings, offering new products and services, and responding more quickly to customer requests, such as approving a car loan on the spot rather than asking the customer to wait several days for approval or processing a mortgage application in minutes rather than weeks.

For most organizations, being adaptive means that the organization's senior management must delegate, or decentralize, decision-making responsibility to more people in the organization. **Decentralization** allows the organization members to identify changing customer tastes quickly and gives front-line employees the authority and responsibility to develop plans to react to those changes.

There are many degrees of decentralization. Some organizations restrict most decisions to senior and middle management. Other organizations delegate important decisions about how to make products and serve customers to the employees who perform those activities. The amount of decentralization reflects the organization's trust in its employees, their training, and their ability to make the right choices. It also reflects the organization's need to have someone who can make decisions quickly.

Decentralization
The strategy of delegating decision-making responsibility from senior management to employees at lower levels of the organization.

OPERATIONS AND FINANCIAL CONTROL

Chapter 11 discussed the consequences of decentralization on organization control. Decentralization requires that if someone is given the responsibility to make decisions, that person should know what is important to the organization's success, have the information to help evaluate alternatives, and have the skill to evaluate alternatives and choose the appropriate course of action. Chapter 11 discussed the role of information relating to critical success factors in a system of operations control that focuses on using operating information to choose the appropriate course of action.

In this chapter, we look at control from a different perspective. Operations control looks at control from the perspective of process improvement; **financial control** assesses the organization's financial success by evaluating the financial facets of the organization. Operations control focuses on finding the best operating decisions; financial control focuses on an overall assessment of how well the systems of operations control are working in the organization to create financial results. Financial control identifies situations in which poor financial results suggest that the systems of operations control are not working well and need to be studied and improved.

Financial control
The formal evaluation of some financial facet of an organization or a responsibility center.

The indices used for financial control vary. The most widely used alternatives are cost, profit, and return on investment. Basic to the application of financial control is the idea of dividing the organization into responsibility centers. Before we can discuss financial control, we must understand the role of responsibility centers in organizations.

THE ROLE OF RESPONSIBILITY CENTERS

Responsibility center
An organization unit for which a manager is accountable in the form of cost (a cost center), revenue (a revenue center), profits (a profit center), or return on investment (an investment center).

A **responsibility center** is an organization unit for which a manager is made responsible. Examples of responsibility centers include a store in a chain of sporting goods stores, a station in a production line manufacturing automobile batteries, the data processing group in a government office that handles claims for payment from suppliers, a claims processing unit in an insurance company, or a shipping department in a mail-order business.

A responsibility center is like a small business, and its manager is asked to run that small business to promote the interests of the larger organization. The responsibility center's manager and his or her supervisor establish goals for the responsibility center to give the manager and other employees of the responsibility center a direction or focus. Goals should be specific and measurable so that they provide specific guidance and direction to all employees of the individual responsibility center. These goals should promote both the long-term interests of the larger organization and the coordination of each responsibility center's activities.

■ The Importance of the Coordination of Responsibility Centers

Consider the operations of a nationwide courier such as Federal Express. Nationwide couriers use local terminals to dispatch trucks to pick up or deliver shipments. Shipments bound for other terminals are sent to the Federal Express hub in Memphis where they are sorted and redirected. The formula for success in the courier business is very simple and involves two key elements: (1) meeting the service commitment to the customer (politely, on time, and without damage) and (2) controlling costs. The only way to achieve success in the courier business is to ensure that all the pieces of the system work together effectively. Suppose that management has determined that each terminal will be treated as a responsibility center. How should the company measure the performance of each terminal, its managers, and its employees?

First, we can measure the things that the terminal does to promote efficiency (cost containment) in the system. To focus on efficiency, we might measure things such as the number of parcels picked up, sorted, or delivered, per route, per employee, per vehicle, per hour, or per shift. To focus on efficiency *and* customer satisfaction, we might include only those shipments that meet customer requirements in the productivity calculations.

Second, because the ability to meet the service commitment to customers in a highly integrated operation like a courier business reflects how well the pieces fit together, we must measure how each group contributes to the organization's ability to meet its commitments to customers. A courier operation has 2 important facets of terminal-hub interaction: (1) the proportion of the time that the terminal met its deadlines, that is, whether the trucks and containers were packed and ready to leave for the hub when they were required to leave and (2) when terminals are required to sort shipments, what the sorting error rate was that resulted in shipments going to the wrong place or traveling by the wrong mode.

Third, it is important also to measure service to the customer at a more detailed level. We could measure (1) how many complaints the terminal operations group receive, (2) the average time taken by the operations group to respond to complaints, and (3) the number of complaints of poor, or impolite, service received by the company's customer service line.

■ Accounting for Responsibility Centers

As mentioned earlier in this chapter, organizations use financial control to provide a summary measure of how well their systems of operations control are working. When organizations use a single index to provide a broad assessment of operations, they usually use a financial figure such as cost, profit, or return on investment.[1]

The accounting report prepared for a responsibility center reflects whether the responsibility center manager controls revenue, cost, or investment. When preparing accounting summaries, accountants classify responsibility centers into 4 types: cost centers, revenue centers, profit centers, and investment centers.

COST CENTERS

Cost centers are responsibility centers whose employees control costs but do not control their revenues or investment level. Virtually every processing group in service operations, such as the cleaning plant in a dry cleaning business, or manufacturing operations, such as the saw group in a sawmill, is a candidate to be treated as a cost center.

Cost center reporting reflects the perspectives and uses the reporting methods described in Chapters 6 and 7. Cost standards and variances figure prominently in these reports.

■ Comparing Budgeted and Actual Costs

Suppose that the cost budget shown in Exhibit 12–1 was prepared for the manufacturing unit in Moncton Carpet Products, a manufacturer of carpet cleaning products. This budget represents a cost target for the cost perfor-

OBJECTIVE 12.2
The issues and basic tools used in assessing the performance of a responsibility center

OBJECTIVE 12.3
The common forms of the responsibility centers

Cost center
A responsibility center whose manager and other employees control costs but not its revenues or investment level.

[1]Some organizations believe that financial control is inappropriate and refuse to use financial numbers for control. Instead, they use performance measures such as quality, cost, or service defined by customer requirements believing that, if customers are satisfied, financial results will follow. Organizations that use financial control believe that it is an overall test of the balance that the organization has struck between quality and service objectives. Most organizations use a combination of both types of control.

EXHIBIT 12–1
Moncton Carpet Products: Master Budget

	Product 1	Product 2	Product 3	Product 4	Total
Units made	245,000	385,000	636,000	1,250,000	
Units per batch	500	2,500	1,500	5,000	
Number of batches	490	154	424	250	
Cost per unit	$5.40	$3.20	$4.25	$1.45	
Cost per batch	$325.00	$680.00	$400.00	$135.00	
Unit-related costs	$1,323,000	$1,232,000	$2,703,000	$1,812,500	$7,070,500
Batch-related costs	159,250	104,720	169,600	33,750	467,320
Product-sustaining costs	125,000	168,000	256,000	355,000	904,000
Facility-sustaining costs					1,450,000
Total cost center costs					$9,891,820

mance of the manufacturing group and shows that total center costs are budgeted at $9,891,820. Suppose that the actual costs reported by the manufacturing group were $9,952,041. Exhibit 12–2 provides details of these actual costs. The evaluation of this cost center involves identifying the causes for the differences between the budgeting costs in Exhibit 12–1 and the actual costs in Exhibit 12–2. Exhibit 12–3 provides a summary of these cost differences. The variances reported in it equal the actual cost minus the budgeted cost.

Because the reported variance equals actual minus budgeted cost, a positive variance means that the actual cost was more than expected. As we saw in Chapter 6, a variance is unfavorable when the actual cost is higher than the planned cost, and a variance is favorable when actual cost is less than planned cost. Therefore, *positive variances are unfavorable and negative variances are favorable.*

EXHIBIT 12–2
Moncton Carpet Products: Actual Results

	PRODUCT 1	PRODUCT 2	PRODUCT 3	PRODUCT 4	TOTAL
Units made	295,000	345,000	675,000	950,000	
Units per batch	600	2,300	1,800	6,000	
Number of batches	492	150	375	159	
Cost per unit	$5.43	$3.18	$4.33	$1.40	
Cost per batch	$335.00	$670.00	$387.00	$144.00	
Unit-related costs	$1,061,850	$1,097,100	$2,922,750	$1,330,000	$6,951,700
Batch-related costs	164,820	100,500	145,125	22,896	433,341
Product-sustaining costs	133,000	163,000	259,000	362,000	917,000
Facility-sustaining costs					1,650,000
Total cost center costs					$9,952,041

EXHIBIT 12-3
Moncton Carpet Products: Simple Cost Analysis

	MASTER BUDGET (FROM EXHIBIT 12–1)	VARIANCE	ACTUAL RESULTS (FROM EXHIBIT 12–2)
Unit-related costs			
Product 1	$1,323,000	278,850	$1,601,850
Product 2	1,232,000	(134,900)	1,097,100
Product 3	2,703,000	219,750	2,922,750
Product 4	1,812,500	(482,500)	1,330,000
Total	$7,070,500	(118,800)	$6,951,700
Batch-related costs			
Product 1	$159,250	5,570	$164,820
Product 2	104,720	(4,220)	100,500
Product 3	169,600	(24,475)	145,125
Product 4	33,750	(10,854)	22,896
Total	$467,320	(33,979)	$433,341
Product-sustaining costs			
Product 1	$125,000	8,000	$133,000
Product 2	168,000	(5,000)	163,000
Product 3	256,000	3,000	259,000
Product 4	355,000	7,000	362,000
Total	$904,000	13,000	$917,000
Facility-sustaining costs	$1,450,000	200,000	$1,650,000
Total costs	$9,891,820	$60,221	$9,952,041

Exhibit 12–3 reports a mix of positive and negative variances. For example, for products 1 and 3, the unit-related costs were higher than planned, and for products 2 and 4 they were lower than planned. In total, the unit-related costs and the batch-related costs were lower than planned and the product-sustaining and facility-sustaining costs were higher than planned.

We might conclude, based on this initial analysis, that the manufacturing group at Moncton Carpet Products was able to control unit-related and batch-related costs but did not do so well controlling product-sustaining and

Acting on the need to control the unit-related costs of filling a customer's prescription, Medco developed this computer-controlled pill-dispensing machine to reduce errors and to cut back on the labor and material cost of filling mail-order prescriptions at its huge distribution center. (© Jeffrey MacMillan/U.S. News & World Report)

facility-sustaining costs. A closer examination of Exhibits 12–1 and 12–2, however, casts doubt on the validity of these conclusions. We can see by comparing line 1 of these exhibits that the number of units *actually* made differed from the planned number of units for each product. Similarly, as we can see from line 2 of these exhibits, the actual number of units per batch differed from the planned number of units per batch for each product. Because of these volume differences, it is inappropriate to compare the cost targets in the master budget with the actual cost results. To accurately assess the situation when actual volume differs from planned volume, accountants have developed the flexible budget.

■ Using the Flexible Budget

A flexible budget recasts cost targets in the planned or master budget to reflect the achieved level of production. The flexible budget develops the cost target levels based on the *actual level of activity*. Exhibit 12–4 presents the flexible budget for Moncton Carpet Products. The cost standards in this exhibit reflect the same cost per unit or cost per batch standards as the master budget.[2] The only difference here is that volume levels are adjusted to reflect the achieved level of activity. For example, Moncton Carpet Products *actually made* 345,000 units of product 2. At the standard batch size of 2,500, there should have been 138 (345,000/2,500) batches of product 2 made. At a standard unit cost of $3.20 and a standard batch cost of $680, the unit-related and batch-related costs for product 2 should have been $1,104,000 ($3.20 * 345,000) and $93,840 ($680 * 138), respectively. We can now adjust the master budget targets for the changes in volume to provide a volume-adjusted cost standard to compare with actual costs. This is done in Exhibit 12–5.

Exhibit 12–5 reconciles the actual cost to the master budget target through the flexible budget. The variances between the master budget (column 1) and the flexible budget (column 3), which accountants call *planned variances* (column 2), reflect the cost adjustments needed to show the differ-

[2]Recall that *standard* refers to the cost per unit, whereas *target* refers to the product of the standard cost per unit and some activity measure (number of units).

	PRODUCT 1	PRODUCT 2	PRODUCT 3	PRODUCT 4	TOTAL
Units made	295,000	345,000	675,000	950,000	
Units per batch	500	2,500	1,500	5,000	
Number of batches	590	138	450	190	
Cost per unit	$5.40	$3.20	$4.25	$1.45	
Cost per batch	$325.00	$680.00	$400.00	$135.00	
Unit-related costs	$1,593,000	$1,104,000	$2,868,750	$1,337,500	$6,943,250
Batch-related costs	191,750	93,840	180,000	25,650	491,240
Product-sustaining costs	125,000	168,000	256,000	355,000	904,000
Facility-sustaining costs					1,450,000
Total cost center costs					$9,788,490

EXHIBIT 12–5
Moncton Carpet Products: Flexible Budget Cost Analysis

	(1) MASTER BUDGET	(2) PLANNING VARIANCE	(3) FLEXIBLE BUDGET	(4) FLEXIBLE BUDGET VARIANCE	(5) ACTUAL
Unit-related costs					
Product 1	$1,323,000	270,000	$1,593,000	8,850	$1,601,850
Product 2	1,232,000	(128,000)	1,104,000	(6,900)	1,097,100
Product 3	2,703,000	165,750	2,868,750	54,000	2,922,750
Product 4	1,812,500	(435,000)	1,377,500	(47,500)	1,330,000
Total	$7,070,500	(127,250)	$6,943,250	8,450	$6,951,700
Batch-related costs					
Product 1	$159,250	32,500	$191,750	(26,930)	$164,820
Product 2	104,720	(10,880)	93,840	6,660	100,500
Product 3	169,600	10,400	180,000	(34,875)	145,125
Product 4	33,750	(8,100)	25,650	(2,754)	22,896
Total	$467,320	23,920	$491,240	(57,899)	$433,341
Product-sustaining costs					
Product 1	$125,000	–0–	$125,000	8,000	$133,000
Product 2	168,000	–0–	168,000	(5,000)	163,000
Product 3	256,000	–0–	256,000	3,000	259,000
Product 4	355,000	–0–	355,000	7,000	362,000
Total	$904,000	–0–	904,000	13,000	$917,000
Facility-sustaining costs	$1,450,000	–0–	$1,450,000	200,000	1,650,000
Total costs	$9,891,820	($103,330)	$9,788,490	$163,551	$9,952,041

ences in production volume between the master budget and the flexible budget. This planning variance is computed by subtracting the flexible budget amount from the master budget amount for each item. Therefore, a negative variance means a cost reduction due to a lower volume and a positive variance means a cost increase because of a higher volume.

Planning variances have little meaning in themselves. Their value is to suggest the effect on revenues, costs, and profits of the volume change and to adjust the master budget target amounts for differences between planned and actual volumes to make the cost targets comparable to the actual cost levels.

The flexible budget variances are the focus of cost control in a cost center. We can see that the flexible budget variance for unit-related costs for product 1 was $8,850 (column 4) signaling that cost expenditures for unit-related items relating to product 1 were $8,850 higher than they should have been given the level of volume achieved. This flexible budget variance is the sum of the price and quantity variances developed in Chapter 6.

For batch-related costs, the flexible budget variance reflects a mix of the difference between the planned and actual cost per batch and the number of batches given the actual level of activity. Note that the variance for batch-related costs for product 1 was −$26,930 (column 4). This is a favorable variance indicating that batch-related costs were $26,930 less than the target specified in the flexible budget.

This favorable variance was the result of two factors. First, as we can see by comparing the cost targets in Exhibit 12–1 with the actual costs in Exhibit 12–2, the standard cost per batch and actual cost per batch for product 1 were

$325 and $335, respectively. Therefore, the batch-related costs for product 1 reflect an increased, or unfavorable, cost, which equals the increased cost per batch of $10 multiplied by the actual number of batches $4,920 ($10 * 492).

Second, we can see that when comparing the actual results in Exhibit 12–2 with the flexible budget amounts in Exhibit 12–4, given the achieved level of activity, the actual number and standard number of batches were 492 and 590, respectively. The manufacturing group increased the average batch size for product 1 from 500 to 600, thereby reducing the number of batches, to create part of the reported savings in batch-related costs.[3] By reducing the number of batches by 98 (590 − 492) from the planned level, the manufacturing group saved $31,850 ($325 * 98) in batch-related costs.

Therefore, the total flexible budget variance for the batch-related costs for product 1 is −$26,930 ($4,920 − $31,850) and reflects the combined effect of fewer than the standard number of batches given the production level achieved and a higher than standard cost per batch.

In a similar way, we could investigate the cause of the other flexible budget variances reported for the various costs for each product. In Chapter 6, we saw the way that accountants decompose the flexible budget variances for unit-related cost into price and quantity components. The analysis of the flexible budget variances for batch-related, product-sustaining, and facility-sustaining costs is not formalized and proceeds on an ad hoc basis that reflects the circumstances of the analysis.

■ Addressing Other Issues in Cost Center Control

Many organizations make the mistake of evaluating a cost center solely on its ability to control costs. Yet quality, response time, the ability to meet production schedules, employee motivation, employee safety, and respect for the organization's ethical and environmental commitments are other critical measures of a cost center's performance. If the cost center is evaluated *only* on its ability to control costs, its members might sacrifice unmeasured attributes of performance. Therefore, organizations should never evaluate cost centers using only the center's cost performance. Cost center performance measures should reflect the contributions the cost center makes to the organization's success.

REVENUE CENTERS

Revenue center
A responsibility center whose employees control revenues but not manufacturing or acquisition costs or the level of investment.

Revenue centers are responsibility centers whose members control revenues but not the manufacturing or acquisition cost of the product or service they sell or the level of investment in the responsibility center.

Some revenue centers control price, the mix of stock carried, and promotional activities. In these centers, revenue measures most of their value-added activities and is a broad measure of how well they carried out their various activities.

Consider the activities of Dartmouth Service Center, a gasoline and

---

[3]It would be interesting to determine whether these savings were accomplished at the cost of increased warehousing costs.

automobile service station owned by a large oil refiner. The service center manager has no control over the cost of items such as fuel, depreciation on the building, power and heating costs, supplies, and salary rates. This manager has a minor influence on the total labor cost through scheduling and staffing decisions. Level of gasoline sales and repair activities determine all the other costs. The service manager has no control over the price of the gasoline or of automobile repairs or salary rates; the head office staff controls them. The central marketing staff controls all promotional activities. The major controllable item in this service station is customer service, which distinguishes the gasoline sales and repair services offered in this outlet from similar outlets and helps to determine this service station's sales levels.

The revenue center approach evaluates the responsibility center based solely on the revenues that it generates. Most revenue centers incur sales and marketing costs, however, and have varying degrees of control over those costs. Therefore, it is common in such situations to deduct the responsibility center's traceable costs, such as salaries, advertising costs, and selling costs, from its sales to compute the center's net revenue.

PROFIT CENTERS

Profit centers are responsibility centers whose manager and other employees control both the revenues and costs of the product or service they deliver. A profit center is like an independent business except that senior management, not the responsibility center manager, controls the level of investment in the responsibility center. For example, if the manager of one outlet in a chain of discount stores has responsibility for pricing, product selection, and promotion, the outlet meets the conditions to be evaluated as a profit center.

Most individual units of chain operations, whether they are stores, motels, or restaurants, are treated as profit centers. It is doubtful, however, that a unit of a corporate-owned fast-food restaurant, such as Burger King, or a corporate-owned hotel such as Holiday Inn, meets the conditions to be treated as a profit center because the head offices makes most purchasing, operating, pricing, and promotional decisions. These units are sufficiently large, however, that costs can vary due to differences in controlling labor costs, food waste, and the schedule for the facility's hours. Moreover, revenues can shift significantly based on the unit's service level. Therefore, although on the surface these organizations do not seem to be candidates to

Profit center
A responsibility center whose employees control revenues and costs but not the level of investment.

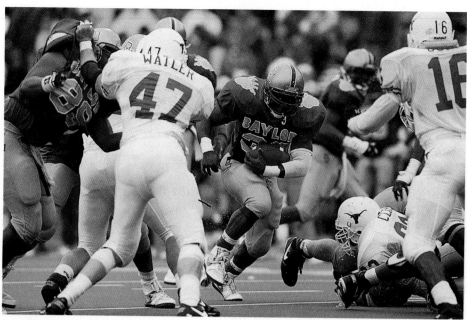

Faced with rapidly increasing costs, many universities have reorganized discretionary operations, such as football teams, into profit centers. These units are evaluated based on their ability to cover all their costs and contribute to the university's overhead. Some universities have dropped intercollegiate team sports that do not cover their full costs. *(Bob Daemmrich/Stock Boston, Inc.)*

be treated as profit centers, enough local discretion affects revenues and costs so that it is useful to treat them as profit centers.

Therefore, many organizations evaluate units as profit centers even though many facets of their operations are controlled by the corporate office. The profit reported by these units is a broad index of performance that reflects both corporate and local decisions. If unit performance is poor, it may reflect poor conditions that no one in the organization could control, poor corporate decisions, or poor local decisions. For this reason, organizations should not rely *only* on profit center results for performance evaluations. Instead, detailed performance evaluations should include quality, material use (yield), labor use (yield), and service measures that the local units can control.

INVESTMENT CENTERS

Investment center
A responsibility center whose employees control its revenues, costs, and the level of investment.

Investment centers are responsibility centers whose manager and other employees control revenues, costs, and the level of investment in the responsibility center. The investment center is like an independent business.

In 1993 Canada Post, Canada's national postal service, purchased Purolator Canada Limited, a courier service, and announced that Purolator would continue as an independent operation with its own management and policies. This is an example of investment center.

Exhibit 12–6 summarizes the characteristics of the various types of responsibility centers.

EXHIBIT 12–6
Summary of Responsibility Centers

TYPE OF RESPONSIBILITY CENTER				
FACTORS	**COST CENTER**	**REVENUE CENTER**	**PROFIT CENTER**	**INVESTMENT CENTER**
Controlled by center management	Costs	Revenues	Costs, revenues	Cost, revenues, and significant control over investment
Not controlled by center management	Revenues, investment in inventory and fixed assets	Costs, investment in inventory and fixed assets	Investment in inventory and fixed assets	
Measured by the accounting system	Costs relative to some standard (usually a budget)	Revenue relative to some standard (usually a budget)	Profit relative to some standard (usually a budget)	Return on investment relative to some target level
Not measured by the accounting system	Performance on any critical success factors other than cost	Performance on any critical success factors other than revenue	Performance on any critical success factors other than profit	Performance on any critical success factors other than return on investment

EVALUATING RESPONSIBILITY CENTERS

■ Using the Controllability Principle to Evaluate Responsibility Centers

Underlying these accounting classifications of responsibility centers is the concept of **controllability**. The *controllability principle* states that the manager of a responsibility center should be assigned responsibility only for the revenues, costs, or investment that the responsibility center personnel control. Revenues, costs, or investments that people outside the responsibility center control should be excluded from the accounting assessment of that center's performance. Although the controllability principle seems to be appealing and fair, it is very difficult and often misleading and undesirable to apply in practice.

A significant problem in applying the controllability principle is that in most organizations, many revenues and costs are jointly earned or incurred. Consider the operations of an integrated fishing products company that is divided into 3 responsibility centers: harvesting, processing, and marketing and distribution. The harvesting group operates ships that go out to sea and catch various specie of fish. The ships return to 1 of the company's processing plants to discharge their catches. The plants process the fish into salable products. Finally, the marketing and distribution group sells products to customers. Like most organizations, the activities that create the final product in this company are sequential and highly interdependent. The product must be the right specie, quality, and cost to be acceptable to the customer.

OBJECTIVE 12.4
The issues and problems created by revenue and cost interactions in evaluating the performance of an organization unit

Controllability
A principle that asserts that people should be held accountable only for results that they can control. The main application of this principle is that a manager should not be held accountable for revenues, costs, investments, or other factors outside her control.

Harvesting, processing, and marketing and distribution jointly determine the organization's success.

Evaluating the performance of harvesting, processing, and marketing and distribution involves considering many facets of performance. For example, harvesting's operations could be evaluated by using the following measures: (1) ability to catch the entire quota allowed, (2) ability to minimize the waste and damage done to the fish caught, (3) ability to minimize equipment failures, and (4) ability to control the costs associated with operating the ships. Similar measures might be developed for processing, and the evaluation of marketing and distribution might be based on the ability to meet delivery schedules and improve market share.

As part of this performance evaluation process, the organization might want to prepare accounting summaries of the performance of harvesting, processing, and marketing and distribution to support some system of financial control. The accountant undertaking this task immediately confronts the dilemma of how to account for highly interrelated organization centers as if they were individual businesses. For example, the costs in harvesting are easy to determine, but what are the harvesting revenues? Harvesting does not control sales or prices. Its role is to catch the fish, maintain raw material and product quality, and meet the schedules determined jointly by it, processing, and marketing and distribution. So perhaps harvesting should be evaluated as a cost center. If this is done, however, what about indirect organization costs such as corporate administration that reflect overhead resources that the cost center uses and other important performance facets such as maintaining quality, catching the full quota of fish, and delivering the required specie of fish, when required, to the processing group? Should harvesting be asked to bear some of the costs of the head office groups such as personnel, planning, and administration whose services it uses? If so, how should its share of the costs of those services be determined?

For the same reasons, we could probably conclude that processing should be evaluated as a cost center. However, what about the marketing and distribution group that, through its general marketing efforts, probably has the most direct impact on sales? However, what costs does it control? It does not control harvesting and processing costs. The only costs that marketing and distribution controls are marketing and distribution costs that, in most integrated fishing products companies, are less than 10% of the total costs. You might argue, however, that harvesting, through its ability to catch fish and maintain its quality, and processing, through its ability to produce quality products, are also influential in determining the organization's sales level.

■ Using Performance Measures to Influence Versus Evaluate Decisions

Some people argue that controllability is not a valid criterion to use in selecting a performance measure. Rather, they suggest that the performance measure should be chosen to influence decision-making behavior. The following situation describes what these people have in mind.

A dairy faced continuing problems developing performance standards in the face of continuously rising costs. Because the cost of raw materials, which

To provide their drivers with an incentive to use and maintain their vehicles properly, many companies have begun programs that pay bonuses to employees based on their ability to avoid costly equipment failures and repairs. Many people complain about these programs, however, citing situations in which responsible employees had vehicle failures that were not their fault while irresponsible employees experienced no vehicle failures. *(D. Hudson/Sygma)*

were between 60% and 90% of the final costs of the various products, were thought to be beyond the control of the various product managers, people argued that managers should be evaluated based on their ability to control the *use* of raw materials rather than their cost.

Senior management of the dairy announced, however, that it planned to evaluate managers on their ability to control costs. The managers quickly discovered that one way to control raw materials cost was to make judicious use of long-term fixed price contracts for raw materials. They began to do this, and soon raw materials cost, as a percentage of what costs would be if the raw materials were acquired as before, began to fall. It was then possible to project product costs several quarters into the future, which promoted stability in planning and product pricing.

■ Using Segment Margin Reports

Many problems occur as a result of using the profit center approach to evaluating performance. These problems concern identifying responsibility for the control of sales and costs, in particular, how to assign the responsibility for jointly earned revenues and jointly incurred costs. Therefore, as we now consider the form of the accounting reports that accountants prepare for responsibility centers, we should remember the important assumptions and limitations that underlie these reports.

Despite the problems of responsibility center accounting, many organizations believe that it is useful to identify profit centers and compute profit center profits. Because most organizations are integrated operations, one of the first problems that designers of profit center accounting systems must confront is handling the interactions between the various profit center units.

To address this issue, consider the activities at Earl's Motors, a full-service automobile dealership organized into 5 responsibility centers: new car sales, used car sales, the body shop, the service department, and leasing. Each responsibility center has a manager who is responsible for the profit reported for that unit. The responsibility center managers report to Earl using the quarterly reports such as the one shown in Exhibit 12–7.

Exhibit 12–7 illustrates a common form of the segment margin report for an organization that is divided into responsibility centers. There is 1 column for each profit center. The revenue attributed to each profit center is the first entry in each column. Variable costs are deducted from its revenue to determine its contribution margin, which is the contribution made by operations to cover costs that vary in proportion to the number of batches and product-sustaining and facility-sustaining costs.

Next, each unit's batch-related, product-sustaining, and facility-sustaining costs ("other costs" in the exhibit) are deducted from its contribution margin to determine that unit's **segment margin**, which is the focus of profit reporting for a responsibility center. The unit's segment margin is the measure of its *controllable* contribution to the organization's profit. Allocated avoidable costs are the organization's administrative costs, such as personnel-related costs and committed costs for facilities, that could be avoided if the unit were eliminated and the organization had time to adjust its capacity levels by selling excess facilities or by reducing the number of administrative staff. Allocated avoidable costs are deducted from the unit's segment margin to compute its income. Finally, the organization's unallocated costs (sometimes called *shut-down costs*), which are the organization's administrative and overhead costs that would be incurred regardless of the scale of operations,[4]

Segment margin
The level of controllable profit reported by an organization unit or product line.

[4] For example, the president's salary and the cost of administrative staff who are unrelated to the operations of the individual responsibility centers are unallocated costs.

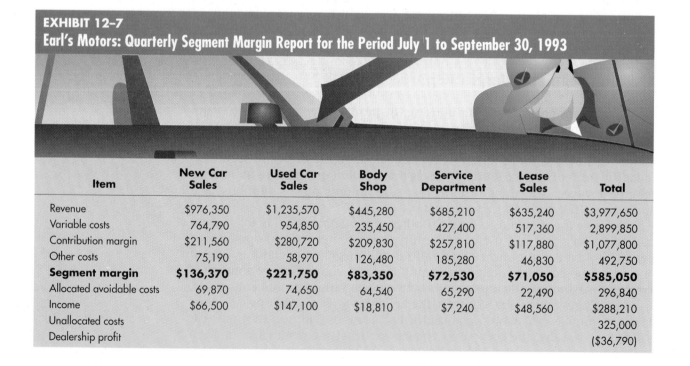

EXHIBIT 12–7
Earl's Motors: Quarterly Segment Margin Report for the Period July 1 to September 30, 1993

Item	New Car Sales	Used Car Sales	Body Shop	Service Department	Lease Sales	Total
Revenue	$976,350	$1,235,570	$445,280	$685,210	$635,240	$3,977,650
Variable costs	764,790	954,850	235,450	427,400	517,360	2,899,850
Contribution margin	$211,560	$280,720	$209,830	$257,810	$117,880	$1,077,800
Other costs	75,190	58,970	126,480	185,280	46,830	492,750
Segment margin	**$136,370**	**$221,750**	**$83,350**	**$72,530**	**$71,050**	**$585,050**
Allocated avoidable costs	69,870	74,650	64,540	65,290	22,490	296,840
Income	$66,500	$147,100	$18,810	$7,240	$48,560	$288,210
Unallocated costs						325,000
Dealership profit						($36,790)

are deducted from the total of the unit incomes to determine the dealership's profit.

EVALUATING THE SEGMENT MARGIN REPORT   What can we learn from the segment margin report for Earl's Motors? First, we know that conventional accrual accounting reports a loss of $36,790 for this quarter. This loss may signal a long-term problem or it might have been expected. Perhaps this quarter is a traditionally slow quarter and operations in the year's other three quarters make up the deficiency. Perhaps there is a disproportionate amount of committed costs incurred in this quarter and they will be less in subsequent quarters.

As we look at the statements for the individual responsibility centers, we can see that each one showed a positive income. The contribution margin for each responsibility center is the *value added* by the manufacturing or service-creating process before batch-related costs and the committed costs related to product-sustaining and facility-sustaining activities.

A unit's segment margin is an estimate of its short-term effect on the organization's profit, and the negative of the unit's segment margin reflects the immediate effect on corporate income if the unit were shut down. The unit's income is an estimate of the long-term effect of the responsibility center's shutdown on the organization's profit, after fixed capacity is allowed to adjust. For example, if the lease sales operation were discontinued, the immediate effect would be to reduce the profit at Earl's Motors by $71,050 after some period of time, however, perhaps a year, or even several years, when capacity has been allowed to adjust for this loss of activity, the estimated net effect of closing the lease operation would be to reduce corporate profits by $48,560. The difference between the unit's segment margin and income reflects the effect of adjusting for facility-sustaining costs, which are committed.

Organizations use different approaches to evaluate whether the segment margin numbers are good or bad. The most popular sources of comparative information are (1) trends of past performance, that is, is performance this period reasonable given past experience and (2) comparisons to comparable organizations, that is, how does performance compare to similar organizations? These evaluations include comparisons of absolute amounts, such as cost levels and revenue levels, and relative amounts, such as each item's percentage of revenue.

For example, in evaluating the performance of Earl's Motors, the manager of the service department might note that variable costs (the costs of flexible resources) are about 62% of revenue. This may compare favorably with past relationships of variable cost to revenue. By joining an industry group that provides comparative information for dealerships in similar size communities, however, Earl's Motors might find that, on average, variable costs in automobile dealerships are only 58% of revenue. This suggests that Earl's Motors should investigate why its variable costs are higher than the industry average. Similar evaluations can be made of all the cost items in this report.

INTERPRETING SEGMENT MARGIN REPORTS WITH CAUTION   At first, the segment margin statement might seem to be a straightforward and interesting approach to financial control. Segment margin statements should be interpreted carefully, however, because they reflect many assumptions that may disguise underlying issues.

First, as with all approaches to financial control, segment margins present an aggregated summary of each organization unit's performance. It is important to consider other facets relating to critical success factors, such as quality and service. For example, companies might use customer surveys to establish a customer satisfaction index for each department or compute quality statistics, which report error or recall rates, for each department.

Second, the segment margin report contains numbers that can be quite arbitrary because they rest on subjective assumptions over which there can be legitimate disagreement (what accountants often call **soft numbers**). As we proceed down the column for each responsibility center, each subsequent amount shown becomes less controllable by the responsibility center's manager and is affected by the assumptions used in allocating costs. Although a unit's segment margin is assumed to be controllable, the manager may have less than complete control over the costs that are used to compute it and almost no control over the costs that are allocated to compute the unit's income. In a typical refinery (Exhibit 12–8), for example, joint use of facilities creates cost allocation problems.

Third, and perhaps most important, the revenue figures reflect important assumptions and allocations that sometimes can be misleading. These assumptions relate to how the revenues the organization earned are divided among the responsibility centers, an issue called *transfer pricing*.

Soft number
A number that may be unreliable because it rests on subjective assumptions over which there can be legitimate disagreement.

TRANSFER PRICING

OBJECTIVE 12.5
Transfer pricing

Transfer pricing
A set of tools and methods (rules) used by the organization to allocate jointly earned revenues to organization subunits. Common transfer pricing approaches are cost, market, negotiated, and administered.

Transfer pricing is the set of rules an organization uses to allocate jointly earned revenue among responsibility centers. These rules can be very arbitrary if there is a high degree of interaction among the individual responsibility centers. Exhibit 12–9 shows the possible interactions among the responsibility centers at Earl's Motors.

To understand the issues and problems associated with allocating revenues in a simple organization like Earl's Motors, consider the activities associated with a new car transaction. The new car department sells a new car and takes in a used car as trade. Then the used car either must be sold to the used car department or sold externally in the wholesale market.

The value placed on the used car transferred between the new and used car departments is critical in determining the profitability of both the new car and used car departments. The new car department would like the value assigned to the used car to be as high as possible because that makes its reported revenues higher; the used car department would like the value to be as low as possible because that makes its reported costs lower.

The same considerations apply for any interaction between any two internal departments. The rule that is used to value the internal transactions will allocate the organization's jointly earned revenues to the individual responsibility centers and affect each center's profit.

Organizations choose among 4 different broad approaches to transfer pricing to develop the transfer pricing rules that they use: (1) market-based

EXHIBIT 12–8
The Operation of a Typical Mobil Corp. U.S. Refinery

CRUDE INPUT

LPG

CRUDE DISTILLATION
Distillation separates the crude into fractions based on boiling range. The crude is heated until each fraction boils off as vapor, then condensed and subject to further processing.

NAPHTHA

DISTILLATE

REFORMER
Reforming is important because it enables refiners to produce the high-octane gasolines required by some of today's cars. Reforming rearranges gasoline molecules into forms with a higher octane rating.

GAS OIL

Mobil's U.S. refineries are designed to process low-cost, high-sulfur crude oil to make high-value premium gasoline, distillate, and lube products.

ALKYLATION
In an Alkylation unit, light olefins from the FCC are reacted in the presence of an acid catalyst to produce high-octane, premium-quality gasoline blending stock.

GASOLINE

HYDROCRACKING
Hydrocracking is catalytic cracking performed under high pressure in the presence of hydrogen to yield products of higher quality and lower sulfur content.

RESIDUALS

Catalytic Cracking is the primary means of upgrading heavy oils into higher value light products. A catalyst breaks down large hydrocarbon molecules in heavy oil into a mixture of smaller molecules that can be separated by distillation into lighter products like liquefied petroleum gas (LPG), naphtha (raw gasoline), and heating oil. The gasoline produced by catalytic cracking has a high-octane rating.

FLUID CATALYTIC CRACKER
In a Fluid Catalytic Cracker (FCC), gas or air is forced through a bed of finely powdered catalyst to flow like a liquid. In large units, the catalyst recirculates through the system at up to 80 tons per minute.

GASOLINE

DISTILLATE SULFUR REMOVAL
Distillate Sulfur Removal typically occurs when sulfur is catalytically removed from distillate streams using fixed bed reactors in the presence of hydrogen. Products include high-quality kerosene, heating fuel, and diesel.

DISTILLATE

DISTILLATE

COKER
The Coker converts residual fuels to lighter components, such as gasoline and diesel oil, using high temperature, and also produces a solid material called coke, which is typically used as industrial fuel. All Mobil U.S. refineries have cokers.

NAPHTHA

DISTILLATE

SULFUR RECOVERY
Very pure sulfur from the Sulfur Recovery Unit is the result of the various sulfur removal processes in the refinery. Effective sulfur removal/recovery permits the processing of low-cost, high-sulfur crudes.

SULFUR

GAS OIL

LUBE/WAX PRODUCTION BLENDING & PACKAGING
Lube/wax units produce a wide range of lube products at two of Mobil's U.S. refineries. Heavy gas oils go through an extraction and dewaxing process to produce lube blend stocks. These are the basestocks that are blended into a variety of high-quality finished lubes and waxes.

LUBE/WAX

COKE

This graphic, developed by Mobil Corporation, shows the processing activities used in a typical U.S. refinery to refine a barrel of crude oil into its resulting, or joint, products. The complex and interrelated nature of the products simultaneously produced in a refinery creates profound problems in determining the individual costs of those products. *(Courtesy Mobil Corporation)*

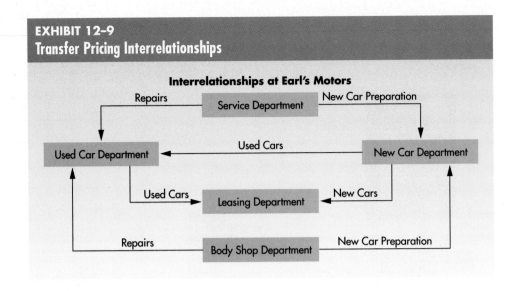

EXHIBIT 12–9
Transfer Pricing Interrelationships

Interrelationships at Earl's Motors

transfer prices, (2) cost-based transfer prices, (3) negotiated transfer prices, and (4) administered transfer prices. Each of these transfer prices has unique implications for the type of behavior it elicits in an organization.

■ Market-Based Transfer Prices

If the organization is committed to the spirit of determining the income of each responsibility center, market prices are the most appropriate basis for transferring goods or services between responsibility centers. The market price provides an independent valuation of the transferred product and results in a distribution of jointly earned revenue in a way that reflects the market's assessment.

Unfortunately, market valuations seldom exist. Consider Earl's Motors. Dealers trade used cars in well-organized markets that publish prices. A given used car could be valued using this information. The wholesale value of a used car depends, however, on its mechanical condition, which is only imperfectly observable and at a cost. In addition, the used car's value depends on its visible condition, which is a matter of subjective judgment. Therefore, it is not clear that a wholesale price can be determined objectively for a given used car.

Some dealerships avoid this problem by asking the used car manager to value any used car being taken in on trade. The value given by the used car manager becomes the transfer price. Because people often react to risk and uncertainty by requiring a margin of safety, the used car manager might discount the perceived value of the used car to provide a margin of safety to cover the repair of any hidden problems that become evident when the car is prepared for resale. If the value is excessively low, however, the new car manager complains that this is impeding the ability of the new car department to sell new cars. Therefore, the new car manager might take a potential used car around to used car dealers to find the best price it would get.

■ Cost-Based Transfer Prices

When a good or service has no market price, one alternative to consider is a transfer price based on cost. Some common transfer prices are variable cost, variable cost plus some percentage of markup, full cost, and full cost plus some percentage of markup.

Proponents of each of these transfer prices have arguments to support their respective choices. Economists argue, however, that any cost-based transfer price other than marginal cost leads organization members to choose a lower than optimal level of transactions, causing an economic loss to the overall organization.[5] The dilemma here, however, is that if the supplying division charges marginal cost as the transfer price and if marginal costs are falling, the marginal cost will be less than average cost, and the supplying division will always show a loss.

Another problem with cost-based approaches to transfer pricing is that they get away from the intent that the transfer pricing mechanism will allow computation of unit incomes. Interestingly, many organization units believe that they are not as important if they are cost centers rather than profit centers.

A final problem with cost-based approaches is that they do not provide the proper economic guidance when operations are capacity constrained. When operating at capacity, decisions should reflect the most profitable use of the capacity rather than simply cost considerations. In this case, the transfer price is the sum of the marginal cost and the opportunity cost of capacity where opportunity cost reflects the profit of the best alternative use of the capacity.

One interesting cost-based approach to consider is to charge the consuming department the target variable cost, that is, the number of standard hours allowed for the work done multiplied by the standard cost per hour for the work, and to allocate to that department a share of the supplying department's committed costs to reflect its proportional use of the supplying department's capacity. For example, if the service department acquired capacity expecting to supply 10% of its service capacity to the new car department, the new car department receives a lump-sum allocation of 10% of the service department's capacity costs. In this setting, the service department's income is the difference between the actual and target cost of the work it completes.

You should be aware that cost-based transfer prices raise performance measurement, equity, and behavioral issues. Such issues are addressed more thoroughly in advanced texts.

■ Negotiated Transfer Prices

In the absence of market prices, some organizations allow supplying and receiving responsibility centers to negotiate transfer prices. Negotiated transfer prices reflect the controllability perspective inherent in responsibility cen-

[5]For example, if the transfer price is higher than the marginal cost, the supplying unit wants to supply more than the optimal quantity and the purchasing unit wants to purchase fewer than the optimal quantity. Because supply and demand must be equated, the amount that is ordered and supplied is the lower amount.

ters. Some theoreticians object, however, to negotiated transfer prices because the resulting profits of the responsibility centers reflect both economic considerations and negotiating skills rather than just economic considerations.

Net realizable value
The difference between a product's selling price and the additional costs needed to put it in the customer's hands.

In an economic sense, the optimal transfer price is chosen when the purchasing unit offers to pay the supplying unit the **net realizable value** of the last unit supplied for all the units supplied. The net realizable value of a unit of transferred material is the selling price of the product the buyer will make from that material less all the costs that remain to prepare the final product for sale. If the supplying unit is acting optimally, it chooses to supply units until its marginal cost equals the transfer price offered by the purchasing unit. This results in the optimal quantity of the transferred units being supplied. Appendix 12–1 presents an example of these calculations and the determination of the optimal quantity to transfer.

Problems arise when negotiating transfer prices because this type of bilateral bargaining situation causes the supplying division to want a price that is higher than the optimal price and the receiving division to want a price that is lower than the optimal price. When the actual transfer price is different from the optimal transfer price, the organization, as a whole, suffers because it transfers a smaller than optimal number of units.

■ Administered Transfer Prices

Administered transfer prices—say, market price less 10%—are set by an arbitrator or by the application of some policy and are popular because they are easy to administer. Such transfer prices are unpopular because they reflect neither pure economic considerations, as market-based or cost-based transfer prices do, nor accountability considerations, as negotiated transfer prices do.

Returning to the example of Earl's Motors, Earl might decree that the transfer price for body shop work is 80% of the normal market rate. This may seem reasonable and might reflect a practical approach to dealing with the issues associated with market-based and cost-based transfer prices, but this rule is arbitrary and, therefore, provides an arbitrary distribution of revenues and costs between the body shop and whatever units it deals with. Administered transfer prices inevitably create subsidies among responsibility centers. When subsidies exist, they obscure the normal economic interpretation of responsibility center income, and they may provide a negative motivational effect if members of some responsibility center believe that the application of such rules is unfair. Exhibit 12–10 summarizes the 4 major approaches to transfer pricing.

■ Assigning and Valuing Assets in Investment Centers

When we use investment centers to evaluate responsibility center performance, we have to deal with all the problems associated with profit centers[6]

---

[6]These problems relate to identifying the costs and revenues that belong to each profit center.

EXHIBIT 12–10
Summary of Transfer Pricing Approaches

	MARKET-BASED	COST-BASED	NEGOTIATED	ADMINISTERED
Measure used	Market price	Product cost	Direct negotiations	Application of a rule
Advantage	If a market price exists, it is objective and provides the proper economic incentives.	This is usually easy to put in place because cost measures are often already available in the accounting system	Reflects the accountability and controllability principles underlying responsibility centers.	This is simple to use and avoids confrontations between the two parties to the transfer pricing relationship.
Problems	There may be no market or it may be difficult to identify the proper market price because the product is difficult to classify.	There are many cost possibilities and any cost other than marginal cost will not provide the proper economic signal.	Can easily lead to decisions that do not provide the greatest economic benefits.	This tends to violate the spirit of the responsibility approach.

and the problems unique to investment centers. The additional problems associated with investment centers concern how to identify and value those assets used by each investment center. Here we encounter troubling questions that have no definitive answers.

In determining the level of assets a responsibility center uses, it is necessary to assign the responsibility for (1) jointly used assets, such as cash, buildings, and equipment, and (2) jointly created assets, such as accounts receivable. Once the decision makers have assigned the organization's assets to investment centers, they must determine the value of those assets. What cost should be used? Historical cost, net book value, replacement cost, and net realizable value are all costing alternatives for which supporting arguments are developed in advanced cost accounting texts.

■ Cost Allocations to Support Financial Control

Despite these difficulties, many organizations develop responsibility center income statements to help evaluate center performance. These income statements should be designed and presented to isolate the discretionary components included in the calculation of each center's reported income. Refer back to Exhibit 12–7, which presents 1 possible format.

The format shown in Exhibit 12–7 helps to identify what the center controls directly (the revenue and variable costs) from the other costs of the profit calculation (indirect costs). As with the allocation of jointly earned rev-

If senior management of McDonald's decided to evaluate this restaurant in Tokyo using return on investment, it would immediately be faced with determining its value. Some common alternatives that analysts use to value the investment are market value less selling cost, replacement cost, historical cost, and net book value. *(George Holton/Photo Researchers, Inc.)*

enues, the allocation of joint costs can cause considerable distortions and can misdirect decision making.

Consider the operations of Shirley's Grill and Bar, which has 3 operating units: a restaurant, a billiards room, and a bar (see Exhibit 12–11). The segment margin of $110,256 reported for the restaurant includes all the revenues from selling food, all the food costs, all the costs of kitchen and serving staff, and all the costs of equipment and supplies relating to the kitchen and the seating area. These revenues and costs are directly attributable to the operation of the restaurant. Indirect costs that are included in the $87,791 allocated to the restaurant operations include depreciation and taxes on the building, advertising, and franchise fees.

EXHIBIT 12–11
Shirley's Grill and Bar:
Responsibility Center Income Statements
Indirect Cost Allocation Based on Benefit

	RESTAURANT	BILLIARDS	BAR	TOTAL
Attributed revenue	$354,243	$32,167	$187,426	$573,836
Less segment costs	243,987	12,965	127,859	384,811
Segment margin	110,256	19,202	59,567	189,025
Less allocated costs	87,791	15,289	47,430	150,510
Segment income	$ 22,465	$ 3,913	$ 12,137	$ 38,515

In general, many activity bases could be used to allocate indirect costs—for example, a responsibility center's direct costs, floor space, and number of employees. Suppose that Shirley's decides to allocate indirect costs in proportion to the presumed benefit, measured by segment margin, provided by the capacity these allocated costs reflect. Many people believe that allocating indirect costs in proportion to benefit is fair; it is a criterion widely used to evaluate an indirect cost allocation.

This result may seem straightforward and reasonable, but, like all results involving indirect cost allocations, it needs to be interpreted carefully.[7] Suppose that a cost driver analysis revealed the following:

1. A significant portion of total indirect costs reflects depreciation on the building.
2. Allocating building costs based on floor space is considered to be the most reasonable approach to handling building costs.
3. The amount of floor space occupied by the restaurant, billiards, and bar operations is 40%, 25%, and 35%, respectively.[8]

An allocation of costs based on floor space occupied yields the results summarized in Exhibit 12–12.

Do these alternative results mean anything? On the one hand, we might argue that the indirect cost allocations based on floor space provide more meaningful economic results because the floor space allocation reflects depreciation, the major component of indirect costs, and its driver, floor space. This empirical issue requires verification by a special study. Even if floor space is the cost driver for indirect costs in the short term, however, the revised results may suggest nothing significant because the allocated costs include items such as depreciation, which are likely to be committed and cannot be avoided in the short-term.

The allocations based on floor space might seem to suggest that the contribution to profit per square foot of floor space is lowest in the billiard oper-

[7]Note that the segment margin for the restaurant is 58.3% ($110,256/$189,025) of the total business segment margin. Therefore, the restaurant is allocated 58.3% of the total allocated costs.

[8]Therefore, following this method, because the restaurant occupies 40% of the floor space, it is assigned 40% of the allocated costs.

EXHIBIT 12–12
Shirley's Grill and Bar:
Responsibility Center Income Statements
Indirect Cost Allocation Based on Floor Space Occupied

	RESTAURANT	BILLIARDS	BAR	TOTAL
Attributed revenue	$354,243	$32,167	$187,426	$573,836
Less segment costs	243,987	12,965	127,859	384,811
Segment margin	110,256	19,202	59,567	189,025
Less allocated costs	60,204	37,627	52,679	150,510
Segment income	$ 50,052	−$18,425	$ 6,888	$ 38,515

Insurance companies that reimburse hospitals for the cost of services provided to customers require that the hospitals compute the full cost of a given procedure. Hospitals are then faced with the problem of answering questions such as this one: What portion of the cost of the hospital building should be allocated to an X ray, blood test, or heart bypass surgery? *(Ettore Malanca)*

ation and the scope of the billiard operations should be reduced in favor of adding more floor space to the bar or restaurant. This conclusion does not necessarily follow, however. Suppose that without the billiard operation the bar sales would be cut in half. How could the responsibility center income statements reflect this? They probably cannot. With this information, we could determine the economic effect of closing the billiards operation. The interactive effects of such actions, however, cannot be captured by conventional segment margin statements.

The message of this discussion is that responsibility center income statements have to be interpreted with considerable caution and healthy skepticism. Responsibility center income statements may include arbitrary and questionable revenue and cost allocations and often disguise the interrelationships between the responsibility centers.

OBJECTIVE 12.6
The use of return on investment and residual income as financial control tools

■ Efficiency and Productivity Elements of Return on Investment

Referring back to the discussion in Chapter 1 about the Dupont Company, recall that one of Dupont's major challenges was to develop the means to manage the complex structure caused by its diverse activities and operations. In the early 20th century, most organizations were single-product activity operations. These organizations approached the evaluation of the investment level by considering the ratio of profits to sales and the percentage of capacity used. Dupont, however, being a multiproduct firm, pioneered the systematic use of return on investment to evaluate the profitability of its different lines of business. Let's develop in more detail Dupont's approach to financial control, which is summarized in Exhibit 12–13. (At Dupont, the actual exhibit used to summarize operations was extremely detailed and contained 350 large charts that were updated monthly and permanently displayed in a large chart room in the headquarters building.)

Recall from Chapter 1 that return on investment is the ratio of operating income to investment. The Dupont system of financial control focuses on return on investment and breaks that measure into 2 components: a return measure that assesses efficiency and a turnover measure that assesses productivity. The following equation illustrates this idea:

Return on investment (ROI) =

$$\frac{\text{Operating income}}{\text{Investment}} = \frac{\text{Operating income}}{\text{Sales}} * \frac{\text{Sales}}{\text{Investment}}$$

$$= \text{Return on sales} * \text{Asset turnover}$$
$$= \text{Efficiency} * \text{Productivity}$$

The ratio of operating income to sales (also called *return on sales* or *sales margin*) is a measure of **efficiency**, the ability to control costs at a given level

Efficiency
A measure of an organization's ability to control costs at a given activity level. In financial control, this is the ratio of earnings to sales, or operating income to sales.

EXHIBIT 12-13
The Dupont Return on Investment Control System

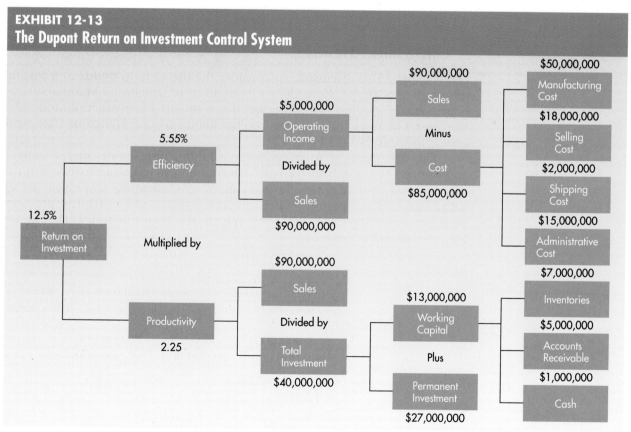

of activity. The ratio of sales to investment (often called *asset turnover*) is a measure of **productivity**, the ability to generate sales for a given level of assets.

The Dupont approach to financial control develops increasingly more detailed subcomponents for the efficiency and productivity measures by focusing on more detailed calculations of costs and different groups of assets. The upper portion of Exhibit 12–13 provides the efficiency measure factored into its components, and the lower portion of the exhibit provides the details of factoring the productivity measure into its components. For example, by looking at the efficiency ratio of operating income to sales, we can examine the various components of costs (manufacturing, selling, shipping, and administrative), their relationship to sales, and their individual trends to determine whether each is improving (see the next section). Comparisons of these individual and group efficiency measures can be made to similar organization units or to competitors to suggest where improvements might be made.

Looking at the productivity ratio of sales to investment, we can develop separate turnover measures for the key items of investment: inventories, accounts receivable, cash (the elements of working capital), and the elements of permanent investment (such as equipment and buildings). Comparisons of these turnover ratios with those of similar units or those of competitors can suggest where improvements are required.

ASSESSING RETURN ON INVESTMENT

■ Using Ratio Trends

Let us expand this discussion to consider the use of ratio trends in assessing return on investment. Consider the operations of Dorchester Manufacturing, which makes custom windows for the residential construction industry. Dorchester Manufacturing's most recent balance sheet and income statement appear in Exhibits 12–14 and 12–15.

The first decision to make when applying the return on investment approach to financial control is to determine how to define investment. In this example, we will measure investment as total assets employed net of accumulated depreciation.[9] With this assumption, and using the previous equation for calculating ROI, the return on investment for Dorchester Manufacturing is

Return on investment =

$$\frac{\text{Operating income}}{\text{Investment}} = \frac{\text{Operating income}}{\text{Sales}} * \frac{\text{Sales}}{\text{Investment}}$$

$$= \frac{5,000,000}{40,000,000} = \frac{5,000,000}{90,000,000} * \frac{90,000,000}{40,000,000}$$

$$= 0.0555 * 2.25$$

$$= 12.5\%$$

[9]Other possibilities to measure the investment level are total assets at historical cost, total assets at replacement cost, total assets at net realizable value, and shareholders' equity.

EXHIBIT 12–14
Dorchester Manufacturing
Balance Sheet

Cash	$ 1,000,000	Accounts payable	$ 2,000,000
Accounts receivable	5,000,000	Other liabilities	1,000,000
Inventory	7,000,000	Long-term debt	7,000,000
Plant and equipment (net)	27,000,000	Shareholders' equity	30,000,000
Total	$40,000,000	Total	$40,000,000

EXHIBIT 12–15
Dorchester Manufacturing
Income Statement

Sales		$90,000,000
Less cost of goods sold:		
Materials and Supplies	$25,000,000	
Labor	10,000,000	
Overhead	15,000,000	50,000,000
Gross margin		$40,000,000
Selling expenses	20,000,000	
Administrative expenses	10,000,000	
Taxes	5,000,000	35,000,000
Net income		$ 5,000,000

Dorchester Manufacturing earned a return of 12.5% on the net book value of its assets invested. Net income was 5.5% of sales, and sales were 2.25 times total assets. It is possible to evaluate trends for these numbers and to make comparisons with other organizations, as shown in Exhibit 12–16. This form of financial benchmarking is common.

Turn to the top two lines of Exhibit 12–16, which show that Dorchester Manufacturing is earning a lower return on investment than its competitor. The efficiency and productivity portions of the exhibit explain why. The middle portion of Exhibit 12–16 shows that the efficiency of operations (return on sales) at Dorchester Manufacturing is declining while the competitor's efficiency is improving continuously. The bottom portion of the exhibit shows that Dorchester's productivity (asset turnover) is lower than its competitor's. Therefore, both components of ROI, efficiency and productivity, are lower for Dorchester Manufacturing than for its competitor.

The efficiency and turnover ratios can be further examined by decomposing them into their individual components. Exhibit 12–17 summarizes the individual components of costs as a cumulative percent of sales for Dorchester Manufacturing and compares these numbers to those of its best competitor.

We can see from the bar chart for Dorchester Manufacturing that materials, labor, overhead, selling, and administrative costs are approximately 28%, 11%, 17%, 22%, and 11% of sales, respectively, and approximately 30%, 9%, 14%, 20%, and 8%, respectively, at the best competitor. These figures suggest that labor, overhead, selling, and administrative costs, in total, are too high at Dorchester Manufacturing relative to the competitor's costs and that

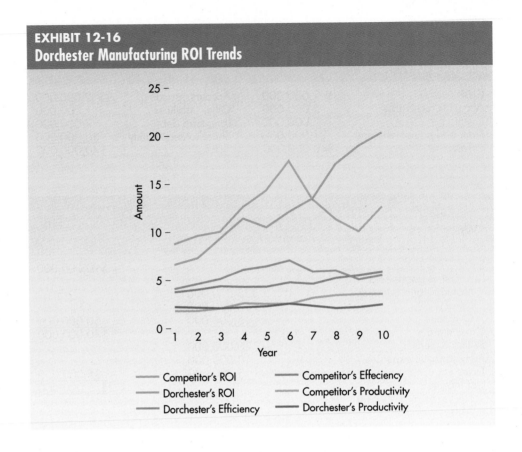

EXHIBIT 12-16
Dorchester Manufacturing ROI Trends

Competitor's ROI
Dorchester's ROI
Dorchester's Efficiency
Competitor's Effeciency
Competitor's Productivity
Dorchester's Productivity

it might be advisable for Dorchester to conduct an investigation to determine why these differences exist.

Exhibit 12–18 summarizes the ratios of sales to assets, the productivity contribution to the return on investment, for individual asset accounts and compares these ratios to those of Dorchester's best competitor. It shows that the ratio of sales to cash and sales to inventory are, respectively, about 90 and 15 for Dorchester Manufacturing and about 100 and 55 for the best competitor. This comparison suggests that, given its level of sales, Dorchester Manufacturing holds too much cash and inventory compared with its competitor. Perhaps the competitor is using just-in-time production to reduce costs, reduce the investment in inventory, improve quality, and increase return on investment. This is an important manufacturing strategy that Dorchester Manufacturing might consider.

This discussion illustrates two important attributes of the Dupont method of financial control. First, these measures are most useful when evaluating trends and when comparing the numbers with those belonging to the best competitor.[10] Second, these comparisons do not identify the problem or how to solve it. Rather, they suggest where to look for a problem.

[10]Recall from Chapter 2 that benchmarking is used to identify best practices in any organization, regardless of whether the organization identified as best at doing something is in the same line of business. Financial information is usually used differently. In comparing financial results, direct aggregate comparisons are made between competitors in order to rank them. Unlike conventional benchmarking, there is no intent here to identify and adapt best practices.

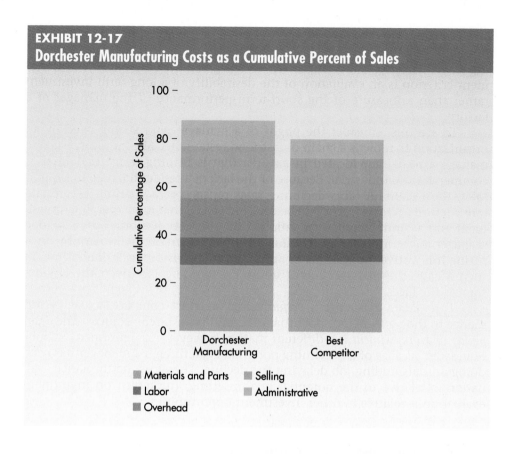

EXHIBIT 12-17
Dorchester Manufacturing Costs as a Cumulative Percent of Sales

Legend:
- Materials and Parts
- Labor
- Overhead
- Selling
- Administrative

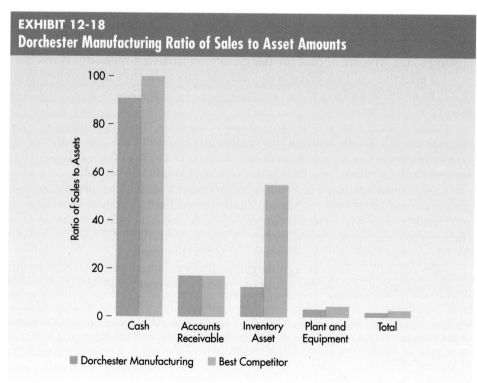

EXHIBIT 12-18
Dorchester Manufacturing Ratio of Sales to Asset Amounts

Legend: Dorchester Manufacturing / Best Competitor

For most organizations, a major portion of the investment number used to compute return on investment is the commitment made for long-term capacity.[11] Therefore, it is important to recognize that the return on investment criterion is an evaluation of the desirability of a long-term investment rather than a measure of the short-term performance of the manager of a facility.

To see this, consider the plight of a manager who is employed by an organization that owns a chain of fast-food restaurants. She has been asked to manage a restaurant located in an area that is turning from residential to commercial and industrial. Because of the lack of a residential base to support sales, the restaurant faces declining sales prospects. As a result, the restaurant's return on investment will be low, indicating that it is a marginal investment and a candidate for liquidation if the property has other uses. A good manager might mitigate or slow the decline of return on investment by organizing innovative promotions to attract business customers at lunchtime. In such a case, the manager might do an outstanding job given the circumstances she faces.

To evaluate a manager's performance, we must compare actual performance to the performance potential inherent in the circumstances. The *desirability of an investment* is a different matter, however. An investment may be liquidated because of its declining potential even though a manager has been doing an outstanding job delaying the decline. Therefore, performance evaluation is relative to the potential in the setting; the return on investment evaluation is relative to other investment opportunities.

■ Using the Residual Income Approach

Despite its relative popularity, many people have criticized using return on investment as an approach to financial control. Some critics have argued that any approach to control that focuses purely on financial measures is too narrow for effective control. They argue that the most effective approach to control is to monitor and assess the organization's critical success factors, such as quality and service.

Other critics who accept the need for financial measures have criticized the economic basis of return on investment focus. This objection is an important criticism of the return on investment perspective and calls into question the relevance of many practical applications of financial control.

Their criticism is an economic argument that begins by observing that profit-seeking organizations should make investments in order of declining profitability until the marginal cost of capital of the last dollar invested equals the marginal return generated by that dollar. Unfortunately, financial control based on return on investment may not yield this result.

For example, consider a manager who is evaluated based on the return on investment of her division. Suppose that the current return on investment

---

[11]The other significant investment for most organizations is inventory, which reflects the nature of the process the organization uses to make products. In this sense, inventory is a long-term investment as well because inventory investment usually changes only when the production process itself changes.

is 15% and the manager is contemplating an investment that is expected to return 12%. She would be motivated to decline this investment opportunity because accepting it would lower the division's return on investment. If the organization's cost of capital were only 10%, however, she would probably decide to accept the investment because its expected return exceeds the investment's cost of capital.

People have responded to this criticism by creating a different investment criterion. **Residual income** equals actual income less the economic cost of the investment used to generate that income. For example, if a division's income is $13,500,000 and the division uses $100,000,000 of capital, which has an average cost of 10%, the residual income can be computed as follows:

$$\text{Residual income} = \text{Accounting income} - \text{Cost of capital}$$
$$= \$13,500,000 - (\$100,000,000 * 10\%)$$
$$= \$3,500,000$$

Like return on investment, residual income evaluates income relative to the level of investment required to earn that income. Unlike return on investment, however, residual income does not motivate managers to turn down investments that are expected to earn more than their cost of capital. Under the residual income criterion, managers are asked to do whatever they think is necessary to make residual income as large as possible.

> **Residual income**
> Actual income less the economic cost of the investment used to generate that income; corresponds to the notion of economic income.

■ Using Shareholder Value Analysis

Although return on investment and residual income were originally designed to evaluate the desirability of a level of investment, a new application of residual income recently has attracted considerable attention. **Shareholder value analysis**, also known as *economic value analysis*,[12] identifies how each product contributes to owner wealth. Shareholder value analysis computes the residual income for every major product or product line and evaluates a product line's long-term financial desirability by using its residual income.

Organizations are beginning to use shareholder value analysis to identify products or product lines that are not contributing their share to organization return given the level of investment they require. Shareholder value analysis can be used to make strategic decisions about the organization's product line.

Shareholder value analysis can also be used to evaluate operating strategies. Quaker Oats Company, a food manufacturer, used shareholder value analysis to support its decision in June 1992 to cease trade loading, which is the food industry's practice of using promotions to obtain orders for 2 or 3 months' supply of food from customers. Trade loading produces quarterly peaks in production and sales and requires

> **Shareholder value analysis**
> Evaluates a product line's financial desirability using its residual income; also known as *economic value analysis*.

[12]Shawn Tully, "The Real Key to Creating Wealth," *Fortune* (September 20, 1993), pp. 38–50.

> **C**ONSIDER THIS . . .
>
> ### Shareholder Value Analysis at Coca-Cola
>
> In the late 1980s, after applying shareholder value analysis to its product lines, Coca-Cola decided to refocus its attention on its soft drink business and eliminated investments in many other businesses, including pasta and wine.

large inventory storage facilities, which create nonvalue-added activities and excess costs that customers eventually support. An article in *Fortune* magazine[13] estimated that trade loading is primarily responsible for the $75 to $100 billion in groceries that are in transit between manufacturers and consumers and that supporting this inventory "adds some $20 billion to the $400 billion that Americans annually spend on groceries."

Quaker Oats shareholder value analysis suggested that even though sales levels might be lower by refusing to offer the price reductions associated with trade loading, it would be more profitable for Quaker Oats to eliminate these large inventories and the related required warehouse space and to produce food at even levels rather than in peaks. Quaker Oats motivated managers to end trade loading by basing bonuses on efficiency and cycle times rather than annual sales.

These results are exciting and interesting, but they should be treated with caution. As with return on investment calculations, shareholder value analysis requires difficult and arbitrary allocations of assets, revenues, and costs and arbitrary valuations of assets in ongoing use.

OBJECTIVE 12.7
The limitations of using financial controls

THE EFFICACY OF FINANCIAL CONTROL

Although financial control is widely practiced, many people have questioned its true insights and effectiveness. Critics have argued that financial information is secondhand information about how well the organization is doing in meeting its commitments to its stakeholders and that it is better served by measuring what really matters.

Some observers believe that financial control is an ineffective control scorecard for 3 reasons. First, financial control focuses on financial measures that do not measure the organization's other important attributes, such as product quality, the speed at which products are developed and made, customer service, the ability to provide a work environment that motivates employees, and the degree to which the organization meets its legal and social obligations to society. Because these facets, and others, are important to the organization's success, they also deserve to be measured and monitored. The argument is that financial control measures only the aggregated results of *how* the organization achieved its target financial performance.

Second, because financial control measures the financial effect of the overall level of performance achieved on the critical success factors rather than the performance achieved on the individual critical success factors,

---

[13]Patricia Sellers, "The Dumbest Marketing Ploy," *Fortune* (October 5, 1992), pp. 88–94.

many people believe that financial control does not provide direct insight into how to improve those performances or financial performance. At best, critics argue that financial results are only a broad signal of how well the organization is managing the tasks that create success on the critical success factors that result in financial returns. The argument is that effective control begins with measuring and managing the critical success factors that result in financial returns, rather than measuring the financial returns themselves.

Third, financial control, *although it need not be,* is usually oriented to short-term profit performance. It seldom focuses on long-term improvement or trend analysis but instead considers how well the organization, or one of its responsibility centers, has performed this quarter or this year. This is the result of the *misuse* of financial control rather than an inherent fault of financial control itself. The preoccupation with short-term financial results is debilitating, however. It motivates an atmosphere of managing short-term financial results that provides disincentives for the types of management and employee initiatives that promote long-term success, particularly in the area of investing in training, equipment, and process changes. One of the major reasons for taking public organizations private is to provide senior management with the opportunity to manage for long-term results rather than being inappropriately concerned with short-term performance.

In summary, how should we interpret these facets of financial control? Financial control is an important tool in the process of control. If interpreted properly, financial results are crucial in assessing the organization's long-term viability. It is a tool, however, that needs to be used along with other tools because it is a summary of financial performance. Financial control does not try to measure other facets of performance that may be critical to the organization's stakeholders and vital to the organization's long-term success. It can, however, provide an overall assessment of whether the organization's strategies and decisions are providing acceptable financial returns.

Financial control also can be used to compare 1 unit's results with another (financial competitive benchmarking). This financial signal indicates whether the organization's operations control systems, which seek to monitor, assess, and improve performance on the critical success factors that create the financial results measured by the financial control system, are operating well.

FORD MOTOR COMPANY REVISITED

After they were hired by Ford Motor Corporation, the group of 10 were dubbed the "whiz kids" by an admiring press. The whiz kids quickly introduced many of the financial control tools described in this text. These financial controls replaced the highly centralized, informal, intuitive, and sometimes paranoid management practices that had characterized the company. These financial controls provided a basis for accountability and highlighted unprofitable practices and products that were quickly changed or eliminated. These actions improved the company's profit performance. In 1955, just 9 years after the whiz kids were hired, Ford reported a profit of almost $1 billion and had a market share of about 31%.

Among the whiz kids were Robert McNamara, who resigned as the pres-

CONSIDER THIS . . .

Managing for Long-Term Results at Harley Davidson

Commenting on the reasons that he and a group of executives at Harley-Davidson purchased the company from its owner AMF, the President, Vaughn Beals observed: "We suffered serious losses in 1981 and 1982. If we had still been under AMF's wing, it would have done what any corporate parent would do—replaced Harley-Davidson's senior management—perhaps not an unreasonable decision, but one that probably would have been fatal to Harley's long-range interests. An experienced, closely knit management team would have been replaced by people who didn't know the motorcycle business at all—and the long-term values of the company would have gone down the drain."

Source: Peter C. Reid, *Well Made in America: Lessons from Harley-Davidson on Being the Best* (New York: McGraw-Hill, 1990).

ident of Ford to become the U.S. secretary of defense, and Arjay Miller, another former Ford president, who became the widely admired dean of the business school at Stanford University.

However, this extraordinary financial success sowed the seeds for future problems at Ford Motor Corporation by implying that decision making based solely on financial numbers could eliminate study and knowledge of employees and customers and could, and should, replace intuition based on experience. Buoyed by the success of this numbers-oriented approach to management, a culture quickly developed at Ford Motor Corporation, and in most other organizations, that financial management was the key to organization success.

In a book describing the whiz kids, John Byrne[14] observed

> [the whiz kids] persuaded themselves and others that a professional manager can and must control everything without knowing anything about the products the company produces. . . . The whiz kids dragged Ford and all of American industry into a modern world but not without some dire consequences. . . . For the efficiencies of cutting costs and gaining control, we sacrificed all notions of product quality and customer satisfaction. . . . Together at Ford [this] group refined and built a mystique for the methods of rational management they invented during the war. . . . Some would say that they lobotomized business, and in truth, they drove emotion and chaos out of decision-making.

Many auto industry experts believe that this exclusive focus on managing financial results and the loss of focus on customers and quality was responsible for the decline of the North American automobile industry during the 1970s and 1980s and provided the opportunity for lower cost, higher quality Japanese automobiles to invade the North American market.

The message of this chapter is that financial controls are an important element of organization control. Financial controls provide invaluable insights by suggesting problems and opportunities for improvement. However, financial controls must support, not eliminate, judgment that is based on a detailed knowledge of the details of operations and customer requirements.

[14]John A. Byrne, *The Whiz Kids* (Garden City, N.Y.: Doubleday, 1993).

SUMMARY

We began this chapter by reviewing the motivation that drives organizations to decentralize decision-making responsibility. Decentralized decision makers create the need for control, and one approach to control is financial control.

The foundation of financial control is the concept of a responsibility center that is an organization unit assigned the responsibility to achieve specified financial results. Responsibility centers are classified and evaluated based on the presumed control that their members exercise over cost, revenues, profits, and return on investment.

A major tool used in financial control is the segment margin report, which computes responsibility center profit. The segment margin provides insights into the financial contribution, or drain, attributable to a particular responsibility center. Because of the assumptions that underlie these reports, particularly relating to cost and revenue allocations, however, they must be evaluated carefully and with an understanding of the potential for distortion caused by the allocations that are used to compute the responsibility center profits.

Transfer pricing is an important tool used to allocate revenues to responsibility centers. Transfer prices can be based on market prices, costs, or negotiation, or they can be set using arbitration.

Return on investment is a widely used tool in financial control and, when used properly, can provide insights into the profitability of invested assets. Residual income and shareholder value analysis are two approaches to financial control that have been developed to mitigate some of the problems associated with the return-on-investment criterion.

In summary, the chapter argues that financial control is an important facet of control that focuses on financial results. Financial control is properly used with other control tools that monitor and assess the organization's performance on its other critical success factors.

KEY TERM LIST

Centralization, p. 488

Controllability, p. 499

Cost center, p. 491

Decentralization, p. 489

Efficiency, p. 513

Financial control, p. 489

Investment center, p. 498

Net realizable value, p. 508

Productivity, p. 514

Profit center, p. 497

Residual income, p. 519

Responsibility center, p. 490

Revenue center, p. 496

Segment margin, p. 502

Shareholder value analysis, p. 519

Soft number, p. 504

Transfer pricing, p. 504

APPENDIX 12-1

Finding the Optimal Quantity to Transfer

Suppose that the cost function for the supplying division in a transfer pricing situation can be approximated as

$$\text{Total cost in supplying division} = \$250,000 + 20x - 0.0001x^2$$

where x is the number of units made and transferred to the receiving division. The marginal cost of the supplying division is found by taking the derivative of its total cost function with respect to x and equals

$$\text{Marginal cost in supplying division} = 20 - 0.0002x$$

Note that the marginal cost in the supplying division decreases as x increases. This guarantees that a cost-based transfer price will create negative profits for the supplying division.

Suppose that the receiving division has committed costs of $200,000 and incurs $48 of cost per unit to sell the product into a market where the price is

$$\text{Market price} = \$100 - 0.0005x$$

Therefore, the net revenue equation for the receiving division is

$$
\begin{aligned}
\text{Net revenue of receiving division} &= (\text{Price} * \text{Quantity}) - \text{Costs} \\
&= (\$100 - 0.0005x)x - \$200,000 - \$48x \\
&= (\$52 - 0.0005x)x - \$200,000
\end{aligned}
$$

The net realizable value for a unit that is transferred into the receiving division is found by taking the derivative of the receiving division's net revenue equation with respect to x and equals

$$\text{Net realizable value of unit } x = 52 - 0.001x$$

The optimal quantity is found when the marginal cost of the supplying division equals the net realizable value in the receiving division

$$
\begin{aligned}
20 - 0.0002x &= 52 - 0.001x \\
0.0008x &= 32 \\
x &= 40,000 \text{ units}
\end{aligned}
$$

Therefore, the optimal quantity is 40,000 units. We can find the optimal transfer price by substituting 40,000 in either the marginal cost equation of the supplying division or the net realizable value equation of the receiving division.

$$\text{Transfer price} = \$20 - (0.0002 * 40000) = \$12$$

or

$$\text{Transfer price} = \$52 - (0.001 * 40000) = \$12$$

Total corporate profit is the net revenue in the receiving division less the total cost in the supplying division.

$$
\begin{aligned}
\text{Total corporate profit} &= \text{Net realizable revenue of} \\
&\quad \text{receiving division} - \text{Total cost of supplying division} \\
&= ((\$52 - 0.0005x)x - \$200{,}000) - \\
&\qquad\qquad\qquad (\$250{,}000 + \$20x - 0.0001x^2) \\
&= -0.0004x^2 + 32x - \$450{,}000
\end{aligned}
$$

Substituting 40,000 for x in this equation, we find that the maximum total corporate profit is \$190,000.

The profit reported by the supplying division equals the number of units transferred multiplied by the transfer price minus its costs:

$$
\begin{aligned}
\text{Profit in supplying division} &= (\text{Units} * \text{Transfer price}) - \text{costs} \\
&= (x * \$12) - (\$250{,}000 + 20x - 0.0001x^2) \\
&= 0.0001x^2 - 8x - 250{,}000
\end{aligned}
$$

Substituting 40,000 for x in this equation, we find that the loss in the supplying division is \$410,000.

The profit reported by the receiving division equals its net revenue minus number of units transferred multiplied by the transfer price.

$$
\begin{aligned}
\text{Profit in receiving division} &= \text{Net revenue} - (\text{Units} * \text{Transfer price}) \\
&= ((52 - 0.0005x)x - \$200{,}000) - (x * \$12) \\
&= -0.0005x^2 + 40x - \$200{,}000
\end{aligned}
$$

Substituting 40,000 for x in this equation, we find that the profit in the receiving division is \$600,000.

ASSIGNMENT MATERIAL

QUESTIONS

12–1 What is decentralization?

12–2 What does control mean in a decentralized organization?

12–3 What is a responsibility center?

12–4 What does the controllability principle require?

12–5 How do responsibility centers interact?

12–6 What does *financial control* mean?

12–7 What is a cost center?

12–8   What is a flexible budget?

12–9   What is the assigned responsibility in a revenue center?

12–10 When do organizations use profit centers?

12–11 What is an investment center?

12–12 What is a contribution margin?

12–13 What does *segment margin* mean?

12–14 What is a transfer price?

12–15 What are the 4 bases for setting a transfer price described in the text?

12–16 What is a soft number in accounting?

12–17 Why must organizations allocate revenues to responsibility centers?

12–18 Why must organizations allocate costs to responsibility centers?

12–19 What is return on investment?

12–20 How does efficiency affect return on investment?

12–21 How does productivity affect return on investment?

12–22 What does residual income mean?

12–23 What is the role of shareholder value analysis?

EXERCISES

12–24 What control problems does decentralization create in organizations?

12–25 Give an example of a responsibility center in a university.

12–26 Based on your understanding, which of costs, revenues, profits, and investment does the manager of a cinema control and what does she not control?

12–27 Suppose that you are the manager of a fitness center that is 1 of many in a chain. Give 1 example of a cost that you control and 1 example of cost that you do not control. Why is it important to distinguish between costs that are controllable and costs that are not controllable in this setting?

12–28 Identify 3 responsibility centers in a fast-food restaurant and explain how they might interact.

12–29 Is financial control sufficient in itself as an organization control tool? Explain.

12–30 Give an example in which a responsibility center is properly treated as a cost center.

12–31 An organization plans to make a product in batches of 25,000 units. Planned production is 1,000,000 units and actual production is 1,125,000 units. What are the planned number of batches and the flexible budget number of batches?

12–32 Give an example in which a responsibility center is properly treated as a revenue center.

12–33 Based on your understanding of how they are managed, would you agree or disagree that 1 outlet of a large department store chain should be treated as an investment center? What about the maintenance department within that outlet? What about a single department within the store?

12–34 Many multinational companies create wholly owned subsidiaries to do business in the countries or regions where they operate. Are these wholly owned subsidiaries examples of investment centers? Explain.

12–35 A home services company offers renovations, heating, air conditioning, and plumbing services to its customers. Imagine that you are in the process of computing the income for the renovations division. What problems might you encounter in computing this income?

12–36 How might a transfer price be chosen for logs in an organization that cuts down trees and processes the logs in a sawmill (to make lumber) or in a pulp mill (to make paper)?

12–37 In a fishing products company, the harvesting division catches and delivers the fish to the processing division that, in turn, delivers the processed fish to the selling division to sell to customers. How would you determine the appropriate transfer price between harvesting and processing and between processing and selling?

12–38 Why did accountants develop the expression *soft number*?

12–39 A store is divided into 4 departments: automotive products, home products, paint, and lumber. How would you assign the building costs (such as depreciation) to each of these departments?

12–40 A business reports an income of $1,000,000. How would you compute the return on investment for this business?

12–41 All organizations face a requirement to earn at least a minimum level return on investment. Some businesses rely on high ratios of profits to sales; other businesses rely on high ratios of sales to investment. Give an example of each of these businesses and explain what this characteristic implies about the business.

12–42 Why is it important to look at the trend of a ratio rather than simply 1 value of it?

12–43 A business whose investors require a return on investment of 8% after taxes reports an after-tax income of $1,500,000 on an investment of $20,000,000. What is the residual income for this business?

12–44 Based on an analysis of operations, a company making sporting goods has determined that the income provided by its golf, ski, tennis, and football product lines are $3,500,000, $7,800,000, $2,600,000, and $1,700,000, respectively. The accountant believes that the investment levels in these product lines are $35,000,000, $50,000,000, $45,000,000, and $23,000,000, respectively. Use a shareholder value analysis to evaluate the performance of each of these product lines, assuming that the organization requires a 10% return on investment.

PROBLEMS

12–45 For many years, automobile companies have been highly decentralized in terms of functions. The most obvious effect of this heavy decentralization of function is apparent when all the groups must work together to accomplish a goal. The highest order of integration occurs in the design of a new automobile.

Reflecting the functional decentralization of automobile manufacturers, the conventional approach to automobile design is for the marketing group to identify a concept. The design group then creates an automobile that reflects the marketing group's idea but incorporates engineering requirements and aesthetics identified by the design group. The purchasing group then identifies the parts required by the design and makes further modifications to it to incorporate parts that can be made or purchased. Finally, the manufacturing group modifies the design to reflect the nature and capabilities of the production process. This process takes up to 4 years and usually results in a vehicle that is far removed from the initial design.

What went wrong here? How might this process be improved?

12–46 Researchers have identified 2 extreme forms of organizations. Organic organizations are highly decentralized with few rules. Most people agree that software development companies are very organic. Mechanistic organizations are highly centralized and use many rules to prescribe behavior. Most people agree that government agencies are very mechanistic.

Do you agree with these examples?

12–47 For each of the following units, identify whether the most appropriate responsibility center form is a cost center, a profit center, or an investment center and why you have made that choice.

(a) A laboratory in a hospital

(b) A restaurant in a department store

(c) The computer services group in an insurance company

(d) A maintenance department in a factory

(e) A customer service department in a mail-order company

(f) A warehouse used to store goods for distribution in a large city

12–48 One of the most widely accepted and longest held beliefs is the responsibility principle, which says that organization units and people should be held accountable only for things that they can control.

REQUIRED:

(a) For any job you choose, give 1 example of something that the person should be expected to control and 1 example of something that the person should not be expected to control.

(b) Can you think of an example in which making somebody responsible for something that he cannot control would promote a desirable activity?

12–49 Some people and organizations have observed that the discussion of controllable and uncontrollable events is distracting in the sense that it encourages finger-pointing and an excessive preoccupation with assigning blame. These observers argue that it is more important to find solutions than to identify responsibility for unacceptable or acceptable events.

REQUIRED:

(a) What do you think of this argument?

(b) As an organization moves away from assessing and rewarding controllable performance, what changes would you expect to see in its organization structure?

12–50 For Moncton Carpet Products, the flexible budget example given in the text, analyze the flexible budget variances for products 2, 3, and 4 using an analysis similar to that used for product 1 in the text.

12–51 A bank is thinking of using shareholder value analysis to identify services that require improvement or elimination. What problems might the bank have in computing the residual income of any of the services that it offers to its customers?

12–52 You are the controller of a chain of dry cleaning establishments. You are computing the return on investment for each outlet.

Outlet A located in a city core reported a net profit of $130,000. The land on which Outlet A is located was essentially rural when it was purchased for $100,000. Since then, the city has expanded and the land is located in the population center. Comparable undeveloped land in the immediate area of the outlet is worth $2,000,000. The net book value of the outlet building and equipment is $400,000. The replacement cost of the building and equipment is $1,200,000. If the outlet building, equipment, and land were sold as a going concern, the sale price would be $1,500,000. It would cost $250,000 to demolish the building and clear the property for commercial development.

REQUIRED:

(a) What is the return on this investment?

(b) How would you decide whether this outlet should continue to be operated, sold as a going concern, or demolished and the land sold?

12–53 You have decided to divide a factory into cost centers. How would you allocate depreciation expense on the factory building to its individual cost centers?

12–54 Many people believe that, in a successful organization, the focus of control reflects the strategic initiatives in the organization. For each of the following organizations, identify what you think are the 3 most important items assessed by the organization's financial control system and why each is important. For each organization, what critical information is not assessed by the financial control system?

REQUIRED:

(a) A company selling cable television services to its subscribers

(b) A symphony orchestra

(c) An organization selling canned soup

(d) A government agency responsible for finding jobs for its clients

(e) An auditing firm

(f) A company selling high-fashion clothing

12–55 Bennington Home Products sells home products. It buys products for resale from suppliers all over the world. The products are organized into groups. A few examples of these groups are floor care products, kitchen products, tool products, and paper products. The company sells its products all over the world from regional offices and warehouses in every country where it operates. Because of differences in culture and taste, the product lines and products within those lines vary widely among countries.

The regional offices have administrative staff that manage the operations, do the ordering, and undertake the usual office administrative functions and a sales staff that does the selling directly to stores within that country. The regional offices are evaluated as investment centers because they have responsibility for revenues, costs, and investment levels. The regional offices make suggestions for new products.

The corporate or head office manages the regional offices and places the orders received from the regional offices with suppliers. The corporate office does the ordering for 3 reasons. First, it is believed that 1 ordering office eliminates duplication in ordering activities. Second, it is believed that 1 office ordering for all the regional offices gives the organization more power when dealing with suppliers. Third, it is believed that 1 office can develop the expertise to find and negotiate with suppliers of unique and innovative products.

(a) Describe an appropriate system of financial control at the regional level.

(b) Describe an appropriate system of financial control at the corporate or head office level.

(c) Explain why the 2 systems of financial control should or need not mesh.

12–56 The owner of a chain of fast-food restaurants has decided to use residual income to evaluate the performance of the managers of each of the restaurants. What do you think of this idea?

12–57 As a result of a shareholder value analysis, the owner of a company that makes and installs swimming pools has decided to shut down the manufacturing operations, which show a negative residual income for the current year. Is this *necessarily* the proper response to this information?

12–58 You are a government controller. A division manager being audited objects to the transfer price he is being charged by the audit group for the audit services. The manager observes, "If I have to pay for these services, I should be allowed to buy them from an outside supplier who is prepared to offer them to me at a lower price." You have been asked to mediate this dispute. What would you do?

CASES

12–59 You are a senior manager responsible for overall company operations in a large courier company. Your company has 106 regional offices (terminals) scattered around the country and a main office (hub) located in the geographical center of the country. Your operations are strictly domestic. You do not accept international shipments.

The day at each terminal begins with the arrival of packages from the hub. The packages are loaded onto trucks for delivery to customers during the morning hours. In the afternoon, the same trucks pick up packages that are returned to the terminal in late afternoon and then shipped to the hub where shipments arrive from the terminals into the late evening and are sorted for delivery early the next day for the terminals.

Each terminal in your company is treated as an investment center and prepares individual income statements each month. Each terminal receives 30% of the revenue from packages that it picks up and 30% of the revenue of the packages it delivers. The remaining 40% of the revenue from each transaction goes to the hub. Each terminal accumulates its own costs. All costs relating to travel to and from the hub are charged to the hub. The revenue per package is based on size and service type (there are 2 services: overnight and ground delivery, which takes between 1 and 7 days, depending on the distance traveled) and not the distance that the package travels.

All customer service is done through a central service group located in the hub. Customers access this service center through a toll-free telephone. The most common calls to customer service include requests for package pickup, requests to trace an overdue package, and requests for billing information. The company has invested in complex and expensive package tracking equipment that monitors the package's trip through the system by scanning the bar code placed on every package. The bar code is scanned when the package is picked up, enters the originating terminal, leaves the originating terminal, arrives at the hub, leaves the hub, arrives at the destination terminal, leaves the destination terminal, and is delivered to the customer. All scanning is done by hand-held wands that transmit the information to the regional and then central computer.

The major staff functions in each terminal are administrative (accounting, clerical, and executive), marketing (the sales staff), courier (the people who pick up and deliver the shipments and the equipment they use), and operations (the people and equipment who sort packages inside the terminal).

This organization takes customer service very seriously. The revenue for any package that fails to meet the organization's service commitment to the customer is not assigned to the originating and destination terminals.

All company employees receive a wage and a bonus based on the terminal's residual income. This system has promoted many debates about the sharing rules for revenues, the inherent inequity of the existing system, and the appropriateness of the revenue share for the hub. Service problems have arisen primarily relating to overdue packages. The terminals believe that most of the service problems relate to missorting in the hub, resulting in packages being sent to the wrong terminals.

REQUIRED:

(a) Explain why you believe that an investment center is or is not an appropriate organization design in this company.

(b) Assuming that this organization is committed to the current design, how would you improve it?

(c) Assuming that this organization has decided that the investment center approach is unacceptable, what approach to performance evaluation would you recommend?

12–60 Baden is a city with a population of 450,000. It has a distinct organization group, called the Public Utilities Commission of the City of Baden (called the Baden PUC), whose responsibility is to provide the water and electrical services to the businesses and homes in the city. Baden PUC's manager is evaluated and rewarded based on the profit that Baden PUC reports.

Baden PUC buys electricity from a privately owned hydroelectric facility several hundred miles away for resale to its citizens. Baden PUC is responsible for acquiring, selling, billing, and servicing customers. The maintenance and moving of electric wires within the city are, however, the responsibility of the City of Baden maintenance department (called Baden Maintenance). Baden PUC pays Baden Maintenance for work done on its electrical wires.

Over the years, there have been may squabbles between Baden Maintenance and Baden PUC. These squabbles have usually involved 2 items: complaints by customers about delays in restoring disrupted service and complaints by Baden PUC that the rates charged by Baden Maintenance are too high. The most recent debate concerns a much more serious issue, however.

On July 12, at about 10:30 a.m., a Baden city employee working in the parks and recreation department noticed an electrical wire that seemed to be damaged. The employee reported the problem at about 12:15 p.m. to Baden Maintenance during his lunch break. The report was placed on the maintenance supervisor's desk at 1:15 p.m. where it was found at 2:05 p.m. when the supervisor returned from lunch. The maintenance supervisor then called the Baden PUC dispatch office to report the problem and request permission to investigate the report and make any required repairs. The request for repair was placed on the Baden PUC service manager's desk for approval at 2:25 p.m. The service manager received the message when he returned from a meeting at 4:00 p.m., approved the work, and left a memo for a subordinate to call in the request. The request was then mistakenly called in as a request for routine service by a clerk at 4:50 p.m. and logged by the dispatcher in Baden Maintenance. A truck was dispatched the following day at 3:50 p.m. When the repair crew arrived at the scene, it discovered that the wire was indeed damaged and, if any of the children playing in the park had touched it, it would have caused instant death.

The incident went unreported for several days until a reporter for the Baden *Chronicle* received an anonymous tip about the episode, verified that it had happened, and reported the incident on the front page of the paper as an example of bureaucratic bungling. The public was outraged and demanded an explanation from the mayor, who asked the city manager to respond. The initial response from the Baden City manager that everyone had followed procedure only fanned the furor.

REQUIRED:

(a) Was what happened inevitable given the City of Baden's organization structure? Explain.

(b) Given the existing organization structure, how might this incident have been avoided?

(c) How would you deal with this situation now that it has happened?

(d) Would a change in the organization structure help prevent a similar situation from occurring in the future? Explain.

12–61 Peterborough Food produces a wide range of breakfast cereal foods. Its granola products are two of its most important product lines.

Because of the complexity of the granola production process, the manufacturing area in the plant that makes these 2 product lines is separated from the rest of the plant and is treated as a separate cost center. Exhibit 12–19 presents the activity and cost data for this cost center for the most recent quarter. The plan data in Exhibit 12–19 reflect the master budget targets for the quarter.

The factory accountant estimates that, with the increased production in line 1, the labor-related product-sustaining costs and the other product-sustaining costs for line 1 should increase by $20,000 and $100,000, respectively. The factory accountant also indicated that the decreased production in line 2 would require several quarters to be reflected in lower product-sustaining costs.

The factory accountant indicated that the labor-related facility-sustaining costs and the other facility-sustaining costs should increase by $0 and $140,000, respectively, given the net increase in production.

Prepare an analysis of costs for the granola line cost center.

EXHIBIT 12-19
Peterborough Food: Granola Line Products

	LINE 1 PLAN	LINE 1 ACTUAL	LINE 2 PLAN	LINE 2 ACTUAL	TOTAL LINE 1 PLAN	TOTAL LINE 1 ACTUAL	TOTAL LINE 2 PLAN	TOTAL LINE 2 ACTUAL	TOTAL PLAN	TOTAL ACTUAL
Number of boxes	945,000	1,200,000	1,175,000	945,000						
Number of batches	189	200	235	210						
Units per batch	5,000	6,000	5,000	4,500						
Unit-related costs										
Materials										
Grams per box	500	515	350	375						
Cost per gram	$0.0030	$0.0027	$0.0050	$0.0055	$1,417,500	$1,668,600	$2,056,250	$1,949,062	$3,473,750	$3,617,662
Packaging										
Units per box	1.0000	1.0600	1.0000	1.0450						
Cost per unit	$0.0450	$0.0420	$0.0380	$0.0410	$42,525	$53,424	$44,650	$40,489	$87,175	$93,913
Labor										
Hours per box	0.013	0.011	0.009	0.010						
Cost per hour	$18.00	$18.25	$18.00	$18.25	$221,130	$240,900	$190,350	$172,463	$411,480	$413,363
Batch-related costs										
Materials										
Per batch	$1,200	$1,325	$1,525	$1,495	$226,800	$265,000	$358,375	$313,950	$585,175	$578,950
Labor										
Hours per batch	12	11	16	18						
Per hour	$18.00	$18.25	$18.00	$18.25	$40,824	$40,150	$67,680	$68,985	$108,504	$109,135
Product-sustaining costs										
Labor					$256,000	$287,000	$305,000	$323,000	$561,000	$610,000
Other					$2,054,000	$2,123,000	$1,927,000	$2,005,000	$3,981,000	$4,128,000
Facility-sustaining costs										
Labor									$145,000	$152,000
Other									$4,560,000	$4,740,000
Total all costs					$4,258,779	$4,678,074	$4,949,305	$4,872,949	$13,913,084	$14,443,023

COMPENSATION

This chapter will introduce you to:

1. the importance of understanding the role of motivation in organizations
2. the elements of 2 important theories of motivation
3. the different approaches to rewarding performance and the nature of intrinsic and extrinsic rewards
4. the characteristics of effective reward systems
5. the guidelines that organizations might use to design reward systems
6. the broad types of monetary rewards that organizations use

CHAPTER 13

Choosing a Method of Compensation: The Situation

Consider the following events concerning a small appliance dealer whose owner, Arthur Friedman, decided to let the employees set their own pay.[1]

Friedman first unleashed his proposal at one of the regular staff meetings. "Decide what you are worth," he said, "and tell the book-keeper to put it in your envelope next week. No questions asked. Work any time, any day, any hours you want. Having a bad day? Go home. Hate working Saturdays? No problem. Aunt Ethel from Chicago has dropped in unexpectedly? Well, take a few days off, show her the town. Want to go to Reno for a week, need a rest? Go, go, no need to ask. If you need some money for the slot machines, take it out of petty cash. Just come back when you feel ready to work again."

This is what happened.

"It was about a month before anyone asked for a raise," recalls Stan Robinson, 55, the payroll clerk. "And when they did, they asked Art first. But he refused to listen and told them to just tell me what they wanted. I kept going back to him to make sure it was all right, but he wouldn't even talk about it. I finally figured out he was serious."

"It was something that I wanted to do," explains Friedman. "I always said that if you give people what they want, you get what you want. You have to be willing to lose, to stick your neck out. I finally decided that the time had come to practice what I preached."

Soon the path to Stan Robinson's desk was heavily travelled. Friedman's wife, Merle, was one of the first; she figured that her contribution was worth $1 an hour more. Some asked for $50 more a week, some $60. Delivery truck driver, Charles Ryan, was more ambitious; he demanded a $100 raise.

(© Edward L. Miller/Stock, Boston)

In most companies, Ryan would have been laughed out of the office. His work had not been particularly distinguished. His truck usually left in the morning and returned at five o'clock in the afternoon religiously, just in time for him to punch out. He

[1] Martin Koughan, "Arthur Friedman's Outrage: Employees Decide Their Pay."

dragged around the shop, complained constantly, and was almost always late for work. Things changed.

"He had been resentful about his pay," explains Friedman. "The raise made him a fabulous employee. He started showing up early in the morning and would be back by three o'clock, asking what else had to be done."

Instead of the all-out raid on the company coffers that some businessmen might expect, the fifteen employees of the Friedman-Jacobs Company displayed astonishing restraint and maturity. The wages they demanded were just slightly higher than the scale of the Retail Clerks union to which they all belonged (at Friedman's insistence). Some did not even take a raise. One serviceman who was receiving considerably less than his co-workers was asked why he did not insist on equal pay. "I did not want to work that hard," was the obvious answer.

THE ROLE OF COMPENSATION IN ORGANIZATION CONTROL

Chapter 12 presented some of the important issues in financial control. Recall from Chapter 11 that control consists of the tools and methods that an organization uses to keep it on the path toward achieving its objectives. An important element of control is motivating employees to pursue the organization's interests as they undertake their daily jobs. In turn, an important element of motivation is compensation, which is the topic of this chapter.

As we have just seen in the story of Arthur Friedman, compensation is both an important and delicate subject. In this chapter we will consider some of the foundation issues in compensation. The experience of Friedman's employees in being allowed to determine their own pay is not typical of most organizations. Let's consider what happened at this company within the larger framework of what motivates people.

OBJECTIVE 13.1
The importance of understanding the role of motivation in organizations

THEORIES OF MOTIVATION

In most organizations, pay is more than simply what is required to keep the person from leaving the organization. It is part of the complex bundle of factors that motivate people to work in the organization's best interests. Therefore, we must consider pay issues within the larger context of motivation.

People who study human behavior have developed many alternative theories to explain what motivates behavior (see Exhibit 13–1). We will discuss 2 of the theories that have been offered to explain individual motivation: Herzberg's 2-factor theory and Vroom's expectancy theory. You should not assume that because this text singles them out, these 2 theories are necessarily the most widely accepted. However, they do provide a good framework for our discussion of pay systems.

EXHIBIT 13-1

"There will be something extra for you if you handle this job as well as we think you can, Smithers."

Many approaches that organizations use to motivate their employees are crude and foster resentment because employees feel that they are being manipulated.

■ Herzberg's Two-Factor Theory of Motivation

Frederick Herzberg developed a theory of motivation that he called his **two-factor theory**.[2] Based on interviews with hundreds of people, Herzberg came to believe that 2 groups of factors affect behavior: hygiene factors and satisfier factors. Exhibit 13–2 summarizes these factors.

    Hygiene factors relate to the job context and define the individual's work environment. Herzberg believed that when hygiene factors are poor, the person becomes dissatisfied and job performance suffers. He believed that improving hygiene factors makes employees less dissatisfied but that hygiene factors do *not* motivate or satisfy them. Hygiene factors establish the potential or environment for motivation, but they do not provide motivation in themselves. We can think of hygiene factors as things that turn people off their jobs.

    Satisfier factors relate to the job content and define how the person feels about her job. Herzberg believed that when satisfier factors are poor, the employee derives no satisfaction from the job and has no motivation. He believed that improving satisfier factors makes employees more satisfied with

[2] Frederick Herzberg, "One More Time: How Do You Motivate Employees," *Harvard Business Review* (January–February 1968), pp. 53–62.

EXHIBIT 13–2
Herzberg's Two-Factory Theory of Motivation

HYGIENE FACTORS	SATISFIER FACTORS
Working conditions	Achievement
Base pay	Recognition
Organization policies	Responsibility
Interpersonal relationships	Opportunity for growth
Supervisory quality	

OBJECTIVE 13.2
The elements of 2 important theories of motivation

Two-factor theory (Herzberg's)
A theory that argues 2 groups of factors, hygiene and satisfier, with different roles motivate individual behavior.

Hygiene factors
A group of factors in the Herzberg theory that relate to job context and define the environment. They are thought to be necessary to provide the environment for motivation rather than being motivators themselves.

Satisfier factors
A group of factors in the Herzberg theory that relate to job content. They are thought to provide motivation when the environment for motivation has been properly prepared.

their jobs and more highly motivated. Satisfier factors can motivate performance if hygiene factors are in place to provide the potential for motivation. We can think of satisfier factors as things that turn people on to their jobs.

Pay has 2 roles in Herzberg's theory. Base pay is a hygiene factor. If an employee believes that his base pay is too low, he will be dissatisfied with his job, and satisfier factors will be unable to motivate performance. Any discretionary part of pay that is perceived as an achievement or a recognition of performance is a satisfier factor.[3] However, if the discretionary part of pay is perceived as an extension of base pay, it is a hygiene factor, not a motivating factor.

■ Vroom's Expectancy Theory

Victor Vroom[4] developed a model of motivation that he called *expectancy theory*. Exhibit 13–3 shows the relationship of various elements in Vroom's **expectancy theory,** which includes the following:

➤ **Expectancy**—the individual's expectations about whether the application of skill and effort will affect measured performance

➤ **Instrumentality**—the relationship between the individual's measured performance and the outcomes provided by the organization, such as pay for performance or recognition

➤ **Valence**—the value assigned by the individual to the outcomes

In the expectancy model, *effort* is the amount of skill and time the person gives to the job, *performance* refers to the results of the person's skill and time that the organization's performance measurement system captures, *out-*

Expectancy theory (Vroom's)
A theory that argues that motivation is a product of expectancy, instrumentality, and valence.

Expectancy
The relationship that a person perceives between effort and skill and the results measured by the organization's performance measurement system.

Instrumentality
The relationship between measured performance and the outcomes provided to individuals.

Valence
The value that a person assigns to the outcomes provided to the individual by the organization as a result of formal performance measurement.

[3] A sense of achievement and recognition can also come in many other forms that do not involve pay, such as personal satisfaction and commendations from superiors. This is important to remember. Many people assume that the only way to provide motivation is to provide people with monetary rewards.
[4] Victor H. Vroom, *Work and Motivation* (New York: Wiley, 1964).

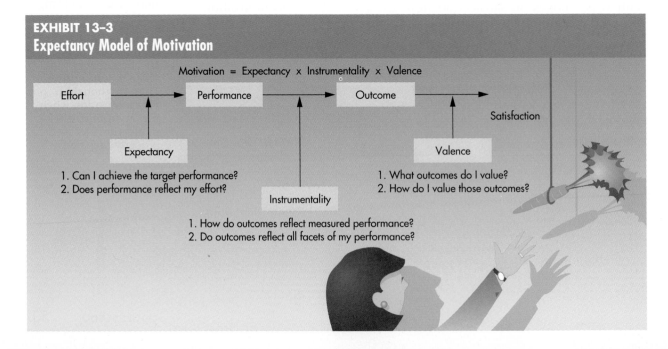

EXHIBIT 13–3
Expectancy Model of Motivation

Motivation = Expectancy x Instrumentality x Valence

Effort → Performance → Outcome → Satisfaction

Expectancy
1. Can I achieve the target performance?
2. Does performance reflect my effort?

Instrumentality
1. How do outcomes reflect measured performance?
2. Do outcomes reflect all facets of my performance?

Valence
1. What outcomes do I value?
2. How do I value those outcomes?

This Ford Motor Corporation employee was a member of a team that streamlined the ordering process for dealers, thereby improving service while reducing costs. This employee may have been motivated by being given the responsibility to make changes and from succeeding in improving a customer-related process. *(Courtesy Ford Motor Company)*

come is the set of rewards that the person experiences or receives as a result of measured performance, and *satisfaction* is the result of value of the outcomes to the person.

This expectancy model is 1 approach to explain how employee skill and knowledge; the organization's performance measurement and reward system; and the individual's personal values combine to determine individual motivation. A **motivation system** is a performance measurement and reward system that provides employee benefits or recognition. The key in designing a motivation system is to tie individual objectives to the organization's objectives so that, as the employee pursues individual objectives, the organization also achieves its objectives.

Motivation system
A system of performance measurement and rewards that provides employee benefits or recognition based on measured performance.

FACTORS AFFECTING INDIVIDUAL MOTIVATION

The Herzberg and Vroom theories offer different, but reinforcing, perspectives on rewards. What is critical in the Herzberg theory is the recognition that hygiene factors are not motivators, but that their existence only provides an environment in which the satisfier factors, or motivators, can have their effect. As we will see, many current debates about motivation focus on whether a particular reward is a hygiene factor or a satisfier factor and on the strength of satisfier factors in motivating performance. For example, most of the articles written about the motivational potential of employee empowerment focus on the value and role of opportunity for personal growth as a motivator.

The importance of the Vroom theory is that it provides a specific structure in which to consider the role and effect of the key management accounting function of performance measurement. We can see from Exhibit 13–3 that the performance measurement system is the heart of the motivation system. If performance measurement is tied directly to outcomes valued by the employee, the employee substitutes performance measures for outcomes, and the performance measures become the employee's goals because valued outcomes follow directly. Therefore, according to this theory, the key is to ensure that while pursuing performance measures, the employee takes actions that meet the organization's objectives.

◼ Intrinsic Rewards

Organizations use 2 broad types of rewards to motivate employees: intrinsic and extrinsic. We can say that people experience, rather than are given, intrinsic rewards. **Intrinsic rewards** relate to the nature of the organization and the design of the job that people experience. They come from inside the individual and reflect the satisfaction that a person experiences from doing her job and the opportunity for growth that the job provides. One of management's most important tasks is to develop an organizational environment and culture wherein employees value intrinsic rewards.

◼ Extrinsic Rewards

An **extrinsic reward** is based on performance and is any reward that one person provides to another person to recognize a job well done. Examples of commonly used extrinsic rewards are meals, trips, cash bonuses, stock bonuses, and recognition in the organization's newsletter and on plaques.

Extrinsic rewards, such as cash bonuses, meals, and trips, are impersonal rewards that tend to reinforce the notion of the employee being distinct from the organization. These types of extrinsic rewards reinforce the common perception that the wage compensates the employee for a minimally acceptable effort and the organization must use additional rewards or compensation to motivate the employee to provide effort beyond the minimal amount the contract of employment implies or requires.

◼ Choosing Between Intrinsic and Extrinsic Rewards

Many compensation experts believe that organizations have not used intrinsic rewards enough. They claim that, given proper leadership, intrinsic rewards may have as strong, or even stronger, motivational effects than extrinsic rewards. In the context of the Herzberg model, these experts argue that organizations have undervalued the importance of the job's structure (a hygiene factor) and the motivational effect of designing a job that promotes employee satisfaction and personal growth in the job. In the context of the expectancy model, we would say that organizations have undervalued the valence that people have for intrinsic rewards relating to pride of accomplishment.

The issue of the effectiveness of intrinsic and extrinsic rewards is a topic of heated debate in the management literature. This is one of the many areas of judgment in management in which we each must evaluate opposing arguments to form our own opinion of what seems appropriate. Here, very briefly, are the opposing arguments prompted by a single article on this topic.

In a provocative article,[5] Alfie Kohn argued that conventional incentive

---

[5] Alfie Kohn, "Why Incentive Plans Cannot Work," *Harvard Business Review* (September–October 1993), pp. 54–63.

plans that tie rewards to measured performance are fundamentally and irreparably flawed. Kohn observed, "At least two dozen studies over the last three decades have conclusively shown that people who expect to receive a reward for completing a task or for doing that task successfully do not perform as well as those who expect no reward at all." Kohn argues that although this result holds over a wide range of tasks, people, and rewards, the result is strongest when the job requires creative skills. Kohn's explanation for these results is that "pay is not a motivator," which echoes the Herzberg argument that pay is a hygiene factor, not a satisfier (motivator) factor. Kohn cites studies that suggest that pay is well down on the list, often the fifth or sixth item, of important job characteristics.

Kohn's argument is essentially that the preoccupation with extrinsic rewards undermines the effectiveness of reward systems and that organizations and jobs should be designed to allow employees to experience intrinsic rewards. Kohn urges organizations to spend more time developing an environment in which employees are empowered and can collaborate and in which the job content offers the potential for personal growth. These are conditions that allow employees to experience intrinsic rewards.[6]

Like all commentaries in this area, Kohn's observations generated many responses, some strongly supporting his views and some fiercely rejecting them.[7] While some responses to Kohn failed to deal with the substance of his argument, others argued that he was naive, and that[8] their personal experience suggested that extrinsic, particularly monetary, rewards are the most effective motivators of performance.

The issue remains unresolved. However, one thing is clear. *Most* organizations have ignored, and continue to ignore, the role of intrinsic rewards in motivation and blindly accept the view that people must be provided with explicit extrinsic rewards to be motivated. Many people believe that extrinsic rewards are both necessary and sufficient to motivate superior performance. Both systematic and anecdotal evidence suggest, however, that extrinsic rewards are not necessary to create effective organizations and that performance rewards do not necessarily create them. Whether intrinsic rewards are more or less effective than extrinsic rewards in motivating behavior is unresolved. Intrinsic rewards do have a role to play in most organizations, however.

Beyond the debate about the relative effectiveness of intrinsic and

> ### CONSIDER THIS . . .
> ## Recognizing Employee Contributions
>
> Wheeling-Pittsburgh Steel Corporation recognizes employee contributions in its employee publication *Windows,* which features the pictures and contributions of employees. Not only does this recognition acknowledge the contribution of the named employees but also provides a description of their ideas, which, in turn, suggests to others the contributions that they might make. In a similar way, McDonnell Douglas developed the Golden Eagle President's Award to commend employees for outstanding performance. An important feature of the McDonnell Douglas award is that fellow employees nominate the recipients.

---

[6] Alfie Kohn, "For Best Results, Forget the Bonus," *The New York Times,* October 17, 1993, p. F11.

[7] "Rethinking Rewards," *Harvard Business Review* (November–December 1993), pp. 37–49.

[8] One respondent called Kohn a communist; another suggested that Kohn was a self-promoter seeking consulting opportunities. Unfortunately, these types of responses are typical of the poor quality of debate surrounding this issue.

This Harris Corporation employee was part of a team that produced integrated circuits (ICs) used in Ford Motor Corporation automobiles. The Ford assembly operations began to reject many ICs supplied by Harris Corporation, which led to downtime, missed production schedules, and income losses for the Ford employees. This employee of Harris Corporation said that she "felt terrible about how they [the Ford employees] thought about us" and joined a team that worked with the Ford production workers to solve the problem. This cooperative venture went so well that the Ford workers asked that Harris Corporation become the exclusive supplier of the part. This employee was motivated by pride in her work, an intrinsic reward, and by how the employees at Ford felt about her work, an extrinsic reward. *(Theo Anderson/Harris Corporation)*

extrinsic rewards, some people argue that incentive compensation programs, in any form, are unacceptable. They suggest that organizations must strive to be excellent to survive in a difficult and competitive world. Therefore, these people argue that superior and committed performance is necessary for organizations to survive and is part of the contract of employment, not something that merits additional pay.

Because of the lack of systematic evidence about the role and effectiveness of intrinsic rewards, this chapter focuses on extrinsic rewards, particularly monetary rewards. This does not mean, however that intrinsic rewards are unimportant but that extrinsic rewards tend to be based on more formal systems that require more explanation.

EXTRINSIC REWARDS BASED ON PERFORMANCE

Incentive compensation
See *pay for performance.*

Pay for performance (incentive compensation)
A system that provides rewards for performance to motivate achieving, or exceeding, measured performance targets.

Incentive compensation or pay-for-performance systems are rewards systems that provide monetary (extrinsic) rewards based on measured results. **Pay for performance** systems base rewards on achieving or exceeding some measured performance. The reward can be based on absolute performance or performance relative to some plan. Examples of rewards based on absolute performance include those tied to the number of good units made (such as a piece-rate system), to the organization's results (such as profit sharing), and to the performance of the organization's share price (such as a stock option plan). Examples of rewards based on relative performance are those tied to the ability to exceed some performance target level (such as paying a salesperson a bonus for sales above a quota or paying a production group a bonus for beating a benchmark performance level) and those tied to the amount of a bonus pool (such as a sharing in a pool defined as the organization's reported profits less a stipulated return to shareholders).

To reward performance, organizations need to develop performance measurement systems that provide realistic means to gather relevant performance information.

Beginning in 1994 in the United States, most organizations cannot claim as an expense for the purpose of computing taxable income the portion of any employee's salary that exceeds $1 million. This will certainly (1) *reduce* the use of salary and perquisites (such as company cars and club memberships) and (2) *increase* the use of monetary rewards based on performance.

EFFECTIVE PERFORMANCE MEASUREMENT AND REWARD SYSTEMS

OBJECTIVE 13.4
The characteristics of effective reward systems

When the organization has decided to reward performance, it turns to the management accountant to design the performance measurement systems needed to support the reward system. A systematic approach to rewarding performance has 5 broad attributes designed to ensure that the performance measurement system has the effect of motivating desired performance.

First, the person must *understand the job* and the reward system and believe that it measures what she controls and contributes to the organization. This attribute ensures that the employee perceives the reward system as fair and predictable. In expectancy model terms, this establishes the expectancy between effort and performance and the instrumentality between performance and outcome.

If the employee does not understand the job or how to improve measured performance, a reward system based on performance measures is ineffective because that employee perceives no relationship between effort and performance and, ultimately, outcomes. Similarly, if the reward system is complex, the employee will be unable to relate perceived performance improvements to changes in outcomes, and the motivational effect of the reward system will be lost. Finally, if the reward system does not measure the employee's controllable performance, he will rightfully consider it to be independent of his efforts and, again, the incentive effect of the reward system will be lost. Specifying and developing a clear relationship among effort, performance, and outcome and ensuring that all employees understand this relationship is a critical management role.

Therefore, the centerpiece of incentive compensation systems is the performance measurement system, which becomes the focus of

CONSIDER THIS . . .

Providing Results-Based Extrinsic Rewards

Lincoln Electric, a manufacturer of electrical components, has carried rewarding performance to the limit. Its production workers are paid on a piece-rate system. These workers receive no holiday pay, sick leave, or family leave, nor do they receive medical or other benefits. Piece-rate workers at Lincoln Electric are literally paid only for the work that they do. Workers who are highly trained, skilled, motivated, and who can work fast find the Lincoln Electric system very attractive. The company claims that its production employees are the highest paid in the world.

Despite the high rate of pay, the turnover rate is 20% because many new workers find adapting to the rapid pace of work difficult. Some social commentators have observed that, in general, piece-rate systems are socially undesirable because, if workers slow down due to health or age, they suffer financially through no fault of their own.

Abandoning Individual Rewards in Favor of Group Rewards

In 1992 Hoechst Celanese, a manufacturer of chemical and pharmaceutical products, announced that "in order to focus more attention on employee performance and development, the (individual) performance rating categories (Exceptional, Quality, or Requires Improvement) are being eliminated. . . . The elimination of these categories is consistent with the company's Quality Values, which place a high degree of importance on continual improvement, teamwork, and participative goal setting."

the employee's attention. The decisions that the employee makes in pursuing the performance measures that ultimately provide valued personal outcomes move the organization toward achieving its goals if the performance measures are aligned with the organization's goals.

Second, the elements of performance that the performance measurement system monitors and rewards should reflect the *organization's critical success factors*. This attribute ensures that the performance system is relevant and motivates intended performance, that is, performance that matters to the organization's success. Moreover, the performance measurement system must consider all facets of performance so that the employee does not sacrifice performance on an unmeasured element for performance on an element that the reward system measures. For example, if a supervisor tells a telephone operator that productivity such as the number of help requests handled per shift, is important, the operator might sacrifice the quality and courtesy of the help offered to customers in order to handle as many questions as possible.

Third, the reward systems must set *clear standards* for performance that the employee accepts. In the context of the expectancy model of motivation, this helps the employee to assess whether his skill and effort will create results that the performance measurement system will capture and report as outcomes. This attribute determines the employee's beliefs about whether the

---

This team of Unocal employees earned a team bonus for designing a system to reduce the time taken to perform the annual maintenance on a natural gas liquids plant from 8 days to 3.5 days. The faster turnaround saved Unocal maintenance costs and reduced the amount of lost production time. Asked to describe his reaction to the reward, the employee shown on the far right seemed to derive more satisfaction from having his views "listened to and acted on" than from the monetary reward. The satisfaction expressed by this employee is a form of intrinsic reward related to satisfaction from a job that provides an opportunity for thinking and contribution. *(Alan Whitman/Unocal)*

performance system is fair. If performance standards are either unspecified or unclear to the employee, the relationship between performance and outcome will be ambiguous and, therefore, will reduce the motivational effect of the performance reward system.

Fourth, the performance measurement system must be able to *measure the objects of measurement systematically and accurately.* This attribute ensures that the performance measurement system establishes a clear relationship between performance and outcome, which, in expectancy theory terms, will improve instrumentality.

Fifth, when it is critical that the employee coordinate decision making and activities with other employees, the reward system should reward *group,* rather than individual, performance. Many organizations now believe that to be effective, employees must work effectively in teams. These organizations are replacing evaluations and rewards based on individual performance with rewards and evaluation based on group performance.

■ Conditions Favoring Incentive Compensation

Some organization tasks are better suited to incentive compensation than others.[9] The incentive compensation system designer must consider many facets when evaluating an incentive compensation system's potential to motivate performance. Moreover, the organization's culture must support the application of any incentive compensation system.

Not all organizations are suited to incentive compensation systems. Recall our discussion about organizations that have centralized most of the important operating decisions in the head office. They are not well-suited to incentive compensation systems because employees in these organizations are expected to follow rules and have no authority to make decisions.

Incentive compensation systems work best in organizations in which employees have the skill and authority to react to conditions and to make decisions. We previously discussed organizations that face environments that are changing continuously—ones in which it is either impractical or impossible to develop standard operating procedures to deal with these changing conditions. Such organizations can develop incentive compensation systems to motivate employees to identify different situations, to apply their skills and knowledge accordingly, and to make decisions that best reflect the organization's goals.

When the organization has empowered its employees to make decisions, it can use incentive compensation systems to motivate appropriate decision-making behavior. In these organizations, enforcement rules change from telling people what to do to asking employees to use their skills and delegated authority to do their best to help the organization achieve its objectives. If the employee does not effectively control the decision, incentive compensation will have no purpose.

---

[9] One of the first, and most definitive, discussions of when incentive compensation plans do and do not work well can be found in Arch Patton, "Why Incentive Plans Fail," *Harvard Business Review* (May–June 1972).

■ Incentive Compensation and Employee Responsibility

Expanding on the idea that the incentive compensation system must focus on the performance that the employee controls, consider an incentive compensation plan that rewards the performance of a production worker for sales. Because the sales department, rather than production, controls sales, such a plan would be ineffectual. In expectancy theory terms, this incentive compensation plan is low on expectancy. The production worker controls quality, the amount of resources used, and the delivery date of the production. Therefore, these items, to the extent that they are important in determining the organization's performance, should be the focus of the production employee's performance incentive system.

An employee's incentive compensation should reflect the nature of her responsibilities in the organization. Employees whose roles are to plan, coordinate, and control day-to-day activities should be rewarded based on their ability to manage these daily operations effectively and to make the best short-term use of available resources. Their rewards should be tied to short-term performance measures such as efficiency and the ability to meet customer quality and service requirements.

John Deere & Co. has signed a union contract in which some hourly employees are given pay raises after they complete technical courses and put their new learning into practice. With diversified skills, these employees undertake roles usually not associated with production line workers. The employee shown in this picture is a production line worker who has been temporarily assigned to demonstrating the company's new products to its dealers and customers.
(© Michael L. Abramson)

Employees whose roles are to plan intermediate-term projects, such as putting equipment and systems in place, should be rewarded based on their ability to identify, plan for, and install equipment and systems that improve the organization's performance. Their rewards should be tied to measures of the system's adequacy in meeting cost and response time targets, results of postimplementation audits of the project's effectiveness, and comparisons with the operating results of other organizations.

Employees whose roles are to undertake the organization's long-term planning should be rewarded based on the long-term growth or improvement in the organization's operations that results from their strategic choices. These rewards should be based on the organization's performance compared with similar organizations.

■ Rewarding Outcomes

The previous section argued that an employee's rewards should reflect his responsibilities in the organization. A second consideration in the design of effective incentive compensation systems concerns *how* the incentive compensation measures performance.

As we discussed in Chapter 2, organizations should reward employees based on the *outcomes* they create for the organization's stakeholders rather than the employees' outputs. This principle reflects the observation that the success in using the time and skills that the employee brings to the organization, not the amount of time and skill used, is the proper focus of an incentive compensation system. Moreover, incentive compensation based on outcomes requires that organization members understand and contribute to the organization's objectives. When it is impossible to measure outcomes consistently and at a reasonable cost, rewards are based on inputs.

As we just mentioned, an employee provides 2 types of inputs to an organization: time and skill. Input-based compensation measures the time and the skill level that the employee brings to the job, with the expectation that the unmeasured outcome is correlated with these inputs.

Many organizations use some form of *knowledge-based* remuneration that pays the employee an hourly rate of pay that reflects her training and job qualifications, which can be upgraded by on-the-job training. The employee's compensation is the product of the number of hours worked (time input) and the hourly rate (a reflection of the deemed level of skill input). Organizations use knowledge-based pay to motivate employees to continuously upgrade their job skills, thereby allowing them to receive a higher base pay.

■ Managing Incentive Compensation Plans

Considerable evidence indicates that organizations have systematically mismanaged incentive compensation plans, particularly those relating to senior executives. Many articles have appeared in influential business periodicals arguing that executives, particularly executives of U.S. corporations, have been paid excessively for mediocre performance.

Some experts stand on both sides of the question of whether conventional incentive compensation systems are effective (that is, whether they motivate goal-seeking behavior) and efficient (that is, whether they pay what is needed and no more). Some studies have shown positive correlations between executive compensation and shareholder wealth.[10] Other studies report finding no or even *negative* correlations between organization performance and executive compensation.[11] Consider the following observation:[12]

> From 1966 to 1970 corporate performance and shareholder value began to decline. And, since 1970, shareholder value has drifted steadily downward, while executive compensation has climbed ever higher. In light of the prospects that the trend in rising CEO pay will continue, it is particularly inappropriate for companies to continue operating compensation systems in which executive rewards bear no relation to corporate performance.

Rosabeth Moss Kanter summarized[13] the issues:

> Every year, routine company surveys show fewer employees willing to say that traditional pay practices are fair. In particular, top management compensation has been assailed as unjustifiably high, especially when executives get large bonuses while their companies suffer financial losses or are just recovering from them.

> Despite economic data showing an association between executive compensation and company performance, many professionals still argue that the amounts are excessive and reflect high status rather than good performance.

[10] See, for example, Kevin J. Murphy, "Corporate Performance and Managerial Remuneration: An Empirical Analysis," *Journal of Accounting and Economics* (April 1985), pp. 11–42.

[11] See, for example, a summary in Alfie Kohn, "Why Incentive Plans Cannot Work," *Harvard Business Review* (September–October 1993). The different conclusions reflect different assumptions and different measures of performance that have been used in the various studies.

[12] Louis J. Brindisi, Jr., "Creating Shareholder Value: A New Mission for Executive Compensation," Chapter 19 in *Corporate Restructuring and Executive Compensation,* ed. Joel M. Stern, G. Bennett Stewart III, and Donald H. Chew (Ballinger Publishing Company, 1989).

[13] Rosabeth Moss Kanter, "The Attack on Pay," *Harvard Business Review* (March–April 1987), pp. 60–67.

These beliefs reflect broadly based feelings of unfairness and cynicism about incentive compensation that organizations must address to restore the motivational effect that incentive compensation is intended to create.

Guidelines for Effective Incentive Compensation Systems

Over the years, managers, compensation consultants, lawyers, and philosophers have proposed broad guidelines for incentive compensation systems. Four broad guidelines have long-standing support, thereby meriting serious consideration.

> *Fairness*—many experts believe that the total pay, including salary, benefits, and rewards of the highest-paid person in the organization, should not be more than about 20 times the total pay of the lowest paid person in the organization. In a cover story describing the issues concerning executive pay, *Business Week* made the following observations:

Management guru Peter Drucker expressed his misgivings in the mid-1980s by suggesting that the CEO shouldn't earn much more than 20 times as much as the company's lowest paid employee. [In 1990] . . . the average chief executive of a major corporation earned 85 times the pay of a typical American factory worker. In Japan, by contrast, the boss receives only 17 times the pay of an ordinary worker.

Drucker worried that the widening gap was harming the morale not only of the rank and file but also of other professionals and managers. And Drucker was hardly the first observer to fret over the gap between the shop and the top. Plato believed that no one in a community should earn more than 5 times the pay of the ordinary worker.[14]

This equity principle concerning relative pay levels relates to fairness. Supporters of this fairness criterion consider it important because it creates a favorable climate in the organization. In the Herzberg theory, pay structure relates to organization policies, a hygiene factor, which is reflected in the comments from the *Business Week* article. Support for this principle in one form or another dates back many thousands of years.

[14] "The Flap over Executive Pay," *Business Week* (May 6, 1991), pp. 90–112.

CONSIDER THIS . . .

Base Pay and Organization Policies

Some critics believe that perquisites, such as private aircraft, limousines, and club memberships, enjoyed by senior executives create an impression of different classes within the organization that can lead to bitterness and resentment.

Many organizations are now dealing with image problems created by a group of employees with special rights. For example, the General Motors Trim Plant in Windsor, Ontario, maintained an underground parking garage and a separate dining room for its executives while other employees parked in outside lots and ate in a cafeteria. To eliminate this image of 2 classes of employees, when General Motors redesigned the plant for synchronous manufacturing and participative decision making, it converted the parking garage to a health club that was available to all employees and converted the executive dining room into meeting rooms available to the organization's new work teams.

OBJECTIVE 13.5
The guidelines that organizations might use to design reward systems

Applying this principle can create practical problems in the competitive market for employees. For example, Ben and Jerry's Homemade, Inc., a Vermont-based manufacturer of dairy products, began with a policy that the ratio of the salaries of the highest- to lowest-paid employees should not exceed 5:1. This policy created problems in attracting and keeping senior management personnel. Eventually the ratio was adjusted upward to 7:1, but the principle of maintaining a balanced salary structure remained.

➤ *Participation*—If the organization uses incentive compensation, many experts believe that all employees should participate, although they do not have to be in the same plan. As mentioned earlier in this chapter, each employee should understand the provisions of the plan to which he is subject. Every incentive plan should be documented clearly and should focus on performance that the employee controls and that helps the organization achieve its goals.

➤ *Basic wage level*—Each employee should be paid a basic wage that reflects the market assessment for her skills and experience. Organizations should not use incentive compensation to reduce the employee's basic wage. Expert opinion varies, but many agree that the incentive compensation should vary between 20% (at junior levels in the organization) and 50% (at senior levels of the organization) of the employee's basic wage.

➤ *Independent wage policy*—Although senior management has the responsibility to develop wage and incentive compensation policy in the organization, it should not set its own wage and incentive compensation. A board of directors' compensation committee should design the incentive compensation plan for senior management. It is imperative that this committee operate independently, and that it appear to be independent of senior management's direction and influence. The compensation committee should operate with its own staff, including lawyers and compensation consultants, if necessary, that is independent of the staff used by senior management.

■ Issues in Designing Incentive Compensation Plans

An incentive compensation plan must identify *what performance to measure* and the *appropriate standard against which it compares measured performance*. Beyond identifying relevant performance and performance targets, the designers of an incentive compensation plan must make other important choices.

A major issue to resolve in the design of incentive plans involves whether the compensation system should base incentive compensation on individual or group performance. Rewards based on individual performance are usually implemented in the context of a management-by-objectives program. Rewards based on group performance are usually based on segment margin or corporate profit. The advantage of measuring and rewarding individual performance is that the individual perceives a clear relationship between performance and outcome. The advantage of measuring and reward-

This Wheeling-Pittsburgh Corporation employee is operating the computerized system that controls the process of rolling steel into the desired thickness. The productivity, yield, and quality of the work done in this mill relies on both this employee, who operates the equipment, and the employees shown in the background, who maintain and set the machines that do the work. (*Courtesy Wheeling Pittsburgh Steel Corporation*)

ing group performance is that the incentive compensation plan encourages coordination and group-oriented behavior by individuals.

Incentive system designers must decide on the form of monetary rewards. That is, should the incentive compensation plan be in the form of cash, perquisites, or equity? Incentive compensation systems tied to identified and measured critical performance indicators should be based on formal awards such as cash or equity. Organizations often use cash awards when the performance measures focus on the short term, and they use equity rewards when the measures focus on the long term or financial results. Organizations can use nonmonetary extrinsic rewards for exceptional behavior that is not captured formally by an incentive compensation system.

Compensation system designers must decide whether the incentive compensation plan should pay its rewards immediately or defer them. Organizations should pay rewards that relate to short-term performance immediately and defer payment of rewards related to long-term performance improvement. The advantage of deferring a reward is to allow time to measure the performance result accurately. An additional consideration in deferring rewards is to tie the individual to the organization, thus restricting rewards available to long-term employees.

OBJECTIVE 13.6
The broad types of monetary rewards that organizations use

■ Types of Incentive Compensation Plans

The most common incentive compensation plans are cash bonuses, profit sharing, gain sharing, stock options, performance shares stock, stock appreciation rights, participation units, and employee stock ownership plans (usually called ESOPs).

Cash bonus
A cash award based on some measured performance.

Profit sharing
A cash bonus system in which the total amount available for distribution as cash bonuses is a function of the organization's, or an organization unit's, reported profit.

CASH BONUS   A **cash bonus**, also called a *lump-sum reward, pay for performance,* and *merit pay,* is a payment of cash based on some measured performance. They are one-time awards that do not become part of the employee's base pay in subsequent years.

Cash bonuses can be fixed and triggered when performance exceeds the target, or they can be proportional to the level of performance relative to the target. They can be based on individual or group performance and can be paid to individuals or to groups.

For example, in the late 1980s, General Motors eliminated automatic salary increases based on increases in the cost of living and replaced them with a pay-for-performance system that rewarded managers based on their results. Each superior was required to group her employees into 3 groups: high performers (the top 10%), good performers (the next 25%), average performers (the next 55%), and the low performers (the last 10%). Supervisors used these groupings to award merit pay and to enforce salary differences based on assessed performance.

PROFIT SHARING   **Profit sharing** is a cash bonus that reflects the organization's, or an organization unit's, reported profit. Therefore, profit sharing is a group incentive compensation plan focused on rewarding short-term performance.

All profit-sharing plans define what portion of the organization's reported profits is available for sharing, the sharing formula, the employees who are eligible to participate in the plan, and the way the plan determines each employee's share.

Many profit-sharing plans stipulate that the reported profit will be reduced by some percentage (say 20%) of the market value of the outstanding stock. This allotment provides the

CONSIDER THIS . . .

Cash Bonuses at Chrysler Corporation

In February 1994, Chrysler Corporation announced that it would give many of its executives cash bonuses for performance during 1993. For the 200 most senior executives, the cash bonuses were about 100% of salary. For the next 100 executives, the bonuses amount to about 80% of salary. Lower-level executives received much less.

The Chrysler bonus plan rewards performance on quality (measured by warranty claims), customer satisfaction (measured by surveys), and profitability. The size of the bonus pool available for distribution reflects whether performance targets are met in all 3 areas. If performance targets are not met in some areas, the bonus pool is reduced proportionately. If goals are exceeded in all 3 areas, the bonus pool expands to 125% of its original size. The bonus pool for 1993 achieved the maximum amount.

shareholders their required return on investment. The resulting pool is to be shared between employees and shareholders on some fractional basis, such as 40/60. The plan also may provide for a limit on the total amount of profits that can be distributed to employees.

Finally, the profit-sharing plan specifies how it will distribute the money in the pool to each employee. Some plans provide equal distribution; others distribute the bonus pool based on the employee's performance relative to individual performance targets.

In the performance compensation approach, each employee receives a performance score that reflects how well that employee achieved specific performance goals for that year. The employee's score divided by the total of the scores of all the employees in the profit-sharing agreement is the individual's share of the pool total. Some profit-sharing plans distribute rewards to each employee proportionally to the base wage or salary because their designers believe this reflects the employee's contribution to the overall result.

GAIN SHARING   **Gain sharing** is a system for distributing cash bonuses from a pool when the total amount available is a function of performance relative to some target. For example, employees in a designated unit receive bonuses when their performance exceeds a performance target. Note that gain sharing is a group incentive, unlike the pay-for-performance cash bonus that is an individual reward.[15]

In its usual form, gain sharing provides for sharing of financial gains in organizational performance. The gain-sharing plan usually applies to a group of employees within an organization unit such as a department or a store. Gain sharing uses a formula to specify the amount and distribution of the rewards and a base period of performance as the benchmark for comparing subsequent performance. This benchmark is not changed unless a major change in process or technology occurs. When performance exceeds the base period performance, the gain-sharing plan pays a bonus pool.

Gain sharing promotes teamwork and participation in decision making. It requires that employees have the skills to participate and that the organization encourages participation. Consider these companies that have used gain sharing effectively:

➤ The Herman Miller Company, a furniture manufacturer that is frequently rated as one of the 10 best-managed U.S. corporations, has used a gain-sharing plan for many years. The company also uses a strategy of employee involvement that supports and enhances the motivational effect of the gain-sharing plan.

Gain sharing
A cash bonus system in which the total amount available for distribution as cash bonuses is a function of performance relative to some target (usually the difference between the actual and the target level of labor cost).

---

[15] For a detailed discussion of gain-sharing approaches to motivation, see Robert L. Masternak, "Gainsharing: Overcoming Common Myths and Problems to Achieve Dramatic Results," *Employment Relations Today* (December 22, 1993).

CONSIDER THIS . . .

Gain Sharing at A&P

When A&P, a large grocery chain, faced a need to reduce costs, it developed and put in place a gain-sharing plan. This plan provided employees in individual stores a bonus of one percent of store sales when employee costs were kept below 10 percent of sales. This plan lowered employee costs and increased profits dramatically.

This employee is part of a gain-sharing plan at Georgia-Pacific, a paper products manufacturer. The plan pays employees cash bonuses based on productivity improvements. A motivationally desirable feature of the Georgia-Pacific gain-sharing plan is that it pays these productivity bonuses even when the company's net income is negative. *(© John Chiasson/Gamma Liaison Network)*

➤ Grumman Corporation developed a performance bonus plan for the crew in its Long Life Vehicle project that it used in conjunction with its Grumman Quality program. Employees focused on processes that involved rework, scrap, and excessive maintenance costs. Half the savings from improved performance were divided equally among the crew working on the project.

The 3 most widely used gain-sharing programs are Improshare, the Scanlon plan, and the Rucker plan.

➤ Improshare (Improved Productivity Sharing) is a widely used gain-sharing program that determines its bonus pool by computing the difference between the target level of labor cost given the level of production and the actual labor cost. Recall from Chapter 6 that this difference is the direct labor efficiency variance. The plan specifies how the difference will be shared between the shareholders and the employees and how to calculate the amount distributed to each employee.

➤ The Scanlon plan is based on the following formula computed using the data in some base period.[16]

$$\text{Base ratio} = \frac{\text{Payroll costs}}{\text{Value of production or service}}$$

For example, if in the base period payroll costs are $25,000,000 and the deemed value of production or service is $86,000,000, the base ratio would be 0.29 ($25,000,000/$86,000,000).

In any period in which the ratio of labor costs to the value of production or service is less than the base ratio, the deemed labor savings are added to a bonus pool. Therefore, continuing the above example, if, in a subsequent period, actual payroll costs were $28,000,000 in a period when the deemed value of production was $105,000,000, the amount added to the bonus pool would be

Amount added to bonus pool
= (value of production this period * Base ratio) − Actual payroll costs
= ($105,000,000 * 0.29) − $28,000,000 = $2,450,000

When labor costs are more than the base ratio, some organizations deduct the difference from the bonus pool. Periodically, usually once a year, the pool is apportioned between the company and the employees in the pool using the plan ratio, which is often 50/50.

➤ The Rucker plan is based on the following formula, which reflects the data from a representative period:

$$\text{Rucker standard} = \frac{\text{Payroll costs}}{\text{Production value}}$$

where production value is measured as (Net sales − inventory change − materials and supplies used). As in the Scanlon plan, the idea in the Rucker plan is to define a baseline relationship between payroll costs and the value of production and to reward workers who improve efficiency, measured as lowering the ratio of payroll costs to the value of production. When actual labor costs are less than the Rucker standard, the employees receive a bonus.

STOCK OPTIONS AND OTHER STOCK-RELATED COMPENSATION PLANS

Stock options are the most widely known, misused, and maligned approach to incentive compensation. A **stock option** is the right to purchase a unit of the organization's stock at a specified price, called the *option price*.

A common approach to option pricing is to set the option price at about 105% of the stock's market price at the time the organization issues the stock

Stock option
A right to purchase a stated number of the organization's shares at a specified price (the option price).

[16] This plan, developed by Joseph Scanlon during the 1930s, promotes and recognizes employee contributions through suggestion systems and participation with management in analyzing and improving operations.

Like their counterparts in most large corporations, these senior executives at ASARCO International, a producer of nonferrous metals, are members of a stock incentive plan designed to reward them for actions they take to increase the firm's market value. *(Chris Jones/ASARCO, Inc.)*

option.[17] This is intended to motivate the employee who has been granted the stock options to act in the long-term interests of the organization, thereby increasing the value of the firm so that the market price of the stock will exceed the option price. For this reason, compensation system designers usually restrict stock options to senior executives because they believe that senior executives have the greatest effect on increasing the market value of the organization. Some people have argued, however, that although operations staff are primarily responsible for carrying out short-term operating plans, they, too, can make significant and sustainable process improvements that provide the organization with a competitive advantage, thereby increasing the organization's market value.

Critics have argued that organizations have been too generous in rewarding senior executives with stock options. For example, the organization may issue a senior executive many thousands of stock options with an option price that is very near, or even below, the market price at the time the stock option is issued. This is a practice issue that is not a fundamental defect of stock options. Some critics have argued, however, that stock price increases often reflect general market trends that have nothing to do with the performance of the individual organization. For this reason, many incentive compensation experts have argued that the stock option price should be

---

[17] This choice reflects both motivational issues (to encourage the employee to work to improve the market's valuation of the organization) and taxation issues (to avoid having tax authorities deem that the organization has given the employee something whose value does not depend on the employee's subsequent actions).

keyed to the performance of the organization's shares *relative to the performance of the prices of comparable shares.* Therefore, the stock option would be valuable *only* if the organization's share price increases more rapidly than the share prices of comparable organizations.

Many other forms of stock-related incentive compensation plans are used, including performance shares stock, stock appreciation rights, participation units, and employee stock ownership plans, which are beyond the scope of issues in management accounting. All these plans provide incentive compensation to the participants when the stock price increases. The idea behind such plans is to motivate employees to act in the long-term interests of the organization by doing things to increase the organization's market value. Therefore, all these plans assume that stock markets will recognize exceptional behavior in the form of increased stock prices.

The use of employee stock ownership plans is based on the belief that employees will work harder when they have an ownership stake.[18] Avis, the automobile rental company, used an employee stock ownership plan to improve employee motivation, which, in turn, resulted in both higher sales and a higher margin on sales.

Salomon Brothers, a Wall Street investment house, provided huge bonuses for high-performing employees during the 1980s and early 1990s. For example, one bond trader was paid a $23 million bonus in 1990. Reacting to this, Salomon Brothers' largest shareholder, Warren Buffett, whom *Forbes* magazine identified as the wealthiest person in the United States in 1993, became interim chairman and indicated that he wanted Salomon Brothers' employees to earn rewards through owning shares, not by free riding on the owners' investment. To align the interest of the firm's employees and its shareholders and to provide for more reasonable performance rewards, Mr. Buffet, through the Salomon Brothers' Compensation Committee, developed an incentive plan that paid employees up to half their pay in company stock, issued at below market prices, that could not be sold for at least 5 years after issue.

FRIEDMAN-JACOBS COMPANY REVISITED

Recall our introductory discussion of Arthur Friedman's appliance dealership. Charles Ryan was clearly an unhappy and unmotivated employee, as every facet of his behavior suggested. In fact, most organizations would not have tolerated his behavior. The Herzberg theory of motivation suggests that poor

---

[18] Of course, as owners, the employees should have some say in how the company is run. Therefore, a real system of employee involvement should accompany the use of employee stock ownership plans.

hygiene factors and his own attitudes explain Charles's behavior. In the matter of having employees determine their own pay, 1 employee, George Tegner, 59, an employee for 14 years, observed: "You have to use common sense; no one wins if you end up closing the business down. If you want more money, you have to produce more. It can't work any other way. Anyway, wages aren't everything. Doing what you want to is more important."

Arthur Friedman's style for and approach to dealing with the pay issue reflected and determined the working conditions, organization policies, interpersonal relationships, and supervisory quality in this organization. The clear signal from Arthur Friedman to the employees was, "I trust you to do the right thing. I want to give you what you think is fair."

Arthur Friedman believed that the poor hygiene factor for Charles was his feeling that his base pay was too low. Once the base pay problem was corrected, Charles became a model employee. Because there is no evidence that any other conditions were changed, the other hygiene factors in this organization seemed to have been acceptable to Charles.

Given that the removal of the poor hygiene factor relating to base pay caused such an improvement in motivation, we assume that the satisfier factors must have already been in place. Certainly, a high element of responsibility was evident here after employees were allowed to determine their own pay. In any event, this anecdote shows, for one employee at least, how 1 poor hygiene factor can prevent all the positive satisfier factors from motivating an employee. When the poor hygiene factor was removed, the satisfier factors provided for a satisfied and highly motivated employee.

This was a unique experiment that we should be careful in generalizing to other organizations. It seems that most employees at Friedman-Jacobs were happy with their base pay; the company had objective evidence in the form of union pay scales that the employees were relatively well paid. It had a positive organization culture that included mutual respect and trust between Arthur Friedman and the employees. This was a small company and everyone knew each other. Arthur Friedman's offer was an extension of trust that employees seemed to feel self-conscious about breaching. This implies that the employees had a positive attitude toward their work and that there was a group norm that they should be paid only for the value of their work. Note that the company had no measurement system to enforce pay for performance, as evidenced by the serviceman who turned down a raise because he felt that he did not deserve it.

The article about Arthur Friedman summarized the results following the point in time when he had implemented his unique wage policy:

> In the past five years, there has been no turnover of employees. Friedman estimates that last year his 15 workers took no more than a total of three sick days. It is rare that anyone is late for work and, even then, there is usually a good reason. Work is done on time and employee pilferage is nonexistent.

> As part of the new freedom, more people are given keys to the store and the cash box. If they need groceries, or even some beer money, all they have to do is walk into the office, take what they want out of the cash box and leave a voucher. Every effort is made to ensure that no one looks over their shoulder.

There has only been one discrepancy. "Once our petty cash was $10 over," recalls Friedman. "We could never figure out where it came from."

Skeptics by now are chuckling to themselves, convinced that if Friedman is not losing money, he is just breaking even. The fact is that net profit has not dropped a cent in the last five years; it has increased. Although volume is considerably less (the store discontinued selling televisions and stereo equipment to concentrate on refrigerators, washers, and dryers) and overhead has increased at what some would consider an unhealthy rate, greater productivity and efficiency have more than made up for it.[19]

SUMMARY

One of senior management's most important leadership roles is to design and manage reward systems that appropriately measure and reward superior performance and to create an organization environment where employees experience intrinsic rewards.

The chapter presented 2 significant theories of motivation. The Herzberg theory argues that 2 types of factors affect motivation. One group, the hygiene factors, provides the framework for motivation. The second group, the satisfier factors, provides the motivation itself. The major insight of the Herzberg theory is that only satisfier factors provide motivation, although hygiene factors must be present to allow the satisfier factors to have their effect. Another important motivation theory, expectancy theory, argues that motivation is a function of expectancy, instrumentality, and valence. The organization's performance measurement system has a critical effect on expectancy and instrumentality, thereby having a critical effect on motivation.

Effective reward systems are clear and unequivocal and focus organization employees on the relevant and measured performance that they control. Organizations that face rapidly changing external environments and give the employees the authority to use their knowledge and skills are the best candidates for incentive compensation systems.

Effective incentive compensation systems reflect employee responsibilities. Therefore, incentive compensation systems for employees who focus on the effective and efficient management of daily activities will be different from incentive compensation systems for employees who identify and implement tactical-level or strategic-level strategies, which are longer term.

Incentive compensation systems should, if possible, reward results rather than work done and should clearly distinguish between base salary, which reflects market conditions, and incentive rewards, which reflect measured performance. Depending on the employee's contribution and the organization's needs, rewards can reflect either individual or group performance and focus on short- or long-term results. An incentive compensation system's

---

[19] Martin Koughan, "Arthur Friedman's Outrage."

effectiveness can be judged by sampling employee attitudes about its relevance, fairness, and comprehensiveness.

The most common forms of incentive compensation are cash rewards based on short-term performance and stock-related rewards for long-term performance. An ideal combination for many organizations is to use a combination of profit-sharing or stock-related plans to encourage coordination and companywide thinking and gain-sharing plans to encourage and reward local initiatives.

KEY TERM LIST

Cash bonus, p. 552

Expectancy, p. 538

Expectancy theory (Vroom's), p. 538

Extrinsic rewards, p. 540

Gain sharing, p. 553

Hygiene factors, p. 537

Incentive compensation, p. 542

Instrumentality, p. 538

Intrinsic rewards, p. 540

Motivation system, p. 539

Pay for performance (incentive compensation), p. 542

Profit sharing, p. 552

Satisfier factors, p. 537

Stock option, p. 555

Two-factor theory (Herzberg's), p. 537

Valence, p. 538

ASSIGNMENT MATERIAL

QUESTIONS

13–1   What is the Herzberg theory of motivation?

13–2   What is a hygiene factor?

13–3   What is a satisfier factor?

13–4   What is the expectancy theory?

13–5   What does *expectancy* mean?

13–6   What is instrumentality?

13–7   What is valence?

13–8   What is an intrinsic reward?

13–9   What is an extrinsic reward?

13–10   What is incentive compensation?

13–11   What are the 5 attributes of effective performance measurement systems?

13–12   What type of organization is best suited to incentive compensation? Why?

13–13   What are the 4 guidelines for designing effective incentive compensation systems?

13–14   What is a cash bonus?

13–15 What is profit sharing?

13–16 What is gain sharing?

13–17 What is a stock option plan?

EXERCISES

13–18 Explain, in everyday words, Herzberg's 2-factor theory of motivation.

13–19 Explain how hygiene factors and satisfier factors combine to provide motivation.

13–20 How do satisfier factors motivate?

13–21 Explain how Vroom's expectancy theory specifies the attributes of an effective performance measurement system.

13–22 Do you believe that people value intrinsic rewards? Give an example of an intrinsic reward that you would value and explain why. If you value only extrinsic rewards, explain why.

13–23 How do leaders provide an environment within which employees experience and value intrinsic rewards? Give an example of such a leader.

13–24 The text claims that providing extrinsic rewards or employment benefits such as parking and dining facilities to 1 group of employees tends to alienate employees who are not in that group. Do you agree or disagree? Why?

13–25 Why are extrinsic rewards important to people?

13–26 Why is it so important that people understand what performance is measured, how performance is measured, and how outcomes (employee rewards) relate to measured performance?

13–27 Why should performance measurement systems and rewards focus on performance that employees can control?

13–28 Why is it important that the performance measurement system include all the elements of employee performance? Can you give an example of the consequence of not including some element of performance in the performance measurement system?

13–29 Why are incentive compensation plans unsuited to organizations in which employees, for the most part, are simply expected to follow rules? Can you give an example of such an organization?

13–30 In a company that takes telephone orders from customers for general merchandise, explain how you would evaluate the performance of the company president, a middle manager who designs the system to coordinate order taking and order shipping, and an employee who fills orders? How are the performance systems similar? How are the performance systems different?

13–31 Why is it important to reward outcomes rather than outputs or inputs?

13–32 Can you give an example of knowledge-based pay?

13–33 Do you believe that organizations should pay extra for superior performance?

13–34 You work for a consulting firm and have been given the assignment of deciding whether a particular company president is overpaid in both absolute terms and relative to presidents of comparable companies. How would you undertake this task?

13–35 What do you think of the principle of keeping the ratio of the highest pay to the lowest pay in the organization below some target value like 20?

13–36 Is it important for employees to believe that the incentive compensation system pays for measured, relevant, and controllable performance? Explain.

13–37 When should an organization use a cash bonus?

13–38 When should an organization use profit sharing?

13–39 When should an organization use gain sharing?

13–40 When should an organization use stock options?

13–41 How would you reward a group of people that includes product designers, engineers, production personnel, purchasing agents, marketing staff, and accountants whose job is to identify and develop a new car? How would you reward a person whose job is to discover a better way of designing crash protection devices in cars? How are these 2 situations similar? How are they different?

PROBLEMS

13–42 Tambrands, Inc., a manufacturer and distributor of personal hygiene products, made the following disclosures about its compensation program

> Our compensation philosophy is based on 2 simple principles: (1) we pay for performance; and (2) management cannot benefit unless our shareholders benefit first.

> Executive compensation at Tambrands consists of 3 elements: base salary, bonus, and stock awards. Frankly, we see base salaries and the underlying value of restricted stock as what you have to pay to get people in the door—fixed costs, if you will. Incentives, in the form of annual cash bonuses and gains tied to increases in the price of our stock, are the performance drivers of our pay equation—the variable costs.

> The first element is base salary. Our philosophy is to peg salary levels at median competitive levels. In other words, we pay salaries that are sufficient to attract and retain the level of talent we require.

> The second element of our executive compensation is our bonus plan. This plan is based on management by objectives. Each year, the compensation committee approves objectives and performance measures for the corporation, our divisions, and our key individual managers. At year-end, bonuses are paid on the basis of measurable performance against these objectives.

> The third element of our executive compensation program is stock incentives, namely, restricted stock and stock options.

> Our restricted stock program is very straightforward. Stock option grants are made each year at market value. Our options vest over time periods of 2 to 6 years, to encourage long-term equity holding by management.

> In 1991, we instituted an innovative stock incentive plan called the Stock Option Exchange Program. Under this program, management can purchase stock options by exchanging other forms of compensation, such as the annual bonus or restricted stock, for the options. The price charged for the options is determined by an independent investment banker using standard pricing mechanics.

> Our compensation committee is made up entirely of independent outside directors. There are no interlocking directorates, in which I serve on the compensation committee of one of my director's companies and he or she

serves on mine. The compensation committee uses outside advisers chosen independently to ensure that recommendations are fair to all shareholders.

What do you think of this incentive compensation plan?

13–43　Hoechst Celanese, a pharmaceutical manufacturer, uses a profit-sharing plan, which it calls the Hoechst Celanese Performance Sharing Plan (PSP), to motivate employees. The Hoechst Celanese Executive Committee sets a target earnings from operations (EFO). This target is based on the company's business plans and the economy's expected performance. The Performance Sharing Plan also uses 2 other critical values: the earnings from operations threshold amount and the earnings from operations stretch target. The targets for 1994 are shown in the accompanying figure.

If earnings from operations fall below the threshold value, there is no profit sharing. If earnings from operations lie between the threshold amount and the target, the profit-sharing percent is prorated between the threshold award of 1% and the target payment of 4%. For example, if earnings from operations were $285 million, the profit-sharing percent would be 2.5%

$$\text{Profit-sharing percent} = 1\% + 3\% * \left[\frac{285 - 250}{320 - 250} \right] = 2.5\%$$

and the profit-sharing pool would be $7,125,000

$$\text{Profit-sharing pool} = 2.5\% * \$285,000,000 = \$7,125,000$$

If earnings from operations are between the target and the stretch target, the profit-sharing percent is prorated between the target payment of 4% and the stretch-sharing payment of 7%. For example, if earnings from operations were $350 million, the profit-sharing percentage would be 5.29% and the profit-sharing pool would be $18,500,000

$$\text{Profit-sharing percent} = 4\% + 3\% * \left[\frac{350 - 320}{390 - 320} \right] = 5.29\%$$

$$\text{Profit-sharing pool} = 5.29\% * \$350,000,000 = \$18,500,000$$

If earnings from operations equal, or exceed, the stretch target level, the profit-sharing pool would be $27,300,000

$$\text{Profit-sharing pool} = 7\% * \$390,000,000 = \$27,300,000$$

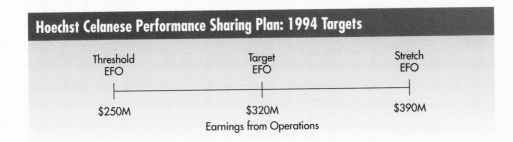

Hoechst Celanese Performance Sharing Plan: 1994 Targets

Threshold EFO	Target EFO	Stretch EFO
$250M	$320M	$390M

Earnings from Operations

(a) List, with explanations, what you think are the desirable features of the Hoechst Celanese Performance Sharing plan.

(b) List, with explanations, what you think are the undesirable features of the Hoechst Celanese Performance Sharing plan.

13–44 Suppose that you are the owner/manager of a house/cleaning business. You have 30 employees who work in teams of 3. Teams are dispatched to the homes of customers where they are directed by the customer to undertake specific cleaning tasks that vary widely from customer to customer.

Your employees are unskilled workers who are paid an hourly wage of $8. This wage is typical for unskilled work. Turnover in your organization is quite high. Generally, your best employees leave as soon as they find better jobs. The employees that stay are usually ones who cannot find work elsewhere and have a poor attitude.

The hourly rate charged customers per team hour is $40. That is, if a team spends 1.5 hours in a customer's home, the charge is $60.

You want to develop an incentive system to use in your organization. You would like to use this incentive system to motivate good employees to stay and motivate poor workers either to improve or to leave. What type of system would you develop and, if the system relies on any measurements, indicate how you would obtain these measurements?

13–45 Darlington Engineering is a research and development company that designs equipment for nuclear generating stations. The company consists of an administrative unit, a research laboratory, and a facility used to develop prototypes of new designs. The major costs in this company are the salaries of the research staff, which are substantial.

In the past, the research scientists working at Darlington Engineering have been rewarded based on their proven scientific expertise. Salaries of these research scientists are based on the level of education achieved and the number of research papers published in scientific journals. At a recent board of directors meeting, an outside director criticized the research and development activities with the following comments:

> There is no question that we have the most highly trained scientists in our industry. Evidence of their training and creativity is provided by the number of research publications that they generate. However, the knowledge and creativity are not translating into patentable inventions and increased sales for this company. Our organization has the lowest rate of new product introduction in our industry, and we have one of the largest research and development teams. These people are too far into basic research, where the rewards lie in getting articles published. We need these people to have more interest in generating ideas that have commercial potential. This is a profit-seeking organization, not a university research laboratory.

REQUIRED:

(a) Assuming that the director's facts are correct, do you agree that this is a problem?

(b) The board of directors has ordered the president of Darlington Engineering to increase the rate of new products and the time for new product development. How should the president go about this task?

13–46 Peterborough Medical Devices makes devices and equipment that it sells to hospitals. The organization has a profit-sharing plan that is worded as follows:

The company will make available a profit-sharing pool that will be the minimum of the following two items:

(1) 25% of profits in excess of the target profit level which is 22% of assets or

(2) $7,000,000.

The individual employee will receive a share of the profit-sharing pool that is equal to the ratio of that employee's salary to the total salary paid to all employees.

REQUIRED:

(a) If the company earned $23,000,000 of profits and had net assets of $78,000,000, what would be the amount available for distribution from the profit-sharing pool?

(b) Suppose that Marg Watson's salary was $68,000 and the total salaries paid in the company were $15,000,000. What would Marg's profit share be?

(c) What do you like about this profit-sharing plan?

(d) What do you dislike about this profit-sharing plan?

13–47 Lindsay Cereal Company manufactures a line of breakfast cereals. The production workers are part of a gain-sharing program that works as follows. A target level of labor costs is set based on the achieved level of production. If the actual level of labor costs is less than the target level of labor costs, the difference is added to a cumulative pool that is carried from year to year. If the actual level of labor costs exceeds the target level, the amount of the excess is deducted from the cumulative pool.

At the end of any year if the balance of the pool is positive, the employees receive half the balance of the pool as part of a gain-sharing plan and the balance of the pool is reset to zero. At the end of any year, if the balance of the pool is negative, the employees receive nothing and the negative balance is carried to the following year.

In any year when the target level of costs exceeds the actual level of costs, the target level for the following year is based on the actual level of cost performance in the previous year.

REQUIRED:

(a) Suppose that the target level of performance is set using the following labor use standards: (1) 0.12 labor hours per case of cereal A, (2) 0.05 labor hours per case of cereal B, (3) 0.18 labor hours per case of cereal C, and (4) 0.22 labor hours per case of cereal D.

During the last year, production of cereal A, B, C, and D were 150,000 cases, 174,000 cases, 145,000 cases, and 212,000 cases, respectively. There were 90,000 labor hours used during the year, and the average cost of labor was $16 per hour. What is the amount available for distribution to employees under this gain-sharing program?

(b) What do you like about this program?

(c) What do you dislike about it?

13–48 Belleville Fashions sells high-quality women's, men's, and children's clothing. The store employs a sales staff of 11 full-time people and 12 part-time people. Until recently, all sales staff were paid a flat salary and participated in a profit-sharing plan that provided benefits equal to about 5% of wages. Recently, the manager and owner of Belleville Fashions announced that in the future, all compensation would be commission based. The initial commission rate was set equal to the rate that would have caused the actual wage bill based on the old system to be equal to what the wage bill would have been under the commission system. Profit sharing was discontinued.

REQUIRED:

    (a) What do you think of this change?

    (b) Describe some of the reactions that the owner might hear from the sales staff when this change was announced.

    (c) Do you think that the method of determining the commission rate was appropriate?

    (d) Describe what you think will happen under the new system.

13–49 Sam Walton, the founder of the Wal-Mart chain, was an inspirational leader. Although some industry surveys suggest that Wal-Mart employees were paid salaries that were lower than the average salaries paid in the department store industry, the employees were enthusiastic and productive supporters of the organization and its objectives.

REQUIRED:

    (a) What is management's role in motivation?

    (b) How do inspirational leaders lead? Why are employees sometimes willing to work for less than what they could earn elsewhere?

    (c) Could an inspirational leader like Sam Walton be successful in any organization? For example, if Sam Walton had been made the president of IBM, could he have created the same success there as he did at Wal-Mart? Explain.

13–50 Intrinsic rewards are rewards that people value because of their commitment to their job or pride in their work. Examples of intrinsic rewards include pride in a job well done and value placed in personal growth in a job.

REQUIRED:

    (a) Why do intrinsic rewards work?

    (b) Do intrinsic rewards work for everyone? Why or why not?

13–51 Identify an organization that is hierarchical and leaves little discretion for employees to exercise. Explain why an incentive compensation system is, or is not, well suited to the organization that you have identified.

13–52 Complete the following table.

Organization Unit	What Is an Appropriate Incentive System?	What Behavior Should Be Rewarded?
A symphony orchestra		
A government welfare office		
An airline complaint desk		
A control room in a nuclear generating facility		
A basketball team		

13–53 In an effort to cut costs, a company in the Bell Telephone system developed productivity standards for its employees. Each employee was expected to deliver services to customers within the allowed time. As part of this process, installers were allowed a certain amount of time to install residential telephones. A new customer in a home that was already wired requested a service connection.

Because the home was already wired and the customer indicated that the telephone jacks were already in the house, the installer was allowed 30 minutes to visit the customer, give the customer the telephone, and ensure that the line had been activated properly.

When the installer arrived at the customer's home, the customer asked about having a second line installed. The installer inspected the lines in the home and told the customer that the second line into the home had a short-circuit and that a second line could not be installed. The installer left the customer's home.

About a year later, the customer was experiencing problems with the line and an installer was dispatched to fix the problem. In the course of identifying the problem, the installer discovered an old transformer that had been used by a previous owner of the home plugged into an electrical outlet in an unused corner of the basement. It turned out that this transformer was causing the short-circuit associated with the second telephone line into the home. Shortly after, the second line was installed in the home. The customer had been without a second line, for which the monthly rental was about $15, for a year. When asked why the first installer had not taken the time to find the cause of the short-circuit, the second installer replied:

He was probably a new fellow who was rushing to meet the productivity standard for the call. Finding the short-circuit would have solved your problem but created problems for him since the system would not have given him credit for doing that work. I don't care. I have been around too long to worry about productivity measurement systems. They are not going to fire me; I have too much seniority.

REQUIRED:

    (a) What do you think of this Bell Telephone Company's performance measurement system? What went wrong?

    (b) Recognizing the need to have a system that provides the proper motivation for customer service and for truthful reporting, what type of performance measurement system would you recommend?

13–54 Marie Johnston, the manager of a government unemployment insurance office, is paid a salary that reflects the number of people she supervises and the number of hours that her subordinates work.

REQUIRED:

    (a) What do you think of this compensation scheme? What incentives does this compensation scheme provide to Marie?

    (b) What would you recommend as an appropriate performance measurement and reward system?

13–55 Many compensation experts have proposed a 20:1 compensation rule for the sake of equity. The idea is that the total compensation paid to the highest-paid person in the organization must not exceed 20 times the total compensation paid to the lowest-paid person in the organization. *The Wall Street Journal* (April 13, 1994) estimated the average ratio of the salary of a chief executive to the average worker's pay to be about 117.

Ben and Jerry's Homemade, Inc., is a manufacturer and distributor of dairy products located in Vermont. The compensation ratio at Ben and Jerry's Homemade, Inc., has been set at 7:1.

REQUIRED:

    (a) Do you think that compensation rates reported by the *Wall Street Journal* article could create motivational problems?

(b) Do you think that there could be some practical problems using a compensation rule like the one that Ben and Jerry's uses?

13–56 Experts in incentive compensation argue that rewards should be based on group performance when people must work together to achieve some objective and rewards should be based on individual performance when work can be decomposed into autonomous work units.

REQUIRED:

(a) Identify a situation that you think is well suited to using a group reward (that is, a reward based on the performance of the overall group). Indicate why you think a group reward is appropriate in this situation and precisely how you would divide the rewards among the individual members of the group.

(b) Identify a situation that you think is well suited to using individual rewards (that is, individuals are rewarded based in their individual performance). Indicate why you think individual rewards are appropriate in this situation and precisely how you would reward each individual.

13–57 During the late 1970s, Harley-Davidson, the motorcycle manufacturer, was losing money and was very close to bankruptcy. Management believed that one of the problems was low productivity and asked middle managers to speed up production. The employees who made the motorcycles were told that the priority was to get the motorcycles made and shipped on schedule, which was usually very tight. Middle managers were judged by their ability to meet shipment schedules.

REQUIRED:

(a) What is the rationale that would lead to a desire to speed production in the face of increasing costs and declining productivity?

(b) What type of behavior do you think that this performance measurement system would create in the sense of the priorities that middle management would establish for the production process?

(c) What type of problems would this performance measurement system create?

(d) How, if at all, would you modify this system?

13–58 Bathurst Company manufactures household paper products. During a recent quarter, the value of the products made was $36,540,000 and the labor costs were $4,202,000. The company has decided to use a Scanlon plan with this quarter being used to establish the base ratio for the plan.

The formula is to be applied quarterly with differences, positive or negative, added to the bonus pool. The pool is to be distributed on a 40/60 basis between the employees and the company at the end of the fourth quarter.

The following production and cost levels were recorded during the first year of the plan's operation.

Quarter	Production Value	Payroll Costs
1	$43,578,000	$5,447,000
2	$34,670,000	$3,520,000
3	$38,450,000	$3,851,000
4	$41,800,000	$5,016,000

(a) How much would be distributed to the employees at the end of the year?

(b) What assumptions does the Scanlon plan make about the behavior of payroll costs?

(c) What formula should be used to determine each employee's share?

(d) Management proposes to adjust the base ratio using the lowest ratio experienced in any year. Do you think this is a good idea?

13–59 These are the four broad approaches to distributing the proceeds of a bonus pool in a profit-sharing plan:

(1) Each person's share is based on her salary.

(2) Each person receives an equal share.

(3) Each person's share is based on his position in the organization (larger payments to people at higher levels).

(4) Each person's share is based on individual performance relative to some target.

REQUIRED:

(a) For each of these alternatives, give 2 reasons to support that alternative.

(b) For each of these alternatives, give 2 reasons against that alternative.

(c) Pick the alternative that you think is best and support your choice with an argument of no more than 100 words.

CASES

13–60 Dorothy Webster was the supervisor of a special claims processing group in the Eastern Insurance Company. This group processed medical claims that involved complex injuries and claims that involved elective surgery. One of the group's major roles was to respond to requests seeking authorization for cosmetic surgical procedures.

The claims processing clerks in Dorothy's department were all highly experienced. Most had worked in the company's regular claims processing group for at least 5 years. The clerks needed a comprehensive knowledge of the company's different insurance plans and the options in each plan. They needed good general medical knowledge since they often had to read and discuss medical reports with physicians who submitted proposals for elective surgery.

The clerks had to make 3 determinations when processing a claim. For claims involving required surgery, the clerks had to verify that the claimant's insurance covered the claim, that all procedures were necessary given the nature of the accident or illness, and that the charges reflected the plan's reimbursement schedule. The same considerations applied to claims for elective surgery, with 2 additional considerations. First, any elective procedure costing more than $3,000 had to be approved in advance by a special claims processing unit. Second, each procedure in an elective surgery and its rate had to be approved separately.

The insurance company dealt only with companies that established medical plans for their employees. The role of the insurance company was really that of an administrator rather than an insurer. The annual premiums charged each company reflected that company's claim experience and the insurance company's administrative costs in dealing with claims from that company. On average, the margin provided by each company's business was about 3% of premiums collected from that company. That is, 3% of the insurance premiums from each customer went toward covering the insurance company's general overhead.

The insurance business was very competitive. There were 3 critical success factors: (1) response time and accuracy in dealing with a claim, (2) keeping administrative costs low so that premiums would provide an adequate margin, and (3) rejecting invalid, unauthorized, or excessive claims to keep the group's claims experience as low as possible, thereby minimizing premium increases.

The clerks in Dorothy's department were the highest-paid nonsupervisory staff in the company. Their average pay was about $65,000 per year. The pay consisted of an annual salary of about $40,000 and incentive pay that averaged $25,000 per year. Incentive pay was proportional to the number of points that the clerk earned. Dorothy rated each claim on a scale of 5 to 10 points, depending on the claim's complexity. The processing clerk earned that number of points when the claim was completed. Points for claims that proved later to have been processed incorrectly were deducted from the clerk's accumulated total. In addition, a penalty was deducted for incorrectly processed claims. A manual described each type of error and the penalty that would result from it. The clerks understood the incentive and penalty scheme and were satisfied with it. Turnover in the group was less than 5%. Most clerks who left the company went to supervisory positions in similar groups in other insurance companies. The clerks in the special claims processing group were widely regarded in the medical insurance industry as the best-trained and most highly motivated.

During the past year, several changes had taken place in the special claims processing group. First, the company had grown rapidly through several acquisitions, and the number of clerks in the group had increased from 73 to 104 in less than 1 year. Dorothy had assigned each new clerk to an experienced clerk for 1 month's training and supervision. This role had cut down on the experienced clerk's ability to earn bonuses, and the average incentive pay had fallen 20% to $20,000. This had created considerable discontent. Second, a study of the group's operations had proposed a major change. The study suggested that the group's response time was below the industry average and needed to be improved.

One of the problems was the excessive amount of time required to process the most complex claims involving elective surgery. These claims often involved conferences with the insurance company's medical staff, which often took days to schedule and usually required travel to another office for the meeting. It seemed that these claims became orphans in the system and, eventually, Dorothy herself processed many of them. The study proposed that clerks work in groups with representatives from other company groups, including medical, legal, and sales, to improve response time for these claims. When asked, the clerks admitted that they avoided these claims because, relative to the huge amount of time they consumed, the clerks received relatively little credit for processing them. Moreover, the most experienced clerks who did the majority of these claims objected to Dorothy's practice of giving them the claims because they were the most experienced. For the first time ever, the special claims processing group was experiencing requests for transfers to other groups within the company and, this year, 7 experienced claims clerks left the company.

Using the expectancy theory model, discuss the incentive plan used in the special claims processing group.

13–61 In 1983 Johnson Controls Inc. developed a 7-year performance plan for 2 of their most senior-level executives. In each of the 7 years, the base amount of the plan (consisting of $300,000 and $100,000 for the 2 executives, respectively) is multiplied by a percentage that varies between 0 and 150 percent. The determination of each percentage is based upon the ratio of the average annual total shareholder return for Johnson Controls (over the 10-year period ending with the current year) to the average total shareholder return for a peer group of Fortune 500 companies over the same period. Then, each of the yearly awards is invested in a hypothetical portfolio consisting of the stock of Johnson Controls. The payment of the total value of this hypothetical portfolio is deferred until the end of the 7-year performance period.

There are several interesting aspects of this performance plan. First, the term of the contract extends approximately 3 years beyond the retirement of the 2 executives. This feature appears to be an attempt to lengthen the decision-making horizons of the 2 executives—especially in the case of those near retirement age. This contract explicitly motivates the executives to consider the impact of their decisions on the company after they leave the corporation.

Second, the scorecard for the annual changes in the value of the performance plan is formally tied to changes in shareholder wealth over the prior 10 years. This is unusual because performance plans are typically based on earnings per share or return on equity growth rates. One explanation for the choice of changes in shareholder wealth is that the board of directors is attempting to lengthen the executive's decision-making horizon by selecting a scorecard that has a longer performance evaluation horizon than yearly accounting numbers.

Finally, the performance plan is based on relative changes in shareholder wealth. This appears to be an attempt to isolate that portion of changes in shareholder wealth that is under management's control from economy- and industrywide effects. The choice of a 10-year period for assessing the performance of the company may be an attempt to wash out other random effects that affect performance in a single year.

Comment on this incentive compensation plan. Identify what you like and what you do not like about it.

Source: Richard A. Lambert and David F. Larcker, Executive Compensation, Corporate Decision-Making and Shareholder Wealth: A Review of the Evidence, Chapter 17 in *Corporate Restructuring and Executive Compensation,* ed. Joel M. Stern, G. Bennett Stewart III, and Donald H. Chew (Ballinger Publishing Company, 1989).

BEHAVIORAL AND ORGANIZATIONAL ISSUES IN MANAGEMENT ACCOUNTING AND CONTROL SYSTEM DESIGN

LEARNING OBJECTIVES

This chapter will introduce you to:

1. managerial approaches to motivation and, in particular, the Human Resources Model
2. the characteristics of well-designed MACS and the links among the concepts of motivation, ethics, control, and performance and the design of management accounting and control systems (MACS)
3. the behavioral consequences of poorly designed MACS
4. the human factors to consider when implementing a new MACS or changing current ones

CHAPTER 14

Implementation of ABC/ABM: The Dilemma

Syd Chan had just heard the news. Within the next 2 weeks, implementation of the new activity-based costing and management (ABC/ABM) system would begin. As senior manager of a division that manufactures electronic components, and because his division was rated as 1 of the bottom 3 divisions regarding product line profitability, Syd knew that implementation was inevitable.

Two years ago, Syd implemented an integrated just-in-time manufacturing system and a total quality management (JIT/TQM) system, which were partially successful at reducing costs and improving quality. Six months after the installation of these systems, however, management told him that his division's product performance was still not good enough, and, to save money, his budget would be cut by 30%. It was up to him to find ways to reduce costs and improve performance. The management mandate mentioned that 40% of his cuts had to come from personnel. This meant that he had to inform 30 of the 150 employees in his division that they no longer had their jobs.

After Syd implemented cuts, morale was extremely low. The 20% reduction in the workforce meant that everyone remaining in the division had to do the work of those who were let go. His employees worked very hard, some out of fear of losing their jobs in the future, and others because they knew that the work had to be done. Pressure to perform was very high, which resulted in a new problem. Syd found that certain work groups had falsified production data. He knew exactly which work groups were involved, but this knowledge posed an ethical problem for him. Two of his good friends were in one of these work groups. Should he confront them and try to resolve the issue, or should he report them to the vice president of manufacturing?

Faced with this uncertain environment in which there were significant productivity demands on a reduced workforce, Syd knew that many of his managers and employees would resist any new changes that came along. Although he felt that the ABC/ABM system would be a hard sell, he also knew that in his 5 years as senior manager, he never quite had a handle on his product costs. Over these years,

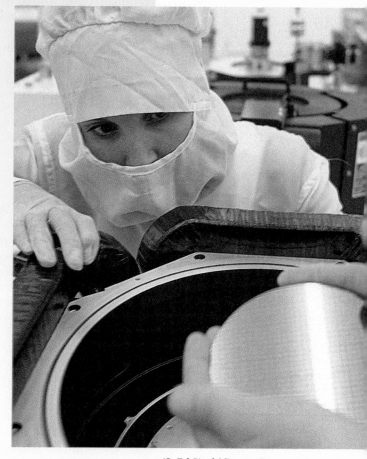

(© Ed Kashi/Image Resources)

573

both the costs and the profitability of the five major product lines varied considerably. Perhaps the ABC/ABM system would help him understand what was going on. Syd was convinced that he had to support the change. Now it was time to implement the ABC/ABM system. How was he going to convince the remaining employees that ABC/ABM could help the entire organization? And what was he going to do regarding the work groups that had falsified production data?

THE MANAGEMENT ACCOUNTING AND CONTROL SYSTEM AND BEHAVIORAL SCIENCE

In previous chapters, our discussion of management accounting presented many aspects of management accounting information from a conceptual and technical point of view. By way of review, the goals of a management accounting and controls system (MACS) are as follows:

1. To aid the organization in *planning* for the future
2. To *monitor* events in the external environment and their effects on the design and functioning of the MACS
3. To *measure* and *record* the results of activities occurring inside the organization to ensure that decision makers are well-informed.
4. To *motivate* individuals and groups who are affected by and who affect the MACS
5. To *evaluate the performance* of individuals and groups in the organization

Because people are involved with each of these goals, we must connect the study of management accounting methods and systems to the study of human behavior. Many accounting scholars have focused their attention on applying theories from sociology, organizational behavior, and social psychology to questions related to management accounting.[1] These disciplines have contributed to our understanding of the way individuals and groups are motivated, the way to evaluate their performance, and the way to coordinate their actions.

This chapter focuses on the behavioral and organizational issues that affect the aforementioned goals through the design and use of the management accounting information and the overall MACS. The opening vignette to this chapter highlights the types of issues that are becoming more commonplace in the working environment, especially during uncertain economic times. Our discussion will focus on the implications of introducing a new MACS to resolve these issues.

We begin by presenting some fundamental ideas about human motivation and then link these ideas to the characteristics of a well-designed MACS and the behaviors that a well-designed system promotes. Next, we discuss the consequences of poor MACS design, especially the lack of goal congruence

[1] An important book in this area is A. G. Hopwood's, *Accounting and Human Behavior* (Englewood Cliffs, N.J.: Prentice Hall, 1976). In addition, the British journal, *Accounting, Organizations and Society* (Pergamon Press) publishes a great deal of research in this area.

and the failure to follow ethical guidelines. Finally, in the last section of the chapter, we consider behavioral factors that companies should address when they alter their existing MACS.

MANAGERIAL APPROACHES TO MOTIVATION

In Chapter 13, we discussed 2 psychological theories of *individual* motivation: Herzberg's Two-Factor Theory and Vroom's Expectancy Model. In contrast, there are also numerous theories of *management thought* regarding the way to best motivate people to improve their performance at work. This chapter emphasizes the way that management thinking has evolved over the past 80 years regarding people and work and how these changes affect MACS design.

The assumptions that the theories made about people's preferences and tastes for work distinguishes the earlier attempts to explain motivation from more recent models. These assumptions have shifted from a viewpoint of valuing employees primarily for their physical contribution to seeing them as an important intellectual and creative force. The earliest model of motivation, developed at the turn of the century in accordance with the **scientific management** *school of motivation,* assumed that most people found work objectionable, that money was the driving force behind good performance, and that individuals cared little for exercising creativity on the job. The task for management was to tightly monitor and control employee behavior and to break down tasks in such a way that employees would have no ability to make decisions. Management believed that with very little discretion, employees would focus their attention exclusively on improving production.

The second significant development in motivational theory arose with the **human relations movement** beginning in the late 1930s. This movement's major contribution was the recognition that people have needs that go well beyond a simple repetitive task at work and that financial compensation was only 1 aspect of what they desired. Employees wanted respect, discretion over their jobs, and a feeling that they contributed to the organization. Thus began a focus on developing interpersonal relations, improving morale and increasing job satisfaction.

The most recent model of motivation, based on the **human resources model,** advances our understanding even further. This model combines aspects from the earlier models and has been influenced strongly by Japanese management practices, such as the high level of employee participation in decision making. The central assumptions underlying this model are that people do not find work objectionable and that they want to participate in developing objectives and attaining goals in a work environment that has grown increasingly complex. The model further emphasizes that individuals have a great deal to contribute to the organization in terms of the information and knowledge they possess about their jobs, that they are highly creative and responsible, and that they desire opportunities to bring about change in their organizations. The task for management is to understand that a mix of psychological factors—such as the supervisory approach, the nature of working conditions, and individual needs—and economic factors that influence motivation. In this chapter, we use the human resources model as the basis for understanding the design of the MACS.

OBJECTIVE 14.1
Managerial approaches to motivation and, in particular, the human resources model

Scientific management
A school of motivation in which people are viewed as finding work objectionable, motivated only by money, and as having little knowledge to contribute to the organization.

Human relations movement
A model of human motivation that considers that people have many needs and aspirations at work, and that they are motivated by things other than money.

Human resources model
An approach to human motivation that emphasizes that individuals do not find work objectionable, that they have knowledge to contribute, and that they are creative.

With the *human resources model* in mind, managers usually focus on 3 key aspects of employee motivation: *direction,* which occurs when an employee focuses attention at work; *intensity,* or the level of effort the employee expends; and *persistence,* or the duration of time that an employee will stay with a task or job. As mentioned previously, the ideal situation for management occurs when employees have aligned their individual goals with those of the organization, so that they can attain their goals as they perform their jobs well. We refer to this situation as achieving **goal congruence.** If goal congruence is possible to attain, then managing direction, intensity, and persistence is easier. But if goal congruence cannot be attained, which is often the case, management's task becomes more difficult.

Creating goal congruence for employees involves many factors. Among these are strong organizational leadership, satisfying work, appropriate rewards, opportunities for advancement, and a supportive work environment. The MACS can help individuals achieve goal congruence if it is well-designed and functions well. We present the characteristics of a well-designed MACS next.

Goal congruence
The alignment of individual and organizational goals.

OBJECTIVE 14.2
The characteristics of well-designed management accounting and control systems (MACS) and the links among the concepts of motivation, ethics, control, and performance and the design of MACS

Multiple perspectives approach
The development of a consistent organization-wide management accounting system that also allows for local input and tailoring.

CHARACTERISTICS OF MACS

The characteristics of a well-designed MACS include the following:

1. A consistent, *global,* technical structure that also allows for flexibility at the *many local levels* (specific groups or operating units) in the organization, and a structure that fosters continuous improvement. We label this the **multiple perspectives approach**

2. The incorporation of the organization's code of *ethical conduct* into system design to motivate appropriate behavior

3. The development and use of both *quantitative and qualitative information* in a timely fashion for control, motivation, and performance evaluation

4. The *participation and empowerment of employees* in systems design and improvements and in continuous education to understand how the system functions and how to interpret the information meaningfully.

5. Development of mechanisms such as *reward systems* tied to performance to promote motivation and goal congruence between the organization and employees to reduce non–goal congruent behavior.

■ The Multiple Perspectives Approach to MACS Design

Traditionally, in many organizations the controller's office has had responsibility for MACS design. One of the controller's main responsibilities is to provide overall information system design, which includes the management accounting and control function. The controller and other members of the MACs design team have two tasks as they implement what we call the *multiple perspectives approach* to system design. First they must structure the MACS

This employee of Marine Atlantic, a Canadian Crown Corporation charged with providing ferry service in Atlantic Canada, is part of a company program called performance management, which provides for employee participation and empowerment. Employees participating in this program have identified and implemented ideas that have saved Marine Atlantic hundreds of thousands of dollars in operating costs each year. Their rewards? Commemorative key chains and public recognition of a job well done. Why do they do it? Because the recession and other factors have put their jobs in jeopardy. *(© Brian Atkinson/The Globe & Mail)*

to *provide a consistent framework* for information that can be applied globally across the units or divisions of an entity. Consistency means that the language used and the technical methods of producing management accounting information *do not conflict* with various parts of an organization. For example, having 2 divisions with different costing systems makes it more difficult to understand and compare results across divisions. If 1 division of an organization uses activity-based costing principles, but another division (especially one that is very similar in goals and function to the first) uses volume-based overhead allocation methods, the organization is not operating under the same MACS philosophy.

MACS designers, however, also must allow for flexibility with the available information. If flexibility is not possible, an employee's motivation to make the best decision may not be appropriate for the decision at hand, especially if units engage in different types of activities. For instance, one division located in Columbus, Ohio, may be involved in new product development; another division in Cleveland may perform final assembly. Each division will probably have different data needs and may use different cost drivers in making its decisions. The critical success factors for managing new product development in Columbus will be quite different from the factors that the Cleveland assembly division must manage effectively. A well-designed MACS should allow for these multiple perspectives. If it does not, inaccurate *ad hoc* local systems may develop, which can lead to poor decisions and confusion between the division and upper management.

For management accounting information to be useful, it must meet the needs of as many parties involved as possible. Thus, the first step is to agree on the underlying philosophy of the MACS. The second step is to tailor local systems to the specific needs consistent with the already-agreed-upon underlying philosophy of the MACS. Fortunately, as we mentioned in Chapter 1, managers in every organization can become party to the multiple perspectives approach because they can devise their own systems for internal decision making. This flexibility does not apply to systems designed to produce information to comply with external financial reporting requirements.

Earlier, we stated that the controller's office traditionally has been responsible for MACS design. Since the early 1980s, however, employees who were frustrated with existing systems and were working in various functional areas of companies began to develop their own formal and informal management accounting systems. For example, in many companies, industrial and design engineers or manufacturing managers have taken the lead in developing their own costing systems due to the inadequacy of existing systems. Initially, in some organizations, the development of local *ad hoc* systems caused conflict between their users and those formally charged with MACS design due to both technical and political reasons. Developers of the new costing systems, such as activity-based costing, believed that many management accountants were inflexible regarding change and that financial reporting requirements would keep management accountants from being able to make key cost management changes. In other organizations, management accountants embraced the changes because they knew that the existing systems were obsolete. They also realized that without adopting new systems, they would be hindering progress. In many organizations today, both sides seem to have realized that they are all better off by joining forces and agreeing on how changes should be made. We discuss the topic of managing these changes more fully later in this chapter.

■ Ethical Considerations in MACS Design

The second characteristic of a well-designed MACS is the incorporation of the principles of an organization's code of ethical conduct into system design to affect the behavior of both system designers and users. We will define *ethics* as a discipline involved with the study of standards of conduct and moral judgment.

For system designers such as management accountants, apart from their organization's code of ethical conduct, the Institute of Management Accounting (IMA) has established ethical standards. Certified Management Accountants (CMAs) are required to be competent and to always maintain confidentiality, integrity, and objectivity.[2] This is extremely important because having a clear set of ethical standards guides motivation, especially in regard to the direction of effort, and should help reduce dysfunctional behavior by users. The specific roles that management accountants might undertake in helping to design a MACS based on ethics include ensuring that

➤ The organization has formulated, implemented, and communicated to all employees a comprehensive code of ethics.

➤ All employees understand the organization's code of ethics.

[2] See "Standards of Ethical Conduct for Management Accountants," *Management Accounting* (February 1992), p. 11.

➤ A system exists to detect and report violations of the organization's code of ethics.

Although management accountants may find some variations in codes of ethics in various countries, such codes are remarkably similar in purpose.

System design influences the behavior of all users. The key user group, managers, interacts a great deal with the MACS. Managers are often subject to intense pressures from their jobs and from other influential organizational members to suspend their ethical judgment. These pressures might include (1) requests to tailor information to favor particular individuals or groups, (2) pleas to falsify reports or test results or approve false reports or claims, (3) requests for confidential information, and (4) pressures to ignore a questionable or unethical practice.

AVOIDING ETHICAL DILEMMAS   Most organizations attempt to avoid ethical dilemmas by developing a code of ethics. Although there is no universal hierarchy of ethical principles, these five categories capture the broad array of ethical considerations.

1. Legal rules
2. Societal norms
3. Professional memberships (CPAs, CMAs, etc.)
4. Organizational or group norms
5. Personal norms

In this hierarchy, a norm or rule prohibits all the actions or behaviors beneath it. For example, an action that is prohibited by law should be unacceptable by society, by one's profession, by the organization and, finally, by each person. An action that is legally and socially acceptable, such as strategically underestimating the product costs, may be professionally unacceptable, however, and, in turn, unacceptable to the organization and to the individual. Unfortunately, any hierarchy of this sort has a number of gray areas, but, in general, it provides guidelines for the organization in understanding and dealing with ethical problems.

The hierarchy presented above provides a set of constraints on a decision. In this scheme, ethical conflicts arise when 1 system of values diverges from a more fundamental system of values. For example, suppose that the organization's code of ethics commits it to meeting only the letter of the law regarding disclosure of a product fault of one of its manufactured goods that could prove to be hazardous to consumers. A broader societal expectation is, however, that organizations be aggressive in identifying and disclosing potential product problems. Thus, an individual decision maker may face an ethical conflict when dealing with a situation in which the organizational code of ethics implies doing nothing, since there is no definitive evidence of a product problem. Broader societal expectations imply that disclosure is necessary, however, because there is persistent evidence of a problem.

DEALING WITH ETHICAL CONFLICTS   When organizations develop a formal code of ethics, they create the potential for explicit conflicts to arise.

The conflicts that tend to appear most in practice are conflicts between the law and the organization's code of ethics, conflicts between the organization's practiced code of ethics and common societal expectations, and conflicts between the individual's set of personal and professional ethics and the organization's practiced code of ethics.

Organizations that formulate and support specific ethical codes can create an environment to reduce ethical conflicts by avoiding ambiguity or misunderstanding. One step in creating this environment is to ensure that the hierarchical ordering identified in the previous section exists. That is, the organization's stated code of ethics should not allow any behavior that is either legally or socially unacceptable. Because most professional codes of ethics reflect broad moral imperatives, such as loyalty, discretion, and competence, an organization would create public relations problems for itself if its stated code of ethics conflicted with a professional code of ethics. Another critical variable to consider is the tone that the behavior of the chief executive and other senior managers set. If these individuals demonstrate exemplary behavior at work, others will follow.

The conflicts that remain relate mainly to the potential for conflict between personal values and the organization's code of ethics and its existing norms before adopting its code of ethics.

CONFLICTS BETWEEN INDIVIDUAL AND ORGANIZATION VALUES
People bring personal codes of ethics with them into the organization. If the organization's code of ethics is more stringent than the individual's, there can be a problem. However, if adherence to the organization's ethical code is required and enforced, it is possible to diminish the problem. This can be accomplished if, as part of the contract of employment, the individual is asked and expected to pursue a more stringent code of ethics.

Difficult issues may arise when the individual's personal code of ethics prohibits certain types of behavior that are legal, socially acceptable, professionally acceptable, and acceptable to the organization. The conflict in such a situation will arise when the action that is unacceptable to the individual is desirable to the organization. In this case, the individual is confronted with a personal choice. Working for the organization will require that the person, under certain circumstances, do things that he or she finds normally unacceptable. Moreover, there is no authority to appeal to for help since the law, society at large, the profession, and the organization have different views. Thus, the individual must decide what is important.

As an example, the employee may have deep religious objections to undertaking business, in any form, on a holy day. Unfortunately, the employee may have little institutional support in this situation but can lobby within or outside the organization to prohibit the behavior, which may be effective, or he or she may choose not to work for that organization.

CONFLICTS BETWEEN THE ORGANIZATION'S STATED AND PRACTICED VALUES   This type of conflict is the most difficult because the organization is misrepresenting its ethical system, which forces the employee to make a choice between going public or not. In this setting, the employee is in the position of being a whistle-blower, which many have found to be a unique and lonely position. In many instances, though, whistle-blowers have chosen personal integrity over their loyalty to the organization.

Experts who have studied this problem advise the individual first to make sure that the facts are correct and that there is, indeed, a conflict between the organization's stated ethical policy and the one it practices. Second, the individual, by speaking with superiors, should determine whether this conflict is institutional or whether it reflects the interpretation of a few zealots.

Faced with a true conflict, the individual has many choices. The following are some of them.

1. Point out the discrepancy to a superior and refuse to act unethically (this may lead to dismissal, resignation from the organization, or the experience of suffering hidden organization sanctions.)

2. Point out the discrepancy to a superior and act unethically (the rationale, which is incorrect, for this choice is that the employee believes this affords protection from legal sanctions)

3. Delay taking action and take the discrepancy to an ombudsperson in the organization, if one exists

4. Delay taking action and work with respected leaders in the organization to change the discrepancy between practiced and stated ethics

5. Delay taking action and go outside the organization to publicly resolve the issue

6. Delay taking action and go outside the organization anonymously to resolve the issue

7. Resign and go public to resolve the issue

8. Resign and remain silent

9. Delay taking action, do nothing, and hope that the problem will go away

Although most experts recommend following the course stated in item 4 on this list, it is not the place of this chapter to discuss the efficacy of any of these alternatives other than to mention that the circumstances can make any of the actions on the list appropriate. If the organization is serious about its stated code of ethics, it should have an effective "ethics control system" to ensure and provide evidence that the organization's stated and practiced ethics are the same. Part of this control system should include a means for employees to point out inconsistencies between practiced and stated ethics without fear of retribution. Any organization that does not provide a system to protect employees in these situations is either not taking its code of ethics seriously or has an inadequate ethics control system. We next turn to a discussion of the ethical control system.

THE ELEMENTS OF AN EFFECTIVE ETHICAL CONTROL SYSTEM   To promote ethical decision making, management should implement an **ethical control system.** The elements of this ethical control system should include the following:

Ethical control system
A system that reinforces the ethical responsibilities of all firm employees.

1. A *statement* of the organization's values and code of ethics stated in practical terms and with examples so that the organization's employees can relate it to their individual jobs.

2. A clear statement of the employee's *ethical responsibilities* for every job description and a specific review of the employee's ethical performance as part of every performance review.

3. Adequate training to help employees identify ethical dilemmas in practice and to learn how to deal with those that they can reasonably expect to face.

4. Evidence that senior management expects organization members to *adhere* to its code of ethics. This means that management must

   ➤ Provide a statement of the consequences of violating the organization's code of ethics.

   ➤ Establish a means of dealing with violations of the organization's code of ethics openly, promptly, ruthlessly, and consistently with the statement of consequences

   ➤ Provide visible support of ethical decision making at every opportunity

Many organizations use management accountants to design and audit sensitive systems of internal control. In auditing these systems, which organizations use to protect their assets, management accountants may encounter inducements to overlook improper actions. Consider, for example, how you might react if a close friend asked you to ignore something that your job and profession expect you to report.
(© Charles Gupton/The Stock Market)

5. Evidence that employees can make ethical decisions or report violations of the organization's stated ethics (the whistle-blower) without fear of *reprisals* from superiors, subordinates, or peers in the organization. This proof usually takes the form of an organization ombudsperson who has the authority to investigate complaints, wherever they lead, and to preserve the confidentiality of people who report violations.

6. Providing for an ongoing *internal audit* of the efficacy of the organization's ethical control system

STEPS IN MAKING AN ETHICAL DECISION   Formal training is part of the process of promoting ethical decision making. After gathering the facts surrounding a particular decision and evaluating the alternative courses of action, the decision maker can eliminate possible courses of action that are ethically unacceptable. The decision model in Exhibit 14–1 is one approach to eliminating unacceptable alternatives.[3]

In summary, MACS represents one of the organization's central information systems. Hence, the organization's code of ethics must underlie its design. Both designers and users of the system should remember this and rectify any deviations from the code of ethics that the system explicitly or implicitly promotes.

[3] This decision model was developed initially to teach cases in accounting with an ethics perspective.

EXHIBIT 14–1
Decision Model

1. **Determine the Facts—What, Who, Where, When, How**
   What do we know or need to know, if possible, that will help define the problem?

2. **Define the Ethical Issue**
   (a) List the significant stakeholders
   (b) Define the ethical issues
   Make sure precisely what the ethical issue is—for example, conflict involving rights, question over limits of an obligation, and so on.

3. **Identify Major Principles, Rules, Values**
   For example, integrity, quality, respect for persons, profit.

4. **Specify the Alternatives**
   List the major alternative courses of action, including those that represent some form of compromise or point between simply doing or not doing something.

5. **Compare Values and Alternatives, See if Clear Decision**
   Determine if there is one principle or value, or combination, which is so compelling that the proper alternative is clear—for example, correcting a defect that is almost certain to cause loss of life.

6. **Assess the Consequences**
   Identify short and long, positive and negative consequences for the major alternatives. The common short-run focus on gain or loss needs to be measured against long-run considerations. This step will often reveal an unanticipated result of major importance.

7. **Make Your Decision**
   Balance the consequences against your primary principles or values and select the alternative that best fits.

Source: William W. May (ed.), *Ethics in the Accounting Curriculum: Cases and Readings.* American Accounting Association, 1990, p. 1. Reprinted with permission.

■ Developing and Using Both Quantitative and Qualitative Information

The third characteristic of a well-designed MACS is to ensure that both quantitative and qualitative information is developed and used for decision making.

THE NEED FOR MULTIPLE MEASURES OF PERFORMANCE   There is a saying in business that "what gets measured gets done." In other words, the ways in which organizations and individuals use management accounting and other types of information, and the particular kinds of measures that the organization establishes, send signals to all employees and stakeholders about the organization's motivation and what it considers important. For many years, it has been recognized that without well-defined measures of performance, employees will engage in *non–goal congruent behavior*. For instance, if a firm uses management accounting information to set up a performance evaluation system that rewards a vendor *only* for the on-time delivery of merchandise, this will be *the* variable on which employees will focus. Since the quality of the goods sent is not considered important in the evaluation, vendors who supply the merchandise may sacrifice quality for the sake of meeting delivery dates—the measured variable—or they may quote excessively long lead times. Either act could work to the long-term detriment of the organization and the vendor.

Department stores have found that when salespeople are compensated solely by sales commissions, their attention will be focused on selling as much merchandise as possible. Employees faced with such a situation may find initially that their sales volume is increasing. But, as the competition for customers develops, the work environment may become hostile as disputes arise over whose customer a person was or who "really" made the sale. Another consequence of relying solely on commissions as a motivating tool is that other aspects of the sales function, such as straightening up merchandise after customers have been browsing or restocking shelves, may become low priorities for salespeople. Ultimately, the department store could be heading for trouble in such circumstances.

Given the problems of using a single performance measure that these examples illustrate, it seems clear that, in many cases, organizations should evaluate employees by using more than a single performance measure. Not only will this expand employee vision, but it also might motivate employees to perform acts congruent with organizational goals. It is important to use multiple measures that are consistent with the complexities of the work environment and the variety of contributions that employees make. In some modern manufacturing and service environments, many employees (or associates or operators, as they are often called) are being cross-trained to perform a variety of tasks. Further, some employees are organized into self-managed work teams, or they follow a product's manufacture from beginning to end. Thus, organizations have an opportunity to design multiple measures to assess the work that is actually being done. Having multiple measures also will cause employees to recognize the various dimensions of their work and to be less intent on trying to maximize their performance on a single target at the expense of other aspects of their jobs. We will discuss this issue in more depth when we talk about information manipulation later in this chapter.

QUALITATIVE AND QUANTITATIVE MEASURES   Our discussion implies that the individuals who design MACS must think very carefully about the organization's mission, and the organization's objectives and the way to operationalize them as stated in Chapter 2. Additionally, the challenge for managers has been to expand their views of the kinds of information to supply for effective control, motivation, and performance evaluation. For instance, only within the past few years have management accountants become aware of the need for measures of *quality, speed to market, cycle time, flexibility, complexity,* and *productivity.* Historically, some of these measures, such as quality, were in the hands of industrial engineers, while others, such as speed to market or flexibility, were not measured directly.

There are other new organizational realities that also should be remembered. Faced with increasing competitive pressures, many organizations have begun to move away from traditional, hierarchical organizations with many layers of management (sometimes referred to as "tall" organizations) to those with fewer and fewer management layers (or "flat" organizations). General Electric, for example has reduced its hierarchical structure significantly. As functional areas, such as engineering design, manufacturing, accounting, finance, and marketing are being broken down, employees are working increasingly in cross-functional teams. Another significant corresponding change involves business process reengineering, where designers begin with a vision of what organizational participants would like their process or product to look like or how they would like it to function and then radically redesign it. Such an approach is significantly different from starting with the product or process and then making slight incremental changes. These organizational design changes also have led to the need for new informational requirements and measures related to the costs and benefits of innovation. Thus, the development of new measures of performance must move away from a focus on individual performance measures to consider group-level performance measures as well as new ways of thinking about business processes and organization.

The traditional focus of performance measures in management accounting has been to develop quantitative, rather than qualitative, measures. However, many of the key variables mentioned above that contribute to organizational performance are not quantitative in a traditional sense. One needs only to read the business press on just about any day to see how important qualitative measures of performance are. For instance, variables such as the *image* or *reputation* of a product or service, the level of *caring* of the staff in a hospital, or the *flexibility* of a manufacturing process are crucial variables to an organization's long-term success. Are such variables the responsibility of management accounting?

Organizations vary as to how they view the nature of the MACS. Some attempt to develop and integrate both quantitative and qualitative measures into the MACS. Others may keep certain types of measures distinct from the MACS. If management believes, however, that the organization is not being supplied with the key information it needs to be competitive, it should not let tradition stand in the way and should help supply the most pertinent information to the MACS.

Whoever supplies information for the organization must be cognizant that some parts of an organization care about the quality of their goods and services, but that others do not. Organizations have no need for different groups to develop different measures, especially when they are essentially measuring the same variables! Rather, it is important to coordinate who is producing and providing various kinds of information and whether the producers are supplying information consistent with the needs of decision makers in a timely and reliable fashion.

■ Participation, Empowerment, and Education of Employees in MACS Design

The fourth characteristic of a well-designed MACS is providing employees the opportunity to participate in decision making and empowering them in the workplace.

PARTICIPATION AND EMPOWERMENT   Organizations often do not realize that, in many cases, their greatest asset is the people they employ. Except in highly automated industries, people still perform the major portion of work and have the best understanding of how jobs get done. Thus, those who perform tasks have the most information about the nature of their work and how to improve products and processes. Asking people to participate in decision making and empowering workers to suggest and make changes is central to fostering all aspects of motivation as well as to good MACS design.

For example, employees in the Poughkeepsie branch of Company B will know more about the way their branch functions than will central headquarters located in New York, and MACS designers should strongly consider enlist-

As organizations empower employees to make decisions, they must provide these employees with the statistical and analytical skills to develop and interpret data. *(Matthew McVay/Stock Boston, Inc.)*

ing the participation of the Poughkeepsie employees. The same concept applies within a division. Assembly line operators usually will know more about the process on which they work than their managers do. Apart from being consistent with the multiple perspectives approach, research has shown that participation and communication between local and central offices and between superiors and subordinates will result in the transmission of critical information to which central management would otherwise not have access. Research also has shown that the equally important benefit of participation in decision making can lead to greater motivation, job satisfaction, improved morale, and greater commitment to decisions.

CONTINUOUS EDUCATION AND UNDERSTANDING INFORMATION   It is also important for organizations to address another key issue—whether employees understand the information that they use and on which they are evaluated. Many superiors believe that management's understanding of the information generated by the MACS is sufficient to run an operation effectively. However, lately there has been a growing realization that employees at *all levels* of the firm must understand what performance measures mean or how they are computed to be able to take actions that will lead to superior performance. Thus, if employees do not understand how their actions affect a variable such as cycle time (the time it takes for a product or service to be produced or performed from start to finish), for instance, then it is not sufficient that the manager understands this measure because employees working on the shop floor do not know how to alter their actions to improve performance on the cycle time measure. For example, if employees in a manufacturing plant are performing unnecessary actions on an assembly line or are idle, the cycle time performance of their group will be affected. Similarly, at the point of service (where organizational employees interact with customers), delays in the processing of claims will increase cycle time as well.

Consider a bank that wants to improve its public image. Some banks from time to time ask customers to fill out a customer satisfaction survey. If bank tellers have not been educated regarding how each of his or her actions with a customer directly affect customer satisfaction, the bank has failed to educate its tellers regarding one of its key indicators. The same is true in many other types of service organizations. In restaurants or department stores, customers often can become frustrated with the level of service. For example, assigning waiters and waitresses in a restaurant too many tables, can cause them to forget customer requests or, if they have annoying personal habits or if they are extremely clumsy, customers will remember the experience and may not return. Consider a department store in which sales personnel may be

---

CONSIDER THIS . . .

Employee Empowerment

Joseph F. McKenna commented in a noteworthy article that all employees, regardless of the type of jobs they perform and the level of their skills, can be empowered. McKenna interviewed Paul J. Giddens, manager of HR planning for General Electric Aircraft Engines in Ohio, who stated that, businesses and industry have to "nurture the environment where people can contribute to the limits of their abilities and get the motivation to improve their competence." Further, the empowerment plan must be well articulated to everyone in the organization, and the organization must emphasize how important its employees are to it.

Source: Joseph F. McKenna, "Smart Scarecrows—The Wizardry of Empowerment," *Industry Week* (July 16, 1990), pp. 8–19. Reprinted with permission from *Industry Week*. Copyright Penton Publishing, Inc., Cleveland Ohio.

too pushy, difficult to find for service, or too arrogant. A customer may become very irritated and vow never to shop there again. Unless restaurant owners and department store managers take the time to educate their employees about how their actions affect customer perceptions of service quality and repeat business, the energy devoted to improving customer satisfaction is wasted. Studies have shown that, on average, 5 times as many customers who are dissatisfied with a product or service will tell other people about their experience than customers who are satisfied with a product or service. Thus, the reputation of organizations that offer a poorly produced product or a poorly delivered service can be ruined very quickly.

In order for MACS to function well, employees have to be constantly reeducated as the system changes. One difficulty that system designers face is that in the United States, employees, in general, are undertrained. In trying to compete with the rest of the world, the U.S. business environment is constantly in a state of flux. Without continuous updating of everyone's education, the United States (and all other countries for that matter) will not be able to keep up or lead in international markets. In the United States the problem of the lack of training is quite severe. Some studies have shown that U.S. employees receive only about one-tenth of the training that Japanese employees do. Thus, U.S. management cannot ask its employees to compete if they do not supply the necessary training to do so.

■ Reward Systems for Goal Congruence

In Chapter 13, we spent a lot of time discussing reward systems. A few additional points are worth considering regarding overall MACS design, however. The backbone of most MACS consists of the many types of performance measures they generate. Throughout this book, we have discussed a variety of them, including budgets, standards, measures of quality, and productivity. But the art involved in this aspect of MACS design is attempting to understand what standards to use and where the level of these standards should be set for motivational purposes.

System designers have many types of mechanisms that they can use to resolve these issues. One mechanism that we have already talked about is the use of participative decision making. By allowing subordinates to participate in standard setting and budgeting, management can obtain a better understanding of what kinds of standards should be used and how motivated subordinates are to achieving certain levels of performance. The other mechanism is to design incentive systems that are tied to standard or budget attainment. Academics in management accounting have spent a great deal of time devising such systems. Typically, incentive system designers are concerned with the level of uncertainty associated with particular degrees of difficulty regarding standard attainment. They also try to consider the risk attitudes and work ethic of individuals when devising these systems.

 The fifth key characteristic of a well-designed MACS is developing appropriate reward systems to foster goal congruence between employees and the organization. Goal congruence implies that the actions that employees take and their personal goals are consistent with those of the organization. In today's uncertain work environment, it is unrealistic to simply hope that employees will inherently have goals that are congruent with those of the organization. Thus, choosing the reward system that is most motivating for the individual or group and consistent with organization goals is very difficult.

The problem is complicated further once employees are organized into teams. Teams of employees can still have goal congruence problems, both within the team and with the organization, especially if MACS design has not been accomplished well. In the following section we discuss some of the behaviors that can occur when system design is flawed and/or when employees lack goal congruence with their organization.

■ Behavioral Consequences of Poorly Designed Measurement Systems

OBJECTIVE 14.3
The behavioral consequences of poorly designed MACS

Up to this point, we have discussed 5 key characteristics in the design of an effective MACS. These characteristics were (1) a consistent, global, technical structure that also allows for flexibility at local levels of the organization; (2) the incorporation of the organization's code of *ethical conduct* into system design to motivate appropriate behavior; (3) the development and use of both *quantitative and qualitative information* for control, motivation, and performance evaluation; (4) the *participation and empowerment of employees* in system design and improvements and continuous education of employees; and (5) development of mechanisms such as *reward systems* tied to performance to promote motivation and goal congruence between the organization and employees to reduce dysfunctional behavior.

What happens, though, when the system is poorly designed or does not promote the kinds of motivation and behaviors that the organization desires? In this section, we address the issue of poor MACS design. Our working definition of *poor design* is a system that lacks at least one or a combination of the 5 key characteristics previously discussed.

Employees can become upset or dissatisfied with a MACS for many reasons. Clearly, if the system produces inconsistent information, gathers only quantitative information when a mix of quantitative and qualitative information is desirable, does not operate under the organization's code of ethics, omits participation and input on the parts of employees in decision making, and does not reward good performance, it will reduce motivation and increase nongoal-congruent behavior. In this section, we present 3 behaviors that employees use to manipulate their way around the MACS for their own ends. Keep in mind these 3 questions as we discuss these behaviors. First, are these behaviors unethical? Second, what are the consequences of these behaviors? Third, is it possible to design MACS so that employees will not be tempted to engage in these behaviors?

NONGOAL-CONGRUENT BEHAVIOR For any number of reasons, subordinates engage in a variety of behaviors to improve their situation in an organization. For example, if employees believe that they are not getting the rewards that they deserve for their performance or that they are not being heard by their superior, they may resort to attempting to increase their bonuses or improve their position in the organization by trying to outwit the MACS. The MACS may be manipulated in such a way that the reports or information generated will affect a superior's behavior. Numerous methods allow the manipulation of information; these include *smoothing, gaming,* and *data falsification.*

Smoothing

The act of affecting the preplanned flow of information without altering actual behavior.

Smoothing occurs when individuals either accelerate or delay the pre-planned *flow* of data without altering the organization's activities. For example, a manager who is close to meeting his or her performance target, such as a net income or ROI number, may decide to defer expenses incurred in the current period to a future period. Similarly, he or she may attempt to book future revenues into the current period to increase net income. Over the long term, such behavior will lead to the same bottom-line financial outcomes, but the cost to the organization is that it does not obtain a clear picture of performance for a defined time period. Excessive amounts of smoothing are probably the result of inappropriate standards or a poorly conceived reward system.

Gaming

An alteration of an employee's planned actions as a result of a particular kind of performance indicator.

The technique of **gaming** is said to exist when a subordinate alters his or her actions specifically in an attempt to *manipulate a performance indicator* through job-related acts. Gaming differs from smoothing in that it does not alter the flow of information but the actions taken toward key indicators. We illustrate gaming within the domain of budgeting.

A BUDGETING EXAMPLE   In Chapter 5, we stated that budgets communicate the organization's goals to its members. Budgets consist of specific and measurable financial targets, the attainment of which helps to achieve an organization's goals. The two most common methods of setting budgets are known as *imposition* or *participation.* **Budget imposition** means that a superior simply tells subordinates what their budget will be. The benefit to the organization is that the process is straightforward, takes little time, is conducive to assigning high budget targets and to achieving overall coordination among divisions in the organization. The downside of imposing the budget is that superiors may have no idea what the appropriate level of the budget should be for the motivational purposes, and subordinates may become frustrated and debilitated, especially if the budget is impossible to achieve. In such a case, motivation can decrease significantly, and individuals and the organization can fail to attain their goals. Research in budgeting has shown that the most motivating types of budgets are those that are "tight"—those that stretch employees—but are most often attainable.

Budget imposition

A situation in which a superior simply tells a subordinate what his or her budget will be, without any input from the subordinate.

Budget participation

A joint decision-making process in which all parties agree to the levels of the budget.

The second method of budget setting, **budget participation,** involves a *joint decision-making process* in which all parties agree to the levels at which the budget should be set. Allowing employees to participate in decision making has many benefits for employees, such as increasing feelings of commitment to the budget resulting in a higher level of motivation and, in some cases, financial rewards, to attain a budget. Research has shown that employees also experience increased morale, greater job satisfaction, due primarily to having greater feelings of control over their jobs, and, in some instances, higher levels of performance.

There is a potential downside to participation from the organization's point of view. Participation provides employees the opportunity to affect their budgets in ways that may not always be in the best interests of the organization. For instance, a risk in allowing subordinates to participate is that they will ask for *excess resources* above and beyond what they need to accomplish their budget goals, resulting in a misallocation of resources for the organization as a whole. Another risk is that subordinates will withhold information and claim that they are not as efficient or effective at what they do as they really are, thereby attempting to lower management's expectations of them. Again, the organization suffers because it is not obtaining the most accurate information that is available to improve its operations. Both of these acts fall under the heading of creating **budget slack.** From the subordinate's viewpoint, he or she wants some cushion in case there is an unforeseen change in the work environment that detrimentally affects resources or impairs his or her ability to meet the budget.

As an example, a manager may be worried that a supplier is unable to deliver raw materials at a price that has historically been budgeted. The manager may decide to build slack into this line item by increasing the amount of money requested for raw materials. Further, subordinates also may be concerned about standards or budgets that are too difficult to attain, and, if their bonuses are based on attaining budget, then they will opt for an easier budget. To counter this problem, management may design an incentive system that provides higher levels of bonuses based on attaining higher targets. This may counteract the problem of setting low targets.

Data falsification or illegal acts occur when someone falsifies a piece of information. Data falsification takes many forms. However, the MiniScribe Corporation situation exemplifies one of the clearest forms. In the late 1980s, senior management at MiniScribe, feeling enormous pressure to meet sales targets imposed on them by their autocratic CEO, engaged in a series of illegal acts. For instance, senior managers packed bricks in crates and shipped them as computer disk drives or shipped faulty disk drives. Then they recorded the shipments as sales. When the shipments were returned, MiniScribe added the shipment to its inventory of disk drives, further inflating inventory. They also accumulated scrap components that had been written off and then added these to inventory. This massive fraud led MiniScribe to file for bankruptcy and both the firm and their auditors to pay bondholders millions of dollars in settlement.

Smoothing, gaming, and *data falsification* result from the pressures that come with having to meet performance targets, many of which are designed by the management accounting system or from having inadequate reward systems. Certainly we will never to able to completely eliminate these behaviors, but the system should be designed well enough so that individuals are not inclined to spend their time worrying about how to manipulate the performance indicators.

Are all of these behaviors unethical? Certainly the last action, *data falsification,* is both illegal and highly unethical. If ethical principles are not internalized by employees and evident in MACS design, the type of behavior that occurred at MiniScribe will be repeated over and over again. *Smoothing* and *gaming,* on the other hand, may violate an individual's code of ethics and the organization's values, but they are not really illegal. One could argue that as long as employees are meeting the targets specified by the organization, neither of these actions is unethical. *Smoothing,* however, does involve altering the preplanned flow of information. For example, if an employee does not defer revenues into the next period, the organization would book these revenues and increase sales. Gaming, in the form of building in slack resources, also can be viewed as a way for subordinates to deal with the risk involved of

Budget slack
Excess resources beyond those needed to accomplish the goals set forth in the budget.

Data falsification
The act of knowingly falsifying information.

OBJECTIVE 14.4
The human factors to consider when implementing a new MACS or changing current ones

meeting performance targets. Slack resources allow some leeway for the employee in case something unforeseen occurs in the work environment. Once again, if performance indicators are met, it is difficult to say whether gaming is unethical. The organization may experience increased costs or inefficiencies in the form of wasted resources, but employees also may be able to function better at work knowing that there is some cushion in case the work environment changes significantly.

BEHAVIORAL CONSIDERATIONS WHEN IMPLEMENTING NEW MANAGEMENT ACCOUNTING SYSTEMS

Today, many firms use management accounting systems that are not keeping pace with all of the changes occurring in their industries and around the globe. Since the late 1970s and early 1980s, however, many other firms have changed their accounting systems. In this section, we will focus on the behavioral factors to consider when changing from an existing MACS to new systems, such as an activity-based costing and management system. An understanding of these factors has become even more relevant with mixed results about the relative success of many new management innovations, such as total quality management and reengineering efforts.[4]

■ Activity-Based Costing and Management

Since the late 1980s, an enormous amount of interest has developed in implementing activity-based costing (ABC) and activity-based management (ABM). Implementing ABC has been difficult for many of these organizations, in part because they did not have an integrative set of performance measures or because their performance measures were not clearly tied to organizational strategy. However, research has identified a number of factors that organizations should consider *before* they actually begin to implement such systems to facilitate the change.

■ Behavioral Factors Relating to Changing to a New MACS

Two different groups can express the need to change to a new system: senior management, and people using currently generated information who realize that the current system is obsolete and needs changing. In some instances, a

[4] See Fred. R. Bleakley, "The Best Laid Plans—Many Companies Try Management Fads, Only to See Them Flop," *The Wall Street Journal* (July 6, 1993): A1.

With participation and empowerment, employees make their own choices about what information and decision-making approaches they will use to undertake their assigned tasks. The role of the management accountant is to support empowered decision makers by providing them with the information that they want and, in some cases, to help them develop the statistical skills they need to analyze data. *(© Ed Kashi)*

change in manufacturing or service technology brings the need to change to the surface. In others, a benchmarking result is the reason for suggesting a modification.

Regardless of why changes are taking place, one thing is certain. Changing to new MACS can be accomplished more easily if the original system was constructed using the 5 key characteristics that we mentioned previously. This is so, in part, because these characteristics themselves are often goals of new systems. However, very few systems, especially those that were developed before the early 1980s have these 5 characteristics.

Researchers have studied the process of implementing new MACS and have identified variables that should to be considered before implementation.[5] We will discuss these variables next.

COOPERATIVE BENCHMARKING   As described previously, benchmarking is a process by which firms strive to use the best practices of others both within their own and other industries to improve their own organizations. One way for organizations to begin the process of MACS change is to engage in benchmarking activities with other organizations. Benchmarking can occur in numerous ways. Some methods involve organizations tying themselves into a database of other firms and learning from the practices of these

[5] See M. D. Shields and S. M. Young, "A Behavioral Model for Implementing Cost Management Systems," *Journal of Cost Management* (Winter 1989), pp. 17–27.

firms. Companies also can work directly with each other to learn how to make changes.[6] This *cooperative benchmarking* approach involves much more face-to-face contact among firms and can lead to more trust on the part of the host organization and, ultimately, to better information regarding what to do.

We discuss a number of specific factors to study for benchmarking purposes in the following sections.

Organizational culture
The mindset of organizational participants including goals, values, and attitudes.

KNOWLEDGE OF ORGANIZATIONAL CULTURE **Organizational culture**[7] can be described as the "mindset of employees, including their shared beliefs, values and goals." Before making changes to a MACS, it is important for an organization to develop a clear understanding of the kind of culture that currently exists. Although cultures can vary a great deal, 3 general types emerge: (1) strong functional, (2) strong dysfunctional, and (3) ill-defined. Some believe that the "ideal" culture is a strong functional one. This culture has clearly articulated beliefs, values, and goals or a clear organizational mission statement. Often these goals are expressed in slogans such as General Electric's "We Bring Good Things to Life" or Digital's "Putting Imagination to Work," which serve as rallying points for employees and clearly define the firm's mission and focus to external stakeholders. A great deal of employee involvement, goal congruence of subordinates and managers, strong feelings of teamwork, work stability, and continuous improvement characterize a strong functional culture.

At the other extreme is a strong dysfunctional culture. This type of culture is characterized by internal conflict between superiors and subordinates, typically arising from stringent top-down control of employees by management. With little employee involvement, poor worker attitudes and behaviors and low morale can result. Often employees are scared to voice their opinions and do not feel a strong commitment to the workplace. Interestingly enough, performance can be high under this type of culture because people sometimes work hard due to fear. The third type of culture is labeled "ill-defined." Such cultures have employees who do not have a sense of mission and whose beliefs, values, and goals are not congruent. Leadership is often lacking in these firms, and they tend to plod along without clear direction.

For those interested in making changes, knowing the existing type of organizational culture is critical. If the culture of an organization is not assessed or if it is misread, it is doubtful that successful changes will occur. Furthermore, experience has shown that strong functional cultures can be changed more easily than either strong dysfunctional or ill-defined cultures.

KNOWLEDGE OF CURRENT MANUFACTURING AND SERVICE PRACTICES One of the initial problems that faced employees who desired to change MACS was how the changes would fit with existing technology. One prominent example occurred as organizations switched from traditional manufacturing methods to the just-in-time (JIT) manufacturing philosophy, which we discussed previously.

[6] One organization that has played a significant role in benchmarking is Consortium for Advanced Manufacturing-International (CAM-I) of Arlington, Texas, which initiated benchmarking activities for MACS in the mid-1980s.

[7] This discussion follows Shields and Young, "Behavioral Model," quite closely.

Researchers found that early attempts to implement JIT were quite successful from a technical point of view. In other words, it was possible to change the actual methods of production with the appropriate level of effort and resources. What organizations did not realize was that many other aspects of their entities, including the existing MACS, were not automatically changing with the adoption of JIT. Instead, they used existing MACS to measure, control, and evaluate performance. As a result, it was hard to clearly evaluate whether the implementation of their JIT system was successful because the use of the current MACS was not appropriate for assessing performance measurement for the new system. As one example, an underlying principle of the JIT system, in its purest form (also known as the *zero inventories system*) is to have virtually no raw materials on hand and no work-in-process or finished goods inventories at the end of a production period. (A central feature of the traditional cost accounting model is the tracing of the flow of inventories through the system. With no inventories, the old MACS either was unsure of what to record or it was attempting to record tens of thousands of inventory transactions as material flowed continuously through the plant on a JIT basis. In either case, the system was producing irrelevant and useless information, and employees became frustrated because it was not possible to evaluate their work efforts clearly.

Another set of issues related to the motivational and control aspect of the JIT system. Unlike many U.S. firms, the JIT system developed in Japan relied on a different kind of cultural control than did traditional U.S. manufacturing. In the United States, most workers adhere to the notion of **primary control** (or rather have it hard wired into them). Under a system of primary control, individuals try to modify the existing social and behavioral factors surrounding them (their environment), including attempting to influence other coworkers or their bosses. Or they may try to alter specific events in their favor. By shaping their environment, individuals in the United States believe that they will increase their rewards.

In contrast, in Japan, under secondary control, individuals increase their rewards and are motivated in a completely different manner. **Secondary control** calls for employees to accommodate *themselves* to the current environment by adjusting their expectations, their goals, and their own attitudes. In other words, individuals subordinate their needs to those of their work group and their organization. The principles that underlie the JIT system rely on the notion of secondary control. For instance, the idea of cross-training of workers in work groups relies on a sense of group cooperation, not on notions of "every individual for him- or herself." It is quite easy to see that attempts to introduce the system to U.S. employees who have not been brought up or trained with secondary control ideas might be met with resistance, which certainly was the case.[8]

Thus, the mixed success of the JIT system in the early 1980s was due, in part, to inappropriate MACS design and to system designers who were not aware that the types of cultural control used in Japan were different from those used in the United States. Adapting to JIT systems, though, may not be

Primary control
A method of control in which employees further their own ends by trying to influence their environment.

Secondary control
A method of control in which employees adapt themselves to their environment rather than trying to change the environment.

---

[8] This issue is discussed at length in S. M. Young, "A Framework for Research on Successful Adoption and Performance of Japanese Manufacturing Practices in the United States." *Academy of Management Review* (1992), pp. 677–700. The paper is included in *Readings in Management Accounting*.

an isolated situation. As benchmarking increases, organizations will attempt to implement new manufacturing and service practices and procedures, not only from companies within their own industries but also from firms in other industries and other countries. This means that system designers have to become fully aware of the ramifications of these changes before they proceed with implementation.

MACS champion
An individual who takes the initiative and risk to develop a new management accounting system.

CHANGE CHAMPION   We use the term *champion* to describe the key person or persons who lead change. Typically, a **MACS champion** is an individual who sees the need for significant change. The champion will often be someone who is very intrapreneurial and entrepreneurial as well as a risk taker. Usually, the champion has to be someone at a reasonably high level within an organization who has the authority and influence to foment any major modifications. In some instances, the champions are at the middle-manager level, but often such managers are responsible for changes only in

Faced with increasing difficulties in competing in the small-volume niche characteristic of the seed-planter market, the John Deere Harvester Works refocused its layout from a process flow to a product flow. This initiative involved employees at all levels of the organization and required major changes in attitude, management, training, and compensation systems. The change was managed by consultants provided by Deere's corporate office. This picture shows the new main assembly line, which is fed from the right by six sublines that make the six modules that go into every seeder. By varying the modules made by each of the six sublines, the final product is customized for each niche market. This change allows John Deere Harvester Works, if required, to make every product different and at a lower cost, higher quality, and faster cycle time than under the old system. *(Courtesy John Deere & Co.)*

their divisions. Regardless of who the champion is, this person must garner the support of top management. Without the backing of very senior managers, change champions, no matter who they are, may lack credibility with many organizational members.

The champion must be very politically savvy and know her way around the organization. This person must obtain the requisite level of financial resources. Without the money needed for personnel, the development of software, and so on, the change will not occur. The champion must develop a team of individuals from various functional areas to aid her by providing various types of information and support. If the champion is not a management accountant, and in many cases she is not, management accountants must make their presence known to the champion and become part of the change team. Often management accountants are overlooked because they are perceived as not being open to change. However, management accountants have a great deal of information about the existing cost system, which should be useful for the champion.

CHANGE PROCESS   The *actual* **change process** includes the procedures and actions by which organizations implement change and is probably the most complex and difficult aspect to consider because it must have a number of ingredients to work. As we previously mentioned, securing top management support of the change is absolutely essential. This action will strengthen the influence of the champion and her team relative to those who may strongly resist the change.

Resistance to change is the *biggest stumbling block* that change agents will face, as we noted in the discussion about overcoming resistance to change in Syd Chan's company. Such resistance was his biggest concern as you will recall from the opening vignette. The difficulties are (1) the defensive response when people and organizations set in their ways are forced to change, (2) the cost of change, which can be very high, both in terms of employee compensation and other rewards and in the amount of time it takes to make change, and (3) the shift in an organization's balance of power. As an example, consider a product line manager who historically has been incorrectly allocated a small amount of the factory overhead. This manager has been operating his business unit for 10 years and, because of the favorable allocation of overhead, has been able to show very good bottom-line results. If an ABC system more accurately reflects cost drivers and changes the allocation of overhead to this person's product line, the business unit's product line will look unprofitable (which indeed it is). This manager will probably resist any of the changes that the new ABC system calls for because such changes will affect the unit's profit and, potentially, the level of expected bonus. In the worst case, the entire business unit could be dropped due to poor profitability.

Another reason that employees resist ABC/ABM is that many of them do not necessarily want their superiors to know what they do. Many managers value their privacy relative to their superiors. Thus, when employees reflect on their original job descriptions, it is highly unlikely that what they actually are doing on the job is reflected in their initial job description, which may be many years old. Some employees may have chosen to engage in more tasks to advance in the organization while others may be shirking their

Change process
The procedures and actions by which change is implemented.

Resistance to change
The act of psychologically refusing to accept the changes brought about in an organization.

responsibilities by doing fewer. The threat to managers is that one of the first things that activity analysis does is to assess how people are spending their time. This analysis is intended to uncover many actions and behaviors that employees at all levels of the firm would prefer to hide. Those who are engaging in additional activities may become concerned that there will be a reallocation of these activities elsewhere or that the activities will become part of their formal job description. Those who know that their activities are being subsidized by others may fear they will have more work to do.

For example, it is not uncommon in manufacturing firms for managers to engage in some customer service because part of their jobs is to understand what customers desire. Some customer service is necessary to maintain customer relations, but the sales and customer service departments usually perform this function. However, some manufacturing managers may spend as much as 30% of their time performing duties, such as service, that someone else should be doing. If the customer service manager is short staffed, she relies on the help from the manufacturing manager, but if the activity analysis identifies this, he will be *unable* to continue to provide service. This will occur because the purpose of the activity analysis is to detect people who are not performing their assigned duties.

One of the most notable reasons for resistance to ABC/ABM relates to employees' fears about cost cutting. Beginning in the late 1970s and continuing through to the present, many organizations have engaged in significant, if not continuous, cost-cutting activities. In the United States, this most typically has occurred by laying off personnel. Even in Japan where so-called permanent employees were supposed to be guaranteed lifetime employment, and at IBM, a company that had an implicit system of permanent employment, employees are being laid off in large numbers. What are the results of these kinds of layoffs and cost-cutting decisions? First, organizational decision makers may be making a tremendous mistake by eliminating people and jobs arbitrarily. However, from both strategic and human resource perspectives, cutting people first is not at all desirable, but it is easy. Employees have a great deal of information about how work gets done, and they develop substantial knowledge about their work domain. Employees also develop working networks within and across their divisions and with other organizations of which upper level management may not be aware. If management uses information about the cost of the employee without considering each person's tangible and intangible worth to the firm, the organization will lose vital resources. Cost cutting of this kind, then, may have short-term benefits, such as reducing costs, but the organization may be severely damaged in the long term.

Another disadvantage to layoffs from the payroll is that in many cases, unless the need to do the work has been eliminated, other individuals will have to pick up the work of the laid-off worker. The negative effect of layoffs on motivation can be devastating because, at least in the short term, employees may be willing to pick up extra work. Eventually, they will burn out if the anticipate no relief. Recall this type of situation highlighted in this chapter's opening vignette. Further, laying off people does not help to build trust among remaining organization members, and the level of efficiency at work may decrease due to concerns regarding who is next to be laid off. The human resources model of motivation on which we have relied focuses a great deal on building and fostering work groups and teams. Often the seemingly arbitrary firing decisions can adversely affect the gains made from adopting this view of the contribution of people to the organization.

The *scope of change* is another critical variable. Organizations and managers often make the mistake of trying to make too many changes simultaneously in too many areas of their organizations. Some organizations implement change beginning in a single work group of business unit. In some instances, the old MACS are run alongside the new system. In this manner, it is possible to work out many "bugs" before changing the entire organization. If attempts to complete conversion to a new system across all functions and divisions simultaneously should fail, the organization may never have the opportunity again to make the change.

Overcoming resistance to change is critical to the success of the new system. Syd Chan and thousands of managers like him face the problem of overcoming resistance constantly because there are ongoing suggestions for organizational innovations. One of the best approaches to use to overcome resistance to change is to introduce the overall philosophy of the new method or innovation to all employees through educational programs and training seminars. These programs should begin well before the changes are to occur. Everyone should understand the reason that the changes are necessary, including the benefits that all employees will realize as a result of them. The benefits include a more secure work environment; a better run and more profitable organization, a fairer performance evaluation system, and a stronger tie between each employee's contribution and organizational rewards. Then each operating unit should develop several attainable goals, which are consistent with the changes. After the company attains these goals, managers and employees begin to build confidence that more significant changes are possible.

COMMITMENT AND CONTINUOUS EDUCATION   Once both top management and other employees have committed to the change, the immediate quest for change is significantly complete. The most difficult aspect of **commitment** is sustaining it. Changing to new management accounting systems is costly, both in monetary and personal terms. However, the level of energy required to change can be staggering on the parts of everyone in the organization. Commitment can quite easily slip; therefore, it is important to consider commitment to require an ongoing effort.

Commitment
The implicit pledging of organizational participants to a course of action.

As described for all the variables presented, employees need to have information about advances, both in what they do and how their MACS operate. Perhaps the most effective way to ensure that employees receive such information is through **continuous education**—a commitment to provide educational programs for employees on an ongoing basis. Employees' skills can erode or become outdated very quickly given the many changes occurring in technology and information systems. Providing employees with the needed skills also fosters more commitment on their part because they believe that the organization is investing in them.

Continuous education
A commitment on the part of the organization to provide educational programs for employees on an ongoing basis

COMPENSATION   Often before an organization implements an ABC/ABM system, it performs an activity analysis. A common outcome of this analysis is that work is reorganized around teams of individuals and away from individuals. As work reorganization occurs, performance becomes tied directly to team effort. Thus, compensation systems must be designed to reward team performance.

As an example, the design, manufacture, costing and pricing, and sales of a product under the former system was done in a linear, step-by-step fashion. Design engineers designed a product and passed it to manufacturing engineers, who laid out the shop floor to produce the product in an efficient manner. Once the product was completed, it was costed by accountants. Then marketing personnel determined the price and salespeople sold the finished product. In today's manufacturing environment, this linear process has changed substantially. The new work environment involves teams of design, manufacturing, and industrial engineers; accountants; operations individuals; and marketing people meeting together to share their information and expertise about all aspects of launching a new product. Not only does this improve the product's chance of appealing to the market (due to consideration of marketing research on what features customers want and costing information during the design phase), but also it often increases the speed with which it reaches market.

Many other types of teams exist. We have already described how employees on shop floors or in service organizations are organized in "cells" to perform specific jobs. Members of these teams are cross-trained so that they can perform the jobs of several others in their team.

Numerous types of compensation systems currently exist to reward team performance. In Chapter 13, we discussed profit-sharing and gain-sharing plans. In the examples just given, the team involved with new product development might be compensated based on how quickly the new product can be brought to market or on the number of parts reduced on an existing product to make manufacturing less complex. It is important to realize that each new situation in organizations, especially ones involving major changes, deserves special consideration regarding development of the most motivating kind of compensation system.

SUMMARY

Our focus in this book has been on a new view of management accounting. This view incorporates the disciplines of strategy, operations management, ethics, and the organizational sciences, with a perspective on management accounting that is organized around the activities that occur in the organization. In this chapter, we have presented the Human Resources model of human motivation and discussed how the design of a management accounting and control system should be consistent with this model.

Additionally, because many traditional management accounting systems have and will be changing to an activity-based approach, we have discussed issues and variables related to the change process. Because the implementation of ABC/ABM can meet with resistance, cost management champions and their teams should pay a great deal of attention to behavioral and organizational issues to increase their chances of being successful.

KEY TERM LIST

ASSIGNMENT MATERIAL

QUESTIONS

14–1 What are the goals of a management accounting and control system (MACS)?

14–2 What was the scientific management view of motivation?

14–3 What was the human relations school view of motivation?

14–4 What is the human resources view of motivation?

14–5 The human resources view of motivation focuses on 3 key aspects of motivation. What are they?

14–6 What is goal congruence?

14–7 What are the 5 characteristics of well-designed MACS? Describe them.

14–8 What is the multiple perspectives approach to MACS design?

14–9 What are the 4 requirements of ethical conduct by which certified management accountants (CMAs) must abide?

14–10 What are the choices that individuals can make when ethical conflicts arise?

14–11 What is an ethical control system?

14–12 What are some quantitative measures of performance?

14–13 What are some qualitative measures of performance?

14–14 What is employee empowerment?

14–15 What is the working definition of poorly designed MACS?

14–16 What is smoothing?

14–17 What is gaming?

14–18 What is data falsification?

14-19 What is participation in setting the budget?

14-20 What is imposition of the budget?

14-21 What is budget slack?

14-22 What is cooperative benchmarking?

14-23 What is a strong functional culture?

14-24 What is a strong dysfunctional culture?

14-25 What is primary control?

14-26 What is secondary control?

14-27 What is a change champion?

14-28 What is resistance to change?

EXERCISES

14-29 How do the scientific management, human relations, and human resource schools differ regarding their views on human motivation?

14-30 Why is having a multiple perspectives approach important in MACS design?

14-31 List and describe the hierarchy of ethical considerations.

14-32 What should a person do who faces a conflict between his or her values and those of the organization?

14-33 What should a person do when the organization's stated values conflict with its practiced values? What are the individual's choices?

14-34 What is the advantage of having multiple measures of performance?

14-35 What are the advantages for the individual in being able to participate in decision making in the organization?

14-36 What are the advantages for the organization in allowing the individual to participate in decision making?

14-37 What are the behavioral consequences of a poorly designed MACS?

14-38 Should reward systems be tied to performance for goal congruence? Explain.

14-39 Are gaming and smoothing illegal activities? Explain.

14-40 What distinguishes data falsification and gaming activities?

14-41 What are some methods of creating budget slack?

14-42 Can gaming and smoothing ever be completely eliminated in organizations?

14-43 Can you think of instances in which gaming behavior is appropriate in an organization?

14-44 How do strong functional cultures differ from strong dysfunctional and ill-defined cultures?

14-45 How does primary control differ from secondary control?

14-46 What factors will help a change champion to be successful?

14-47 What is resistance to change and how can it be overcome?

PROBLEMS

14–48 Why is an understanding of human motivation essential to MACS system design?

14–49 Lido Co. has been using the same management accounting system for the past 25 years. Faced with increasing international pressure, Sally Lido, president of the company, has decided that one of the major changes that she must make is to implement a new management accounting and control system.

What key variables does President Lido have to manage very carefully during this transition?

14–50 List the characteristics that will lead to good MACS design. What are the benefits of each?

14–51 Denver Jack's is a large toy manufacturer. The company has 500 employees who are involved with 7 product lines, including the production of toy soldiers, dolls, and so on. Each product line is manufactured in a different city and state. Jack has decided to make all of the budgeting decisions for the toy lines himself, including which products to eliminate. The managers of each toy line believe he is making a mistake.

What are the pros and cons of Denver Jack's budgeting approach?

14–52 Describe the acts of smoothing, gaming, and data falsification. Are they unethical? How can they be overcome?

14–53 Archer Company, a high-tech manufacturing firm, has faced severe losses over the past 3 years. Archer's stakeholders have demanded that the company make some significant changes and improvements to its operations over the next 2 years. Faced with a very hostile group of shareholders at a board meeting, Archer's president, Roger Slothand, quickly lays out a plan to lay off 20% of its workforce. The thinking is that this reduction in people will make their financial statements look better. The irate shareholders seem to believe that this plan may work.

What are some likely results of Slothand's actions? Will the shareholders be happy two years from now?

14–54 Under what circumstances should both quantitative and qualitative performance measures be used to evaluate employee, work group, and divisional performance? Provide examples to justify your answer.

14–55 Is it possible to design a single performance measure to capture all aspects of an employee's performance? If your answer is yes, provide a context and an example.

14–56 What are the pros and cons of tying an individual's pay to his or her performance? Write an essay citing concrete examples of both pros and cons.

14–57 During data collection for the transition from an old management accounting system to a new ABC system, you see a manager's reported time allotments. You know that the data supplied by the manager on how she spends her time are completely false. You confront the manager who states that she is worried that if she reports how she spends her time and resources truthfully, her job will be altered and it will be found out that she is really not performing very well. She implores you not to tell anyone. What action should you take?

14–58 As a management accountant working in the controller's office, a very powerful executive approaches you in the parking lot and asks you to do him a favor. The favor involves falsifying some of his division's records on the main computer. The executive states that if you do not do as he asks, he will have you fired. What do you do?

14–59 Write an essay discussing the key variables that system designers must consider when trying to implement an ABC/ABM system.

14–60 Write an essay discussing the pros and cons of participation in the budgeting process versus imposition of it.

14–61 You are the change champion for the new MACS (an ABC system) that your organization is going to implement. You have been working on the change for 18 months and firmly believe that it is the best system for your organization. Along the way you have met with a great deal of resistance to change, primarily from managers who fear that their product line profitability will change as a result of the ABC system.

REQUIRED:

(a) Discuss how you would deal with the managers. What key arguments would you use to convince them that they should lower their resistance to the new system?

(b) What steps would you take to make the transition to the new system easier?

CASES

14–62 Thomas Company is an insurance company in Oberlin, Ohio. Thomas hires 45 people to process insurance claims. The volume of claims is extremely high, and all claims examiners are extremely busy. The number of claims with mistakes runs about 10%. If a claim has an error, it must be corrected by the claims examiners. Recently, Mike Blue, senior manager of the division, has not been satisfied with the volume of claims processed, however. He instructed Doreen Yonger, the manager, to motivate the claims examiners to work faster. Doreen believes that the claims examiners are working as fast as they possibly can. She is also concerned that, by working faster, the number of errors will increase.

REQUIRED:

(a) How should Doreen Yonger handle this situation?

(b) On what performance measures is the organization relying?

(c) What performance measures should the organization use?

14–63 Lucy Bond, vice president of manufacturing of Marx Plastic Company, has been asked to implement an activity-based costing and management system in her organization. Lucy has had some training in ABC/ABM, but all of her managers know nothing about the method. Jack Rostoy is the manager of the best performing division of Marx Plastics. Two of his 10 product lines, SuperX and SuperY, make the most money of any products in the entire company. For years, Jack has boasted endlessly about the success of these products, and he gets a great deal of satisfaction knowing that these are the company's most successful products.

Recently, Lucy has begun to wonder about SuperX and SuperY. As she has begun to learn more about ABC/ABM, she realizes that she has been using direct labor as an allocation base for overhead in all of her divisions and for all of her products. She now realizes that two other drivers seem to be the most appropriate for Jack's division—direct materials and machine hours.

Her preliminary figures show that if she uses these drivers to compute the costs of producing both SuperX and SuperY, the costs are higher than anyone ever thought. In fact, they are so high that, at the current price, they lose money. Some of his other products, though, begin to look a lot more attractive. Lucy has a hunch that Jack will strongly resist the ABC system, given his strong ego involvement with SuperX and SuperY.

REQUIRED:

(a) How should Lucy approach this problem?

(b) What should she tell Jack?

(c) What if he is adamantly opposed to changing to different allocation bases?

14–64 You are employed as a senior manager in an insurance organization. One of your responsibilities is to randomly review claims for reimbursement that have been submitted by people who have traveled on the organization's behalf.

By accident, you have pulled a claim that was submitted by Susan, one of your closest friends. You decide to confront your friend with your findings. Susan, knowing you are a friend, replies, "Sure the claim contains false items. Everybody does it and it is almost expected!"

Stunned by her confession, you tell her that she has to resubmit an accurate reimbursement claim. Susan responds, "Look Mark, I don't feel that I get paid enough in this lousy organization and this is my way of getting a few extra dollars each month. You know how they have been working all of us to death after the layoffs. I'm entitled to this, and I refuse to resubmit the claim."

REQUIRED:

(a) What do you think of Susan's argument?

(b) Should you have approached her differently?

(c) What should you do now?

GLOSSARY

activity A unit of work, or task, with a specific goal. Examples of activities are grading a student's examination, issuing a medicare check, and painting an automobile. (p. 44)

activity analysis An approach to operations control that involves the application of steps of continuous improvement to an activity; also known as *value analysis*. (p. 64)

activity cost driver Unit of measurement for the level (or quantity) of the activity performed. (p. 102)

activity improvement Improving the performance of an activity in terms of the organization's objectives. (p. 47)

activity overhead rate Ratio of the cost of resources to provide an activity to the level of the capacity made available by those resources. (p. 106)

activity-based costing A procedure that measures the costs of objects, such as products, services, and customers. Activity-based costing (ABC) first assigns resource costs to the activities performed by the organization. Then activity costs are assigned to the products, customers, and services that benefit from or are creating the demand for the activities. (p. 23)

activity-based costing systems Costing systems based on cost drivers that link activities performed to products and allocate overhead activity costs directly to products using these cost drivers. (p. 291)

activity-based management The management processes that use the information provided by an activity-based cost analysis to improve organizational profitability. Activity-based management (ABM) includes performing activities more efficiently, eliminating the need to perform certain activities that do not add value for customers, improving the design of products, and developing better relationships with customers and suppliers. The goal of ABM is to enable customer needs to be satisfied while making fewer demands on organizational resources. (p. 24)

administrative and discretionary spending plan An operating plan that summarizes administrative and discretionary expenditures. (p. 197)

aggregate planning An approximate determination of whether the organization has the capacity to undertake a proposed production plan (also called *rough-cut planning*). (p. 204)

annuity A contract that promises to pay a fixed amount each period for a stated number of periods. (p. 413)

appropriation An authorized spending limit in a government department. (p. 220)

avoidable costs Costs that are eliminated when a part, a product, a product line, or a business segment is discontinued. (p. 372)

balanced scorecard A set of performance targets and an approach to performance measurement that stresses meeting all of the organization's objectives relating to its critical success factors. (p. 445)

batch-related activities Activities whose levels are related to the number of batches produced. (p. 100)

benchmarking Studying how other best-performing organizations, either internal or external to the firm, perform similar activities and processes. (p. 14)

breakeven chart A set of graphs depicting the sales revenues and fixed, variable, and total costs. The breakeven point is the point of intersection of the sales revenue curve and the total cost curve. (p. 164)

breakeven point The level at which profits from 2 alternative options are equal. (p. 136)

budget imposition A situation in which a superior simply tells a subordinate what his or her budget will be, without any input from the subordinate. (p. 590)

budget participation A joint decision-making process in which all parties agree to the levels of the budget. (p. 590)

budget slack Excess resources beyond those needed to accomplish the goals set forth in the budget. (p. 591)

budgeting The process of preparing budgets. (p. 193)

budgets A quantitative model, or summary of the expected consequences of the organization's short-term operating activities. (p. 193)

business-level strategy Developed by middle-level management, a statement of how the organization has chosen to compete in its chosen markets. A decision to be the low cost producer is a business-level strategy. (p. 444)

capacity constraints Limitations on the quantity that can be produced because the capacity committed for some activity resources (such as plant space or number of machines) cannot be changed in the short run. (p. 144)

capital budget The management document that authorizes spending for resources, such as plant and equipment, that will have multiyear useful lifetimes. (p. 16)

capital budgeting The collection of tools that planners use to evaluate the desirability of long-term assets. (p. 407)

capital spending plan An operating plan that specifies when long-term capital expenditures such as acquisitions for buildings and special-purpose equipment must be made to meet activity objectives. (p. 197)

cash bonus A cash award based on some measured performance. (p. 552)

cell manufacturing A means of organizing a production activity so that all the equipment needed to make a good or service is grouped together. (p. 69)

cellular manufacturing Organization of the plant into a number of cells so that within each cell, all machines required to manufacture a group of similar products are arranged sequentially in close proximity to each other. (p. 375)

centralization Reserving decision-making power for senior management levels. (p. 488)

centralized control The management process by which senior executives receive periodic information about decentralized divisional operations to ensure that division managers are making decisions and taking actions that contribute to overall corporate goals. (p. 17)

certified supplier A specially selected supplier who is assured a high level of business for conforming to high standards for quality and delivery schedules. (p. 375)

change process The procedures and actions by which change is implemented. (p. 597)

charting Identifying each activity in the value chain and visually depicting it. (p. 46)

chase demand strategy A policy of producing for demand. When production occurs exactly, and only, when the units are required, this strategy is called a *just-in-time production strategy*. (p. 204)

commitment The implicit pledging of organizational participants to a course of action. (p. 599)

committed resources Resources made available for an activity prior to knowing the demand for it. These resources cannot be reduced in case the demand turns out to be less than the capacity made available by the committed resources. (p. 155)

community Defines the legal, moral, and social norms that constrain an organization's activities. (p. 42)

competitive benchmarking An organization's search for, and implementation of, the best way to do something as practiced by another organization. (p. 56)

compounding effect (of interest) The phenomenon of earning interest on interest previously earned. (p. 409)

concurrent control An approach to control that relies on detecting problems when they are happening so that the process can be adjusted to prevent further undesired outcomes. (p. 452)

continuous budgeting A budgeting process that plans for a specified period of time, usually 1 year, and organized into budget subintervals, usually a month or a quarter. As each budget subinterval ends, the organization drops the completed subinterval from the budget and adds the next budget subinterval. (p. 221)

continuous education A commitment on the part of the organization to provide educational programs for employees on an ongoing basis. (p. 599)

continuous improvement The ongoing processes by which employees continually problem solve and search for methods to reduce and eliminate waste, improve quality and reduce defects, shorten response and cycle times, and design products that are simpler to manufacture, deliver, and service. (p. 25)

contribution margin per unit Difference between the price and variable cost per unit. (p. 163)

contribution margin ratio Contribution margin expressed as a percentage of sales. (p. 165)

control The set of methods and tools that organization members use to keep the organization on track toward achieving its objectives. (p. 54)

controllability A principle that asserts that people should be held accountable only for results that they can control.

The main application of this principle is that a manager should not be held accountable for revenues, costs, investments, or other factors outside her control. (p. 499)

conversion costs Costs of production labor and support activities to convert the materials or product at each process stage. (p. 262)

corporate-level strategy Developed by upper-level management, a broad statement of the type of product or service markets in which the organization has chosen to compete. For example, a decision to compete only in the domestic household appliance market is a corporate-level strategy for an appliance manufacturer. (p. 444)

cost Efficiency to the provider of a product; that is, using minimum resources to achieve objectives, and price paid to the purchaser of a product. (p. 49)

cost behavior Description of how costs change with changes in an activity cost driver or production volume. (p. 154)

cost center A responsibility center whose manager and other employees control costs but not its revenues or investment level. (p. 491)

cost curve Graph of costs plotted against activity cost driver or production volume. (p. 144)

cost of capital The minimum return that the organization must earn on its investments to meet its investors' return requirements. (p. 414)

cost variances Differences between actual and standard costs. (p. 117)

critical performance indicators Performance measures used to assess an organization's performance on its critical success factors. (p. 47)

critical success factors The elements, such as quality, time, cost reduction, customer service, or product performance, that create long-term profitability for the organization. (p. 13)

customer costing The process of assigning marketing, selling, distribution, and administrative costs to individual customers so that the cost of serving each customer can be calculated. (p. 14)

cycle time The total time the organization needs to complete an activity or a process. (p. 67)

data falsification The act of knowingly falsifying information. (p. 591)

decentralization The strategy of delegating decision-making responsibility from senior management to employees at lower levels of the organization. (p. 489)

decentralized responsibility Senior corporate managers give local division managers the rights to make decisions on pricing, product mix, customer relationships, resource acquisition, materials sourcing, and operating processes without having to seek approval from higher-level managers. Decentralized responsibility allows local managers to make decisions rapidly based on their superior access to information about local opportunities and threats. (p. 17)

demand forecast An estimate of the market demand, or sales potential, for a product under specified conditions. (p. 202)

Deming wheel A means to organize process improvements, which involves a continuous cycle of planning, doing, checking, and action. (p. 57)

direct allocation method A simple method to allocate service department costs to production departments that ignores interdependencies between service departments. (p. 281)

direct costs Costs that can be traced easily to the product manufactured or service rendered. (p. 95)

discount rate The interest rate used to compute present values. (p. 413)

discounting The process of computing present value. (p. 412)

discretionary costs Costs that result from managers' strategic and tactical decisions, such that the expenditure levels chosen influence the production volume instead of production volume influencing the consumption of activity resources. (p. 155)

diseconomies of scale Increasing average costs with increases in production volume. (p. 144)

economies of scale Decreasing average costs with increases in production volume. (p. 144)

effective A process that meets its objectives. (p. 46)

effective rate of interest The actual annual rate of interest earned on an investment. (p. 410)

efficiency A measure of an organization's ability to control costs at a given activity level. In financial control, this is the ratio of earnings to sales, or operating incomes to sales. (p. 513)

efficient A process that uses the fewest possible resources to meet its objectives. (p. 46)

elasticity of demand Demand is elastic if a small increase in price results in a large decrease in demand. (p. 342)

employee empowerment Managers give employees, who are closest to operating processes, customers, and suppliers the rights to make decisions. Employees are encouraged to solve problems and devise creative new approaches for performing work and satisfying customers. (p. 25)

Engineered expenditure An expenditure whose short-term cost is directly determined by the proposed level of activity. Engineered expenditures reflect product design and process design (e.g., materials costs and the cost of casual labor). (p. 205)

environment Those elements outside the organization that affect the organization's ability to achieve its goals. (p. 454)

ethical control system A system that reinforces the ethical responsibilities of all firm employees. (p. 582)

expectancy The relationship that a person perceives between effort and skill and the results measured by the organization's performance measurement system. (p. 538)

expectancy theory (Vroom's) A theory that argues that motivation is a product of expectancy, instrumentality, and valence. (p. 538)

extrinsic rewards Rewards, based on performance, that are provided to the individual by the organization. (p. 540)

facility-sustaining activities Activities performed to provide the managerial infrastructure and to support the upkeep of the plant. (p. 101)

feedback control An approach to control that reports data on completed activities to decide whether they were completed as planned. (p. 452)

feedforward control Often called *preventive control*, this approach to control focuses on preventing an undesired outcome and occurs before the activity is undertaken. (p. 451)

financial accounting The process of producing financial statements for external constituencies, such as shareholders, creditors, and governmental authorities. This process is heavily constrained by standard-setting, regulatory, and tax authorities and the auditing requirements of independent accountants (contrast with management accounting). (p. 5)

financial budget A budget that summarizes the expected financial results from the chosen operating plans. (p. 196)

financial control The formal evaluation of some financial facet of an organization or a responsibility center. (p. 489)

first-level variance Difference between actual and estimated costs for a cost item. (p. 255)

fixed costs Costs that are independent of the level of production. (p. 137)

flexible budget A forecast of what expenses should have been given the actual volume and mix of production and sales. (p. 18)

flexible resources Resources that are acquired as needed and whose costs vary with production activity. (p. 154)

full costs Sum of all costs (direct materials, direct labor and overhead) assigned to a product. (p. 337)

functional-level strategy A statement of how the organization carries out its business-level strategy daily at the operational level. Using just-in-time manufacturing is an example of a functional-level strategy. (p. 444)

future value The amount to which an amount invested today will accumulate over a stated number of periods and at a stated rate of interest. (p. 408)

gain sharing A cash bonus system in which the total amount available for distribution as cash bonuses is a function of performance relative to some target (usually the difference between the actual and the target level of labor cost). (p. 553)

gaming An alteration of an employee's planned actions as a result of a particular kind of performance indicator. (p. 590)

goal congruence The alignment of individual and organizational goals. (p. 576)

goals The long-term results sought by an organization. (p. 444)

human relations movement A model of human motivation that considers that people have many needs and aspirations at work, and that they are motivated by things other than money. (p. 575)

human resources model An approach to human motivation that emphasizes that individuals do not find work objectionable, that they have knowledge to contribute, and that they are creative. (p. 575)

hygiene factors A group of factors in the Herzberg theory that relate to job context and define the environment. They are thought to be necessary to provide the environment for motivation rather than being motivators themselves. (p. 537)

incentive compensation   See *pay for performance*. (p. 542)

incremental budgeting   An approach to developing appropriations for discretionary expenditures that assumes that the starting point for each discretionary expenditure item is the amount spent on it in the previous budget. (p. 222)

incremental cash flow   Cash flows that change as a result of acquiring or disposing of a long-term asset. (p. 415)

incremental costs (or revenues)   The amount by which costs (or revenues) change if one particular decision is made instead of another. (p. 337)

indirect costs   Costs that cannot be traced easily to products or services produced; also referred to as *overhead costs*. (p. 96)

inflows   The incremental cash inflows associated with an asset. (p. 411)

instrumentality   The relationship between measured performance and the outcomes provided to individuals. (p. 538)

internal control procedures   Systems and rules used to enforce or promote task control. (p. 455)

intrinsic rewards   Rewards relating to the nature of the organization and the design of the job that people experience without the intervention of anyone else. (p. 540)

investment   The monetary value of the assets that the organization gives up to acquire a long-term asset. (p. 408)

investment center   A responsibility center whose employees control its revenues, costs, and the level of investment. (p. 498)

job bid sheet   Format for estimating job costs. (p. 242)

job cost sheet   Format for recording actual job costs. (p. 253)

job costs   Total of direct material, direct labor, and overhead costs estimated for or identified with a job. (p. 244)

job order costing system   System for estimating costs of manufacturing products for a job. (p. 242)

just-in-time or JIT   Making a good or service only when the customer, who may be internal or external, requires it. (p. 72)

labor hiring and training plan   An operating plan that schedules the hiring, releasing, and training of people that the organization must have to achieve its activity objectives. (p. 197)

line of credit   A short-term financing arrangement, with a prespecified limit, between an organization and a financial institution. (p. 214)

long-term or capital assets   Equipment or facilities that provide productive services to the organization for more than 1 accounting period. (p. 406)

MACS champion   An individual who takes the initiative and risk to develop a new management accounting system. (p. 596)

make-or-buy decision   Decision either to make a part or

component in-house or to purchase it from an outside supplier. (p. 372)

management accounting   The process of producing financial and operating information for organizational employees and managers. The process should be driven by the informational needs of individuals *internal* to the organization and should guide their operating and investment decisions. (p. 4)

management accounting information   Output from a management accounting system (e.g., calculated cost of a product, an activity, or a department in a recent time period). (p. 4)

management accounting system   An information system that collects operational and financial data, processes it, stores it, and reports it to users (workers, managers, executives). (p. 4)

management by objectives   A control system that uses the idea of self-control in an environment of employee involvement to promote results control. (p. 466)

management control   The process of providing information about the performance of managers and operating units. (p. 14)

manufacturing costs   All costs of transforming raw materials into finished product. (p. 94)

manufacturing cycle efficiency   The ratio of the time required by value-added activities in a value chain to the total time required by all activities in the value chain. (p. 67)

manufacturing overhead costs   Indirect cost of transforming raw materials into finished product; indirect manufacturing costs. (p. 100)

marginal revenues (costs)   The increase in revenues (or costs) for a unit increase in the quantity produced and sold. (p. 349)

markup or margin   Amount of profit added to estimated job costs to arrive at bid price. (p. 244)

markup rate   Ratio of the markup amount to the estimated costs for a job. (p. 244)

materials purchasing plan   An operating plan that schedules purchasing activities. (p. 197)

materials requisition note   A note instructing the stores department to issue materials to the shop floor in order to commence production. (p. 252)

mission statement   The organization's statement of purpose and commitment to its stakeholders. (p. 449)

mixed costs   Costs comprising both fixed and variable cost components. (p. 141)

model   A representation. (p. 193)

motivation system   A system of performance measurement and rewards that provides employee benefits or recognition based on measured performance. (p. 539)

multiple perspectives approach   The development of a consistent organizationwide management accounting system that also allows for local input and tailoring. (p. 576)

multistage process costing system   System for determining product costs in multistage processing industries (p. 261)

net present value The sum of the present values of all the cash inflows and cash outflows associated with a project (also called *residual income, economic income,* and *economic value added*). (p. 415)

net realizable value The difference between a product's selling price and the additional costs needed to put it in the customer's hands. (p. 508)

nominal or stated rate of interest The stated annual rate of interest. (p. 410)

nonmanufacturing costs All costs other than manufacturing costs. (p. 94)

nonvalue-added activity An activity that presents the opportunity for cost reduction without reducing the product's service potential to the customer. (p. 61)

normal unit cost of an activity Average cost at the point where activity demand equals available capacity; regular cost of providing the resource capacity made available for an activity. (p. 150)

objectives The broad purposes of an organization or process. Objectives reflect the stakeholder requirements that the organization is committed to achieving, such as employee safety, profitability, and customer satisfaction. (p. 40)

operating budget The document that forecasts revenues and expenses during the next operating period, typically a year. The operating budget also authorizes spending on discretionary activities, such as research and development, advertising, maintenance, and employee training. (p. 16)

operating overhead Indirect costs of producing services in a service organization. (p. 113)

operational control The process of providing feedback to employees and their managers about the efficiency of activities being performed. (p. 14)

opportunity A change in the organization's environment that enhances its ability to achieve its goals. A change in customer tastes is an opportunity. (p. 443)

opportunity cost The potential benefit sacrificed when, in selecting one alternative, another alternative is given up. (p. 335)

organizational culture The mindset of organizational participants including goals, values, and attitudes. (p. 594)

outcome The value attributed to output by the customer, for example, the number of good units of production and the amount of client satisfaction generated by a service. (p. 52)

outflows The incremental cash outflows associated with an asset. (p. 411)

output A physical measure of production or activity, such as the number of units produced or the amount of time spent doing something. (p. 52)

outsourcing Purchasing a product, part, or component from an outside supplier instead of manufacturing it in-house. (p. 372)

overhead cost pools Identified categories of overhead costs; each category has a separate rate, that is used. (p. 244)

overhead rate The rate at which overhead costs are applied to individual jobs. It is the ratio of the normal cost for a support activity accumulated in a cost pool to the normal level of the cost driver for the activity. (p. 244)

partners The suppliers and distributors that an organization uses to achieve its objectives. (p. 41)

pay for performance (incentive compensation) A system that provides rewards for performance to motivate achieving, or exceeding, measured performance targets. (p. 542)

payback period The number of years taken for the cash inflows associated with a project to recover the initial investment. (p. 407)

penetration pricing strategy Charging a lower price initially to win over market share from an established product of a competing firm. (p. 344)

performance measurement Measuring the performance of an activity or a value chain. (p. 46)

period costs Costs treated as expenses in the period in which they are incurred because they cannot be associated with the manufacture of products. (p. 94)

period length The time period over which interest is computed (e.g., monthly, quarterly, semiannually, or annually) in a capital budgeting analysis. (p. 415)

periodic budget A budget that is prepared for a specified period of time, usually 1 year. As each budget period ends, the organization prepares a new budget for the next one. (p. 221)

planning The way that organizations set their goals and objectives. (p. 443)

postimplementation audit Reevaluating a past decision to purchase a long-lived asset by comparing expected and actual inflows and outflows. (p. 425)

present value The current monetary worth of an amount to be paid in the future under stated conditions of interest and compounding. (p. 412)

Price setter A firm that sets or bids the prices of its products because it enjoys a significant market share in its industry segment. (p. 329)

price taker A firm that has little or no influence on the industry supply and demand forces, and, consequently, on the prices of its products. (p. 328)

primary control A method of control in which employees further their own ends by trying to influence their environment. (p. 495)

process layout A means of organizing a production activity so that all similar equipment or functions are grouped together, for example, a university where faculty are housed by department. (p. 68)

product costing The process of measuring and assigning the costs of the activities performed to design and produce individual products (and services, for nonmanufacturing companies). (p. 14)

product costs Costs associated with the manufacture of products. (p. 94)

product layout A means of organizing a production activity so that equipment or functions are organized to make a specific product, for example, an automobile assembly line. (p. 69)

product-sustaining activities Activities performed to support the production of individual products. (p. 101)

production cycle time Time elapsed beginning with the receipt of raw materials and ending with the shipment of the final product. (p. 368)

production departments Departments directly responsible for some of the work of converting raw materials into finished products. (p. 278)

production plan An operating plan that identifies all required production. (p. 197)

production volume Overall measure, such as number of units, of various products manufactured in a given time period. (p. 92)

productivity A ratio of output to input. In financial control, this is the ratio of sales to investment and represents the ability to generate sales for a given level of assets. (p. 514)

profit center A responsibility center whose employees control revenues and costs but not the level of investment. (p. 497)

profit sharing A cash bonus system in which the total amount available for distribution as cash bonuses is a function of the organization's, or an organization unit's, reported profit. (p. 552)

pro forma statement A forecasted or estimated statement. (p. 196)

project funding An approach to developing appropriations for discretionary expenditures that organizes appropriations into a package that focuses on achieving some defined output. For example, an organization might fund a project designed to identify and evaluate its practiced organization ethics. (p. 223)

quality The similarity between the promised and the realized level of service. (p. 48)

rate of return Ratio of net income to investment (also called *return on investment*). (p. 244)

reciprocal allocation method A method to determine service department cost allocations simultaneously, recognizing the reciprocity between pairs of service departments. (p. 281)

relevant costs (or revenues) The costs (revenues) that differ across alternatives and, therefore, must be considered in deciding which alternative is the best. (p. 339)

relevant range The range of production levels over which the classification of a cost as fixed or variable is appropriate. (p. 145)

residual income Actual income less the economic cost of the investment used to generate that income; corresponds to the notion of economic income. (p. 519)

resistance to change The act of psychologically refusing to accept the changes brought about in an organization. (p. 597)

responsibility center An organization unit for which a manager is accountable in the form of cost (a cost center), revenue (a revenue center), profits (a profit center), or return on investment (an investment center). (p. 490)

results control A system focused on results or outcomes

that is designed to motivate decision-making behavior to achieve the organization's behavior. (p. 454)

return on investment The calculation that relates the profitability of an organizational unit to the investment required to generate that profitability. Often written as the return on sales multiplied by the ratio of sales to assets (or investment) employed. (p. 16)

revenue center A responsibility center whose employees control revenues but not manufacturing or acquisition costs or the level of investment. (p. 496)

sales plan A document that summarizes planned sales for each product. (p. 197)

satisfier factors A group of factors in the Herzberg theory that relate to job content. They are thought to provide motivation when the environment for motivation has been properly prepared. (p. 537)

scientific management A school of motivation in which people are viewed as finding work objectionable, motivated only by money, and have little knowledge to contribute to the organization. (p. 575)

second-level variance analysis Analysis of a first-level variance into efficiency and price variances. (p. 257)

secondary control A method of control in which employees adapt themselves to their environment rather than trying to change the environment. (p. 595)

segment margin The level of controllable profit reported by an organization unit or product line. (p. 502)

self-control The ability of a system to accept objectives and regulate itself as it seeks to achieve those objectives. (p. 462)

sensitivity analysis An analytical tool that involves selectively varying key estimates of a plan or budget. Sensitivity analysis allows planners to identify the effect of changes in estimates on decisions. If small changes in plan parameters (estimates and relationships) produce large changes in decisions or results, the plan is said to be sensitive to the estimates. (p. 218)

sequential allocation method A method that recognizes interdependencies between service departments and allocates service department costs, 1 service department at a time, in a sequential order. (p. 281)

service The product's tangible and intangible features promised to the customer; also known as *value in use*. (p. 47)

service departments Departments performing activities that support production but are not responsible for any of the conversion stages. (p. 278)

shareholder value analysis Evaluates a product line's financial desirability using its residual income; also known as *economic value analysis*. (p. 519)

signal Information provided to a decision maker. There are two types of signals: (1) a warning that there is a problem and (2) a diagnostic that identifies the problem. (p. 53)

Skimming pricing strategy Charging a higher price initially from customers willing to pay more for the privilege of possessing a new product. (p. 344)

smoothing The act of affecting the preplanned flow of information without altering actual behavior. (p. 590)

soft number A number that may be unreliable because it

rests on subjective assumptions over which there can be legitimate disagreement. (p. 504)

stage 1 allocations Identification of costs with individual production and service departments (step 1), followed by allocation of service department costs to production departments (step 2). (p. 281)

stage 2 allocations Assignment of production department costs to jobs and products when they are worked on in the departments. (p. 284)

stakeholders Groups of people who have a legitimate claim on having an organization's objectives reflect their requirements. Stakeholders include customers, employees, partners, owners, and the community. (p. 41)

standard costs Efficient and attainable benchmarks established in advance for the costs of activity resources that should be consumed by each product. (p. 116)

step fixed costs Costs that increase in relatively wide discrete steps. (p. 146)

step variable costs Costs that increase in relatively narrow discrete steps. (p. 146)

stock option A right to purchase a stated number of the organization's shares at a specified price (the option price). (p. 555)

strategic information Information that guides the long-term decision making of the organization. Strategic information can include the profitability of products, services, and customers; competitor behavior; customer preferences and trends; market opportunities and threats; and technological innovations. (p. 14)

strategic planning The tools and processes an organization uses to identify its goals. (p. 444)

strength A characteristic or resource that offers the organization an advantage in successfully pursuing its goals. Highly motivated employees are a strength. (p. 444)

sunk costs Costs of resources that have already been committed, and, regardless of what decision managers make, that cannot be avoided. (p. 369)

task control Systems or procedures designed to ensure that employees follow stated procedures or rules. (p. 454)

threat A change in the organization's environment that diminishes its ability to achieve its goals. A new competitor is a threat. (p. 443)

time value of money The notion that, because money can be invested to earn a return, its value depends on when it is received. (p. 408)

time zero (or period zero) The point in time when the investment is undertaken. (p. 412)

total quality A management philosophy that attempts to eliminate all defects, waste, and activities that do not add value to customers; also refers to an organizational commitment to customer satisfaction. (p. 26)

total quality management Also known as *total quality control* and *TQM*, this is a results control system that is widely used, in various forms, to focus an organization on meeting customer requirements. (p. 470)

transfer pricing A set of tools and methods (rules) used by the organization to allocate jointly earned revenues to organization subunits. Common transfer pricing approaches are cost, market, negotiated, and administered. (p. 504)

two-factor theory (Herzberg's) A theory that argues 2 groups of factors, hygiene and satisfier, with different roles motivate individual behavior. (p. 537)

unit-related activities Activities whose levels are related to the number of units produced. (p. 100)

valence The value that a person assigns to the outcomes provided to the individual by the organization as a result of formal performance measurement. (p. 538)

value chain A sequence of activities whose objective is to provide a product to a customer or provide an intermediate good or service in a larger value chain. (p. 44)

value-added activity An activity that, if eliminated, would reduce the product's service to the customer in the long run. (p. 60)

variable costs Costs that change proportionally with production volume. They represent resources whose consumption can be adjusted to match the demand placed for them. (p. 137)

variance The difference between a plan, or target, and a result. Variances provide a warning that operations did not go as planned. (p. 194)

variance analysis Decomposition of differences between actual and estimated costs into amounts related to specific factors causing the variance between actual and estimated costs. (p. 255)

weakness An organization characteristic or liability that inhibits the organization as it pursues its goals. A bad public image is a weakness. (p. 444)

what-if analysis A strategy that uses a model to predict the results of varying a model's key parameters or estimates. (p. 217)

worker time card Record of hours spent by each worker each day or week on different jobs. (p. 253)

zero-based budgeting An approach to developing appropriations for discretionary expenditures that assumes that the starting point for each discretionary expenditure item is zero. (p. 222)

SUBJECT INDEX

Behavioral implications of management accounting information, 29. *See also* Management accounting and control system (MACS)
Behavioral science, MACS and, 574–75
Beiner, Stanley C., 200
Benchmark budget targets, 207
Benchmarking, 14, 62, 299, 516n
  competitive, 55, 56
    financial, 521
  cooperative, 593–94
  long-term benchmark prices, 351
Bidding, decisions on, 13
Board of directors compensation committee, 550
Bonus, cash, 552, 553–55
Breakeven analysis, 161–70
  breaking even, 167–68
  capacity utilization and, 168
  cost variability and level of analysis, 169–70
  evaluation of business venture with, 163–64
  target profit, 164–65
Breakeven chart, 164
Breakeven load factor, 136
Breakeven point, 136, 161, 162, 163
  on breakeven chart, 164
  in dollars, 165–67
  step fixed costs and multiple, 168–69
Brindisi, Louis J., Jr., 548n
Brown, Donaldson, 17–18
Budget committee, 224
Budgeted and actual costs, comparing, 491–94
Budget imposition, 590
Budgeting cycle, 217
Budget participation, 205, 590–91
Budgets and budgeting, 190–239
  budgeting process, 195–216
    aggregate planning, 204
    annual operating, 17–18
    capacity levels, choosing, 206–9
    cash flow statement, understanding, 211–15
    demand forecast, 201n, 202–3
    financial plans, 211–16
    illustrated, 197–216
    managing, 223–24
    production plan, 197, 203–4, 210–11
    projected results, using, 216
    spending plans, developing, 204–6
  capital. *See* Capital budgeting
  computer and, 194–95
  defined, 193
  discretionary expenditures, controlling, 222–23
  ethics in, 221
  financial, 192, 193n, 196, 197
  flexible, 18, 494–96
  in government, 200, 220
  in high-technology organizations, 217
  incremental, 222
  level of difficulty of, 207
  master budget outputs, 196–97
  operating, 16, 17–18, 192, 196, 197

  participative, 205, 590–91
  periodic and continuous, 221–22
  planned and actual results, comparing, 219
  role of, 193–94, 219–20
  source of budget information, 221
  standard cost accounting system for, 116
  what-if analysis, 216–19, 423
    evaluating decision-making alternatives, 217–18
    sensitivity analysis, 218–19, 423
  zero-based, 222
Budget slack, 591
Budget targets, 207
Budget team, 223–24
Buffett, Warren, 557
Business-level strategies, 444
Business partners, 41
  as stakeholders, 445
Business process reengineering, 585
Business segment evaluation, 299
Buiness Week, 549
Byrne, John, 522

C

Canada Post, 498
Canadian Department of Veterans' Affairs, 463
Capacity
  surplus, 337–39
  unused, 156
Capacity constraints, 144
Capacity expansion, decisions on, 12, 13
Capacity levels, choosing, 206–9
Capacity utilization, 168
  monitoring, 12
Capital, cost of, 414–15
Capital assets, 406–7, 423–24
Capital budgeting, 16, 404–39
  budgeting discretionary spending proposals, 425
  defined, 407
  investment and return, 407–8
  long-term (capital) assets, 406–7, 423–24
  postimplementation audits and, 424–25
  strategic considerations in, 423–24
  time value of money. *See* Time value of money
  what-if and sensitivity analysis, 422–23
Capital spending plan, 197, 205
Carnegie, Andrew, 9
Carr, Lawrence P., 173
Cash bonus, 552
  gain sharing and distribution of, 553–55
Cash flow(s)
  comparisons at different points in time, 371
  incremental, 415
    tax effects and, 420–22
  inflows, 411
  outflows, 411
Cash flow analysis, projected, 343
Cash flow statement, 211–15
  cash inflows section of, 213

Cost(s)
  avoidable, 372–74
    allocated, 502
  budgeted and actual, comparing, 491–94
  conversion, 262–65
  critical performance indicators for, 50
  defined, 49, 93
  direct, 95, 96
    direct labor costs, 95, 99, 147–49,
      151–52, 155–56, 243, 259
  discretionary, 155
  engineered, 222
  facility-sustaining, 381
  financing, 381–82, 388
  fixed. *See* Fixed costs
  full, 337
    pricing decisions using, 340–42
  how activities create, 60
  incremental, 325, 337–39, 379
  indirect, 96, 98–99
    operating overhead, 113
  inventory-related, 71–72
  job, 244
  manufacturing, 94–95
  marginal, 349
  mixed, 140–42
  nonmanufacturing, 94–95
  normal, 149–51, 160–61, 244–45
  opportunity, 335–36
  overhead. *See* Overhead costs
  as performance measure, 49–50
  period, 94
  product, 94, 116, 326–27, 338
  relevant, 339, 369–71, 378–82
  shut-down, 502
  standard, 116
  sunk, 369
  total, 142, 164
  variable. *See* Variable costs
Cost allocation to support financial control,
    509-12. *See also* Activity-based costing
    (ABC) systems; Two-stage cost alloca-
    tion method
Cost-based transfer prices, 507, 509
Cost behavior, 134–89
  activity resources
    commitment versus consumption of,
      147–51
    expenditure versus consumption of,
      159–61
  breakeven analysis, 161–70
    breakeven point in dollars, 165–67
    breaking even, 167–68
    capacity utilization and, 168
    cost variability and level of analysis,
      169–70
    evaluation of business venture with,
      163–64
    step fixed costs and multiple breakeven
      points, 168–69
    target profit, 164–65
  defined, 154
  planning model and, 170–74
  production volume and, 136–46
    costs in economic framework,
      144–45

fixed versus variable costs, 137–40,
    142–44
  mixed costs, 140–42
  step function cost curve, 145–46
resource flexibility and cost variability,
    151–59
  multiple products and activity costs,
    156–59
  overhead cost variability, 154–56
Cost centers, 491–96, 499
  comparing budgeted and actual costs,
    491–94
  defined, 491
  flexible budget, 494–96
  performance measures for, 497
Cost concepts, 90–133. *See also* Product cost-
    ing systems
  activity-based analysis of costs, 99–111
    activity cost drivers, 102–6, 123,
      142–44, 156
    determining overhead rates, 108–11
    identifying activity costs, 106–8
    types of production activities, 100–102,
      104, 114, 115
  functional cost classifications, 93–99, 123
    traditional cost classification, 94–97
  need for cost information, 92–93
  for service organizations, 111–16
  standard cost accounting systems, 116–21
    choosing level of standards, 117
    determination of standards, 118–21
    limitations of, 121
  summary example of, 121–23
Cost curve, 144
  step function, 145–46
Cost cutting, resistance to change for fear
    of, 598
Cost driver, 147, 292, 295
  activity, 102–6, 123, 142–44, 156
  allocation of costs and, 281–84
  normal level of, 244–45
Cost driver analysis, 511
Cost of capital, 414–15
Cost performance measures, 58–63
  efficient and inefficient activities and,
    62–63
  information about activity costs, 59
  reasons for using, 60–62
  understanding causes of costs and,
    58–59
Cost pools, 248, 249, 252, 301
Cost sampling method, 299
Cost structure, change in, 98
Cost variances, 116. *See also* Variance analy-
    sis
Crane, Michael, 299
Credit, line of, 214-15, 216
Critical performance indicators. *See*
    Performance measures (critical perfor-
    mance indicators)
Critical success factors, 13–14, 47–50, 449,
    460, 461
  communicating, 465
  defined, 13
  multiple perspectives on, 577
  organization unit's role in, 462–63

Goal congruence
  defined, 576
  nongoal-congruent behavior, 589–92
  reward systems for, 588–89
Government, budgeting in, 200, 220
Grant, Chuck, 217
Gross margin, 8
Group performance, rewarding, 544, 545,
    550–51

H

Hale, R.L., 383
Hardy, A., 293
Heisenberg uncertainty principle, 29
Herzberrg, Frederick, 537–38, 539, 549, 575
Hierarchical structure, 585
High-technology organizations, budgeting
    in, 217
Hiring, team, 462
Hiring freeze, 60
Hiromoto, T., 289
Hobdy, T., 290
Hoelscher, D.R., 383
Holmes, Marjorie E., 343
Hopwood, A.G., 574*n*
Hughes, John S., 150, 342, 351n
Hughes, Vernon H., 338
Human relations movement, 575
Human resources, leveraging, 299
Human resources model of motivation,
    575–76, 598–99
Hygiene factors, 537, 538, 540, 549
  removal of poor, 558–59

I

Iacocca, Lee, 467
Illegal acts, 591
Improshare (Improved Productivity
    Sharing), 554
Incentive compensation, 542–57
  conditions favoring, 545
  defined, 542
  effective performance measurement and,
    543–45
  employee responsibility and, 546–47
  guidelines for effective, 549–50, 551
  issues in designing, 550–52
  managing plans, 548–49
  rewarding outcomes, 547–48
  types of, 552–57
Income statement
  pro forma, 218
  projected, 211, 213
  responsibility center, 509–12
Incremental budgeting, 222
Incremental cash flow, 415
  tax effects and, 420–22
Incremental cost per unit, 325
Incremental cost (revenues), 325, 379
  with available surplus capacity, 337–39
  defined, 337
  with no available surplus capacity, 339

Independent wage policy, 550
Indirect cost allocation, 511–12
Indirect costs, 96, 98–99. *See also* Overhead
    costs
  operating overhead, 113
Individual performance, rewarding, 550
Inefficient activities, 62–63
Inflows, 411
Inform-and-improve philosophy, shift
    toward, 25–26, 27
Information. *See also* Management account-
    ing information
  activity, developing, 59
  budget, source of, 221
  cost, need for, 92–93
  financial, sharing with employees, 26–28
  frequency of, 11–12
  nonfinancial, role for, 26
  operational control, 28
  quantitative and qualitative, 584–86
  strategic, 14
Innovation, standard cost accounting sys-
    tem and, 121
In-process materials, 101
Input activities, 45
In Search of Excellence (Peters), 383
Institute of Management Accounting (IMA),
    32, 578
Instrumentality, 538, 543
Integrated systems for control, 470–71
Intensity of competition, 342
Interest
  compounding effect of, 409
  effective rate of, 410–11
  nominal (stated) rate of, 410–11
Internal constituencies, 6
Internal control procedures, 455
Internal control systems, 582
Internal rate of return. *See* Return-on-invest-
    ment (ROI)
Intrinsic rewards, 41*n*, 540–42
Inventory
  process cycle time and, 72. *See also*
    Production cycle time
  process layout system and, 69–70
  work-in-process. *See* Work-in-process
    inventory
Inventory policy, 203-4
Inventory-related costs, 71–72
Inventory stock turns, 8–9
Investment. *See also* Capital budgeting
  criteria used for justification of, 417
  defined, 408
  desirability of, 518
  return and, 407–8
  return on. *See* Return-on-investment (ROI)
  technological risk and, 406, 407
Investment centers, 498, 499
  assigning and valuing assets in, 508–9

J

Japan, secondary control in, 595
Job bid sheet, 242–44
Job cost, 244

COMPANY INDEX

Stanley, 220
Steel Company of Canada, 463–64

T

Tater Tot, 471
Teijin Electronics Corporation, 375
Teijin Seiki Co., Ltd., 373
Tektronix, 22
Teledesic Corporation, 405, 425–26
Telemark Corporation, 391–92
Tennant Company, 383
Texaco, 557
Texas Instruments, 22
Texcel Company, 330–36
Timber River Metal Windows, 39, 74–76
Toyota Corporation, 22
Trane Company, 118
Treadwell Electric Corporation, 375–83

U

United Airlines, 111
U.S. Air, 96

Unocal, 544
Upjohn, Inc., 281
UPS, 21

V

Victory Memorial Hospital, 65

W

Walt Disney, 65
Weirton Steel, 339
Wheeling-Pittsburgh Steel Corporation, 285, 541, 551
Whirlpool Corporation, 92
Woolworth, 8

X

Xerox Corporation, 22, 25, 56